ITALY AND THE GREAT WAR

ITALY AND
THE GREAT WAR

Politics and Culture, 1870–1915

JOHN A. THAYER

Madison and Milwaukee, 1964

THE UNIVERSITY OF WISCONSIN PRESS

Published by
THE UNIVERSITY OF WISCONSIN PRESS
Madison and Milwaukee
Mailing address: P.O. Box 1379, Madison, Wisconsin 53701
Editorial offices: 430 Sterling Court, Madison, Wisconsin

Printed in the United States of America
by North Central Publishing Company, St. Paul, Minnesota

Library of Congress Catalog Card Number 64-17768

FOR DORAN

PREFACE

Within the framework of European history, the decades from the emergence of the new Continental nations to the outbreak of the Great War have an established place in historical literature. With respect to the history of Italy, the years from the occupation of Rome to the intervention of 1915 constitute a historical unit of more than conventional significance.

This is due to the intimate connection which many Italians themselves saw between the two events. The year 1870 marked not only the beginning of national existence; it was the end of the Risorgimento. With Rome the capital, the heroic era closed, or, as Victor Emmanuel put it, the age of prose had replaced the age of poetry.[1] The very choice of words was suggestive of a self-conscious awareness of a loss of ideals, of a decline in those intellectual qualities which were the glory and the romance of the struggle for unification. Natural as it might seem to statesmen, the custodians of Italy's fragile existence, that a period of more ordinary character devoted to administrative problems at home and a necessarily modest foreign policy abroad should follow now that unity had been achieved, the question for many educated Italians was whether the nation's existence had proved itself worthy of the idealism that had gone before. The problem of what Luigi Salvatorelli had called the "continuity" between the Risorgimento and the Postrisorgimento[2] was raised.

During the half century following the occupation of Rome, this problem was the cause of relentless dissatisfaction, particularly among Italian intellectuals. Between the accomplishments of the new regime, the material facts, and the doubts whether Italy had fulfilled the promise for which its heroes had lived and died, an antagonism emerged that was never completely put to rest. For many articulate Italians, the age of prose had never replaced the era of poetry. For them, the Great War was the deed which would justify and reaffirm the Risorgimento.

This may be seen by turning briefly to 1915. During the session of the Chamber of Deputies that committed Italy to the war, Paolo Boselli, chairman of the parliamentary commission which granted the Government's request for full powers, spoke for the older generation. In their name he gave his blessings to Italy's youth whose impassioned ideals recalled the revolutionary battles of Solferino, Calatafimi, and Bezzecca. It seemed, he said, as if the great shades of Italy's creators were present in the Chamber.[3] Boselli was old enough to have participated in the struggle for unity. This, and the emotionalism of war, may explain his rhetoric but not deny its significance. Younger deputies, like Salvatore Barzilai, a boy of ten when Rome was occupied, spoke of the unredeemed lands left behind in 1866, lands that were "in the vision of Dante."[4] Only now, "when Italy in their name takes up the torch of life that had fallen from her hands . . . the thought of her future and her mission in Europe," only now were they to be "gathered up in the religion of the *patria*."[5]

The elders who had experienced the Risorgimento relived their youth. The generation of the Postrisorgimento, raised by their fathers to revere Italy's heroes,[6] also kept alive the problem of the nation's historical continuity. For Barzilai, a native of Trieste and leader of the Republican Irredentists, the significance of the war was clear. Irredentism, however, was but one facet, and by no means the most important, of the political and cultural crisis of the Great War. The issues that were debated during the months of Italy's neutrality covered every aspect of the nation's history since 1870. Because intervention was regarded as the necessary and natural outgrowth of the Risorgimento, it was also, by implication or expressed intent, a rejection of the years from 1870 to 1915. The war, and not fascism, Federico Chabod has written, was the turning point for modern Italy.[7]

The truth of this is borne out by a division among historians between those who portray the years 1870–1915 in a negative light and those who praise the work of Cavour's successors. For the former, the war is a redeeming act, the just and proper conclusion to the Risorgimento. Foremost in this camp are Volpe, Salvemini, and Albertini. For the latter, intervention was both unnecessary and a breach of the political, cultural, and diplomatic traditions of the past. In this group, the names of Salvatorelli and Croce stand out. For all five, their historical outlook is tied to personal participation in the events of 1914–15. The same division, however, continues to exist among historians of later generations. The scholarly debate goes on in Chabod's defense of Croce's history of Italy and in the recent work of Mack Smith.[8]

In order to grasp the importance of the crisis of May, 1915, it will be necessary to analyze the fundamental issues which arose after 1870 and which became the basis for the journalistic propaganda of neutralists and interventionists. It is also hoped that some light may be thrown on another vexing question — over which the historical camps are equally divided — namely, what caused the sudden collapse of the Giolittian regime. Knowledgeable foreign observers were impressed by the advances made in all areas of Italian life during the prewar decade. Their opinions have been corroborated since by students of the Giolittian age. Yet the whole edifice seemed to crumble before the attacks of the interventionists, and this despite the fact that war was opposed not only by Giolitti but by the Socialist party, the Vatican, the great majority of the Chamber of Deputies, and the Italian people. To Guglielmo Ferrero, writing at the time, it seemed as if a "cyclone of hatred"[9] had welled up against Giolitti and the parliamentary system with which his name had become synonymous. War was a revolutionary action for Italy. The question remains how it ever came to be at all, unless the nation was in fact built on sand, unless the praise that Croce had for the Postrisorgimento was unjustified.

If the Great War was a political revolution, it also involved a radical change in the intellectual history of modern Italy, or at least gave great prestige and glamor to irrational currents which had flowed, now submerged, now breaking out into turbid streams, throughout the decades under consideration. The claims of the interventionists, with few exceptions, far from being based on a rational assessment of the European situation in 1914–15 were set forth in the language of late nineteenth-century literature and thought. In this, the war was not only a departure from the tradition of good sense, of political pragmatism, that, with momentary lapses, had guided the policies of Italian statesmen during the Postrisorgimento; it was also a betrayal of the intellectual traditions of Italy's leading thinker.

Italian intervention in 1915 was a shock to the academic revival of idealism associated with the work of Benedetto Croce. What had begun as a disciplined intellectual struggle to counteract the prevailing application of scientific methodology and analysis to all branches of human life and thought ended in a mysticism that seemed to have lost all regard for verifiable facts. Nowhere was this made more apparent than in the literary arguments in support of the Great War. Italian intellectual history shared in the general European reaction to those attitudes which have been generically labeled "positivism." This reaction has been examined for Western culture as a whole in a recent study by H. Stuart Hughes. Hughes has chosen what he considers to be the *via regia* of intellectual history: the study of ideas as they were expressed by men who belonged to the "higher" level of cultural history, the men who made "intellectually clear and significant statements." As for what Croce termed "ethico-political" history, its inadequacy for the intellectual historian, according to Hughes, lies in the necessity it imposes to revert to the historian's traditional concentration on political activity. This is due, he feels, to the fact that save for periods of unusual ideological integration, the stock of convictions held by individuals varies markedly from person to person. The most reliable indicator of men's ideas, therefore, is not what is said but what is done. But in this way, he concludes, we are led directly back to the history of action rather than of thought.[10]

Yet is it not precisely because of this that one should attempt to integrate ideas and politics? Hughes himself has raised questions that cannot be explored without returning to the history of political action. Speaking of Germany, he notes that the "central paradox" which tormented the minds of Ernst Troeltsch and Friedrich Meinecke was this: why was it that from "shallow" philosophies of history and society Britain and France were able to develop political practices that were both viable and humane, whereas the Germans, with their "deeper" understanding, not only failed to achieve a social equilibrium but, as the twentieth century advanced, were ever more obviously succumbing to the demon of naked physical power? While in the dominant Anglo-French tradition, utilitarianism and positivism, democracy and the natural sciences went together, in Germany the paradox remained — indeed was intensified. Intellectual creativity and destruction flowed from a common source. It is that which suggests to Stuart Hughes why any pragmatic judgment on the German idealist tradition must necessarily be ambivalent.[11]

This statement, however, implies a causal relationship between ideas and politics, and suggests as well a possible judgment as to the positive effect of intellectual movements on society. In order to assess the validity of the proposition, even to find whether a paradox did exist, one must of necessity return to the historian's traditional materials. It is hoped that the following pages may be of some help in clarifying the origins and political significance of this problem within the context of a national history.

ACKNOWLEDGMENTS

I wish to thank the staff of the American Commission for Cultural Exchange with Italy for their many kindnesses during my stay in Italy under the terms of a Fulbright scholarship.

I particularly wish to thank the Stack and Reader Division of the Library of Congress for access to the Library's materials.

To the *Istituto italiano per gli Studi Storici* I am obligated for financial support which enabled me to continue research on this topic. To the Institute's Director, the late Federico Chabod, I am indebted for scholarly encouragement while sharing in the larger debt which all students of the field owe to his work.

Above all, I should like to express my appreciation to my teachers, George Mosse and Robert Reynolds.

J. A. T.

Washington, D.C.
January, 1964

CONTENTS

CONTENTS

LIST OF ILLUSTRATIONS

ITALY AND THE GREAT WAR

·1·

THE OCCUPATION OF ROME AND THE CONCEPT OF THE POSTRISORGIMENTO

A history of united Italy devoted exclusively to domestic and foreign affairs would begin more properly with 1860 and the destruction of the Bourbon regime in the South than with 1870. The decade of the 1860's was to see decisions made which would influence the course of Italian history down to our own day. No discussion of the problems of administration, education, Church-State relationships, or diplomacy can avoid going back to the 1860–70 period in search of the roots of later issues. The present work offers no exception to this rule.

When one turns from political history to the study of intellectual currents, however, the continuity which seemed so well established with 1860 as its point of departure is broken, and the year 1870 becomes a dividing line separating the era of the Risorgimento from a new age which began with the occupation of Rome, the age of the Postrisorgimento. This partitioning of the history of united Italy was particularly noticeable in the writings of those Italians who judged their country in the light of what it should have become, who found its destiny foreshadowed in the records of its past or in manifestations of cultural and spiritual values. For men who took this view, the years 1860–70 belonged to the older, heroic age. Italian political life was then still enhanced by the same glowing qualities of mind and deed that had illumined the pages of the history of the Risorgimento. The War of 1866, and Garibaldi's fight for the Trentino; the revolts of Palermo; even the life of those brigands whose forays tested the skill of Cavour's successors — in all these events there were signs of passion and drama which resembled the romance of the era of national revolution.

No less vital for some were regional sentiments, the free play of untrammeled local forces seeking constitutional recognition in the decade after 1860, only to be set aside in favor of administrative centralization. All of Europe seemed to be following the same straight and narrow path toward uniformity. From his Swiss retreat, Jacob Burckhardt looked

3

northward to Prussia and came to much the same conclusion. German unity had blown sky high all those small centers of culture. The chief consequence of the ensuing centralization was spiritual mediocrity, obliging scholars to cling more fervently to their ideals, emphasizing cultural history in an age of masses and commercialism. "Europe without an amusing France," he exclaimed "Phew!"[1] When Burckhardt wrote his classic study of the Renaissance, it was to Venice's bureaucratic, political structure that he attributed a thwarting of the Italian genius. Among modern Italians a similar theme would be repeated in varying forms by those who believed in the concept of a Postrisorgimento. Here it would be Piedmontese rule which had done the work of Bismarck's Prussian in Germany and also in France. Just as the valor of the *Furia francese* failed before the material might of Prussian arms, just as the Commune — last stronghold of local revolutionary patriotism — had fallen, so it seemed to many Italian intellectuals that Italy in 1870 had lost the spirit of old.

This outlook was by no means the prevailing one. There was also a far more practical attitude to compete with it, particularly among the men who were responsible for preserving Italian unity. Italian statesmen, with important exceptions, recognized that problems had to be faced as they arose, seized with regard to the existing realities rather than in response to a theory of historical and cultural development. Nonetheless, a cleavage of opinion did come to being in 1870. From the occupation of Rome, wrote Federico Chabod, there emerged two opposing mentalities. There was on the one hand the viewpoint of the "new Italian" who had come forth from the struggles of the past prepared to take up the difficult tasks that lay ahead, who hoped for a period of quiet, convinced that the age of heroes must be left behind if progress were to be made. On the other hand, there was also the Italian who felt himself equal to the past, who, having achieved freedom too rapidly, was not prepared for this modest outlook, and whose head was full of scholastic memories, a literature of grandeur.[2]

There was nothing grand about the occupation of Rome on September 20, 1870. What, in the minds of some, should have been a triumphant conclusion to the struggle for liberty and unity, proof as well that Italy was decidedly not a negligible quantity, seemed instead to those who would not abandon their fondest memories a lackluster diplomatic maneuver achieved at the expense of France. Government policy was obviously one of hesitation and delay in the hope of reaching a peaceful settlement with the Papacy. Victor Emmanuel, inclined to a superstitious view[3] of the power of the Vatican's religious weapons, refused to take the final step.

Only after Sedan, when Napoleon III, his partner in the game of royalist diplomacy,[4] had fallen did he agree to move. Now that the Emperor, whom he had looked upon as a force for conservatism, had been replaced by a radical government, he might explain his actions to Pius IX in terms of a desire to protect the Papacy from the forces of revolution. This he did in almost pleading terms, offering the Pope the Leonine City, independent of all human sovereignty.

This direct appeal from the King met with the same response that had been given his personal emissary, San Martino, who had been sent to Rome in order to arrange a compromise. The Leonine City was not enough. If Rome were to become Italian, it would have to be occupied. General Cadorna was ordered to march south, slowly. There was always hope that a spontaneous popular uprising might offer the Government the pretext that its action was necessary to restore order.[5] There was really little likelihood that the Pope's subjects would rise up to defend him. Catholic writers had been aware since 1848 of the anticlericalism of the inhabitants of the Papal States, an area that had given many partisans to the cause of the Risorgimento.[6]

Foreign intervention was even less likely. The Papacy had isolated itself completely by the proclamation of infallibility.[7] This dogma, already applied to spiritual matters by the Doctrine of the Immaculate Conception, was now extended to the political sphere, thereby seriously weakening support of the Papacy among European Catholics. Cardinal Antonelli and his backers had defeated the liberal prelates at the Vatican Council of 1870. As Gregory XVI had sacrificed Lamennais, it was later written, so Pius IX sacrificed Döllinger and the German clergy.[8] In Italy as well, patriotic clerics who regarded the temporal power as a hindrance to the faith, who hoped to see the liberal faction win out at the Council, were disappointed. When the temporal power had fallen, in fact if not in theory, one of them, Luigi Tosti, Abbot of Monte Cassino and a distinguished church historian, wrote that the loss would prove beneficial to the Church as well as to the united nation of Italy.[9] For the rest of his life, Tosti was to labor in vain for a reconciliation between his church and his country.

The one country from which support of the papal position would have been expected had been rendered impotent at Sedan. In the hope of salvaging something for future diplomacy, France sent generous but at the time quite meaningless expressions of esteem coupled with an offer to receive Pius IX on French soil.[10] In these circumstances, the Italian government at Florence could not delay. The moment was ripe and had to be seized before the Franco-Prussian War ended. Even the Italian Minister of Foreign Affairs, Emilio Visconti Venosta, attached though he was to France and to French culture and, so far as the Papacy was concerned, reluctant to the end to take forceful measures, recognized the need for swift action. He was won over to this policy in part by Count Beust's friendly attitude at the critical juncture, but also by the proddings of Italy's ambassador at Vienna, Marco Minghetti.[11]

When the Italian troops arrived in Rome, there was no resistance. Nothing about the occupation even faintly recalled the legendary exploits of Garibaldi. It seemed instead that the Government had been forced to act. "Events did everything for us, and we ourselves did little or nothing." So wrote the director of the moderate *Opinione*, Giacomo Dina. Sir Augustus Paget, British minister at Florence, cabled London that the Italian government had acted in good faith, not wishing to attack Rome. It had, however, been "carried away by the force of circumstances, and by public opinion, resistance to which might have produced revolution."[12] The final step in the process of unification thus appeared the child of historical inevitability rather than of choice. For many who measured Italian capabilities by the criterion of action, it was an ominous suggestion that the future of united Italy would be dictated by a negative exploitation of the balance of power rather than by a positive assertion of rights. Forty years after Rome was taken, the phrase "historical inevitability" was made a catchword by the nationalist-imperialist press[13] in order to downgrade the achievements of the Giolitti government during the Tripoli campaign, portrayed by harbingers of national greatness as an undertaking which, like 1870, expressed the lifeless character of the Postrisorgimento.

Once Rome had been entered there remained the problem of the plebiscite scheduled for October 2. The *Destra*, then in power, held back. Wishing to avoid any suggestion of Italian infringement on the Pope's spiritual authority, which no one questioned, these moderates advised that the plebiscite be worded so as to include references to the Papacy's spiritual independence. The opposition party, the *Sinistra*, which claimed to represent the revolutionary traditions of the Risorgimento, attacked this proposal as offensive to national dignity. The Government finally gave way, partly for fear of playing into the hands of the Italian radicals were it to insist on its original position. There also remained the question of the Leonine City, which the Government had never intended to occupy under any circumstances.[14] But as matters then stood, that area of Rome was included within the terms of the plebiscite. Reports reached Florence that Pius, prodded by the Jesuits, as a protest against the plebiscite would leave Rome secretly by a boat which had been concealed along the Tiber for that purpose. Giovanni Lanza, the Prime Minister, instructed General Cadorna to be conciliatory when dealing with the Pope, who was to be treated with all the consideration due a sovereign. Cadorna's comportment, and that of Baron Blanc, Secretary General of the Foreign Office, was all that the moderates in Florence could have desired. On the Vatican side, Cardinal Antonelli praised the conduct of the Italian troops.

But the fear that Pius IX might flee Rome weighed heavily on the decisions made at Florence. Visconti Venosta turned to Vienna for help in dissuading the Pope from this drastic move. Cadorna and Blanc at Rome worked feverishly to prevent a flight. On September 28 Antonelli told Blanc that the Pope was not thinking of leaving for the time being. He could not, of course, give any assurances for the future. As to the Leonine City, it had been occupied originally on the request of the Cardinal Secretary of State, who stated that he feared disorders in the absence of protecting troops. He was also greatly concerned by a store of powder that had been left unguarded in the Castel S. Angelo. Baron Blanc made it quite clear, however, that the Italian government was still willing to leave that part of Rome to the Papacy. He very carefully pointed out that if Italian troops were to remain there, it was not to be construed as a sign that his Government no longer thought it practical to relinquish the Leonine City.[15]

Cardinal Antonelli's gesture in inviting the Italians into the grounds of the Vatican itself has been interpreted as a device to provoke foreign intervention and as a decision predicated on his conviction that Italian unity would not last in any event.[16] If that were his attitude, the utter isolation in which the Vatican found itself, plus the obvious restraint shown by the Italian government in every aspect of the occupation, soon proved him wrong. The fear that the Pope might some day leave Italy or that he could successfully call on foreign aid remained essentially a minor one, save to those Italians whose policies were grounded on anxiety. Only a disastrous blunder on Italy's part could have called forth any great tangible support for the self-styled prisoner of the Vatican, or could have induced the Powers to permit the destruction of Italian unity. That this unity was still fragile depended essentially on domestic matters. For those who had hoped for less circumspection and more flourish in 1870, however, policies devoted primarily to the domestic field were hardly satisfying. Nor was the eminently conciliatory attitude of the Destra towards the Vatican to be forgotten. In 1895, when some of the documents re-lating to the diplomacy of 1870 were printed, significant passages which demonstrated Italy's willingness to give up the Leonine City were de-leted.[17] By that time it was far too late for any such solution. It was also the era of Francesco Crispi, who self-consciously represented the spirit of the Risorgimento as opposed to the drabness of the Postrisorgimento.

Having acquired full control of Rome at the suggestion of an enemy of national unity, the Government called for a plebiscite. It was held without incident and gave, as was to be expected, clear popular sanction to Italy's action. When it came to moving the capital from Florence, how-ever, there was considerable resistance from conservative and moderate politicians. During the Senate's discussion of the question of the transfer, Gino Capponi expressed the view that the Vatican would always tower over all other buildings in Rome; but were it ever to be empty, it would give the appearance of a "fearful loneliness" in the midst of the city. The noted conservative Catholic layman, Stefano Jacini, Sr., raised the ques-tion of the dogma of Rome as Italy's capital. Cavour's celebrated insis-tence on this, he said, should be taken as a momentary concession to political feelings and not as an expression of his true convictions.[18] These debates during the winter of 1870 threatened to divide the governmental majority. The premier, Giovanni Lanza, and with him Visconti Venosta, who was by then one of Italy's most distinguished diplomats, advised de-lay. But the Sinistra, as in the case of the plebiscite formula, demanded action. In this they were supported by a prominent leader of the Destra, later to become premier, Quintino Sella. Lanza himself was willing to the end to grant the Leonine City to the Pope if it would bring peace. The advocates of action won. Rome was to be the capital. But the Govern-ment's hopes for conciliation even at that late date were again made evi-dent by the decision to postpone the King's entry into his new capital until the following year.[19]

To those who recalled the dramatic days of the struggle for liberty and unity, the last stages of the Risorgimento were "shorn of their due meed and glory." Venice and Rome were acquired in a "backhanded manner," wrote Trevelyan.[20] Garibaldi's sympathetic biographer shared the view of those Italians who would continue to see in the pragmatic rather than rev-olutionary policy of Italian statesmen after 1870 a debasement of the lofty sentiments of their hero. The hesitation with which Italy occupied Rome certainly contrasted with the exploits of the Thousand. But was this not as well an indication of the nature of Italy's new position in Europe, and of the less heroic policy she would be obliged to follow? A significant camp among Italian political leaders would insist, moreover, that it was wise to accept the more modest, hence more realistic, situation. In the debates on the future of Rome, this opinion was expressed by such men as Jacini and Visconti Venosta, who pointed out the danger of a myth of Rome, the perils of a literary infatuation associated with history.[21] That their qualms reflected in part religious and essentially northern conservative scruples does not detract from the wisdom of their counsels: Italians should face the facts and be discouraged from excessive expectations. In the decades to follow Porta Pia, these men would note with alarm the tangible results of diplomatic extravagance and seek to curb such passions or counteract the dangerous effects which they had produced.

Their fears were not unfounded. As the date for the King's visit to Rome approached, the grandiose plans being made indicated a far less prudent vision of Italy's place in the world. The Roman Commission for the Conservation of Monuments suggested that the King ascend the Campidoglio by way of the *via sacra*. In this way, the marvels of the past would be joined to the triumphs of the present, both united in the nation. The *Opinione*, reflecting the Government's views, quickly dampened such enthusiasms, pointing out the ridiculous anachronism involved. The King, it wrote, would enter Rome as citizen monarch, not Roman emperor.[22]

In fact, Victor Emmanuel came to Rome in a way no one had foreseen. A flooding of the Tiber during the winter of 1870 offered the occasion for a modest, inconspicuous royal visit which might be justified by the royal wish to inspect the scene of the disaster. Visconti Venosta saw the chance to make the move with as little fanfare as possible.[23] On the morning of December 31 the King arrived, signed the bill annexing the city to his kingdom, and left the same evening. Gregorovius wrote that the event marked the close of the Middle Ages.[24] Another witness, however, took a much less flattering view. Alfredo Oriani, a little known novelist and historical essayist until after his death, when anti-Giolittian and, later, fascist writers made of him a "precursor,"[25] described it as follows:

The King arrived in the afternoon. There were very few waiting to meet him in the station square, and these were more a common crowd than the people, because all were concerned by the hardships and dangers of the flood. When the King stepped down from his carriage at the entrance to the Quirinal, turning to La Marmora like a traveler bored by the trip, he murmured in Piedmontese, "Here we are at last."

In all this, wrote Oriani, there was no touch of greatness.[26]

Implicit in this description were many of the doubts of those who tended towards a negative view of the Postrisorgimento. Equally present are indications of some of the real problems whose undeniable existence offered concrete support for scornful rhetorical flourishes: regionalism underscored by dialectal differences; the dramatic comparison of the *plebe* and the *popolo*, indicative of the need for a greater national cohesiveness. And the monarchy? This was the king who had absorbed, or perhaps betrayed, the revolution. Oriani's description of the incident was too pointed to be mistaken. Here was a king who arrived after the deed was done, who had received his kingdom from the hands of the hero, a theme later exploited by D'Annunzio.[27]

To sustain a sensation of frustrated heroism, the living symbols of the Risorgimento were there, men whose day was over in fact but whose reputation, for many people, counted more than did realities. Mazzini's bitterness was immense as he viewed Italy in 1871. His Italy, he wrote, was one that would rise up through the sacrifices and virtues of the people, its wrongs purified by an expiation of three centuries, splendid in its enthusiasm and its faith, strong in the awareness of the battles fought. What he saw was a falsification of the true Italy: Trent, Trieste, and Nice in foreign hands; a corrupt administration copied from a foreign model (French); a mosaic of lands put together by battles waged for reasons of dynastic egoism, servile to France, until she lay prostrate, and then Rome taken; Lissa and Custoza, the results of ineptitude and worse on the part of its leaders. It was only a shadow of Italy. His followers, many of whom had turned to socialism as a new ideal capable not only of meeting material problems but of restoring the fervor of the Risorgimento, agreed. In Romagna a local socialist, Alessandro Mussolini, Benito's father, wrote that this was certainly not the Italy desired by Carlo Pisacane, Mazzini, and Garibaldi.[28]

Mazzini's laments were understandable. But as the legitimate heroes died, more important were the men who perpetuated this view of the Postrisorgimento, men who themselves were born too late for the saga. Oriani was one such, and his growing reputation in the early twentieth century is a significant indication of the function of these transmitters in carrying on the tradition of derision for the new nation. In the decades following 1870, however, Giosuè Carducci was more important, his artistic reputation having been established. Carducci's violent anticlericalism in the *Hymn To Satan* (1863) — in which he referred to the Pope as an "infamous old priest" — abated somewhat as the years passed.[29] Those "excommunications of the Pope," as Croce called them,[30] found less appeal as strident anticlericalism softened towards the close of the century. His denunciation of the new Italy, however, lost none of its edge. In this respect, Carducci helped establish a tradition, however much it was later to be corrupted by his self-proclaimed successor, D'Annunzio.[31] Carducci's own description of the King's arrival in Rome, like Oriani's, derides the lack of greatness, the obvious reluctance of the Government to act.[32] In a speech commemorating the death of Garibaldi, the poet asked sarcastically what flags would fly over the hero's grave. Perhaps those used in the recent demonstrations against the assassins of Marseilles. They had already been put away while Italians were being hunted down in foreign streets. Or those which saluted the departure of the King for Vienna. Or should Italy assure Europe, swearing upon his tomb, that it renounces Trieste and Trent? Or to placate the spirit of the victor of Bezzecca and Dijon, the vanquished of Mentana, should Italians merely mutter boldly that France's isolation in Egypt repays us for the humiliation of Tunis; that we, if not the descendants of Camillo and Caesar or Machiavelli's grandsons, are Bismarck's friends and flunkeys?[33] Again, speaking at Pisa in 1886: "Oh radiant days, the freedom and the glory of 1860; Oh, the titanic clash of Garibaldi and Cavour. And what have we become!"[34]

This was the stuff on which dissatisfaction fed. A cultural attitude towards politics was taking shape after 1870 which worked to undermine the prestige of the nation as it existed in fact, an attitude which at times became a rival to government for the affections of educated Italians, the very segment of the population on which the strength of Italy's constitution depended. Dissident literati were certainly not an Italian peculiarity. France had already produced Lamartine and the revolution of contempt. The Third Republic would yet have Maurras, Barrès, Péguy, and Sorel, whose corrosive impact on French political life would eventually be felt. In England, Kipling's imperialism sounded not unlike that of Enrico Corradini in Italy or those poetic naval odes of D'Annunzio.[35]

There is nothing novel in the Italian intellectual's discontent with his society after 1870. He is often but illustrating the general tension in Western Europe, and in England as well, between what Raymond Williams called culture and society. If Italy's share in this cultural response to bourgeois, technological society is in no way unique, it is, however, more virulent and politically more significant than it was in England or France. For one thing, Carducci's mordant criticisms could exploit many hard facts whose undeniable existence made a sorry showing when seen through eyes still blinded to realities by the lingering glare of the "titanic" era in Italian history. The answer of the moderates, of men like Stefano Jacini, would be that Italy could not afford England's greatness. This was not a satisfactory reply to those who viewed the present in terms of history and culture rather than realities. And although it was true that Italy could not afford England's imperial greatness, she could and did produce her own Kiplings. But here it is important to note a difference between the English imperialist and D'Annunzio or Corradini. Kipling identified himself with England's ruling power. For all his heroics, as George Orwell observed, Kipling was a conservative. He was not one to *épater les bourgeois*. He had a grip on reality. A similar characterisic has been observed in Carlyle, whose career in other respects reflected a dangerous tendency to lose the balance between the claims of culture and the necessities of society, moving steadily towards a form of mysticism, the idealization of power, which we will meet with many times in Italian history.[36]

In France as well, the tension between the intellectuals and the Third Republic does not share some of the important characteristics of the same contest in Italy. A prominent Italian journalist, the eccentric and thoroughly antibourgeois ultramontane Mario Missiroli, examining the flowering of the Italian Nationalist Movement in 1911, noted that French nationalism was superior in content because it rested on a great monarchical tradition. In Italy, he wrote, when we speak of our "historical problem" we speak of that which is yet to be made.[37] But it was just the urge to form the tradition that was lacking which made much Italian thought extremely dynamic, highly resistant to immediate satisfactions, and quite subversive. That France's intellectual and political atmosphere differed from Italy's was also perceived by Georges Sorel. In the latter country, where he was more widely read (as he himself had predicted he would be), monarchy was not, as with Maurras, a wish, but a reality. And this reality, Sorel observed, was tied to the middle class.[38] How dim a view many Italian intellectuals were inclined to take of that bourgeois monarchy which slipped meekly into Rome has been seen.

In Italy, expressions of disdain for existing society, and for the Government which was the reflection of that society, became more intense despite material advances made precisely because this hostility was based on a total opposition to the existing political framework while having no stable roots of its own. Where Frenchmen, of extreme left or extreme right, could look back either to the great King or to the great Republic, in Italy both radicals and conservatives who held to the concept of the Postrisorgimento as a betrayal of ideals looked back for inspiration to the same era — of revolutionary nationalism. Men of the most divergent political persuasions shared the belief that the continuity of Italian history had been shattered. It was easier, therefore, to join forces against the Government. Sorel's conversion from syndicalism to monarchism was itself an illustration of this sort of total rejection of society, be it a rejection from the right or from the left. His belief that Italian intellectuals would find more of interest in his works than would his countrymen rests on his awareness of a specifically Italian problem, while among Italians the same historical problem will give rise to more than one Sorelian shift of political position.

The discontented voice in Italy was also strengthened by the existence of an exceptionally large white-collar proletariat, full of frustration at having arrived too late at the "banquet of nations."[39] The tendency to avoid professional training was a problem with which the Piedmontese were concerned before unification. Each year produced a new crop of indigent, dissatisfied youth who despised the trades. On the eve of unification, 40 per cent of university students were studying law.[40] Francesco De Sanctis, in 1878, when Minister of Education, was concerned with the lack of practical scientific studies in Italy. The situation did not improve. From 1880 to 1890 the number of students in classical schools doubled; the number in technical schools increased by 50 per cent. This meant thousands of poor doctors and lawyers,[41] fertile ground for the sense of pessimism and literary heroics already represented by Carducci and Oriani.

This section of Italian society has been aptly referred to as a "humanistic petty bourgeoisie." Its importance for the rise of fascism was analyzed in 1921 by Luigi Salvatorelli with prophetic insight.[42] Its influence during the years 1870-1915 was no less significant. Through the pages of the small reviews, which were such a common feature of European society, this segment of Italy's educated population not only served as the transmitter of a negative, pessimistic concept of the Postrisorgimento but also perpetuated, in lofty defiance of the material realities, the "style" of the Risorgimento itself. While never sufficiently numerous or politically influential to make policy for Italy, this diffuse and disorganized group, lacking any apparent unity of purpose, always worked as a goad, urging Italy's leaders to greater deeds. That statesmen were unable to satisfy these critics of society was partly due to the total opposition to the spirit of the Postrisorgimento which motivated many of them. But it was also apparent that the intimate relationship between the world of ideas and the world of politics was the very source of the concept of the Postrisorgimento.

From the beginning, the problem was both cultural and political. As long as this remained true, as long as men persisted in viewing politics in the light of cultural values, so long would many Italians refuse to take that grip on reality which made Kipling safe for English government as well as a politically satisfied artist. In order to trace the development of this competition, it will be necessary to examine the essentials of Italy's political, economic, and diplomatic history after 1870, seeking to uncover the continuing affinities between the worlds of ideas and politics.

·2·

FUNDAMENTAL PROBLEMS
OF THE POSTRISORGIMENTO

Economic Challenges

Much of the criticism of the failures of the Postrisorgimento reflected an unrealistic desire to recapture the romance of the past, to direct united Italy's policy along lines that were no longer feasible. Moreover, the critics too often forgot the very great achievements of Cavour and his successors. Few Europeans felt that Italy would ever be united at all, or that unity could last if achieved. Nassau William Senior's conversations with prominent men bear this out. General Fénélon remarked, in 1861, that if Napoleon III should allow Italian unification, it would only be so that Italy would remain dependent on France for fifty years. Besides, he added, no one expected unity to last. There would be instead a sort of *gâchis*. The French would stay in Rome to prevent the Papacy from ever falling under Piedmontese protection. Naples would become Bonapartist. Piedmont might be extended as far south as the Marches. As for Venice, should Piedmont ever attack Austria, she would be disgraced. The General was sure of this, for he shared the opinion of many that Italians were poor fighters. Charles de Rémusat considered the lack of Venice a positive blessing for Italy. Should Italy acquire it, she would split up. Thiers told Senior that his own dislike for Italian unity was common to all educated Frenchmen. But there was no fear of this. It would never happen.[1] Lamartine wrote Dumas, who was covering Garibaldi's Sicilian expedition for the French press, that while he felt as much Italian as French, it would not be patriotic to hope to see the creation of a power at France's door. As an "Italian at heart," he felt that a unified state would break apart at the first battle lost. A confederation would be lasting.[2] Similar dire predictions were voiced by Russians, English, and Germans. Even Bismarck, in 1868 after Venice had been won, although less pessimistic felt that the process of consolidating the new nation had made less progress than the friends of Italy might have wished.[3]

The correspondence of the British ministers at Turin and Naples in

1860 with Lord John Russell shows clearly how little these friends of Italy desired unification, until Garibaldi's campaign settled the issue. At that point even Palmerston was willing to concede that unity was the best arrangement. But these dispatches point out as well the very difficult problems involved in a unification of the North with the backward and corrupt Neapolitan kingdom.[4] In Italy itself there were many who agreed. Marquis Giorgio Pallavicino-Trivulzio, patriot of the Risorgimento and veteran of Spielberg prison, told Senior in 1861 that he had never dreamed of uniting the "three countries" of Italy, Piedmont, and Central and Southern Italy. Cavour himself had said that the task of putting the North and the South together presented as many difficulties as a war with Austria and the struggle with Rome.[5]

In this light, the achievement of unification was deserving of far more credit than Carducci was willing to grant. When the Italian poet, in 1882, was lamenting the diplomatic failures of the Berlin Congress, the occupations of Tunis and Egypt, and the loss of Savoy and Nice, he was expressing the understandable but quite unrealistic bitterness of men who had grown to manhood during the heroic age. As for the Berlin Congress, it was no small matter that Italy's presence there as an accepted power among her former enemies was, itself, proof that she had defied the prophecies of doom. For the first time at a major gathering of the powers, the "Italian question" was not discussed. That the new nation had survived this long was a tribute to the efforts of Cavour's successors. Historians who tend to take a positive view of the accomplishments of the Postrisorgimento have justly defended the heroic character of their work.[6]

While for our purposes a detailed account of the economic and administrative problems which constituted an unrelenting threat to national unity is neither necessary nor possible, it is essential for any evaluation of the conflict between the new national government and its domestic critics to examine these problems in their main lines. And this for two reasons: to make clear the existence of material realities that gave support to the laments of the intellectuals, and to demonstrate the tenacity of dissatisfaction among educated Italians in the face of the creditable record established by the men who inherited Cavour's mantle.

Finance was the overriding issue. To it the Destra was forced to devote its major energies. The national debt was unified in 1861. The expenses of the War of 1848, the Crimean War, and the struggle for the South in 1859-60 brought the deficit by 1861 to over 500,000,000 lire. Quintino Sella, Minister of Finance in the Rattazzi Cabinet, spoke in 1862 of the task of achieving a balance between revenue and ordinary expenses by 1864 as a matter of life and death. By 1864, however, despite the most stringent economies, the imposition of new taxes, and frequent recourse to foreign loans, the deficit was still over 300,000,000 lire. To the already shaky finances the Austrian War would add the crushing expense of 800,-000,000 lire. There was also the immensely complicated and politically hazardous job of unifying the chaotic tax structure. Although twenty-two separate land tax registers were in existence, they covered only one half the total surface area of the peninsula.

Through a policy of "economies to the bone," Sella was able to take some satisfaction in announcing that the deficit, as far as ordinary expenditures were concerned, had been reduced by 1866 to 261,000,000 lire. The defeats of the war left a feeling of deep discouragement in Italy, which soon had its effect on the economic front; nonetheless, encouraged by the drop in the deficit, Sella went ahead with the campaign aimed at the one great goal of achieving a balanced budget. His plan was to increase government revenue through an enforced, progressive income tax.

The idea of progressive taxation was always to meet stubborn resistance. Giolitti would revive it in 1892 during his first premiership, only to see it lost in the confusion of the Roman Bank Scandals. In Sella's case, coupled with the resistance to any new taxes and to chronic tax evasions was the loss of prestige that followed the War of 1866, which forced him to look elsewhere for sources of desperately needed revenue. It was only the dire necessity of meeting the financial crisis that induced him to institute in 1869 the *macinato*, a tax on the milling of grains, which was bound to cause popular resentment. Unquestionably, the tax hit the poorest Italians the hardest. Sella was aware of this.[7] But whether the new nation could survive without an assured source of extra income at that time was doubtful. As it turned out, the macinato failed to deliver the anticipated revenues until 1872, when it brought in 60,000,000 lire. Another unpopular feature of the Destra's finance policy was the *corso forzoso*, the compulsory circulation of nonconvertible paper money, which lasted from 1866 to 1881. Revenues from the sale of church lands put up for auction in 1867 failed to take the Government out of the red, because of the lack of available purchasing capital. Although reliance on indirect taxation was a constant irritant to the poor, provoking popular uprisings throughout Italy,[8] it can be shown that indirect taxes accounted for less of the total tax revenue during the years in which the Destra was in power [9] than after 1876 under the Sinistra. As for revamping the tax registers and effecting collections, which varied in method from region to region, Sella found it difficult to keep his agents on the job. Giolitti, then a young Piedmontese official, was asked by Sella to assist in this project. His memoirs have left a well deserved tribute to his chief's efforts, as well as a first-hand account of the difficulties the hated tax officials encountered.[10]

In the field of communications, local facilities, and industry the ledger was no brighter. Statistics seemed to bear out the predictions of foreign observers that Italy could not stay united. The whole Kingdom of Naples had less than 100 kilometers of railroad track when it became part of united Italy. Nationally, illiteracy of those six years old and above stood at 68 per cent in 1872. Of 1,848 southern communes in 1860, 1,621 had no paved roads and were almost without public fountains.[11] Sidney Sonnino later remarked that had those in power realized the immensity of the problems which faced them in the first three decades of united Italy, it was doubtful whether they would have had the courage to face the tasks that lay ahead.[12]

With this beginning, the advances made in the first decades following Porta Pia were a credit to the new nation and its leaders. Railroad track increased from 1,758 kilometers in 1860 to 10,000 in 1885. Coal production rose from 51,386 metric tons in 1868 to 341,327 in 1898. Illiteracy had decreased from 68 to 43 per cent by 1901. Hygiene and clothing among the peasant population improved. Pellagra and malaria were being brought under control. The mortality rate dropped from 30/1000 in 1872 to 21/1000 in 1897. A moderate protectionism begun in 1878 was beneficial, as was indicated by increased imports of industrial materials. From 1879 to 1883 coal imports were doubled, steel tripled. By 1876, when the Destra fell from power, never to return, the budget had been balanced. It is true that the extreme economies of Sella had inhibited industrial expansion. There were critics within his own party. Under the leadership of the Sinistra after 1876, a more liberal policy of government support for industry wiped out the balance achieved by the Destra but did give a boost to Italian industry.[13]

Foreign observers returning to Italy were impressed by the material advances made. Gladstone, for whom the Bourbon regime had been an abomination, was enthusiastic when he visited Naples in 1888. Treitschke noted, in 1877, what had been achieved since his last visit to Italy ten years before. Beneath the literary polish of Norman Douglas' recollections of his hikes through Calabria, significant observations on recent accomplishments emerge side by side with his descriptions of persistent poverty.[14] Less friendly visitors were repeating the dire predictions of Senior's time.[15] And much remained to be done. What is interesting to note, however, is the criticism from within Italy, particularly in regard to military power.

It was clear that an economic situation of the seriousness which these statistics reveal did not permit lavish military expenditures. The military budgets were reduced in the decade following the War of 1866, reaching the lowest percentage of the total state expenditures in the history of the nation. However much Carducci might have wished it otherwise, a choice had to be made in favor of internal over foreign policy, in the belief that the former was critical for the nation's survival. But Carducci's regrets that Italy had become Bismarck's flunkey — which was not the case — indicate the sense of frustration that undermined the accomplishments of the Postrisorgimento. And if a poet may be permitted his excesses, it is more difficult to pass over the attacks of the Sinistra on the question of military preparedness. For Crispi to say that Italy must "arm, arm, arm," as he did in the Chamber in 1872,[16] was scarcely realistic.

Between Sella, a mining engineer turned financial expert in years of national crisis, and Crispi, ex-Garibaldian leader of the political opposition, the difference in temperament was so marked that the former might be taken as a model of the prosaic age that had arrived, while the latter was in fact to become a symbol of the age of poetry that had been left behind. There was nothing colorful about Sella. Simple of speech, orderly in his personal life, he lacked all outward show of the revolutionary nationalist. Yet no one had pressed harder for the occupation of Rome nor fought the finance battle with greater determination. Crispi, on the other hand, was rather flamboyant in dress, rhetorical in speech, given to dramatic pronouncements that revealed the self-conscious hero. His private life was most irregular, characterized by romantic liberties with accepted moralities. This and his equally erratic personal finances contrasted sharply with Sella's staid existence and laborious attention to the state's ledgers.

The contrast between Sella and Crispi involved more than financial policy. It was always bound up with and affected by the parallel cleavage between those who took a cultural view of Italy's destiny and those whose outlook was bureaucratic and utilitarian. For the former, the age in which they lived was a Postrisorgimento, while for the latter the continuity of history was made apparent daily by the problems of administration which went back to 1860 and unification, rather than to the occupation of Rome.

This clash of views, already noticeable in the 1870's, was not to abate; indeed, it became more and more intense. At the close of the century it would come back full force. By then, Sella was dead, but Crispi lived on — more than ever the embodiment of the past as the men of his generation died off — a lonely figure whose memories were peopled by the noble spirits of his youth. He and younger men who shared and admired his dynamic qualities found their target in Giolitti. For although Giolitti by then had become a leader of the Sinistra, he possessed the same sober, thrifty, and eminently bourgeois traits he had so much admired in Sella,[17] under whom he had learned the techniques of administration. It was not surprising that when Giolitti entered the Chamber of Deputies in 1882 as representative of the Piedmontese electoral college of Cuneo, he was soon marked as a man of the Postrisorgimento by those fiery young politicians who preferred Crispi's grand manner, however much they opposed his foreign and domestic policies.

It was in part because of this somewhat romantic criterion for statesmanship that Giolitti was never to get his due recognition, despite the material advances made under his leadership. A stigma attached to his reputation and to that of the Chamber of Deputies with which his name was to become almost interchangeable. But this political attitude, so persistent in the face of economic improvements, rested as well on a very real issue, which was to become almost insoluble as the years passed, and which also, by its very nature, encouraged a cultural response to Italian politics. This was the problem of the administrative system. It was extremely difficult to tamper with the decisions taken in the 1860's, which created a centralized rather than a federal system. Fear that any loosening of the reins would lead to secessionist activities upon which France and the Vatican would capitalize — to say nothing of Italian radicals who had never wanted a constitutional monarchy — inhibited every effort at reform from the start.

Yet it was also clear that the sudden application of Piedmont's laws and bureaucracy to Central, Southern, and insular Italy had caused widespread resentment. Increased taxes were an immediate source of complaint. Many Northerners as well felt the loss of political power when the center of government was moved south, first to Florence and then to Rome. Some Catholic conservatives also regretted that a federal arrangement had not been created which would have been more acceptable to Pius IX. There were also political theorists who tended to agree with the pessimistic predictions of the French concerning the frailty of the unitarian structure.

These men, rather than reform the state in the direction of regionalism, looked to more forceful, even authoritarian ways of creating a greater degree of centrality.

In many cases, however, one could see the same sort of cultural distaste for Piedmontese hegemony that Burckhardt felt for the rule of Prussia over the Germanies. Because of what seemed at the time a callous disregard for local traditions on the part of Cavour and his heirs, Italian unity could be viewed as the product of a coldly rational, scientific, and thoroughly unromantic snuffing out of potential regional energies, or worse, the corruption of these native political virtues for the sake of party rule. All these criticisms of the political life of the Postrisorgimento, however, had in common a dislike of the Italian parliamentary system as it existed. The arguments raised against the system varied widely, from extreme radicalism to authoritarianism; even so, the Chamber, and later Giolitti, came under relentless attack during the Postrisorgimento. Fundamental to this attack was the regionalist issue generally, and the more important aspect of it which was to be known as the Southern Question.

The Regional Question

In 1884 the moderate *Nuova Antologia* wrote with obvious pride about Italy's material achievements, then on display at the Turin Exposition. What was particularly gratifying was not so much the signs of increased prosperity but the pilgrimage so many Italians had made to the tomb of Victor Emmanuel. According to the influential political and cultural review, this demonstrated affection for the monarchy and was proof as well of Piedmont's contribution to Italian unity.[18]

Many were less pleased with Piedmont's role in the process of unification. The regional issue — the charge that Cavour would Piedmontize Italy, not unite it — was not dead. Traces of it linger to this day.[19] The beginnings of such discontent, which would flare up into near civil war, went back to the first months of unity. The Duke of Castel-Cicala, Viceroy of Sicily when the island was joined to Italy, was convinced that the union would not last. The Sicilians, he told Senior, fought for Garibaldi only out of hatred for Naples. The noted federalist, Francesco Ferrara, wrote Cavour the same thing during the Garibaldian occupation of Sicily.[20] Even those historians who tend to maximize the amount of popular support for Garibaldi take note of the reluctance of Sicilians to cross the Straits with their hero, and of the signs of civil war which broke out when the King came south to assume leadership of his new kingdom.[21]

Regionalist sympathies were not slow to reveal themselves. The application of the macinato resulted in increased brigandage. Nor was this the result necessarily of pro-Bourbonist sentiments among the contadini.[22] By 1861 Crispi was accusing Sicilian priests, many of whom had backed the revolution, of inciting the peasantry against the nation. In 1866 the charge was repeated by General Cadorna during the Palermo revolt of that year. This uprising, which followed an outbreak of cholera that claimed 4,000 lives — an epidemic said to be a plot of the Government — showed the rancor and contempt among the poor for the new nation. Men spoke of the betrayal of Sicily. Cardinal Antonelli, encouraged by these signs of imminent collapse of the nation, predicted to foreign representatives at Rome the secession of the Kingdom of Naples.[23] Those patriotic priests whose faith in unity survived a decade of turmoil conceded that the Neapolitans needed a hard hand. Dictatorship, wrote Luigi Tosti, was more in keeping with their temperament than any sort of liberal government.[24]

Despite evidence of improved economic conditions, in the 1860's the Italian government looked as if it were about to collapse.[25] The regionalist solution, which might have reduced popular resentment of centralized administration and taxation, had been dropped under the pressures of events. One authority has ascribed most of the trouble to Cavour's arrogance, and to his reliance on men who were not likely to assuage the wounded feelings of the Garibaldians.[26]

To speak of arrogance is too anti-Cavourian and too simplified. Cavour had approved the regional administrative policy set forth by Marco Minghetti.[27] Far from being advocates of extreme centralization on the French model, the Moderates admired English local government. Cavour's Cabinet put forth proposals for an administrative system allowing considerable local autonomy, with hints of the formation of possible regional bodies. At the time this plan was suggested, however, Italy would have included Lombardy, Emilia, and Tuscany, areas in which the Moderates were the dominant political force, but not the Mezzogiorno. A commission was chosen to discuss the project. It met from August to October, 1860, the very months in which Garibaldi's victory in the South had completely altered the nature of Italian unity. The fear of extending local powers to an area outside the control of the Moderates was only one factor in changing the Government's attitude. Cavour felt that the inhabitants of the South, lacking political experience, would fall under the sway of communal tyrants — the village dottoruzzi — while on the diplomatic front a quick solution was needed to prevent any foreign interference. Another factor that must be weighed when judging Cavour's handling of the situation is that of the Bourbon reactionaries, who were espousing decentralization in the hope of clinging to their own powers. Cavour's agents were generally ignorant of the Mezzogiorno, it is true; but reports from Garibaldians, while these may show a greater humanitarian spirit, are equally unrealistic when it comes to their descriptions of the South's material conditions.[28]

The fear that unity would be compromised at its inception, and the emergence in Italian history of the Southern Question, whose importance will be considered in another place (Chapter 6), were at the root of the decision to extend the Sardinian communal and provincial laws of 1859 to the whole Peninsula. This was done by the decrees of October 9, 1860, handed down by Baron Ricasoli's government, which had taken over after Cavour died. It was nonetheless true that Italian unity had the appearance of an improvisation, and was suggestive of that gâchis which hostile French observers had predicted.

It was also true that many southern patriots had turned to Piedmont late in the day, when the government of Ferdinand II proved immune to suggestions of an understanding with enlightened middle-class leaders. De Sanctis noted the existence of regional jealousies that could be enflamed if the role of Piedmont in Italian unification, which he himself had accepted, were understood as the primacy of Piedmont over the other areas of Italy. He was told, coming north, to watch out lest he be taken in by the Piedmontese.[29] Not unlike the manner in which Rome was to be taken, the extension of Piedmont's control to the Peninsula as a whole could be interpreted as an unholy compromise of the revolutionary ideals and sacrifices of the Risorgimento. Mazzini had insisted on unity. His disgust with the false Italy was in part the result of this bureaucratization of the unitarian revolution, the extension of a foreign system to Italy for reasons of dynastic egoism.

Total unification was also resisted by prominent Northerners. This opposition stemmed from two fears which, in some cases, were related: the fear of losing Piedmontese power and primacy through the absorption of the politically and economically backward South, and the realization by Catholic conservatives that total unification with Rome as capital would compromise the chances of conciliation with the Papacy. Massimo D'Azeglio, as early as 1859, before the Garibaldian expedition, had expressed the hope of Catholic reformers. Realizing that the temporal power was an anachronism, that the Papal insistence upon it only weakened the faith, he advised leaving Rome to the Pope in the form of a free city. A reform of the Church might follow were the incumbrances of the Papal States to be taken from it. This was essential, he wrote, since Protestantism would never penetrate into Italy. Following the plebiscites which annexed the Papal States, D'Azeglio continued to oppose the myth of Rome as the capital of Italy, but in a manner that revealed his northern fears as well as his religious scruples. What had Rome to do with modern life, with industry and liberal thought? To insist on it was to exploit rhetoric and not realities. D'Azeglio also feared that a hostile Papacy would prove a threat to a united Italy. Was it advisable to "take in tow that leaky southern barge"? In 1863 D'Azeglio again proposed his solution of Rome as a neutral city, with the Pope the nominal sovereign but the residents Italian citizens. His essential conservatism made him fearful of the radical, antimonarchical, as well as anticlerical propaganda associated with the cry "Rome Capital of Italy." [30]

Stefano Jacini, later prominent in the *Lega Nazionale*, which sought conciliation in the decades after Porta Pia, also thought it unwise for the Subalpine Parliament to have voted for making Rome the capital. What Cavour wanted, Jacini wrote in 1863, was the use of moral force, not physical pressure, to acquire Rome by means of conciliation. Jacini advocated an international guarantee for Rome. The city itself would remain under the Pope. Since the French would probably stay there, there was little chance in any case of acquiring Rome.[31] But when, in 1864, the September Convention stipulated that the capital would be moved to Florence, Piedmontese fears became realities. The dominance of Turin was over, and it was this fear, as one deputy wrote Crispi in 1860, which had been driving the parliamentary majority crazy.[32] Riots broke out, sparked not only by regional susceptibilities but by the economic crisis as well, caused by the new taxes needed to pay the costs of the national struggle.[33] Prominent among the pamphlets attacking the September Convention were those of Piedmontese authorship. Some expressed the suspicion that the Convention was a prelude to the cession of Piedmont to France.[34] Jacini was grieved by the loss of Piedmontese leadership, so essential to the keeping of order in the midst of revolution. By 1870, however, he recognized that the cause of federalism had broken on the rock of national unity. Nonetheless, until his death in 1891 he regretted the transfer of the capital to Florence and then to Rome and continued to speak for administrative decentralization and conciliation with the Vatican.[35]

Parliamentary debate on the regional question did not stop. But the fear of compromising national unity was too strong. Many of the suggestions proposed were also vague, and with the occupation of Rome the Roman Question was to complicate the issue. All the pre-1870 schemes for a neutral state were ruled out by the Pope's insistence on the temporal power. Pius IX had confided to others his own reluctance to repossess the estates of the Church. These, he said, he would refuse even if they were offered to him. But at least a *petit coin de terre* was essential for the full exercise of his spiritual functions.[36] These minimal territorial requirements of the Papacy after 1871 made conciliation impossible. And since many conservatives were obviously looking for an accord with the Vatican in order to use the Church's power as a political weapon against revolutionaries, many federalists of radical and republican persuasion began to question the wisdom of weakening the national framework as it existed.

Much of the literature between 1860 and 1870 that was devoted to the liberal Catholic position (which sanctioned Italy's nationalism but wished as well to placate the Vatican) included in its program some sort of federalism. Moreover, following 1870, France appeared the chief European champion of the Papacy. Patriots recalled the ideas, attributed to Napoleon III, which appeared in 1859 under the authorship of Viscount Arthur de La Gueronnière. At that time, prior to the plebiscites, the Emperior rejected unity as impossible because of the presence of Austria, and suggested an Italian federation under the Pope. Following the invasion of the Romagna, an anonymous pamphlet — attributed to the French ruler but actually the work of Count Persigny, the Minister of the Interior — conceded the loss of the Papal States. But Italy was still to be federal, Rome guaranteed by the European Catholic powers.[37]

Intransigent clerical writers also tended to stress the incompleteness of national unity, the historic regionalism of the Peninsula. This did much to create a patriotic opposition to any sort of decentralization. It was true, however, that the rapid extension of Piedmontese laws and institutions to the whole Peninsula was resented by many who were equally opposed to clericalism. The regional and federalist issue remained. It was another dissident current, a reason for dissatisfaction with the outcome of the Risorgimento. In particular, as will be seen, the Southern Question became a constant reminder of the insufficiencies of the Postrisorgimento. There was something unplanned and often unwanted in a regime thrust upon Italy by the force of circumstances. And in Italy, unlike France, no one city had ever established its primacy in the Peninsula. Rome was undeniably a Risorgimental ideal which had been fulfilled; but to make it a center of economic, political, and cultural life was not in keeping with Italian tradition. There was a tendency to see bureaucratic delays, taxes, and Parliament itself as results of the somewhat artificial imposition of Rome upon the more traditionally communal pattern of Italian life.

As for Sicily in the decades following unification, movements for regional autonomy cropped up, but they did not have the support of the majority of the people. Nonetheless, the outbreak in Palermo was indicative of a lingering resentment that was felt not only by the brigands, whose activities were obvious in 1866, but also by the educated and patriotic classes.[38] The truth was that unification had created economic burdens unfamiliar to Sicilians. In 1860 taxes on real property amounted to 7,676,000 lire. By 1877 the figure had climbed to 22,000,000 lire. Confiscations of church properties were regarded by Sicilians as pure theft. The reaction of the lower clergy was not surprising. As for the general populace, lack of any affection for the National Government was demonstrated by chronic evasions of military conscription.[39]

The impact of unification on the South generally was no less pronounced. The Mezzogiorno paid a heavy price in the form of taxes. Italy had become the most heavily taxed nation in Europe by 1900, and a marvel of patience to foreign observers. By that date Italians were paying at a rate of 25 per cent on property and income, while the English were paying one-half that amount.

Despite material advances, the economic gap between North and South appeared to be widening from 1860 to 1900. The Basilicata between the years 1885 and 1897 had three times the number of seizures for tax arrears as had all the northern provinces. Yet the population of the Basilicata was less than 5 per cent of that of the northern provinces. In 1897 the same southern region had more deaths from malaria than all Northern Italy combined, although it comprised less than 2 per cent of the national population.[40] Education statistics reveal similar disparities. On the national level illiteracy did drop significantly, but a regional breakdown in 1901 showed a wide variation — from 17 per cent in Piedmont to 78 per cent in Calabria. Further, the statistics of literacy concealed large numbers of semiliterates, while the over-all decrease in illiteracy was less than one per cent a year.[41]

One of Italy's earliest investigators of economic and social conditions in the Mezzogiorno, Leopoldo Franchetti, noted that by 1873–74, while the middle class was undoubtedly strengthened economically, fourteen years of unity had entailed an incredible pauperization of the contadini and city poor.[42] Pasquale Turiello, who was to become the severest critic of the feebleness of the nation's solidarity, took note of the estrangement of the contadini of the Mezzogiorno from the Government, the result of worsening of economic conditions. The contadini, he reported, spoke of the good old days under "Franceschiello."[43] In assessing Turiello's opinions, one must take his political philosophy into consideration. His dislike for the liberal regimes of the Postrisorgimento, his antiparliamentary doctrines, prompted him to take a negative view of the new Italy. But his first-hand reports cannot be discounted. What he wrote in 1882 was no different from the reports Luigi Farini sent back to Cavour in 1860 during the first months of Piedmontese rule in the South.[44]

So it was muttered that things were "better when they were worse" — that is, before unification. Actually, while the Bourbon regime was an anathema to liberals like Gladstone, it was of necessity paternalistic. Its middle class, moreover, was rather blissfully free from taxation. Comparing the South with the northern and central regions in 1860, one finds that the South had a lower tax rate, a greater monetary circulation, and a bureaucracy half the size of that of Tuscany alone. If industry was lacking, enlightenment was repressed, and education was retarded under the Bourbons, the South also had paid heavily for unity.[45]

The effect of southern economic backwardness on federalist proposals was bound to be negative. In his study of the social, economic, and administrative problems in Sicily, published in 1877, Franchetti emphasized the material roots of Sicilian discontent. He did not, therefore, ascribe the troubles in the Island to domestic subversives, whether clerical, socialist, or anarchist. Franchetti also refused to find an easy way out in imposed dictatorship. Here he was in the tradition of Cavour, who, although prepared to use the Government's legal powers to ensure strict law enforcement, had on his death bed ridiculed those who would resort to the expediency of martial law. Just as Cavour had wanted to "moralize" the land by setting an example of justice and honest administration emanating from the Central Government, so Franchetti advised continued reliance on noninsular officials. Because of what he regarded as a highly individualistic sense of southern justice, which made it impossible to turn over the local bureaucracy to Islanders, he concluded in favor of more rather than less centralization.[46]

Nevertheless, very limited concessions to demands for loosening the tightly organized bureaucracy were made. The law of February 10, 1889, granted the power to communal councils in provincial capitals and in cities over ten thousand in population to choose their own mayors. This scarcely satisfied the opponents. When Giolitti formed his first government in May, 1892, he came before the Parliament with a platform of wide administrative reform. Demands for decentralization soon followed from both sides of the Chamber. Two of the most colorful orators of the extreme left, Edoardo Pantano and Giovanni Bovio, called for the liberation of those "vital forces" latent in the provinces, forces that had been stifled by the system created in the 1860's. Italy, said Bovio, had become fat and sickly under the power of Rome. Moderates, headed by Tommaso Tittoni, later Premier and Minister of Foreign Affairs, insisted that the new law of February, 1889, be extended to all communities. He also pointed out that Italian governments were getting an undeserved reputation as manipulators of local elections. Even though this was not the case, people tended to believe it because of the close ties that existed between Rome and communal administrations.[47]

The chief spokesman for federalism, Pietro Bertolini, had a conservative voting record during the upsurge of conservatism which came in the 1890's. Yet he, too, joined the forces pressing for reforms. In 1892 he traced the whole question of Minghetti's plans for the creation of local self-government, and summarized the factors that had forced the Government to abandon the idea in the 1860's. Now that Italian unity had been firmly established, however, he saw no reason why fear of compromising nationhood should operate against decentralization. Giolitti admitted that the plan for the election of the mayors should be studied, but advised that the powers which these newly elected officials would have should be carefully weighed. Here Giolitti touched on one of the chief causes of anxiety: the fact that local clerical groups exploited communal elections for their own ends while boycotting the national elections. This was an unwise argument. It emphasized a problem hopelessly beyond rapid solution and played into the hands of men who used such fears to create a sense of national insecurity on which to base very illiberal programs. Giolitti saw that all too soon. When answering Bertolini, he studiously avoided the question.[48] And it is notable that after 1892–93, his first ministry, he never raised the issue again.

The situation was complicated in the winter of 1892 by the first reports from Sicily of the widespread discontent among the sulphur miners, and of the formation of the Sicilian *Fasci*. By the time Giolitti's government fell, largely because of the Bank of Rome scandals, the unrest in Sicily had become the chief topic in the Chamber. With what amounted almost to desperation, the Deputies turned to the aging Francesco Crispi, a native of Sicily. His government, established in December, 1893, lasted until 1896, when the defeat at Adowa finally ended his sway over the nation. In this three-year tenure Crispi, who himself in 1886 had made bold speeches calling for the liberation of the Sicilian poor from the oppression of the middle class, used military tribunals, troops, and censorship laws aimed at suppressing socialist, republican, clerical and anarchist propaganda. As if panicked by events in Sicily, the old Garibaldian called for a great unitarian party, a "Truce of God," which would save imperiled unity. He lashed out furiously against what he claimed were secessionist plots being hatched in Sicily. And as the unrest spread across the Straits and up the Peninsula, he wildly ascribed the whole crisis to the machinations of an unlikely combination of Italian anarchists and socialists, the French and Russian governments, plus the Vatican.

In reaction to what amounted to an unconstitutional regime, the radical elements of the extreme left, the same men who had done their best to ruin the Giolitti government, and who had joined in welcoming back the old hero to power, now turned on Crispi. As the debate became more heated, Crispi tended increasingly to fall back on his role as a maker of Italian unity, to refer to the Risorgimento as if it were still going on. He compared his methods with those used by Garibaldi in 1859–60, or those used to meet the Palermo revolt of 1866. To the objection that higher interests, the wars with Austria, had demanded stern measures which could scarcely be justified in 1893, Crispi simply did not reply. He claimed he had documentary proof to support his charges of socialist-anarchist intrigue. When the leaders of the extreme left demanded to see it, they were held off with the pronouncement that "Francesco Crispi has never told a lie in his life." Felice Cavallotti, the artist-politician bard of the dwindling democratic faction — later to become Crispi's bitter enemy — compared his policy to Napoleon III's "Crime of December 2," and told Crispi that despite his great past services to the nation he was dreaming of an age that was no more.[49]

The incredible authority that Crispi held, by virtue of his grand manner and his historical role, enabled him to override all logical objections. But the debates themselves show that his fears were quite unrealistic. It was clear, even from speeches of observers who voted for Crispi's government, that the Fasci had risen spontaneously. The Socialists had had nothing to do with starting the movement. Giuseppe De Felice, leader of the southern Socialists, had gone to the Island, where Crispi had him arrested despite his being a Deputy. But in the Chamber his fellow Socialists, a handful of men by 1894, cited facts to prove that Crispi's description of the unrest in Sicily was alarmist, that they, the Socialists, had done much to restore order among the Fasci and would have eventually calmed down violent factions in the Island had not the Government resorted to brutal and unconstitutional means. They also protested their unswerving loyalty to a united Italy, denying as well that there was any tangible evidence of a separatist movement among the Fasci. No less a moderate than the Marquis Di San Giuliano, Minister of Agriculture in the Giolitti cabinet and a Sicilian, agreed that the basic cause of unrest was economic and social, although he did feel that the Socialist party had tried to exploit the chaotic situation after the Fasci had arisen.[50]

As long as Crispi dominated the Chamber there would be no concession to decentralization. Even though many of its advocates were quite conservative and willing to support his government generally, the fears that seemed to possess the mind of the aging statesman, his apparent conviction that Italian unity was at best a shaky and incompleted thing, ruled out any administrative reforms. When, in March, 1896, the old patriot fell from power, never to return, the new premier, Antonio di Rudinì — a man who represented the oligarchic traditions of the old Destra — extended the law of February, 1889, to all communes. Rudinì spoke of this as a return to the ideas of Marco Minghetti. But farther than this no government would go. The same issues that had been raised against federalism since the 1860's were still being voiced. In 1896, when the anti-French policy of Crispi was being dropped by his successors, and with it one of the favorite Crispian arguments against decentralization, Bertolini continued to find that the fear of weakening the nation in the face of domestic clerical and radical propagandists overrode all his arguments in favor of changes in the bureaucratic structure established in the 1860's.[51] During the crisis of 1898–1900, marked by a new outbreak of violence stemming again from economic problems, these same fears were used to justify the harsh policies of General Pelloux. Sidney Sonnino, who from the floor of the Chamber managed Pelloux's attempt to crush the constitutional opposition by means of royal decrees, defended the Government against charges of tyranny. Neither he nor Pelloux, said Sonnino, was a tyrant. The real threat to liberty came from the collectivist radicals and the theocratic clergy.[52]

It is clear that the regionalist question could give rise to decidedly authoritarian political responses, frequently the product of a sense of national insecurity. This tended to confirm the radicals in their belief that the Postrisorgimento was a betrayal of the popular forces of democracy, socialism, or republicanism. There were, however, excellent arguments in defense of the existing system which were not necessarily justification for illiberal policies and theories of government. In answering his critics in the Chamber, Giolitti had observed that Italy was simply not ready for decentralization in 1893. Its effect, moreover, had it been achieved in the 1860's, would have been to place extra financial burdens on the provinces and communes while depriving backward areas of public works projects without which they would not have progressed as rapidly as they had. His passing reference to backward areas was quickly taken up as offensive to the South by Napoleone Colajanni, one of the most tireless southern radical orators in the Chamber, showing just how delicate regional sensitivities had become. But Colajanni had little concrete ammunition with which to counter Giolitti's position. It was obvious that however insufficient the Government's labors for southern development had been since 1860, much had been achieved which would have been highly improbable under a federal system. Colajanni therefore shifted his attack to the Giolitti government's suppression of civil liberties, a charge which was almost always linked to the attack on centralization.

In his parliamentary reply, Giolitti defended the use of existing laws to prevent violence, maintaining that exceptional measures were quite unnecessary. He also upheld the right to strike, petition, and peacefully demonstrate. Quite unlike many conservatives, he insisted that the extent of disorder in Sicily had been exaggerated. In two memorable speeches to his electors, the Premier, as if answering those who condemned the age of the Postrisorgimento as lacking a heroic imprint, paid his respects to the generation that made Italy but emphasized that the more modest task of consolidating its structure through attention to primarily material challenges was no less important. The material welfare of the country was a great coefficient of moral and political progress. Giolitti continued to call for progressive legislation, graduated income taxes, and increased inheritance taxes, while at the same time defending civil liberties against those who would respond to the violence of the Fasci by methods that would deny the necessity for the growth of democracy. Given the existing political situation, he warned Italian liberals to be on guard against unpleasant surprises.[53]

Defenders of centralization could also be found in men whose writings emphasized the economic disparities between North and South. Outstanding among these was the future premier, Francesco Nitti. Nitti's economic studies of the problem concluded that the costs borne by the South were fully justified by the fact that unity had been reached, as it would not likely have been without the leadership of the North.[54] To the claim that all this leadership came to was Piedmontese aggrandizement, there was the ready answer — one which Giolitti had confronted Colajanni with — that northern voters had had to be reminded that they were expected to pay for a national program. It was apparent that Piedmont had also renounced northern interests, dynastic and otherwise, by accepting the challenge of total unification. If inhabitants of the former Bourbon kingdom were forced to help pay the bill for a national unity too few of them wanted, Piedmont as well made great material sacrifices.[55]

From the vantage point of a century of Italian unity, the essential wisdom of the solution of the 1860's can be defended. Considering the diplomatic situation of the times, the need for swift action, seizing the moment which might never return, it is hard to find a plausible alternative. What is defensible in retrospect, however, has no weight when dealing with the doubts of many political figures of the Postrisorgimento, doubts which deepened as all attempts to relax the bonds holding the nation together were thwarted. It was these doubts, often expressed in passionate parliamentary and journalistic rhetoric, that were to have such far-reaching effects on Italian political history after 1870, particularly in regard to the waning prestige of the parliamentary system of government among many highly educated Italians. That there was a link between the regional question and the Chamber's reputation had already been grasped by Tittoni. With the extension of the prefectural system throughout the Peninsula and Sicily, the cry for a federal structure allowing local autonomies — as distinct from true regionalism, which had less and less backing after 1870 because of the unitarian ideal it would negate — often became equivalent to the demand for the destruction of what some looked upon as a parliamentary dictatorship based on a permanent majority recruited in the South. This charge was leveled at the Government by Stefano Jacini, a conservative Catholic layman; but it was also raised by influential politicians of republican and socialist convictions, notably Gaetano Salvemini and Arcangelo Ghisleri.[56]

The impact of the regional problem on conservative political theory was equally significant. Where the radicals, the federalists, looked on the prefectural mechanism as intrinsically undemocratic, conservative and authoritarian spokesmen saw nothing but national weakness resulting from the persistence of a historic provincialism. Something of this has been seen in Pelloux's and Sonnino's reaction to the 1898–1900 crisis. For men of the right, parliamentary government had promoted not too much centrality but rather a dangerous fragmentation, or at least allowed that condition to go unchecked. To Pasquale Turiello, for example, the essential problem was too little national cohesiveness. Turiello's views were to be influential not only on the philosophy of the Nationalist Movement of the Giolittian period following 1900, but on the theories of Gaetano Mosca.[57] Because of this, his ideas, and the related topic of antiparliamentary literature, will be discussed in detail in their proper place. But it is important to note that the problem of the regions had called forth programs from the political extremes which, however opposed in theory, shared a common opposition to the constitutional as well as the physical framework of Italy in the Postrisorgimento.

There is one more fundamental theme pertinent to the era of the Postrisorgimento that must be touched upon before proceeding to an analysis of Italian political thought. It, too, grew out of the Regional Question. Among those who regarded the unification of Italy as a "royal conquest" by the Piedmontese it was fashionable to add that the true Risorgimento had not been fulfilled — it was, indeed, still going on. Italy, Giovanni Bovio declaimed in the Chamber, was made by "gentlemen wearing white gloves."[58] The people were absent. The whole edifice after 1870, therefore, was false, lacking its proper roots. The period of the Postrisorgimento, for those who shared this feeling, was an age of waiting, waiting until the moment rolled around again at which the popular element could be fused with the nation as it existed in theory. In this theme of the "revolution that failed," moreover, one may discern the beginnings of a merging of extreme positions that were largely the outgrowth of the material problems thus far discussed, and which were to become the source of future political ambiguities.

The Revolution That Failed

The contrast between the "real" Italy, a product of history with its provincial characteristics and virtues, and the administrative system, a product of political expediency that had been put together in the 1860's, was a reflection of the more fundamental distinction between Risorgimento and Postrisorgimento. That basic cleavage was also to be reflected in a debate closely related to the Regional Question: that of Italy's diplomatic rather than revolutionary birth. Those Piedmontese administrative practices which were looked upon as a mechanistic humiliation of vital local forces could also be portrayed as a great net in which the nation's revolutionary flight and impetus were trapped and brought down to earth. Garibaldi's savage attack on Cavour in 1861 was not forgotten. The "Hero of Two Worlds" had charged the statesman with diplomaticizing the revolution. In the Chamber at Turin the Premier was accused of provoking fratricidal war. In the final moments of the Risorgimento the "nation in arms" was absent. Garibaldi spoke with bitterness of his legions being "put at the tail end." [59] As if to discredit by personal valor the government's lack of dynamic action, he went to fight for France in 1870, thus keeping alive the fire of action and revolution then symbolized by the Commune. At the same time, the Italian government was moving with diplomatic caution, taking Rome when France was beaten.

In truth, there had been little mass support for the national revolution. Of Garibaldi's volunteers, most were northern. In effect they were an elite, there being no contadini among the Thousand, and only twenty-eight Sicilians.[60] No attempt had been made to capture the peasantry for the Risorgimento. Mazzini neglected them prior to 1860. After that date he was reluctant to condone revolutionary action which would be aimed, now that unity had been achieved, at economic and social ends. In the years to come the Italian socialists also neglected the great bulk of southern agrarian workers.[61] It was this lack of a popular base for Italian political institutions that Count Sforza considered one of the country's fundamental weaknesses.[62]

It would have been unrealistic to expect anything other than a middle-class revolution. To lament the absence of the "people" in the creation of national unity, Salvemini and Chabod wrote in 1952, was unhistorical; for in no nineteenth-century nation did the people, if this includes the lower classes, participate in public affairs. Salvemini insists, however, that if the Risorgimento was a revolution, it was essentially a conservative victory in which the illegal, truly revolutionary impulse acted as a spur to legal, diplomatic action. The politicians and diplomats triumphed, and in so doing produced a vast change in the pre-existing situation. Hence, Salvemini would not accept the view that the Risorgimento was a revolutionary failure.[63]

But in the decades of the Postrisorgimento, this historical perspective was not likely to satisfy the longing to repair what many — including a younger Salvemini — believed to have been a defect of national unity. In time, a literature devoted to the question of whether the Risorgimento had been a royal war or a people's war took shape. Garibaldi became the symbol of the voluntaristic element in the nation's birth. His being placed at the tail end by the Piedmontese suggested a betrayal of the revolutionary spirit. Carlo Pisacane was to become another precursor of the populist concept of the nation. For Pisacane, national independence without liberty, and without the active participation of the masses, was useless. Better to remain under Bourbon rule than to achieve unity under the House of Savoy. At least the Bourbon reactionaries aroused men's passions; the rule of the Piedmontese would only deaden them. In his *Guerra combattuta in Italia negli anni 1848–49* (1850), the romantic patriot extolled the virtues of the people who had sparked the revolutions of 1848. He charged the Republicans with having prevented the spread of revolutionary socialist ideas among the masses. Charles Albert, invincible when backed by his humble subjects, had turned on them in fear. The monarchy at that point passed from "poetry to commerce." [64]

Pisacane's thoughts, imprecise as they were, changed significantly after 1850. The Bonapartist *coup d'état* in France, followed by the abortive Milan uprising of February 6, 1853, caused him to lose faith in the revolutionary virtues of the people. And yet, what was the nation to become without the masses? Pisacane turned to the ideas of Rousseau, proposing a *patto sociale* in which the immutable constitution would be established in accordance with the laws of nature. The creator of this eternal bond was to be the "genius legislator." Pisacane insisted that this was not to be a dictatorship. The role of the masses, however, had become that of a spontaneously revolutionary force, moved not by the love of liberty, much less democracy, but by purely physical wants. It was because of this that he placed his hopes in the peasants of the Mezzogiorno. In 1857, his quixotic revolutionary expedition came to a tragic end when the contadini, as well as the Bourbon troops, turned on him.[65] His death marked another failure for a people's war of national redemption. The collapse of the federalist solution to Italian unification, in which Pisacane also believed, came a few years later. In time the lonely hero of Sapri was to take his place in the ranks of the martyred prophets of a revolution that had failed.

After 1860 regional resentment of Piedmont served to perpetuate the idea of an unfulfilled nationhood. Local sentiments as well as economic hardships were behind the Palermo uprising in 1866. Romagna too became a center of resistance to central authority. Despite the fact that

Republican strength was waning, it became a badge of honor in Romagna to be placed on the police surveillance lists. It was recognized by anarchist leaders that much revolutionary activity in the Postrisorgimento was more than a reflection of increased economic burdens. One of these leaders, Francesco Merlino, writing in 1889, noted that the popularity of anarchism in Romagna was the result not so much of greater financial drain as of regionalist hatred for Piedmont. The Government, he wrote, treated Romagna like a conquered province. It and Sicily were Italy's two Irelands.[66]

The Republican party continued to call for action, for the "second revolution." [67] Popular revolutionary ferment, however, was for the Mazzinians too often tied to regionalism. Their unitarian tradition made it difficult for them to capture a great following after 1870. The decline of the Republicans as a party would be due in part to the appeal which the anarchists, with their opposition to the "State," were able to make to this anticentralist feeling, particularly in the Mezzogiorno.

The myth of revolution as an essential of national status remained a source of dissatisfaction with the Postrisorgimento. What was meant by revolution was clearly not the profound change in the political structure which had been effected under northern leadership, prodded by the daring of Garibaldi. What had taken place was an undeniable reality; for many, however, it was only a bureaucratic readjustment. What was lacking was the popular element. Because of this it was possible for dissatisfied spirits to seek means of utilizing the people, for the sake of the unfulfilled nation, which were not necessarily democratic, nor even political. Pisacane's pessimism after 1851, his ill-defined concept of the "genius legislator," and the permanent social contract that harnesses the masses to the nation are illustrative of one alternative. It was also possible to convert militant populism into war, which, like revolution, could be conceived as a mass undertaking for the consecration of the nation. The revolutionary failure, in the minds of some, and the wish to rub out the memory of Lissa and Custoza, could become interchangeable.

It is interesting to note that this equating of war and revolution was appreciated by foreign observers. In 1888 a dispatch from Baron Karl Bruck, ambassador at Rome, to Count Gustav Kálnoky, the Austro-Hungarian Minister of Foreign Affairs, contains a shrewd analysis of this problem, with a suggestion as to how the revolutionary impetus might be channeled into acceptable conservative paths. Vienna recognized Italy's need for a military victory. It was possible to fulfill this need and at the same time satisfy the revolutionary past of Italy's Premier, Francesco Crispi, by encouraging Italy to seek her outlet in Africa. What was to be avoided was anti-Austrian irredentism, in itself a part of the revolutionary drive of the Risorgimento. Crispi's radical past could be harmonized with the conservative nature of the Triple Alliance through war.[68]

Implicit in this policy is the recognition that war could be a substitute for political radicalism. In Crispi, an ex-Garibaldian, Vienna perceived the agent of a conservative siphoning off of revolutionary and irredentist energies. This was a very astute evaluation of Crispi's character. In fact, the revolutionary had embraced the monarchy as early as 1865, writing to Mazzini that the republic would divide Italy, the monarchy unite it. By 1888, he had already made his celebrated visit to Bismarck at Friedrichsruh. And in later years, looking back on Bismarck's policy, he would criticize the Chancellor for not having tried to promote a monarchical restoration in France. But it was also true that Crispi had told Mazzini that Garibaldi's war was a popular triumph over the Bourbons — that in the South the people alone had overthrown an ancient dynasty. While insisting on a unitarian rather than federalist solution, the Sicilian patriot spoke of his resentment of the plebiscite, which seemed to imply a supine yielding to Piedmontese annexation. "Our country must not *give* herself to another, must not *annex* herself, which verb savors overmuch of servitude." He advocated the use of Bourbon administrative and legal instruments as the basis for the united nation, rather than those of Piedmont which, despite the greater liberty of the North, were archaic.[69] For all of Crispi's conservatism, the strain of the southern regionalist remained, and with it the concept of a people's war which Garibaldi's expedition symbolized.

Crispi was to become ministerial, parliamentarian of necessity, and a defender of the monarchy. But, as will be seen, his vision of the military possibilities of the Triple Alliance betrayed his revolutionary, popular past. His role in the Postrisorgimento might be described as that of uniting the nation through mass military rather than political action. This urge for action which Crispi converted from revolutionary to diplomatic methods had its fascination as well for men who refused to abandon popular radicalism. Felice Cavallotti was to become Crispi's most outspoken critic. His democratic faith refused to bend to the cause of monarchy. Yet Cavallotti could speak in 1881 in terms no less illustrative of the conversion of revolution into war. Italy after fifteen years of unity still paid the bitter price of military failure. Until success in war came to her through some "bloody baptism," she would not have that place among nations worthy of her new destiny. Crispi had said much the same thing, and D'Annunzio would later add his poetic touch.[70]

It is worthy of note that the baptism of blood theme was present long before D'Annunzio and his cultural offspring in the art of irrational politics made their appearance. In the age of prose, the decades of Lanza, Sella, Depretis, and Giolitti, such phrases were not yet the common stock of the "humanistic petty bourgeoisie." The prevailing mood was one of material achievements, seeking the good and comfortable life. There was not that myth of action which had been described as one of the most dangerous aspects of Italian political life.[71] A thirst for action and violence was present, but only as a minor note. It remained for a new generation, born too late for the real revolution, to seize upon all the deficiencies of the age of commerce and clerks as fuel for the journalistic fires of national redemption.

What is apparent in the theme of a *rivoluzione mancata* is that the nation as legally constituted did not represent the country as embodied in the the people. How deep this sense of incompleteness went may be seen by turning from revolutionary to conservative spokesmen. Moderate voices of discontent were also to function as purveyors of dissident opinion. While rejecting the revolutionary or militaristic solution to Italy's ills, men like D'Azeglio and Jacini coined phrases that could be put to decidedly subversive use. D'Azeglio's oft-quoted remark — now that Italy was made, the job was to make Italians — could be turned to radical purposes. If the process of infusing the people of the Peninsula with a sense of the *patria* were to be one of war or revolution, or both, rather than progressive reforms, that epigram could become the motto of popularism as well. That it was not merely a rhetorical figure of speech, moreover, was clear. The Palermo revolts of 1866, Merlino's reference to Sicily and Romagna as Italy's two Irelands, the high incidence of desertion among the military, the apolitical discontent of the southern contadini — these realities gave substance to the statement.

The same may be said for another stock expression that became a catchword of the disillusioned. As in the case of D'Azeglio, the author was a conservative. Jacini was certainly not given to Crispian diplomatic melodramatics. We have seen that he opposed the transfer of the capital to Rome, as did D'Azeglio, and hoped to see federalism rather than administrative centralization win out in Italy. Later, when Crispi was Premier and Foreign Minister, Jacini wrote one of the principal attacks on the policy of seeking redemption through war, accusing Crispi of megalomania in politics and diplomacy, as well as with excessive anticlericalism. But in an earlier book, describing Italian political and social conditions after 1866, Jacini found that the nation rested on a false foundation. Despite economic advances, despite the fact that Italian unity was accepted by the powers, Italy, he wrote, was afflicted with "an indefinable, terrible sickness." Its cause was not to be sought in brigandage, in sporadic popular demonstrations. Italy was not in a state of rebellion, as some thought. Nor Did Jacini subscribe to D'Azeglio's views about the necessity of creating Italians. The problem lay, he felt, in the excessive centrality of Italy's administrative and parliamentary systems. "There is," he wrote, "a *real* Italy which is not the *legal* Italy." [72]

Incompleteness was felt by both radicals and conservatives. It was also a factor, as will be seen, in the ultraconservative doctrines that were later taken up by the Nationalist party in the Giolittian age. Jacini's catchword would be carried over into the new generation, where its function would be anything but conservative. A "real" and a "legal" Italy — or "official" Italy, as it would later be called — seemed to exist side by side. For those who shared the mentality of the continuing sense of revolution, who burned with a desire to return to Italy's origins (to borrow a phrase from Giovanni Gentile[73]), the job was to put the two together by some act of fusion that would fulfill the promise of the past.

The question was, what agency would effect this desired drawing of the people closer to the constitutional framework of government? Speculation on this subject was to produce political theories on both the right and the left which claimed to solve what their authors considered to be the great historical problem of modern Italy. Before turning to these theories, however, it is essential to look at the role of the Parliament itself, both as it existed in fact and as it was often seen by men who were dissatisfied with the results of the wars for Italian unity. Here was the constitutional mechanism which was the proper and legal vehicle for the growth of greater mass participation in Italian politics after 1870. However it, too, was to feel the effects of the dialogue between culture and society and the corresponding Italian clash between the memory of the Risorgimento and the existing climate of the present.

PARLIAMENT IN THEORY
AND IN PRACTICE

Parliament and Its Critics

No other facet of Italian politics served the critics of the Postrisorgimento as well as the parliamentary system. It became the accepted target for all who lamented the passing of the heroic age. Following unification, a vast quantity of antiparliamentary literature was produced. When the constitutional system was gone, those who sympathized with the dictatorship pointed to the early antiparliamentarians as precursors of fascism, as if they had seen the truth and formed a bridge between the Risorgimento and the new regime. Parliament, according to this view, was no more than a necessary experiment which had been tried because time was short, events were pressing. Italy had not had the chance to work out a form of government suitable to her particular needs and traditions.[1]

As Croce has written, had the Italian antiparliamentarians looked about them, they would have seen that the system was being subjected to the same sort of criticism everywhere in Europe. Intellectuals were bemoaning the decline of noble ideals, the absence of moving oratory which had once vitalized the representative assemblies of the Continent.[2] It was true of most Italians who were hostile to parliamentary government that they failed — either because their primary concern for Italian problems narrowed their vision or because they were blinded by frustration — to examine realistically the functioning of their own institutions. Invidious comparisons drawn between the Chamber of Deputies and the House of Commons seldom pointed out that there were sessions of the Commons which were no better attended than those at Rome. That English politics revolved around a clear-cut party structure was assumed.[3] Since the failure of two-party government in Italy was a source of much criticism, the prestige of the Chamber would have benefited had the English system been investigated. And as for its legendary corruption, Italian politics was at least a cut above the "era of good stealings" which followed the Civil War in the United States.

Foreign visitors to Italy noted from the outset of the Postrisorgimento that the critics of Parliament were given to unreasonable faultfinding. Émile de Laveleye, an experienced student of Italian affairs, found it strange that so many influential Italians were dissatisfied with the regime. Italy, he wrote in 1870, was blessed by the absence of any dynastic party struggle, quite unlike France. All factions accepted the House of Savoy, with the exception of the Republicans, and they were losing ground. There was neither a clerical nor a legitimist party to worry about. Yet this good fortune — for so it seemed to the Belgian observer — was looked upon as the very cause of Parliament's failure to function properly. For those who had Italy's real interests at heart and not her vanity, there could be no cause for complaint.[4]

To many Italians, however, less compromise and more drama would have been preferable. Those "radiant days" of Garibaldi and Cavour of which Carducci spoke exerted an understandable attraction, as the debates of the Chamber never could. It was simply not in the nature of parliamentary government to be "heroic." De Laveleye also put his finger on a very sore point when he wrote that had Italy won at Lissa and Custoza and taken Venice by force of arms, a military dictatorship rather than a representative government would have been established.[5] He was, of course, defending the parliamentary solution, but the implication was that the institution itself was the child of military failure and exceeding good luck. For a Deputy like Felice Cavallotti, who preached a resurgence of Italian greatness, a recapturing of the fervor of the Risorgimento, Parliament hung over Italy like a cloud, obscuring clear distinctions of politics and philosophy. Constant reminders of a greater age worked to create a vision of Italy's position and destiny with which the accomplishments of Italian governments after 1870 could not compete. It was especially true of the intellectuals, the journalists, that they were forming an almost literary view of an imagined nation which had little to do with the facts. Salvemini, one of the harshest critics of Giolittian Italy, could write later, once fascism had run its course and following his years of exile in the United States, that it seemed as if nothing could satisfy them.[6]

There were those, however, whose objections to the way Parliament functioned had nothing to do with a desire for military victory, for a "test of arms and blood." Jacini was one of the earliest to examine the question of Italy's institutions. The Northern conservative was a foe of those who demanded an aggressive foreign policy, or spoke of the "Roman mission." His strong regional attachment, his belief in federalism, made him critical of the excessive centralization imposed on Italy by the Chamber of Deputies. Part of the "indefinable illness" he observed in Italian politics he attributed to the artificiality of centralized government. His plan for administrative decentralization would, he hoped, lessen the concentration of power in Rome. Jacini proposed a system of local assemblies which would be chosen by indirect universal suffrage. Illiterates would be chosen by indirect universal suffrage. Illiterates would be admitted to the lists on the local level. Here their competency was assured by intimate acquaintance with their own milieu. One of the benefits that would result from this reform, according to Jacini, would be the drawing of the people, the "real" Italy, into the orbit of the nation's public life. It was significant that Jacini also linked the regime to Italy's military failures. Had the wars of the Risorgimento been won, a federal rather than a centralized system would have followed. Although he rejected any dictatorial solution to the problem of Italian politics as being inconsistent with the liberal ideals of the Risorgimento, it was clear that for the conservative federalist the existing government was an expedient born of defeats on the battlefield.

Jacini, unlike the authoritarians and militarists, refused to condone a radical purge of the system. Moreover, he was not given to that sort of polemical and uncritical condemnation of Parliament. Rather, he offered a federalist alternative which would heal the sickness without destroying constitutional government. Jacini, setting down these views as early as 1866, also touched upon another facet of Italian politics. He recognized that the press had a penchant for constant and often unjustified criticism. Italians, he wrote, are prone to destructive faultfinding. To listen to the press, all Italian politicians were corrupt. The public grasps at every idle rumor. Jacini saw all too well that this sort of muckraking constituted a great source of danger to orderly government, encouraging disrespect for "legal" Italy. One of the benefits of administrative decentralization would be to check popular belief in hearsay by giving the people a stake in local government where daily experience would breed a greater sense of responsibility. Irresponsible criticism would then subside.[7]

The derisive habit of the Italian press, however, was not to lessen as years passed. Resentment for "official" Italy seemed to increase. By 1889 Jacini himself was less moderate in his criticism of the parliamentary regime. While still maintaining his belief in true representative government, he rejected the pseudoparliamentary system that had been established in Italy as a falsification of the properly decentralized organization. What had come about was a ponderous bureaucracy that had not in fact killed off regional sentiments but only converted them into political clienteles, which were in turn exploited by politicians. The outcome was to be seen in unnecessary public works, superfluous railroad construction, and behind-the-scene political intrigues, which had become all too common. Public life was almost a closed circle, from which the people were excluded. Gone were the great ideals that had once inspired parliamentary debates. In the place of all that should be, a type of ministerial dictatorship ruled over Italy. Jacini's resistence to antiparliamentary cures for Italy's ills was weakening. He looked for some "farsighted and synthetic" mind, a new Cavour to restore Italian political life to its old luster.[8]

Jacini's views were in part the expression of the northern conservative's reaction to the loss of political control which followed 1870. He speaks in 1889 of a return to the cautious policy of the Destra,[9] the heirs of Cavour. But in one so moderate and generally reasonable in his criticism, the growing dissatisfaction is an indication of a deepening of the scorn for the parliamentary system between 1870 and 1890. When Jacini wrote of a decline in the great moving ideals of the past, he was but echoing Carducci's laments, all the more significant in a man of balanced judgment. Even he seemed to be taking on some of the characteristics of the hypercritical intellectuals whose excesses he had once condemned. And it was the intellectuals, not the apolitical population, who were fast creating an image of Parliament that would endure despite all positive achievements of later Italian governments. Representative institutions have little to recommend them to poetic fancies. From Lamartine to D'Annunzio the literati have taken delight in stirring up trouble with which statesmen must deal as best they may, armed with the weapons of politics, which often have little effect against the rhetoric of poets. In Italy, moreover, the picture of Parliament as a source of contagion and corruption was created not alone by the artistic community; prominent political figures also lent a hand in the steady devaluation of the Chamber. Frequently political reformers who believed in democracy unwittingly served its enemies, and their own, by joining the chorus of derision.[10]

That Jacini had become less willing to put up with the law's delay and the insolence of office during the first two decades of Italian unity testifies to a dangerous tendency to flee from reformism and towards idealized solutions. This shift was paralleled by a decline in general public interest in politics, as reflected by the circulation of journals and newspapers. The percentages of eligible voters using the ballot also fell off, although not drastically. The figure never went above 60 per cent in the late nineteenth century. But had Italian commentators looked abroad to other countries having similar forms of government, they would have seen this was not at all out of keeping with the nature of representative regimes.[11] In a country whose history had so ill prepared the people for political responsibility, it was not a bad showing. It was significant that among the generation of the Postrisorgimento there were few who viewed politics within this wider framework. A flight from realities was given added encouragement by the growing disillusionment of great personalities. Pareto left Italy, fed up, he said, with politics. Carducci had campaigned for the Chamber of Deputies in 1876 on the ground that it is one's civic duty to take an active role in politics. This was particularly true of intellectuals, he said. But in 1876 the Sinistra had triumphed, breaking the monopoly of the Destra. Politics still seemed vital. In 1882, on the other hand, Carducci refused to become a candidate. He could not, he told his backers, subject his untamed intellectual independence to the dominance of others.[12]

It was soon apparent that the victory of the Sinistra in 1876 was anything but revolutionary. Carducci's retreat from politics expressed the artist's disgust with what seemed a tarnishing of dramatic beauties which true political conflict engendered. A relaxing of political tensions culminated in 1882, when the chief of the victorious Sinistra, Agostino Depretis, came out with a bipartisan platform, inviting all liberals to join forces. This marked the official birth of the system known as *trasformismo*. In effect, it was not a new policy but the result of a parliamentary situation which had been obvious for some time. Depretis in 1882 merely recognized an existing reality. But his public confession that the age of party strife was over seemed to justify the loathing for politics on such a low key which many felt. Trasformismo, according to Carducci, was an "ugly word for an even uglier thing." [13] The poet's label soon became a commonplace among Italian intellectuals. It helped leave a stain on the reputation of Italian parliamentary government that survives to this day in the judgment of many prominent students of the period. Not infrequently, moreover, the era of trasformismo is linked to positivism, to the general decline of culture, and to the loss of ill-defined spiritual values, which many sensitive Europeans regretted.[14]

It would be well to examine briefly the process which gave rise to trasformismo. How much did the practice justify Carducci's attack? How much did the attack itself reflect an aesthetic view of politics, thereby encouraging a sinister current of dissidentism, sinister precisely because it was based on cultural and historical standards that could prove totally unresponsive to the facts of political life? The examination is also necessary as a background for the discussion of the many, often paradoxical alternatives to trasformismo, particularly those put forward by conservative spokesmen who insisted that the system instituted by Depretis was stifling Italian politics, depriving it of the always necessary vitality. In order to rid Italy of this pallid, anemic existence, a return to clear-cut party lines was considered essential. This, in turn, would require the formation of a conservative party to replace the fallen Destra. Because of the manner in which Italian unity was won, in particular because of the inescapable religious factors that emerged after 1870, Italian conservatives of all camps were obliged to work out theories of government and of society rich in ambiguities, and important for later devolopments in Italian politics.

For the development of trasformismo itself, one must return to the nature of government under the successors of Cavour. The energies of the Destra were directed primarily to the solution of administrative and economic problems. Under Lanza and Sella, the financial threat to the nation's existence was given top priority. To those who found this program mundane Sella, speaking in the Chamber in 1872, answered that progress had been made. Italy was never more productive. He asked whether his critics wanted a political life of constant street demonstrations. He was undoubtedly expressing the opinion of the majority of the population. The desire for peace in Europe and order with liberty at home was of greater importance to most Italians than a revival of the tumultuous clashes that had been so much a part of the Risorgimento. The new spirit was one of material interests, the fulfillment of immediate physical needs. It was true, however, that the Destra appeared more and more a narrow group, a political clique not only cut off from the people but excluding the representatives of the revolution from power, those men who, it was said, had bled for Italy. The opposition party, the Sinistra, spoke for the popular cause, but also for the Mezzogiorno, since the Destra's ranks were filled primarily by northern and central politicians. Those Southerners who were in the Destra were often converts to Piedmontese leadership. For many, the Sinistra seemed to represent the feelings of the lower classes, which were beginning to protest the rule of the "optimates." [15]

The elections of 1874 reflected this discontent. The Sinistra won 232 seats in the Chamber of Deputies, the Destra 276. Most of the opposition's strength lay in the South and in the Islands. Somewhat greater interest in this election was shown by a slight rise in the percentage of the franchised using the ballot, an increase from 45.8 per cent in 1870 to 55 per cent in 1874. In the course of the election campaign the Destra committed a breach of civil liberties by arresting twenty-eight prominent Republicans who had met at Villa Ruffi near Rimini. The move was impolitic not only because of the issue it provided the opposition but because the group's leader, Aurelio Saffi, had come out against violence, breaking with the anarchists, and had called for the common defense of the patria.

The Sinistra kept up its attack, concentrating on the Villa Ruffi scandal and on the hated macinato, which was taken as proof of the Destra's class favoritism. The ministry was also severely criticized for what was claimed to be its lenient attitude toward the Church despite the clerical threat to the nation. That the two major political factions were not as opposed on principle as this campaign oratory suggested, however, could be seen in 1876. When the Destra lost its grip on the majority, the vote that tipped the scales in favor of the Sinistra involved no fundamental split on policy but a defection of the Tuscan members of the Government's coalition for purely regional motives.[16] Neither party was at all solid. Local interests were divisive. Moreover, the method of election that was used until 1919, save for a brief experiment in the years 1882–91, was not likely to encourage the formation of national parties. Only one candidate was elected from each of the 508 electoral colleges. There being no proportional representation, the votes given the loser were never represented in the Chamber. This method retarded the formation of a more cohesive party structure, each incumbent deputy concentrating only on his own locality, building up a constituency that would assure his re-election. Jacini counted sixty ex-ministers who had been returned over the years and were Deputies in 1870.[17] Rather than organized parties, the political contests centered around these notables in each of the two major factions and, this in turn tended to weaken the majority's position, leading to frequent ministerial crises caused by individual defections.

In the elections of 1876, which were called after the vote ending the rule of the Destra, the Sinistra's power in the South was shown to be overwhelming. Of the 200 southern deputies returned, only four were in the Destra. Indicative of the great importance placed on the election was the rise of the percentage of those using the vote to 59.2. In France in the same year the figure stood at 74 per cent.[18] The Italian electorate was extremely narrow, some 2 per cent of the total population. Given the social and political background of the Italian people and the fact that the election of 1876 was viewed as a true revolution (having turned out the party of Cavour), the acceptance of the constitutional verdict by the monarchy and former majority was a significant victory for representative government.

Those who saw 1876 as a revolution were soon to be disillusioned. However bold the Sinistra in its attack while a party of opposition, its revolutionary spirit was soon tamed by the responsibilities of office. Times were changing. Debate was losing its grandiose, rhetorical character. Parliament mirrored the trend away from heroics and towards science, technology, fact. Garibaldi's political utterances were becoming a bit out of place.[19] Old revolutionaries like De Sanctis, Minister of Education in the government of the Sinistra, had already spoken out for the acceptance of the age of prose, and for that good sense which was in the best Italian tradition. Political compromise, rather than being a desertion of principle, was to be commended as a sensible search for the middle ground. Looking back on what we were in 1860, he said, and recalling the feelings and aspirations of those days, the present may pale. The abuses, the scandals of contemporary politics would once have been thought intolerable, provoking general indignation. The necessity of accustoming oneself to the real, if more ordinary, existence, however, has meant that the once lively sense of indignation has become a wistful smile that says, "this is the way things must be."[20]

It would be well to stop a moment to consider these remarks made in the Chamber by the patriot scholar. De Sanctis took stock of the growing desire for new things, and also of the manner in which this desire was being translated into doubts as to whether Italy's political institutions were satisfactory. His advice was to get on with the job, to stop wasting time in useless exchange of sarcasms. It has been said that in an age which failed to appreciate men of "large vision," the age of the "deftly corrupting Depretis," De Sanctis seemed to stand out against the general sterility, both political and intellectual.[21] This association between cultural tastes and political facts could have extremely damaging results for parliamentary government in Italy. One reason was that men who defended political liberty were also prone to ridicule their parliamentary leaders for their lack of cultural attainments,[22] thereby serving liberty's foes. Inasmuch as De Sanctis can be taken as his generation's chief spokesman for a revival of idealism — that is, the freeing of literary criticism from the excesses of pedantry associated with what was loosely termed "positivism" — it should be noted that he himself rejected this illicit mixture of art and political action, and along with it that sort of snobbery which discredited politicians merely for their literary shortcomings. De Sanctis represented the mentality that had come forth from the hard struggle of the Risorgimento, prepared to get on with the real, if less glorious, tasks ahead. In the ranks of the conservatives, as will be seen, this same realism distinguished Silvio Spaventa from a newer variety of theorist who was looking for violent rather than constitutional answers to the problems of the Postrisorgimento. Not by chance, the intellectual and political descendant of them both, Croce, published these speeches of De Sanctis in 1913, when young rebels who claimed to have inherited the tradition of the late critic were crying for more blood, unsatisfied by the Tripoli War.

The spirit of accommodation which trasformismo represented was already being felt before Depretis formally initiated the policy. The new outlook was in part an expression of the general reaction to the period of dash and flourish. As such it was a healthy indication of a wish to get to work, putting aside recollections of political strife which no longer corresponded to realities. It was obvious that the differences dividing the two parties before 1876 were more verbal than real. The Sinistra had attacked the majority party for its clerical sympathies. Yet Sella had been most insistent that Rome be occupied. Some felt he really belonged in the ranks of the Sinistra. Lanza had defended the rights of the civil authority as established by the Guarantees, particularly that of the *exequatur* which recognized the civil power in the confirmation of benefices, something the Church tried to avoid whenever possible. If infringements were overlooked at times in the interest of peace, in general the Destra's firmness represented a victory for the principle of civil law as defined by the acts of Parliament. In regard to the suppression of the theological faculties in universities and the extension of the law of 1866 disbanding religious orders to the city of Rome itself, concessions were made which irritated outspoken anticlericals of the Sinistra, such as Pasquale Mancini, who considered antipapalism a part of the Italian character. All in all, however, the Destra had been courageous in its defense of the rights of the civil authority,[23] and this in a period beset by great internal problems quite apart from the Church-State issue.

When the Sinistra triumphed, there was no radical shift in the matter of anticlerical legislation. The civil marriage bill, for which the Sinistra had pressed prior to 1876, was not immediately taken up. Proof of the fundamental agreement between the two parties on this question could be seen in the Vatican's attitude toward the election of 1874. When the

Catholic Congress met that year, there were those who suggested relaxing the *non expedit* which ordered Catholics to boycott national elections in order to support the conservative Destra, to prevent the rise to power of what appeared to be a faction imbued with revolutionary teachings. Reaction to this idea was negative. The Unità Cattolica expressed the opinion that the Destra was worse than the Sinistra. At least the latter was openly anticlerical. After the elections, the *Osservatore Romano* echoed this feeling. The language of Depretis was clear, unlike the fictions and hypocrisies[24] of the Destra. There was a firmness of purpose and a long-tried experience in the party of Cavour which gave its leaders a prestige and sense of duty not easily compromised. And in the political philosophy of Silvio and Bertrando Spaventa, the leading statesmen and theoreticians of the Destra, the "State" was in itself a metaphysical entity, standing not as a neutral force outside the individual but within him. This State was modern, having cast off the yoke of theology. There could be no conciliation with the Vatican, according to Silvio Spaventa, until the State was strong enough to parry all clerical thrusts.[25] This sort of political philosophy, of Hegelian origin, challenged Catholic theology with a new civil theology. To Catholic thinkers this was far more insidious than the strenuous but often inconsequential anticlericalism of the Sinistra.

Neither was there to be a significant change in military and foreign policy after 1876. The low military budgets of the Destra, necessitated by the chaotic state of Italian finances, had provoked the Sinistra, and particularly Crispi, into calling for a tougher diplomacy and a stronger military machine. Depretis, although a former Garibaldian, had left his revolutionary past behind him, as had De Sanctis. Essentially a calm and circumspect man, the leader of the Sinistra had that good sense which was ready for compromise and adverse to rapid shifts and starts. Nor was he interested in the "Roman dream," the imperial mission. There was also the fact that although the Sinistra was in power after 1876, the Destra's leadership was not entirely destroyed. In the field of foreign affairs especially, Visconti Venosta remained to give advice to the new government, instructing Depretis as to what he should tell the Chamber about the Balkan crisis of 1877. Until 1881, when Mancini took over the Foreign Office, Italian diplomacy was directed by the experienced representatives of Piedmontese bureaucracy. Visconti Venosta saw all too clearly that Italy and Europe needed peace. It was no time for the new nation to go about trying to make a name for herself. As for the crown, the King tended to tighten rather than relax his personal control over foreign policy after 1876,[26] checking any dangerous flights by the new "revolutionary" government of the Sinistra.

It was much to Depretis' credit that he recognized the realities of power and did not allow himself to be driven into perilous adventures abroad by more sanguine colleagues within his own party. When relations with France were strained, Crispi pressed for a German alliance. Depretis allowed him to go on his famous tour of Europe's capitals in 1877. Crispi's admirers made much of this bit of personal diplomacy, claiming as well that Victor Emmanuel was ready to fight for Italian honor, with Crispi as his trusted statesman. There was reason to believe, however, that the trip was a convenient way of getting an embarrassing critic out of Italy until things cooled down.[27]

The same caution could be seen in the Sinistra's handling of the Irredentist Question. This had become the chosen field of the radicals, in particular of the Republicans. Depretis was met by an outbreak of anti-Austrian demonstrations when he took office. Garibaldi lent his name to a press campaign for the recovery of Trent and Trieste. Since the great hero had run for the Chamber in 1874 as a Sinistra candidate, the moment was a test of the new ministry's authority. Depretis made it clear that his government would not tolerate such activity. The Destra took note, chiding the Sinistra, once so outspokenly irredentist, for its sudden awareness of the sobering influences of office.[28] When the Government passed from the hands of Depretis to those of the more radical Benedetto Cairoli, the moderate trend continued. Many would insist that it went too far. It was during the Cairoli administration that Count Corti went to the Berlin Congress, returning to Rome with his hands clean but empty.

In internal affairs, save for the 1877 law requiring three years of elementary education and the 1881 reform that increased the electorate from 600,000 to 2,000,000, the Sinistra's program was anything but revolutionary. The macinato remained, despite charges that it gouged the poor and favored the rich. When Cairoli's finance minister, Bernardino Grimaldi, realized that the nation's finances forbade its repeal, something the Sinistra had promised, he resigned, with the statement that arithmetic was not a matter of opinion. The phrase caught on; better than Carducci's public declarations, it reflected the down-to-earth spirit of the new age. The Sinistra, however, did not forget its promise. The macinato was voted out in 1880, repeal to take effect in 1883. The loss of revenue, plus increased military expenditures, ended the balanced budget left by the Destra. Taxes increased under the new regime.[29] Although the Sinistra had seemed the party of the poor, nothing could blot out the same harsh realities with which Lanza and Sella had had to deal in the days of the Destra.

The other burning domestic issue was that of political liberty. That it should be increased was a maxim of the Sinistra. In the national elections of 1876, however, the new minister of the interior, Giovanni Nicotera, seemed to be adopting the tactics of his predecessors. His removal, following public disclosure of illiberal activities which were reminiscent of the Villa Ruffi scandal, brought Giuseppe Zanardelli into the Cabinet. Zanardelli's political motto — repression but not prevention — was designed to grant the widest possible political freedom to all Italians. The theory of the watchdog state ran up against the same sort of problems that had curbed the Government's optimism in all other fields. An attempt on the life of the new King, Humbert I, and anarchist activity in Florence, made stricter police measures imperative. Depretis became anxious about the possible effects of the entry of the lower classes into politics. The Sinistra was accused of showing excessive tolerance toward subversives, and not all of these charges came from the opposition party. Depretis spoke out against theoretical conceptions of political freedom, advising a more elastic approach to the problem of liberty and authority.[30]

By 1882, political differences did not seem sufficient to maintain the ideal of a two-party system. Trasformismo seemed the best means of creating more durable government, drawing on all constitutional factions. It has been suggested that the real reason for the merging of Italy's historic parties was their common fear of the Republicans and of the rising socialist movements.[31] The Sinistra and the Destra drew upon the same middle-class elite. In the opinion of later Marxist critics, both camps were essentially authoritarian in spirit. The electorate was narrow and socially homogeneous. The nobility was disorganized. Great industrial magnates did not yet exist. The clergy was organized, and certainly conservative, but the *non expedit* theoretically placed them outside the sphere of national politics, however much they operated in local elections. Under such circumstances, a frankly conservative and openly progressive party merged into a large center group. Silvio Spaventa, even before 1876, had observed that for all their public rivalry the two parties were gathering together in a large center group, both conservative and progressive, monarchical and liberal, rejecting the extremes of political action.[32]

That the men who governed Italy feared the subversive elements of the extreme left is true. To see trasformismo as an authoritarian answer to revolution, however, seems hardly justified. To link it with the reactionary policy of General Pelloux which closed the nineteenth century, or with the fascist regime,[33] is to lapse into a rigid, partisan view according to which the middle-class "oligarchy" consciously frustrated all popular aspirations. In a nation which still knew the meaning of brigandage, with a population 60 per cent illiterate, it was neither economic exploitation of the poor nor political reaction to tread cautiously the path of that *buon senso* which De Sanctis, an old revolutionary, praised as being in the best Italian tradition. In truth, Italy did not experience true authoritarianism until the 1920's. One is constantly impressed by the degree of political liberty maintained by the Italian governments after 1870 in the face of the chaotic situation that the generation of the Postrisorgimento inherited. The Crispi and Pelloux intervals were exceptions. That the General left few admirers was partly due to the ambiguous nature of much conservative theory in Italy, which prevented open advocacy of one-man rule, as will be seen; but it is also an indication that the ideals of liberty which were so much a part of the Risorgimento were still widely held. If these ideals were at times set aside in the heat of the moment, as was the case in every representative government of the time, they were never discarded.

Parliamentary government in Italy had its share of corruption. De Sanctis, responsive though he was to the practical demands of government, took note of this. But his remarks make slim pickings for those who would conscript him for the ranks of fascist precursors.[34] It is impossible to prove that political corruption was more flagrant in parliamentary Italy than in other countries governed by representative institutions. On the contrary, there is much to indicate that the Chamber was relatively free of it. The major scandal of the Postrisorgimento, the Bank of Rome affair of the 1890's, which became synonymous with the name of Giolitti, did not involve more than a handful of Deputies, and then only for lapses that were often common practices in other lands. Nor has Giolitti's personal involvement ever been proved, while that of Crispi, the flamboyant patriot dear to nationalist and fascist theoreticians, is well documented. Giolitti's statement to the Chamber that no one, not even his enemies, could say that he profited from public office has never been seriously contested. Even such a frank apologist for fascism as Luigi Villari concedes that Giolitti was not motivated by financial greed. The reason was his petty bourgeois mentality.[35] According to this standard of values, basic honesty was no substitute for Crispi's verve and style. Private virtues had become public vices.

More than an organized political reaction to concrete deficiencies, dissatisfaction with Parliament and with trasformismo came to reflect the growing disgust many harbored for the new climate of opinion, so dull and listless after the idealism and self-sacrifice of the revolutionary era. Just as the vitality of the regions appeared to have been smothered by the bureaucracy of Turin, all political passions seemed depressed by a wave of cultural vulgarity. "The heroes," Oriani wrote, "became soldiers, the martyrs changed into clerks." [36] Positivism, equated with a crude and leveling democracy by Oriani and others, drove the "better minds," that is, those conscious of their superiority (unlike De Sanctis) into a sort of exile. Garibaldi and Mazzini seemed forgotten. The revolution had failed. The "people" were absent from the struggle for the nation. Italy was made by the "heroic imposition" of the few. The Italians were the conquered, not the conquerors. For Oriani, the result was a separation of Parliament from the country, the decline of parties along with all other political ideals.[37] His disciples would continue to associate trasformismo with the historical failure of revolution, with the cheapness of cultural life, the rage for positivism.[38]

Oriani predicted an idealistic revolt, championed by a new elite. Yet while he spoke of liberty as the end and guiding principle of history, and of Hegel as the greatest modern philosopher,[39] Oriani's liberty had little to do with the realities of everyday politics, the endless debates, budgets, and legislation that were the province of the Chamber of Deputies. The new revolution of better minds was never defined, but remained a vague expression of intellectual frustration, a feeling of disquietude. How in fact the idealized government was to function was never made clear. Only the longing for a spiritual liberation, for the return to fashion of ideals that the Postrisorgimento seemed to have cast off, emerges from his work. A dangerous contempt for official Italy was brewing among the intellectual avant-garde, in which culture and politics were being confused, the wistful smile of De Sanctis becoming a sneer.

During the last decade of the nineteenth century the appropriate object for this intellectualized attack on politics arrived on the scene in the person of Giovanni Giolitti. His name was to become synonymous with the Bank of Rome Scandals. However, inasmuch as he became as well the symbol of parliamentary government and of those middle-class values which were frequently bemoaned as a betrayal of culture, his career has a deeper significance. Long before fascist writers made him the epitome of all that their antibourgeois revolution would eradicate, he had already become the recognized evil genius of Italian politics, a man without scruples or erudition whose intimate knowledge of bureaucratic machinery had enabled him to fashion permanent parliamentary majorities by means of election rigging. The movement within Italy to purify the nation of this corrupting influence began in the 1890's.

The Giolittian legend, for such it was, took a firm grip on generations of Italians. Not even the painstaking work of scholars who later tried to correct this historical falsehood has been able to do more than loosen its hold. It is important to examine the evolution of this myth not only because of the impact it was to have on the formation of Italian political theory and practice, but also because many of Giolitti's contemporaries in the Chamber of Deputies and in the world of political journalism were passing through their own apprenticeship in the years when Italy was absorbed by the Bank Scandals. Their own contribution to the drama of the 1890's will have some bearing on later events. Lastly, it is fundamental to an understanding of the ideological debate over the nature of Italian unity as it existed after 1870 and as it ideally should have developed to witness the emergence of another legend, that associated with the great antagonist of the drama, Francesco Crispi.

Giolitti versus Crispi: The Evolution of a Myth

To speak of private virtues and public vices is not to turn a phrase; it is an accurate description of Giolitti's reputation among men whose appraisal of Italy's cultural and political progress during the Postrisorgimento was, and remains, negative. While it is true that the Chamber had already acquired its fame as a fetid place where all virtue languished in an atmosphere of accommodation, the striking thing to be observed was the almost automatic way this predisposition to condemn fastened on Giolitti when he became Premier in 1892. He was the living counterpart of that loss of ideals and glory which the artistic imagination had created. His staid, orderly life, representative of the Piedmontese rural gentry of which his family was part; his low-keyed domesticity, untouched by even the breath of scandal; his clerkish punctuality in office — these were no defense against the growth of the historical fiction according to which he was the cynical master of intrigue. Indeed, as Luigi Villari's disdain for mere private honesty suggests, Giolitti's philistine existence was in itself proof of his official guilt.

Working to encourage the propagation of the myth was his long association with the bureaucracy and professional politics. Giolitti was a politician, as distinguished from a statesman, the latter word in Italy and elsewhere being reserved for men of larger vision. In addition, he was marked from the outset of his career as a man of the Postrisorgimento. He was the perfect foil precisely because his life and personality fit so well with the tension between an idealized historical past and an inferior concrete present. In the Bank of Rome Scandals which dominated the political scene from 1892 to 1896 his suitability as the villain, regardless of tangible evidence, was matched only by the magnificence of Francesco Crispi in the role of the hero.

When Giolitti began the first of his five premierships in May 1892, he was an unvenerable forty-nine. Crispi was then a seasoned seventy-two. Giolitti's administrative experience dated back to the Lanza government in the days shortly after the occupation of Rome when he was a stripling in his late twenties. The appearance of this youngster had been the delight of cartoonists, who drew him wrapped in swaddling clothes. In the Chamber, when he became President of the Council of Minister, a post reserved for the ancients, he got much the same treatment. He quickly became the butt of sallies from the great orators of the extreme left, those tireless defenders of the heroic age. Matteo Imbriani-Poerio, replying to Giolitti's opening policy statement, congratulated the Premier on having survived his appearance before the Senate: he had expected an "infanticide." Felice Cavallotti thought that it would be fitting if some of that past greatness which he and others still cherished were associated with the new leader's name. Giovanni Bovio reminded Giolitti that he should expect the men of the generation which had made Italy to be more pugnacious than those who had no part in the nation's redemption, men who had not yet faced the "test of fire." [40]

It mattered not that these three were themselves Giolitti's contemporaries. With the exception of Bovio, a self-made man whose strident radicalism made up for the lack, they had fought for Italian unity and were recognized literary as well as political celebrities. Imbriani came from a family dedicated to revolutionary activity. He had joined the Thousand at the age of seventeen, fought with the regular army in 1866. Following this, he founded the irredentist journal *Patria degli Italiani* and the *Italia irredenta* society. He was also a minor poet. Cavallotti's biography reads as if he had planned it as a challenge to the very being of the Postrisorgimento. He, too, got to Sicily in 1860 with the Medici expedition. In 1866 he fought alongside Garibaldi. It was at that time that he met the elder Dumas, who launched him on a literary career that was eventually to include a translation of Strauss's *Life of Christ* and a dozen prose and verse dramas. Cavallotti's poetry won Carducci's praise. He was the poet *della bohème*, and managed to live up to the title. Like Imbriani, he was involved in frequent quarrels in defense of his honor. In 1898 he died on the dueling grounds outside Rome. Imbriani's end, no less romantic, came as he was speaking at the dedication of a monument to Garibaldi in 1897.

Giolitti had no credentials save the ink stains won fighting the battle of the budget under Lanza and Sella. Whereas Cavallotti was feted as the Bard of Italian Democracy, Giolitti was known as "Monsieur Travet," or "Old Frock Coat." By popular agreement he was totally ignorant of literature and the arts. The favorite illustration of this was, and still is, his one attempt to quote Dante in a speech before the Chamber — and then he made a mistake. In truth, he was an excellent speaker, ready of wit, in command both of himself and of the facts. But to find Giolitti's talents one must leave the world of art and war and enter the parliamentary arena. It was here that he was at home, and where he sought to make others at home. To Giolitti, the Parliament was Italy. When he spoke of his country's history, Italian liberty began not in 1860 or 1866, but in 1848,[41] the year of the Constitution and the Subalpine Parliament. For the "new man" there was no break in the continuity of Italian history, there was no concept of a Postrisorgimento. The Chamber and the *Statuto* formed the bridge which connected generations past and present, and which would serve to embrace those yet to come.

The program which Giolitti had announced to the Chamber in 1892 was attacked as being too modest, to which he replied that it was in keeping with the realities of the moment. To the Young Turks, led by Cavallotti, he pointed out that if they insisted on rhetoric in place of facts, they should vote against his government, while keeping in mind that rhetoric never saved a nation. How quickly the stage was set for the clash between the new Premier and his critics could be seen by Cavallotti's glib reply, that worse than rhetoric was the "empiricism of practical men" who thought to solve great problems with little means. What Giolitti had recommended were new economies, a limitation on military expenditures consistent with national security and the country's financial resources, a reform of the tax structure plus legislation that would give precedence to civil marriage over the religious sacrament. He contemplated a deficit of fifty to sixty million lire for the coming fiscal year, yet rejected current pessimistic prophecies by noting that Italy had made great strides since the days when deficits ran as high as 485,000,000 lire.[42]

This platform was anything but unrealistic in view of the economic crisis then brewing. A decline in farm prices, beginning in 1882, had reached alarming proportions by 1890. Emigration statistics reflected growing discontent among the poor peasantry, climbing from 83,000 in 1886 to 100,000 by 1890. The situation was aggravated by the collapse of the building boom in Rome, which had strained Italian credit institutions and which was to play a part in the coming Bank Scandals. Once the capital had been moved from Florence, Rome's population rose from 200,000 in 1870 to 400,000 in 1890. Land values soared from fifty cents a square meter to fifty lire. Entrepreneurs were more confident than some statesmen that the city would remain Italian. Loans were made to construct one floor of a dwelling, which was then mortgaged to finance the second story. In order to expand credit, banks — particularly in southern Italy — tended to carry notes, the famous *sofferenze* of the Scandals, far beyond any justifiable term. To make matters worse, the six emission banks, those empowered to print Italian currency, were at war with one another. The stronger banks, notably the National Bank, sought to gather up as many notes of a rival bank as possible and then demand payment. This unmanageable system had almost ruined the Tibernian Bank, which had been bailed out by the Crispi government in 1889 when Giolitti was Minister of the Treasury. But the Bank of Rome was in similar straits and during the building crisis was to be very hard hit.

All competent students of the problem realized the need for new banking legislation. Giolitti, speaking in the Chamber on May 5, 1892, when Antonio di Rudinì was still in power, insisted that economies without a reorganization of the banking system would be useless. It was Giolitti's speech which helped bring down the Rudinì government. It lost a vote of confidence by the slim margin of eight votes. This proved to be almost the same margin which gave Giolitti his first uneasy victory once he had taken over.[43] It was clear, therefore, that he did not possess any following at the outset of his administration. It was also generally known that King Humbert was not happy with Giolitti's political philosophy which he found excessively liberal. When the King asked Crispi during the interval after Rudinì had fallen whom he would recommend, the aging patriot began by painting a bleak picture of Italy's future. Things were worse than after Novara; men talked as if economies were the answer to a moral crisis which amounted to a loss of national confidence. Crispi reminded the King of the Kaiser's error in sacking Bismarck. The King got the point, but Crispi modestly declined. He was too old, and never really thought of himself as a likely successor. As for Giolitti, he lacked "education, experience and knowledge of the administration." [44] Despite this damning verdict, and perhaps to Crispi's surprise, Giolitti was given the task of forming the new Government. Many believed that the Minister of the Royal House, Urbano Rattazzi, Jr., son of the Premier of the 1860's, had induced the King to swallow Giolitti.

Since Giolitti had been trained in the administration, he was a logical choice for a job no other leading political figure relished. Crispi's opinions could scarcely have dented the man's reputation as a skilled and knowledgeable bureaucrat, which was just what was needed. Anyone connected with government knew that the banking structure had been allowed to deteriorate over the past decade. Giolitti's tragedy, however, was that his energetic attempts to do something about it were to uncover startling facts that ended in making him the victim of his own determination to save Italy's financial credit before it was too late. On June 9 he asked for six months' provisional power to deal with the recession. On the next day, in a Chamber still 80 per cent full, he won a clear vote of confidence, 261 to 189. The Chamber then recessed. New elections were scheduled for November, elections which were to be the source of Giolitti's undeserved notoriety as the buyer of corrupt politicians.

When the new Chamber assembled on November 23, 1892, debate was opened on the Government's budget. Although the discussion was heated on the question of increased unrest in Sicily, prompted largely by a rapid decline in the price of sulphur, everything seemed to indicate that Giolitti would be able to carry through his financial program. Aware that the opposition minority, the extreme left, led by Napoleone Colajanni and Giuseppe De Felice, spokesmen for the Sicilian miners and peasants, threatened to tie up the Chamber in a discussion of fraudulent elections, Giolitti demanded that debate be directed to real issues, not sidetracked by personal rancor. Above all, he singled out the need for tax reform, asserting that a democratic country could not afford to have a tax policy which was "progressive in the reverse," that is, one which hit lower-income groups the hardest. To clear the air immediately, putting all on record, he asked for a vote of confidence and won a striking majority, 296 to 82. [45]

This was December 15. The Christmas vacation was approaching. Rumors of grave irregularities in the Bank of Rome's books had already hit the domestic and foreign press, causing an outflow of gold as Italian currency became suspect. During the summer vacation, the Government had extended the emission powers of the banks, which were due to terminate, for six years by royal decree. But the decree had to be sanctioned by the Chamber according to proper parliamentary procedure. Unless some temporary legislation were enacted before the vacation, Italy on January 1, 1863, would not have a parliamentary sanction for its new currency. Giolitti therefore requested the Chamber to grant a three-month extension of the old banking law. This would carry the banks through until spring, and also give the Deputies a chance to debate the six-year bill in detail. Giolitti noted that his government had found the need for a careful investigation of the banks.

These proposals were greeted by lively applause. Unquestionably the great majority present recognized the Government's intention of getting at the root of the matter. All this was about to change, however. On December 20, the Scandal was exploded in the Chamber by Colajanni and Lodovico Gavazzi, a new Deputy. The latter was a member of the important center faction headed by Sidney Sonnino and supported by Sonnino's close friend, Antonio Salandra. Colajanni revealed the existence of an investigation of the banks made in 1889 during the Crispi regime by Senator Giacomo Giuseppe Alvisi. At the time, Giolitti, as Minister of the Treasury, had also loaned a young member of his staff, Gustavo Biagini, to the Government in order to assist Alvisi. The two of them had drawn up a report which showed the emission banks to be grossly mismanaged, having been allowed for years to print currency far in excess of the limit set by the law. According to Colajanni, when Alvisi had tried later to tell the Senate about this, he had been hushed up by the Rudinì government. Gavazzi, for his part, insinuated that Giolitti must have known all about the Alvisi-Biagini report, since he, together with Luigi Miceli, formerly Crispi's Minister of Agriculture and Commerce, had been responsible for the bank bill of 1889. Gavazzi wanted to know how Giolitti, upon becoming Premier, could have selected Bernardo Tanlongo, the Governor of the Bank of Rome, for the high honor of Senator of the Realm, knowing the truth about the bank he headed. The naming of Tanlongo Senator, for which Giolitti accepted full responsibility, was to become the one fact on which the rest of his crimes rested by implication. Gavazzi demanded Giolitti's word of honor that none of this was true before the Chamber would consider his request for a three-month prorogation of the emission powers. With Colajanni, he called for a full-scale parliamentary investigation.

In reply, Giolitti let it be seen that he was incensed by undocumented and slanderous innuendo, by the assumption that he would lie in order to get his request through the Chamber. He warned the Chamber of the evil effects of a "current of defamation" which some were trying to import from abroad, a reference to the Panama Scandals which had just broken in Paris and which had already hurt the prestige of the Third Republic. Giolitti flatly rejected a parliamentary inquest and challenged the opposition to vote against a government it did not trust.[46] He had no fear of being defeated, however, for the obvious reason that no one wanted to replace him at the time, as shown by the fact that men who were later to be Giolitti's most bitter enemies spoke out against Colajanni's demands for a parliamentary investigation. Luigi Miceli, whose office had been responsible for administering the banks in 1889, conceded that Alvisi and Biagini had at first found serious irregularities in the Bank of Rome. In order to check this, the Government had authorized another inspection, under a certain Antonio Monzilli. Monzilli, according to Miceli, proved to everyone's satisfaction that the facts uncovered by Alvisi and Biagini were not true. This was an absolute lie, as will be seen. Crispi also rose to defend the Government against the demand for a full political inquest. It was no time, he said, "for a Committee of Public Safety." Rudinì, always a likely candidate for the Premiership should Giolitti go down on a vote over the bank issue, made a plea for avoiding a vote of confidence. Giolitti, not wishing to elevate the Scandal to the proportion of a cabinet crisis, asked for a vote granting the government authority to investigate the whole matter. He won an overwhelming mandate, 316 votes to 27. On December 30 the Government appointed a commission to make a thorough check on the banks.[47]

As was so often the case with noted scandals of the times, the source of the problem was less outright cupidity than a combination of fear and stupidity. In the background was a decade of incredibly slipshod regulation of the emission banks, and the practice, begun as an emergency measure to uphold Italian credit, of allowing the banks to go over their legal circulation limits. The practice got so out of hand that no government could reform the abuse without discrediting Italian currency at home and abroad. That this was the history of the problem was made quite clear by the speeches in the Chamber, speeches which amounted to attempts by each former minister involved to prove his own innocence. Miceli,

Crispi, and Rudinì all told the same story. Most revealing was the explanation of Bruno Chimirri, Rudinì's Minister of Agriculture and Commerce: from his remarks it was equally apparent that the banks had possession of the plates and control of their own printing presses, so that it was possible to counterfeit legal currency without the Government's finding out. Unfortunately, this had been done, and it was Giolitti's lot to uncover the guilty parties.[48]

Colajanni was absolutely correct about the existence of the Alvisi-Biagini report and about the Government's attempt to keep it quiet. Alvisi, a hard-money man, had been so upset that he broke the news in the Senate in June, 1891. He was told by Luigi Luzzatti, at the time Minister of the Treasury, to remain silent for the sake of the nation's financial credit. Alvisi died a few months before Colajanni exploded the Scandal. What is interesting is Colajanni's source of the truth. By his own admission, he was given a copy of the Alvisi document a few moments before he entered the Chamber on December 20. The copy belonged to Leone Wollemborg, a colleague known for his work in favor of agrarian banks and farm cooperatives, a Deputy not likely to favor the big banking interests.[49] Wollemborg's source is more significant, however. He got the report from the noted Republican and free-trade economist Maffeo Pantaleoni and from his friend and collaborator on the *Giornale degli economisti*, Vilfredo Pareto.

The connection these two had with the Scandals is interesting in view of their later careers. As for Pareto, soon to leave Italy in disgust, the fame of his theories and their impact on parliamentary traditions is well known. Pantaleoni (who was later made a Senator under Mussolini) was to become an ardent anti-Giolittian, especially at the time of the Great War, when he favored Italy's entry. By 1892 both had become convinced of the Giolittian legend, even before the new Premier had had a chance to enact any of his legislative proposals. Pareto and Pantaleoni, in fact, were responsible for the confusion which did so much to strangle any effective reform legislation, reducing the Chamber to chaos and preparing the way for the man of energy, Francesco Crispi. The voluminous correspondence between the two economists reveals the expected contempt for parliamentary majorities and for politicians in general. They were also determined to promote their free-trade theories, and looked for men in the Chamber who were free of the taint of political compromise. These they found in the outspoken renegades of the extreme left, especially Cavallotti, Imbriani, and Colajanni. Pantaleoni did not care for the socialist sentiments of some of these men. But Pareto was putting forth arguments which would lead directly into the elite theory of political action. He told Pantaleoni not to worry about the ideas. If he thought it would be effective, he would even use intransigent clericals to expound his free-trade theories. What counted for Pareto was the power of a man like Cavallotti, the fact that what he said was heard. Ideas were less important. Because the extremists were independent of any organized political structure, they were ideal propagandists. It was becoming increasingly obvious to Pareto that statesmen were limited by the general ideas of the masses. What was needed, therefore, was an elite force within the Chamber which could use that corrupt body to prepare the climate of opinion for change.

It was decided to feed copies of the Alvisi-Biagini report to a few select Deputies. Gavazzi and Colajanni were finally chosen. There was a trace of antiparliamentary obsession in Pareto's letters. He warned Pantaleoni that now that the Alvisi report was to be leaked, his life was in grave danger from the ruling class. Pantaleoni had to guard against assassination. To the end, Pareto remained convinced that Giolitti had known the truth about the Bank of Rome and was paying Tanlongo to keep quiet by making him a Senator.[50]

In the Chamber, when the Christmas recess was over, Giolitti announced the findings of his government's investigation of the banks. A clandestine circulation of 65,784,792 lire had been uncovered. He asked for legislation that would absorb this worthless currency in order to prevent a panic. It was also announced that Tanlongo and his associates had been placed under arrest because of incriminating evidence discovered during a search of their offices. Giolitti was immediately questioned about his knowledge of the Alvisi-Biagini report. He denied that he had seen it, but added that it was not pertinent, as it dealt with the condition of the banks in 1889. Besides, his colleague Luigi Miceli had assured him, as he had assured the Chamber, that there were no irregularities. The Premier could not but believe the word of a fellow minister.[51]

Whether Giolitti was already aware that he had been deceived will never be known. He never spoke of it during his life or in any publication intended for posterity. By January, 1893, however, it was quite clear that the temper of the opposition had changed. Whereas prior to the recess the influential men of the Chamber had wished to prevent an investigation, the extremist minority was now joined by Rudinì, Crispi, Miceli, and Sonnino. Once Giolitti had shown he meant business and would get to the root of the affair, he was made the subject of a steady barrage of vilification which did not let up until his resignation in November, 1893. Sonnino took up Colajanni's demand for a full parliamentary inquest. He also raised the issue of reported abuse of office by the Minister of Justice, Teodorico Bonacci. Rumor had it that the Government had secreted certain bits of evidence. Sonnino's insinuation was to be the basis for a growing belief that Giolitti had set aside damning letters to be used as blackmail should his position become desperate. Rudinì in turn backed the need for bringing the whole subject before the Chamber. Giovanni Bovio insisted that the honor of the Assembly was at stake; the people were beginning to say that the Deputies "represented the nation as the Cardinals represented Christ." This cry for a purification of Parliament became the trademark of all anti-Giolittians. Giolitti continued to assert that he had not been sent a copy of the Alvisi-Biagini report, that he accepted then — and still did — Miceli's statement that nothing serious had been amiss in 1889. Miceli, for his part, showed signs of nervousness. He admitted that Colajanni's version of the report was accurate. But Monzilli had proved that no grave irregularities existed. Then Miceli confessed that when the famous bank bill of 1889 had gone to the Chamber — sponsored, he was careful to note, by himself and Giolitti — he had toned down a resumé of the Alvisi report and sent it to the Chamber's commission that was drawing up new legislation. This produced jeers from the handful of Socialists and Republicans, to which Miceli could only answer that the patria was the result of an ideal that had cost blood and sweat. It could not be compromised.

Miceli never said publicly that he had shown Giolitti the Alvisi-Biagini document. But he did his best to create the belief that he had, by linking Giolitti to the bank bill of 1889 and by emphasizing that Biagini was a member of Giolitti's staff at the Ministry of the Treasury. Giolitti, recognizing that a parliamentary investigation would destroy any hope of getting through desperately needed legislation, tried to prevent one by asking a three-month suspension of the discussion, staking his Cabinet on the vote. Crispi, who had been silent until that crucial moment, then arose to announce his intention of voting against the Government. It is difficult not to conclude that he waited to be sure Giolitti was going to win this test before casting a vote which by implication was in favor of a parliamentary hearing on all the evidence relating to the Bank Scandal. Giolitti had no difficulty winning his appeal for a truce: 274 for the Government, 154 opposed.[52]

On February 1 the Chamber was asked to permit criminal proceedings against Deputy Rocco de Zerbi, already under arrest for his part in the Tanlongo case. On the night of the 19th, De Zerbi died in prison. Giolitti, expressing the Chamber's feelings, remarked simply that before the grave only a man's services to the country were remembered. However, this did not satisfy the intransigents. De Zerbi was lauded as a patriot and artist whose courage had withstood the Government's persecutions. In a bitter speech, a friend of the late Deputy charged that De Zerbi had been the victim of an investigation promoted by a man who had done nothing to serve Italy. De Zerbi was one of the few cases of a Deputy who betrayed his mandate to the banks. But he was also an ex-Garibaldian, and his death set the stage for a concerted attack on Giolitti that dramatized the Premier's unheroic past. De Zerbi was not the only patriot involved. Miceli had fought at Calatafimi, Palermo, and Aspromonte. It was he who had trussed up the lamb for slaughter by involving Giolitti in the manipulations of 1889. It remained for Crispi to dispatch him. Crispi claimed, in an interview to the press, that Giolitti had come to him at 8 A.M., June 14, 1890, and stated that facts had been discovered which justified criminal proceedings against the Bank of Rome. In the Chamber, Crispi feigned reluctance to talk, citing the House of Common's practice that press reports were not to be brought into the Assembly. Giolitti suggested that after two years Crispi might possibly have forgotten the conversation to which he alluded — it seemed rather remarkable that he could be so precise about the time. Undaunted, Crispi arose to reply. "Listen to me, young novices," he began, and to the laughter of his following he went on to lecture the youngsters on how to run the government. He had, he said, taken very precise notes on the talk with Giolitti, as was his habit with all such matters of state. He never produced these notes. With great restraint, Giolitti observed that he would indeed take Crispi's advice in the future, keeping records of all such conversations. Against the minority who flaunted their patents of revolutionary nobility, there was no recourse save in patience and self-control. As one Deputy put it, someone was lying, and he preferred to believe Crispi, who had faith in Italy's destiny.[53]

On March 20 Giolitti delivered the results of the Administration's investigation of the banks to the Chamber. Suddenly the opposition took fright. They realized that the documents might implicate members of their own confused coalition rather than Giolitti. What they needed was a way to protect themselves against that possibility. By taking up Sonnino's charge that Giolitti had stolen important evidence, they could ruin the man and discredit his government's investigation as a whitewash. Sonnino demanded a complete cleansing of the moral atmosphere, recommending the formation of a committee of the house empowered to interrogate witnesses, including members of the Chamber. Giolitti denied he had taken any documents. He warned his colleagues that they were falling prey to excessive nervousness and by so doing were serving only the interests of the yellow press. He also observed that publication of the documents his government had gathered would constitute an unwarranted intrusion into the lives of private citizens. In order to avoid another parliamentary inquest which would block pending legislation, he advised that a group of universally respected men be selected to read the files. This, he said, would prove that claims of widespread corruption were unfounded.[54]

This was the origin of the Committee of Seven, chosen by Giuseppe Zanardelli, President of the Chamber, an ex-Garibaldian himself whose reputation was beyond reproach. The Committee included, as was proper, one of the extremist faction, Giovanni Bovio. Having forestalled his opponents, Giolitti now brought the bank reorganization bill to the floor on June 24. He insisted that Italy's financial integrity demanded its passage before the summer recess. But the minority opposition was not to be thwarted. Cavallotti and Sonnino asserted that there could be no vote on the bill since the Committee was very likely to find that many Deputies, perhaps as many as thirty according to Cavallotti, would be found guilty of political simony. This monstrous assumption of guilt was embellished by Cavallotti with charges so devoid of concrete proof that Zanardelli, in one of his rare interferences with open debate, had to check the speaker. Cavallotti was infuriated because Giolitti's Finance Minister, Bernardino Grimaldi — the same man for whom arithmetic was not an opinion — had refused to release the names of all Italian stockholders in the National Bank. Many believed that the new bank bill was designed by Giolitti to favor this institution and its owners. Unable to document his charges, Cavallotti shifted to the familiar theme of the decline of culture in modern Italy. He spoke of his own youth, of "those beautiful years when first I entered this parliamentary hall, when first I mounted this tribune, my mind filled with classical knowledge on the rights of free assemblies." From legislature to legislature, he went on, his illusions faded. Gone were the days when scandals would have been unthinkable. "Other times, I know. And Giolitti's presence at that bench tells me this." As for Grimaldi, he was one of those men of the *fin de siècle*, proud of his modern culture, unburdened by useless classical erudition.

Above the cries of the minority Giolitti's voice could be heard, repeating his warning that Italy's credit was in danger. The majority heard him, and brought the bank bill to the floor by a vote of 238 to 143, with twenty-eight abstentions.[55] Through the hot summer days, Giolitti resisted all attempts to strangle the bill. Meetings lasted into the night. Giolitti called for Sunday sessions. The opposition tried to prevent passage until the report of the Committee of Seven came in. Every constitutional device was exploited, from the filibuster to innumerable amendments. Antonio Salandra, at the time an undistinguished professor of law, an infrequent speaker who was known to be Sonnino's man, made the absurd claim that Giolitti was preserving the Bank of Rome by having the National Bank absorb the illegal currency. The Bank of Rome had been closed long before, and was not to reopen; but it was not hard to predict what would have happened had its false bills not been honored by other banks. Salandra also took up another argument. Regionalism suddenly blossomed as a convenient pretext. As a Southerner, from Puglia, Salandra defended the banks of Sicily and Naples against the great northern National Bank and against the new Bank of Italy which the Government's proposed legislation would establish. Sonnino, a Tuscan, together with Marquis Filippo Torrigiani, a very conservative Florentine, spoke for the banks of that region. The most ingenious diversionary tactic, however, was to sign up to speak for the bill and then use the floor to attack it. Colajanni, Salandra, and others did this. The minority then claimed that the bill was unpopular because no one from the administration defended it.

Giolitti had little difficulty disposing of these arguments for the simple reason that Sonnino had once been in favor of a single national bank, which would have quite effectively ruined the local banks, while Salandra had been on the committee which drew up the bank bill.[56] This is not to say that the draft measure was flawless. Its responsible opponents insisted on amendments. Maggiorino Ferraris, the noted commentator of the *Nuova Antologia*, Luigi Luzzatti, a former minister, and Giustino Fortunato, a leading student of the problems of the depressed Mezzogiorno, all criticized the bill but without resorting to insinuations or sterile recriminations. In response to their suggestions, a significant faction within the majority put forth compromise proposals which were to win over the responsible voters. This faction was headed by Alessandro Fortis, a veteran of Mentana, whose role in the Giolittian camp was extremely influential. With Giuseppe Marcora, a former Mazzinian, and a few younger men, these ex-revolutionaries had entered the new majority in order to put an end to trasformismo. It must be kept in mind that the Giolitti Cabinet was the first attempt since 1876 to form a government entirely of the constitutional left. Having Fortis on the floor meant that there was a counterweight to Crispi and Cavallotti. Fortis was a man of few words. Some of them he reserved for Cavallotti, whom he told bluntly to stop acting as if he were the only honest man in the Chamber.[57]

By early July the Government had managed to win approval of the separate articles of the bank bill. It now faced the last determined effort to prevent passage of the whole act before the verdict of the Committee of Seven came in. On July 7 the Chairman of the Committee sent Zanardelli a letter informing the Chamber that the investigation was not yet complete. Bovio was furious with Zanardelli for reading the letter to the Deputies. The reason for his anger was simply that the letter made it plain that tales of extensive corruption involving politicians were not true. Bovio tried to reveal secrets from the documents which he, as a member of the Committee, had examined. Apparently Zanardelli managed to reach him during the recess and used all his prestige to prevent the enraged man from betraying his oath of secrecy taken as one of the Seven. On the next day the bill was finally passed, 222 votes to 135, with five abstaining.[58] The Giolittian majority had won a triumph which was at the same time a victory for parliamentary practice. Not once, despite clear majorities and despite the methods of the opposition, was there any suggestion of hurrying the passage of this critical piece of legislation by use of unconstitutional expedients.

During the summer recess the Fasci suddenly flared up in Sicily. The Aigues Mortes riots between French and Italian workers seemed to confirm the claims of those who painted France as Italy's eternal enemy. Domestic unrest, international tension over France's attempts to build a great naval base at Bizerte, and the growing belief in the dishonesty of Italy's government all were working to prepare the way for the return of Crispi to power. Giolitti took advantage of the holiday to call a political rally at Dronero, his constituency. His enemies predicted a fiasco, but over 200 Deputies and 80 Senators showed up. The influential *Nuova Antologia* likened it to Gladstone's Midlothian campaign.[59] The basis for the formation of a national party along liberal-progressive lines was being established.

When the Chamber reconvened in November, the Committee of Seven sent in its findings. The report was a model of probity and good sense. Criteria for a judgment of political corruption were carefully defined so as to exclude needless and unjustifiable exposure of the innocent. Not

only politicians but journalists were investigated and questioned. No parliament of the time could boast of a more determined effort to get at the
truth. In answer to the charges of political simony, the Committee —
with Bovio dissenting — found no evidence among living men. Beyond
the grave it would not go. Several Deputies, some of them ex-ministers,
were censored or admonished for having sofferenze, or notes, long over-
due. Chief among these were Francesco Crispi and Luigi Miceli. Others,
including Di San Giuliano, were criticized for having recommended
friends for loans. In effect, the worst charge that could be brought against
all but a very few men was that they were lobbyists for the banks. The
Committee found no proof that Giolitti had borrowed money to rig the
elections of 1892. His testimony that a loan had been made to the Government for the financing of the Columbian Exposition of that year has never
been refuted. To additional charges that he might have had other secret
funds, the Committee replied, "not proved." It also made clear that the
administrative report which Giolitti had ordered was extremely thorough,
not in any sense a cover-up. But on the one remaining accusation — that
he had known of the Alvisi-Biagini report when he nominated Tanlongo
Senator — the Committee voiced disapproval while making clear, however, that its source of this information was one man, Luigi Miceli.

The next day Giolitti resigned on the grounds that he and his colleagues
wished to be free to answer all charges made against them.[60] This resignation was to be the source of one aspect of the Giolittian myth. He has
frequently been portrayed as a man who dumped power on others when
things became difficult, craftily waiting until his successor ruined himself
politically in an attempt to solve problems he inherited. This appraisal
of Giolitti's character — which has become standard in histories of the
period — is destroyed by the records of the debates of the Chamber,
which show instead that he endured a year of abuse while refusing to give
way until Italy had new banking legislation and an honest version of the
extent to which political corruption had spread. After his resignation,
Giolitti went abroad to visit his daughter and her German husband. This
"flight to Berlin" was also to figure in the evolution of the myth, particularly during the months of Italian neutrality at the time of the Great War.

The Chamber, shaken by a year of scandal, unsure of itself, morally
weakened by the work of the extremists, turned to Crispi. The old lion
called for a return to the spirit of the Risorgimento. "From 1859 to 1870,"
he told the Deputies, "we worked for the attainment of the patria's material unity; and now we will have to work to cement its moral unity, so

that the edifice for which our martyrs shed their blood may be consolidated." Using threats to national security by the Russians, the French, and Italian Socialists as an excuse, Crispi tore up the Statuto. Cavallotti, Imbriani, and others of the old anti-Giolittian alliance now attacked their former chief as they had once attacked Giolitti. But what a difference when challenging Crispi, whose "artistic life," in Cavallotti's words, would yet become a legend, marred only by his fantastic imagination of constant plots. It was not Crispi but his advisors who were really to blame for the reactionary policy in Sicily. The extremists made the lesser members of the new government the real villains. It was true that the new Minister of Justice, Calenda Di Tavani, was an out-and-out reactionary, quite willing to suspend the Constitution in the name of order. But Cavallotti in a letter to Crispi suggested that the man most responsible for leading Crispi down the path of reaction was Sidney Sonnino.[61]

Sonnino had become Crispi's Minister of the Treasury, dragging Salandra along as Undersecretary. How much his advice counted in the formulation of Crispi's policies will probably never be known. It is significant, however, that when first taking power Crispi did not immediately move to crush the Fasci. General Pelloux, Giolitti's Minister of War, defending his handling of the Sicilian outbreak, told the Chamber that the fleet which had been stationed at Palermo in case of possible emergencies had been withdrawn by Crispi. Later, however, while the Chamber was enjoying the December holiday break, the new government had suddenly shifted to a policy of force which included the proclamation of martial law and the use of military tribunals. When the Chamber met again in February, 1894, Sonnino's voice became increasingly evident. Whereas Crispi used plots from foreign and domestic enemies to intimidate those who counseled moderation, Sonnino used the budget message to frighten the Chamber into compliance. It is impossible to avoid this conclusion. Cavallotti and Imbriani had tried to force debate on the Government's breach of constitutional rights, only to be checked by Crispi's insistence that the floor be cleared for a report on the budget. Sonnino had then delivered a long, detailed analysis of the disastrous state of Italian finances. The Chamber listened in stunned silence, punctuated by murmurs of disbelief, as the young minister spoke of an impending deficit of 155,000,000 lire.[62] This seemed to challenge the sober but far less pessimistic analysis which Giolitti had turned in the year before. But by then Giolitti was no longer there to reply.

Sonnino's speech did much to inhibit a parliamentary rising against the dictatorial press and security laws which were in the offing. Crispi also capitalized on an attempt on his life. As word spread through the Chamber that the former Garibaldian was unscathed, he strode into the hall and was greeted by the thunderous applause of his colleagues. The new President of the Chamber, Giuseppe Biancheri, an old companion in arms who was to show decided partiality to the dynamic Premier throughout his last ministry, asked him to accept the moving demonstration of esteem as a sign of affection from the representatives of the Italian people. Crispi obliged, in a theatrical manner which was certain to evoke memories of the plebiscites of the Risorgimento. On July 11, in a Chamber half attended, the Government put through the final article of its new security law by a clear majority, 204 to 40. The law, a shocking departure from previous legislation, authorized up to three years' imprisonment for anyone who had shown "clear intention to commit overt acts against the social structure."

During the summer of 1894 Crispi used this law to close down socialist clubs and newspapers, betraying his previous promise — that his only aim was to strike at criminal and anarchist elements in league with foreign agents to subvert Italian unity. By the following year he had forgotten this assurance. He blandly reminded the defenders of liberty that they themselves had agreed to the new laws in the first place.[63]

By December, however, the Bank Scandal had come home to roost at last. The documents and testimony amassed by the Committee of Seven were printed and placed on record. There had been some question whether they should ever be made public. No sooner had Crispi replaced Giolitti than the issue as to what disposition to make of them had been debated, with Cavallotti and Colajanni insisting as always that everything be released in order to save the Chamber's reputation. Certainly they had assumed that publication would put the finishing touches to Giolitti's career. There was one notorious anti-Giolittian, however, who had been strangely reluctant to authorize their release. This was Bovio. He, unlike his friends, had seen the documents and heard the witnesses, and he must have recognized that only Crispi would suffer by an official publication. But the Government could scarcely make a fight of it. The ministerial party abstained. The vote to print the minutes of the Committee of Seven was carried 142 to 24.[64] This vote meant essentially that those who still trusted Giolitti — and they were many, even though their voice had been muted — were not afraid to expose him as well as themselves to the light of truth.

When the Deputies met again in Rome in December, 1894, they had all either read the official volumes or been told of their contents. It was clear, save to those who refused to abandon their illusions, that Giolitti and the overwhelming majority of the Deputies were innocent. Most damning, however, was the evidence relating to Luigi Miceli. He had not toned down the Alvisi-Biagini report, as he had stated in the Chamber; the report had been intentionally suppressed. Poor Biagini was forced to swear never to reveal the truth to anyone, even his own superiors. Reasons of state commanded silence, and Biagini obeyed. As for Monzilli, it was obvious that he and Miceli had worked together to smother the facts. Alvisi's death might have made concealment possible had he not given a copy of his own findings to friends, from whose hands it passed into the possession of Pantaleoni and Pareto.

But the testimony of Pietro Tanlongo, son of the notorious banker, was most enlightening. It was clear that he and his father had been able to prevent great numbers of private letters from falling into the hands of Giolitti's investigating commission. These had then been offered to all influential parties, including Giolitti, in an obvious effort to foster suspicion, befuddle the Chamber, and take the pressure off the guilty. Here was the source of the *plico*, Giolitti's collection of incriminating letters which Sonnino and others believed he had stolen in his official position as head of the Government. Giolitti had cautioned his colleagues against listening to "voices from the jails." That this warning was not heeded was apparent from the exhibition of political irresponsibility which followed.

However, Crispi also was furnished with letters relating to the loan for the financing of the Columbian Exposition. The man who acted as Tanlongo's messenger was Count Pietro Antonelli, nephew of the late Cardinal Secretary of State, a prominent advocate of African colonialism who was to become Crispi's Undersecretary of State for Foreign Affairs. Pietro Tanlongo had told the Committee of Seven that Crispi had requested this blackmail to be used if necessary against Giolitti. When asked about this, Antonelli had refused to reply, much to the disgust of some members of the Seven. As for Colajanni, so bold in the Chamber with his rash accusations, he squirmed when questioned by the Committee, because he was privately in debt to the Bank of Rome. He tried to implicate Zanardelli in the scandal, and all in all proved a rather unpleasant witness.

Whether Crispi had in fact made overtures to acquire the blackmail letters cannot be proved. But the documents did show that he had for years lived royally by means of extended loans from the Bank of Rome which were never repaid. Giolitti was as clean as a whistle, and moreover was a very forthright witness. He took full responsibility for the nomination of Tanlongo to the Senate, even though it was quite apparent that when the choice was made Tanlongo, who was also President of the Rome Chamber of Commerce, was a logical candidate in good standing.[65]

The men who had originally fomented the scandal, Colajanni and Cavallotti in the lead, perhaps still believing in Giolitti's guilt but also prepared to press the issue because of Crispi's illiberal domestic policy, now demanded that the Government try Giolitti and his agents for the theft of the plico. Although some of the detectives who had searched Tanlongo's residence were under indictment, they had not been brought to trial. Colajanni wanted to know why not. No one could fail to note the delay. It looked as if the Government had no desire to press the case. Crispi blithely replied that he knew nothing about secret packets of documents. He insisted, a bit tardily, that he trusted all his colleagues until they were proven guilty. Colajanni shot back that if the trials were not carried out Italians would say that Francesco Crispi was afraid of the truth. Crispi retorted grandly that the word fear was not in his vocabulary. But it was too late for phrases. The session was interrupted by the Socialist Deputy, Camillo Prampolini, who challenged the Government to tell the whole truth once and for all, but he was cut off by the President of the Chamber, Biancheri. This precipitated such wild confusion that the session was suspended.

On the next day, December 11, Giolitti returned to the Chamber to answer Colajanni's charges that he, his colleagues, and the police of Rome had concealed official evidence. Biancheri made a desperate attempt to prevent the question from coming to the floor. He literally begged Giolitti not to speak. But Giolitti, who had resigned a year before in order to be free to defend his administration, who had suffered political extinction in silence, could no longer submit to scandalous attacks. Had Colajanni and others allowed the matter to drop, it is very likely that Giolitti would never have spoken. Now that men were suspended from their jobs, under indictment for crimes that never came before the bench, he felt he had to be heard. The plico contained the proof that there had been no theft. Prior to going before the Chamber he had asked the opinion of the most distinguished leaders of every sector of the assembly, including Cavallotti; they all agreed that the packet could not remain secret. Giolitti placed it on Biancheri's desk, but the President of the Chamber refused it. An old and loyal friend of Crispi's, Biancheri recognized that the last shreds of the hero's reputation were safer in the hands of Giolitti than in those of the scandalmongers who had done so much to bring Crispi back to power.

For the diehard anti-Giolittians, however, there was one last hope. If the former Premier could be brought before the courts immediately, the plico would be *sub judice*, kept in the possession of the judges. The arch conservative theorist Ruggero Bonghi and Crispi's Minister of Justice Calenda Di Tavani moved that this be done. But the Chamber decided overwhelmingly against it, voting instead to choose yet another Committee to read the documents. When Biancheri tried to stall the selection of this new Committee of Five on the ground that the matter was not on the agenda, the Deputies mustered the needed three-fourths majority to enter the question immediately.[66]

The Committee of Five, which included Cavallotti, sat through the night of December 11 reading the plico. On December 13 they reported to the Chamber. This report was only a description of its contents; the actual documents were not yet released, and Crispi still hoped to stop their distribution to his colleagues. He brought suit for slander against Giolitti on the same day. When the Chamber met on the 14th, he tried to alter the agenda, claiming as a good parliamentarian that royal military decrees issued during the summer had to be converted at once into law. This was scotched by General Pelloux, who denied that any emergency existed. On December 15 the printed edition of the plico was distributed. Crispi claimed it was a tissue of lies. Biancheri refused to permit any debate on the documents. But the opposition to Crispi was growing. Rudinì, his most probable successor, now went over to the side of the extremists. A vote taken to inscribe the discussion in the agenda for the same day failed to get the required three-fourths majority, but was a defeat for Crispi, since 188 spoke for the motion, 179 against. This having failed, the Florentine Deputy, Count Francesco Guicciardini, moved that the affair be taken up the next day. Knowing that this motion would get the simple majority needed, Crispi declared that he was completely disinterested.[67]

That same evening, by royal decree, the Chamber was prorogued. Papers reported that Crispi had obtained the decree days in advance to be used in case of emergency. The Bank of Rome Scandal had now become a constitutional issue. On December 16 leaders of the Chamber met in the *Sala Rossa* of the Parliament building and approved Rudinì's statement deploring an unjustified interference with the freedom of the Parliament. This meeting was attended as well by some prominent Socialists. Giolitti was not present personally, although in spirit he was very much so. The

Sala Rossa rising of the opposition was the germ of the later coalition between his liberal-progressive majority and the Italian Socialists which was to take shape at the turn of the century in order to save the Parliament from the reaction of the Pelloux government. Giolitti was emerging as the leader of this coalition by virtue of his conduct during the years of the Scandal. While many would always cling to the myth, the great majority of the Deputies could not fail to appreciate his striking qualities of character and political wisdom.

Had the plico added new crimes to the long list of Crispi's indiscretions, one might understand Giolitti's historical reputation as an unprincipled politician who tried to destroy a tottering giant. Reading its contents, however, only shows why Giolitti tried to suppress it. There was nothing in it which added significantly to the previously published dossier of the Committee of Seven. Although the extent to which a few known culprits were involved with the banks was shown in greater detail, new crimes were not revealed, as the yellow press and some excitable politicians had hoped. In fact, the plico did not contain original documents, but rather copies made by the Ministry of Justice of originals which had been turned over to the courts. The exception to this was a series of letters from Tanlongo, some addressed to Giolitti. Far from proving Giolitti's guilt, these showed, as he had always insisted, that the banker was ready to implicate all manner of men to save himself. In a piteous letter, Tanlongo implored Giolitti to remember his long services to Italy, his large family. In the tortured syntax of a provincial businessman who had risen too rapidly in Roman circles, the jailed man tried to insinuate himself into Giolitti's confidence, offering, as if he himself believed the myth, anything the Premier needed to destroy his enemies. Giolitti had acted in the best interest of all honest men in not permitting these letters to be revealed. In his own letter to Biancheri which accompanied the plico, he advised taking its contents with a grain of salt. Among the other documents that came to Giolitti, there was a note from Crispi's wife. While it added nothing new, it mercilessly told the story of the warrior's fall from valor: "Power had ruined us. I pray God that my husband may be relieved of it."[68]

The plico was not to be printed as part of the Chamber's official acts until 1895. In the meantime, during the long and quasi-constitutional recess which lasted until June of that same year, Cavallotti released his manifesto "To the Honest Men of All Parties" to the press. Actually a lengthy *j'accuse* aimed at his former friend, it turned on Crispi the same sort of innuendo, insinuation, and assumption of evidence with which Giolitti had been long familiar. Cavallotti followed this up with a volume devoted to the "moral question of Francesco Crispi." He protested that his attack was justified by evidence of new crimes. In truth, he offered nothing that all but the most deluded politicians did not already know about Crispi. His principal charge was that Crispi had sought to profit by getting the King to bestow Italy's highest decoration on Cornelius Herz, partner in crime to Julius Rheinach of the Panama Scandals. Yet even this had been touched upon by the Committee of Seven. If Crispi was reluctant to withdraw the decoration once Herz's true character was known, there was no proof that he intended to profit personally. Certainly Cavallotti's public revelation of information his colleagues had entrusted him with was vicious. He raked up Crispi's tussle with the law in 1878 over the charge of bigamy, an old and well known blot. Crispi was also accused of having been a pro-Bourbon lawyer prior to 1860, and with having been a physical coward during the Sicilian expedition.[69]

After the long, quasi-constitutional recess, Crispi faced Cavallotti in the Chamber on June 24, 1895. "At my age," he said, "after having served the country for fifty-three years, I have the right to believe myself invulnerable and above insults and defamation." The majority chose to show charity to the old statesman, voting a six-month suspension of the question of the plico's contents. By this action, the Deputies wished to put an end to a miserable affair in which they had allowed themselves to succumb to suspicion. Since Giolitti did not protest, taking no part in the vote, it was easier to bury the whole rotten business. However if the victim was willing to drop the matter, Crispi's own friends were not. And they were joined by his most vitriolic enemies. Count Tommaso Cambray-Digny, later to become with Sonnino the architect of Pelloux's heavy-handed policies, found himself oddly in agreement with the tireless Imbriani in demanding that Giolitti still face trial. Whereas Imbriani wished to ruin Crispi's last vestige of power, Cambray-Digny obviously hoped to prevent publication of the plico. But the Court of Appeals decided that Giolitti could not be judged for acts committed as head of the Government without infringing on the separation of powers. Tragically, this left those indicted but yet to be tried — those whom Crispi surely would never try if he could avoid it — in an impossible position. Therefore Giolitti's Minister of the Interior, Pietro Rosano, demanded that the trials go on. If they should not, he threatened to ask justice of the Chamber. Having himself ordered the search of Tanlongo's home, he felt morally responsible for the men who had lost their jobs and yet could not clear their names. Calenda Di Tavani, in the past never reluctant to whet the Chamber's appetite for scandal, now claimed that the grave financial situation argued against tying up the legislature with new investigations.

It was too late for this feeble tack to work. Rosano's plea made the injustice of the delayed trials so patent that something had to be done. From the right, Rudinì called on the Government to produce the evidence that the courts, having declared themselves incompetent, no longer could keep sub judice. Salvatore Barzilai, a young Irredentist of the left, con- curred. This forced Crispi to promise to deliver the evidence. To satisfy the other side of this strange alliance that threatened Crispi with ultimate catastrophe, a new Committee was empowered to argue whether the courts had the constitutional right to avoid the responsibility of indicting Giolitti. Cambray-Digny was the heart and soul of what was to be the last committee of inquest of the four-year-old affair.[70]

That was on July 22, 1895. The court records did not reach the Chamber until November 21. In the interval, Africa became the great topic. The Crown speech of June 10 opening the new legislature had been laced with references to Italy's glorious mission in the Dark Continent. Disquieting news of an Italian penetration of the Abyssinian highlands, extending the Italian coastal position at Massawa dangerously deep into the interior, began to reach home. Rudinì, in an open bid for power, demanded a policy of consolidation, not penetration. He prophesied unhappy experiences if this were not done. Crispi denied that he was furthering adventurous claims in the Red Sea area; besides, he said, a great country could not be concerned with Africa. The contemptuous insouciance that was leading Italy to the humiliation of Adowa and the end of Crispi's career was already present. Nonetheless, Crispi's word was accepted. This was made the easier by Sonnino's stress on economies. Had not the financial prophet of doom spoken of the benefits of peace?[71]

On December 9 the news of the defeat of Italian troops at Amba Alagi hit the Chamber. Imbriani cried out against the loss of Italian blood not shed for the patria. The newly elected President of the Chamber, Tommaso Villa, ordered the remarks stricken from the minutes. At a very opportune moment Cambray-Digny rose and asked to read his Committee's report on the Giolitti case. Giolitti immediately asked to speak, but Villa chose to give the floor to Cambray-Digny. The report proved to be an act of pure desperation. In a tediously learned discussion of constitutional theory, the Committee sought to prove that the Chamber could prevent the courts from declaring incompetence. But the report also let out the incredible fact that Giolitti had twice asked to be questioned under oath by the Committee in order to prove that there was no case of theft. He had never been permitted to testify.[72]

On December 13 Giolitti finally had his chance before the Chamber. In a masterful address, fully documented, unmarred by rhetoric or vindictiveness, he proved that his administration and the bureaucracy generally had been innocent of the charges. He also sought to demolish the legend that his government had tampered with the courts in order to spare those under indictment for fraud. After denying that any judges had been pressured, he quoted a remark that Calenda Di Tavani had let slip in an unguarded moment when defending the Crispi government for permitting a long delay in the trials of Giolitti's supposed accomplices. The Minister of Justice had cited the need to "prepare the milieu" before the trials could take place. As Calenda Di Tavani spoke in rebuttal, it dawned on the Chamber that his defense was instead the clearest admission that the regime, doubtless believing the myth that justice under Giolitti was not possible, had shifted the judges, replacing those who had handled the Tanlongo case with others. This speech amounted to a confession of executive interference with the bench. It provoked shouts of rage from the same men who had done most to assassinate Giolitti's character, who now found that the government which arose to purify Italy was unable to hide its own disregard for judicial independence.

When the shouting had died down and calm was restored, Giolitti's old majority began to come back into its own. In a brilliant speech a young Deputy, Emanuele Gianturco, demolished the Cambray-Digny report and called on the Chamber to investigate Giolitti's case. Cavallotti, Imbriani, and Colajanni simply could not bring themselves to confess their own folly. They continued to cry for a resolution of the moral issue. Greater courage than that they did not possess. By a vote of 167 to 145, eleven abstaining, the Gianturco motion was defeated. That vote, however, marked the real end of Crispi's power and the beginning of Giolitti's rise as Italy's leading parliamentarian. Six of the twelve sponsors of the Gianturco motion had been willing to vote confidence in Crispi a week before. A dozen other Deputies, including Di San Giuliano and Luzzatti, defected from the majority. Three members of the old Committee of Seven voted to continue the investigation. Had Giolitti, who abstained, wished to press the issue then and there, he doubtless could have forced the Chamber to take up his case. He did not do so. Having from the outset maintained that the scandal was essentially political in nature, he refused now to take part in the blatant hypocrisy of the incorrigibles who spoke so piously of purifying the Chamber only to do serious damage to the entire parliamentary system. Therefore he said nothing, nor complained when he was denied the chance to clear his name forever. Never would Giolitti raise the subject of Crispi, Miceli, and the Bank of Rome. In his memoirs, his old adversary is described as an ardent patriot though an emotional statesman.[73]

Because he was silent, the legend of the Minister of Corruption survived in the minds of men for whom Giolitti could do no right and Crispi no wrong. However, for the majority of the Deputies who lived through the days of scandal, Giolitti's lofty conduct must assuredly have constituted the basis for the respect that conferred on him such great authority in the decades preceding the Great War. The Age of Giolitti, as it came to be known, rested on a foundation of trust; it was not mired in the mud of deceit, as many would claim. But in the country at large — among the journalistic intelligentsia, the humanistic petty bourgeoisie, and for some unconvinced politicians—the damage had already been done. Giolitti was to remain the cynical pragmatic schemer. When he was dead, and fascism ruled Italy, the Scandal of the Bank of Rome was dug up again in a ponderous work distinguished by its assumption of his guilt in the face of all the evidence. To the author, Crispi still represented the spirit of the revolution that failed, his mystical powers offering the shining contrast to the nullity of the new men of the Postrisorgimento who had atomized all ideals, reducing grandeur to minuscule problems of economics. That new class, according to the fascist view, had been unable to replace the cultural elite of the Risorgimento.[74]

The debates in the Chamber in the winter of 1895 were held in an atmosphere of uncertainty. Crispi was still in power and able to exert his highly personal will despite the damaging effects of published documents. It was understandable that the Deputies did not wish to trample on him now that Cavallotti had unleashed his spectacular condemnation and Giolitti had shown his willingness to let the matter sink slowly into oblivion. But the African campaign began to creep into the hinterland with the occupation of the Tigré. The Government called for emergency funds and was greeted by massive opposition from all sides. Crispi seemed shaken, unsure of himself, even showing signs of not being fully in control of his faculties. An old, broken man, he made a pathetic figure compared to the Crispi of memory. He begged his critics not to interrupt him; he was not well, Africa had never been his idea, he had opposed the Massawa expedition in 1885. He laid the blame at the door of General Oreste Baratieri, commander in the field, for not having asked for sufficient supplies. The Government, he said, was ready to furnish anything needed to do the job. This seemed to contradict his and Sonnino's stress on economies. Crispi ended his confused speech by promising "neither imprudence nor cowardice." On that note he won his last vote of confidence, 255 to 148. This time, however, the minority was joined by Giolitti, Luzzatti, and Di San Giuliano. When a motion condemning colonial expansion came up, it went through by the almost unprecedented margin of 301 to 36, a staggering figure because some of the thirty-six negative votes were from the extreme left, from anticolonialists who wished to stress their total opposition to the Government.[75]

The Chamber left for the Christmas holidays on December 19. On March 5 the members were hastily summoned to hear Crispi's resignation following the Adowa catastrophe. There was no doubt that the majority had been betrayed. Only a policy of utmost prudence and withdrawal from dangerously exposed inland positions was compatible with the Government's mandate. The Deputies had trusted Crispi, and Italy had paid for it. Yet who could have believed that such folly was possible with Sonnino so prominent a member of the Cabinet? His constant pleas for thrift and peace were hardly compatible with the African debacle. It has been suggested that he was kept in the dark by Crispi. This is possible. However, Crispi need not have feared that Sonnino was a convinced anti-Africanist. In 1890 Sonnino had written of the necessity of getting into the Abyssinian highlands to protect trade routes. His article, like his speeches, was characterized by the straight-laced, methodical prose that had become his hallmark. There was no D'Annunzian rhetoric. Nonetheless the message had been quite clear and quite consistent with the program that had led to to Adowa.[76] Behind the taciturn facade for which he was famous — he was known as "Sidney the Silent" — and behind his carefully polished reputation as the strict moralist of the Parliament, Sonnino acted with a lack of consistency that was more than the product of ordinary political maneuvering, making him one of the most enigmatic figures in modern Italian history.

Crispi's fall brought Rudinì back to power. Though a prominent conservative, the new Premier was obliged to give evidence of a more liberal direction, liquidating his predecessor's government of force. De Felice was granted amnesty. More important, the new Cabinet included men who had been part of Giolitti's majority; some of them had backed him in his bleakest hour. Gianturco became Minister of Education; Admiral Brin returned as Secretary of the Navy, a post he had held under Giolitti; and Guicciardini took over the Ministry of Agriculture and Commerce, which had charge of the emission banks. What of the firebrands? They had apparently learned nothing from the last four years. In one of his last oratorical flights, the artist-politician Cavallotti again drew the distinction between culture and modern society, between ideals and narrow, particularistic materialism. To the essentially positivistic temper of the 1890's he linked the failure of regionalism, the decline of the spirit of the patria, and the rise of egotistical parliamentary politics.[77] Crispi was gone, but the tastes and intellectual values which had furthered his almost magical sway were still very much alive.

Having examined the operations of the Parliament and witnessed the emergence of Giolitti from within the framework of domestic Italian politics, something must be said in conclusion about two important facets of the myth and also about the role of Crispi in the history of Italian political theory.

No belief concerning Giolitti was more resistent to disproof than that he used the Prefects to make elections and was therefore master of trasformismo which he elevated into a theory of government. Taking up the question of the Prefects, the growth of that falsehood was in part a response to the imposition of the French administrative system that Piedmont had inherited on the Peninsula. Noted federalists, from Imbriani to Ghisleri and Salvemini, were important purveyors of the idea that Giolitti had perfected the standing practice of using the centralized apparatus to kill off his political rivals. If one looks at the record, however, it is unmistakably clear that when these charges were brought up in the Chamber they were never founded on facts. Of course, those who remain convinced of the legend may reply that evidence of the facts was suppressed by the Government. But this is not very satisfactory to the historian, who could reasonably suspect that even so efficient a system of political oppression as Giolitti's was supposed to have been could not have concealed all the evidence.

On the other hand, there is much evidence to the contrary in the parliamentary debates. Giolitti's guilt was accepted as an established fact even before he had organized his first Cabinet. He had been in power less than a month when Imbriani accused him of plotting to rig the forthcoming elections of November, 1892. Those elections became tangled up with the Bank Scandals. The same men who exploded the Alvisi-Biagini report cried fraud as soon as the new Chamber had assembled in December. Colajanni referred to telegrams which a Prefect had sent to the mayors of his province in favor of a governmental candidate. He never produced the telegrams, while Giolitti produced the logical reply that the candidate in question was in fact known to be opposed to the Government's program. Unabashed by this, Colajanni insisted that his case was airtight, since the loser had been Imbriani, who was even more opposed to Giolitti.[78] This was true; but alas for the fiction, Imbriani was eventually elected despite the network of devoted Prefects.

Far from allowing fraud to go unchecked, the Chamber's standing committee that reviewed all cases of disputed elections established an admirable record for thoroughness and good sense which is available to anyone who cares to read it. Days out of each legislature were spent presenting the detailed conclusions of these investigations, called for usually by the defeated candidate or by his backers in the Chamber. As an example, it was scarcely disregard for honest politics in the 1890's that led to annulment of the election of a candidate who won by a plurality of 2000 votes in a total of 4750 because there had been twenty deceased electors still on the lists and a few hundred illiterates illegally entered. Giolitti, speaking of Italy's bureaucracy, noted that there was not one case of embezzlement, and defied any other government to match the record.[79] There is as yet no proof that the same cannot be said for the quality of political justice in the Postrisorgimento.

That local abuses existed it would be absurd to deny. But that the Central Government was a cesspool of intrigue presided over by a man who knew every man's weakness is equally ridiculous. And it was just this view of centralized crime which was being spread by the extremists. In a speech full of venom, De Felice added another touch to the myth, accusing the Government of shooting down the unarmed and innocent, of assassinating its political enemies. The Sicilian Socialist made it clear that all this was "prepared in high places." At one point his denunciation became so outlandish that Zanardelli, patient up to that point, accused the speaker of not even believing himself what he was saying, but of saying it merely for the sake of speaking.[80]

Defending himself and his colleagues against such violent diatribes, Giolitti showed remarkable composure, asking again and again that proof be brought before the Chamber. It was impossible to assail his own statistics. Of the 508 elections of 1892, 448 were never contested by the defeated candidate; fourteen of those investigated by the Chamber were validated and only nine were annulled, three of which involved Deputies who had voted with the majority. To the charge that he had shifted the Prefects in order to have his men in crucial electoral colleges, Giolitti offered the easily verified reply that every Prefect was at the same post he had held when the new cabinet was installed. It was no coincidence that, whenever the house Committee certified the contested election of a known opponent of the Government, no stir was heard from the anti-Giolittians. One of the more outspoken of these, Palamenghi-Crispi, who had been enraged at previous examples of what he believed to be governmental electioneering, never spoke about his own election, which was contested on the ground of governmental interference in his behalf and cleared by the Chamber. In order to punish the Committee, presided over by Fortis, the irresponsibles once refused to allow the annulment of a contest in which local criminal elements were involved. This prompted Fortis to resign; he failed to understand, he said, how men could continually speak of the need to cleanse Italian politics, making a show of their own honesty, and then permit open corruption to triumph.[81]

In all fairness, it must be pointed out that once Crispi had embarked upon his reactionary policy he got the same treatment. Pelloux's government, at first regarded as a step in the direction of greater freedom, fared no better once he, too, installed a near dictatorship. Political expediency certainly entered into the picture. Men who were possible successors or who wished to weaken the position of a hostile regime could always exploit the oratory of the extremists in the hope of toppling the Cabinet. But it is also true that many came to believe Italian politics hopelessly corrupt by virtue of constant repetition of the legend. It was this assumption that did much to damage parliamentary government in the Postrisorgimento, encouraging the search for alternatives.

Giolitti's reliance on trasformismo holds up no better when confronted with reality. His first Ministry, destroyed by the Bank of Rome affair, had departed from the policy begun by Depretis in that the entire Cabinet was composed of leftists. Giolitti even induced such notable ex-revolutionaries as Luigi Ferrari to take posts in his administration. Giuseppe Zanardelli backed the majority, as did Fortis, Marcora, Giuseppe Mussi, and Ettore Sacchi. These men represented the legalitarian or constitutional wing of the declining Democratic, Radical, and Republican parties. From the outset, however, there was a studied attempt to prove that this government was not at all a revival of the old Sinistra that had been the parliamentary opponent of Cavour and his successors. The men who emphasized this point were the same incorruptibles who posed as the purifiers of the Chamber, who did most to keep the scandals alive. It was quite common to see men of the legalitarian left being twitted by gadflies of the extremes for having lost their virtue by entering the Giolitti majority. In this the extremists were joined by Sonnino, by Ruggero Bonghi, and by the noted Neopolitan political theorist, Giorgio Arcoleo.[82]

When Crispi returned, he in effect restored trasformismo. Yet he was praised for this by the same men who insisted that it was representative of that suppleness of thought, lack of clear positions, both political and philosophical, and dearth of erudition common to the climate of opinion of the 1890's. Fortis asked how men who had for years attacked trasformismo as the cause of political degeneracy could now prefer Crispi's coalition government to that of Giolitti.[83] The truth was that trasformismo was indispensable to those solitary heroes of the Chamber who, like Carducci, could not subject their savage independence of mind to the rule of others. Were a party machinery to develop around Giolitti, or any other leader, the elite of the Chamber — those same men to whom Pareto looked for uncommon courage of conviction — would have lost their power, a power which rested on their highly individualistic and even anarchic parliamentary tactics. It is extremely important to see the beginnings of this idea that power and political sincerity could not survive together within any organized system. As we move into the Giolittian Age, this flight from formalism will take on all the characteristics, in thought as well as in politics, of a romantic struggle to protect the vitality of the isolated man from the contamination inherent in political compromise. It was Giolitti and his new techniques, as exemplified by the Dronero Rally of 1893, who represented a threat to this artistic appreciation of the lonely genius. The more he came to personify the Parliament itself, the more it became true that singular men feared for their reputations as charismatic leaders of the real Italy should they become part of the Chamber or of any tightly organized group.

In his own day and for later theoreticians, Crispi was the outstanding example of the pure hero. His moral and political tragedy were converted into sure signs of a higher truth. Adowa became a victory in that it bid bold defiance to the pusillanimous majority of the Chamber which captured the essence of the inert bourgeois mind, so attached to the hearth and to material wants. His was a virtue to a thousand faults conjoined. But because in practice he also promoted blatantly unconstitutional methods of government, the question arises whether he was a forerunner of fascism. That the Fascists would deify him is true. Whether he helped prepare for their arrival is another matter.

Both Croce and Count Sforza have denied any fundamental link between Crispi and the totalitarian regime that they lived to experience.[84] The reason they give is that the former Garibaldian was a parliamentarian, proved by his admiration for English constitutionalism. This rejection of the fascist version of Crispi as a precursor is part of Croce's and Sforza's own defense of the Postrisorgimento. They would not allow their enemies to lay claim to the past. It is also quite true that Crispi was an admirer of the House of Commons. He referred to it and to English law so often that it became a trade-mark. However, it would be quite wrong to take this as proof that he was in fact a good parliamentarian in his homeland. Indeed, when he, Colajanni, Imbriani, or Cavallotti referred to the Mother of Parliaments, and they all did frequently, they were in effect attacking the Chamber of Deputies.[85] England was to have an important place in the fabrication of an idealized political environment in which freedom and glory went hand in hand. The Commons became a mirror which, like the Risorgimento, reflected all that was considered deficient in the "falsified" Italy that began in 1870.

From the debates of the 1890's the concept of a theoretical and national parliament emerges which has little to do with the concrete Chamber of Deputies. What does not emerge, however, is an attack on the idea of parliament itself. The reason for this was that the critics of the Postrisorgimento, having put themselves forward as men who would recapture the spirit of the past, could not discard the constitutional system which was an inheritance of the age of revolution. What was needed to solve this dilemma was a political theory that would preserve parliamentary monarchy but destroy the mechanism of the Chamber. One step in this direction was to invent new words that permitted men to be at once good patriots and effective antiparliamentarians. In Italy, as in other countries governed by representative systems, legislators could proclaim the Parliament dead and when challenged for this blasphemy quickly assert that they meant not Parliament but parliamentarianism.

Crispi's importance in the growth of this political outlook cannot be overlooked, not so much for what he wrote about the theory of government, but for what his life and actions came to stand for. It was his style, as Chabod has written,[86] that was so significant, and that was to become so appropriate for later nationalist hagiographers. However, there was another function for an idealized legislative body and a romanticized leader who could embody the spirit of the past. One of the sources of dissatisfaction with the Postrisorgimento was the sense of revolutionary failure that has been touched upon. The "people" were as yet not part of the "state"; the Deputies represented the real Italy just as the Cardinals represented Christ. The question was how the fusion between the two was to take place while at the same time retaining one of the legacies of the Risorgimento, that same Chamber where Cavour and Garibaldi had clashed during the age of giants. In Pisacane's idea of the Genius Legislator, and in the suggestion from Vienna that Crispi might convert domestic revolution into war, we have already encountered two possible solutions. There was also the possible solution of politics, the evolution of a party apparatus which could draw Italians slowly into the orbit of legal government. It is to these alternatives that we must now turn.

POLITICAL ALTERNATIVES

The Role of the Socialist Party

It would be wrong to dismiss epigrams such as those coined by Massimo D'Azeglio and Stefano Jacini as mere clichés. Hard facts supported the observation that there was a "real" and an "official" Italy. The lack of mass support for the Risorgimento; the narrow franchise under the constitutional monarchy; the persistence of brigandage which was not, despite claims to the contrary, organized class warfare that might serve as an instrument of political education — these realities testified to the need for closing the gap between the people and the government. Local uprisings in the 1870's were exploited by the Bakuninists, it is true, but they looked more like guerrilla wars than authentic political action. The lack of any tactical direction or party discipline was apparent.[1]

Given this situation, the role of the Socialist party in the history of the Postrisorgimento was crucial. Prior to the formation of the Popular party, and following the decline of the Republicans, the Socialists alone rested on a mass base. It was the most promising organization for the furtherance of the political education of the uncommitted and disinterested bulk of the population. Much depended on the attitude which the Socialist party would take toward the "State." It would not be an exaggeration to say that the very existence of parliamentary government in Italy was bound up with the policy of this party.

Before the formation of the Italian Socialist party in 1892, nascent socialist movements were usually associated with Bakuninist doctrines. It has been said that Bakunin's influence rested largely on the manner in which his propaganda appealed to the tradition of lofty idealism and heroic self-sacrifice which were so much a part of the epic struggles of the Risorgimento. In contrast, Marxist theory appeared cold and impersonal.[2] Bakunin was aware of the similarities between his own theories and the pre-existing tradition of Italian revolutionary idealism. He tried to exploit the political passions associated with the specifically Italian current, winning to his cause men who were dissatisfied with the unitarian settlement and with the general decline of ideals. What success he was to have in the Peninsula depended more upon a spontaneous turning to anarchism — as an answer to specifically Italian problems — than upon a critical appraisal of his ideas. As a result, Italian Socialists might purge their party of anarchism on the theoretical level without destroying its Italian roots, deeply planted before Bakunin came to Italy. This was to be of the greatest importance in the history of the Socialist party, particularly with respect to its attitude toward the constitutional regime.

It is significant that Bakunin first seems to have found a common ground with Italian revolutionaries in the Mezzogiorno. It was in Naples, where Bakunin went from Florence in 1865, that he first began to gather about him a small group of followers. His political philosophy seemed to fit in with the traditions of Pisacane and Cattaneo, with their accent on action in opposition to the centralized state. By 1866 Bakunin was beginning to win over some of the former followers of Mazzini and Garibaldi. Mazzini was aware of the threat posed by the Marxist International, but he refused to compete with Marxism by condoning social revolutionary action. His own insistence on Rome and national unity, which Bakunin opposed, was losing its hold. The War of 1866 with its humiliations further compromised Mazzini's unitarianism. Garibaldi's withdrawal from the Tyrol, his obedience to the monarch, helped discredit another of Bakunin's rivals.[3]

The regionalist issue offered the anarchist a fertile field for spreading his own ideas and exerting his own leadership. How Bakunin's theories could merge with specifically Italian traditions was seen in 1866. In October of that year a propaganda leaflet appeared in Naples that expressed the dissatisfaction of the small Bakuninist group with the Mazzinian program and Garibaldi's attitude toward the monarchy. Mazzini had awakened Italy from her torpor. This was conceded. But his aim was national greatness and the Italian mission. The "people" entered into his formula only as an attractive, high-sounding word. As for his national goal, was it not partly achieved by the monarchy? The difference between monarchical or republican unity was a matter of form. Mazzini's insistence that the social problem required a centuries-long process for its solution made him an ally of the conservatives. And Garibaldi, the sword of the Mazzinian movement, had tricked the people by accepting the monarchy. According to the leaflet only one force could create a great, a free Italy: "The real Italian people . . . We have faith only in the revolution made by the People for their positive and complete emancipation; a Revolution that will make Italy a free republic of free communes in the free Nation . . ."[4]

This revolutionary, anticentralist view tallied with that of Bakunin. It was part of the specifically Italian problem (mentioned above) that had arisen before he visited Italy. But there was one element in the leaflet's program which shows that Bakunin was not its author, although it seems he looked it over before it went to press. This was its patriotism, which was not in accord with his doctrine. The real author, Alberto Tucci, rejected Mazzini's religion of the fatherland, the idea of a national Italian primacy over other peoples. But, as he wrote in 1871, five years after the pamphlet had appeared, he did not reject the patria. "In our view, the fatherland is created spontaneously . . . from the bottom to the top, and it excludes every idea of conquest and forced annexation." While Bakunin might exploit the resentments of the *conquista regia* and the diplomaticized revolution, the patriotic basis of Italian revolutionary thought was another matter. This was the common inheritance of the Risorgimento. It remained a factor in Italian socialism even after anarchism had lost ground.

Also consonant with Italian traditions was the stress on action. What the early socialists wanted was a return to Pisacane's formula of the propaganda of deeds. Bakunin's anarchist theories fell in line with a venerable tradition in this respect as well. The Italian Republican movement had encouraged and even bred political activism as a positive virtue. In capitalizing on this spirit, Bakunin did tend to retard the reception of Marxist theory in Italy. Engels in London was supposedly in charge of the Italian branch of the International. Bakunin and anarchism, however, were winning out over Marxist scientific socialism in the Peninsula by 1872. The Mezzogiorno and Romagna were ripe fields for his activity precisely because of the regionalist question and the growing awareness that unity had worsened existing economic conditions. Bakunin was aware of this. In particular, he realized the importance the struggle of the Paris Commune could have in Italian revolutionary circles. He appealed to a policy of the "Republic-Commune" as against the Mazzinian system of the "Republic-State." It was, in fact, in 1871 that the International first began to take hold in Italy, and the sympathy for the Commune was intimately bound up with this reception. As to the feud which was to come between Engels and Bakunin, the Italian revolutionaries apparently were indifferent to or quite unaware of it. In the Romagna-Emilia area, strongholds of Republican popularity, the socialist movement grew spontaneously, without contact with either Bakunin or Engels. It was sparked by the local Garibaldian forces. But here again, the trend was toward federalism. As for the pre-political peasantry, Bakunin had no more success rousing them than had Pisacane.[5]

Early Italian socialism was following native impulses. As in so many other Italian political movements, foreign ideologies served to buttress and give direction to, but not absorb energies which had arisen from, local problems. By 1876, however, anarchist power was beginning to fade. The legalitarian approach, with its stress on trade-unionism and the necessity of organized political action, began to take its place. More and more, the mood became one of seeking practical, material results and discarding the memories of the heroic age. Italian Socialists moved closer to their European comrades and the Marxist teachings. The influence of Benoît Malon, who arrived in Italy in 1874, along with the failure to stir up a popular revolution, weakened the anarchist hold. By 1879 Andrea Costa was criticizing the excessive concern with revolution. What was needed was greater study of existing economic conditions, greater attention to the people's needs. The first surveys by Sonnino and Franchetti of the Mezzogiorno attested to this same concern among decidedly conservative members of the Chamber for taking a closer look at the facts. In 1882 Costa went to Parliament. Even Cafiero gave way, advising his friends to follow the path of the German Social Democrats, to prepare themselves for the conquest of public power.[6]

The teaching of Marxist theory began in earnest only in the 1890's through the lectures of Antonio Labriola at Rome. The ground had been prepared for scientific as opposed to romantic and libertarian socialism by the decline of the anarchists. In Milan, Anna Kuliscioff, whose contacts with European Marxists were extensive, pulled young Italian revolutionaries away from the ranks of the Democratic and Republican organizations, and into the new Italian Socialist party, which was officially constituted in 1892. Filippo Turati, who was to remain her lifelong friend and companion, joined with her in founding the *Critica Sociale* in 1891. Leonida Bissolati left the dwindling Republican Party to become the first editor of the chief Italian Socialist newspaper — the *Avanti!* — which came out in 1896.

It was the realistic element in the Marxist critique of Italian revolutionary movements that was to have such a healthy influence on the development of politics during the Postrisorgimento. Inasmuch as Marxists attacked exaggerated individualism, the theatrical glorification of the solitary hero, their teachings were more suitable to the country's needs than Cavallotti's rhetoric. Scientific socialism was in keeping with the age of prose. When the Italian Socialist party was organized, it reflected this outlook, breaking with the anarchist and getting down to the problem of building a national organization. The conservative reaction to this new direction on the left showed the possibilities of such political coordination. Commenting on the Socialist Congress at Reggio Emilia of September, 1893, the *Nuova Antologia* was impressed by the high order of discipline and the Party's ability to draw an audience from the surrounding country-side. This worried the conservative journal [7] far more than the old-style radicalism that by the 1890's was championed by familiar personalities, the elite of the Chamber.

On the other hand, memories of the Risorgimento were by no means blotted out by Marxist realism. For all their emphasis on science and materialism, the vast majority of Italian Socialists remained fundamentally patriotic.[8] In this respect, the Party could be viewed as the spiritual off-spring of the age of national liberation. Similarly, Italian socialism never lost its humanitarian idealism. This was in part due to the struggle then going on in academic circles between the idealists and the positivists. Many looked upon the rage for science as the ultimate denial of the noble sentiments that had dignified the wars for independence. Pure Marxism could be construed as the culmination of positivism and the naturalistic view of man.[9] As such it seemed incompatible with the thought and action of Italy's triumvirate, which included, in addition to the technologically oriented Cavour, the bolder figures of Garibaldi and Mazzini.

In the aims of socialism, however, there was much that could be taken up as a response to scientism itself. For intransigent Communists who reject the Marxism of the heart that was so much a part of early social-ism, the leaders of the Italian Socialist party were simply not Marxists.[10] Filippo Turati has been called a humanitarian more than a scientific socialist. His early correspondence shows a fondness for poetry, at which he dabbled, which permitted an appreciation of Cavallotti's blend of art and politics. It was the romance of socialism that inspired the sentimental novelist Edmondo De Amicis to plan a great work, to be entitled "First of May." The novel was never finished; but his letters to Turati, if they reveal the author's meager acquaintance with Marxist theory, show how easily socialism captured the generous impulses of many Italian intel-lectuals.

In Italy, as in Europe generally, the new party preserved much of the passionate, romantic flavor of nineteenth-century revolutionary action while ridding it of what Turati called its verbal revolutionism.[11] Because of this, organized socialism was endowed with a balance between prevailing cultural attitudes and a realization of the material needs of society. This made the Party the most reasonable agent for the political education of the people, as well as a very fruitful outlet for the activities of dissatisfied educated Italians. The rational, hard-headed side of Marxism prevented a total opposition to the age of the Postrisorgimento on primarily aesthetic or historical grounds. On the other hand, many intellectuals — who for want of better might easily have drifted into the company of the politically uncontaminated elite — had an effective platform for political action that satisfied those memories of the heroic age on which they had been raised. The problem was to preserve this balance, to hold out not only against those who rejected all trace of humanitarian idealism, but against the more unsettling faction within the party that demanded a return to the activism associated with the martyrdom of Pisacane.

The beneficial effects of Marxist theory were evident in the Socialists' response to the crisis of the 1890's, which opened with the first Giolitti government and closed with Pelloux's and Sonnino's vain attempt to destroy the power of the Chamber of Deputies. In 1892, at the beginning of the story, the groundwork for later collaboration between the party and the new premier was being laid. The Socialists split from the anarchists. Shortly after becoming premier, Giolitti addressed the members of the Association of Labor at Turin. If the Socialists disavowed individual violence, Giolitti abandoned the fear of the proletariat. He spoke of the need for an improvement of the conditions of labor through meaningful legislation. Giolitti was certainly no Socialist. He believed in the naturalness of private property, opposed ideas of collectivization of the land, and hoped for the spread of intensive small-farmer cultivation. Yet he had recognized the need for tax and land reforms. His confidence in the Parliament as the center of Italian political life, his willingness to see all parties drawn into the constitutional framework, and his defense of the right of peaceful dissent helped Socialists justify their break with the advocates of violence. One of the first questions put to Giolitti as premier was what he intended to do about anarchist activities and about unrest among the Sicilian miners. Refuting the alarmists, he maintained that existing legislation was adequate. He opposed the use of exceptional laws in the name of public order, and defended the right to strike so long as violent methods were not used.[12]

In the Chamber, a handful of socialist Deputies, lead by Andrea Costa

and Camillo Prampolini, voted against Giolitti. But their votes were predicated on the doctrine of class struggle and therefore had little to do with
the scandalmongers. Although they joined in demanding a parliamentary
investigation of the banks, the target was not a man but the whole economic structure. This kept the socialist group relatively free of the highly
personalized invective of the incorruptibles. On the election issue, the
story was much the same. When Colajanni accused Giolitti of interfering
with the right of assembly, preventing hostile political rallies, Giolitti answered that 1893 was the first year in which the May Day celebrations
had not been the subject of a query in the Chamber. No Socialist rose to
challenge his reply. One notable exception to this disciplined opposition
along Marxist lines was a Neapolitan Socialist, Carlo Altobelli, who
leagued with the independents of the extreme left in their attempt to throw
doubt on the sincerity of Giolitti's attempt to end trasformismo.[13] In this,
Altobelli showed his affinities with those who resisted organized political
action. He was to become one of Giolitti's permanent enemies. He also
became a renegade from his party in 1915 when he joined in the cry for
war. It was equally true of Colajanni, De Felice, and Imbriani, who spoke
of themselves as Socialists, that they were never happy within the ranks
of any organized group and always remained on the fringes of the national
party.

Whatever individual Socialists may have felt, the party's position was
that the Bank Scandals were representative of the decadence of an entire
class. There was no rejoicing at the fall of Giolitti, because such glee
would have been a denial of the theory on which the party based its
claims to the future. In this way, orthodox socialism gave little support
to the evolution of the legend of Giolittian corruption. In the Crispi period
that followed, we have seen that the socialist opposition in the Chamber
defended the party against the Premier's charges that they were sub-
verting Italian unity. Nicola Badaloni, Enrico Ferri, Prampolini, Costa,
and Altobelli all stressed their acceptance of national unity and tried to
convince Crispi and the majority of the Chamber that socialism was a
force for civic education in Sicily and throughout the land. Ferri, a noted
criminologist of the positivistic school, offered the proofs of scientific
research to show that crimes were products of environmental and hered-
itary factors, not of Marxist propaganda. Class struggle, he told the Chamber, should not be confused with anarchistic violence. Ignorance and
poverty were behind the Fasci, not the Socialist party. Crispi, who regarded education as safe for cultivated men but considered it dangerous

to let peasants read Proudhon, chose to circumvent this loyal opposition by promising that his new security laws would be used only against foreign plotters and domestic anarchists. At this, Altobelli expressed his willingness to accept the new legislation with amendments.[14] Crispi then betrayed his promise, turning these laws against socialist organizations.

Raised in the era of conspiracy, Crispi was simply unable to see that the evolution of a national party was quite consistent with his own burning desire to keep Italy united. The socialist denial that there was any move afoot to sever Sicily from the mainland had no chance of convincing him. The greater danger for the national state, however, was the persistence of Crispi's attitude, his inability to accept the national significance of the party's role, thereby encouraging it to break into its own regional parts, to abandon Parliament, and to lapse into anarchism. Despite this, by the time Rudinì came to power after Adowa, the Socialists were remarkably well organized for a new party and seemed embarked on a parliamentary course. The Deputies had lined up with Cavallotti in attacking Crispi. When the Rudinì government made its obeisance to liberalism by promoting minimal decentralization and taking known progressives into the Cabinet, the Socialists were again faced with the possibility of greater legal latitude for political action. The party had to decide whether to continue the alliance with the nonsocialist left. This was the great issue before the National Congress that met at Florence in July, 1896. Prior to the Congress, the tactic of alliance with democratic factions had made important converts, including Leonida Bissolati. In certain regional meetings, however, and in the pages of the leading socialist paper, the *Lotta di classe*, the hard line was winning out. This position was given added impetus by a resounding electoral success. In Milan the noted Giolittian progressive, Luigi Rossi, who together with Fortis and Marcora had backed the revival of a one-color government in 1892, was defeated by Turati. Many could argue that a position of absolute independence was justified by this victory. In the end, a compromise, drawn up by Ferri and passed by the Florentine Congress, managed to satisfy the demands of regional branches while maintaining the usefulness of tactical alliances with advanced parties of the bourgeoisie. Perhaps a more important decision of the Congress was one that shunted aside Bissolati's proposal to spread socialism not only among the farm laborers but among sharecroppers and poor farmers. Because this going to the people — to the contadini who were described frequently as the real Italy — was rejected, the party was to come in for increasing criticism on the ground that it, like the

Chamber itself, had lost contact with the latent power of the masses and had succumbed to the fascination of parliamentary politics. The essentially political rather than economic nature of the policy agreed upon at Florence was also evidenced by the decision to found a daily newspaper in the capital. The *Avanti!* came into being as the central organ of the party, but not without grumbling from those who looked to the Lotta di Classe as the original voice of socialism,[15] whose brilliance was not dulled by the Roman bureaucratic milieu.

Rudinì's liberalism did not last out the summer of 1896. The Cabinet was reshuffled to bring in Giulio Prinetti as Minister of Public Works. Whereas Rudinì, a Sicilian nobleman, represented the southern landowner oligarchy, Prinetti, conspicuous for his part in fostering the Bank Scandals in the Chamber, spoke for Milan industrial interests. In January, 1897, Sonnino was to publish his celebrated article calling for a "Return to the Constitution" — that is, to a literal reading of the Statuto of 1848 — which would strip the Chamber of its control over the Ministry, restoring Crown power. Rudinì had anticipated this ultraconservative revival by closing down socialist clubs and seizing editions of radical newspapers. Turati led the Socialists in a parliamentary protest. Their attempt to restore constitutional freedoms by legal means met with a sharp rebuff. Rudinì emphasized in most alarming fashion his full executive powers to use the police in the name of order.

While the Government was moving farther to the right, the electorate was showing signs of an increased awareness that progressive reforms were needed. The general elections of March, 1897, ended in striking gains for the extreme left. Its total forces in the Chamber rose from 63 to 75, while the Socialists alone went from 7 to 16 seats. One of these was won from an entrenched Giolittian incumbent, Edoardo Daneo. During the campaign, Giolitti had called for an end to African expansion, a reduction of military expenses, progressive tax reforms, provincial decentralization, and the breaking up of the latifundia. His speech had warned against the use of exceptional security legislation that only benefited its victims and discredited the country's institutions.[16] By the summer of 1897, the Government was confronted with a series of strikes at Cremona. Rudinì's response was to shut down all socialist clubs in the Bologna province. A new security law, almost identical to that which Crispi had used, was passed over the protests of Cavallotti, Marcora, and Turati. The alliance between the legalitarian left, the progressive Giolittians, and the Socialists was still intact. But the Socialists were being forced to defend political maneuvering in the face of the Government's uncontrollable policy of reaction. The National Party Congress at Bologna in October came up with another compromise, one which gave greater emphasis to the economic foundation of political action and the use of strikes, but also upheld the value of promoting legislation.[17]

Rudinì seemed determined to force the extreme left to abandon constitutional protests. By December, 1897, his methods had forced many Deputies to desert the majority. His margin was cut to ten votes. Giolitti, recognizing that his hopes in the new Government were misplaced, had joined forces with Cavallotti, still the accepted leader of the extremist faction. In the countryside, a poor harvest in 1897 now began to have its effect. The price of bread climbed, nearly doubling in some southern areas; sporadic raids on bakeries, local merchants, and grain elevators broke out in the Mezzogiorno. It was clear that the Socialists had in no way incited these disturbances, and that they were truly spontaneous. The Party in 1898 had neither influence nor control over the rising of the contadini and urban poor in the South. By March the riots had spread from the original centers in Sicily, Puglia, and Calabria into Naples and then to Tuscany, the Marches, and Emilia. Rudinì took halfway measures: he lowered the tariff on grain in late April, and ordered the distribution of state grain stores in Sicily and the sale of bread at 1897 prices.

By May, Italy from south to north was in the grip of the explosion. The major drama, however, was to be played at Milan, not by any means the hardest hit city economically, but far more politically conscious. Several other facts helped make it the scene of the May Days. On March 6 Cavallotti was killed. His funeral at Milan brought out immense crowds. Socialists, Republicans, Democrats, and many moderates mourned the dramatic passing of the Bard of Democracy as Turati draped the red banner of the revolution over his coffin. On March 20 the fiftieth anniversary of the Five Days of 1848 recalled the city's revolt against the Austrians in which Cattaneo had figured prominently. On May 6 a clash between police and demonstrators at Pavia cost the life of a young student, Muzio Mussi, only son of the radical Giolittian Deputy and Vice President of the Chamber, Giuseppe Mussi. News of this sparked the protest that led to the May Days of 1898.

According to government statistics, eighty deaths had occurred in the city by May 9. Radical sources speak of as many as 180. In either case, the fault lay with the Government that had reacted with frantic measures to a dangerous but by no means revolutionary situation. Rudinì's conservative blindness to the true nature of the situation is best seen in his treatment of the Socialists. In Milan, where the Party had far more influence than in the Mezzogiorno, Turati tried to head off mob action. A Socialist manifesto condemning the Government called as well for non-violence, and ended in political demands for universal suffrage and the restoration of constitutional freedoms. Official socialist policy in 1898 was scarcely more subversive than Chartism in 1848. But the Premier was unable to see anything but the impending threat of revolution. He ordered General Bava-Beccaris to keep order in Milan at all costs. Martial law was decreed on May 7 and extended to Florence and Naples on succeeding days. Hundreds of arrests were made, including those of Turati, Anna Kuliscioff, Costa, and Bissolati among the Socialists. The panicky General spared no one who might conceivably be dangerous to national security. Noted Republican journalists and prominent Catholics, among them Don Davide Albertario, were locked up.

The folly of government that had lost its head was dramatized by two ludicrous incidents. One was the arrest of the Republican Deputy Luigi De Andreis, who was found carrying a map of the city's streetcar lines; the General was sure it was the master plan for the seizure of strategic points. General Bava-Beccaris also made prisoners of a group of Capuchins and their mendicant guests, who had been driven from their convent, soup dishes still in hand, by the fire of cannon which the General had zealously employed to quell the uprising.[18]

In the trials that followed, Turati was sentenced to twelve years in prison, though he served only nine months. Rudinì's excesses had produced a rapid collapse of his authority in the Chamber. The socialist Deputy Badaloni called on the Premier to face the alternative of freedom and an organized proletariat or civil chaos. On June 18 the Cabinet resigned without waiting for the vote. From the events of May the Socialists drew the conclusion that the tactic of barricades, as Turati put it, was no longer viable.[19] A defense of liberty through political action became the platform that permitted the Party to engage in the great defense of the Statuto and of the Parliament that closed the century.

As a background for this political struggle, it is important to bear in mind that General Pelloux, who succeeded Rudinì, had a good reputation even among Deputies of the extreme left. As in the case of the succession to Crispi, the Chamber had reason to feel that there would be a change of policy, an end to repression. However dictatorial the Pelloux ministry was to become, it is not to be supposed that he represented at first a continuation of the reaction of 1898. He had been Giolitti's Minister of War, had voted against Crispi, and had used his military prestige to counter arguments that were designed to sidetrack the opposition by appealing to patriot fears for the nation's safety. As premier, however, Pelloux was a fish out of water. He was unable to control his own majority, and was a very inept parliamentarian. Eventually he became the instrument of Sonnino. While Pelloux fumbled in his replies to the opposition, Sonnino, his floor leader, prodded him publicly to be more forceful in meeting domestic threats to the nation. That Sonnino was the real force behind the Government was soon recognized by all who took part during the parliamentary crisis of 1899–1900.[20]

Socialists were in a quandary as to what position the Party should adopt toward the new Premier. As the *Avanti!* editorialized, his was the peculiar instance of a liberal dressed in the uniform of a general. The socialist paper was willing to suspend judgment, offering its sincere applause should he move to restore constitutional law. Within a month, however, the Government presented the Chamber with a series of proposals obviously designed to curb radical protests and to arm the State with new legislation against subversives. Speaking for the Socialists, Ferri in essence repeated Giolitti's advice that the State had sufficient power in existing statutes and would do better to promote economic reforms. Since socialism had nothing to gain from popular insurrection, relying instead on the inevitable economic development of society, Ferri was inclined to dismiss the new draft legislation as immaterial.[21]

As yet, Pelloux's policy was unclear. When the bills came to the floor on June 1, 1899, however, the socialist group was immediately involved in a parliamentary fight to block passage. It allied with the nonsocialist extreme and with Giuseppe Mussi in presenting a prejudicial motion which would prevent the first reading of the bills. Since Mussi had been part of the legalitarian left which had backed Giolitti in 1892–93, this motion brought together again the same parliamentary forces which had tried to check Rudinì. In the vote on the motion, Pelloux won easily, 218 to 73. Giolitti voted with the majority. From the opening day of the crisis he took the stand that all bills, whatever their worth, should be debated. In this, he was and remained opposed to obstructionism. However, he was to be equally opposed to the Government's unconstitutional attempts to destroy the minority's right to defend its philosophy in the Chamber.

Having failed to block the first reading, the opposition then tried to delay it by a suspensive motion. This also lost, but the ranks of the anti-Pelloux coalition grew to eighty-two as Maggiorino Ferraris and the Giolittian Deputy, Francesco Guicciardini, sided with the minority. On June 6 discussion of the new press and security measures opened. From the first day, it was clear that the President of the Chamber, Luigi Chinaglia, was not endowed with the patience and parliamentary prudence which had distinguished Zanardelli's handling of the obstructionist campaign of 1893 against Giolitti's bank bill. Despite the fact that the minority of 1893 had sought only to get at the Committee of Seven reports — they had no constitutional point to defend — Zanardelli had shown great impartiality, while Giolitti had never suggested a limitation of debate, choosing instead to wear down the minority by open argument. In contrast, Chinaglia was frequently to use the chair as a platform for the expression of his own conservative views. Sonnino, a conspicuous obstructionist in 1893, waited only a few days in 1899 before putting forward a motion to alter the rules of the Chamber in order to facilitate a vote of cloture, this to get around the minority's use of filibusters, frequent roll calls, and endless amendments. By June 13 Pelloux had taken up Sonnino's and Chinaglia's line, insisting that his government had been tolerant beyond all reason.[22] Debate had been going on only a week; and the issue in 1899 was no less than the future of the Chamber of Deputies. Such haste, amounting to the same sort of panic that had been disastrous for Rudinì, foreshadowed the hardening of positions which was to produce a parliamentary impasse that forced the Crown and the legislature to choose either constitutional monarchy or absolutism.

On June 14 Zanardelli and Giolitti sought to head off disaster. In a speech essentially favorable to the minority, Zanardelli made an impassioned plea for the preservation of parliamentary government. Much as he disliked obstructionism, which prevented meaningful social and economic legislation from being enacted, he would not support Pelloux's demands for a limitation on debate. The former Garibaldian was saddened that the General's promises of liberal government had been forgotten. Giolitti's speech was one of the most important of his career. It was in part an attempt to convince Pelloux, a former colleague, that he had a glorious opportunity before him — that of providing for the nation's material problems, which had been the real source of the unrest of 1898 and of continuing popular uprisings. Giolitti denied that the disorganized tumults were political in nature. Having appealed to Pelloux to detach himself from those about him who were inclined to see revolutionary theory everywhere, he then warned the Government and the Chamber that the Socialists were drifting away from a policy of political action within the legal boundaries of the law and toward economic class warfare. He recalled his own speech to the Turin Association of Labor in 1897 and asked whether a head of government could still draw the cheers of the proletariat in 1899. Unless the Government adopted that part of the socialist program which was reasonable, Giolitti predicted that the Party would move in the direction of violence.

The speech also underlined the constitutional dilemma. Italy had two paths open to it: trying to draw the masses, upon whom the nation's future depended, toward the country's constitutional institutions; or repression. If absolutist regimes of the past, which had had far more power than the Italian Parliament, were unable to stand up against popular discontent, Giolitti concluded that a policy of toughness, after fifty years of liberty, would encounter insurmountable obstacles. Pelloux's government, he said, had an obligation that was a matter of both morals and justice. When the applause from the left of the Chamber had died away, Giulio Prinetti spoke for the majority. To Giolitti's words he had one reply. Who was Giolitti to speak of morality? Prinetti could remember the bank crash and the name of Tanlongo. Others chimed in, too, in this attempt to use the years of scandal to prevent the evolution of a progressive-socialist coalition. The relationship between the Bank Scandals and anti-parliamentary opinion had become more apparent with the passing of six years. Unmoved outwardly, Giolitti observed in reply that when he had come to power in 1892, none of the guilty parties was in jail. He had put them there, and there they had stayed until he was out of office, when they were released.[23]

Unable to get far in the attempt to discredit the progressives and quash the minority by vilification, Cambray-Digny, a former Crispian now closely associated with Sonnino, presented a draft of amendments to the Chamber's rules. The new rules would permit fifty Deputies to demand a vote on cloture. Speeches would be limited to fifteen minutes when it was apparent that debate was being arbitrarily prolonged, and the use of roll-call votes would be curtailed. By now, however, the opposition had grown to 113. The Socialists continued to obstruct all discussion of the security laws and of the rules changes. But it was significant that their leader, Ferri, having heard the speeches of Zanardelli and Giolitti, chose to stake his defense of the minority's case on constitutional and parliamentary grounds. When Prinetti, claiming to speak for effective parliamentary government, attacked the Socialists as destroyers of the country's representative institutions, Ferri countered by pointing out that obstructionism was a legal right, and that its use had increased the prestige of the Chamber. All eyes were on Rome. Even anarchists, he said, wrote to praise socialist Deputies not for acts of violence but for the legality of their methods.[24]

On the evening of June 22 the Chamber was prorogued for six days. When it reconvened, Pelloux in effect conceded the first round to the obstructionists by withdrawing the security bills and presenting in their place a royal decree. He admitted that this was an exceptional move, a statement that must certainly have angered Sonnino, who wanted the General to operate with less concern for the minority. But the decree had to be sanctioned by the Chamber eventually. This attempt to use the King's hand to weaken the opposition proved even less successful. Now that the King was involved, conservatives and moderates who feared for the Crown itself should the parliamentary crisis continue were to desert the majority. The first important break in the majority's ranks, however, came from Teodorico Bonacci, Giolitti's Minister of Justice in 1893 and later in the Rudinì cabinet, who offered a motion declaring the royal decree null and void. Ascanio Branca, another progressive whom Rudinì had taken as a sop to the anti-Crispians, also turned against Pelloux. The Statuto, he declared, was the pillar of the monarchy and of Italian unity. Turning to Prinetti and Sonnino, he placed the responsibility for Pelloux's reaction squarely on their shoulders. Tyranny from any quarter was inadmissible. "But between the tyranny of Ferri and that of Sonnino," he ended, "I fear the latter considerably more."

Sonnino's rebuttal was remarkable for its lack of logical consistency. He professed to see nothing extraordinary in the Government's legislative proposals; they were designed, he insisted, only to prevent Parliament from committing suicide by allowing itself to be the victim of an impasse created by the excesses of a tiny fraction of the Chamber. In the same breath, he admitted that decree law could be abused and that the royal decree would become law even if the Chamber refused its sanction. For proof of this interpretation he drew upon past cases that referred mainly to financial regulations, bringing forth a sharp retort from the floor. Sonnino's flimsy defense was reminiscent of Crispi's claims that his use of martial law and military tribunals was no different from emergency enactments during the War of 1866. Both comparisons were specious. Sonnino, again like Crispi, ended his speech with reference to the internal threat from the Church and the revolutionaries, and with a salute to the Statuto and national unity that all Italians owed to the lofty patriotism of the Crown. As for practical solutions, he recommended that the decree, together with the original press and security laws and the new rules legislation, be sent into committee with instructions to report back within twenty-four hours. The contradictions between Sonnino's praise of the Parliament and the methods he would use to preserve it were the result of a dilemma already encountered, the necessity of paying formal homage to the institution while seeking ways to emasculate its powers. The distinction between the Parliament and parliamentarianism underlay this speech as it did his political theory. But he was not allowed to get off this easily. Alessandro Fortis delivered a devastating critique that made the contradiction between Sonnino's constitutionalism and his denial of the rights of the assembly inescapable.[25]

On June 28 Pelloux called for a vote to send the security bill to the floor for a second reading. He staked the Government on it. This time the opposition was able to muster 138 votes to the majority's 208. On the next day a separate bill to convert the royal decree into law was read. Pelloux asked that it be placed on the agenda for July 1. Costa, by then a veteran of the Chamber, suggested that the budgets be taken up first. They were, after all, so very important. This remark produced the expected mirthful outburst of all who remembered how often Sonnino had tried to use this same device to block Giolitti's bank bill and later to weaken the opposition to Crispi. Nonetheless Pelloux had his way. The bill was entered on the agenda. On June 30 Prampolini tried to delay proceedings by demanding a roll-call vote. When Chinaglia refused the minority's request the Socialists and allied extremists tipped over the ballot boxes. The King again stepped in by closing the parliamentary session.[26]

There were essentially two choices before the Government in the winter of 1899–1900. Either it could attempt a revolution of the right, hoping to put Sonnino's ideas into practice, or it could abandon the hopeless battle to get the decree through the Chamber. Pelloux did neither. Had he chosen the first alternative, revolution would very likely have ensued. The socialist Deputies would have been unable to control the Party membership. The trend toward violence, as Giolitti had warned, would have become headlong flight from legalitarianism, placing the Crown itself in jeopardy. Yet Pelloux refused to withdraw the royal decree. In Ferri's words, it was as if Sonnino were forcing the Cabinet to commit suicide in order to get power for himself. That the Government's position was hopeless was conceded by one of its own backers, Giorgio Arcoleo. This noted political philosopher lectured Pelloux on the legal as well as political hole into which it had stumbled. Some of the courts had refused to sanction the ordinances contained in the decree, forcing an open confrontation between the executive and judicial branches. Worse, the situation had reached the point of absurdity, since the Parliament now had before it the original security bill, a royal decree, and another bill designed to convert the decree into law. Arcoleo did not suggest a way out, but it was clear that Pelloux had no hope of success unless he gave up the fight in the Chamber. Rudinì, still part of the majority, put it more succinctly: the royal decree had become the General's cardboard saber. Another conservative, Luigi Luzzatti, recognizing that Italy and perhaps the Crown faced disaster, bitterly attacked Pelloux's ineptitude. However, he ended on a softer note, which seemed to confirm Ferri's suspicions. If Pelloux had no interest in becoming the Great Chancellor of Italy, there were perhaps others behind him who did. Here Luzzatti was interrupted by cries from the Chamber, "It's Sonnino! It's Sonnino!"[27]

By March, 1900, it was evident that the game was up. Still Sonnino persisted in the name of the King and the patria. In a war of words with Sonnino, Ferri came around full circle, charging Sonnino with provoking violence and with being not a conservative but an anti-constitutionalist. In turn, Sonnino compared socialist obstructionism to "a poison imported from Vienna," where minorities destroyed the great national purpose. The concept of an idealized national parliament, gutted of its procedural props, was evident from Sonnino's reply. Ferri now took a stand that brought the Socialists into fundamental alliance with Giolitti on the question of tactics. Giolitti, who would not condone obstructionism, asked the Chamber to allow the decree to come to the floor so that all men might take their stand before the country. The Government sought to avoid this clarification, and instead offered the astounding motion, put by Cambray-Digny, that a committee draft new rules which would then be voted on without debate on their merits. Ferri countered with a prejudicial motion on only the second paragraph, which related to the vote without discussion. This was defeated 232 to 116. But Giolitti had cast his vote with the Socialists, while the latter had limited obstructionism by permitting the issue to come to the floor. The minority could still hope to block passage when the rules came out of committee.[28]

On March 29 the crisis reached its final stage. The Government rammed through a vote that would have forced the Chamber to pass on the new rules without discussion. If the majority would hold for this one vote, the rules could go into effect despite the obstructionists. On March 31 the Chamber's new President, Giuseppe Colombo, resigned and immediately gave the floor to Giolitti. Calling for the harmony of all men and for the principles of open debate, Giolitti asked the Deputies to express their esteem for the President of the Chamber. On April 2 Colombo was re-elected to the post by an easy victory over his nearest rival, Giuseppe Biancheri, whose presidency had been instrumental in supporting Crispi's reaction. Colombo's return to office was obviously a vote for Giolitti's plea for a return to parliamentary government. There still remained, how-ever, the vote of March 29 on the rules. Ferri and the minority maintained that the vote was illegal, since they had not been allowed to debate the Cambray-Digny motion. He now offered socialist collaboration with the parliamentary system if the old rules were kept. Recognizing that save in certain areas Italy was not ready for the leap into modern industrialized society and complete democracy, the Party would labor for the peaceful and political education of the Italian people. A gradual development of political consciousness consistent with socialist teachings was acceptable. But Parliament had to be preserved, for what, he asked, were material benefits to the proletariat without the guarantees of parliamentary free-dom? According to Ferri, the Socialist party did not wish to encourage Bourbon reaction by exposing the people to the methods the French had used against the Commune. Modern Socialists, he concluded, had dropped the pose of antiquated rhetoricians of conspiracy and revolution.

Giolitti then offered the Government its chance to escape from the blind alley without losing face completely. He proposed that a commis-sion elected by proportional representation of the Chamber, so as to in-clude men from all factions, be empowered to discuss changes in the rules. By implication, the Government would have to abandon the campaign to get the decree validated or to force through its own rules without dis-cussion. Giolitti made it clear that should Pelloux refuse to compromise, the Government and its majority would be responsible for any new out-break of violence. When Pelloux did refuse, Giolitti withdrew the idea. Remarking that it was a sad day for the history of the Italian Parliament, he expressed the thought of many present, that the General was not his own master.[29]

On May 16, 1900, the Chamber was prorogued. New elections were held. On them, the future of the Parliament rested. The results proved that the days of Rudinì and Pelloux were over. Ministerial candidates received 611,000 votes. The constitutional opposition, headed by Zanardelli and Giolitti, got 340,000. But the extreme left's tally showed a sizable increase. Its candidates polled 345,000 votes, 200,000 of which went to Socialists. On June 28 Pelloux resigned. The King, unwilling to take either Zanardelli or Giolitti, both too progressive for his views, settled on Giuseppe Saracco, a moderate who would serve as a transitional premier, ending the regime of Pelloux and preparing for the government of Zanardelli, which came to power in February, 1901, with Giolitti as Minister of the Interior.

The parliamentary Socialists had preserved the balance between disciplined political action and the idealism of the barricades. Not even the stubbornness of Sonnino and the complicity of Pelloux had been able to drive them into the arms of those among their own ranks who wished to return to the days of pre-Marxist violence, who hoped to relive the days of the Commune, witnessing again the active clash of proletariat and the bourgeoisie. Their work in the Chamber had been an indispensable ingredient in the preservation as well of the Italian Parliament. Not only had they been the leaders of the obstructionists; by tying the existence of the Party to the Chamber, and by resisting the temptations that Pelloux thrust upon them, socialist Deputies had helped to discredit the Government's policy even among conservative and moderate anti-Socialists. On July 29, however, this collaborationism was endangered by the assassination of the King at Monza. The plot, engineered by anarchists, threatened to restore to power the recently fallen advocates of toughness. Turati, in the Chamber, deplored the act as inconsistent with socialist respect for human life. Class war, not individual acts of violence, he said, was the answer to the needs of the masses. When asked to serve as attorney for the assassin, he refused. In the country, the royal armies awaited the command of the new King to invoke martial law. It never came. Victor Emmanuel III spoke of the "plebiscite of sorrow," the national mourning which bound the people to the Crown. On this he based his hopes for the new reign. Italy, he said, must preserve its great conquests of unity and freedom.[30]

The year 1900 in Italian history marked the restoration of Crown and Parliament. On the willingness of the former to reign and not to govern, as Sonnino wished, and on the ability of the latter to take up again the work of social and economic reforms advocated by the progressives, the future of constitutional monarchy depended. That the fate of King and Parliament were henceforth inseparable was recognized in the influential

Milan daily *Corriere della Sera*. By temperament, the new monarch was hardly fit to play the role of the Grand King. He was the good bourgeois ruler in every respect, close to the home and to his hobbies, uncomfortable in the uniform or in the banquet hall. Short and slightly deformed, Victor Emmanuel had indeed hoped to avoid the succession. He had asked his father to pass him over in favor of his cousin. Regicide had made him King, not his own choosing. In 1900, he had taken heed of those who advised that the era of Crispi was gone, and had embarked on his reign as a parliamentary sovereign. History was not to spare this reluctant ruler from decisions on which the life of the Parliament would hang, and with it, in the end, his crown.

As for the Socialists, they too shared in the work of restoration, and showed that they understood it. The question of the monarchy was not pressed in 1900 when the new King was enthroned. At the Rome Party Congress of 1900, and again at Imola in 1902, Turati's "minimalist" program of parliamentary support of progressive legislation won out. In 1903, when Giolitti returned as Premier, Turati was offered a cabinet post. He refused, but the offer itself was indicative of a major shift in the political climate. It was only five years since Turati had been jailed during the May Days. Now he was praising, with reservations, the work of the government that had liquidated Pelloux's reactionary policies.[31] Three times the Socialists voted for the Zanardelli-Giolitti cabinet. Outside Parliament, Italian labor under socialist direction moved away from insurrectional techniques and toward a struggle for material benefits. A national party had been formed capable of breaking down provincialisms and of serving as the instrument by which the amorphous, disaffected Italian people might be brought into personal political contact with the constitutional government. Indicative of this important function was the decline of social banditry, a prepolitical phenomenon closely tied to specific localities, and of the Mafia, which often acted on the local level as sort of a parallel government, both of which followed the creation of the Socialist party.[32] In time, the lingering doubts about Italy's social and political as well as geographical unity might be satisfied through the activity of this party. Its role in achieving that fusion between the people and official Italy which many found wanting was critical to the history of the Postrisorgimento.

Once in the Chamber of Deputies, however, the party's tendency to concentrate on the urban proletariat and to ignore the southern agrarian masses could be taken by opponents of legalitarian methods as a sign of betrayal of the people. Quite as if contact with official Italy exerted a stifling influence, producing that middle-class dehumanization which Sorel was to condemn, the movement, once legalized, seemed to ignore those areas of popular vitality so dear to the anarchists and so much a part of the romance of the Risorgimento. Enemies both of Socialism and of parliamentary government were quick to seize upon this oversight as proof of the Socialist party's inability to act as the instrument for drawing the people into the structure of "legal" Italy. Pasquale Turiello, whose theories foreshadowed those of the Nationalists of the Giolittian era, had written in this vein as early as 1894. The contadini would never follow the call for order, nor the concentration on long-range goals of the Socialists. Having entered Parliament, Turiello wrote, the party will only add to the institution's discredit while weakening its own popularity. "In Italy, more rapidly than elsewhere, socialism is taken over by its antithesis, by admiration for individualistic and artistic boldness, by the anarchic instinct . . . . In Italy the discipline and patience, which the parliamentary Socialists preach out of necessity, can only succeed, in the long run, in depriving them of esteem and a following."[33]

From its very inception the Socialist party was challenged to square its revolutionary heritage with its constitutional position. One can hear in Turiello's predictions the first faint sound of the Fascists' attacks on what they chose to call the Official Socialist party to distinguish it from the true radicalism untainted by the Chamber. Within the party itself there were always those who rejected the collaborationist direction its leaders took in 1900. Debate over tactics never ceased. They were often marked by an excess of vehemence, a rhetorical violence which showed that the longing to return to the poetry of the anarchist period was not dead. In certain areas, notably Romagna, the old Republican and anarchic strain was still quite alive. Two distinct directions always remained within the party. The more modest, practical outlook of Turati was on top. But even he was sensitive to the charge of having betrayed the heroic origins of socialism in return for parliamentary influence. Popular and anarchic tactics condemned in theory were often tolerated in fact for fear of compromising the party's position.[34] The tug of the days of Pisacane was always present. Like Italy itself in the Postrisorgimento, the Socialist party had its two mentalities, the one that had accepted the new order of things and the one that looked back fondly on the colorful period of dynamic populism. In moments of national crisis, the latter attitude, which could claim to represent the idealism of the Risorgimento, was always ready to reassert itself in the name of the continuing revolution.

If anarchic strains persisted within the Socialist party in spite of Marxist realism, more significant were the problems that plagued Italian conservatives. Socialism, however "official" to its critics, was by virtue of local organizations and trade unionism a movement linked to the people. However much Turiello wished to discredit its mass base, the party could not be denied its claim as the leading political spokesman for the wants of the poor. Why an ultraconservative like Turiello found it necessary to find a cleavage between the political apparatus of the party and the masses is of greater import. If the regimes of Rudinì and Pelloux fought to preserve the maximum power for the few while confining the spread of socialism, it was soon apparent that a narrow conservative philosophy was unsatisfactory. What was needed was a conservatism which could claim to express the will of the masses better than either socialism or parliamentary reformism. Pelloux himself became a forgotten man. It is almost impossible to find mention of the General after 1900 as a prominent force in Italian politics. The suddenness with which he faded from the scene was due only in part to his political ineptitude and to the fact that he took no interest in forming a political ideology which might have served as the foundation for an authoritarian revival. The reason later rightist thinkers and political organizers omitted his name from the list of their intellectual ancestors was that his type of authoritarianism lacked any popular base which would satisfy the desire to complete the work of national consolidation. His passing from the public eye did not mean that authoritarian doctrines died with him. They continued to exist and to flourish. But an examination of Italian conservative thought brings to light the manner in which rightist theory had to adapt itself to the historical problem of the Postrisorgimento, giving rise to ambiguities of considerable importance for later Italian history.

Church and State: The Conservative Dilemma

In discussing the Parliament and its critics, one of the chief sources of dissatisfaction with the legislative process was seen to be an inability to preserve two-party government. By 1900, however, with the emergence of the Socialist party and the victory of the anti-Pelloux alliance, the formation of a government of the left, directed by progressives but supported by Socialists in matters of reform legislation, furnished one part of the theoretical dialogue which was to enliven politics once again. The problem was where to produce the antagonist on the right. Conservatives had been just as critical of trasformismo as had radicals. Stefano Jacini, one of the first to take up the question, had observed in 1866 that the Austrian War had had a corrosive effect on the individuality of the Sinistra and Destra. He saw Italy's historic parties breaking apart under the pressure of national emergency, and regretted that the united front needed to win the war had not given way to realignments on the old pattern. At the extreme left, the problem as he saw it was much the same. The Republicans were losing their own identity because of the way in which the Statuto of 1848 was being applied. The King was no more than a chief magistrate, whatever the role assigned to the Crown under the terms of the constitution.

Where could a conservative party get its strength? The logical source was the Church. Jacini's federalism — he realized that a regionalist solution had been abandoned in the name of the struggle for liberation —[35] was in part motivated by his desire to come to terms with the Vatican. A centralized national state would be too hostile to the Church, hence Jacini's reluctance to condone the occupation of Rome. As late as 1869 there had been hope that Italy would not make the move.

After Porta Pia, however, conciliation was far more difficult. That *petit coin de terre* proved an insuperable block in the path toward conciliation and toward the formation of a conservative party along lines envisioned by Jacini. The encyclical *Respicientes ea omnis* of November 1, 1870, proclaimed Pius IX's firm intention of conserving the lands of the Church intact for his successors. All those, regardless of their dignities, who had in any way helped perpetrate the invasion of papal territories were excommunicated. Whatever the possibilities for Catholic participation in Italian politics within the terms of the *Syllabus*, those chances were badly hurt by the events of September, 1870. The Guarantees of the following year were given equal treatment. The Pope, in a letter to Cardinal Antonelli in June, 1872, rejected completely any such protection from the State. In order to stiffen the Church's position, the non expedit was redrafted in 1874 in such a manner as to close any loopholes relative to a clerical participation in the Chamber of Deputies. The lines hardened after 1870. The Church began to organize the faithful through the agency of the Catholic Congresses. On the opposite side, anticlericalism became more pronounced, reaching its peak in 1881 with an attack on the bier of Pius IX as it was being carried to its final place of entombment. In

1882 Leo XIII reaffirmed the non expedit. By 1886 it had become *non licet.*[36]

Many Italians besides Jacini were saddened by the Vatican's position. Liberal Catholicism was far from dead. It had its principal following in Lombardy, home of the Ambrosian church. Here neo-Guelph traditions, the influence of Manzoni, and years of Austrian rule had left a different spirit regarding Church-State relations than in Southern and Central Italy. There was also the more practical factor of regional opposition to making Rome Italy's capital. But even before Rome was taken, lay organizations were springing up, with the Vatican's approval, to check such conciliatory tendencies. Catholic retrenchment was begun in earnest in 1874 with the meeting of the First Catholic Congress, whose refusal to back the conservative Destra has been mentioned. These Congresses set out to deprive the civil government of its popular backing, creating local educational, charitable, and electoral networks. The Church seemed bent on the creation of a state within the State, opening a crusade against the work of the Risorgimento.[37]

There were hopes that Leo XIII might relax his predecessor's intransigence toward the Italian nation. Conservatives could recall that, as the Cardinal Archbishop Pecci of Perugia, the new Pope had shown a singular talent for smoothing over Church-State differences. He had handled with worldly finesse the touchy matter of a circular signed by patriotic priests in which Pius IX was begged to renounce the temporal power. Three of the erring priests were in Cardinal Pecci's diocese. His tactful defense of the Vatican's position while dealing with the civil authorities marked him as a man of uncommon prudence. When Perugia was occupied by Piedmontese troops, he had written an almost ingratiating letter to Victor Emmanuel in which he expressed his personal willingness to receive the King should he come to Perugia. It was unfortunate, the Cardinal concluded, that his own desires had to give way to the larger demands imposed by the conflict between Church and State.[38]

Leo XIII's early encyclicals seemed to confirm conservative expectations of a lessening of papal hostility. In 1879, the second year of his pontificate, the Pope issued the first of his attacks on socialism, *On Socialism*. It was observed that the familiar references to the Church's abnormal position in Italy were passed over, the bulk of the message being devoted to the danger from impious political sects that threatened all authority everywhere. Pantaleoni, Cavour's agent in the fruitless negotiations with the Papacy in 1860, thought he saw a new attitude emerging in Leo's teachings. The old stubbornness that had turned the faithful from their civic duties, he wrote in 1884, might be abandoned. Only fanatical clericals continued to believe in a collapse of Italian unity. The temporal power might be renounced. The Church was moving toward a more modern view of society.[39]

By the time he had become Pope, Gilson wrote, Leo XIII had from direct personal experience acquired wisdom in political problems and in the specific nature of the temporal authority. The word "State" had for him just as concrete a meaning as the word "Church."[40] Many Italian conservatives of the time agreed with this assessment and took note of what appeared to be a new direction. They failed to appreciate the Pope's extremely traditionalist view of society. Cardinal Pecci's secular experience had taught him much about political doctrines that were threatening the faith. As Pope, he set out to combat them, not to come to terms with them. The path chosen was not that of Pius IX's apocalyptical condemnations. Italy had withstood the test of dire prophecies. Meanwhile, there came that "deadly plague," that "sect of men, who, under various and almost barbarous names, are called socialists, communists, or nihilists, and who, spreading all over the world . . . no longer seek the shelter of secret meetings, but, openly and boldly marching forth in the light of day, strive to bring to a head what they have long been planning — the overthrow of all civil society whatsoever." Despite this, rulers, deceived and terrified by threats, have looked on the Church with suspicion, even hostility, "not perceiving that the attempts of the sects would be in vain if the doctrine of the Catholic Church and the authority of the Roman Pontiffs had always survived, with the honor that belongs to them, among princes and peoples." The encyclical *On Socialism* went on to deny man's natural equality in civil society, to reaffirm the doctrine of the divine origin of all authority and the sanctity of private property. The Pope called on rulers to seek refuge in the Church against socialism, and to "restore the Church to the condition and liberty in which she may erect her healing force for the benefit of all society."[41]

While attacking political radicalism, Leo XIII made clear the Church's acceptance of the benefits of science and the modern triumphs of human reason. The encyclical *On Christian Philosophy* of 1879 sought to deny the rationalists' charge that the intellect entered into bondage by subjecting itself to divine authority. That the Pope was not prepared to meet the enemy on its own rational ground, however, could be seen in his return to Christian philosophy as elaborated by St. Thomas. Had not the

very enemies of the faith been compelled to admit the power of the An-
gelic Doctor's reasoning, so much so that leaders of heretical sects openly
declared that were those teachings taken away they could easily do battle
with all Catholic teachers? The reference to heretical leaders, in this case
Martin Bucer, pointed up Leo's extreme conservatism. The roots of modern error and of contemporary subversion of authority lay in the Reformation, not merely in the Enlightenment.[42]

This became clearer in the encyclical *On Civil Government* of 1881.
Society had enjoyed tranquillity and a sufficient prosperity so long as
the civil and religious powers maintained the friendly agreement that had
been established following the fall of the Roman Empire. It was papal
consecration of political power, enhancing the authority of rulers, that
had preserved this society from the revolts and seditions which could be
seen in Germany immediately following the so-called Reformation. Leo
stressed the link between Protestant heresy and the false philosophy of
the eighteenth century, which spoke of a popular authority and which
produced an unbridled license regarded by many as the only true liberty.
Carrying the history of social disintegration down to his own day, the
Pope spoke of the horrors of communism, socialism, and nihilism as out-
growths of the original heresy. Against the "hideous deformities of the
civil society" of his times, the State's coercive laws were insufficient, although Leo was careful to note that rulers were "right to a certain extent"
in making use of these. But only the salutary fear of God could lead men
to duty. The Church offered princes and other rulers of the State the protection afforded by religion against the calamities of society.[43]

There was nothing modern in teachings that took up arguments found
in Joseph de Maistre, save that the power of religion was now made
available to all types of civil authority. It was this the conservatives heard.
Leo had upheld the doctrine of the divine origin of authority regardless
of how the ruler was designated. Designation did not confer the authority,
hence the social contract theory was rejected. But there was no prejudice
against democracy as a form of government. The Church's support in the
struggle against subversion was made available to representative governments as well as to legitimate monarchies. While the Pope restated the
traditional doctrine that men need not obey "when anything is demanded
of them which is openly repugnant to the natural or to the divine law,"
it is wrong to see this as a call to disobedience, as some have done.[44]
Were that the message of the encyclical, the Italian conservatives could
never have responded to the appeal. Gilson is correct when he states that

the refusal of obedience to rulers whose orders are contrary to the law of nature and divine law is very different from an attempt to overthrow by force the established political power. The Pope's language was very pointed here. He cited the patience of Christians in pagan Rome, and concluded with a firm pronouncement on the necessity of obedience. On the relations between Church and State, Leo was equally temperate, respecting the sphere of the civil authority in matters of a secular nature and calling for harmony between Church and State when the decision belonged to both sacred and civil power.[45]

In response to the Pope's apparent wish to play down the Roman Question, a group of conservatives, among them Jacini, founded at Florence a liberal Catholic review, the *Rassegna Nazionale*. Professing their loyalty to the House of Savoy and united Italy, the group tried to induce Catholics to enter national politics. By following the non expedit were they not abetting the advance of socialism, materialism, and positivism? Styling themselves "Catholics and Italians," "conservative friends of progress," the collaborators of the *Rassegna Nazionale* issued a formal program in 1880. The liberal Catholic association was constituted for the purpose of contributing with all its strength to "the preservation of united, free and independent Italy under the rule of the House of Savoy, without any mental reservations: obtaining respect for all rights within the State, first among these that which the Supreme Pontiff has to the free and independent exercise of his apostolic ministry, and the exercise of all the freedoms necessary for a civil people, first among them being freedom of conscience; combatting and destroying any form of despotism whatsoever, may it come from above or below . . . and, first among despotisms, that which invades the rights of the family in those things pertaining to the instruction and education of children." The fact that Leo XIII had not mentioned the Syllabus of Errors may have been the factor that led one of the group, Guglielmo Audisio, to affirm that the Syllabus did not constitute a definition of faith.[46]

This was the platform for a conservative party which would restore a proper balance to Parliament, ending trasformismo. But it met with an immediate response from intransigent Italian Catholics who rejected any departure from the policy of Pius IX. The Fifth Catholic Congress, meeting at Modena in 1879, pointed out the dilemma of liberal Catholicism. Either one was a Catholic and as such worked for the elimination of all laws that contradicted the teachings of the Church, or one was no Catholic at all. As for united Italy, it was, like all nations, a result of divine providence. It could disappear just as easily as it had taken shape. When was Italy more flourishing, magnificent, and glorious than in the days of the Communes? The *Rassegna Nazionale's* antisocialism, its plea for a relaxation of the non expedit in order to combat subversive materialistic philosophies, was a complete contradiction. How could one defend private property and accept spoilation of the lands of the Church? Socialism was a result of the liberal concept of the State. To defend the latter and attack the former was a logical absurdity.[47]

Liberal Catholicism has been called a state of mind or sentiment that was logically a contradiction.[48] Between the encyclicals of Leo XIII, however mild in tone, and the program of the *Rassegna Nazionale*, there was an insuperable barrier. Intransigent Catholics were aware that one could not swear unconditional loyalty to united Italy and insist on the Church's independence. As long as the revolutionary gains of the Risorgimento were to be defended, there could be no conciliation. The Roman Question, as yet unmentioned by Leo XIII in his encyclicals, was always present. It was also plain that many Catholics had not accepted a united Italy as a permanent entity. Allusion to the Communes was a challenge to the nation, to official Italy from its enemies. Liberal Catholicism was dealt a blow within a month after the appearance of the encyclical *On Civil Government* when anticlericals assaulted the coffin of Pius IX. The Freemasons struck a medal in honor of the demonstrators, some of whom had tried to throw the corpse into the Tiber. Leo XIII appealed to Franz Joseph, but to no avail.[49] In 1882, the non expedit was reaffirmed.

The encyclical *On the Christian Constitution of the State* of 1885 departed in significant respects from Leo's earlier teachings. Again the divine origin of all authority — regardless of the form that authority takes — was taught, along with the necessity for obedience. Greater emphasis, however, was placed on the ruler's obligation to make public profession of the true faith and to "shield it under the credit of the sanction of the laws, and neither to organize nor enact any measure that may compromise its safety." Thus far, the message permitted Italian Catholic conservatives to hold on to their hopes. But the encyclical in other respects singled out Italy for special condemnation while encouraging a rapprochement with foreign states. Leo emphasized the Church's sovereignty in international relations and tied this to the civil sovereignty which God's providence had provided as the safeguard of this independence. The overthrow of the temporal power was referred to as an attempt to cramp to the utmost the freedom of the Church. On political activities, Leo allowed a prudent part to be taken in municipal administration. But on the national level, Italy was to be boycotted, whereas Catholics in other lands were permitted to extend their efforts beyond the local level of government.[50] The encyclical answered in effect the pleas of the intransigents who played up Italy's communal pattern prior to unification. Capturing of city administrations by Catholic politicians while keeping clear of national elections to the Chamber would become the pattern henceforth. Nonetheless, to erect a barrier within Italy against radicalism, as the Pope certainly wished, required that some way be found to end the struggle between the two powers that would also satisfy the Church's position on temporal sovereignty. Leo apparently thought he had found the answer; but in attempting to execute the plan he was to find that the Church's influence was almost nil when it ran up against the diplomatic needs of the modern state.

If Italy was to be politically boycotted, the encyclical was obviously designed to further Leo's plans for closer ties with Germany. The sections dealing with Church-State relations mentioned the possibility of formal arrangements between rulers and the Roman Pontiff touching special matters, adding that such relations were possible with non-Catholic nations. While the Church considered it unlawful to place various religions on an equal footing with the Catholic faith, it did not "condemn those rulers who, for the sake of securing some great good or of hindering some great evil, allow patiently custom or usage to be a kind of sanction for each kind of religion having its place in the State. And, in fact, the Church is wont to take earnest heed that no one shall be forced to embrace the Catholic faith against his will."[51]

The "great good" and the "great evil" referred to Bismarck's seven-year military bill and his fears for the rise of the Socialists. Both the Center and the Social Democrats opposed his army budget. And the latter had doubled their strength in the Reichstag in 1884. A flurry of correspondence between the Vatican and the Chancellor took place in 1885–86. Bismarck relaxed some of the May Laws in 1885 in order to woo the Center away from an alliance with the Social Democrats. Leo XIII was called in as arbiter of the Caroline Islands dispute. The Pope wrote Bismarck, addressing him as "Great Chancellor," and emphasized the Papacy as a force of conservatism. Bismarck responded with a vague letter in which Leo was styled "Sire." Ludwig Windthorst, leader of the Center party, was told that the Pope wanted the army budget passed. But the German Catholics balked, and voted against the bill on January 14, 1887. Bismarck called new elections. To compromise the Catholics he published letters from

Cardinal Jacobini, Secretary of State at the Vatican, expressing the Pope's desire that the Center let the army bill go through. These letters apparently were to have been kept secret. Their publication raised a sharp protest in Italy from intransigent Catholics who did not approve of Leo's pro-German policies.[52]

Bismarck got his bill through the Reichstag as the Center abstained. But Leo XIII's diplomacy was to prove a complete failure. He had not only been interested in promoting a conservative barrier in Germany to the spread of radicalism; behind the accord with Germany was the plan to enlist Bismarck's support in settling the Roman Question on papal terms. Italy seemed diplomatically isolated during the first months of 1887. Crispi, who was to become Premier on August 7, did not know that the Triple Alliance had been renewed. He took fright for Italy's security when he saw that Bismarck and the Pope were working together. Unhappily for Leo, he too was unaware of the fact that Italy was stronger diplomatically under the new terms of the Alliance signed on February 20, 1887. In the negotiations preceding the renewal of the pact, Bismarck had in fact exerted strong pressures to induce Austria-Hungary to meet Italy's demands. The army bill passed on March 12, 1887. On March 17, Bismarck began leaking the news of the renewal of the Triple Alliance. But on the same day, Cardinal Luigi Galimberti left for Berlin on his mission to win German support for a solution to the Roman Question. Bismarck managed to evade any commitment, offering only the admission that true independence did not exist without territorial possessions. But he would not be pinned down. It is probable that the Pope was trying to get an international agreement on the Guarantees, and possibly a strip of land connecting the Vatican with the sea.[53] Once he knew of the Alliance, Leo was obliged to press on, having taken up a policy which was by no means popular with the Curia. The Vatican persisted in its hopes that Bismarck would put pressure on Italy until Crispi's visit to Friedrichsruh in October, 1887, dispelled all doubts. The new Italian Premier and the German Chancellor dismissed the Roman Question from their talks. It was a purely Italian issue. Leo was bitter, not only toward Germany, but toward Austria-Hungary, which had been of no assistance. His feeling that Bismarck had tricked him[54] was certainly justified.

By the time Leo XIII learned of the renewal of the Triple Alliance, however, plans for effecting a conciliation with the Italian government had already begun. In December, 1886, Mgr. Geremia Bonomelli, Bishop of Cremona, wrote the Pope of his hopes for peace between Church and

State, the dream of all good men. Leo responded in vague but nonetheless favorable terms. These letters were published by the *Rassegna Nazionale* on February 1, 1887. According to some authorities the Vatican had given official approval for their release. More impressive as a token of the Church's willingness to treat with the Government was the clerical reaction to the Italian defeat at Dogali on January 26, 1887. Moving inland from the Red Sea coastal settlement of Massawa to put down Ethiopian frontier incursions, a column of five hundred men had been ambushed. Bonomelli saluted the fallen Italian troops in a printed pamphlet. Funeral services in Italian churches seemed to have papal sanction. On February 28, in his allocution to the Sacred College, the Pope spoke of the advantages to Italy that would result from recognition of the Papacy's just claims.[55] These were not spelled out. The *Moniteur de Rome*, which reflected the Pope's personal views, in an article on February 13 denied that the Pope's aims were anti-Italian. Peace with the Church would mean political participation of Catholics, hence a source of conservatism, a force for social order. The paper also suggested that the Guarantees were of an international nature. Once the question of their juridical status was properly settled, the enemies of Italy abroad would be deprived of any excuse for interference with Italy's internal affairs.

To this point, the Vatican had been operating on the assumption that Italy was isolated in Europe. Crispi, sharing this belief, was turning to France and away from Germany in order to bolster Italy's forces. He was not in the Depretis government and hence knew nothing of the negotiations with Berlin in progress in February, 1887. By late March, however, the Pope knew that his assumption was false. It is clear that Crispi was unaware of the exact terms of the Alliance even after he had become Minister of the Interior on April 4, 1887. From that post, he tried to direct Italian foreign policy, offering Depretis advice that was in marked contrast with the terms of the Triple Alliance. Depretis died on July 31. Crispi succeeded him.

In order to understand Crispi's part in the negotiations with the Vatican for a settlement of the Church-State issue, it is important to keep in mind that he was extremely fearful for Italy's safety during the spring of 1887. As for the Vatican, even after Leo XIII had learned of the Triple Alliance, he persisted in his conciliatory policy, perhaps because he could not turn back without admitting that the intransigent Catholics were right in opposing any letting up of the total war against united Italy. He also had some reason to hope that Bismarck might yet use his influence at Rome in favor of conciliation. On April 12 the *Unità Cattolica* called on Italians to appeal to the Pope to restore peace between Church and State. No conditions would be placed in the way of conciliation. Leo would prove more generous than Pius VII had been with Napoleon. At the ceremonies for the unveiling of the façade of the Florentine cathedral, the King and Queen were blessed by the Archbishop, Mgr. Cecconi. The Archbishop's pastoral letter written for the occasion, entitled "Peace," was praised by the *Moniteur de Rome.* On May 23 Leo XIII himself raised the hopes of Italian conservatives by speaking of his desire for an agreement with the Italian government, to put an end to the "distressing discord" between Italians and the Holy See. The Pope mentioned the necessity of according the Holy See full freedom. But no specific reference was made to the temporal power. Italy's interests, he said, would not suffer any damage; rather, the nation would benefit by a settlement of this sort.[56]

The high point of the movement for an accord between Church and State was the appearance on May 31, 1887, of Father Luigi Tosti's celebrated pamphlet "Conciliation." In it an imaginary priest, Don Pacifico — obviously meant to be Tosti himself — told of his dream for a solution to the Roman Question, a dream suppressed as long as Pius IX had lived. Under Leo XIII, the Prince of Peace, a new spirit of accommodation gave reason to believe that an end to the struggle was in sight. The articles in the *Moniteur de Rome* and the blessings bestowed on King Humbert by the Archbishop of Florence filled Don Pacifico with joy. He envisioned the Pope borne aloft on the shoulders of 30,000,000 Italians. Tosti did not explain how conciliation was to be effected. But he did make it clear that Rome was Italian. If the attack at Porta Pia had been an ugly business done by a minority of Italians, that minority had created a government, passed laws, and in this way had become the majority. The Pope could not ask the King for the return of the city, for it had become part of the nation.[57]

Father Tosti, abbot of Monte Cassino, papal archivist, and student of Thomistic theology, had long been a friend of Leo XIII. His *History of the Lombard League*, written in 1848, had been dedicated to the Italian nation in whose creation he had played a part. Jailed briefly by the Bourbon regime, he had returned to Monte Cassino, where he devoted his time to scholarship and to the cause of peace between Italy and the Vatican. His correspondence with members of the Italian governments of the 1860's proves his patriotism had not died. He wanted Pius IX to abandon the temporal power for the sake of united Italy. Even the occupation of Rome had not destroyed his loyalty to the national idea.[58] On May 27, 1887,

Tosti went to Crispi, then Minister of the Interior, with a request from the Pope that the basilica of St. Paul Outside the Walls be restored to the Benedictines. Tosti certainly wished to use this concession as a spring-board from which to launch the topic of conciliation. Whether Leo had this in mind as well has never been decided. Crispi later insisted that Tosti gave him to believe that the Pope had approved of this wider mission. In Italy, many felt that Leo had read Tosti's pamphlet before it was published, and hence must have realized the implications of sending the patriot priest to Crispi. Tosti, in a letter to Crispi, mentioned in passing that the Pope had not read the work; but he may well have written that in order to protect the Papacy. Official Catholic sources emphatically deny that Leo had seen the pamphlet, and many students of the affair feel that there was no mutual agreement between Tosti and Leo XIII.[59]

On the very day the "Conciliation" was published there appeared in the authoritative *Moniteur de Rome* an article that did contradict the pamphlet's views on the juridical position of the city of Rome. In response to intransigent clerical journals that had been shocked by the Papacy's apparent surrender to the Italian government and had insisted that the Papal States would have to be restored, the *Moniteur* spoke only of that "little corner of earth." To leave that to the Pope, the journal concluded, would scarcely be harmful to a great nation of 28,000,000 people.

Reduced in size though it had become, the temporal power still re-mained a barrier to conciliation. No Italian government faithful to the ideals of the Risorgimento could give up that bit of land, either to Pius IX or to Leo XIII. Nonetheless, talks between Tosti and Crispi's representa-tive dragged on through the month of June and into July. Neither side would give an inch until assured of what it would receive in exchange. Little was said about out-and-out conciliation, save by Tosti, and he was shortly to be disillusioned. Pressure from French and Spanish as well as Italian Catholics increased. It has been said that the French government, in agreement with clerical leaders, warned Leo that peace with Italy could lead to a schism among French Catholics and that war was imminent in Europe. France and Russia would win, restoring the Papal States.[60] From Germany, on the other hand, there was no help forthcoming. The Pope's diplomacy had ended in a perilous state of isolation. Meanwhile Crispi's fertile imagination began conjuring up visions of plots, useful to justify his crushing of the Fasci in 1894.

To put an end to this intolerable situation, the new Secretary of State, Cardinal Rampolla, drafted a circular to the nuncios. It was dated June

22, a time when Tosti was still dickering with Crispi, and it was to remain secret, to be used only to inform foreign governments that the temporal power was indispensable to the Church's independence. It became public property when the radical *Riforma* printed a copy of it on July 23, causing a furor among anticlericals while dashing the expectations of Italian conservatives. Not only did Rampolla insist on the temporal power; he raised the specter of a collapse of Italian unity. Speaking of "Italy as it is officially constituted," the message went on to say that the nation's true glory consisted in the presence of the Holy See on Italian soil. The same prosperity and greatness could just as well exist should unity disappear.

Once the news was out, the Vatican assured the public that the circular only paraphrased the Pope's own letter on the subject. This was duly published on July 26 in the *Osservatore Romano* and was dated June 15, but may have been written only after the circular became known and predated in order to cover the Pope. There are those who believe Rampolla was the evil genius behind the intransigents' plot to ruin conciliation, that by issuing his circular he had in fact forced the Pope's hand.[61] However, even before the outburst of indignation caused by Rampolla's circular, Crispi, defending the Depretis government in the Chamber against attacks from radicals who rejected any deal with the Vatican, had spoken in such a way as to make peace between the two powers very unlikely. Crispi had praised the Pope's personal qualities, but stressed the autonomy of the modern State. "We don't ask for conciliation, nor do we need it, because the state is at war with no one. Nor do we know or wish to know what the Vatican may think on this subject." The papal letter may have been written as claimed on June 15, five days after Crispi's speech. Sources close to the Curia refuse to see Leo XIII as a pliant tool in Rampolla's hands.[62] As for Crispi, he certainly had acted as if he wished to exploit the Tosti mission. But his own enthusiasm may have cooled off once he was better informed on Italy's diplomatic position, which was far stronger than he had supposed.

Tosti was forced to make public confession of his error. His letter of repentance did not satisfy the intransigent clergy. In a second letter, which he was assured would remain secret, the discredited abbot properly humbled himself, only to see this one published as well.[63] That put an end to the affair as far as the liberal Catholics were concerned. Stefano Jacini conceded that the Church could not become the basis for a conservative party. The patriotic sentiments of Pius IX and Leo XIII had been sacrificed to the Church's universalist character, to the demands of foreign

Catholics. Jacini still maintained that the transfer of the capital to Rome had been a blunder. Now that it was the nation's center, however, it would have to remain so; to give it up would be a disaster. Much as a frankly conservative party was needed to give balance to Italian politics, Jacini realized the fundamental dilemma of the conservatives. The party they sought would have to be national and should be Catholic. But when the Papacy demanded the temporal power, it was in effect threatening the dismemberment of the nation. As a last resort, he suggested an internationalization of the Guarantees. Few Italians, he conceded, would accept such a plan, which would imply foreign interference in Italian internal affairs. It was the French who seemed interested in the scheme.[64] That was scarcely a recommendation.

Essentially, the problem of Italian conservatives who represented the school of liberal Catholicism was that the Church remained politically subversive. Moreover, conservatives who did not share Jacini's regional and religious sentiments feared the "Reds" no more than they feared the "Blacks." Republicans and Socialists opposed in theory the monarchy and the rule of a middle-class oligarchy. But this radicalism was working within the framework of the nation, as part of the existence of united Italy. The Republican tradition was a national heritage of the Risorgimento. And when the Socialists split with the anarchists, they too entered the lists as a national party, committed to legal political action, while carrying over much of the patriotism of pre-Socialist revolutionaries who had fought for unification. This sort of radical political activity was quite different from the organization of Catholic groups on the local level that boycotted Italy by means of the non expedit on the national level. Pantaleoni had been mistaken in thinking that only a few diehards still counted on a collapse of unity.[65] Jacini, pious and moderate though he was, had to accept the fact that Catholicism had retained its antinational purpose. In 1898, during the reaction of the Rudinì government, the threat of the Blacks was met with the same rigor as that of the Reds.[66]

There is no doubt that the prospects of liberalism and democratic reform were furthered by this situation. While recognizing that a generous degree of political freedom was maintained by the governments of the Postrisorgimento despite the absence of a long tradition of political responsibility, one must also take into account the position of those who would have blocked progressive legislation and favored authoritarian rule were it not for their failure to come to terms with the Church. The encyclical On the Christian Constitution of the State had stated that "unrestrained freedom of thinking and of openly making known one's thoughts is not inherent in the rights of citizens, and is by no means to be reckoned worthy of favor and support." [67] This was an invitation to those who feared freedom of speech, press, and assembly to alter the letter and spirit of the Statuto. The failure of conciliation was a blessing to the cause of civil liberty.

But the dilemma of Italian conservatives was more complex than this inability to come to an agreement with the Vatican. Conciliation was conceived not only as a means of creating a political dike against the flood of radicalism. It was often tinged with what appeared to be quite the opposite of a narrow oligarchic outlook — that is, a strain of populism. The reason for this was the need many felt not only to strengthen the Government against subversives, but to solidify the nation by drawing the large bulk of Italy's apolitical and Catholic population into the life of the State. Because of this, conservatives with pronounced anticlerical reputations could leap at the chance of coming to terms with the Vatican in order to put an end to the non expedit. This would end subversion of the nation by the Catholic masses, leaving the radicals isolated. Here was an alternative to a widening of the suffrage and to the creation of national fusion through political reform. In particular, corporative theory, reminiscent of Adam Müller and Louis de Bonald, seemed to permit identification of the people with the nation without involving concessions to parliamentary democracy.

There is some reason to believe that the ingenuous, patriotic Tosti had stumbled unwittingly into a plan that was already being hatched before he wrote his famous pamphlet, but that was motivated by just this sort of antiparliamentary populism. The plan in which the Vatican was interested some months before Tosti approached Leo XIII involved the election to the Chamber of Achille Fazzari in January, 1887. Fazzari was a Garibaldian, a veteran of Mentana and Aspromonte. He had renounced his part as a "Red Shirt," however, and campaigned instead for election on the platform of conciliation with the Church. The radical press wrote that any votes he would get could be attributed only to his revolutionary past. But Fazzari insisted that his campaign was to be interpreted solely as a movement for peace between the Church and the State.

He was elected by a clear majority from the Calabrian town of Catanzaro. In March the *Rassegna Nazionale* took up his cause, calling for the creation of a conservative party drawn from the "majority of the nation, to which majority the halls of Montecitorio have up to now been closed." The *Unità Cattolica*'s noted article of April 12, in which Italians were invited to turn to Leo XIII for a solution to the Roman Question, suggested that Fazzari be the man to negotiate the settlement. It was to the ex-Garibaldian that the *Unità* — the journal of Don Margotti, author of the formula "neither elected nor electors" — was turning in order to make peace with Italy. Fazzari, writing in the *Nazione* of Florence, May 17, 1887, advised the Pope to renounce the non expedit, to make the Government the "real expression of the country." The radicals, led by Giovanni Bovio and Felice Cavallotti, spoke out against this plan for coming to terms with the Church. In the Chamber, Crispi defended the autonomy of the State and the sufficiency of the Guarantees. Two days later Fazzari resigned his seat as Deputy, saying that those who had voted for him in Calabria represented the majority of the country, and that only when their voice was heard would Italy be a great nation. On June 17 the *Moniteur de Rome* exulted at the rise of conservatism in Italy. This was "the real Italy, disgusted by artificial Italy." [68]

Here was the chance to weld the nation together, not through parliamentary reform but through an appeal to the Catholic masses. It is known that Fazzari contemplated conciliation by means of a direct accord between the Pope and the King,[69] avoiding the Parliament which he had accused of rejecting the Pope's overtures. Ultraconservatives who in the past had been outspoken in condemning the Papacy now began falling in line. Ruggero Bonghi, for example, had conceded in 1882 that there could be no conservative-clerical alliance. In 1886 he spoke of the Pope as the world's most obstinate clerical, "the cancer of Italy's public life." Suddenly Bonghi shifted ground, even suggesting a Concordat with the Vatican,[70] something the conservative Destra had never been willing to accept. Into this project Tosti intruded with his pamphlet. Unlike Fazzari, who spoke of the masses being estranged from the nation and urged a fusion of all Italians that would restore the greatness of the Risorgimento, Tosti's "Conciliation" refuted by its very arguments that there were two countries, one "real" and one "legal." A minority had made Italy, but that minority had become the expression of all Italians. That was the great difference between Tosti and Fazzari: the abbot represented the mentality that accepted the Postrisorgimento, while the ex-Garibaldian represented the continuing urge to complete the work of the national revolution.

That Fazzari's plan was feasible for Catholic intransigents, whereas Tosti's was too Italian to be acceptable, might be seen in the way the *Unità Cattolica* took him up. French Catholics, who damned Tosti, continued also to look to Fazzari. In late June or early July, 1887, the nuncio at

Paris, Rotelli, tried to interest the French government in the Fazzari scheme. Émile Flourens, the French Foreign Minister, is reported to have been in favor of conciliation along the lines suggested by Fazzari because it would take on the character of a Catholic plebiscite, weakening rather than strengthening Italy.[71] The Tosti scheme, based on an acceptance of the constitutional framework, would only benefit Italy.

Although more palatable to the intransigents, the attempts of former revolutionaries[72] to unite Italy through an accord with the Vatican had no chance of success as long as the Church insisted on the preservation of papal territorial sovereignty. Church-State relations became strained following the collapse of the Tosti affair. The Permanent Committee of the Catholic Congresses circulated a petition among all eligible voters in which the Pope's rights were upheld in full. It was looked upon as a sort of plebiscite of the "real" Italians. Bonghi now switched back to his former anticlericalism, suggesting that the Government prosecute those who signed the petition. The Crispi government in 1889–90 undertook a much-needed reform of charitable institutions and drafted a new penal code in which stiffer penalties were handed out for abuses of the clerical office. Conservative opposition forced the Government to tone down the sanctions against unpatriotic priests before the bill could pass. But the reaction to the disillusionment of 1887 was generally one of increased diffidence between the Vatican and the Quirinal. Popular anticlerical manifestations culminated in the erection of a statue to Giordano Bruno in the Campo di Fiori, where the martyr to reason had died. It became a tangible remembrance of the bitterness that Tosti had been unable to ease. On the other side, the Crispi reforms were answered with a clerical appeal to "Christian Italy" against the spurious unity of the Postrisorgimento.[73]

In the discussion of conservativism we have considered mainly liberal Catholics such as Jacini and the *Rassegna Nazionale* group, who ardently sought conciliation but not at the expense of the unitarian settlement. What of those conservatives whose religious or philosophical convictions forbade acceptance of Vatican support under any circumstances? For these men Catholicism denied the rational basis of the modern State. The Church was not merely a subversive force in Italy; it stood for the rejection of the proper claims to autonomy by civil authority in the modern world. In examining the concepts of this school, however, the same need to avoid a narrow, oligarchic conception of the State that has been noted among Catholic thinkers could give rise to political theories fundamentally hostile to parliamentary government yet on the surface compatible with democracy. The problem here was how to tap the vitality of the masses in the name of the nation while maintaining the authority of the State.

Ambiguities of the Secular Right

We have met Sonnino as a leading personality in the Chamber during the stormy 1890's. It remains now to examine his theoretical works in the light of his activities as a practical politician. Although his father was a Jew, Sonnino had been raised in the Protestant faith of his Scotch mother. In the Chamber he early distinguished himself as a leader of the moderate center group. He feared the rise of the urban proletariat, which would replace the conservative rural element, yet he spoke out in 1881 against the idea of an alliance with Catholic groups for the purpose of defending the Government's authority against the Left. It has been said that he would have abandoned this secularism in moments of great revolutionary peril; and in truth he was known to speak of the Church as the "greatest Italian institution, the chief agency of 'Italianity.'"[74] In general, however, Sonnino's fear of the Blacks, as has been seen, was such that any flattering remarks he may have made about the Church could not have stemmed from a love of its teachings regarding the civil society. They reflect at best a patriotism, not a religious appreciation, and were made moreover in the years following 1900, when the Church's position in Italy was far weaker than it had been when Sonnino entered politics.

In 1897 Sonnino wrote that the growing network of Catholic organizations was far more insidious than a mere front for papal claims to the "divine law of morality in opposition to individual utilitarianism." They were being forged as a weapon in the war against liberalism. This assessment appeared in Sonnino's celebrated article in which he called for a return to the Statuto — that is, to monarchical government as prescribed by the original document prior to the evolution of parliamentarism. Parliamentary rule was sick, according to Sonnino, not only in Italy but in all Europe. While representative government languished, the disorganized forces of moderate liberalism were being threatened by the Reds and the Blacks. Theoretical liberalism and individualism could no longer hold out against the assaults of the smaller but more closely knit ranks of its adversaries. Sonnino saw an impending crisis of the State's authority, which was disintegrating as a result of the excessive power vested in Parliament. The ministry, a hybrid institution not sanctioned by the Statuto, had usurped the King's executive prerogatives, exploiting the Chamber, which in turn had absorbed the Crown's legislative role in government. Sonnino advocated a restoration of the monarchical principle contained in the constitution. The ministers should be responsible to the King, not to the Chamber. Moreover, the Crown was not only the executive. It should also share with the Chamber the legislative function, having the power to propose laws and possessing, alone, the faculty of sanctioning laws. The King "synthesizes the general interests of the patria, both present and future," Sonnino wrote. This was to be no sort of Caesarism, but rather a return to a healthy political system and a defense of the moderate liberal tradition.[75]

Sonnino spoke in the name of liberalism and against the ultraconservative conspiracy of the Church. He denied having any thought of preaching reaction. Still, there is much to justify the charge that his noted article was a proclamation of the reactionaries.[76] In that it added to the discredit of representative government, it served the enemies of the very liberal traditions Sonnino wished to protect. It is also true that he was an early and consistent backer of the alliance with the Central Powers. The Triple Alliance contained a conservative element in its avowed purpose of buttressing monarchy. Because of this, the return to the Statuto has also been seen as a departure from a parliamentary regime in favor of one modeled on the German pattern.[77] However, these interpretations tend to ascribe too much to foreign influences and to a classical reactionary view of politics, thereby ignoring more significant aspects of Sonnino's position.

It should be recalled that Sonnino put forth his monarchical ideas after having been in favor of universal suffrage. This suggests that the idea of a strict interpretation of the Statuto was the result of a sense of deep pessimism over the prospects of achieving political stability by less conservative means. In 1881, speaking in the Chamber on behalf of the impending electoral reform bill, Sonnino had stated that the great weakness of the State's authority was caused by the absence of any feeling on the part of the majority of Italy's population that it constituted a vital and organic part of the State. The existence of a "real" and an "official" Italy worried Sonnino as it had Jacini. The latter had also approved of a great participation of the people in politics (albeit on the local level), in keeping with his regionalist outlook. Sonnino went much farther in 1881, defending what was then a very radical point of view. Or so it seemed. In truth, his intentions were extremely conservative from the start. To those who argued that universal suffrage was by nature subversive and antimonarchical, Sonnino answered that it would become so only if the State withheld it from the masses, who would then turn to the Blacks or the Reds. At that time the Sinistra was in power. Yet conservatives seemed the more "radical." One explanation of this was the belief of men like Sonnino that universal suffrage would tap the conservative elements of the rural population as a counterweight to the urban proletariat.[78] While professing himself a liberal, Sonnino was able to support Pelloux's government, indeed to become its driving force. His abstract conception of the government, which he viewed as a metaphysical, eternal entity, permitted him to defend clearly unconstitutional and reactionary measures. His defense of universal suffrage, as Luigi Salvatorelli wrote, was motivated by his desire for a strong and stable state.[79]

By 1897, Sonnino's hope of capturing the masses for the State by means of liberal reforms was fading. The Socialist party was a reality, and the Catholic Congresses were threatening to turn the supposedly conservative contadini against the nation. It was almost with an air of desperation that Sonnino took up the monarchist cause. Only in later years, during Giolitti's second ministry when the threat of Reds and Blacks had waned, did he confess that the parliamentary system he had once condemned was the only one to govern Italy.[80] To what extent this confession was in the back of Giolitti's mind in 1915, adding to his misplaced confidence in the Salandra-Sonnino ministry, we will never know. But it is important in assessing Sonnino's actions of that year to note the ambiguity of his parliamentary liberalism prior to 1900, and to recognize how much it was motivated by a conservative fear that the State was too feeble.

Sonnino's was not the only such criticism of parliamentarism during the pre-Giolittian era. Jacini, as early as 1866, had criticized the excessive power vested in the Chamber, not by the Statute but by a loose application of its terms. But Jacini struck to his regionalism. His conservatism was that of the rural Catholic pluralist who feared not that the State was too weak, but that it might become too strong for liberty to survive. Hence he could not approve of enlarging the Crown's power once the monarchy had become centralized and national. Ruggero Bonghi, however, writing in 1893 — four years before Sonnino's celebrated article appeared — had gone Sonnino one better as far as monarchism was concerned, while betraying a similar insecurity based on the separation of the "people" from the "State." It was this anxiety that forced him to swallow his anticlericalism. Bonghi saw the monarch as free from all checks save those prompted by his sense of duty. The Crown, he wrote, exercised a "lofty moral supervision" over the nation. He suggested a privy council from which the

Cabinet would be selected, making the ministers responsible to the King rather than to the Chamber as had been the practice. His monarchist theory was far more "legitimate" than Sonnino's, which was a last-resort expedient. Bonghi spoke of the King as a "symbol of *gentilezza*," a model of artistic and literary culture, the repository of a "depth of feeling" that made him a social and intellectual force. The nation's continuity rested with the dynasty.[81]

Pity the poor king who had to fit this glowing portrait, particularly if he were, like Victor Emmanuel III, shy and devoted to bourgeois pursuits no more lofty than automobiles and coin collecting! As for Parliament, Bonghi was convinced by 1884 that it was dying in Italy. And yet he too sought some way to draw the population of the new nation into a closer relationship with the State. His legitimist vision of the Crown precluded a solution to this problem based on gradual electoral reforms. What did appeal to Bonghi was medieval corporate representation, a system the French Revolution had killed off. Here Bonghi was obviously turning to the ideas of Müller and other Restoration conservatives — minus the Catholicism for apparent reasons. This harking back to medievalism reveals Bonghi's extreme conservatism, as does his view of the monarchy. But the use of such antiquated ideas in 1884 was not at all a romanticist's worship of the past. Corporate theory was encouraged because of the sense of national frustration that Bonghi felt, the fear for Italy's cohesiveness. Corporatism was a means of bringing the government and the governed together in an intimate union without giving way to mechanistic, utilitarian democracy.

More significant than any dependence on German conservative thought was his use of Gaetano Mosca whose principal work came out in 1884. Repeating Mosca's thesis that modern representation was a sham, since only an active minority takes part in it, Bonghi went on to compare this falsification of delegation of powers to the medieval corporation. In the latter, not the individual but the group is represented. Unlike the deputy who is interested only in his own election, the medieval representative expresses the will of the corporation. Regardless of the method of his selection, he is a part of the whole, hence truly representative. The parliamentary system, in contrast, ended in the moral corruption of elected and elector. From time to time a man of genius might arise to seize the helm and guide the ship of state to some safe port; but this was rare, nor was the effect lasting.[82] Bonghi placed little trust in a dictatorial solution. It lacked sufficient power as an instrument of mass action.

At the time Bonghi was writing in this vein, the chances of conciliation with the Vatican seemed very dim. Since he had been one of the men who had drafted the laws of the Guarantees, it would be impossible to place him in the ranks of the liberal Catholics. But his rejection of an atomistic, individualistic society in favor of corporatism was too close to the theologically based social theories of Leo XIII to be mistaken.[83] No sooner had the opportunity for conciliation presented iself than Bonghi took it up, not only in the name of narrow conservatism and legitimacy, but as a means of achieving that true representation of the "whole." There were others, however, whose Hegelian academic background forbade any recourse to the Catholic masses, in whatever extremity the State might find itself. Giorgio Arcoleo, professor of law at the University of Naples — a center of Hegelian and Viconian studies — was one of these. His analysis of the role of the cabinet in parliamentary government, written in 1881, is interesting not only as an early example of antiparliamentary literature; it brings out once more the inherent dilemma of conservative theorists in looking for an answer to specifically Italian problems.

Arcoleo anticipated Mosca's theories. Majority rule rested on a false conception of government that arose during the French Revolution. The government of a state does not draw its power from popular consent any more than the head of a family depends on his children for his authority. Departing from the political commentaries of Rudolf von Gneist, whose *Der Rechtstaat* appeared in 1872, Arcoleo compared Continental representative institutions to the English parliament. The former lacked the English tradition of self-government which permitted the people to be sovereign yet upheld the strength of the state. In keeping with all theoreticians of the strong State, Arcoleo asserts the paradox that true authoritarianism results from a concept of government founded on politics instead of on laws. In Italy, government based on political competition had produced parties that served not the ends of society, of the State, but sought only to win executive power for themselves. This gave rise to a sterile, narrow party struggle within the Chamber, but not to a polity of order. Whereas the English constitution rested on a historic development which promoted both freedom and authority, the problem in Italy was to create an organic government capable of harmonizing respect for law with the influence of political factions. The creation of such an organic government in Italy would have to be the work of science, of applied reason, because the country's history had not created it.[84]

Arcoleo could not accept Sonnino's return to the monarchy as a viable solution to the question of the State. He agreed that the Cabinet should be the fount of executive power rather than the servant of the Chamber. It should also be formed by the King. But in its own sphere it was independent, acting in co-ordination with the Chamber from which its members were to be drawn. The German system, in which the Chancellor represented the Crown and ran the Parliament, was — according to Arcoleo — the one that least corresponded to the nature of constitutional government. In England, the King had influence. In Germany, he had influence and power which were not in keeping with true constitutionalism. In 1900, when Sonnino seemed determined to push Pelloux to the limit, making him Italy's Great Chancellor, Arcoleo broke with the majority he had backed wholeheartedly to that point.

Arcoleo's Hegelian-based view of the modern State was too rational and too secular to accept either Bonghi's recourse to the political museums of the old regime or the liberal Catholics' schemes for conciliation as acceptable responses to Italian political problems. Science was the new gospel. Neither throne nor altar could preserve the modern State. As for his rejection of the German constitutional pattern, the reasons he gives are intimately related to the central dilemma of the Italian Right. In Italy, he wrote, the revolution was first conceived in the mind; it did not develop within society itself. In effect, Italy's constitution lacked a history. It was merely a code of laws, and not a creation from within the national conscience. After Cavour a period of disintegration set in under lesser men. Ministries no longer reflected the Chamber, nor did the Chamber reflect the will of the electorate. Parties arose according to the tendencies of the Deputies and not in response to the interests of the people. The country began to believe itself estranged from the Government, its intervention in politics useless. From these circumstances there arose the doubt whether a "legal country could be formed." [85]

The fundamental problem of the secular conservatives was to achieve the identification of the country with its legal institutions. Sonnino had abandoned his own plans to effect this identification, and had in frustration turned to the Crown. Arcoleo could not exploit a Catholic or monarchist alliance without betraying his Hegelian and scientific theory of the State. The same was true for Silvio Spaventa, the leading southern statesman of the Postrisorgimento and also one of the ablest of the Neapolitan school of political theorists. Spaventa considered the State as a modern metaphysical entity which had replaced traditional theological concepts of society. Conciliation was never therefore a possible answer to the question of how the State's authority was to be strengthened and made part of the social consciousness. He recognized that the non expedit deprived the State of valuable conservative support. For this reason, he envied Protestant countries, where Church-State relations did not operate to the detriment of political authority. A democratic reform, however, was also unacceptable. Spaventa rejected as unsound and pernicious the Enlightenment's view of government, with its emphasis on the individual. The true State was an ethical force that idealized within itself the individual's desire for law and authority. Democracy, on the other hand, stood mechanically outside the individual, indifferent to him. It was therefore illiberal. The liberal State must exist *in interiore homine.*

Spaventa shared the opinion of most conservatives that a two-party system was essential to good government. It was for that reason that he had welcomed the advent of the Sinistra to power in 1876, even though he disliked the presence of what he considered Jacobin, revoutionary elements within the ranks. But the revolution of the Sinistra proved an illusion. Its excessively humanitarian attitude toward criminals, based on what Spaventa called a philanthropic dogmatism, threatened authority, and was a return to eighteenth-century sentimentalism. Spaventa felt that Italy needed more authority, not less. He opposed granting autonomy to Italian universities, on the grounds that they should become centers for inculcating popular awareness of the State's presence, its existence as the idealized force of the collective will. When the Sinistra also failed to produce the two-party system, Spaventa became pessimistic about the future of parliamentary government in Italy.[86] In 1885, by which time trasformismo had become an accepted method of rule, he referred to Italian politics as a quagmire. Quite as if the parties represented the necessary conflicting forces in a Hegelian scheme of government, their absence meant sterility, lack of progress due to the decay of ideal positions.

Yet Spaventa was a strict constitutionalist.[87] He could not return to the archaic idea of a king who governed as well as reigned. Significantly, he came to realize that some extension of the vote was necessary. He could not accept universal suffrage, which would mean granting the ballot to illiterates.[88] That would be a falsification of the privilege itself. It was clearly impossible to create the State in interiore homine, however, as long as the people were one thing and legal Italy another. The secular conservative position contained traces of the same concessions to the masses that were to be found in the ideas of conservative Catholics. Both wished to strengthen the authority of the State. It is equally apparent that the two camps were aware of the separation of the government from the governed, the need to "make the Italians," now that Italy was united.

Because of this, conservative theories that rejected the people in the name of a narrow oligarchy, a rule of the better men only, tended to find little backing even among authoritarians. Mosca's theory is a case in point. He rejected the rights-of-man concept of the Enlightenment as unscientific. It was only a hypothesis, and one that was never founded on historical observation. Since all majorities were passive, it was useless to seek reform through widening the suffrage. Like most conservatives, Mosca agreed that Italian politics was in a state of decline. The parliamentary system drew men into the Chamber only to corrupt them, stripping them of their noble passions. Having rejected any concession to democracy as a means of buttressing the Government, Mosca was left with the alternative of a ruling elite that would be formed outside Parliament.[89]

Although fascist antiparliamentarians cited Mosca's theory as one of the earliest examples of Italian discontent with the fetish of representative government, conservative and authoritarian movements shied away from his aristocratic concept, preferring instead to pass themselves off as spokesmen of the people, the healthy part of Italy as opposed to the sickly and artificial Chamber. But Mosca himself tended to abandon his theory for quite other reasons. He became a Deputy and a Minister, entering that parliamentary "swamp" he had once condemned. By 1904 enemies of Italy's representative institutions were to be disappointed in finding Mosca no longer held to his youthful positions. Parliament could serve the useful function of being the agency for the formation of the political elite. This was a far cry from his earlier work, which had taught contempt for legal paths as a means of increasing the stability of the State.[90]

Mosca was to become responsible. He left his subversive past behind when he became a representative of official Italy. In the Chamber he continued to defend the conservative viewpoint, opposing universal suffrage. His arguments on the floor, as Giolitti noted, were distinguished by their logical and respectable character, whereas many who were certainly conservative pretended to support electoral reforms for fear of being compromised among the voters.[91] Giolitti's distinction between Mosca and the conservatives masked as liberals was a pointed reference to Antonio Salandra as an example of the latter. Salandra's handling of Italy's intervention had opened Giolitti's eyes to the ambiguities of many supposed liberals, men whom he had trusted with the welfare of Italy and the protection of the parliamentary system, only to be deceived. What Giolitti may not have seen, however, was that deeper than the fear of being discredited by Italian voters was the realization among many Italian conservatives that no theory of the nation — of the strong and durable State — could succeed if it left out the masses. This was not peculiar to Italian rightist thought. The *Action française* spoke for the people, and in Germany the leadership principle under National Socialism had to square its elite concept with the popular base [92] essential to all modern national philosophies. At another place (Chapter 7) the prewar predecessors of fascist doctrine, the Nationalist Association, will be examined. These journalists and second-rate novelists turned political pundits were to wrestle with this very problem: how to give authority and direction to the nation, freeing it from the bourgeois restriction of Parliament, while at the same time creating the synthesis between government and governed that the new nation lacked.

In the hands of young intellectuals who were properly of the generation of the Postrisorgimento, born too late to recall the wars for unification, conservative ideology became subversive and revolutionary. Their facile solutions to the self-conscious need for greater cohesiveness, in particular the transference of this domestic problem to the area of foreign policy, the equating of war and national revolution, lost contact with the traditions of Silvio Spaventa, Stefano Jacini, and Gaetano Mosca. These three may be taken as examples of an authentic or loyal conservative tradition because they accepted, for all its faults, the existing political settlement and rejected idealized solutions for concrete problems.

It is true that their political philosophies lent themselves to corruption by less responsible and more opportunistic men. Spaventa's metaphysical *stato volativo* could degenerate, as even his admirers admit, into authoritarianism.[93] Jacini's posing of the dilemma of a real and a legal Italy, his dislike of Piedmontese centralization, also would furnish arguments for subversive, anarchic conservatives in their war with Giolittian Italy. Mosca's elite would remain a weapon in the hands of those who wished to destroy the Parliament of which he had become a part. But these men were too responsive both to the realities of Italian politics and to the obligation for clear discourse to give way to the literary and political irrationalism that flourished during the decade preceding the Great War.

Croce wrote of Marxism that it was less a philosophy of history than a program for revolution.[94] In the respect that many Italian intellectuals thought in terms of creating the as yet unfinished nation, evolving the organic state as Arcoleo put it, the same could be said of Hegelian idealism in the hands of a new generation of dissatisfied Young Turks. The longing for the synthetic whole that the work of the Risorgimento had not produced; the desire to weld people and government together, inculcating a feeling of the State's authority in the minds of the peasants who spoke of a return of the Bourbons — these and the need to baptize Italy in blood gave a dynamic quality to Hegelian concepts. The strict constitutionalism and disciplined conservatism of Bertrando and Silvio Spaventa was corrupted into an eminently radical thirst for action, an idealism which was a cloak for naked power.[95]

It must be made clear that this was a corruption of neo-idealism. Hegel had been an inspiration to older Italian patriots. His works were taken into the Bourbon jails by prisoners, to be read there amid the material proofs of despotism, giving encouragement to the dream of restoring Italy to the family of nations. Bertrando Spaventa used Hegelian philosophy to attack the chauvinism of Vincenzo Gioberti. Silvio, when Italy was united, rejected talk of an African mission or other such historical nonsense as a revival of the Roman Empire. As has been written, it would be hard to think of a volte-face more complete than that which turned the teaching of the nationality of philosophies into the rigors and excesses of a philosophy of nationalism.[96]

What is apparent in much of this conservatism of the Postrisorgimento is the perversion of theories of history, or of traditional conservatism, into justifications for action. The words are often the language of Burke, Müller, and Bonald. The anarchic conservatives speak of the organic society which is stable and offers true freedom, rejecting the mechanical individualism of bourgeois liberalism. But the words are thin veils for the very revolutionary urge for violence and action in order to create the roots that are lacking. This perversion of language is seen as well in radical theory, particularly among the syndicalists. Georges Sorel would give Marxist economic determinism a sense of life, of vitality. But, as A. O. Lovejoy pointed out as early as 1913, there are affinities between Sorel the syndicalist and Henri Bergson the father of creative evolution. While Bergson claimed to shun society's practical problems, the message many got from his paradoxical and many-sided doctrines was one that lent itself to activism. The effect of Bergsonian philosophy was to promote not a conservative climate but one given to emotional reactions.[97] A creative sense of national evolution was precisely what attracted many Italian intellectuals, wounded in pride by the taunts of foreigners who saw a loose, dissolving nation, frustrated by the Church's refusal to draw the people into the life of the nation and fed on a literature of past grandeur. There is more Bergson than Hegel in the militant idealism of Giuseppe Prezzolini and Giovanni Gentile, an activated idealism which they began to elaborate during the Libyan War and which fit in well with the sense of renewal associated with the Great War — a struggle backed as well by many syndicalists who regarded it as the equivalent of revolution. Nor is it historically improper to link the activists of the Right, the anarchic conservatives, with those of the extreme Left. In modern Italy the syndicalists were to get far better treatment in the hands of the ultraconservative Nationalists of the Giolittian period than were the official Socialists who had become part of the system. The affinity of activism plus the common loathing for the artificial, bourgeois, and positivistic Postrisorgimento made political alignments between these extremes possible, and often natural.

This corruption of idealism had begun before the nineteenth century closed. It was indicative of things to come that one of the corrupters came not from the ranks of politics, or even political theory, but from the deracinated literati. Alfredo Oriani has been mentioned briefly in connection with a tendency to apply aesthetic values to politics, thereby encouraging a flight from political responsibility among the intellectual petty bourgeoisie. Oriani's life, like Crispi's, was to become a symbol of the neglected Italian genius in the age of prose and positivism. In the revival of Oriani by the Nationalists, and later by the Fascists, the image of the lonely, solitary prophet in the era of trasformismo became a commonplace theme. The pose of the neglected hero, the cult of strength through solitude, and an autobiographical obsession for outpourings of lofty intimacies would also become fashionable.[98] These essentially neoromantic fancies, reminiscent of Rousseau, were loaded with political significance. In Italy, as elsewhere, they constituted a revolt against the political as well as cultural climate of the times.

Oriani was born at Faenza in the Romagna in 1852, too late for the wars of national liberation. His family was wealthy; they had a villa at Cardello where the young man spent much of his time. He studied law at Bologna and Rome, but never entered private practice. He was never to travel out of Italy. He passed his time in literary pursuits and frequent visits to the town café, where he discussed politics and the latest scandals from Rome with others of the same class of educated but often indolent young men. In time he became something of a recluse, an oddity in his own Romagna, bicycling into town from his country home for evenings of cultural debate. His early novels, which attracted no audience in his own lifetime, were characterized — as even his admirers will admit — by a convulsive, violent, and often vulgar tone.[99] Representative of this phase of Oriani's writing, the novel *Al di là* is a study of lesbianism, promiscuity, and sadism concocted of tortured symbolism and erotic, pornographic description. In 1892 he visited Rome, only to return to Romagna in disgust with the political immorality and pork-barrel legislative practices of the capital. He resisted efforts of friends to have him campaign for the Chamber. He, too, was unwilling to compromise his intellectual independence in the halls of Parliament.

By that time Oriani had made the acquaintance of Angelo Camillo de Meis, a favorite student of De Sanctis and of Bertrando Spaventa, Silvio's brother, the leading Hegelian philosopher of Italy. From De Meis, Oriani imbibed Hegel, and it can be said that the fount was already tainted. De Meis' own literary masterpiece, *Dopo la laurea* (1868-69), is an example of the artistic and rhetorical use of idealism, converting it from a rational philosophy to mysticism. De Meis illustrates the neoromantic revolt against positivism and materialism. A professor of medicine, he spoke of his abhorrence for the deadly laboratory existence of modern man, and advocated seriously that all students of medicine should be required to become poets first. His attempt to prove how the idea became manifest in matter, as Gentile concedes, was never successful. Croce pointedly distinguished De Meis from the Hegelians proper, insisting that the former's idealism was artistically rather than philosophically motivated.[100]

The same could be said of Oriani. Where De Meis put idealism to work as an artistic device, Oriani tended to utilize it as a political weapon. When he wrote that it was difficult for him to choose between the "tempests of Hegel's thought and the storms of Napoleon's wars," one is struck by the confusion of a philosophical view of history and political action. Oriani's heroic self-consciousness emerges from the statement that he would "scale the peaks of metaphysics with Hegel, while the air thins and the bravest companions suffocate and fall to earth." Hegel had indeed been a source of inspiration for nineteenth-century national movements in Europe. In Italy the connection between the stages of Risorgimento and the dialectical process by which the national ideal emerged seemed particularly close.[101] But in Oriani, the theme of the evolving of the State no longer becomes only an explanation of what had taken place prior to 1860. It takes on a prescription for the future manifest destiny of

Italy whose national consciousness was not complete. On the eve of the Italian entry into the Great War, Giuseppe Borgese wrote of Oriani — by then an adopted precursor of the interventionists — that if his work was intellectually weak as a synthetic explanation of past history, it was formidable from a practical standpoint. It had given Italy heart.[102]

Oriani's novels never achieved any success in his lifetime. They are not even mentioned by leading foreign students of Italian literature.[103] He turned to historical essays, publishing a work entitled *Fino a Dogali* in 1889. Taking his inspiration from the defeat of a company of Italian colonial troops at Dogali in 1887, Oriani proclaimed Italy's inevitable mission — the *raison d'être* of the Risorgimento — to be the return to Africa. The resurgence of Italy was part of a great historical design, in which the nation and its people were to play a part. This mission was the civilizing of the Dark Continent. The governments of the Postrisorgimento, having risen to power from the failure of a "true revolution," were unable as yet to grasp the real significance of Italian unification. The return of Italy to Africa after an absence of 2,000 years, according to Oriani, was a disaster because it was carried out by the drab parliamentary regime which was a falsification of the real, the revolutionary Italy. That "vulgar constitutional revolutionary" Depretis, his faculties limited by parliamentary practice, led the nation back to Africa and defeat. Oriani condemned the moral and political atmosphere of the Postrisorgimento, the passing from popularity of the great heroes Mazzini and Garibaldi. Their greatness was "perverted by a vulgar democracy." Describing the death of the company of soldiers in Africa, Oriani made them martyrs to historical destiny. The hill on which they died was an immense altar. "Italy," he wrote, "too easily crushed during the revolutions of 1821 and 1831; defeated in 1848 throughout its cities and countryside; barely victorious in 1859 . . . ; miserably beaten in 1866 on the fatal plains of Custoza and in the waters of Lissa; Italy, into which Garibaldi could not breathe his courage, Mazzini his genius and Cavour his good sense, which entered Rome in 1870 on the sly . . . needed a contingent of its soldiers who, becoming heroes, proved that the Latin blood still coursed in the veins of its people . . . , that the revolution was being continued in Africa." The five hundred who died in Africa represented the new Italy. "But the tragic solemnity of Dogali has not been able to raise the nation from the political mud."[104]

For Oriani 1870 was but a step on the way to the fulfillment of Italy's manifest destiny. The revolution was still in progress which would give

Italians an awareness of themselves and of their mission. The same theme appears in another essay, in which Oriani celebrated the life of Don Giovanni Verità, the obscure priest who had helped Garibaldi on his retreat from Rome in 1849. Here too the author plays on the unfinished internal revolution. In his life the simple priest synthesized the opposing forces of patriotism and Catholicism. Oriani rejected any conciliation between Throne and Altar. The monarchy and the Papacy were dying historical forms. Should the King restore the Pope's political position, he would be going against the revolution which the monarchs had absorbed in the process of unifying Italy. The result of an official conciliation would be the overthrow of the monarchy. Yet Oriani foresees eventual conciliation by the unfolding of the historical process. He predicts the inevitable Republican and anticlerical revolution by which the nation will attain its predestined goal, its self-awareness. Mazzini's republicanism was not felt by the people. The triumph of the monarchy, the conquista regia, followed as a necessary step in order to give Italy independence and an external unity. But an intimate unity, a popular feeling of identification with the regime, would come only when the Republic was proclaimed.

Again the problem was to bring real and official Italy together. The intransigence of the clergy was a negation of the wholeness of united Italy. But when it comes to the question of just how this synthesis is to be achieved, Oriani flees from concrete suggestions and into the woolly reaches of rhetoric. What emerges is the equating of war and revolution. Italy awaited her great battle. "War," according to Oriani, "is an inevitable form of struggle for existence, and blood will always be the best warm rain for great ideas. To the war! And woe to the vanquished, because truth is invincible. Italy's future consists entirely of a war which, while restoring her natural boundaries, may cement within her, by the tragedy of mortal dangers, the Unity of national sentiment."[105]

In 1892 Oriani published, at his own expense, his major work, a monumental history of Italy from the fall of the Western Roman Empire to the period of the Sinistra. The bulk of this study, which took up some nine hundred pages, was devoted to the Risorgimento. It was to be a history on the grand scale, restoring to historiography the romantic sweep that pedantic academicians had stifled. Borrowing heavily from Giuseppe Ferrari's equally ponderous *Storia delle rivoluzioni*,[106] Oriani imposed his own personality on materials furnished by others. This near-plagiarism was itself an example of the liberties with scholarly niceties that were becoming fashionable among men of genius. The reaction of the positiv-

istic academicians was to be expected. Oriani's history, in the words of
one of them, lacked any value — literary, historical, or political. It was
written in the style of De Sanctis at his worst. Oriani was advised to return to writing fiction. Whether the art of the novel would benefit was
something the reviewer could not say. History, however, he was sure,
would not suffer from the loss.[107]

This is too strong, and reflects the bitterness of the war between the
positivists and antipositivists that was ranging at the time. Oriani was no
mean writer. And if, as Croce noted, he was too intentionally original, he
could and did come up with worthwhile historical essays. His essay on
Machiavelli,[108] although written to counteract the positivistic study of
the Florentine by Pasquale Villari, is not without valuable insights into
the work of Machiavelli as compared with that of Guicciardini. In Oriani's
great epic of the Risorgimento, however, the scheme is that of the creation
of Italian unity in accordance with the dialectical process. In particular, a
Hegelian triad is formed by the figures of Mazzini, Cavour and Garibaldi.
Mazzini's idealism, his lack of political finesse, made him a "solitary
apostle." Again the figure of the lonely hero, dear to the Romanticists, takes on a sharper political outline in the hands of a transmitter of
their deeper view of society. On Cavour, Oriani was rather harsh, as was
to be expected. The great statesman lacked the mentality for great philosophical flights. Cold and calculating, his goal was eminently antirevo-
lutionary, hence he could not understand the heroism of the revolution.
But both men were necessary to the Risorgimento. If Mazzini saw farther,
Cavour's good sense recognized the impossibility of Mazzini's dream. The
apostle's transcendental vision and the statesman's very intellectual insufficiencies were equally needed and inevitably antagonistic. These an-
titheses were reconciled, however, in the instincts of Garibaldi.

The outcome of the dialectical evolution of Italy was a compromise in
which republicanism and federalism were set aside. The Piedmontese dynasty triumphed, but only as a momentary synthesis. And with its triumph, the romanticism of the earlier nineteenth century vanished as minor
interests absorbed the attention of the nation. "Patria, liberty, democracy," wrote Oriani, "came down from the luminous realm of principles
to that of facts. . . . The epoch of heroic passions was finished." The
national genius seemed diluted by increased contact with foreign cultures.
Verdi appeared to have preserved the revolutionary fire, but Wagner
eclipsed him in genius. The people had played no part in the revolution.
Yet that too was part of the historical necessity. Without the apathy of

the masses, Oriani taught, the mediocre triumph of the national compromise would have been impossible. Italy's revolution, however, was negated, since the victory came by French arms. Only Garibaldi's daring prevented Cavour's dynastic plans to unite Northern Italy from winning out. In all this, there was no poetry. Italy was made prosaically, by a war of liberation and not a revolution. Blood was not shed, and without blood there are no true revolutions. The King refused to take Rome. Only Garibaldi dared. Aspromonte was the "highest point in modern history," the "Calvary" of the revolution. When the moment did come to take Rome, the "little King of Piedmont" trembled before the Pope. Porta Pia was "too small to be a battle, too bloody for a demonstration."[109]

It is true that Oriani praised Sella and the "heroic" work of the Destra in defense of the nation's economy. Nor did he affirm a chauvinistic policy of Italy's world primacy. Instead, he took up current Pan-Slavist ideas and predicted that the future belonged to Eastern Europe. Italy's mission was in the Mediterranean and in the return of Trent and Trieste.[110] In these respects, he was less immoderate than later nationalist and fascist apologists who elevated him to the status of a seer. Nonetheless, his work encouraged an idealized vision of realities. The Risorgimento was still in the process of unfolding — that was doubtless true — but it was one thing to see the divine plan moving through the past, leading toward what had happened, and another to become its prophet, pointing the way it should go.

If Oriani paid his respects to the material accomplishments of the Postrisorgimento, it was clear that these advances did not dull his political imagination nor make him more responsible as far as the constitutional system was concerned. His last major work, the *Rivolta ideale*, written in 1906, was just as scornful of Giolittian Italy as his earlier works had been of Depretis and trasformismo. In that it discussed internal political regeneration, it was more revealing of the dangers, for the parliamentary regime, of idealism in the hands of novelists. Liberty and the individual are still the irreducible factors of history. But when Oriani speaks of the ideal State, the properly functioning society, both disappear from view as recognizable quantities. A grab bag of prevailing conservative speculation takes their place.

The *Rivolta ideale* exalted the aristocrat, the elite of superior minds whose tragedy it had always been to drag the inert masses along the road to self-identification. From the aristocrat the idea that forms the essence of the people is breathed forth by a spiritual radiation. Democracy is condemned as a fatal leveling of all ideals that produces a tyranny of the masses. But Oriani's conservatism could not leave out the real Italy by proposing a new ruling elite only. He dabbled with the convenient solution of corporate representation, which was less debasing of individual virtues than democratic suffrage. He insists on the romantic notion that the virtues of the nation reside in the people. The people are "vital" and in fact superior to the government. He rails at positivism, the reducing of man to the level of an animal, and rejects any sort of economic or territorial imperialism. Chauvinism is also ruled out. Italy's imperialism, her Mediterranean mission, remains. It is to be an "idealist" imperialism, without crass profit as a goal. But when it comes to the practical achievement, Oriani never explains how this new idealism is to be carried to Africa without playing the game of the positivistic imperialists. He speaks of history as being a struggle of ideas. But the price is blood,[111] shed for the lofty dream of civilization, but blood all the same.

Beneath Oriani's idealism lurks the same fleshy materialism, the same urge for national grandeur of the Social Darwinists he despises. It would be true of the generation of antipositivists who were to come of age in the Giolittian decade that they, like Oriani, masked brute power in the guise of a restoration of ideals and passions. What at first glance might pass for a liberation of man and culture from the narrow and lifeless limits imposed by science was too often but a return to the heroism of the Risorgimento. In the twentieth century, this frequently became a brutal nationalism and imperialism made palatable to the revival of the romantic temper. The liberation to come, moreover, was no longer from the foreign conqueror or the internal reactionary regime, but from the domestic tyranny of parliamentary monarchy conceived as a necessary but transitory phase in the predestined plan of national evolution.

We may begin to summarize this discussion of the ambiguities of Italian politics by saying that a tension, at once artistic and political, existed within the conservative and radical schools. The two mentalities that Chabod described as characteristic of the leading men of the Postrisorgimento can be seen on the one hand in the subversive conservatism of those who would create the roots of the nation-state, and on the other in the words and deeds of the traditional conservatives who, while recognizing the defects of Italian political life, accepted the outcome of the Risorgimento as worthy of respect as well as susceptible to reforms. They can also be seen in the theories of those Socialists who would recapture the romance of the Pisacane episode — to whom the humanizing violence of Sorel would be appealing — and the official Socialists who, whatever their practical reservations born of a need to preserve their revolutionary identity, would defend the constitutional monarchy not only against the Right but against the syndicalists and lonely heroes within their own ranks.

Common to Right and Left were the prophets of action, of a renewal that was both cultural and political. In moments of crisis these kindred spirits joined forces, glibly rising above the logical contradictions of their opposing programs, united by their mutual desire to destroy the reigning political regime and the prevailing climate of opinion. In the figure of Oriani the artist and the political theorist merge. In his works the activist outlook of many conservatives and radicals is given approval by his prophecy of the continuing national revolution, which will reach its climax on some future field of battle.

We have also seen something of the very real domestic problems that served to sustain much of the criticism of Italy's feeble existence in the years after 1870. It is important to keep these material problems in mind when evaluating the impact and persistence of ideas that often appear to be conceived in the nooks and crannies of the neo-romantic imagination. It was the relationships between realities of politics and society on the one hand and the artistic view of life on the other which gave special immediacy to the outpourings of the lonely genius. The links that could be established between politics and culture, between trasformismo and positivism, between the mechanized dehumanization of man that Nietzsche and like-minded intellectuals throughout Western Europe loathed, and the apparent debasing of civic passions through parliamentary compromise, gave concreteness to the works of the little-known eccentric from Romagna.

In the list of these undeniable facts, which worked to feed the subversive artistic imagination of dissatisfied intellectuals, one must include foreign policy in general and two aspects of it in particular: irredentism and the Triple Alliance. Ambiguities similar to those that drew elements of the Right and the Left together in domestic politics can be observed at work in the attitudes of prominent Italians toward these major features of Italian diplomacy. There were those who accepted the necessity of Italy's aspirations within realistic limits, just as they had been willing to accept the outcome of the Risorgimento as viable if imperfect. Indeed, the loyal conservatives whom we have just examined usually proved to be equally rational in their approach to diplomacy. There were also those

— radicals and conservatives alike — who yearned for the vitality of a daring diplomacy reminiscent of the days when Cavour had risked all for the sake of Italy. That same common longing for action that drew political extremes together in internal affairs will be seen in facile shifts from Africanism to irredentism, however much these two poles of Italian interests were opposed by the logic of the balance of power. In Crispi, as the Austro-Hungarian ambassador noted, this transference of action from one sphere to another was already apparent. As for the Triple Alliance, or rather the motives that gave rise to it, there were equally ambiguous attitudes: the pact was essentially defensive, conservative in its terms, while many who favored it did so for reasons that suggested a desire to bring Italy's destiny to its fulfillment through war.

CROSS CURRENTS OF ITALIAN FOREIGN POLICY

Irredentism

There was no more palpable reminder of the deficiencies of the Post-risorgimento than the unredeemed lands left to Austria-Hungary in 1866. Oriani, although he stressed Italy's African mission, made clear the necessity of restoring Trent and Trieste to the nation in order to complete the work of the Risorgimento. This in itself suggests that between Africa and the Adriatic there was a common bond of affection for men who sought Italy's "fulfillment." And if the two spheres seemed unobtainable at the same time, if Africanism was to be associated with a foreign policy tied to that of the Central Powers, and the Adriatic with one leading toward Paris, it was true for the national idealists that either area was an acceptable outlet for the drive toward fulfillment. This would become apparent in 1914–15.

Irredentism was a less constant subject for lament than many others. It rose and fell with the diplomatic and political current, at moments apparently limited to the dwindling ranks of the Republicans, then bursting forth as a challenge to the official foreign policy that linked Rome and Vienna. Since Irredentists were to figure prominently in the campaign for intervention in the Great War, it would be well to place the movement in its proper perspective. How popular was it? What were its traditional aims?

The failure of the Italian government to obtain territories beyond the limitations set by the Prussian alliance laid the basis of the irredentist issue. While it was true that Bismarck refused to include the Trentino among the lands to be won by Italy, he was willing to consider an eventual cession of that area provided the course of the war made this feasible. The Government at Florence was decidedly interested in securing the Trentino. Trieste, on the other hand, was considered only by a minority among Italian leaders. Very few would have gone as far as the intrepid Baron Bettino Ricasoli, who wanted Istria as well. Efforts to secure the

Trentino persisted to the end. Even after the defeats of Lissa and Custoza, not only Ricasoli but the more cautious Visconti Venosta made
the Italian Tyrol — as the Trentino was sometimes called — a condition
for armistice. Although military setbacks weighed heavily on the new
nation's pride, it was not these that forced Italy to abandon the irredenta.
Custoza was no great battle. The Italian fleet still outclassed Austria's.
Everything hinged on the designs of the other powers. Austria refused
an armistice *uti possidetis*, and demanded the withdrawal of Garibaldi's
irregulars from the Tyrol. Bismarck held out some hope that the Trentino
might still be won. His support was contingent upon what France would
do. It was also clear that he wanted an end to the war. From Paris came
word that Napoleon III would not back Italy against Austria. General
La Marmora informed Ricasoli that without French backing the situation
in the field was so grave as to imperil not only Venetia but all Italy.[1] And
the war ended.

Venice came to Italy in the backhanded manner Trevelyan described.
The army, plagued by desertions that ran as high as 75 per cent among
those drafted in some areas of the Mezzogiorno,[2] woefully lacked coordination among its generals, who were resentful of Garibaldi and made a
sorry showing. It seemed as if the hero could have won had not the Government forced him to abandon the fruits of his victory. Officially Italy
did not shine. The idea soon arose that the "real" Italy, represented by
Garibaldi, would have triumphed had not the diplomats had their way.
Considering the reality, however, Italy had not fared badly. It was the
diplomats who had made the war, and it had proved successful in a very
material way. As for Austria, there was also general agreement among
Italian statesmen that she was a needed bulwark against Russian penetration in the Balkans and against Pan-Slavism. This was an old theme,
that of Cesare Balbo's *Speranze d'Italia* of 1843. But it was typical of
those who, like Balbo, spoke the language of reason rather than that of
revolutionary passion,[3] that they were inclined to dwell on unhappy facts,
on Italy's tenuous position. Jacini, writing forty years after Balbo, condemned megalomania in foreign policy, and correctly asserted that an
irredentist war had few backers. That he found it expedient to preface
his defense of a modest foreign and domestic policy with a catalogue of
Italy's narrow escapes and general good luck during the Risorgimento [4]
seemed to tie reasonableness to weakness.

To those who would call upon the energies of the real Italy, diplomatic
realism was galling. Realpolitik for Italy meant not the show of power,

but the more traditional Piedmontese policy of carefully assessing and if possible exploiting the power of others. Yet irredentism was not merely a literary exercise, as witness the efforts to get the Trentino in 1866 through diplomatic channels. What was to emerge after that date was a policy that formally disavowed any connection with irredentism. Any other position would only have proved detrimental to Italy's greatest immediate interest, peace. But Italian leaders never lost hope of satisfying the aims of 1866 should the diplomatic situation offer the chance. This hope meant, however, that no Italian government could turn its back on the movement with any finality. To do so would not only have wounded national pride but would also preclude any diplomatic advantage that might arise. On the other hand, statesmen could never give the Irredentists much encouragement. This ambiguous situation was recognized by foreign diplomats. The British ambassador, Sir Augustus Paget, made this clear to his Austrian colleague when the latter arrived to take up his post in 1877. The Italian government was sincere in its opposition to any irredentist tendency that would prove unpleasant to Austria. Even the Trentino did not concern the great majority of Italians. On this, Paget said, Visconti Venosta and Depretis were agreed. But to get an official disavowal from Rome was quite another matter. The Austro-Hungarian ambassador, Heinrich von Haymerle, got the same advice from the French and German representatives at Rome.[5]

The need to skirt the issue, to avoid commitment to national aspirations out of consideration for diplomatic realities, was not something uniquely Italian. But it did serve to reinforce the impression that Italy's governments were lacking in a just regard for national sentiments. No sooner were men "ministerial" than they seemed compromised, turning their backs on once professed ideals. Benedetto Cairoli was an example. When the Sinistra triumphed in 1876 he remained radical, attacking Depretis. In 1876, during the seven-hundredth anniversary celebration of the battle of Legnano, Cairoli was prominent among irredentist speakers; he called for the redemption not only of Trent and Trieste, but of Nice as well, thus revealing another side of the irredentist problem which, while less significant, should not be forgotten.[6] Once he became Premier, Cairoli shifted ground. Faced with a serious incident in 1880, he assured Vienna, speaking in the Chamber, that he would deal firmly with any action, or preparations for action, by the Irredentists. Crispi from outside the Government denounced this as incompatible with the principles of a free society. All irredentist manifestations should have free rein. When no longer in office, Cairoli again associated himself with Crispi in the Pent-archy, opposing Depretis and trasformismo. The group's paper, the *Tribuna*, proceeded to attack Depretis for having deleted certain remarks hostile to Austria-Hungary from the pages of the parliamentary records.[7]

As for Crispi, his first ministry from 1887 to 1891 was to involve him in two outstanding examples of irredentist activity, both of which he handled with dispatch. He showed his determination not to permit anti-Austrian demonstrations. Vienna was quick to express its gratitude for this decisive move.[8] But now Crispi was attacked by the Irredentists, who were still free of the taint of officialdom. Their leader was Salvatore Barzilai, a native of Trieste, whose election to the Chamber in 1890 strengthened the anaemic Republican forces and provided a forceful irredentist spokesman. When Cavallotti came to write the celebrated anti-Crispi diatribe that grew out of the Bank of Rome Scandals, he included Crispi's handling of the incidents as proof of a patriotism only skin deep.

By 1890 Crispi was speaking of irredentism as an enemy of the nation. In that the movement challenged the European balance, he said, it could imperil Italy's very existence.[9] This was not far from La Marmora's warning of 1866, which had led to the withdrawal of Garibaldi's troops from the Tyrol. Crispi's attack on irredentist activity while Premier was due in part to the necessity of closing the ranks of the Triple Alliance, which he generally favored. But the Alliance itself was bound up with a deeper concern. It was a guarantee, although not territorial as will be seen, against maneuvers at the Vatican. When Crispi spoke out against irredentism in 1890, he mentioned Italy's two enemies. One was the Republican Irredentists, and the other the clericals. It will be recalled that conservatives, such as Sonnino, feared both the Reds and the Blacks. Because Crispi placed Italy's security, as he saw it, above all else, he was inclined to share Sonnino's concern. It was also true that the activities of the Republicans in favor of irredentism, as well as their opposition to the monarchy, placed them in a tacit alliance with the intransigent clericals. Certainly, there was little love between the rationalist Republicans and the theocratic clerical extremists. Nonetheless, their common opposition to the Throne made them strange bedfellows, and was one of the reasons for the waning of republicanism. The fact that Republicans often manifested their opposition to the monarchy by refusing to vote seemed to make them sharers in the non expedit. In certain regions there was evidence to suggest that they were in a more than casual alliance with the Blacks.[10] Furthermore, given Leo XIII's professed indifference to the form of government, an Italian Republic that would leave the Papacy intact was conceivable. Bismarck sensed as much on the eve of the formation of the Triple Alliance. In 1891 an anonymous "Continental Statesman," obviously French, wrote that what the Vatican wanted was not the temporal power, but a new political solution to the Italian question, even a Republican one. To this Crispi answered that republicanism was dead in Italy, adding that it could only benefit France and the Vatican. He referred on more than one occasion to the aid being given the "internal enemy" [11] by those who carried on irredentist activities.

However, things would be placed in a very different light should Italy's allies shown signs of encouraging the Blacks. It would then be difficult for a patriot, and Crispi was certainly that, to crack down on anti-Austrian irredentist groups. Interestingly enough, this seems to have been the case in 1889, the year before Crispi came out with his very strong speech against irredentism. When, in June, 1889, the radical Left led by Cavallotti began stepping up the irredentist campaign, Crispi was far less hostile to the movement. He spoke in the Chamber of Italy's having nothing to lose and much to gain by war, although he ended his remarks with a plea for prudence. He put pressure on Bismarck to induce Vienna to let up on her anti-Italian campaign, with only slight result. The Chancellor did not wish to give the appearance of meddling in Austro-Hungarian internal problems.[12] Crispi took measures against the Irredentists in Italy, but none so strong as those of 1890. What was doubtless at the root of his greater leniency was the fear in 1889 and the first half of 1890 that Vienna was turning to a proclerical policy. If so, the Triple Alliance would lose much of its value for Crispi. We know that the Austrian Prime Minister, Count von Taaffe, was following an anti-German policy. Crispi complained of this and of Taaffe's pro-Slavonic attitudes to his son Herbert in October, 1888, during the state visit of William II to Rome. And Herbert seemed to agree. In May of 1889, when Crispi visited the Chancellor, Taaffe's name was again raised. Bismarck admitted that the Austrian statesman was no friend of the Alliance. By July and August Crispi had become very concerned by Taaffe's clerical and anti-Italian policy. He mentioned this to Count Nigra, the Italian ambassador at Vienna, in strong terms. Nigra tried to convince the Premier that this was not a clerical plot. He finally wired Crispi beseeching him "not to be led to seeing Jesuits even where they are not."[13] That was on August 7, 1890. Crispi's tough handling of Italian Irredentists, accusing them of aiding and abetting the Blacks, followed in October, 1890.

Church-State relations had their effect on Italy's attitude toward irredentism as they did in all other areas of domestic and foreign policy. Signs that Vienna might be adopting an unfriendly view regarding the Roman Question could be expected to produce a certain toleration, at least unofficially, of irredentism. The same result would follow indications that France, after 1870 the one sure defender of the papal claims, was moving away from the Vatican, or that the intransigents in Italy were losing ground. One of the outcomes of the decline in anti-Italian clerical activities during the pontificate of Pius X would be the rise in pitch of Italian irredentist agitation. This was in keeping with the general shift of the diplomatic front that came after the collapse of the French policy pursued by Leo XIII and Cardinal Rampolla. Anticlerical measures taken by the Rudinì government in 1898, coupled with the Dreyfus case, which ended in a failure of French ultramontane power, opened the way for a rapprochement between Rome and Paris. The excessive if not entirely unjustified [14] fears of France that were associated with Crispi gave way to a more elastic diplomacy which sought to balance Italy's position among the Powers. As a consequence irredentism, necessarily opposed by Italian statesmen, including the ex-Garibaldian Crispi, could be expected to find more official sympathy if not outright support once the clerical alliance with France was less of a threat.

It was also true, however, that both Victor Emmanuel II and Humbert I opposed irredentism. Too often the cry "Down with the monarchy" was associated with "Down with Austria." Royal diplomacy after Sedan looked to Vienna rather than Republican and clerical France for its partner in statecraft. This helped to smooth relations with Austria-Hungary, and also to weaken the irredentist campaign. When Victor Emmanuel II met Count Julius Andrássy at Venice in 1875, during Franz Joseph's trip to Italy, he made it clear that in the event special problems arose, Andrássy might come directly to the Throne by way of the King's personal agent. The occasion for doing so soon presented itself. In 1876 an article in the conservative *Opinione* spoke of Italy's right to irredentist lands should Austria-Hungary occupy Bosnia and Herzegovina. This indicated that the Republicans were not alone in pressing for a revision of the boundaries. Tension with Vienna followed. Italy could not afford this, given French attitudes at that time. Victor Emmanuel instructed Depretis what he should say in the Chamber to assure Vienna of Italy's good intentions. The King also personally informed Vienna that a project then under discussion for strengthening the northern defenses had been set aside. And when Baron Haymerle presented his credentials as Austrian Ambassador to the King he was told, according to his report to Andrássy, that the monarch ascribed irredentist activity to Italian hotheads. Victor Emmanuel's language about the movement became not only stronger but rather offensive to Italian dignity. Those who talked of expeditions to the Trentino or Albania, he said, were "dogs." Humbert I, if less aggressive in managing diplomacy, was perhaps even more submissive to Vienna. In 1893 General Baratieri, a native of the Trentino, was being considered as the new Foreign Minister. The King suggested that Vienna be consulted. The Premier designate, Zanardelli, refused to have any part of this. But Italy's ally was informed all the same, and naturally objected. Having offended Zanardelli, as well as having shown subservience to Austria, Humbert wrung his hands until the loyal General solved the dilemma by withdrawing from the scene.[15]

In that the Crown opposed irredentism, it was lending its support to the general policy followed by all the ministries of the Postrisorgimento. But this placed the monarchy in a particularly weak position. Not only did the few remaining Republicans continue to oppose the Throne; it had far less real support from conservatives than might be expected. The theme of a return to the Statuto became almost a fad in the last decade of the nineteenth century. That a truly legitimist party existed in Italy, however, was not the case. Conservatives turned to the monarchy almost in despair, in a period when the crown power was in abeyance. Humbert I did not show his father's interest in politics. In fact when Ruggero Bonghi came out with his almost ultramontane defense of the royal prerogatives, the King was displeased. What had caused the flurry of apparent legitimist theory was the lassitude of Italian politics, in particular the practice of trasformismo. Mosca rightly noted that monarchist sentiment in Italy was based on a skepticism for politics rather than a deeply held conviction.[16]

On the other hand, the Italian monarchy was tied to the revolutionary tradition. Many who gave their allegiance to the Throne despite their antimonarchical past did so with reservations. The monarchy, as Carducci wrote, had two faces: the "people" and the "Crown." It was the "legitimate depository of popular sovereignty." Carducci had accepted the monarchical solution to Italian unity on this basis.[17] This implied a conditional acceptance. The Crown had absorbed the revolution and would have to do its duty by it. This contradiction between the King and the popular element in the creation of Italy was something that unfriendly foreign observers were happy to underline.[18] Within Italy, Oriani for one made clear his reservations concerning the role of the Throne. The Throne would have to fulfill the nation's destiny.[19]

The monarchy's reputation, in short, was often dependent upon its role in the continuing revolution. Its job, for many, was the creation of that synthesis between the people and the State. Irredentism was one very real reminder of the incompleteness of united Italy. In that the Throne backed its ministers in opposition to the movement, it laid itself open to the charge of having betrayed its revolutionary and national origins. When Humbert, addressing the Chamber in 1886, spoke of Italy as being finished, he was told by the Irredentists that this was not at all the case. The royal speech was criticized as an example of the moral impoverishment that had engulfed Italy in the wake of the brightness of the Risorgimento.[20] Given the absence of any substantial ultramontane sentiment in Italy, the Crown was unprotected from the attack by the pseudo-idealists and anarchic conservatives of the Oriani variety as well as by the radical Left. Thus exposed, it was understandably difficult for the King to resist the pressures for dynamic action that originated with the advocates of Italian manifest destiny. Where the Crown was most secure was in alliance with the Parliament. Logically, the enemies of the one institution were often the enemies of the other, as would become obvious during the turbulent months of Italian neutrality. Italian rightists were quite ready to sacrifice the King even though this brought them together with syndicalists, Socialists, and Republicans.

The idea beneath much of irredentism was that of the clash between the national mission and the bureaucratic timidity of official Italy. The contrast was sharpened by the execution of a young Austrian subject, partly Italian by descent, in 1882. Guglielmo Oberdan — or Oberdank as the anti-Irridentists preferred it, since this spelling underlined his Austrian status — became the martyr of irredentism and a symbol of that idealism and self-sacrificing heroism that seemed reminiscent of greater days. His attempt to assassinate Franz Joseph was a lonely, hopeless, even romantic plot. Its very hopelessness appeared virtuous compared to the drabness of the era of positivism. Moreover, it seemed to sanctify the popular native drive behind irredentism to free the movement from the suspicion of serving not Italian but French interests. Whereas Irredentists were often Freemasons — an organization which, for some, represented a French exploitation of Italian passions — Oberdan's youthful figure symbolized the "true" unsophisticated Italy which kept alive the Italian spirit despite diplomatic coolness toward the irredenta.[21]

The day of his execution, December 20, was to take its place in the patriot's calendar alongside the anniversary of Garibaldi's death, June 2, as a time for special irredentist enthusiasm. The great orators, with Cavallotti heading the list, added fire to the cause when these dates rolled round. Carducci lent his talents, dubbing Franz Joseph "Emperor of the Hanged." Even before the execution, Carducci had seized upon the young patriot's boldness in order to attack the baseness of Italian policy. "Oh, poetry of another time. But that one could pluck out its heart and feed it to all the miserable wretches of the patria so that their spirits might grow, that they might find something worthy at last." Carducci spoke for that Roman population of Trieste and Istria that should be Italian in fact as it was in language, origin, culture, and martyrdom. When Oberdan was dead, Carducci, speaking in 1886 at the dedication of a plaque in his memory, returned to the lament for lost ideals. Italy was growing soft, relaxing amid economic improvement, but decadent in regard to political ideals. War was not possible, for Italy was unprepared. The job at hand was to carry on incessant propaganda, to establish the conviction that Italy was neither finished, strong, stable, nor secure, regardless of what the King might say.[22]

The poet had accepted the monarchy, even writing an ode to the House of Savoy. But this did not lessen his insistence that the Crown had yet to fulfill its national mission. And the concession to reality, that war was folly given Italy's position, did not obscure Carducci's disdain for merely material advances made since 1870. Materialism and positivism were the extinguishing forces of idealism. This was implicit in Carducci's irredentist speeches. His language was also similar to Cavallotti's in its incitement to action. In later years, Carducci's works were to be ransacked, as were those of Dante, Petrarch, Cicero, and Manzoni, for references to *Italia irredenta*[23] quite as if the age of cultural nationalism were still alive.

That it was not, even for the Irredentists — however much they might deny the nation's completion — could be seen in the ambiguity of their campaign for rectification of the frontiers. They claimed to be keeping Mazzinian principles alive. But Mazzini had spoken for all peoples. Adam Mickiewicz, for him, had been a great prophet. Now that Italy was in fact a nation, the Pole's mission among the Slavic peoples took on another color, especially since Russia seemed to be taking over Pan-Slavism for her own. Cavallotti might attack Crispi's anti-Irredentism, but he shared Crispi's belief that the Dual Monarchy was needed. It was no longer, he declared, the Austria of Metternich. As for the peoples of the

Balkans, one could speak of them only with certain reservations. When Kossuth died at Turin in 1894 the Irredentists mourned him, although there were no great and moving demonstrations. Kossuth represented Hungary, however. The Slavs, on the other hand, were becoming for Irredentists the chief weapon in the anti-Italian program of Austria-Hungary.[24] Few Irredentists had any desire to see the rise of a South Slav nation to the east in the event of a collapse of the Dual Monarchy. During the months of Italian neutrality, the war parties in Italy shed copious tears for Belgium, but far less was said about the plight of the Serbs. Italy might be proclaimed unfinished by the Irredentists; but fear of the Slavs showed that, even for Cavallotti, she was bound by the realities of power politics and no longer free to risk everything for national ideals as in the days of the Risorgimento. That, in effect, was the substance of Jacini's advice to the Italians in his noted articles attacking Crispi's "megalomania." For a small state like Piedmont to wish to become larger, he wrote in 1899, was plausible. But Jacini as a northern conservative regretted that a considerable faction among Italy's leaders had not realized conditions had changed, that Italy's position in Europe placed limits to her expectations.[25]

While it is too much to suggest that the irrendentist movement would have died out had Austria-Hungary been wise in her handling of the Italian question,[26] it is certainly true that what sentiment did exist was affected markedly by Vienna's policy. In the decade following Porta Pia, Italo-Austrian relations were generally cordial despite the existence of irredentist groups in Italy and in the Dual Monarchy. Not the least factor contributing to this was Andrássy's sensible attitude toward the Irredentists. Rather than a policy of cleverness and chicanery, the Austrian statesman chose to adopt a frank but friendly tone, making Vienna's position unmistakably clear, as shown by the note that Andrássy addressed to the Italian government in 1874, a year in which anti-Austrian feeling was running high in Italy. Times had changed, he wrote, from the days when Austria was isolated in Europe. Whatever factors had once prompted irredentist sentiments, these were no more. Relations between Italy and Austria-Hungary rested on a mutual respect for the borders established between the two countries by treaty. Be they well or badly drawn, Vienna could not accept any criticism of them based on ethnographic principles. Were she to do so, similar demands could then be raised by others within the Empire which it would be almost impossible to deny. Austria-Hungary could not cede Italian-speaking subjects to Italy without causing a centrifugal movement among the subject nationalities. Andrássy conceded that the modern trend toward national states had its *raison d'être*, but to apply this idea in detail would imperil the whole European order. Austria-Hungary had no designs on Italian territory. Past differences were forgotten. United Italy was recognized as an essential guarantee for peace and the European balance. Nothing Italy might wish to gain would be comparable to good relations with the Empire. Andrássy made it clear that Vienna would not demand any formal guarantees against irredentist intrigues. He also made it clear that Austria-Hungary would find the cure for any harm they might cause in her own forces. Although Vienna did not subscribe to the Government opinions in the Italian press, Andrássy did ask that the ministers use whatever influence they might have with certain papers to stop irredentist activities and to recommend quietly to the more or less official press that it avoid anything which could embarrass the Italian government itself. He also requested that Rome help Austria-Hungary discover the promoters of annexationist propaganda within the Empire.[27]

Visconti Venosta, the Italian foreign minister, assured the Austro-Hungarian ambassador that annexationist sentiment in Trieste and the Trentino was weak. This, and the King's reported reaction to the Andrássy note — which was one of complete approval — could not but please Vienna. In years to come, the note took on the quality of a fundamental of Austro-Hungarian policy. Its substance was restated at moments when irredentist activities seemed on the rise. Vienna for its part recognized that the movement was not widespread. But it was the fear of those centrifugal forces that became a nightmare, inducing Austrians to exaggerate every straw in the wind, as may be seen by the personal attention the royal bureaucrat, Franz Joseph, devoted to the particulars of irredentist activity.[28] To counter these alarmist tendencies, Andrássy tried to promote a more sensible appreciation of the scope and significance of the Italian question. An important element in his over-all strategy was his own coolness to Austrian clericalism, his resistance to demands from anti-Italian Church groups within the Empire for a tougher stand on the Roman Question.[29] His attitude toward the Church was linked to his wish to depress irredentist sentiments. Since many anti-Austrian Italians were radical anticlericals, it could be expected that any sign of an Austro-Hungarian proclerical stand would enflame Italian agitation for a conquest of the irredenta. That a departure from Andrássy's wise policy could act to encourage irredentism, even at the government level, has been seen in the case of Count Taaffe and Crispi. In general, however, during the first decade after Porta Pia, a tacit arrangement was taking shape according to which Rome refused to encourage irrendentism while Vienna took an equally negative stand on the Roman Question. This quid pro quo will be examined again within the larger context of the Triple Alliance.

The fundamental realities behind the crisp language of the Andrássy note of 1874 were appreciated even by those Italian diplomats who hoped some day to acquire the Trentino. Count Nicholas Robilant is a case in point. During the critical summer of 1878 Robilant advised the King to accept the fact that even should Austria-Hungary annex Ottoman lands, Italy would have to resign herself to it and not compromise her prestige, perhaps her existence, by fruitless acts. Austria, he said, would never cede a "finger" of the irredenta. What Italy needed were useful, effective alliances, the maintenance of good relations with Vienna, and the avoidance not only of inopportune discussions of the irredentist question, but of all forms of public expression of irredentist sympathies. If such a policy were followed, Italy might face the Eastern question without danger and perhaps even reap some advantages from it. Robilant predicted the day when the Three Emperors League would collapse. The Austro-German alliance he felt would remain. Nor would he have it otherwise. More to be feared was a revived France allied with Austria and backed by Russia. Italy should seek to establish and maintain the Austro-German alliance and then become part of it, in order to secure the peace of Europe.[30]

This was diplomatic realism, as well as a remarkably accurate appraisal of the future possibilities upon which Robilant was to capitalize when he became Foreign Minister in 1885. For those who thought in terms of heroic memories, however, it was a betrayal of the national destiny. Yet Robilant had by no means abandoned the Trentino. Implicit in his advice to the King was the hope eventually of getting it. As he himself made clear in 1886 to Ludolf, the Austrian ambassador, Vienna had no need to fear irredentism as long as he, Robilant, were Foreign Minister and as long as peace reigned in Europe. Should peace be disturbed, on the other hand, he could not answer even for his own feelings on the subject.[31]

Was there no hope, then, that Italy might exploit the balance of power to pry loose, without war, some concession from the ironclad terms of the Andrássy note? If Vienna was unwilling to cede an inch, might not Berlin add some leverage to Italy's benefit? In 1888 it seemed that this might be the case. Germany needed Italy now that the Franco-Russian alliance was in effect. Baron Karl Bruck, representing Austria-Hungary at Rome, sent back a disquieting report to Vienna. The German ambassador, Count

Solms, had apparently recognized the irredentist question in the course of a private conversation, referring to a "regulation of the south Tyrol border." Solms also implied that the Trentino was really of no great significance. Bruck wrote home that while Crispi might satisfy Italy's need for victory in Africa, no one had really forgotten the irredenta. Germany needed Italy and would propose, if necessary, the cession of the Trentino, for which Austria would be compensated elsewhere.

Kálnoky, the Austro-Hungarian foreign minister, answered this report with a restatement of the 1874 Andrássy note. As for the German ambassador's ideas, he assumed Bruck had made it clear that it was not advisable to make such a request at Vienna. Lombardy, he wrote, was lost chiefly because Germany — "or to put it better, Prussia" — left Austria in the lurch against France. The Veneto could be ceded with honor following the victories over the Italian army. But it was madness to think of ceding lands that had belonged to the Hapsburg monarchy for centuries, and to do this not to satisfy but to whet the territorial appetites of Austria's neighbors. Kálnoky closed his reply with a reminder that the Trentino was just about the size of the part of Lorraine that Germany was occupying. Perhaps Berlin would care to enter into discussions relative to a return of that land to France in order to preserve the peace of Europe?

That was putting it on the line. Austria-Hungary would not cede a scrap of the Hapsburg lands, nor admit any discussion of the subject by her allies. Nonetheless, when the question of Lorraine was being argued on the battlefield, Germany might well be forced to raise the question of the Trentino at Vienna. And the Trentino had always been the traditional focal point of Italian irredentist aspirations.[32] Much would depend, however, on whether those aspirations had remained what they once were, or whether the undercurrent of dissatisfaction with Italy's destiny had been swelled to unrealistic and insatiable proportions by the rhetoricians of power abetted by statesmen less sure of united Italy's role in Europe than the cool and confident Robilant.[33]

The Triple Alliance

Oriani wrote that the Triple Alliance represented the last stage of Italy's political inferiority. The official foreign policy of the Postrisorgimento according to the eccentric prophet, stood in marked contrast to the interests and wishes of the real nation. Once Italy had achieved self-consciousness, awareness of her mission, the Alliance would collapse.[34] Here, as in all of Oriani's work, the tendency to view political realities in the light of a predestined historical plan becomes apparent. The dichotomy of the real and the official Italy was applied to diplomacy as to every other area of Italian life.

The Triple Alliance came to be viewed in the light of cultural values as part and parcel of the generation of prose. It has been called a "most grotesque example of intellectual decadence,"[35] quite as if foreign policy were governed by standards of philosophy. A dangerous application of idealistic considerations underlies much of the literature critical of the pact. One reads, for example, that Oberdan's martyrdom in 1882, the year the Triple Alliance was formed, signaled the emergence of a people's foreign policy as distinct from that of the Government. Nor is one surprised to find this evaluation of the Alliance tied to a distinction drawn between a diplomacy which is the product of a mentality — a climate of opinion — and one based solely on material considerations. Gioacchino Volpe whose views these are, completes the familiar picture when he writes that these distinctions relate to a period in Italian history when the Risorgimento barely existed, when the old spirit was no more.

The noted historian's judgments must be seen in the light of his own opposition to Italian neutrality in 1915.[36] Considering the ease with which the Alliance did lose its backers in 1914–15, however, one wonders whether the prophetic insights of Oriani were not valid after all. In the space of weeks, men who for years had written in defense of the pact shifted ground, becoming fervent propagandists of intervention on the side of the Entente. In breaking loose from the system that had been the center of Italy's diplomacy for over thirty years, was the nation then finding herself, and achieving that fusion between the deeper currents of wisdom residing in the people and the formal structure of government? Or was there an ambiguity underlying the Triple Alliance that made these sudden shifts more logical than they appeared at first glance?

As far as irredentism was concerned, the spirit — if not the letter — of the Alliance opposed it. But to make this the central issue, to see the Triple Alliance for Italy as contradictory,[37] is to exaggerate the force behind the irredentist movement. It has been an assumption rather than a proven fact that Italy had a "permanent ill will" toward Austria-Hungary.[38] To say this is to forget the period after Porta Pia when the ties between Vienna and Rome were far more cordial than those between Rome and Berlin, not to mention the friction with the French Republic. Irredentism was always a discordant note. It was not so loud, however, as to drown out the clerical voices coming from Paris, nor Russian talk of

Pan-Slavism. Even those irredentist societies that were founded as a response to Oberdan's execution and that are cited as a popular testimony of anti-Austrian feeling, were no less circumspect in their recognition that the Dual Monarchy formed a barrier to the Slavic east.[39]

As for France, the threat of ultramontane intervention after 1870 was sufficient to drive even those hostile to Prussia and sympathetic to France toward Vienna and Berlin. Thiers shared in the widespread dislike of Italian unity.[40] Although he made it clear that France was obliged to keep peace, and accept Italy, his speech in the Chamber of July 22, 1871, attacked the policy of the Second Empire that had made that unity possible. He also stressed France's whole-hearted devotion to the Pope, to whom the Republic was open should he seek exile. The speech made a bad impression in Italy. Visconti Venosta wrote Robilant, then representing Italy at Vienna, that the "evident antipathies" were not well received by Italian public opinion, even if Thiers had reassured Italy as to impending difficulties. Five months later he again wrote Robilant that only Austria's good will, indicated by her refusal to raise the Roman Question, prevented the French ultramontane party from acting.[41] Visconti Venosta was no admirer of Bismarck, but his sympathies for a France[42] humbled by the force of Prussia could not blind him to the hostility of the French government. In order to offset the shift of Italian opinion toward Germany, Paris appointed a liberal, Hugues Fournier, to represent France in Italy. Suspicion was far from stilled. The Sinistra's more strident deputies spoke of the inevitability of war with France. Visconti Venosta countered for the Government, which he defended from charges of overindulgence to the Vatican. Italy needed peace. She must not play into the hands of the ultramontanes by imprudent actions. But his allusions to Germany, which was having its own problems with the clerical party, were met with general approval on both sides of the Chamber. When Fournier was given an extended leave of absence by the De Broglie government that had followed Thiers, even Bonghi — known for his dislike of Prussia — spoke of a "natural and necessary understanding" between Italy and Germany.[43]

Vienna then invited Victor Emmanuel to visit Austria-Hungary. Berlin followed suit. The King appeared reluctant to make the trip, not so much to Vienna as to Berlin. He had little fondness for Bismarck's new Germany. The May Laws had just been passed. His own religiosity spoke against this obvious recognition of the Pope's chief European adversary. In Italy, Church-State relations were embittered by the bill, passed the previous year, that had suppressed theological chairs in Italian universities. The clash over the *exequatur* had followed. And at the moment the invitation arrived, the bill ending religious orders was being debated. It was passed in June, 1873. The *Osservatore Romano* accused the Italian government of slavishly following Bismarck's orders. It was even reported in the clerical press that Bismarck had intervened to prevent an understanding between Church and State on the exequatur.[44]

The announcement that the King would go to Vienna and Berlin was received with great satisfaction in Italy. Even men whose personal ties with France were strong expressed their approval.[45] Between Germany and Italy there was a natural community of interests that suggested an alliance. Their histories from Utrecht to Sedan seemed to speak of national affinities. Now the *Kulturkampf* underscored the existence of a common enemy. By the appointment of Cardinal Hohenlohe as representative to the Vatican, Germany seemed to recognize the religious rather than temporal nature of that post. And Hohenlohe's brother, later Chancellor, had proposed the campaign in Germany against the Jesuits.[46] In 1872 the Italian Crown Prince and his consort attended the baptism of the daughter of the German Crown Prince and Princess, acting as godparents. French statesmen smelled a German-Italian alliance. And Bismarck made overtures in that direction; he spoke to De Launay, the Italian ambassador, in 1872, of a "predestined" alliance. Repeated suggestions that Italy might take Nice were put forth.[47] The offer was obviously designed to enlist Italian support against France. Bismarck, like a great centrifuge, would create problems elsewhere in Europe in order to protect his own nation. Nice was the bait. Its sacrifice to France was a symbol of the price paid for unification, and it was also Garibaldi's birthplace. Among the Irredentists Cairoli spoke of Nice along with Trent and Trieste. Cavallotti's paper, the *Ragione*, went as far as claiming Malta and Corsica.[48]

For all these affinities, Visconti Venosta and the Destra were not to be lured into a path of adventure that might compromise the nation, already beset with grave social and economic problems. There was also concern for Church-State relations, which would inevitably deteriorate should Italy move toward the leader of the Kulturkampf. Addressing his constituents during the election campaign of 1874, Visconti Venosta characterized Italian policy as a search for the peace and security needed in order to face these domestic problems. He recognized the importance of the royal visit and of the entente among the three powers. It was the best guarantee of that peace. An alliance, however, was premature. Implicit here was the assumption that, diplomatically, Italy could benefit just as much from an entente as from an alliance that would necessarily commit her to larger responsibilities. When the Sinistra was in power, his calm appraisal would be less in evidence. It is important to make this clear in order to understand some of the reasons behind the Triple Alliance when it did finally take shape.

There was also the hope that French policy would shift. De Broglie fell in May, 1874, and the *Orénoque* was recalled the following October 13. This was one month before the Italian elections. The Destra, under attack for its submissive policy toward the Church and France, had insisted on the ship's removal. The French government agreed. MacMahon's note informing the Pope of its recall, however, stressed France's "religious attachment to the Holy Father," while making it known that another ship, anchored at a French port, would be available. Pius IX sent his blessings to the French Republic.[49] For its part, the Destra failed to achieve its political aim. The Sinistra made notable gains in the elections, attesting to the fact that anti-French sentiment was not easily satisfied.

If Rome refused to be enticed into the "predestined alliance" with Germany, it was partly because Italy's relations with Austria-Hungary were far more intimate than her ties with Berlin. A stronger community of interests united Vienna and Rome, in spite of irredentism. Both countries wished to remain on good terms with Germany without committing themselves to the struggle against the Vatican or France. This meant that Vienna must resist any temptation to exploit the Roman Question and that Italy play down irredentism. The irredentist problem has been touched upon. Something more must be said about Austria-Hungary's handling of the Roman Question.

From the beginning Vienna had tended to avoid any semblance of pressuring Italy as regards the Vatican's demands. Austria gave reason to believe she would accept the occupation of France if it were done quickly. This attitude permitted even those Italians who were reluctant to make the move to drop their previously stated willingness to seek an international agreement on the Papacy's place in Italy. When Visconti Venosta, after Porta Pia, still offered to go through with Italy's promise to place the question before the Powers, Count Beust, Austro-Hungarian minister of foreign affairs, did not insist. The Franco-Prussian War absorbed the attention of Europe, and Italy was thus able to avoid a possible international intervention in her domestic affairs. Once the regulation of her relations to the Vatican had been left to Italy, however, any further suggestion that the Guarantees be backed up by the Powers met with widespread resistance in Italy. Those who still recommended an internationalization of the Italian law of 1871 found themselves without significant backing, as Jacini discovered.[50]

Andrássy had become Foreign Minister in 1871 and held that post until 1879. Austria had good reasons of her own for not wanting any part of the Kulturkampf. But Andrássy also resisted ultramontane pressures. His handling of the Roman Question was designed to prevent the Catholic powers from using it as a weapon against the Italian government. In 1873, during an illness of Pius IX, it was reported that should the Pope die the coming conclave might be held outside Italy. Andrássy was most explicit in making known his disapproval of such a plan. He asked the Italian government to show by some statement that it intended to guarantee the conclave's security. Thus the matter was left to the discretion of that Government, and any foreign interference was avoided. In January, 1874, a circular was issued giving the requested assurances. This had been arranged during the royal visit to Vienna. At that time Andrássy had also displayed his willingness to court Italy by turning a deaf ear to anti-Italian clerical demonstrations. He agreed that the Italian monarch should have a military parade. It took place, in fact, on the third anniversary of Porta Pia.

As a Hungarian, Andrássy feared the rise of a strong Slavic state. The Italian government agreed, as he was happy to note in 1876 during the Balkan crisis. As for irredentism, he personally intervened to check the emotional tendency in Vienna to exaggerate its importance.[51] One of his last official acts was to reassure Italy that Austria-Hungary did not share the views expressed in an aggressively anti-Italian pamphlet that appeared in 1879. This work, entitled *Italicae Res*, was written by Colonel Haymerle — whose brother was then Ambassador to Italy — of the Austro-Hungarian general staff. The connection certainly added to Italian suspicions. Colonel Haymerle was an advocate of strong military entrenchment in the Trentino. Andrássy strongly disagreed, and made his feelings known to the Emperor.[52] One sees in this incident the germ of the struggle within Vienna governmental circles between the more circumspect views of Austro-Italian relations, represented by Andrássy, and the aggressive tendencies of the military, a struggle that was to become more pronounced in the decade before the Great War.

It was not Catholic Austria but Protestant Germany whose attitude toward the Roman Question was a source of Italian concern. Bismarck's policy in this matter was to become a great issue among those who opposed the Triple Alliance in 1915. It would be well to see what his motives really were. On the question of the Italian occupation of Rome, William had refused to make a formal protest, although expressing his regrets for the Pope's plight. Bismarck agreed that it was up to Catholic countries to make a protest. He declined to say whether or not Prussia would cooperate in this matter. All this took place in November, 1870. By the following February domestic considerations seem to have had an effect. The Catholics had substantially increased their representation in the Prussian Diet. The King received a delegation of Silesian Knights of Malta who had come to request formal German intervention in the Roman Question. He now spoke of the Italian occupation as an "act of violence." William was careful to add that one would have to wait to see what Italy did in Rome. He did state, however, that he would join other rulers in a *démarche*, but only after the war with France was over. As for Bismarck, he may have been considering intervention in Italian affairs. He was angry with Italy for having permitted Garibaldi to fight in France. Again, domestic concerns made such a policy risky. Bismarck could not afford to involve Germany in foreign squabbles at the time. He was also worried about the political impact of the dogma of infallibility on German Catholics. The Liberals, on the other hand, made gains in the elections of March 3, 1871. It was not wise to take up the Roman Question under these circumstances. The royal address to the Reichstag of March 21 settled the matter. Germany would not intervene.

It is apparent that Germany's handling of the Roman Question was governed by purely German interests from the very beginning. This was true as well of the famous offer of asylum for the Pope in Germany. Bismarck, in making the offer, suddenly reversed his previous emphatic rejection of the idea.[53] Those who see him as a blackmailer, ready to use the Roman Question as a lever to force a reluctant Italy into the Triple Alliance, picture him gleefully contemplating the embarrassment he could cause Italy.[54] It is certainly possible that he enjoyed the prospect, provoked as he was with the Italian government. But the reasoning behind the offer of an asylum at Fulda was nothing so negative as dislike of Italian policy. He could scarcely have afforded to alienate Italy in any case, given the diplomatic situation. His motives reflected not a desire to punish Italy but rather his own political insecurities. Once in Germany, the Pope would show himself for what he was. The sacred aura would wear thin on close inspection. The Poles would be won over. The grateful pontiff would persuade the Bavarian ultramontanes to accept the German Empire. Bismarck also hoped that Pius IX would then use his influence to shorten the war. The Chancellor's oft-quoted remark to Marco Minghetti, that the Pope was never so immune to foreign pressure as under the unilateral Guarantees of the Italian government, with the temporal power gone,[55] showed how much his own Roman Question was at the root of Germany's relations with Italy.

While Andrássy was paving the road from Rome to Vienna, accepting Italy's assurances on the next conclave, Bismarck was handling the problem on the international level. He addressed a note to the Powers in May, 1872, suggesting some agreement on recognition of Pius' successor. States with Catholic subjects, he said, were greatly interested in seeing the next papal election conducted in a fashion that would permit them to recognize it as "valid and regular." His aim, however, was not to raise the international issue in order to force Italy's hand, but to get a less intractable pope chosen when Pius IX died. This method was bound to be offensive to Italy, whose protection of the Papacy was then beyond interference from outside.

It is true, then, that Germany's policy was less acceptable to Italy than Austria's. But the cause for this was Bismarck's own problems. In 1875 the encyclical declaring the May Laws null and void was issued, releasing Prussian Catholics from obedience to them. Bismarck stormed at Italy's refusal to follow the lead of the Kulturkampf. It was at this point that he complained to Minghetti about papal immunity. Visconti Venosta refused to modify the Guarantees so as to allow the Pope less freedom. Bismarck wrote Count Alois Károlyi that he had become absolutely indifferent toward Italy.[56]

In fact he was anything but indifferent. The *Orénoque* had been recalled, which suggested an Italian-French *détente*. Victor Emmanuel's trip to Vienna was followed by Franz Joseph's visit to Venice, where Andrássy and the Italian ruler had their very friendly exchange. As far as Austria and Italy were concerned, the Roman Question seemed put aside. Robilant, from Vienna, informed Visconti Venosta that it was hard for him to bargain for an imperial visit to Rome after the King's warm expressions of friendship for Franz Joseph.[57] Bismarck could see the threads of that Catholic alliance which had been discussed on the eve of the Franco-Prussian War being taken up again. This fear does much to explain the war scare of April-May, 1875. The Center party had increased from sixty-one to ninety-five seats in the general elections of 1874. Bismarck's attempts to deal with Pius IX directly, offering suspension of the May Laws in return for a papal order to the Center that it should back the Chancellor, had failed. Rumors of impending war might discredit the Catholics in Germany while bringing to power a more pliable government in France. When the desired result did not materialize, Bismarck called off the war scare. He now took up French overtures, hoping to avert a Franco-Russian rapprochement. But among the topics discussed between Paris and Berlin was that of the status of the Holy See.[58]

Unquestionably Bismarck's attempts to raise the Roman Question among the Powers annoyed Italians. However, the charge that he did so in order to force Italy into an alliance is quite mistaken. Internal considerations were always at stake. The Chancellor's fears are evident at each turn, far more so than those of the Italian statesmen who dominated their country's foreign policy in the decade after Porta Pia. The reputation of Bismarck as the cool and self-possessed Machiavellian pales considerably while that of Visconti Venosta takes on new luster, the more deserved since Italy was deprived of the luxury of material power with which to back up her diplomacy.

Italy's position was made easier by the tacit agreement with Vienna already touched upon. It amounted to a trade by which the former kept a tight rein on irredentism while the latter checked clericalism. This understanding was to become an unwritten principle of the Triple Alliance. In 1887 a dispatch from Kálnoky to Bruck, Austro-Hungarian minister at Rome, said as much. To ask Austria explicitly to oppose the Papacy would be the same as to ask Crispi, then in power, to declare in the Chamber that Italy not only raised no claims on Trent and Trieste, but also formally renounced them once and for all. This dispatch points up a feature of the Triple Alliance that was not generally known until after the Great War,[59] and that even since then has been sometimes forgotten.[60] Rome was not territorially guaranteed as the Italian capital. Had it been, Kálnoky's dispatch would be self-contradictory, since an Austrian acceptance of Italian sovereignty over the city would have been in fact an official denial of the papal claims. When the truth became known following the publication of *Die Grosse Politik*, critics of the Triple Alliance seized upon it as proof that Bismarck had bludgeoned Italy, threatening an internationalization of the Guarantees should she fail to come to terms.[61] This portrayal of Germany as extortioner rather than loyal ally comes for the most part from the advocates of intervention in 1915. How much patriotic and partisan considerations weigh in this belittling of the Alliance may be seen by the fact that there were those who made the same charge against Bismarck when it was assumed that Rome *was* guaranteed.[62] There is also a tie between much postwar literature discrediting the Triple Alliance and Bismarck's role in its creation, and a wish to defend Sonnino's handling of the negotiations leading up to the London Treaty of 1915, which, by Clause XV, obtained the Entente's assurance that the Papacy would not be allowed to participate in the peace conference once the war was won.[63] The Vatican's opposition to Italian intervention is also behind this blackening of the Alliance. As far as Sonnino's own position is concerned, it is important to recall that he was very fidgety about the possibility that the Vatican might try to exploit the Church's international character. This was true of Sonnino not only in 1914–15, but in the days before the Triple Alliance took shape. He also worried in those early years about German designs for exploiting the Roman Question.[64]

When one examines the documents cited as proof of Bismarck's anti-Italian motives, however, it becomes clear that his primary concern, as far as the Roman Question was involved, was domestic rather than diplomatic. He wanted to settle the quarrel between the Vatican and the Quirinal, it is true; but he was aware that the role of mediator was a thankless one. If he hoped at first to make the Italian alliance conditional on a modus vivendi between the Vatican and the Italian government, it was because he feared that any pact would appear to be aimed at the Church unless this could be arranged. Leo XIII's Christmas message of 1881 had declared the existing situation under the terms of the Guarantees incompatible with the freedom and dignity of the Holy See. Under such circumstances, it seemed unwise for a country with many Catholics to offer a territorial guarantee of Rome. Such a guarantee could also have endangered the peace. However, Bismarck was willing to admit that even the guarantee would be possible if Italy tied the Alliance to the existing pact with Russia.[65]

In short, Bismarck wanted the Alliance but did not want to stir up a clerical wasp's nest in Germany, nor to upset the peace of Europe at Germany's expense. Kálnoky, on the other hand, took a much more circumspect view of the problem, showing again that Vienna's relations with Italy were based on a deeper mutual understanding of the Roman Question. He agreed that a modus vivendi would be the best solution.

But he doubted that the Italian government could ever offer a settlement acceptable to the Vatican. And how, he asked, could Austria-Hungary approach the subject without seeming to interfere in Italian affairs? He informed Bismarck that the Empire wanted no part of the Roman Question. Vienna had maintained a position of benevolent neutrality that would be compromised by any attempt to achieve a conciliation precisely because of the need to contact the Vatican in order to patch up the quarrel. The inevitable result of any such approach would be publicity about Austrian intervention in favor of the temporal power. Besides, he told the Chancellor, what could Italy offer the Vatican? However modest the Pope's demands, one could not, in all fairness, expect the Italian government to accept them. At the very time this exchange of views was in progress, the Vatican was appealing to Vienna in vain for backing following the assault on the bier of Pius IX.[66]

It is interesting to note that Vienna was not at first unconditionally opposed to granting a territorial guarantee. In that case, however, Italy would have to pay a corresponding price. This would have been the final renunciation of the irredenta. Much as Kálnoky disliked getting mixed up in the Church-State issue, the fear of those centrifugal forces which represented Austria's own nightmare seems to have been for a moment even stronger. On Italy's side, the Roman Question apparently far overshadowed irredentist sentiment, as witness the Italian desire to secure a guarantee of Rome, which could only have been bought at the expense of the Trentino. As for Sonnino, in 1881 he was quite prepared to sacrifice that area. Enmity toward Austria on irredentist grounds, he wrote, was artificial and unjustified.[67]

Bismarck dropped his idea of demanding a settlement of the Roman Question before an alliance could be sealed. Pasquale Mancini, the Italian foreign minister, made it clear that no government, regardless of its party, could admit the least interference in a matter that was strictly domestic in nature. Perhaps in reaction to recent Pan-Slavic statements from Russian sources, Bismarck also dropped his other condition, that of tying the Triple Alliance to the duration of the Russian pact.[68] What emerged was a treaty sanctioning the pre-existing quid pro quo that had been the work of the Andrássy period. It was because Rome was not guaranteed that the German ambassador, Solms, could toy in 1888 with the idea of an Austrian cession of the Trentino. Interestingly, there was reason to believe that Solms was also trying to promote conciliation between Church and State in the wake of the Tosti debacle. He was known to be close to Cardinal Rampolla, whereas his predecessor, Keudell, was regarded as a "Lutheran to the bone."[69]

This would make sense, for one could not seriously suggest that Austria abandon the Trentino without getting the expected price: an end to the Roman Question acceptable to the Vatican and to Austrian Catholics. That Vienna rejected any idea of giving up Hapsburg lands proves again that she had not departed significantly from her original stand on the Roman Question. This was essentially the situation in 1882 when the Triple Alliance was formed. Because it was, Italy could bargain for the Trentino in 1914-15, while still an ally of Austria-Hungary, although neutral in accordance with the terms governing the *casus foederis*. During the period of Italian neutrality Matthias Erzberger was to try once more to reach a bargain by which Italy would come to terms with the Pope and get the coveted irredenta in return.[70] His plans were to be ruined by Vienna's refusal to make the sacrifice until the very last moment; by that time the Italian government was decided on war.

It is true that Crispi and later Tommaso Tittoni[71] did make the claim in their speeches that a territorial guarantee was included in the treaty. It has been suggested that the wording of the preamble, with its stress on securing the monarchical principle and internal social order, may have been interpreted as a tacit recognition of the guaranteed status of Rome.[72] That is doubtful, since Vienna had made it quite clear that this was not so. But to suggest that Crispi and Tittoni intentionally falsified the truth is quite unfair. Diplomatic realities justified Italian statesmen in saying that Rome was permanently Italian.[73] Even before the Triple Alliance was sealed, the Italian government recognized that Germany would never stand by and allow a French attack on Italy. Bismarck was aware of this elementary fact. He appreciated that Italians could work upon this fundamental assumption in any negotiations preceding an alliance.[74] It was because of this that a mutual neutrality pact was insufficient basis for a treaty. Italy could count on at least that much, and doubtless more, without a formal alliance.

After the Triple Alliance had been signed, visible proof of the real if not official guarantee of Rome was given by the visit of the German Crown Prince to Italy's capital in 1883. The *Nuova Antologia* made a point of the fact that Frederick William visited the Quirinal and the Pantheon before going to the Vatican. This moderate journal twitted the Blacks by suggesting that Leo XIII might have had an unpleasant surprise in noting the Prince's silence on questions relating to Germany and the Vatican. The *Revue des Deux Mondes*, on the other hand, played up the visit to the Vatican as an indication of the Pope'se increasing prestige. The *Nuova Antologia* not only flatly denied this, but said that the royal visit reinforced the Triple Alliance, not the Papacy.[75] In 1888 the German Emperor himself came to Rome. William II was more secure at home in regard to the Catholic party. (Cardinal Galimberti had run up against a stone wall in trying to enlist Bismarck's support for the Pope. When asked what Austria would do if France attacked Italy in order to restore the temporal power, Bismarck had replied that "one thought first of existing and then of being Catholic.") This was made abundantly clear to the Vatican when, on the very evening following his visit to the Pope, William II toasted the health of the King and of Rome, "Your Majesty's capital."[76]

Italy was never to enjoy a similar testimony from Franz Joseph. The Austrian never returned the Italian King's visit of 1881. No sooner was the Triple Alliance signed than the Italian radical press demanded that he do so. Kálnoky made it clear that a visit to Rome was out of the question,[77] and this was to remain true throughout the life of the treaty. To assert that this fact sorely tried even the most faithful supporters of the Alliance,[78] however, is to overstate the case. Austria's refusal represented a possible source of discord between the allies. It wounded Italy's pride. But for those who viewed diplomacy in the harsh light of facts, this was insufficient motivation for casting aside the greater advantages that rested in the assurance that, visit or no, Rome was Italian and would remain so. Sonnino, however touchy where the Roman Question was concerned, supported the Triple Alliance even after he was in a position that gave him access to the secret of its terms and thus to the knowledge that there was no territorial guarantee of the capital.

Besides, it was the French far more than the Austrians who played upon the Roman Question. Until 1904 and Émile Loubet's visit to Rome, Paris expressed not only reservations but often open hostility toward Italian unity. French ultramontanism weighed far more in the balance than Franz Joseph's refusal to come to Rome, a refusal that was also understandable in view of Austrian Catholicism. And, although Venice was not Rome, he had gone that far, which indicated his personal acceptance of the conclusions of the War of 1866. Only the fall of the French ultramontanes permitted the rapprochement between France and Italy that was officially confirmed by Loubet's visit. That visit, as Giolitti told Bülow, meant that henceforth French backing, real or apparent, of the Papacy in the political field was excluded. According to Giolitti, the Roman Question was dead in 1904.[79]

It was to be expected that this shift in French policy would have its effect on the Triple Alliance. After 1904 the insecurities rising from the fear of French clericalism decreased. As a result, the unwritten understanding between Rome and Vienna was of less moment. Nonetheless, when Italy was obliged to choose between her "allies" and her "friends" in 1914–15, the Roman Question suddenly came to life. Berlin and Vienna, and not Paris, were portrayed by ardent interventionists as the focal point of the Vatican's hope to play its trump card: internationalization of the Guarantees. Conservative newspapers that had always supported the Triple Alliance, and whose social and political programs were viewed in a sympathetic light by the clerical press, suddenly resurrected the corpse whose obituary Giolitti had read in 1904. And since irredentism represented the Italian share in the Italo-Austrian bargain, it was logical that these same papers, but recently anti-irredentist, should become spokesmen for that great mission. One could not breathe life into one corpse without reviving the other.[80]

On the surface, there was something contrived in these sudden shifts. And yet they were carried off with a fervor that belies mere political opportunism, although that element was by no means absent. The Alliance which had served Italy so long suddenly became a massive contradiction, uniting the inimical forces of Austria and Italy, even though those two countries had been bound together for over thirty years by mutual interests. These startling reversals, however, were not the result of a new awareness of any inherent contradiction in Italian diplomacy; rather, they were the logical outcome of an ambiguity that was at the root of the treaty from the very beginning.

It has been said that Italy got from the Alliance something she did not really need, namely the promise of support in case of a French attack. That is true. In 1882 the situation had not changed so radically as to set aside Visconti Venosta's prior reluctance to negotiate that "pre-destined alliance." Bismarck had assured Victor Emmanuel in 1873 that Germany would not permit a French attack on Italy.[81] In 1881 that was still the case, as the Chancellor and Mancini, the Italian foreign minister, both recognized. And yet, when Italy was offered a simple neutrality pact which would not have obligated her to defend Germany in case of unprovoked French aggression, Mancini rejected this. His well-known anticlericalism, and the fact that 1881 was a year of unusually strained Church-State relations, may have had something to do with his attitude. The French occupation of Tunis was also a factor, although of less significance than is usually assumed.

The wounds went deeper than that, as may be seen from Mancini's principal objection to the neutrality pact. He refused it because, for Italy, it would have "given the special conditions in which past events have placed her, almost the meaning and appearance of our reluctance to run the risks of war." This would be "a serious and irreparable moral injury for a power not yet surrounded by that halo of military glory." It was that halo that permitted a nation to preserve its dignity even while refusing to fight, regardless of the circumstances.[82] The pact, in its original draft, secured neither Italy's Mediterranean nor Balkan interests. Its purely defensive nature was apparent in the clause governing the casus foederis and also in the additional declaration that the Alliance could not "in any case be regarded as directed against England." Rome was no more secure from the intrigues of the Blacks than before, not because Bismarck had swindled Italy, but because the prevailing international balance was sufficient guarantee in itself.

There were from the start conflicting attitudes toward the Triple Alliance. On the one hand, it could be viewed as a formal, almost superfluous, addition to Italian security, motivated by a sincere desire for peace. But there were also those who thought of it in terms of a positive vehicle for effacing the memory of Lissa and Custoza. Once those moral wounds were healed by victory, Italy could stand aloof, should she choose to do so, without losing face. In short, Italy could make her own decisions, and not seem to be the impotent subject of forces beyond her control, following history rather than making it.

It was this second "mentality" that Jacini criticized in his penetrating analysis of Crispi's foreign policy. Understandable as it was, he wrote in 1889, that Italians felt the hurt of past failures, of being unable to look others in the face as equals, there was an immense difference between a natural desire to display Italian valor on the battlefield and a policy that sought to create the occasion for doing so, almost as if the occasion itself were necessary for national survival. Jacini regretted that too many Italian leaders failed to grasp the significance of Italy's new position in Europe. They remained rhetorically consumed by a passion for great deeds that had no relation to the realities of Italian strength. What Piedmont could dare, standing as she did a small buffer state between France and Austria, was one thing. But for Italy, completed in 1866, defeat would be disaster. Unless attacked, it would be madness to expose the nation to the risks which Piedmont had taken in the past.

Jacini appreciated, as did Visconti Venosta, that the balance of power was Italy's best guarantee. He was sorry to see that Italy had thrown away her diplomatic freedom by failing to rely on that balance rather than on a treaty. He accepted the Triple Alliance, but only in the spirit of peace. The Massawa expedition of 1885, according to Jacini, was the result of that urge to be great, a megalomania which Italy could not afford. He advised a peaceful settlement of the African war. If that could not be achieved, he recommended that Italy abandon the colony before being drawn into events that could lead God only knew where. As for Italy's Mediterranean interests, Jacini did not ignore their importance. Again, however, the key to Italy's primacy in the Mediterranean was her magnificent geographical position and the balance of power. The latter would work to preserve the status quo, allowing Italy to guarantee her future in the Mediterranean by laboring in peace at home to solidify the nation from within.[83]

Jacini, as we saw, was representative of a nothern conservative tradition and of Catholic federalism. As opposed to his modest view of Italian diplomacy, some writers have ascribed the rise of an African direction in Italian foreign policy to the increasing weight of Southerners in politics after 1876. It has been said that the triumph of the Sinistra marked the beginning of a new direction in foreign affairs and that after 1876 Italy tended to be lured away from the historic Europeanism of Piedmont and toward African imperialism.[84] On the surface, this observation has much to recommend it. Jacini certainly spoke in terms of the traditional Piedmontese suppleness in exploiting the tensions between the Great Powers. It is also true that Mancini was a Neapolitan and was the first Southerner to run the Consulta free of the guiding hands of the old men of the Destra whose influence in foreign affairs had continued immediately after 1876.

But this geographical explanation of the rise of a more heroic concept of Italy's role in the world should not be too greatly emphasized. Jacini himself was aware of Italy's legitimate Mediterranean interests. Nor was Visconti Venosta oblivious to his nation's proper share in the African sphere. Even Mazzini had warned the Italians in 1871 that Tunis was their logical outlet and to beware of the French who had designs on it,[85] although to make him a precursor of imperialism, as would be done later, is quite absurd. Mancini, for his part, was not prepared in 1881 to press for any African claims, and he made his views known to both Vienna and Berlin.[86] No one Italian was to be more identified with Africa than Crispi, a Sicilian. Yet there is no reason to suppose that his remarks to Bismarck in 1888 and 1889, in which he expressed his dislike of the colonial problem that he had had no part in creating, were insincere at the time he made them. An African cult did arise in Italy. Oriani was one of its earliest prophets, and he came from the Romagna. The journalistic centers of later Italian imperialism will be found not in the Mezzogiorno, but in Tuscany. Italy's most prominent southern statesman, with the exception of Crispi, was Silvio Spaventa. But Spaventa rejected any sort of Romanism as a falsification of history. The Empire was dead and buried.[87]

What is more to the point in the modest as opposed to the heroic vision of Italy's diplomatic mission is the divergence of views concerning the Postrisorgimento, which has been the continuing theme of these pages. Jacini spoke of Italy as having been completed in 1866. He accepted the outcome of the Risorgimento, despite his dislike of excessive bureaucratic centralization. The same may be said of Spaventa. He had been won over to the cause of Piedmont's role in unification. Like Jacini, he found Italian politics deficient in many respects. Where the Catholic conservative hoped for conciliation and federalism, the Hegelian theorist of the State wanted more central authority. But both were committed essentially to the nation as it stood, to official Italy.

It is also true that Jacini spoke in terms of realities, of facts that could not be disregarded merely because the glow of some greater idealism seemed to cast a shadow on the tangible results of the Risorgimento. Not inappropriately, his outlook has been linked to the "positivistic" view of man and society,[88] taking this word in the general meaning that it came to have, as referring to a common-sense view of life. Those who spoke of Italy as having been made were able to resist the lure of Africa and action. The job was not to achieve some great synthesizing test of arms, but to effect a greater consolidation from within the already existing structure of united Italy.

For the advocates of a restoration of lost ideals, however, the desire for action was deeply felt and revealed a sense of insecurity, the sensation that Italy was not yet finished. Whether directed toward the irredenta or toward Africa, this passion never changed. That African imperialism was a substitute for irredentism was appreciated by Italy's allies.[89] In 1914–15 the thirst for greatness that had been evident in the formation of the

Triple Alliance would come to the foreground, converting anti-French imperialists into anti-Austrian Irredentists. Many backers of the Triple Alliance would remain quite satisfied until that point was reached at which the defensive nature of the pact threatened to deprive Italy of military greatness, leaving her neutral while others were winning the "halo of military glory."

If Africanism was not the result of a purely geographical pull toward the Mediterranean resulting from the joining of Piedmont to the South, it is nonetheless quite true to say that Mezzogiorno played an important part in the evolution of a diplomacy of grandeur as opposed to the more modest expectations of Jacini and Spaventa. The reason for this, however, is geographical only in the sense that the very feeling of insecurity, of incompleteness, that did so much to undermine the defensive character of the Triple Alliance — to give rise in its stead to dangerous longing for a facile solution to the problem of forming the "organic nation" — had much to do with what was known as the "Southern Question." It is to that we must now turn.

·6·

THE SOUTHERN QUESTION AND
ITS POLITICAL SIGNIFICANCE

The need to develop a greater national cohesiveness was not imaginary. Whether put in the dramatic terms of the artist-politician, or described in the prosaic language of the bureaucrat, the separation of the majority of Italians from the new nation's political life and the persistence of historic localisms within the unified peninsula were evident. Geographical divisions were paralleled by wide social cleavages within the various areas. The former worked to sharpen the latter. As anti-Piedmontese feeling after 1860 grew, local resentment could be exploited to turn the poor into mobs; the dislike of centralization and the taxes it brought were converted into popular riots against the rich. This the anarchists grasped, working in the South where poverty could most easily be tied in with regional resentment of northern political dominance. Local uprisings revealed a serious lack of the political organization necessary if uneducated Italians were to be accustomed to a more sophisticated method of protest that would eventually result in the formation of parties capable of being drawn into the orbit of national politics. Too often revolts followed the pattern of that which took place at San Lupo in 1878. The peasants, led by Carlo Cafiero, a Bakuninist, broke loose from their chief and went about what they considered their main business of burning the land registers.[1]

The more Italian politicians and intellectuals became aware of the problems of the South, the more the necessity of drawing the people of Italy together, identifying their individual lives with the existence of the nation, became an inescapable challenge. What emerges from the literature dealing with the Southern Question, as the topic came to be known during the last quarter of the nineteenth century, is the elaboration of political theories all of which, radical or reactionary, have in common the realization of a great unfinished job to be done. This aspect of the Southern Question, the posing of theoretical solutions and the elaboration of methods of political action, may have had more significance for modern Italian history than the material deficiencies of the South, serious as these were.

173

Realities were subject to practical improvements; but theories in response to the Southern Question tended to influence the direction of Italian politics as a whole. Certainly it is true that the existence of the issue of the South has never ceased to be a source from which the most wide-ranging viewpoints on the history of united Italy have been drawn.[2]

A glimpse of the impact of the Southern Question on political thought is given by Sonnino's reaction to it. He was one of Italy's first serious students of the Mezzogiorno. There is no doubt that the knowledge he gained influenced the direction his political philosophy was to take. In 1881, the same year in which he had spoken in favor of universal suffrage, he also remarked that the great majority of Italians felt estranged from the nation's institutions. The Italian people, he said, "sees itself subject to the State . . . but does not feel that it forms a living and organic part of the State, nor takes any interest whatsoever in its existence or development."[3] Here again, as in the challenge to those conservatives who sought an alliance with the Church in vain, the realization of the "inorganic" nature of the Postrisorgimento settlement is apparent. The absence of the "people" is sorely felt. In this case the impact was perhaps even greater than that caused by clerical boycotting of the nation. Italians had become accustomed to the non expedit; but it was almost three decades after Garibaldi's victories that they became aware of the Southern Question.

One of the reasons for the failure to investigate the problems of the Mezzogiorno was the prevailing myth of the area's natural wealth. Even Sonnino had said, in 1876, that the South would revive if left to its own devices,[4] quite as if the mere destruction of the Bourbon regime would release pent-up energies and untapped resources. Another factor in this blindness to the problem was the historic separation of North and South, caused in part by the intervening barrier of the papal states. Few Northerners visited the regions south of Rome. Unity shattered this mutual isolationism and produced in its place a shock of recognition, often of disgust. Southern patriots who had embraced the national ideal and who had fled north to escape the Bourbon police returned to their southern homes after 1860 and saw, as if for the first time, the true conditions of the Mezzogiorno, the brigands and the blight of inhuman poverty. Northern leaders, on the other hand, when they first ventured into the area, were often insulting in their comparisons between Italy's two major regions, referring to the inhabitants of the South as more akin to the primitive tribes of Africa than to Italians. This reflected an old tradition among

Northerners. Stendhal, during his years in Milan following the Restoration, had heard much the same thing.[5]

If Southerners themselves had devoted little attention to their own region, northern politicians after 1860 paid even less. Cavour, on his deathbed, had spoken of the "poor southerners," a good people corrupted by an evil regime, and had uttered his celebrated warning not to try to change the Neapolitans by force, by absolute government. But his political successors in the Destra could not number among their achievements any great concern for the South. Even Sella's admirers concede that his party tended to overlook the problem.[6] The Sinistra was able to capture the South for itself after 1876.

By that year, however, a group of prominent political figures had begun the examination of the question. Chief among them were the two Tuscans, Sonnino and Leopoldo Franchetti. Their published studies dealing with the South [7] dispelled forever the myth of its being the garden of Europe. Sudden interest in the question that followed their work was partly due to conservative fears. Much of the belated investigating was prompted by the same anxiety Sonnino experienced, the dread of socialistic ideas spread among the peasantry and poor urban proletariat. As if to give official notice of Rome's awareness of the South, a tour of the region was made in 1902 by the Premier, Zanardelli. By that time a significant body of literature dealing with the Southern Question had come out.

Detailed studies by economists, particularly those of Francesco Nitti, indicated a widening economic gap between the two sections. Despite advances in both areas, there was no doubt that the South was farther behind the North in 1900 than it had been in 1860. Nitti justified this as the inevitable price of unification and northern industrial progress.[8] This was his answer to Republican and Socialist critics who claimed that unity had imposed a crushing servitude on the southern debtor class. It was because of this — as one critic, Ettore Ciccotti, wrote — that the Bourbon regime was economically preferable however backward politically.[9]

Ciccotti had joined forces with Napoleone Colajanni in a campaign to drum up interest in the problem of the South. By the time the Southern Question had become a national topic, Colajanni had already gained fame as the man behind the Bank of Rome revelations. Between the Scandals of the 1890's and the sudden interest in the Mezzogiorno there was a close relationship. While Colajanni was accusing Nitti of glossing over economic and political exploitation in the name of national, i.e. northern, patriotism,[10] he and other spokesmen for the South insisted that the whole area had become the stamping grounds of the Prefects. During the debates of the 1890's, as has been seen (Chapter 3), these civil servants were accused of operating under the direction of the Premier to create permanent majorities of supine Deputies. Since the Sinistra had come to power in 1876 largely as a party of southern Deputies, many concluded that the North's stranglehold was the outcome not only of industrial power but of administrative centrality that permitted a yearly harvest of faithful political henchmen. Because of this, the Southern Question was to be taken up as a means of purifying Italy of corruption, freeing latent democratic energies and, in effect, sparking a second revolution directed against northern bureaucrats, of whom Giolitti was taken as the most unscrupulous example.

That a tie existed between the Scandals of the 1890's and the emergence of the Southern Question was also shown by the writings of Gaetano Salvemini. Unlike Colajanni, Ciccotti, and De Felice, Salvemini was never to become a Deputy. He operated as an independent political power in Italy, both in his defense of the southern cause and in his condemnation of ministerial dictatorship. What Salvemini advocated in his first writings on the South, which came out in the 1890's, was a federal reform that would put an end to the established administrative system by which, as he saw it, governmental majorities were recruited among southern politicians. Administrative centralization had created a tradition of political exploitation by the southern ruling class. Governmental favoritism, particularly in regard to taxation, benefited the large landowners of the South who in turn constituted a conservative bulwark on which the administration could count. In this way, ex-Bourbonists were able to protect their local dominance by falling in line with the administration of a united Italy they had once opposed. While recognizing the value of conservative and unitarian studies such as Nitti's, Salvemini felt that iniquities were being accepted in the name of centralization. The answer was federalism, to be achieved by granting local autonomy in matters of roads, tax collection and allocation, water works, and transportation. Salvemini, however, was firmly opposed to regionalism. In fact, his advocacy of administrative decentralization was in part aimed at killing off regionalist sentiments. Parliament would remain the central and national mechanism of political representation. Federalism would in turn permit the free play of popular local forces which were being strangled by the prefectural bureaucracy that had been imposed on Italy by Piedmont.[11]

The year 1900 marked a high point in the campaign to focus public attention on the Southern Question. In that year the *Pensiero contemporaneo* sponsored a survey of the opinions of leading Italian politicians and academicians. Considerable hard feeling had already been aroused by the attitudes of noted sociologists. Anthropologists, among them Cesare Lombroso, ascribed the backwardness of the Mezzogiorno to racial factors.[12] Racist explanations of southern ills reached their extreme in the works of Alfredo Niceforo, whose principal study, published in 1898, referred to the whole area as "barbaric Italy." Niceforo extended his system of classification of human types, which he had first applied to Sardinia, to the population south of Rome. His conclusions, generally prejudicial to all Southerners, were especially severe in regard to the Neapolitans. These people were biologically destined to be ruled over, were incapable of fighting, and represented a "feminine people" of Mediterranean stock as contrasted to the "masculine people" of the North, Celts in origin. Italy's failures since 1860 — the defeat of Adowa was a recent memory when Niceforo published his book — were the result of having taken over these lower types. Neapolitans were characterized by extreme individuality, even by anarchic tendencies, and were therefore unable to evolve a stable society. Given these views, one would expect Niceforo to have been an exponent of extreme centralization under northern leadership. His race theory of the South appeared the ideal justification for absolutism. And yet he attacked Piedmontese centrality.[13] Much as he disliked the Neapolitans, he was at one with pro-Southerners when it came to the unitarian settlement of 1860. His ideas of southern anarchic propensities, however, would be used to defend authoritarianism by other investigators of the Southern Question.

Works of this sort brought forth protests from noted Southerners, among them Salvemini and Croce.[14] This had the effect of soft-pedaling race theory. Lombroso shifted his point of view as if out of deference to southern feelings, directing his attention to such economic factors as the existence of latifundia. He tried to soften the impression of his earlier analysis by pointing out recent advances in literacy and the decline of illegitimacy in the South. Achille Loria, also of the positivistic school of social scientists, carefully noted that northern Italy had a higher crime rate than the European average.[15]

The over-all effect of the great debate was to stress the tenuous nature of Italian unity. Undoubted patriots of southern birth questioned the results of the national revolution. Salvemini spoke in passing of the "so-called united Italy." Another federalist, later to become a Nationalist, Scipio Sighele, made the telling observation that there were in fact two Italies, that everyone recognized this privately while refuting the claim publicly whenever it cropped up in print. A conspiracy of silence reigned, he wrote, resulting from the fear of compromising Italian unity.[16] A French student of Italian affairs who was sympathetic to the southern cause noted the same reluctance to face the problem squarely since it suggested that Italy had been made too quickly.[17] On the opposite side, French observers who favored papal claims, and carried over Thiers' earlier hostility to Italian unity, were happy to utilize the southern problem as confirmation of their prediction that a *gâchis* and not real unity would result from the Risorgimento.[18] Needless to say, Italian clerical writers themselves exploited the issue. Hostile journalists frequently played up the estrangement of the southern masses and the parallel clerical boycott of the nation. Both the failure to resolve the Roman Question and the Government's unpopularity with the contadini were taken up as proof that Italy was as yet unformed.[19]

In view of this, it was not surprising that the idea of decentralization was becoming less popular. Federalist proposals raised in the 1890's were voted down for the very reasons pointed out by French observers, that they would become a weapon in the hands of domestic radicals and the clerical right. In response to Bertolini's impassioned speech in favor of a revival of administrative reforms first broached by Minghetti in the 1860's, Sonnino had experssed his reluctance to compromise forty years of unity. This was the opinion as well of the majority of Deputies, shocked by the rise of the Fasci and the persistent anti-Italian policy of Leo XIII, two threats Crispi insisted were related. That some loosening of the apparatus was deemed essential by the progressives in the Chamber, however, was clear in Giolitti's 1892 platform, in his campaign speeches of 1897, and in the nominal reforms that Rudinì backed in 1897 upon first taking office, in the wake of Crispi's downfall. But in 1898, and again during the May Days of 1899, the governments of Rudinì and Pelloux struck at the Socialist Reds and the clerical Blacks with equal severity.

In governmental circles, the topic of relaxing the hold of the central administration was becoming a great unmentionable. But it was clear that those who refused to tamper with the system also revealed their own uneasiness. A sense of disquiet and a feeling that the nation had to be bound more firmly together were apparent. The question was one of what methods could be used to achieve what Lombroso in 1897 had referred to as that "hoped for unification" that was as yet "more formal than real." What was necessary in any proposed solution was that the largely apolitical population, often illiterate, depressed by poverty, and corrupted by historical traditions scarcely conducive to a healthy political atmosphere, be brought into the orbit of national affairs. To create a greater sense of national feeling, to fuse together the "real" and the "legal" Italy, was the great task. It was a dangerous indication of the depth of discontent with the Postrisorgimento that not only the contadini but the cultural leaders were profoundly hostile to official Italy. Lombroso, publishing in 1897 a work on Calabria written in 1862 while he was in the army, found it necessary to preface the edition with the remark that when he had written it he had been able to wear the uniform without blushing.[20]

By avoiding decentralization the Government was abetting the resurgence of talk about a "lost revolution" and a royal Piedmontese conquest, themes that were central to the writings of Oriani. All this recalled the collapse of the original regionalist plans, which even Cavour had shown an interest in, once Garibaldi had invaded the Kingdom of Naples. But, as Lombroso's comparison between his attitude in 1862 and his shame of the uniform in 1897 show, one could in retrospect justify the decisions of the 1860's on the grounds of national security. It was only after 1870 that the revolutionary impetus no longer seemed alive and worth the submerging of individual sympathies. The Southern Question also served to revive interest in the ideas of Pisacane and Cattaneo, both of whom had stressed federalism as well as the power of the unfettered masses. Pisacane's preference for the revolutionary passions which Bourbon tyranny encouraged as compared to the moral depression that he felt Piedmontese rule would bring was very much to the point in the reaction of southern spokesmen of the 1890's. Many who were inspired by Pisacane's noble sacrifice and by Cattaneo's heroism during the Milan revolt of 1848 agreed that a northern bureaucracy had indeed strangled the "vitality" — a favorite word in much prosouthern literature — that resided in the people.[21]

Emerging from the debate of the 1890's was a faith in the power of the unsophisticated man — a new "Rural Socrates" — and a tendency to idealize the renegade that is quite familiar in the literature of the romanticists who visited Italy before unificiation. Stendhal was struck by the daring, the refinements of cruelty, and the raw beauty of southern bandits. His romanticizing of the heroic robber was to become a feature of late nineteenth-century Italian folklore.[22] During the Postrisorgimento, the real Italy for some lay in the honest, uncorrupted, and eminently unofficial simplicity of those popular heroes who had been for Stendhal the truth of life of which the salons of Paris and Milan gave only the palest reflection. In the age of the Scandals and of Giolitti's political apprentice-ship it was natural that a comparison should be drawn between individual boldness and political pettifogging. Scipio Sighele could write in 1900 that the brigand was more sympathetic than the banker, who ruined men with-out risking his own life. The Scandals of 1892-96 were less repellent to him than the murders committed by a notorious southern outlaw. Ac-cording to De Felice, Socialist Deputy and leader of the Fasci, the Mafia was preferable to the common run of criminals; at least there was a cer-tain chivalry in its code of conduct.[23] When Crispi cracked down on the Fasci and the anarchists, Giovanni Bovio, another prominent figure in the bank exposé, defended those whom the Government accused of being apologists for crime on the ground that Schiller, Byron, and Hugo had also defended bold spirits. Suppress those eloquent witnesses of human passion in the courts, he told Crispi, and you will have destroyed the most beautiful, vital pages of universal literature.[24] In his important study of government and administration in Sicily, Franchetti was shocked to find that educated, wealthy Sicilians often shared with the local peasantry a frank admiration for famous outlaws. This would be understandable, he wrote, in a professor of European literature. But that large landowners also helped pomote the legend of the brigand type was something Fran-chetti could only ascribe to the Sicilian's highly individualistic sense of law and justice.[25] It was this extremely personal, disorganized sentiment that prompted Franchetti to advise against any relaxation of the central administration of the Island.

On the cultural level, the love of the singular and the colorful in pref-erence to the rage for science and uniformity was part of the European reaction to positivism. This intellectual revolt was always capable of po-litical adaptation, whether in Burckhardt's and Cattaneo's dislike of Prussian and Piedmontese centrality, or in the glorification of the pure Italian peasant and his brigand benefactor. Moreover, because of the an-thropological works of Niceforo, Lombroso, and Enrico Ferri, the cul-tural manifestation had a particularly pointed application to the Southern Question. These studies were offensive at once to southern pride and, in their most outlandish form, to human intelligence. In defense of his earlier work on "barbaric Italy" already mentioned, Niceforo published a second volume in 1901 in which the latest tool of the anthropologist was brought into play. This was the cephalic index based on the works of another

Italian, Giuseppe Sergi. Niceforo went into raptures over this final, perfect method of determining human types. With unbounded confidence in this system, he made all Italians subject to the latest in scientific research, with results no different from those in his earlier work. Northern Italians suddenly became little different from Anglo-Saxons, something that must have surprised Anglo-Saxon racists. As for Ferri, the Socialist leader's own work on homicide proved, through measurements of 411 "normal" men, that the northern male cranium was larger than the southern. Among such scientific attempts to establish biological division between North and South, few were more revealing of the stultifying effects of positivistic methods when carried to the extreme than Niceforo's tables, which showed that northern females began to menstruate at an average age of fourteen years and eight months as compared to fourteen years and ten months in the Mezzogiorno.[26]

In the revival of the romantic temper, which worked to salvage southern pride while freeing men from naturalistic laws, it was apparent that this valuable corrective to exaggerations by anthropologists could easily become a veneer beneath which an equally superficial and often brutal love of violence was hidden. This was especially true where the anti-positivistic revolt dovetailed with existing political dissatisfactions, exacerbated by the decade of scandals and the growing legend of Giolittian corruption. Once the Southern Question was viewed in the light of a liberation not only from the new science but from the Italian bureaucracy, it would be more difficult to satisfy the material needs of society by means that were compatible with organized politics, or to preserve a balance between culture and bourgeois society. Romantic individualism encouraged a flight from systematic political action and toward anarchy, and thereby weakened the chance that Italian governments would ever be able to capture the support of the leading defenders of the South by convincing them that the best agency for promoting change was the Chamber of Deputies. Conversely, those critics who did become part of the system were always open to the charge of having abandoned their sincerity as well as their contact with the power and purity of the masses. This was certainly the case with the Socialist party, which by 1900 had become quite constitutional in practice, yet which also had within its ranks — though more often on its hazy perimeter — men who took an artistic view of political action that was bound to imply rejection of party leadership. That Ferri was both a positivist and a parliamentary Socialist was symbolic of the link between a climate of opinion and political compromise.

Something of this can be seen in the works of Gaetano Salvemini, who was to become Italy's foremost voice not only of the southern position but of the need to cleanse Italian politics. For Salvemini, universal suffrage was one answer. This would destroy the alliance that had evolved between the northern-dominated governments and the southern aristocracy. He discounted conservative and moderate insistence on literacy as a prerequisite for the vote, placing his faith in the natural intelligence of man. Everyone, he wrote, could think of ten illiterates who showed good horse sense, and ten professors who were perfect idiots outside their special fields of study and perhaps even in them. But the system that had risen from the Risorgimento legalized oppression and reaction. It also failed to utilize a great treasury of energy by disregarding the voice of the people.

However, universal suffrage alone was insufficient, according to Salvemini. He doubted whether it would be enough without a corresponding federalist reform of the administration. He placed his hopes at first in the Italian Socialist party. But the party must be federalist in nature, repeating Proudhon's dictum that "liberty is federalism, federalism is liberty."[27] He campaigned tirelessly to induce the Socialist party leadership to regard the Southern Question as indispensable to its cause, warning that unless the party's northern proletariat rank and file used their power in the Government to effect the needed reforms, the contadini would turn to reactionary leaders in the Chamber. When the Socialist party failed to take up the southern cause and federalism, Salvemini split off and became in effect a party unto himself, attacking the party's northern narrowness first in the pages of the Florentine review, *La Voce*, and later in his own journal, *Unità*,[28] founded in 1911.

Salvemini's position in the campaign for southern regeneration is of the greatest importance, not only because of his personal qualities, which inspired so many Italian intellectual and political leaders, but because his own failure to find a legal, an official outlet for southern populism was indicative of a major crisis in the Postrisorgimento. It must be made clear that Salvemini did not share anarchic hopes in the undirected blind fury of the peasantry. The apolitical violence of the Sicilian Fasci of 1893 was a reaction to poverty, not a step toward political education. What the southern proletariat needed was political experience and direction. The problem was to open up legal channels [29] for those treasures of energy that resided in the people.

Nonetheless, Salvemini had a decidedly romantic outlook. To link his name to that of Voltaire [30] is to mistake his ideological roots. His empiricism and abiding suspicion of idealistic philosophy, of "Panglossian" historicism, do indeed owe much to the age of reason. However, he shared in the romantic heritage of the Enlightenment as well. Here he parts company with those who would keep the canaille in place. His confidence in the abilities and natural intelligence of man, even the brigand were he but given an outlet for his virtues by society, placed Salvemini closer to Rousseau than to Voltaire. Only in later years would he qualify this optimism.[31]

Because of this aspect of his thought there was a strain of passionate activism in Salvemini's earlier writings that could shade over into revolutionary violence. It is true that he ultimately rejected any facile or romanticized solution to the moral and political cleavage of the Postrisorgimento. Writing toward the end of his life, he denied there was historical justification for speaking of the "revolution that failed." By 1952 Salvemini could say that in comparing the condition of Italy's poor in the years 1860 and 1900, one was passing from night to a promising dawn, if not the bright light of day.[32] The frustration of seeing the doors of official Italy closed to the people, however, and of observing reaction rise in the last years of the nineteenth century, had prompted him to write in 1900 that since the Government had not only not prevented but encouraged oppression for forty years, the only remedy for a politically and morally intolerable state of affairs was to leave oppressed and oppressor face to face. Either by elections, or by guns, a solution would come sooner or later.[33]

Symptomatic of the growing, rather than fading, contempt for official Italy during the prewar decade was the fact that Salvemini and other leading exponents of the southern cause rejected Giolitti's governments as a viable means of achieving a legal solution to the problem of drawing the southern proletariat into the arena of public life. In 1910 Salvemini published his study of Giolitti's reputed corruption of the electoral mechanism. *Il Ministro della malavita* traced the political career of a southern Deputy, Vito De Bellis, from 1885 to 1909. His triumphs at the polls in 1904 and 1909 were ascribed to the operation of Giolitti's henchmen, the Prefects, leagued together with local criminal elements. For Salvemini, this Deputy was a symbol of an Italian institution, "Giolittism," which, although not invented by the statesman, was perfected by him.[34] In 1909 the Chamber of Deputies upheld the election of De Bellis. Having lost faith in the Socialist party, finding no legal yet uncorrupted channels for political action, Salvemini now advocated violence. As long as there might be one legal and peaceful path open, to speak of violence, he wrote, would be criminal and stupid. But when violence had become the tactic of a permanent parliamentary majority of proven delinquents, its use by the opposition was not only a right but a duty. No honest man could condemn him for it under these circumstances.[35]

A similar flight from legal paths of political action was displayed by another champion of the South, Giustino Fortunato. Unlike Salvemini, Fortunato was opposed to federalism on the ground that it would weaken the nation in the face of its internal enemies. Nonetheless, one of Fortunato's principal reasons for opposing administrative decentralization was the existence of corrupt political practices. In a notable speech in the Chamber, which Salvemini later reprinted in his *Unità*, Fortunato attacked the Central Government for its manipulation of local criminal and reactionary clienteles.[36] In 1911, writing in the Florentine review *La Voce*, Fortunato continued to oppose federalism. But what he had to say on the question of the position of the Mezzogiorno in the unitarian framework attests to the persistence of the sense of national weakness. For Fortunato there were two countries. Racial, climatic, economic, and historical factors worked to preserve this division. Political unity, he wrote, had not been followed by moral unity, by the feeling of national existence among the people. Nationalism he defined as the completion of unity by means of the elevation of the South. Taking a page from the anarchist Merlino, whose political theories Fortunato scarcely shared, he wrote that Ireland was to Great Britain what the Mezzogiorno was to Italy.[37] In 1912, in the pages of Salvemini's journal, Fortunato spoke of the impossibility of utilizing the constitutional mechanism to achieve the reforms that would elevate the South and hence achieve moral unity. It was interesting, moreover, that Fortunato praised the Deputies, of whom he was one, as being generally honest men. The mechanism of bureaucracy, however, was the force that stifled true representation. No clearer expression of the theme of a "real" and "official" Italy could be found than this antibureaucratic view, unless perhaps it was Fortunato's advice that the great task ahead was the creation of an Italy that existed outside the sphere of the administration.[38]

These remarks are highly significant in that they were made after the introduction of a universal suffrage bill by the Giolittian ministry in 1911. This reform, which became law in June, 1912, opened the Chamber to the great majority of the adult male population, including illiterates who had fulfilled their military requirements or were thirty years of age. The electorate rose from about 3,000,000 to almost 8,500,000. The success or failure of Giolitti's governments, and hence of official Italy, to capture the sympathy of the critics of his system could be judged by the reaction of the southern reformers to this momentous legislation. Salvemini, who had fought so long for extension of the vote to the poor, was caught off balance. He felt, he wrote, like a man served a large meal at breakfast when his stomach was unprepared. He recognized, however, that here was the means of achieving the true revolution, the revolt of the *cafoni*, whereas 1860 was only the "superficial" act of the "gentlemen." But he was clearly dissatisfied with the official rather than revolutionary manner in which the great weapon of popular redemption had been won. He could not deny its great importance, but he wrote that it would have been better had it been won by the slow process of propaganda and extraparliamentary action. Suspicious of Giolitti's Italy, he wondered whether this "gift" from the "minister of corruption" was not a swindle; whether "in our political life which seems to be fecund of nothing save miscarriages, universal suffrage as well may not be destined to add to the already long list of untimely births and deformed fetuses." Salvemini still referred to the Giolittian majority as a "base heap of smugglers, blackmailers, and henchmen."[39] Nor was the gap between real and official Italy closed. There did not as yet exist a true nationality. Half the nation, Salvemini wrote, was ruled by incompetents who thought of nothing save exploitation and inhibited by a subjected class that was tied to the patria by no bond of affection. This subjected class regarded the Government as an enemy to avoid, or as an obstacle to destroy whenever the opportunity arose.[40]

Giolitti's major political reform had not lessened the sense of revolutionary failure nor the frustration of wounded national pride. Between governed and government a chasm was seen by many influential political observers. The reaction to universal suffrage is more significant in that it seems to accept the virtues of a legislative reform that was anything but narrow or timid under the circumstances, while refusing to grant the merits of the parliamentary regime that made it possible. So tainted had the legal channels of political action become that many tended to reject out of hand, or accept with reluctance, anything emanating from the halls of the Chamber. Official reform lacked the vitality of revolutionary victory that marked true social advance.

This was true not only for radical and quasi-socialistic reformers but for advocates of the power state. Not the least significant aspect of the over-all response to the problem of the South was that it included solutions from the far Right and the far Left, which were in harmony on one point: the unsatisfactory nature of the nation as it existed. This frequently led to unholy alliances against Rome, the Chamber, and Giolitti. A meeting of the extremes, however, was to become more than the casual pragmatic assault on government so often observed in the heyday of parliamentary liberalism. In the writings of some students of the Southern Question, a full-blown political theory began to take shape that would reconcile under one banner a faith in the hidden powers of the masses with a program for building up the authority of the State. Something of this could be found in the meandering works of Oriani. But a more cogent foundation for a theory of national democracy was apparent in the writings of Pasquale Turiello, until recently[41] a slighted figure in the history of Italian political thought.

Turiello we have met in connection with the rise of the Socialist party. His prediction that the party would lose its dynamism as well as its prestige among the contadini once it entered the Chamber was very much a fore-shadowing of Salvemini's split from organized socialism after the party failed to heed his appeal for a breaking down of its northern base. What was interesting in Turiello's attack on the party hierarchy was that he seemed to be worried not only about socialism as a revolutionary and subversive force, but about the conservative alternative to this separation of the people from their national leaders. The title of his principal work, published in 1882, proclaimed the existence of those two Italies that had been noted since the 1860's when Jacini first examined the subject.[42] There was, according to Turiello, a "government" that was quite distinct from the "governed." Unlike the conservatives of Jacini's school, however, and quite unlike the federalist libertarians who derived much of their theory from Pisacane and Cattaneo, Turiello opposed any increase in local self-government. The decentralized libertarian solution to the problem of the Postrisorgimento found no theoretical response in his work. From his viewpoint — and it was that of a Southener — the Italian people suffered from excessive individualism. This was, he felt, particularly the case with southern Italians. The lack of cohesiveness, the presence in the Italian character of what Turiello like Franchetti before him called a certain "looseness," required not more local autonomy, but less. The Government had erred in giving too much power to the communes in 1860. Because of this, a new sort of feudalism had emerged, in which local political clienteles had risen to replace the Mafia and Camorra. Operating in alliance with the Deputies at Rome, these local groups perpetuated a historical lack of civic cohesiveness. The effect was a reduction of centralized authority which, if not restored, promised to ruin the Nation-State.

Turiello's low opinion of Italian public morality was no different from that of De Felice, Colajanni, Salvemini, and other reformers who had lived through the decade of the 1890's. This opinion had become an assumption rather than a proven fact, as witness the debates in the Chamber concerning contested elections. Turiello did not even bother to offer proof of his claims. That the Prefects were all electoral agents, he wrote, was so well known that any demonstration was superfluous.[43] But where Republicans and Socialists regarded chicanery among Prefect, Deputy, and local criminal elements as a legalized stifling of the treasures of energy latent in the people, Turiello feared instead for the solidarity of the central apparatus, for the State. It is also interesting that Turiello, like the libertarians, relied heavily for his material on the investigations of the Southern Question, particularly those of Sonnino and Franchetti. Moreover, he was himself among the first generation, as it were, of investigators of the social and political conditions of the Mezzogiorno. He traveled extensively in the southern provinces, taking notes from local papers on brigandage, social unrest, and economic problems that attested to the existence of a social question ignored by Rome. Anticipating Gaetano Mosca, Turiello insisted that the southern contadini had been deprived of justice as it existed under the old Bourbon regime. The presence of an immediate authority, hence an immediate security, had been done away with in 1860. Desiring more than the abstract freedoms offered in theory by doctrinaire liberals, the real Italy — that is, the contadini — awaited the return of "Franceschiello." In the face of this manifest lack of organic unity, he agreed with Sonnino that Italy's very existence was being threatened by two great internal enemies: the Marxist International and the Vatican.[44]

What was needed, according to Turiello, was the creation of the "organic" state. Again he was not far from Sonnino, nor from the Hegelian Arcoleo. Turiello also foreshadowed Sonnino's later views by calling for a revival of the Crown's power at the expense of political parties. Local political authority should be reduced. But Turiello went much farther in the direction of a formulated theory of the State than would Sonnino. He called for the selection of a ruling class in accordance with individual merits rather than by means of democratic franchise. Implicit in all of Turiello's work is a rejection of liberalism and the traditions of the Enlightenment. Theoretical concepts of freedom had but produced a lessening of the State's power. This could be seen in the weak penal laws based on untenable humanitarian principles. While social chaos reigned in Italy, particularly in the Mezzogiorno, the Government remained calm, confident in its theoretical liberalism.

In his proposals for the reorganization of government — rather one should say the creation of the State out of the existing mechanism of government — Turiello was in fact elaborating a corporate state theory, representation to be by interests under the rule of the intelligent elite.[45] In this, and in his objections to doctrinaire humanitarianism, Turiello shared the views of other conservative liberals of the Hegelian school. Silvio Spaventa also decried the mildness of penal law in Italy.[46] And Federico Persico, another of the Neapolitan school of political theorists, had called for a representation by interests and classes in order to achieve a greater sense of national unity.[47] In these respects, and in their mutual rejection of eighteenth-century individualism, Turiello had much in common with the Hegelian and Viconian traditions centered at Naples. There are, however, significant differences between Turiello and Silvio Spaventa. The latter, as has been seen, was a strict constitutionalist, a "loyal" conservative. It is true, nonetheless, that a bond did exist based upon a refutation of abstract democratic ideals and an awareness of the inorganic nature of Italian unity. It was this that encouraged the corruption of neo-idealism, as witness the ideas of De Meis and Oriani. In Turiello the results became more obvious.

Not surprisingly, Turiello regarded the army as the only existing agency of national cohesiveness. He suggested that mass gymnastics, choral work, and all other suitable forms of group activity be utilized to overcome the Italian people's *scioltezza*, their natural "looseness."[48] Similar proposals were sponsored by another and more prominent figure of southern Italian origin, Francesco de Sanctis. That De Sanctis was himself imbued with the idealistic philosophical traditions current in Neapolitan intellectual circles points up again the relation between existing social and political problems and purely speculative thought. But Turiello, unlike De Sanctis,[49] tended to subscribe to that literary "idea of Rome," the pernicious influence of which had played a part in the fears of conservatives like Jacini and Silvio Spaventa. In Rome, according to Turiello, there was discipline. He became an advocate of imperialism, hoping that Italy's internal problems might be solved in a sphere of activity outside the Peninsula freed from the corrupting influences of parliamentary cliques.[50]

It is true that Turiello also reflects the intellectual climate of his day, the ideas of the "generation of materialism," Social Darwinism, and the rising authoritarian spirit. He certainly shared in current European intellectual and political refutations of parliamentary government and liberalism. He asserts the necessity of struggle, and ridicules the philosopher's dream of an international brotherhood. The names of Spencer and Gneist appear in his major work.[51] But it is more to the point to take stock of the problems that were all too present in the Italian Postrisorgimento, problems that were recognized by radicals, liberals, and authoritarians alike. It was their unavoidable existence that gave rise to spontaneous Italian theoretical responses, supported by but not derived from ideas of foreign import. Had the latter been true, it is doubtful that the roots of political frustration would have survived, much less deepened, during the age of Giolitti. To attach too much importance to non-Italian intellectual and political influences to look to France, as Croce did,[52] for the source of the Nationalist party's program that blossomed forth on the eve of the Libyan War, is to forget that the essentials of that program were implicit in Turiello and Oriani.

Because the common issue was the estrangement of the masses from the legal framework of united Italy, theoretical political positions were seldom without ambiguities. The revolutionary tradition, which was not satisfied with the outcome of unification, carried over its patriotic Risorgimento verve into the decades following 1870. In the literature of libertarians, the word *patria* remained as a reminder of the unfulfilled task. The Republican *Popolo d'Italia*, founded in 1860 at Naples, continued to stress the failure of government to express the "instincts, desires, and needs of the people." But it also insisted that the aim was the true liberty of the patria suffocated by exaggerated administrative centralization.[53] Cavallotti's cry for a "bloody baptism" makes it clear that the revolutionary strain could be converted into militarism. And something of this has been seen in the life of Crispi.

It would be improper, certainly, to carry the point too far, to identify essentially democratic theorists as hidden authoritarians. Between Salvemini and Turiello there was a fundamental difference arising from their conflicting intellectual heritage. For Salvemini, the word "State" was to become anathema. His confidence in the good sense of the unlettered masses and his essential humanitarianism have little in common with Turiello's political philosophy. Like Carducci, with whom he has characteristics in common — if we rule out the poet's Roman heroics — Salvemini detested the "subtle Minerva of the philosophers,"[54] and was suspicious of metaphysicians of politics who spoke of liberty but had tyranny in their hearts.

Ambiguities, however, did exist and worked to confuse Italian political thought and action. More of this will be seen when we examine the reaction to the Tripoli War among the radical publicists of the Southern Question. As for Turiello, he could speak in a vein that was ripe with libertarian suggestions. Italy, he wrote in 1892, was always united in the temper of the people. Since the nation resided in the people, it might be better served from without the Chamber of Deputies. How many talents were wasted in Parliament! The vital forces resided in the masses. To uplift the nation, one must turn not to the Parliament but to the "fresh will of the country." Turiello suggested the use of a national referendum, a return to the Latin plebiscite. He spoke of a coming new order to be effected through the leadership of some great man. His authoritarianism was theoretically opposed to the libertarian view, which had its point of departure in the people, not in the State. Yet the germ of a proletarian nationalism was already present in Turiello's writings. What Italy needed, he wrote, was a "new and virile resurgence, a second test of arms and blood."[55] The end was the powerful State; the means to that end was for the people to become soldiers once again. The popular element was always there. Because of this, the conventional figure of the man on horseback must, in Italy as elsewhere, claim to represent the people. Italian Nationalists will, like the *Action française*, speak for the workers and the contadini. A military rule simply, a narrow dictatorship, had no place in Italian rightist thought. Something much wider and deeper than Pelloux's state-of-siege tactic was needed to solve the moral crisis of the Postrisorgimento. In a very real sense, as far as the theorists were concerned, the revolutionary aspects of nineteenth-century nationalism remained alive following 1870, but were now turned toward a liberation from the existing mechanics of government and were turned against Italy as it had been officially constructed.

It has been said that Italian conservatism always had an anarchic cast.[56] It was this underlying impulse that rendered much Italian conservative thought, and its followers, resistant to the lures of office and unsatisfied with the accomplishments of the parliamentary governments of Giolittian Italy. That the paths of legalized, constitutional action failed to attract eternally restless revolutionaries who chided the Socialist party for its loss of virtue is not surprising. That this was true as well of advocates of national power, imperialism, and the State is more revealing. A flight from formal positions and the mechanisms of organized politics was harder to square with a political philosophy which demanded that the apparatus of the central administration be put to use to achieve glory and give the nation its predestined identity. This was the dilemma of the extreme right. To see it, one must look at the disciples of Turiello, the leaders of the Italian Nationalist Association.

The Nationalist party was founded at Florence in 1910. The first expression of the movement, however, can be found in the pages of a small Florentine review, the *Regno*, which began publication in 1903 under the direction of Enrico Corradini and Giovanni Papini. Turiello had died in 1902. The first issue of the *Regno* (November 29, 1903) contained a tribute to the southern theorist. In later years he was to be ignored, Nationalists turning for inspiration to the "great solitary heroes," Oriani and Crispi. But there is no question that Turiello, who, unlike Crispi and Oriani, had attempted to formulate a plan of political action, was a steppingstone. It was also to be true that the Nationalists would absorb the problem of the regions and the Southern Question, much as he had done, into the larger context of an aggressive foreign policy. War was to become the alternative of the far Right to a revolutionary welding together of government and the governed.

THE ITALIAN NATIONALISTS

The Literary Phase

The life of Enrico Corradini, the *Regno's* editor, could well be taken as a pattern for the biographies of many deracinated intellectuals who found their way into politics after having tried their hand at literature with only moderate success. Corradini was born in 1868, a time, according to his fellow Nationalist and biographer P. L. Occhini, that marked the end of the "lyrical" period in Italian history.[1] He was, quite literally, a child of the Postrisorgimento. His career, in both art and politics, suggests that he regretted the natural tragedy of his birth that prevented him from having conspired in the formation of the nation, and that he set out to make up for this by conspiring against the work of his elders. After a fling at teaching he turned to writing, producing a half dozen novels of no great literary merit but of some interest to the student of Italian history who would seek to uncover the cultural roots of dissident political movements. Largely in response to what was considered the cultural emptiness of positivistic philosophy and literary realism, the "intellectual petty bourgeoisie" were turning to profound pessimism in literature as a means of filling the "spiritual void."[2] In keeping with this neoromantic trend, Corradini became a novelist of despair. His first work, *Santamaura*, published in 1896, was a study in the futility of philanthropic humanitarianism. The following year his *La gioia* came out, a novel peopled by neurasthenics, lost souls unable to find an outlet for their talents and tormented by a sense of impotency. The hero, wandering in utter dejection, squanders his life and brings misery to his lovers. The same theme, that of the sensitive aesthete in the harsh world of materialism and science, was taken up by another future leader of the Nationalist Association, Luigi Federzoni.[3] With young men of similar outlook, Corradini brought out a literary review, *Il Marzocco*. Its contents were aimed at an artistic minority whose tastes were "elevated and intensely expressive."[4]

Tiring of literature of morbid passivity and unrequited love — the theme of his *Dopo la morte,* a play first performed in 1895 — Corradini blossomed forth as a bard of the heroic. In his new phase those "strange, bizarre and monstrous flowers" which one French critic found characteristic of his work[5] disappeared. The influence of Ibsen, which was apparent in his early work, seemed to have lost its hold. Ibsen's scorn for futile idealism and humanitarianism had been taken up by the young Italian pessimists. Their lives, in the words of Corradini's biographer, seemed an Ibsen drama. Existence was futile, and the Italian environment of the Postrisorgimento a prison.[6] In the new heroic phase Corradini's hero was no hapless purveyor of reform, no fated idealist, but the self-made man who defies society, rejecting the softening influences of passion for a bold toughness. Corradini had become, we are told, a "professor of energy." The pale, pessimistic strain of D'Annunzio was also left behind.[7] It had not been abandoned, to be sure; but the intellectual Young Turks were always sensitive about their inability to compete with the "Poet" in his own kingdom. They preferred to write him off as a dandy, a literary fop, or, as Corradini put it, "an effeminate Franco-Russo-Abruzzese novelist."[8]

Nor was it true that Ibsen had been discarded in favor of a more positive view of life. From profound pessimism Corradini made the not very startling leap to uninhibited exaltation of power and the cult of heroes. Ibsen himself had written, in *An Enemy of the People,* that the most powerful man was he who was most alone. And in the Postrisorgimento, as seen by romantic pessimists, there were enough examples of this lonely, defiant type. Corradini, in *La guerra lontana* (1911), seized upon Oriani as the model for one of the novel's principal characters, Vincenzo Orio. The Italian translation of Carlyle in 1897 was followed up by the writer of the *Marzocco,* who made a vogue of great men. The cry was for a new Plutarch to sing of heroes. Corradini obliged with his *Giulio Cesare* in 1902. The political implications of this Caesar, a man of action imposing his will on local clienteles, were obvious. This was not the politician Caesar, but the "Roman Caesar of the Roman people."[9] D'Annunzio was at the same time describing the modern version of military imperialism, drinking in the wine of power, admiring the might of Germany as he journeyed along the Rhine. The "Poet" rhapsodized that "German instinct for supremacy," the expansive power of Kipling's England which was "opening its jaws to devour the universe." "Never," wrote D'Annunzio, "had the world been so ferocious." What of Italy? Would she grasp the necessity of sweeping out the heap of soiled imbecility that held her back?[10] Corradini followed suit with a proclamation in the *Marzocco* that henceforth his works would not be merely literary, but would be a literature that expressed life.[11]

In 1903, attracted by the linguistic dash and violence of a new Florentine review, the *Leonardo*, Corradini enlisted the support of its editors, Giovanni Papini and Giuseppe Prezzolini, in a new journalistic venture. The *Regno*, as Corradini's political review was called, was to be the voice of those who lamented the baseness of Italian life, of those who scorned the ruling bourgeoisie, which had become soft under the corrosive influence of liberal and internationalist ideas. "All the signs of decrepitude, sentimentalism, doctrinairism, immoderate respect for fleeting life and for the weak and lowly . . . are exhibited in the intellectual life of the Italian middle class which rules and governs." For the "ignoble Socialists" who had cast their lot with the parliamentary system, working for reform, Corradini had equally harsh words. But it was indicative of much Italian conservative thought that the *Regno*'s chief from the first showed a certain admiration for those Socialists who were not "debased," whose stomachs also turned at the spectacle of Italian degeneracy. Corradini wrote of a "civilized barbarism" worse than the savage, infantile barbarism that had destroyed Rome — worse because it destroyed the lofty values of man and nation.[12] This was another way of stating the anarchist Merlino's contempt for the rule of Piedmont, which had "deadened the passions" where the Bourbons had at least engendered hatred. Papini, whose facile mind and pen were to do so much toward the creation of a cult of heroism and violence in Giolittian Italy, joined in this derisive chorus. "Human life," he wrote, "is sacred; the breath of some insignificant creature more precious than an empire; the lives of a few thousand savages greater than the power of a nation. Fear of blood has become the incubus of modern men who are pursued like so many women, little nineteenth century Lady Macbeths, by the spectre of death. . . . The principle of right to life is utterly without rational justification. The word 'right' is a verbal travesty. I have a right to do something when I *can* do it, when I have the means, the *power* equal to the deed."[13]

The young men of the *Regno* had not left their literary past behind them when they took up politics. Their political theories and their vision of Italy's possibilities were more artistic than feasible. With the defeat at Adowa (1896) a fresh memory, Corradini "embraced life" by affirming the necessity of imperialism as a cure for domestic problems as well as a means of foreign expansion.[14] Less sanguine spirits conceded that a peaceful economic expansion might be justified, but that Corradini's insistence on military imperialism was absurd. To this the "professor of energy" replied that such opinions only reflected the essential defect of Italian public opinion, excessively absorbed in philosophical speculations. It was, he insisted, precisely because of Italy's industrial backwardness that expansion must be military. As proof of this he cited the example of agricultural Russia's nineteenth-century imperialism — soon to be unmasked at Tsushima Straits. The same sort of logic was applied to the arguments of those who suggested peaceful expansion through emigration. This too would require a national strength that was lacking. The advantage of military action lay in its power to unite the people while checking the advance of antinational socialism. This had been the theme of Turiello's last work, published posthumously in 1902.[15]

The danger of a literary view of politics is all too clear. Rather than accept the existence of undeniable economic problems, Corradini and the young lions of the *Regno* sought to create power through war, unleashing those "spiritual" forces which, by some mystical chemistry, produce material results. That war did in fact have a leavening effect on the economy of nations seemed a reasonable political philosophy with the outbreak of the Russo-Japanese War. The *Regno* greeted the event with rapturous hymns to violence. It proved for Corradini that war was the essence of the modern age, a fact that sentimentalists, humanitarians, and evangelists of peace failed to appreciate. Mario Morasso, another prominent imperialist, took up the shopworn theme of nature red in tooth and claw. Man in the colonial environment returned to his savage, virile, natural self, shedding the veneer of civilization. Corradini wrote of modern mechanized warfare as a source of new beauty in the world, foreshadowing F. T. Marinetti's "Futurist Manifesto"[16] of 1909. Giuseppe Borgese, nominaly the *Regno's* literary critic, capitalized on the Russo-Japanese War to berate Italians for their lack of courage. Tales of Japanese self-sacrifice, he said, and of women bearing arms, must have shamed Italian mothers who had gone into the streets when the news arrived from Adowa not to cry for revenge, but to weep for their fallen sons. Unity through bloodshed became a prominent feature of the *Regno's* imperialism. It surpassed itself when an earthquake in Calabria prompted the observation that "only terrible crises of destruction and blood can save and give new vigor to the life of sick social organisms."[17]

There was nothing original in this exaltation of violence. It was part of the general European intellectual anarchy of the prewar decade. The impact on politics of neoromanticism, Bergsonian philosophy, and mysticism was becoming an accepted field of study even then. The repetitious works of Ernest Seillière, whose harvesting of European expressions of political aesthetics made him the foremost archivist of irrationalism, attest clearly to the widespread exploitation of violence and activism as a weapon of realpolitik.[18] It would be an error to dismiss the Italian exponents of these ideas as literary dabblers, avant-garde dilettantes. Unquestionably they were that. But a deeper importance emerges when one considers the manner in which Italian political and economic realities offered a fertile field for the seeds of neoromanticism, permitting intellectual currents to bear upon existing material and social situations. The noted Italian literary critic Francesco Flora, who lived through the prewar decade, was correct when he wrote that this was more than mere aestheticism. The urge for artistic renewal was a social movement.[19]

The ease with which even the wildest cultural and philosophical concepts merged with political movements may be seen in the *Leonardo*, Papini's and Prezzolini's review that ran concurrently with the *Regno*. Unlike Corradini's journal, the *Leonardo* was primarily devoted to cultural problems. It specialized in the antipositivist crusade which, in Papini's hands, branched off into mysticism. But Papini's diatribes against Italian politics were illustrative of the transference of philosophical anarchy to the familiar theme of the political as well as cultural decadence of the Postrisorgimento.[20] "The generation which followed that of the Risorgimento," Papini wrote in 1905, "has been unequal to its task. It has succeeded in organizing an enormous bureaucracy (also one which is lazy and undisciplined); it has built railroads (too few and very uncomfortable); filled the archives with forgotten laws and unobserved regulations; it has even raised the economic standard of life. It has failed to give national life that content, those attitudes and ideals which are the expressions of a great culture." Papini declared as his intention the renovation of Italian culture. Italy lacked that "elementary, supreme virtue of courage." The leaders of the age that opened in 1870 had been satisfied with the creation of an officialdom. The movement for national renovation must come from the outside; it must be "ever less official." While insisting on the purely spiritual character of his campaign for national redemption, and making clear his disdain for politics, Papini also wrote: "Give me a few men who feel and understand what I wish to do, and with their contagion they will change the moral climate of the country, and the contagion of this country will change the world." He spoke of restoring the primacy of Rome, "for

Rome has always had a universal and ruling mission."[21] Like Corradini, Papini portrayed himself as a child of despair, frustrated by the society into which he had been born, a great iconoclast and self-styled solitary hero.[22] When the *Leonardo* and *Regno* had collapsed, Papini wrote for the *Voce*, whose propaganda in behalf of the Mezzogiorno did signal service to the cause of Italian political and economic reforms. Much of the heady and irrational aestheticism of the *Leonardo* was momentarily dropped for a more constructive sort of criticism. Nonetheless Papini could still write in the old vein. "Only a Bonaparte could enter the bureaucracy, smash it and go on."[23]

The rather hackneyed contradiction between real and official Italy was made much of by the *Regno*. Borgese claimed that Italy was divided between a "government" and a "people," thus repeating Turiello's idea. Prezzolini wrote of two Italies, the active, producing part, and the Italy of words, again a familiar idea. Action must come, but from outside Parliament. "If one wishes to act, it is not necessary to begin from the shell, to turn to the mechanism of the State. Rather one must turn to the active, vital part." According to Prezzolini, this active Italy consisted of the workers, manual and intellectual. Italy's progress came not from government, but from the port of Genoa, from the factories of Milan. "Between these two Italies we must be the force which destroys the former and enlightens the latter. We must be a torch which burns and illumines" As for Parliament, Prezzolini considered it a fetish that would go the way of other democratic mythologies "I dare dream of no greater liberation of the patria," he wrote, "for no greater conquest could I hope, than the awareness of the evil of Parliament." In substitution for the legal mechanism of government, Prezzolini conceived of a direct rule of free organizations of industries and labor.[24] Papini took up the idea of physical fitness, proposing the formation of an unofficial army of athletes. During the 1904 elections the *Regno*'s editorial read: "We, in truth, do not await the returns from the polls with that nervous veneration with which those who see only Parliament in the nation's existence await them. . . . The real Italy is not there, amidst clever lawyers, cynical opportunists, politicians. . . . That is the weak, sickly part of the country. . . . Italy's life rests in those courageous industrialists of Milan . . . in those contadini of Puglia, and among the agricultural laborers of Romagna and Venetia."[25] Following the elections, the noted popularizer of this sort of academic bellicosity, Rastignac (the *nom de plume* of Vincenzo Morello) wrote in the *Tribuna* that the electoral process had deformed the new people of Italy at their very birth, and would continue to do so unless the "cure of fire" came to restore their backbone, crushed by prolonged political corruption.[26]

Violence and syndicalism were at the root of the *Regno*'s attack on official Italy, and this four years before Sorel's *Réflexions sur la violence* (1908). Unquestionably the *Regno* had an authoritarian air about it. But, as in the case of Turiello, the "fresh will of the country" could not be ignored. Corradini's journal was harsh with the Socialist party leadership because of its essentially bourgeois, legalitarian program. It agreed with Vilfredo Pareto that the revolutionary wing of the party represented the only vital force in Italian politics.[27] Corradini was sensitive to the charge of being conservative or reactionary. He tried to avoid it by stating that his imperialism and his demands for a revitalization of the Italian middle class were anything but conservative. He also conceded that the Socialists had the great advantages of being in touch with the people and possessing a "collective conscience."[28] But it was absurd to campaign for military imperialism as a means of achieving national greatness and to deny the mechanism of government at the same time. Syndicalism and imperialism were strange bedfellows. Much as Corradini would try to obscure the difference betwen them, he could not. After flirting with the vague syndicalist suggestions of Papini and Prezzolini, he was forced to part company with them and with their ideas. Expansion through war would unite the country, he claimed. But the direction must necessarily come from the Government. When in September, 1904, Italy's first general strike was promoted by the victorious left wing of the Socialist party, Corradini called on the Government to take up arms against the revolutionaries. The mushrooming of voluntary citizen antistrike brigades, which should have pleased a true syndicalist, found Corradini opposed. They were a necessary evil, but an evil nonetheless. Instead he demanded that Giolitti, then in power, use the troops against the strikers. Giolitti wisely chose to let the general strike burn itself out.

Corradini's essentially authoritarian outlook became clearer in articles written after the strike had failed. Imperialism was hard to square with revolutionary socialism. But Corradini could not abandon his revolutionary position and accept the legal orbit of the constitutional monarchy as the necessary vehicle for expansion. What was needed was a concept of the State that permitted him to appear both revolutionary and nationalistic. A plea for oligarchic conservatism was ruled out by the traditional rejection of official Italy. As in Turiello, the problem was to fuse the popular element of the continuing revolution with the demand for increased power of the centralized government. In response to the syndicalist challenge, he outlined his own concept of the State. Liberty was always properly proportionate to the State's authority. In Italy, however, liberty had become directly proportional to the State's weakness. This could lead only to the collapse of the whole structure of the regime. Challenged by the superior organization and the popular drive of the socialist movement, the State must fight back or be destroyed.[29] What was needed was a return to Mirabeau's concept of liberty as the exclusive rule of law. Instead of this, Giolitti offered only a program of permissiveness in the face of anarchy, a regime of politicians in an artificial, rootless Parliament. The nation, not the individual nor the class, was the dialectical entity of history. Its mission traversed centuries and collectively embodied the destinies of individuals. Beyond the nation there was no higher international collectivity that could prevent the inevitability of war.[30]

There is not one idea here that is original. From Burke, Hegel, Fichte, Treitschke, and Gneist as well as from Silvio Spaventa and Turiello, Corradini drew forth the elements of this grab-bag theory of the nation and war. But when Corradini, obliged by Italy's particular political situation to maintain his radical and dynamic position, insists that the nation must have a revolutionary consecration, he reveals the sense of unfulfillment that gave twentieth-century Italian conservatism its dynamic character. Those who would link Corradini's nationalism to the traditions of the Destra,[31] to the ideas of Spaventa, fail to make the necessary distinction between traditional conservatism and the variety that finds much of its inspiration in Oriani and Turiello. When Russia lost at Tsushima Straits, Papini, for all his syndicalist rhetoric, seemed the more conservative, speaking of Russia as a bastion of tradition, authority, and European culture. The "Little Father" and the Cossacks would take care of the revolution of the *muzhiks*.[32] For Corradini, on the other hand, Russia's collapse was proof of the nonnational character of the Russian state. The failure of war to consolidate the Russian people resulted from the old regime, the prerevolutionary basis of the nation. France, he wrote, had not become a nation until the Revolution freed her from her feudal past. The Russian Revolution of 1905 would not be checked by a constitutional solution; it would be carried to the end. Nicholas II, like Louis XVI, would fall before the historical force of the patria.[33] It might be pointed out that if war is a source of national cohesion, while revolution is necessary for the creation of the nation, one is faced with the logical conclusion

that war must be revolutionary in scope in order for it to work the won-
derous chemistry of Corradini's political vision. By 1905, then, the interventionist battle cry "War or Revolution," which Mussolini's *Popolo
d'Italia* was to make its stock in trade, was already enunciated. Indeed, it
was always present as an implicit theme in Oriani.

Corradini's revolutionary nationalism inevitably made him a very ambiguous defender of monarchy. The *Regno* was too conservative to be
openly antimonarchial. It was critical, however, of the bourgeois nature
of the Italian crown. A king who follows the lead of individuals and cliques
rather than that of the nation, Corradini wrote, can be a bad monarch.
Monarchy per se was not at fault. But a throne enslaved to the middle
class and to Parliament was not fulfilling its duty. Someone in Italy must
repeat the words of Louis XIV, "I am the State." But, Corradini adds, if
that proclamation does not come from the throne it will have to come
from the citizens. When Victor Emmanuel III addressed Parliament in
1904, the *Regno* heard only the usual platitudes of peace and liberty. It
denounced the Government for having so little respect for the monarchy
as to make it the mouthpiece of eternal sermons.[34]

In that Corradini would have the King assert himself as the leader of
the nationalist and imperialist cause, he was not prejudiced against monarchy as a form of government. But his monarchist sentiment is quite
clearly conditional upon the Crown's willingness to take up Italy's imperial mission. This must be stressed in order that the specifically Italian
nature of the *Regno*'s conservatism be distinguished from contemporary
French political theory. The Italian journal was unquestionably sympathetic to French rightist literature. The works of Daudet, Bloy and Barrès,
and Bourget were favorably reviewed in its pages. This has led some
critics, particularly Croce,[35] to the erroneous conclusion that Italian nationalist thought derived from foreign sources. It is true that admirers of
Italian nationalism — and Croce was not one of these — admit to French
influences while insisting that the Italians were less literary, more active.[36]
This is Gentile's view. It only repeats the careful distinction that the Italian
nationalists themselves insisted upon for fear of being demoted to the role
of political dilettantes, followers of D'Annunzio rather than active leaders
of the nation. The *Regno* was also sensitive to the charge of being dependent upon foreign ideologies. Prezzolini felt it wise to point out the Italian
origin of the *Regno*'s theories, referring to Mosca and Pareto. There was
no need, he wrote, of a Barrès or an H. S. Chamberlain.[37]

In assessing Croce's judgment of Italian nationalist literature, it must be kept in mind that he himself was profoundly patriotic. The Risorgimento he regarded as a healthy reaction to foreign intellectual influences, particularly French abstractionism.[38] Hence any reliance on French ultramontane theories was bound to be resented, and rejected as a new intrusion out of keeping with the best traditions of Italian thought. But it is clear that any utilization of French political literature had little to do with Italian problems. It was these that were at the heart of the matter, and not any convenient exploitation of contemporary rightist and antiparliamentary theories. Italian nationalists could scarcely turn to a historical monarchy for inspiration. French nationalists were happy to point this out as a defect in the Italian movement. Italy had had no Louis XIV, as one of them wrote.[39] It was this important difference that whetted Sorel's expectations. Monarchy was not a dream, as with Maurras, but an existing reality shorn of its true valor by the bourgeois, constitutional settlement of the Risorgimento.[40] Corradini reflects this in his scorn for the program of the Young Monarchist groups in Italy. In reply to one Young Monarchist, Aldemiro Campodonico, he pointed out that for all their talk of a national redemption, they were essentially pacifists. More pertinent, however, was the attitude of Campodonico himself. He betrayed his own revolutionary view of monarchy by writing that Italy was still a nation in the process of formation.[41]

Mosca was quite right. There was no legitimism in Italian monarchist sentiment. The appeal is to an idealized monarch who will take up the revolutionary banner of the Risorigmento, fulfilling the king's historical function. Oriani's description of the royal visit to Rome, where he was greeted not by the "people" but by a disorganized "crowd," is very much a part of this. As for the other pillar of the legitimist solution, the Church, it was treated by the *Regno* with sympathy but also with suspicion. No factor was more conducive to the ambiguities of Italian conservative thought than that of the Church's position in respect to the State. The *Regno* opposed anticlericalism, and spoke of the Church as an instrument for gathering the Italian people together. It was a great Italian and Roman institution,[42] and as such was looked upon with favor by the Nationalists. The *Regno* was also opposed to Freemasonry, as was the later *Idea Nazionale*. Unquestionably the Italian conservative and authoritarian school would have welcomed the backing of the Church in giving Italy that solidarity between the governed and the government that was felt to be lacking. But, as in the period 1870–1900, the threat of a subversive Church prevented this logical and admittedly desired result. The days of the patriot priests, of the lower clergy who had backed the Risorgimento, were over. Garibaldi's protector, the good Don Giovanni Verità immortalized by Oriani, had been forced to choose between the nation and the Vatican by the events of 1870. Following the visit of Loubet to Rome and the lifting of the non expedit by Pius X, the *Regno* sounded the alarm. The Nationalists feared the rise of an antinational political movement directed by the Vatican.[43]

In addition, the Nationalists could hardly preach of the mysterious powers of war and violence without rejecting the Christian view of peace and humility. A D'Annunzian, Nietzschean pose of neopaganism was very much in evidence among the imperialists. Papini in the *Leonardo* indulged in this, scoffing at what he called *pecorismo nazareno*. Corradini spoke of Christianity as "pathological and economic," whereas life consisted of conquest and struggle. In this, Papini and Corradini, as well as D'Annunzio, were capitalizing on Carducci's "Romanism" as expressed in the *Odi Barbare*[44] long after Carducci himself had abandoned the idea as artistically sterile. Beneath the literary heroics, however, there was the traditional fear of the Church that always plagued Italian conservatives. The Vatican's theoretical refusal to recognize the nation's existence deprived the Nationalists of a clear-cut political doctrine. Much of the pseudo-revolutionary and anarchic content of Italian rightist political thought resulted from the ambiguous position in which its exponents found themselves because of the Vatican's failure to come to terms with the Risorgimento.

What of the Mezzogiorno and the Southern Question? The *Regno* took no apparent interest in it for the simple reason that domestic problems were to be solved by a dynamic foreign policy. In that the Nationalists seemed to ignore fundamental problems within Italy, it is partially true, as Croce charges, that they were really antinational.[45] But Croce's dislike of escapism missed the real point. Corradini's insistence on military imperialism certainly ignored the existence of internal economic and social problems that had to be faced before any move in Africa was feasible. It is also true, as Luigi Russo noted, that in a generation of autobiographical neoromantics, the greater artistry of Italy's foremost writer, Giovanni Verga, was given only cold recognition. Papini's mysticism was more in keeping with the intellectual climate. Irrationalism was an easy solace for Nationalists who saw too clearly in Verga's novels the truth about the Mezzogiorno.[46] With *Mastro-don Gesualdo*, Verga had abandoned the pale lost lillies of his earlier works such as *Eros*, and had turned to a realism that Papini and Corradini chose to avoid; they converted their literary pessimism into political dynamism. But beneath the literary escapism there was also a convenient political device by which the Southern Question was made a source of power. As in Turiello, the people were never far behind the imperialist façade. The proletarian element in the *Regno* had been absorbed into military action. Since the fundamental problem of the Mezzogiorno was the popular disaffection for the nation which it represented, it would be wrong to miss the implications for Italian internal politics of this outward avoidance of a major domestic issue. The *Regno*'s preference for syndicalism as the dynamic form of socialism reflected in part the wish to avoid anything that resembled the bureaucratic and parliamentary program of the Italian Socialist party. It also was related to the fact that syndicalism maintained its quality of being a vital link with the undisciplined and apolitical population of the South while condoning violence. It was the violence of war that the imperialists chose to close the gap between the State and the people. The syndicalists themselves were often in accord. As one of them, Angelo Oliviero, put it, "a people which cannot make war cannot make revolution."[47]

It has been seen, in connection with Turiello's political theories (Chapter 6), that the need for a mass base for any national movement precluded a frankly reactionary approach. This was true as well of the *Regno*. Nowhere in the early Nationalist review, nor in the later *Idea Nazionale*, did General Pelloux become a symbol of political wisdom, even though Pelloux's China policy should have made him acceptable to the Nationalists. The reaction of 1898 was erased from the imperialists' calendar. It was because of the absence of anything that could be called a police-state theory in Italian politics that Pareto had once predicted the eventual triumph of the Socialists.[48] It was that triumph which Corradini feared. His fright during the general strike of 1904 proved that he was just as willing to condone reactionary methods as Pelloux. But it was impossible to narrow the base of nationalism without appearing official. In later years he would be forced to face the same dilemma, to strain the logic of his authoritarianism so as to incorporate the popular element, thus giving rise to a political literature far more insidious, because far less coherent, than an out-and-out demand for military dictatorship.

By December, 1906, the *Regno* was showing signs of a financial strain. It began reprinting old articles from the *Leonardo*, and then went out of existence. By that time, relations between Corradini and Prezzolini had deteriorated. The latter twitted the *Regno* for its "literary imperialism."[49] Corradini gave up editorship of the *Regno* in 1905, although remaining

a prominent contributor. The *Leonardo* came to an end in 1907. Prezzolini became the editor of the *Voce*, which came out in 1910. This journal
opposed imperialism as dangerous to the nation, luring Italy into under-
takings beyond her capabilities. Whereas the *Regno* had ignored the
South, the *Voce* made the Southern Question a national problem. In doing
so, it seemed, as Croce noted, to be coming down to earth, passing from
the philosophical excesses of the *Leonardo* to the investigation of concrete
matters. The undoubted seriousness of the *Voce* attracted a wide and distinguished following.[50] Croce's own contributions were evidence of its
importance as an outlet for informed public discussion.

The demise of the *Leonardo* and the *Regno* was in itself a healthy sign,
indicative of the intellectuals' turning away from rhetoric and preciosity.
In the midst of Italy's economic progress under Giolitti's guidance, Papini's mysticism sounded false. It would be quite proper to say that among
Giolitti's triumphs one should list the fading away, at least for the moment,
of the sort of journalistic and intellectual bombast represented by these
small reviews. Because the effect of the *Leonardo* and the *Regno* was partly
that of seducing a highly literate minority into the paths of implacable
opposition to the Italian government, thus depriving the constitutional regime of potential leadership, their passing from the scene was a hopeful
indication of greater political responsibility. No sooner did the Government stumble, however, than a new batch of dissident political and cultural journals arose to carry on the fight against official Italy. The Bosnia
and Hercegovina crisis of 1908 was followed by a rash of small imperialist
and irredentist papers which decried the baseness and cowardliness of
Italian foreign policy. The crisis was also followed by D'Annunzio's *La
Nave*, with its final chorus representing the popular demand for the redemption of the Adriatic. A bronze wreath, bearing the date 1908 and
the appropriate irredentist quotation,[51] was placed beside Dante's tomb
at Ravenna. It was clear that Giolittian Italy was hard put to still the
voices of discontent.

Nonetheless, between 1907 and the Libyan War of 1911–12 there
were strong indications that a more amenable intellectual atmosphere was
offering respite to the hard-pressed bureaucracy. D'Annunzio's popularity
was on the wane. The poet took himself off to exile in France, pursued by
creditors. His French admirers found themselves in the position of defending him against the neglect shown him in Italy.[52] Borgese could write
by 1909 that there were perhaps more anti-D'Annunzians than D'Annun-

zians left in Italy.[53] That the poet had left his mark, however, was apparent in the writings of the same anti-D'Annunzians. Many who rejected the fallen idol showed traces of his exotic and richly festooned style.[54] Giolittian Italy was by no means quit of its nemesis, but seemed at least to be absorbing the poisons of political irrationalism. This was in keeping with a general trend in Europe. As time elapsed without any visible effects of his blows against democracy and Christianity, Nietzsche was also becoming a subject for tolerance and compassion, a literary curiosity.[55] Bourgeois values were still in the lead, and parliamentary government was moving ahead. The intellectual elite had not had its victory over materialism, positivism, and soul-stifling democracy. But the glorification of action and the spiritualizing of power was in the air. If the moderate forces of slow reform and practical achievements were to preserve the society of the Giolittian image, statesmen would have to preserve as well the conditions in which men will wait, trusting in liberalism, and not create by their folly the horrors of butchery that could only justify the scorn of the artist-politician, making real his hymns to violence.

If the antibourgeois iconoclasts were forced to come down to earth, this did not mean that they had abandoned their past. With the collapse of their early reviews, which were transparent in their love for shocking the middle class, a drift toward organized political activity could be noted. This in itself was a victory for official Italy. Just as the decline of anarchism and the advent of scientific socialism had been a healthy political sign, giving rise to a party apparatus that in time could accustom Italians to national politics, so the formation of the Nationalist Association, in 1910, seemed a trend in the direction of less literature and more political awareness. But in examining the birth of the Nationalist Association and the pages of its paper, the *Idea Nazionale*, we will note that the literary devices of neoromanticism, the hatred of formulas, of systems, of positivism, and the urge to live intensely — so characteristic of the extreme individualism and linguistic unclarity of much late nineteenth-century thought — were carried over into the "organized" phase of Italian Nationalism. Here these devices worked to smooth over fundamental contradictions. The results were political doctrines containing the same view of life that had been the stock in trade of their creators during their purely literary days. Now they dressed as legitimate politicians. Parliament might absorb them and their party; but in so doing it would have to take in the artistic temperament as well and tame its subversive outlook.

The Challenge of Organized Politics

Following the period of the *Regno*, Corradini busied himself with travel and writing, visiting South America, the French colony of Tunis, and the irredentist areas of the Austro-Hungarian Empire. In the course of this footloose interval before returning to political journalism, he wrote two novels, *La patria lontana*, published in 1910, and *La guerra lontana*, which came out in the next year. Both of these works express the familiar theme of the redeeming qualities of war. The latter sought to capture the romance of Italy's great solitary heroes, men whose patriotism and national vision clashed with the false pacifism and political degeneracy of their milieu: Crispi, Carducci, and Oriani. The battle of Adowa was depicted as a symbol of the betrayal of Italian virtues by the corrupt bourgeoisie whose narrow egoism was permitted to corrode the nation because it was shared by the ruling political factions of official Italy. The defeat, however, was also the seed of regeneration, awakening the dormant patriotic energies of a new generation, of which Corradini sought to make himself a prominent spokesman, a new bard of the patria.

In all, Corradini was a prolific writer, producing a dozen plays and as many novels, to which must be added another dozen volumes of collected speeches and articles on politics. Yet no one could grant him a prominent place in the field of Italian literature. His works were far too derivative and propagandistic to leave any lasting artistic impression. The leading French critic, Maurice Muret, could at best give him brief mention among Italian writers.[56] Although never abandoning the world of letters completely, Corradini was more interested in an active political career. Unlike Papini, whose interest in art was stronger than any occasional dabbling in politics, he had elaborated a concept of political action which, however confused and unoriginal, required an organization with which to penetrate the apparatus of government.

Between 1908 and 1910 the opportunity for achieving this foothold presented itself through the formation in northern and central Italy of small nationalist groups. Corradini became one of the leaders of the Florentine nucleus of the later Nationalist Association. Also from the ranks of secondary writers came Luigi Federzoni, then known as Giulio de Frenzi in his capacity as a member of the editorial staff of the prominent paper *Il Giornale d'Italia*. Whatever the outward appearance of a more down-to-earth approach to politics, the old literary swagger was still there. Federzoni wrote of humanitarianism as the fleeting utopia of childish poets and positivist thinkers. "Hatred is no less necessary than love to

breed civilization." When the Ligurian, Tuscan, and Lombard Nationalists merged, they adopted as their motto the concept of the nation as the
"final and greatest union of collective existence," and as their cult, "the
tradition of heroes, the Roman mission."

In December, 1910, the Nationalist Association was founded at Florence under the leadership of Corradini, Scipio Sighele, Maurizio Maraviglia, Francesco Coppola, Federzoni, and other exponents of national
rejuvenation. From the first, the taint of conservatism was avoided by a
proclamation of the proletarian character of Italian imperialism. "We are a
proletarian people in respect to the rest of the world. Nationalism is our
socialism. This established, nationalism must be founded on the truth that
Italy is morally and materially a proletarian nation."[57] On March 1, 1911,
fifteenth anniversary of the battle of Adowa, the Nationalists' weekly paper
appeared in Rome. The first edition of the *Idea Nazionale*, continuing the
literary tradition of the great solitary hero, adopted Francesco Crispi as
its precursor. It was an indication of the abiding hostility to the Italian
government that the Nationalists chose to surround with a halo of grandeur
a man whose political career was marked by failure. In the first issue of
the paper Luigi Federzoni extolled Crispi's virtues. Taking as a model for
his essay a memorial written by another nationalist idol, Oriani, Federzoni
affirmed Italy's need for a great national act, a gesture that would consolidate Italian unity. This had failed at Adowa because of the nation's betrayal by the democratic and moderate parties and the monarchy's weakness in refusing to support Crispi in his hour of defeat. The vanquished,
however, were not General Baratieri and Crispi. What the blood of Adowa
had destroyed was the "weak, incoherent, pale unitarian sentiment of this
Italy, which, from the incidents and coincidences of European policy and
the heroism of a small minority . . . received the gift of independence."
In the proud silence of defeat, vituperated, abandoned by all, Crispi had
died alone, an exile in his own land. That noble silence was Crispi's legacy
to Italy, to the patria that mourned him secretly.[58]

Departing from the Crispian hagiology, the *Idea Nazionale* called for
the assertion of Italy's just claim on Tripoli. Tracing the history of Italian
diplomacy since the formation of the Triple Alliance, the paper pointed out
that a heavy price had been paid to assure this last Mediterranean outlet.
After sacrificing Tunis and Morocco to France, and Egypt to England,
Italy had still to obtain a guarantee of her Mediterranean position from
her allies. The Triple Alliance had the virtue of ending Italy's isolation in
Europe. But Tripoli had to be won. The nationalist paper denied that

Tripoli was the "gnawed bone" some claimed. The Anglo-French control of the hinterland caravan routes had not divested the coastal area of its great importance. Tobruk remained a strategic that must not be allowed to fall to France. Should it do so, Italy would be encircled by the French holdings at Tunis and Corsica, as well as by the English position at Malta.[59]

The Nationalists were in the dark as to whether the Triple Alliance had been renewed. They were correct, however, in their surmise that no Mediterranean guarantee had yet been wrung from the Central Powers. The text of the 1901 version of the Alliance, which had been automatically renewed in 1907, added only the note by which Austria-Hungary declared disinterest in Tripoli and Cyrenaica and promised not to thwart Italian interests in the Mediterranean. Being supporters of the Triple Alliance, although far less fervid since the occupatiion of Bosnia and Hercegovina,[60] the Nationalists had to counter the argument that any hostile move might shake the Ottoman Empire and thus permit possible new French advances in the Mediterranean. This was done by claiming that an Italian occupation would in fact strengthen the Alliance by removing the equivocal nature of Italy's role that had become evident at Algeciras. Italy's failure to take steps to enforce her rights in Tripoli weakened the Alliance by rendering it devoid of meaning.[61]

More was involved, however, than the need to justify the Alliance. At the core of the matter was the necessity of glossing over a fundamental split within the ranks of the Nationalist Association. At the first Congress at Florence the disagreement between the Africanists and Irredentists was evident. This was healed by the general enthusiasm of the meeting, which permitted both sides to have their day. The *Idea Nazionale* admitted this internal quarrel. It sought to solve or at least forestall the dilemma by the dubious argument that the Dual Monarchy opposed Italy's advance in Africa in order to offer Tripoli in return for Italy's renunciation of the Adriatic sphere.[62] The argument of the Africanist wing was that if Tripoli were seized the Alliance would no longer be a barrier to an active irredentist policy. Austria would be deprived of bargaining power. This was absurd, as the paper's editors well knew. Italy's former foreign minister, Tittoni, had made it clear in 1905 that Italy's prior rights on Tripoli were assured by all interested powers, while advising against any occupation on the ground that it would disturb Italian relations with the Ottoman Empire, whose integrity was the "unshakable foundation" of Italian foreign policy.[63] What was at the heart of the Nationalists' demand for Tripoli was the realization that war with Austria-Hungary was simply out of the question, while Tripoli had been a possible battlefield ever since the rapprochement with France of 1901–4. Even those Nationalists who, like Sighele, believed that the natural grouping of European powers would place Italy together with France and England, defended the Triple Alliance as a practical necessity. The practicality, as Sighele expressed it, consisted of the fact that nature's law was one of competition. "To live — for the social as for the individual organism — means to expand." [64] Beneath the rational surface of the *Idea Nazionale*'s diplomatic analysis there lurked the urge of war and glory of the defunct *Regno*. Action was the key word. The sphere was a minor consideration.

The psychological rather than materialist motivation behind the Tripoli venture was apparent in the Nationalists' weak attempts to sustain the economic advantages of Tripoli. Citations from Herodotus of the wealth of North Africa were scarcely in keeping with the supposed diplomatic realism of the *Idea Nazionale*, something the *Voce* [65] was only too happy to point out. Corradini went to North Africa whence he sent back dispatches that were a mixture of political reporting and literary sentimentalism. Descriptions of Roman ruins had little to do with economic imperialism, but were compatible with the principal imperialist aim: that of creating a greater unitarian feeling at home. This sort of journalism recalled Corradini's heroic novels and suggested that the Nationalists would manage to find fault with any action the Government might undertake in Tripoli. Literary Africanism was not limited to the new and scarcely influential *Idea Nazionale*. The *Stampa* of Turin, one of Italy's best dailies, printed similar fare from its correspondent Giuseppe Bevione. Bevione indulged in classical scholarship on North Africa, and added the dubious prophecy that the Arab population would not resist European intervention.[66] Far more hardheaded was Gaetano Mosca, then a Deputy in the Chamber. His own views on Tripoli threw cold water on the idea of its economic possibilities as well as on the contention that the Arabs would offer no resistance, and tried to prepare the public for a hard campaign. Mosca, to be sure, accepted the war, but was frank enough to justify it on the more plausible ground that Italy could not afford to come out of the power struggle in the Mediterranean without a crumb.[67] That, in fact, was to be the Government's position when the war was launched.

As the summer of 1911 wore on without noticeable activity on the part of Giolitti's ministry, the *Idea Nazionale* stepped up its campaign. Less was said about any economic possibilities. More was written about the role of the military as a force of national solidarity, recalling the days of the Risorgimento. In D'Annunzian prose, the glory of the Italian navy, the hoped-for vindicator of Lissa, was described. There was something sinister in the Nationalists' harping on the primacy of spiritual and moral values. "The Italian people, although having made marvelous progress in all fields of labor, of economic production . . . has allowed the spirit of expansion, the indispensable condition for existence, to weaken; and has permitted the decay of that military spirit which is the necessary weapon of any struggle." By September, the *Idea Nazionale* was demanding immediate occupation. The threat — hardly worthy of serious consideration — that if the Government did not act the nation would[68] foreshadowed the days of May, 1915, when similar claims were to be made against the Salandra-Sonnino ministry.

What of the Mezzogiorno? It is interesting that in the first issues of the *Idea Nazionale* a very sober note was struck, one quite in keeping with the articles in defense of internal reforms then appearing in the *Voce*. But the flurry of interest was short-lived. The question was dropped almost as soon as it was raised. The Nationalists returned to the original theme of imperialism as the panacea for domestic ills.[69] Not that the South was forgotten. As in the *Regno* it was absorbed into that larger vision of the cohesive nation. In subtle ways the imperialists tried to link the cause of the Mezzogiorno with Crispi, a Sicilian. Federzoni's evocation of Crispi's memory included the assertion that the hero had been betrayed by the Socialists and the Lombard bourgeoisie, while the people of southern Italy were behind him.[70] This was, of course, false. Italians in general had been unwilling to carry on after Adowa. But what the Nationalists resented was the historical reluctance of northern interests to part with their economic and political primacy through a total unification of the Peninsula. It was not forgotten that one of the leading spokesmen of the northern conservative and Catholic tradition, Stefano Jacini, had also been among the first to accuse Crispi of megalomania.

The imperialists were disturbed by the same scioltezza, the persistence of localisms, of the Italian people that Turiello had noted a decade before. Pride in one's city, *campanilismo*, wrote Sighele, was a noble sentiment. The aim was to transform this feeling into a national pride. The Nationalists, therefore, had not ignored domestic problems, and in particular the problem of the Mezzogiorno. According to this one-time federalist, they sought solutions abroad, in foreign expansion.[71] Indeed, the great attraction of warmongering was that it did rise above regionalism. Had African imperialism been tied to any geographical shift of Italy's center, as some historians claim, the facility with which the anti-Entente Nationalists of 1911–14 became pro-French interventionists in the period of neutrality would be harder to explain. But it was clear from the aggressive interpretation the Nationalists placed on the Triple Alliance — it must bear territorial fruits — that their support of it was always dependent on its being a vehicle for war.

It was the fear of incompleteness that tormented the Nationalists as it had Turiello before them. Where Turiello only suggested a proletarian national-imperialism, the *Idea Nazionale* sought to elaborate a coherent political theory that would include both the power State and the popular will. The latter was an unavoidable ingredient because of the uncommitted forces, what the *Idea Nazionale* called the "healthy and vital life of the people," suppressed by an artificial government organization.[72] Corradini's revolutionary concept of national genesis had paved the way for this doctrine. But the ingenious political philosophers of the *Idea Nazionale* were now obliged to call upon all their rhetorical resources in order to square their view of the State with a libertarian, even democratic tradition that was a common heritage of the Risorgimento.

Another contradiction taxed the intellectual agility of the novelist-politicians: that of clamoring for an African invasion while condemning official Italy. It was manifestly impossible to preach immediate war and deny the existing administrative structure without which war was inconceivable. This logical puzzle was solved by the use of a vocabulary more reminiscent of literature than political science. If one were to seek a geographical explanation for the rise of the cult of Rome and Africanism, it would perhaps be more fruitful to concentrate on a linguistic shift from Piedmont and Lombardy toward Tuscany. It was in Florence, not in Naples, that the major outpouring of imperialism had its fount. The clean, unadorned style of Giolitti, compared with that of any one of the intellectual Young Turks, tells more of the causes of political irrationalism than does the pulling of Italy south into the sphere of the Mediterranean. The vocabulary of neoromanticism became the language of diplomacy.

Programmatic confusion encouraged the use of highly imprecise language to obscure obvious differences of opinion among the nationalist membership. It was apparent at the first Congress of the group that no agreement could ever be reached that would satisfy the many currents represented: Monarchists and Republicans, Irredentists and Africanists, protectionists and free-traders. The only point of agreement was that Italy should be stronger. From the first, however, the Nationalists were skittish about the incubus of organization. They preferred to call themselves an association rather than a party. Political platforms were too reminiscent of official Italy, and of the once heroic socialism that had lost its drive and spontaneity by becoming a well-knit camp. Nationalists were not politicians, Sighele wrote. "They are men of faith who express freely what they feel and think in order to reinvigorate our weak political life." In the words of Gualtiero Castellini, nationalism was more than a party. It was a tendency and a hope, reflecting a general state of mind as interpreted by young Italians.[73] In this way, fundamental political distinctions were obscured. The *Idea Nazionale* recognized that there was no essential agreement among its followers on the ultimate political direction of the movement. But, as in the case of the *Regno*, the problem of juggling authoritarian militarism and a certain populism soon presented itself. The paper's editors achieved this feat by calling for the formation of a conservative party while denying that they were in fact conservatives. This logical sleight of hand was accomplished by distinguishing between ideal conservatism, which was truly national, and existing conservative politicians, who were in fact betraying the national cause. As for democracy, the *Idea Nazionale* accepted it in theory, but opposed Italian democratic parties. The conclusion would be that the Nationalists were theoretical democratic conservatives. The paper's phrasing of this paradox, however, revealed the source of the confusion. In a country in which only two parties, clerical and Socialist, were well organized, and in which "the principle of political continuity of the State is not represented and guaranteed by a suitable constitutional structure, but must rest on spontaneous factors expressed directly by the popular conscience, a strong conservative party is not only useful but beneficial . . . "[74]

At the root of all this was the old problem of the separation of the governed and the government. Both were indispensable for the nationalist creed. Hence the State was exalted in ultraconservative fashion, and the people were made the expression of the nation along libertarian lines. It was impossible, however, to subdue distinction forever. Not all the editors of the *Idea Nazionale* were ready to abandon their own points of view in the name of harmony. It was perhaps a benefit — if only as an undisguised point of reference — that one of them, Francesco Coppola, chose to make his own out-and-out reactionary theories known. Whatever may be said about the impact of French rightist thought on Nationalists in general, there was little doubt about Coppola. His first articles were inspired by ultramontane sentiments and anti-Semitism. It should be said here that expressions of anti-Semitism were rather rare in modern Italian history. Coppola's use of it, in an article dedicated to Maurras, caused a widespread reaction within the ranks of the Nationalist Association. Resignations followed, and Coppola was obliged to deny that he was advocating anti-Semitic ideas. That he was indeed became clearer in the article in which he sought to refute the charge.[75] It was a masterpiece of self-contradiction.

Sighele, despite his former willingness to gloss over distinctions, now objected to the antidemocratic stand the paper seemed to be taking. He insisted that the Nationalists make up their minds just where they stood. He published a telling critique exposing the contradictory attitudes that were lumped together within the Nationalist Association. It had become a conglomorate of reactionary, syndicalist, irredentist, imperialist, and democratic thought. He demanded an open debate to decide whether the movement would become a reactionary or a democratic party. According to Sighele, the source of confusion resulted from the absence of a clear philosophical point of view upon which all political action must be based. He put his finger on the essential similarity of Sorel's syndicalism and the classical conservatism of Maurras. Both opposed democratic individualism. Hence their ultimate compatibility as allies against all democratic principles. Sighele now came out in defense of representative government. Any defects in the system were the result of corruption that could be done away with by reform legislation. Theoretical arguments rejecting democracy as the rule of the incompetents were specious. Oligarchies as well had proved themselves to be incompetent. With Salvemini, Sighele called for universal suffrage.[76]

This cutting through the layers of political sophistry, demanding clear definitions, was at first glance a healthy reaction to nationalist rhetoric. But a closer look at Sighele's democratic beliefs shows that he, too, tended to speak in suggestive rather than precise terms. His own "positivistic" background — he was a noted criminologist — did not prevent him from using the vocabulary of the aesthetes. This was true of his critique of foreign policy. He had backed the imperialist campaign for Tripoli even though his own inclinations were in the direction of the Trentino as the focal point for a vital national foreign policy. The reason for this was his wish to elevate the "collective feeling" of the Italians above narrow, regionalist viewpoints. Like Turiello, Sighele hoped to creat a greater national sentiment, to break down provincialisms. Promoting a popular interest in foreign policy was a means of preventing Italy from becoming resigned to her internal weakness. As to the functioning of Italy's domestic political system, Sighele's views were closer to Corradini's than at first appeared. What Sighele found most objectionable in Coppola's French nationalists doctrine was the fact that it left out the popular will. Italian nationalism, he wrote in 1909, had nothing to do with anti-Semitic, legitimist, clericalist reaction. Sighele recognized, as had Sorel, that in Italy ultramontane theory was an alien intrusion. Barrès was an admirable artist, but Italians could not defend his ideas without blushing. "In Italy, therefore, Nationalism is not nor cannot be . . . anything save a liberal party, sincerely and boldly liberal, seeking to awaken slumbering national energies." [77]

Sighele's democratic beliefs had little to do with any utilitarian resistance to the State conceived as a metaphysical entity. Liberty and authority were quite as confused in his own view of Italy's future as they were with Corradini. His support of democracy, representative government, and universal suffrage rested on the same historical dissatisfaction with the Postrisorgimento, its failure to "create Italians" once Italy had been created. Regarding the role of the people, Sighele betrayed his own ambiguities by quoting Barrès: "The people always speaks an admirable synthetic language." Was Sighele himself a devotee of French political theory? Only in that it served his purpose. More significant was his return to Vincenzo Gioberti for a defense of democratic nationalism. In his *Del rinnovamento civile d'Italia*, Gioberti had written of expansion as a leavening force of national greatness. Here, wrote Sighele, was Corradini's imperialism anticipated by sixty years. In response to the antidemocratic wing of the Nationalist Association, he cited Gioberti's dictum: "The people is the heart and nerve of nations." It was democratic nationalism that had created Italy. It was the same movement that would transform the weak uncertain nation into a greater Italy. Democracy, according to Sighele, was "that social organization which tends to promote to the maximum the civic conscience and responsibility of each individual. . . . And how could one give all citizens a 'sense of the nation' . . . that is teach them sacrifice and discipline for the supreme good of the patria if Nationalism were antidemocratic, if it prevented participation in public life of a significant part of the Italian population?" [78]

Seeing his Giobertian democratic nationalism betrayed by the ultraconservative wing of the party, Sighele resigned from the Central Committee. He defended universal suffrage, whereas the *Idea Nazionale* belittled electoral reforms as serving other purposes than that of offering

Giolitti a wider field for election-rigging.[79] But Sighele was not so far from the Nationalists as might be supposed. His own view of Giolitti, of official Italy, was quite in keeping with that of the conservative wing of the party. "No patriotic halo surrounds this man," he wrote of Giolitti. His youth was "bureaucratically gray." Lacking any intellectual interests, "he is the minister farthest removed from literature." Lacking those "adamantine qualities before which the crowd bows," his genius instead is that of political manipulations, the creation of a "parliamentary dictatorship." "There are two ways to get ahead in the world: either by means of brilliance of mind or by shady efforts of corruption. One must penetrate the masses like a cannon ball, or insinuate oneself like a poison. Giovanni Giolittli is — politically speaking — that poison." Sighele granted Giolitti's political abilities. Corruption alone was not the explanation for his success, which was founded on his ability to preserve a liberal policy of peaceful economic progress at home while refusing to press a dynamic foreign policy abroad. Giolitti, according to Sighele, was the mirror in which Italy saw its own personality. This was essentially the language of the anti-Giolittians of the 1890's.

One would think that this was high praise indeed, that Giolitti had in fact governed Italy in accordance with the wishes of the majority of the nation. Nowhere did Sighele deny that progress had been made under his ministries, 1903–05 and 1906–09. And yet Giolitti was "the symbol of the antinomy which exists between the nation and Parliament." Universal suffrage would cure the ills of parliamentarism. Recalling Sighele's romantic portrayal of the southern brigand, more noble than the crass banker who stole without risk, it is clear that his democratic fervor is quite subversive of the legal paths of political action. That Sighele dropped his earlier interest in southern reforms illustrates again the manner in which the Mezzogiorno had become for the Nationalists a great "unmentionable," but also an anarchic source of popular energy remaining to be tapped. Although he defended the cause of democratic reforms against the authoritarian philosophy of Coppola, Sighele could also quote, revealingly, that "great antidemocratic philosopher, Friedrich Nietzsche, who himself could not help recognizing that 'to mingle and talk with the people is like contemplating a potent and healthy plant.' " The anarchic cast of Sighele's own brand of nationalism comes out clearly in a review he wrote of D'Annunzio's *The Fire*, a play that expressed "in marvellously lucid prose the unconscious power of the mob." [80]

What at first appeared a logical critique of nationalist political sophistry ended up an ambiguous defense of democracy and universal suffrage. In returning to Gioberti, Sighele betrayed his own sensitivity about being labeled a cosmopolite, a purveyor of French ideas. It was more significant, however, that in the midst of undoubted domestic progress, the Post-risorgimento was found to be "spiritually" insufficient. Lauding Gioberti meant returning to the heroic age of Italy's drama. For Sighele, as for all Nationalists, that drama was still in the process of unfolding. The heroic element had been dulled by the "bureaucratic gray" personified in Gio-litti. It continued to thrive, untainted by the poison of Rome, in the people. Romantic nationalism of another age was very much a part of this political theorizing.

What of the *Idea Nazionale* itself? Had it really gone over to French ultramontane theory? It had not, for the very reasons that Sighele pointed out. Neither Corradini nor Federzoni could defend a frankly rightist view-point. Coppola did, it is true. In this he was joined by Maurizio Maraviglia. But important as their writings are, they always strike a discordant note, not only because of Coppola's anti-Semitism, which found little response among Italians, but because their failure to incorporate those spontaneous popular forces compromised them from the start. How the subtle political writers of the nationalist paper succeeded in squaring the circle, in meeting Sighele's insistence on a clear-cut choice between democacy and reaction, without committing themselves to either alternative, is worth considering. Out of the debate on political positions, an idealized and somewhat literary program of political action emerged that permitted the Nationalist to be all things to all people. Coppola's views, on the other hand, were striking in that they at least took a stand firmly behind ultramontane theory. In this they were an anomaly rather than typical of extreme Italian conservatism.

In 1909 the Italian edition of Sorel's *Réflexions sur la violence* ap-peared. By that time, Sorel was perhaps better known in Italy than in France. He had been a contributor to Italian reviews, and some of his works had been published originally in Italian.[81] Corradini, as has been seen, flirted with syndicalism until the general strike of 1904 forced him to show his authoritarian colors. No imperialist could hope to mount an African invasion without a solid governmental structure. But when the Nationalist Association was formed, the proclamation of the proletarian nation showed that the imperialists were not yet ready to embrace authori-tarianism publicly. In response to Sorel's book, Corradini attempted to absorb the syndicalist theory of violence and mass action within the frame-work of national imperialism. Beginning with the admission that imperial-ism and syndicalism were incompatible, a logical conclusion that even

Corradini could not avoid, he went on to show that there were certain affinities between the two camps. The three elements of syndicalism were the union, direct action, and the general strike. The unions were comparable to the army. The method of warfare was one of direct action. And the general strike was the final battle against the enemy, that is, against the capitalist regime. Since syndicalism refuted pacifism, humanitarianism, reform legislation, Parliament, and any hope of international peace, it was the only means left by which European nations could rediscover their ancient vigor. Being antidemocratic, syndicalism represented for Corradini the "first declaration of an aristocratic will to be made since the French Revolution." Moreover, it arose on the periphery of socialism, from the manual laborers and not from the bourgeois leadership of the Socialist party. Here was that contact with the vital element, the people, that was dear to the Nationalists. In that syndicalism demanded discipline, patience, and sacrifice Corradini could compare the striker to the soldier who died on the battlefield.

Having exploited the antidemocratic, antibourgeois character of the syndicalists, Corradini was left with the contradiction between his national imperialism and a doctrine of international class war. He denied that he was himself a syndicalist, and then proceeded to face this contradiction armed with the weapons of literature, if not those of logic. "Keep in mind," he tells us, "that a doctrine, any doctrine, exists not so much in its program as in the power of action which its program can release. . . . This being accepted, then, we can imagine a syndicalism which stops at the nation's shores and does not proceed farther; which ceases to operate internationally, but instead works on the national level. The workers unite, no longer on a world-wide basis, but within the confines of the nation. They unite to win power, not throughout the world, but nationally. If, then, this were to happen, the principal point of opposition between the two doctrines would be suppressed."

This imagined syndicalism of the patria, however, did not solve the problem of imperialism. Many, Corradini conceded, would accept nationalism but reject military imperialism. But imperialism was not so limited. It was of many sorts. Syndicalism, for example, was class imperialism. There was also a European imperialism, as the rapid extension of European rule and techniques throughout the world demonstrated. This was, in turn, a manifestation of what Corradini called "civilized imperialism." In the final analysis, however, what Corradini posed as the unifying factor of all imperialisms, including syndicalism — i.e. class imperialism — was the common aspect of man's love of conquest that each revealed. The Nietzschean theme of the will to power became a convenient rhetorical device by which Corradini, in D'Annunzian language, escaped the logical contradictions of his political theory. "If we could have the power of vision of one hundred thousand eagles concentrated in our eyes; if we had the power of flight and breath of one hundred thousand eagles to raise ourselves on high, we would see the earth pass below us tormented by this unrelenting human will to domination . . . this tragic imperialism of man over nature." Imperialism was not a particular doctrine. It was a "universal doctrine" inherent in man. Whether syndicalist, national, or European, imperialism was a "rebirth of the collective values of existence." And in all its forms it was antibourgeois and heroic.[82]

In the last analysis, the novelist's talents came to the fore in response to the problem of reconciling contradictions. Beneath the "heroic sublimity" and similar literary shortcuts, however, there was the essential task of harnessing the masses to the imperial chariot. It was also wise to avoid any precise definition of policy. The Nationalist Association was obviously composed of internecine factions that would fly off in their many separate directions at the first sign of a more detailed elaboration of theory. According to Corradini, nationalism, unlike all existing political parties, had no program because it was a moral force, a state of mind, a liberation from the fixation of parties. The only formula that could be applied to it was that it alone was truly antisocialist. But Corradini was quick to add that nationalism was not opposed to the proletariat as such. It merely sought the means of uniting the workers with all other classes in defense of the nation.[83]

Ironically, Corradini had already gone too far in the direction of a political program to satisfy some. On the eve of the First Nationalist Congress at Florence, Giovanni Amendola, writing in the *Voce*, stated what he considered the only valid basis for a nationalist movement. The creed of the nationalist position must be that "our ideals of public and private life, our intellectual, political, and moral values are not those of the men who today constitute the ruling class." By accepting a limited political program, the individual ideal was lost. The only hope lay in "the strict and absolute opposition to everything which is representative of that Italy of which we disapprove and from which we wish to remove ourselves." This opposition must be radical and irreconcilable. Corradini, Amendola wrote, had once expressed the same view, if in somewhat literary terms. But he had then expounded a theory of the proletarian-national state. This might lead to the formation of a political party and support of a particular ministry, but could not carry on the strictly un-official opposition necessary to cleanse Italy. Sighele was also distressed by the fact that the Nationalist Association's directorate seemed to be backing the conservative faction within the Chamber,[84] thus entering into the recognized political arena and losing its revolutionary spirit.

The Nationalists were faced with the uncomfortable alternatives of entering party politics, and by so doing being marked with the stigma of official Italy, or remaining a vociferous but sterile intellectual movement. Since imperialism was their one distinguishing political feature, it was illogical to shun the paths to power that alone could lead to directing the machinery of government, that hated bureaucracy without which Afri-canism was meaningless. However, the heterogeneous following thus far attracted to the movement was by no means agreed on this. The summer of 1911 was spent debating political tactics as well as theory. The im-portance of the debate was enhanced by the return to power of Giolitti in March of that year. The infamous political wizard presented the Chamber with a program of wide social as well as political reforms. Besides universal suffrage, it included a plan for a national monopoly on life insurance, the revenues from which were to be applied to old-age and disabled worker pensions. In this way, Giolitti said, the proceeds derived from policies taken out by the well-to-do could be used to increase the pensions of less fortunate Italians without unbalancing the budget. In the Chamber, Giolitti could count not only on his traditional majority, but on the votes of the Left, including those of the Socialists. He had tried unsuccessfully to induce Leonida Bissolati, one of the founders of Italian socialism, to join his Ministry. Bissolati considered the party as yet unprepared for ministerial collaboration. Such a move could produce a schism within its ranks, whereas support from the floor of the Chamber would be of greater benefit to the Ministry.[85]

Giolitti has been described as a political opportunist, a pragmatic bureaucrat lacking the lofty vision of a true statesman. His detractors, as Sighele makes clear, found him utterly unheroic. Even those who praise him question what they choose to call his empirical[86] view of political action. That any active politician — and Giolitti was certainly that — could be labeled an "empiricist" with effect is evidence of the abiding sense of frustration of Italian intellectuals who anathematized Parliament as a great slough where lofty ideals were swallowed up. But it must be said that Giolitti did have a fundamental principle upon which he based his whole career. One would hesitate to call it anything so grand as a lofty vision, a synthetic view of the State. These are expressions that suit neither his mode of speech nor his realistic regard for politics; they are expressions drawn from the vocabulary, literary and political, of his enemies. Simply stated, it was to bring within the orbit of Italy's constitutional institutions men of all parties, regardless of their political past.[87] In his program of 1911–12 Giolitti was following just that plan. In a much more important sense, he was effecting through legal means the solution to the major problems that weighed so heavily on the intellectual and political consciousness of the Postrisorgimento. Universal suffrage and wide social reform legislation were the parliamentary response to those who spoke of a needed fusion of real and official Italy. There was a third point in the Giolittian program: the Libyan War. This remained, for excellent diplomatic reasons, a well-guarded secret. Here was that "test of arms and blood" that would erase the blot of Adowa. The war in Libya was to force the Nationalists into a corner from which they could not escape. In effect, their reaction to the colonial campaign was to ruin them as leaders of anarchic conservatism, leaving the field open for others who were to adopt many of their ideas, capturing for themselves the leadership of disgruntled intellectuals and amateur politicians.

The Nationalist Party and the African War

The period of the African War, 1911–13, was a turning point in the history of the nationalist movement. Together with the passage of the bill granting universal male suffrage, the Tripoli expedition placed the authoritarian imperialists in the position of choosing between political extinction and a frank declaration of extreme conservatism, dropping their pose as bearers of the popular will. One wing of the Nationalist Association was to choose the only road to survival left open to them. By so doing it entered the parliamentary system, there to do battle on the terms set down by official Italy. It even seemed, for a moment, as if the Nationalists were to become the core of a monarchical conservative party drawing its support from clerical forces, solving the dilemma that had defeated the Right in the days of Leo XIII. In that the literary and fundamentally subversive Nationalists were forced to become part of the legal apparatus, this was a victory for the Giolittian policy of drawing all factions, however opposed in principle to representative institutions, within the framework of constitutional government. The coming of the Great War, however, would see the inherently anarchic temper characteristic of so much of the Italian right making its appearance again, adding thereby to the revolutionary nature of Italian intervention and foreshadowing the eventual crisis that was to destroy Giolittian Italy.

Corradini had never openly opposed Parliament as an institution. Imperialism forced him to stop short of anticonstitutional theory. He agreed with Prezzolini that Parliament stood between the nation and the people. In response to Giolitti's proposed reforms, Corradini could do no more than avoid the issue by distinguishing between the ideal Parliament and the existing sham. "Parliament in a democratic regime," he wrote in April, 1911, "should be the instrument of the national will." Giolitti's parliament, on the other hand, was a confusion of oligarchical interests — bourgeois, industrial, or socialist."The dictatorship of Giovanni Giolitti leaves out two simple things: the monarchy and that other thing which parliamentarians and journalists call the country, which our elders called the people and which we call the nation." Nationalism alone had arisen to combat all oligarchies and demagogues allied within the walls of Parliament. The great weapon of this struggle was Tripoli. The war would involve a great domestic reform as well: the destruction of Giolitti's parliamentary dictatorship.[88]

This was not only a facile way of escaping the dilemma. It was an anarchic, militaristic substitute of mass action for democratic legislation, preserving the popular base of nationalist theory without committing the movement either to destroying Parliament or to entering it. Within the Chamber of Deputies, however, a strong conservative reaction to the insurance monopoly bill sparked a revival of the Liberal party. Federzoni — still going under his pen name Giulio de Frenzi — attended a meeting in Rome of one of the leaders of this revitalized group, the Deputy Romeo Gallenga-Stuart. The *Idea Nazionale* attacked the insurance bill as interference by the State with the free economic development of the nation. In the Chamber the leader of the opposition, Antonio Salandra, made this the theme of an important speech in which he accused Giolitti of creating a monstrous state capitalism and of betraying the liberal tradition of Cavour. Salandra defended liberty. But Giolitti's suspicion that behind the attack on the insurance bill there lay the real target, universal suffrage, which a cabinet crisis might well have killed,[89] is borne out by the *Idea Nazionale*'s sudden concern for the doctrines of nineteenth-century liberalism.

An alliance between the Nationalists and the liberal — i.e. conservative — faction within the Chamber now became possible. This frightened some Nationalists, who foresaw a loss of idealistic purity, a threat to the dynamic individuality of the movement should it enter organized politics. The editorialists of the *Idea Nazionale* were hard put to answer this. The paper made it clear that the Association was not going to be sunk in the mire of politics. Federzoni's support of the Salandra faction was indicative only of the Nationalists' disapproval of Giolitti. The Liberal party had an ignoble record, as had all factions within the Chamber. Nonetheless, a flame had been kindled by Salandra's speech attacking Giolitti's opportunistic maneuvers; this was clear from the *Idea Nazionale*'s remark that one could not take a completely Buddhist attitude. Salandra had to be commended for his stand. As for universal suffrage, it was hard indeed to come out flatly against it after having talked so long of the fresh will of the country, the latent power of the masses. And Giolitti had made opposition more difficult by proposing that military service be recognized as a substitute for literacy. Fearing the reactionary tag, the *Idea Nazionale* once more denied that it was opposed to democratic reforms.[90]

The anti-Giolitti Liberals continued to bid for the support of the Nationalist Association. Gallenga-Stuart in particular insisted that "good Liberals" — that is, those uncorrupted by Giolittian tactics — should work together with the Nationalists. A similar appeal came from the Liberal Union, which would have the Nationalists join them in strict opposition to universal suffrage.[91] In reply, in an unsigned article, the *Idea Nazionale* tried to clarify its position on parliamentary democracy. It was obvious, the writer admitted, that one could not be imperialist and antidemocratic in a country ruled by democratic institutions. To take an anticonstitutional stand and demand foreign expansion at the same time was a contradiction. "In the history of Italy we cannot find any other institutions to which to tie the patria's destiny more profitably. In France, the historic tree felled in 1789 may sprout anew. But in Italy, that which was destroyed in 1860 is, fortunately, gone forever. We, therefore, are loyally faithful to the existing political arrangement." Parliament being a national institution, Nationalists could have no prejudices against democratic institutions nor classify themselves as absolutely opposed to democracy. Not unlike the pseudo-parliamentary theorists of the 1890's, the Nationalists were hard put to find a way of creating the power State while preserving the shell of a parliament whose roots went back to 1848 and the national revolution.

Classify was the dreaded word. And events were pressing the Nationalists to do just that, as seen by Sighele's critique of the incoherence of nationalist doctrine. Conservatives and authoritarians though they were, the imperialists were trapped by their own foreign policy and by the common parliamentary heritage of the Risorgimento. They accepted Parliament as a national ideal, but opposed its actual functioning. Democracy was also a national ideal. This forced them to pay lip service to "true democracy." But the Nationalists made their antidemocratic convictions obvious by opposing all progressive parties within the Chamber.[92] For some, however, this verbal maneuvering was not sufficiently bold. An "authentic" ultraconservative, Mario Missiroli, writing in Sorel's *Indépendance*, criticized the Nationalists for not having taken a moral stand, on principle, against all parties and against Parliament. The Nationalists must be a party representing class interests, refusing political alliances of any sort. Answering Missiroli, the *Idea Nazionale* rejected such a narrow view of its role in Italian politics. Nationalism must represent the nation which transcends all classes, not an elite.[93] In order to satisfy the authoritarian desire for a compact State, while holding to Parliament as a national institution incorporating all strata of Italian society, Maurizio Maraviglia concocted a blend of corporate state theory and parliamentary government. Parliament, he wrote, was the common heritage of the nation. No party could enter the government and hope to change its institutions. Only in its origins, however, was Parliament democratic. Democracy had served its purpose. In the modern concept of the State the ballot was conceived not as an exercise of a right but as the observance of a power that belonged to the State. Whereas democratic-socialism promoted class interest, even if that of the most numerous class, nationalism furthered the fortunes of the "National Corporation." Individualism, the creed of the Enlightenment, was an arbitrary and false assumption.

The very existence of the isolated individual is a pure fiction, which not only has no reflection in reality, but of which it is impossible to conceive even theoretically. One cannot imagine the human individual free from those very attributes . . . which presuppose the existence of society. The rights that belong to individuals can only be *positive* rights which the State confers on them, limiting itself. . . . The individual, therefore, far from being considered the possessor of any part whatsoever of the popular sovereignty, as if armed with an *imperium* against the State, is to be restored to his place as subject, from whence the democratic illusion tried to take him in order to elevate him to the rank of sovereign. He is subject, however, to no other master save the State which can confer on him, temporarily or permanently, public functions and even sovereign functions.[94]

As in the case of Ruggero Bonghi and other conservatives of the late nineteenth century who had faced a similar problem, corporatism was a solution to the problem of creating the organic nation, which was inconceivable as long as the real Italy remained estranged from the State. An elite was still unacceptable. But with the coming of the Libyan War, the situation changed radically. Maraviglia, joined by Coppola, committed himself to an out-and-out rejection of democracy. He declared his opposition to universal suffrage and went so far as to take up the doctrine of the political elite from which the Nationalists had shied away in favor of syndicalism. This clarification of political positions split the Association. Sighele and others[95] extolled the virtues of popular action as seen on the battlefields of Libya. The truth was that Giolitti's program had deprived the Nationalists of their one acceptable form of populism. The war had taken the wind from their sails, something the *Idea Nazionale* could not hide, and which its rival, the *Voce*, was pleased to point out.[96] By 1912 it seemed that the paper would follow the *Regno* into oblivion.

One way to avoid going under was to form a political alliance with conservatives in the Chamber, to enter the legal orbit of Giolitti's Italy. But the Nationalists were to cling to their lofty, isolated freedom from official contamination as long as possible. By December, 1912, when the Second Nationalist Congress met at Rome, the Association was badly split between the conservative wing, in which Coppola was emerging as a leader, and the democratic faction, championed by Sighele. Corradini, back from Africa where he had gone as a correspondent for the *Illustrazione Italiana* to observe war's virtues, told the assembled Nationalists: "We have finally the courage to declare ourselves antidemocratic." Not to be accused of denying the people, however, he added a reference favorable to that violent element of socialism, the doctrine of class war, which had escaped the stifling tactics of the reformist branch of the party operating from within the Chamber.[97]

Following the Rome Congress and the splitting off of the Sighelian Nationalists, the remnants of the Association, admittedly few in number, chose the only remaining alternative: that of entering the political lists. It was ridiculous to preach war and shun power, the *Idea Nazionale* wrote. It would have been more accurate to say that having no war to call for there was nothing else to do but give in to official Italy. Not surprisingly, some democratic elements remaining within the Association objected that organized politics would kill the movement which should seek power not in Parliament but in the "nation's energies," the people. Federzoni, the politician of nationalism, chose to run for the Chamber despite this. He was elected in 1913. The Nationalists came out for protective tariffs and apparently were given financial backing by some Italian industrialists.[98] From 1913 to the intervention in the World War, the *Idea Nazionale* made an open bid for clerical support in the hope of creating a strong conservative party. This was a shift of direction more apparent than real, reminiscent of the days of Leo XIII and Tosti. As long as Italian clerical groups had displayed their traditional hostility toward united Italy, the paper had attacked them as subversives, defending instead the strictly lay character of the State, in the manner of Silvio Spaventa. At the same time, however, the *Idea Nazionale* spoke of the valuable contribution of religious sentiment to the life of the healthy society. Their defense of the autonomy of the modern State was far less hostile to possible collaboration with Catholic political groups than was Spaventa's. The paper was careful to show itself opposed to anticlericalism. It attacked Freemasonry, which Coppola linked to international Jewry.[99]

It was apparent that the Nationalists would welcome clerical support if this could be had without compromising their own patriotism. The reaction of clerical journals to the Libyan War offered the Nationalists the chance to do just that. In spite of the Vatican's orders, the patriotic response to the war even among members of the Curia showed that Pius X's attempt to control the political direction of Italian Catholicism was failing. Intransigent Catholics, those customarily most hostile to Italy, deluded themselves into conceiving of the war as a new crusade against the Turks! The flag of Don John of Austria that flew at Lepanto was raised at Gaeta. The Pope sternly warned the flock against such false enthusiasm. Nonetheless, semi-official organs reflecting the views of the Catholic hierarchy succumbed to the "winds of Africa." The truth was that the bitterness had been largely removed from Church-State relations since the days of Leo XIII.[100]

In 1913 prominent Catholic laymen had agreed upon a policy of furnishing in the forthcoming elections Catholic votes for candidates who agreed, if elected, to vote against anticlerical measures in the Chamber of Deputies. The successful candidates would principally try to block legislation relating to divorce, abolishing of religious instruction in the public schools, disbanding of religious brotherhoods, or tending to hinder private education. The stipulations were mild enough to be acceptable to many liberal and moderate candidates. The agreement became known as the "Gentiloni Pact," taking its name from the Director of the Catholic Electoral Union. It was partly a reaction to signs that the Italian Socialist party had taken a bolder, more violent direction. The ranks of the party were growing. Its chief organ, the *Avanti!*, now edited by Mussolini, was on its way toward tripling its circulation. Many liberals were happy to accept Catholic backing at the polls in the face of this socialist revival, particularly since the price to be paid was that of opposing anticlericalism, in which they did not believe, rather than that of promoting clerical bills. Count Gentiloni's political activities were anything but clandestine. The *Corriere della Sera* of Milan had alerted its readers to the danger of clerical electioneering before the polls had opened. The existence of the pact, however, did not become public knowledge until after the elections were over. The *Idea Nazionale* reacted favorably, welcoming Catholic political action as long as it served national interests. The nationalist newspaper minimized all expressions of clerical opposition to the Guarantees, or in favor of the temporal power, as verbal formulae without concrete significance.[101]

The aim of the right wing of the Nationalist Association was to assume direction of a new conservative party, frankly bidding for Catholic support. Nationalism, unlike moribund Italian liberalism, the *Idea Nazionale* editorialized, posed no theoretical barrier to collaboration with Catholicism. Federzoni pronounced the Liberal party dead. Only nationalism could carry on the defense of Italy's political institutions, defending the national principle against the radical subversion of the Left and embracing all patriots within its ranks. It was admitted that Federzoni had been helped in his own campaign by the Gentiloni Pact. The idea was to capitalize on the Catholic Alliance, discrediting at the same time those liberals who attacked the Pact, thereby replacing the disorganized Liberal party with a disciplined conservative organization. The *Idea Nazionale* carefully avoided the Church-State question. Their aim was "the maximum idealization of the historical national principle," gathering together "all historical forces of the nation understood in its material and spiritual unity." This was language vague enough to skirt the Roman Question, or so the Nationalists hoped.

On the eve of the Third Congress at Milan, held in May, 1914, the *Idea Nazionale* made its play for leadership of the new rightist party. Federzoni and Maraviglia, speaking in behalf of the antidemocratic leadership of the *Idea Nazionale*, accepted Catholic action as compatible with a defense of the nation. All lingering expressions of clericalism emanating from prominent Catholic laymen were dismissed or glossed over. Those who spoke of

Catholic antipatriotism were playing into the hands of subversives. As for anticlericalism, it was an anachronism. This was too strong for some Nationalists, who continued to look upon the Vatican as a subversive force to be combated along with Italian Socialists, Republicans, and Radicals. Roberto Forges Davanzati, one of the founders of the Association, answered this by calling their view "Masonic." That insult widened the schism that had already shown up in the ranks. The liberal elements bolted at the Milan Congress just as the democratic faction had split off at the Rome Congress. The Nationalists now were left to fend as best they could. They made the final move in the direction of legal political action by dropping the term Association and calling themselves a party. Their constitution was modified to exclude members who were enrolled in other parties.[102]

The Nationalist party now abandoned its proletarian, populist approach. In general, as has been noted,[103] more emphasis was to be placed on the elite, and on the military leader during the ensuing period of Italian neutrality, 1914–15. This was already true of the *Idea Nazionale* at the time of Libya and the passage of universal suffrage. War and the political franchise had stolen the show from the anarchic reactionaries. It was also obvious that the few remaining within the *Idea Nazionale* circle could hardly do much else than play up the elite theory of national rejuvenation. Indicative of the waning of the Nationalists was Corradini's return to literature. He produced a play in 1913 dealing with the trials of the emigrant whose patriotism was fired by the news of Libya.[104] In any event, the flirtation with syndicalism was over as far as the Nationalist's journal was concerned. Alfredo Rocco and Coppola with their Corporate Nation doctrine assumed a more conspicuous place in its pages. Liberalism, democracy, individualism, and the philosophical heritage of the Enlightenment came under steady attack. In June, 1914, the anarchists and radical socialists, encouraged by Mussolini's proddings in the *Avanti!*, tried to exploit a general strike called by the Italian Confederation of Labor in protest against the sentencing of some soldiers who had opposed the Libyan War. In Romagna, where republicanism was still alive, the revolution was proclaimed. The Red Week that followed before the Salandra government, installed in March, could restore calm was greeted by the Naalists with an appeal for popular physical reaction to the revolutionaries. The *Idea Nazionale* did not hide its counterrevolutionary propaganda. This flurry has been compared to the work of the fascist *squadristi*.[105]

It is interesting to see the response of the so-called liberal wing of the

Nationalist party to the decision to abandon populism and enter the Chamber. On the eve of the Milan Congress the Liberal Nationalists came out with their own journal, the *Azione*, directed by Paolo Arcari and Alberto Caroncini. If one could believe its first editorial, the review was dedicated not to literary fancies, but to an "austere awareness of the unlimited responsibility connected with the written word." Although a cultural review, it was not to be precious or unrealistic. Rather an interest in everything "which ennobles, spreads and disciplines sports, elevating them to the service of military preparation, will not in fact prove foreign to our way of understanding and living literature; the way, that is, which the Greeks and Leopardi understood it." The editors concluded this dubious defense of linguistic clarity and political realism with a justification of the political sovereignty of the individual. Attacking Rocco, Caroncini pointed out that one could not be a Nationalist and deny liberalism, which was part and parcel of the Risorgimento. As might be expected, the *Azione,* while anti-Socialist, tended to praise the more vital elements represented by Mussolini. His attack on the Reformist wing of the Italian Socialist party was not "lacking in a certain greatness" that might prove salutary in its practical effects on Italian political life. The Liberal Nationalists were but taking up Corradini's earlier proletarian-nationalism, returning to the "fresh will of the country." The error of the Nationalist party, according to Arcari, was that it had abandoned the great hope of furthering the "entry of the people in national politics." The turn to French rightist theory was criticized on the familiar ground that whereas French Nationalists could deny the French Revolution and still have centuries of historical greatness to return to, in Italy to deny the revolution would mean denying the Risorgimento. From the First Congress at Florence, where the Nationalists had attacked parliamentarism and clerical intrigues, the movement had degenerated into a conservative parliamentary party allied with the clericals through the Gentiloni Pact. The ideals of the original movement, Luigi Valli wrote, had been corrupted by electioneering. One could "smell the odor of elections." [106]

As far as Giolittian Italy was concerned, the blatantly authoritarian wing of the Nationalist party had succumbed to the lure of power. It would have to do battle from within the Chamber, whereas the Liberal Nationalists kept alive the anarchic purity of the original Florentine movement by refusing to fight the infamous "Minister of corruption" on his own grounds. Once the Nationalist party had taken its stand, its future depended on clerical backing. Corradini ran in the by-elections of 1914.

Throwing aside his earlier neopaganism, he actively supported the Church's position on private education, the sanctity of the family, and the right of religious association. Even with active clerical support, he lost. But it was clear that the Nationalists' ultraconservative platform had attracted widespread sympathy among Catholic groups.[107]

All this was very much like Crispi and Bonghi, both of whom could indulge in anticlericalism and, when the opportunity offered, seek an alliance with the Blacks. The same Crispi who had accused the Vatican of working with France and Russia to stir up the Fasci had later attacked the anarchists on the ground that they knew neither "God nor Country." If the failure to reach a settlement of the Roman Question in the nineteenth century was a blessing to civil liberties, it was certainly no less so in the case of Corradini and the Nationalists.

What ruined the game this time was the Vatican's response to the World War. The Nationalists, not surprisingly, had switched from their customary defense of the Triple Alliance to the cause of the Entente. Once official Italy had proclaimed its neutrality, it would have been inconsistent to do anything else. Besides, the "halo of military glory" could not be won by sitting on the sidelines. All hinged on the attitude of Benedict XV, who succeeded Pius X in the summer of 1914. The *Idea Nazionale* withheld judgment[108] of the Pontiff. By September, 1914, however, the first oblique references to the Church's pro-Austrian neutralism appeared in its pages. On September 17 the *Idea Nazionale*'s editorial spoke of the antipatriotism not only of the Socialists' *Avanti!* but of the clerical *Unità Cattolica*. The Nationalists tried to play down the[109] importance of Benedict's first encyclical, *Ad beatissimi*, of November 1, 1914. As was to be expected, the Pope called for peace. If his reference to the "abnormal state" of the Holy See under the terms of the Guarantees was no more than a customary protest, the fact that the Pope had tied the question of Italian neutrality to the necessity of resolving the Roman Question[110] was another matter. It was impossible to uphold intervention and appeal to the Church for political backing. The *Civiltà Cattolica* refused to let the Nationalists obscure this essential contradiction. It underlined the connection between neutralism and the outrageous position of the Vatican, referring to the Guarantees as a "miserable illusion" of freedom. In January and February, 1915, the *Civiltà Cattolica* devoted two articles to the Nationalists in which it made clear that while it had seen in nationalism a generous refutation of old prejudices, free of the filth of socialism and radicalism, Nationalists were in error when they exalted the State. Catholics had joined its ranks, it was true. Now, however, the Nationalists were aligned with Masons, Socialists, and Liberals in their preaching of war, which, although not a sin in itself, was always a scourge to be justified only in defense of one's offended rights. Because of this, Catholics could praise Giolitti for his opposition to war as a human misfortune.[111]

This last remark was a bitter pill for the Nationalists. Giolitti, in a letter made public with his consent, had suggested that Italy might gain "much" through neutrality, whereas war was never to be counted a fortune. In the published version, the "much," felt to be too binding, was changed to "quite a bit" (*parecchio*). In the interventionist press, parecchio became a badge of dishonor. For the *Civiltà Cattolica* to defend the arch villain was to cut all ties with the Nationalists. The Jesuit journal also touched a very sore point by claiming that Bismarck had once warned Crispi that an Italian breach of the Triple Alliance would mean the restoration of the temporal power. Remarks of this sort seemed to raise the threat of diplomatic exploitation of the Roman Question, something many radicals and some noted conservatives — among them Sonnino — feared. Coming from Catholic sources, such threats worked to goad the interventionists to greater action while justifying war as a means of preserving the civil authority against its internal enemy. These allusions also paved the way for postwar interventionist literature describing the Alliance as a piece of Prussian blackmail from which Italy had been liberated by going into the war.[112] More important, these ill-conceived menaces, in addition to the Vatican's pronounced neutralism, were to have considerable influence on the deliberations of the Salandra government in 1914–15.

As far as the Nationalists were concerned, the stand of the Catholic press ruined their bid for leadership of a revived conservative party based on Church support. It was impossible to make intervention compatible with the Pope's stated opposition to the war. Appealing to the patriotism of Italian Catholics only made the Nationalists' problem more obvious. Portraying the war as a new crusade against the infidel[113] after Turkey entered was simply ludicrous. During the Libyan War, when enthusiasm had swept up many churchmen, such a ploy was at least clever. In 1914, however, the great majority of Catholics were neutralist. Coppola insisted that this was not true. How false his claims of clerical war sympathy were could be seen later when he deleted them from the collected edition of articles he had written during neutrality.[114]

Having become a political party with representation in the Chamber of Deputies, and having lost their liberal and democratic wings by embracing reactionary theories, the Nationalists were finished as a nucleus around which disgruntled anti-Giolittian intellectuals could gather. They had turned against that populism so essential to any successful nationalism, while becoming part of that "gray mass" over which Giolitti ruled. They now stressed the role of the elite. This was in keeping with the fact that the interventionists were a decided minority. However, it should be kept in mind that the Corporate Nation was still a response to the problem of escaping the conservative label. It was designed to avoid the taint of narrowness. But entering the Parliament and allying with the clericals was too much for the Liberal Nationalists to swallow. The Nationalists were forced by a logic greater even than their literary skill to defend Italy's institutions. How little their National Parliament had to do with that lifeless hall over which Giolitti presided is apparent from their fundamental opposition to anything that was done there. The Nationalists were basically subversives caught in their own imperialist snare. As neutrality dragged on, that subversive quality came to the surface. Corradini, speaking to an interventionist rally in Rome, threatened an antimonarchical revolution unless the war were proclaimed. So Mussolini's *Popolo d'Italia* reported it. The *Idea Nazionale* in its account took pains to soft-pedal the speech's revolutionary parts. Federzoni, a practical politician by then and a Deputy (whereas Corradini was still a journalist and second-rate author), knew too well that such remarks only played into the hands of the leftist interventionists. He scotched any talk of backing a revolution.[115] Mussolini was delighted at this since it proved the Nationalists to be conservatives, while he was the true revolutionary.[116] History would show, however, that the Nationalists' pseudo-parliamentary corporatism contained all the materials Mussolini would use to solve his own dilemma after he as well had been drawn into the halls of Montecitorio. The forging of fascist doctrine was not done, as some claim, in the postwar years; all its essentials, ideologically speaking, were elaborated between 1870 and 1915. The one new element, and it was crucial, was the war itself. Without it, parliamentary government in Italy had given every indication of being sufficiently rooted against the gales of intellectual ridicule. And it was to the common experience of the Great War that Mussolini was to turn when the familiar rhetoric of the old Nationalists proved impotent.[117]

Mussolini was fooling no one by claiming to be Italy's only true revolutionary. He had seen the impending collapse of the anarchic wing of the nationalist movement once the bid for official power had been made, and sought to avoid a similar fate for himself. He realized that the Socialist party's own involvement with the parliamentary majority would threaten his very existence as a political individualist. His belated break with the party's neutralist platform in 1914 and his attack on the Nationalists reflected a shrewd analysis of the crisis which the Tripoli invasion and universal suffrage had created among extremists of right and left. But the Nationalists, even those who had frankly entered the lists as candidates for the Chamber, also saw that they were caught in the mire of parliamentarianism. They, too, would use the coming of the Great War to recapture their earlier total opposition to legal Italy.

The period from the Tripoli War to the outbreak of European hostilities in 1914 was a turning point in the struggle between the leaders of bourgeois society and the journalistic purveyors of a literary, philosophical, and historical view of Italian destiny. By 1912 it seemed as if the artist-politicians had been obliged to come to terms with official Italy, to get a grip on reality. The evolution of the Nationalists from unimportant novelists to an informal association and then to a party within the Chamber was one sign of this coming down to earth. D'Annunzio's "exile" and his waning popularity at home, the failure of syndicalism, and the control that Turati continued to maintain over the violent elements of the Socialist party were also indicative of increased political stability within the constitutional framework. That a just balance between the claims of a cultural revival and the utilitarian demands of society was being maintained could also be seen in the decline of such iconoclastic, neoromantic reviews as the *Leonardo* and the *Regno* and the publication by the same young men of the more responsible *La Voce*. But in the over-all response among intellectuals to the Tripoli War and universal suffrage the loss of this precarious balance could already be felt, setting the stage for the parliamentary, diplomatic, and cultural revolution of 1915.

·8·

FROM AFRICA TO THE GREAT WAR

Tripoli: The Turning Point

It was the outbreak of the Great War that restored the original focus of the Nationalist party, allowing its leaders to recapture their dynamic aura as spokesmen for the true Italy that existed outside the halls of Parliament. The war, by rekindling all the irrational political embers that had been damped but not extinguished by the concrete achievements of the Postrisorgimento, paved the way for the crisis of 1915. There were signs even before Sarajevo, however, that dissident currents were becoming stronger; that the Giolittian program of 1911–12 had stimulated rather than depressed the imagination of Italy's "humanistic petty bourgeoisie." In order to see this clearly, one must examine the eventual reaction among Nationalists and radical southern reformers to the political and diplomatic events of the years between the African campaign and the proclamation of Italian neutrality in August, 1914.

As for the Nationalists, the taking of Tripoli seemed at first to be their undoing and Giolitti's triumph. In the wake of the Government's bold bid for the last scrap of North African territory not possessed by France and England, it was difficult to call for a vindication of Adowa, for a war that would justify Crispi's "martyrdom" to bourgeois Italy. But the limited African war served only to stimulate their appetites, the more so because they soon saw that anything but a complete rejection of the undertaking would mean their own death as a potential political power. When considering the logic the Nationalists were to use when they turned against the African campaign, it is important to keep in mind the diplomatic steps which led up to Italy's assertion of its claims on Libya. Reaction to the war was to be influenced and even prompted by the manner in which the Government handled the matter.

As early as December, 1910, during the Luzzatti ministry, which lasted from March, 1910, to March, 1911, Vienna and Berlin were informed that Italo-Turkish relations had worsened to the point of threatening war. In January, 1911, an incident involving a South American resident at

Tripoli, accused of promoting anti-Italian propaganda, resulted in a squabble between Turkish and Italian authorities at Tripoli. Italy threatened to take serious steps to counteract Turkish disregard for her rights. Giolitti again became premier in March, 1911. By July, Rome was preparing the ground for an eventual solution to the Tripoli question by notifying European governments that Turkish actions could lead to hostilities. Italy's allies, Germany and Austria-Hungary, however, were treated with great reserve, since their interests in the Ottoman Empire clashed with Italian designs on Tripoli. Nonetheless, Berlin and Vienna were made aware of the possibility of military action in the near future. According to Giolitti's account of his Government's handling of the war, maximum secrecy was demanded in order to prevent the Ottoman Empire from placing the issue before a European Congress, thereby frustrating a rapid solution and allowing time for a military buildup in Libya. Although the European powers sounded out in 1911 did not deny that Italy had legitimate complaints about Turkish hostility to her interests in Libya, there was a general fear that war might lead to complications, particularly in the Balkans, and in the Ottoman Empire generally. England was concerned over the embarrassment that annexation of Tripoli would pose to powers with Muslim subjects. Italy was cautioned from all sides against any extreme action.[1]

Giolitti appreciated the possibility of wider complications developing from an attack on Tripoli. He was especially concerned about the course of the Second Moroccan Crisis, realizing that Italy could not afford to be pinned down in North Africa if war should break out in Europe. When, on September 23, the preliminary accord was signed between Germany and France, he felt that the time was ripe. Italy delivered her ultimatum to Constantinople on September 28. It offered the Ottoman Empire the choice between surrender and war. Last-minute concessions were excluded. War was declared September 29. Military plans drawn up during that summer went into operation.

Because of the necessity for absolute secrecy, in order to forestall delaying tactics at Constantinople, neither of Italy's allies was given advance notice of the ultimatum.[2] Moreover, the Italian public was kept in the dark. Giolitti and the Italian foreign minister, Di San Giuliano, left Rome to give the impression of quiet on the diplomatic front. So successful was the ruse that the Italian press criticized them for what seemed inattention to pressing affairs. Apparently the Government's intentions were withheld even from members of the Cabinet until late in the game. Nitti, Minister of Agriculture, seems not to have been aware of the pending war as late as August — perhaps because he was known to be opposed to African imperialism.[3]

Whatever one may think of the ethics of imperialism, it is refreshing to read Giolitti's unvarnished statement of the reasons that demanded the occupation of Tripoli. Compared to the flood of literary heroics that greeted the invasion, his own justifications for it had at least the merit of being straightforward. Aside from a passing remark about intolerable conditions in Libya that Europe could not accept, he made no attempt to drape the action in either humanitarian or chauvinistic garb. Italy simply had to put an end to the ambiguous situation in Tripoli before that area went the way of Tunis — this, he wrote, was something Italians would not accept. It has been conceded that Italy was doing no more than cashing in on her diplomatic rights. These had been recognized by the powers and fortified by economic penetration.[4] Giolitti did just that, and in a way which makes him stand out as a realistic statesman among so many poets of toughness. His diplomatic maneuvers, however, deceived not only Europe but Italians as well. The war caught them off guard, and gave the appearance of being a poorly conceived impetuous act. In appraising the final Italian reaction to the war among Giolitti's critics, this fact must be kept in mind. Although Giolitti never thought of war as an alternative to domestic reforms, and in fact pointedly rejected that nationalist outlook, the diplomatic situation that cramped Italy's freedom of action served as a springboard for those who were to deprive the colonial venture of any patriotic, regenerative virtues. It was in the process of the devaluation of the Tripoli campaign, which followed hard upon a wave of bipartisan enthusiasm, that the ground was prepared for the explosions of anarchic and chauvinistic wrath during the 1914–15 crisis. It is also important to consider the enthusiasm for the war that preceded intentional downgrading of the effort. While much of it was colored by excessive optimism, it is impossible to discount the positive statements in favor of the parliamentary regime called forth by the landings in Tripolitania.

Those who had predicted a disaster, who expected to see Italy lapse into anarchy, were quickly disappointed. A decade of domestic progress on all fronts had prepared the nation for its first successful military venture since the defeat of 1896. In 1911 Trevelyan could write that Italy's edifice was as safe as any in Europe. Other foreign observers familiar with the recent course of Italian economy were not surprised, whatever their own countymen might think, by Italy's ability to bear the costs of the undertaking.[5] For some whose knowledge of Italian affairs was more intimate, the war was seen in relation to the "spiritual crisis" of the Postri-sorgimento. An English Italophile, Richard Bagot, likened the war to a "second unification." Significantly, he quoted D'Azeglio's epigram, "Now that Italy is made, one must make the Italians." Bagot then went on to write: "It is not too much to say that, in the short space of the last four months, Italy has passed through a period of reunification. It may even be said, indeed, that she has achieved what she had not completely attained in the course of the last forty years." Albert Dauzat, a prominent French student of Italian affairs, praised the planning and execution of the campaign, and added: "In general, the nation has regained confidence in herself. A breath of pride and victory has passed over her as in the days of the Risorgimento." To Sorel, the war represented "Italy's greatest day." [6]

Divisive forces at home were too feeble to detract from the first wave of enthusiasm with which Italians responded to the news. Papal attempts to dampen Catholic expressions of patriotism proved fruitless. On the radical side, many southern reformers conceded the advantages of a war they had opposed. More important, the Southern contadini, whom the anti-imperialists hoped to spare the sacrifices of war, did not lag behind their protectors in meeting the test. In regions where Garibaldi had had no support, Count Sforza later wrote, volunteers for the African army were numerous. [7] The days of the Palermo riots, of high desertions, of Verga's Sicilian fishermen for whom the Kingdom of Italy meant higher taxes and the deaths of young men at an unknown place called Lissa, were seemingly history.

One of the more significant testimonials of the general support for the war came from Mosca. The theoretician of the elite, by 1911 a seasoned politician, no longer could be counted among those who ridiculed the nation's institutions. His pessimistic forebodings on the eve of the war, written to inform Italians of the real difficulties that lay ahead, were dispelled by the generous popular rally in favor of the government's decision.

The nation's spirit has remained undaunted, ready for even greater sacrifices. . . . The country knows it can await the outcome of the undertaking without trepidation. It is the first time that all regions, all classes of the people have shown such unanimity of sentiment and opinion. During the struggle for the nation's Risorgimento, numerous examples of individual heroism and sacrifice undoubtedly were seen. But only certain sections of the population and certain cities participated in its most rugged tests. Garibaldi had to take note then that among his volunteers there were scarcely ever any contadini. . . . Today, on the other hand, hundreds and thousands of young men leave their families to go off to fight in Africa, without any vain swaggering and without regret. Today, the same sure resolve is seen in great cities and in remote villages, in the poor man's hut and the rich man's palazzo. And the few voices of discord, heard at the war's beginning, still remain isolated. The nation takes stock of the results achieved. When the poet, whose recent tomb we honor, wrote that now the Italians were made, he expressed an idea which all felt to be true.[8]

The *Idea Nazionale* seemed to join the general applause, even though it was for official Italy. It admonished its readers to fulfill their civic duty, to back up the Government, and to refrain from exaggerated journalistic coverage of the war. Nationalists were also encouraged to counteract the activities of "bad Italians," an obvious reference to the Socialist party, which had opposed the expedition. This new-found civic responsibility was not so deep as to let pass an opportunity for inciting popular reaction against subversives. On the other hand, the Nationalists praised those syndicalists who, like Arturo Labriola, defended the war as a national revolution against the hegemony of England and Germany.[9] This was early in the war, before possibility of a Catholic Alliance had materialized. The flirtation with syndicalism was still on. The rapid collapse of the general strike called by the Socialists to protest the invasion deprived the Nationalists of a chance to flex their muscles in defense of social order. The Government's leadership of the campaign, and the favorable national response, obliged the imperialists to let up in their fierce attack on Giolittian Italy. Following the votes in the Chamber of February 22 and 23, 1912, by which the decree of sovereignty over the North African colony was converted into law, Corradini wrote of the new spirit of concord embracing Parliament and the country, a "concord consecrated by the blood of its sons who are fighting in Africa." Even Giolitti was praised, but in a manner that could not have pleased the prosaic bureaucrat. Describing the popular ovation the Premier received as he left the Chamber after the vote, Corradini called it a "Roman triumph." Italy was united at last. "Today a historic period is closed. Today the faction is defeated and the patria triumphant. Today the once victorious demagogues are isolated. Today everything is renewed, liberated, redeemed, purified. The people, the government, the mob, youth, the King, Rome, and Italy are all redeemed." [10]

The imperialists spoke of their confidence in Italy's government.[11] Oriani and Turiello, the prophets of the coming baptism of fire which would fuse people and State, would seem to have been reduced to the role of Giolitti's precursors. But the style, the flourish, the journalistic ferocity accompanying much of this sudden praise was indicative of a stimulated thirst for greatness that the limited colonial war could not satisfy. The press inflated each skirmish to unlikely proportions. Letters from soldiers became a prominent feature in newspapers. The *Idea Nazionale* chided this indulgence in mock heroics, war being but an ordinary aspect of life. This pose did not prevent its own writers from extolling the undreamed-of virtues and sincerity illustrated by letters from the front, testimonials of "war's purifying aura. . . . Millions, blood, victims are a small matter compared to this work of self redemption." [12] Coppola raked the European Jewish press for its hostile attitude toward the Italian campaign. His own response was a hymn to Italy's liberation from the

shameful reign of vile pacifism, from the subversive camorra to which we have been obscenely enslaved since the last decades of the nineteenth century by timid, cynical, bourgeois individualism and idiotic humanitarian falsehoods. War and even more the will to war, is the only inexorable force which has ripened all humanity's fertile seeds, which has generated all civilizations and human morality. . . . The national conscience which Italy has lacked is being born from this feeling for struggle. . . . HINC INCIPIT NOVA ITALIA! [13]

D'Annunzio, from his debtor's exile, was not to be excluded from a literary banquet for which he had prepared the guest list prior to leaving his homeland. Having had no part in the imperialist campaign, and out of touch with Italian politics, he did his best to bone up on recent events, cribbing from Corradini's African dispatches and those letters from the troops so prominently displayed in Italian papers. From such sources he composed his own glorification of the war, the *Canzoni della gesta d'Oltremare*. These war songs, each designed to fill a page in his newspaper, were commissioned by Luigi Albertini, director of the great Milan daily, the *Corriere della Sera*. The war dragged on through the winter of 1911–12, limited in its operations by Austria-Hungary, which had placed the Adriatic out of bounds to the Italian fleet. D'Annunzio burst forth with a metrical challenge to Italy's ally, Franz Joseph, "the angel of the everlasting gallows," and his "two headed eagle which like the vulture vomits up the corpses' undigested flesh." Africa was but the preparation for greater conquests, these being the irredentist lands. At this, Albertini drew the line. The offensive lines were not published in his paper. The Giolitti government censored them out of the first published edition of the *Canzoni*. But they found their way into other papers;[14] soon they were known all over Italy. It was scarcely proof of civic virtue, to say nothing of soldierly patriotism, that a prominent publisher included in the second edition, in place of the missing lines, the notice that: "This song of the disappointed *patria* was mutilated by the policeman's hand, by order of Giovanni Giolitti, Esq., head of the Italian Government." [15]

Spiritually, D'Annunzio returned to Italy. Physically, he stayed abroad, perhaps sensing that the mood in Italy was not yet quite ready for his brand of subversion. Besides, an American publisher, Hearst, was offering more for his wares than he could get at home.[16] Other expatriated artist-politicians followed his lead and capitalized on the revival of literary violence in Italy. From Paris, the Franco-Italian Futurist leader, F. T Marinetti, penned a defense of the Libyan War, dedicating his work to

war the World's only hygiene and breeder of morals. Let the individual and the people be granted all freedoms save that of cowardice. Let it be proclaimed that the word ITALY reigns over the word LIBERTY. Let the tedious memory of Roman greatness be cancelled out by an Italian greatness a hundred times greater. Italy has for us today the power of a beautiful dreadnought. . . . Poets, painters, sculptors and musicians of Italy! Put down your verses, brushes, chisels and orchestras for the war's duration! The ruddy vacation of genius has begun! Today we can admire nothing save the formidable shrapnel symphonies and the mad sculpture wrought in the enemy's masses by our expert artillery.[17]

If the decline of D'Annunzio's popularity in Italy had been symptomatic of a lessening of journalistic ferocity in the years leading up to Tripoli, the return to favor of his and his disciples' rhetorical stimulus suggested a resurgence of a dangerous state of mind that dreamed of glories beyond Italy's real capabilities. It was not without significance that his attack on Franz Joseph came while the African War was in progress. As has been seen, those who saw the Triple Alliance as a vehicle for promoting a Great War rather than as a security pact were prone to take up either African imperialism or anti-Austrian irredentism. D'Annunzio's poetic challenge to Vienna recalled Carducci's glorification of Oberdan. It also foreshadowed the Nationalists' sudden shift from Africanism to irredentism, which was to come when the World War began and Italy remained neutral. The Libyan War also saw a revival of interest in Oriani, or rather it was at that time that the hitherto obscure writer was elevated to the rank of a neglected prophet. His works were reprinted in 1913. By 1915 he would have become the solitary hero of the Postrisorgimento. The fact — which Croce pointed out[18] — that by the time of his death in 1909 Oriani had himself gone a long way toward accepting the regime of official Italy and had muted his earlier opposition to the political arrangement of the Postrisorgimento was ignored by the anti-Giolittian intellectuals and occasional politicians who rifled Oriani's works for verbal weapons in their war against the parliamentary regime. It was true, however, that Oriani had laid out a vast diplomatic program for Italian redemption, and that

it included Africa and irredentism. Before Tripoli was secured, the cry
for war with Austria was being taken up, in total disregard of the realities
of diplomacy. This literary warmongering set the stage for the interventionist rally of 1914–15.

If the Nationalists were momentarily caught off guard by the Tripoli
invasion they had always recommended, more significant was the manner
in which the campaign was received by Italian publicists of the Southern
Question. While the imperialist *Idea Nazionale* had avoided mentioning
the problems of the Mezzogiorno, looking to the Mediterranean for answers to domestic ills, the men who had continued the work of the southern
reformers of the 1890's placed particular stress on the democratic and
socialist potential associated with a revitalization of the South. Because of
this, they had opposed imperialism from the start, not only as a betrayal
of the real needs of the Italian people, but as a frankly authoritarian movement. Their response to the war when it came, however, revealed a
fundamental point of agreement with their enemies. Both detested the
bureaucratic regime and its acknowledged master Giolitti. Where the Nationalists would have destroyed parliamentary inefficiency by substituting
a regime capable of mounting a successful war, the radicals would use the
rising of the contadini, federalism, and socialism to uproot what they continued to look upon as a parliamentary dictatorship. The alliances between
independent Socialists, Republicans, and Democrats who expressed the
hopes of the South, and Nationalists, who sought to play down any internal
weakness, was to be one of the most obvious contradictions of the months
of Italian neutrality when both camps demanded war. This unholy union
had begun to take shape by 1912.

Prior to the Libyan War, the *Voce*, directed by Giuseppe Prezzolini,
had opposed the demands of the nationalist-imperialist press for a return
to Africa. This was consistent with the campaign for the reclamation of
the Mezzogiorno in which the *Voce* played a prominent role. In an editorial of May 18, 1911, four months before the Italian government began
the Tripoli campaign, the *Voce* took the imperialist writers of *Idea Nazionale* to task for ignoring internal problems, for staking all on the mirage
of colonial adventure. Citing reports of the Jewish Territorial Organization, a group then investigating possible sites for a future Jewish homeland,
the Florentine review denied that Tripoli was of any real economic value.
Love of the patria meant a desire to spare Italy disastrous and shameful
adventures the *Voce* wrote, begging the Nationalists to reflect on what
they were doing. A writer familiar with the motives of the Jewish Terri-

torial Organization testified to the credibility of its negative report on Tripoli.[19] Salvemini, while making it clear that he did not reject a future move in Africa, pointed out that an attack on the Ottoman Empire would strengthen Austria's hand, giving her the chance to move in the Balkans toward Salonica. After the war was on, Salvemini continued to demolish the Nationalists' arguments as to the economic advantages to be won, questioning the authenticity of recently published correspondence between Crispi and the explorer Gerhard Rohlfs that painted a glowing picture of Tripoli's material prospects.[20]

But there was even in the opposition to the war a suggestive note that foreshadows the eventual reaction to it. The *Voce* doubted whether a country so badly organized could pretend to organize others. While opposing the imperialist writers of the *Idea Nazionale*, Prezzolini also praised them for focusing attention on Italian foreign policy, which had been in a state of baseness and abjection since the days of Crispi. It was the undeniable lack of organization, the diffidence of the people for the State, that made war impossible. Armaments alone without discipline were insufficient, the *Voce*'s editor wrote. A serious foreign policy would be possible once Italy was endowed with the ethical and economic values to back up her claims. Less than a month before the embarkation of Italian troops for North Africa, Salvemini cited riots in a southern commune as indicative of the persistent lack of national cohesion. The peasantry, he said, attributed an outbreak of cholera to drugs distributed by the Government — drugs intended, according to Salvemini, to keep down the birth rate. The sense of unity that Italy lacked could not be achieved by any magical action, but only by slow progress and political activity.[21] The *Voce* maintained its opposition to the imperialist idea to the very eve of the war.[22] But it was also clear that a desire to avoid the test rested in part on a sense of national frustration that the anti-Africanists shared with the Nationalists.

When the war for Tripoli came, this hidden longing for a challenge that would find Italy united weakened the barrier between the Africanists and the southern reformers of the left. Salvemini blamed the war on an imperialist press and on the do-nothing policy of the Socialist party, which had placed too great trust in Giolitti. He conceded, however, that the country was behind it, including a good part of the proletariat. Now that it had come, he wrote, it must be exploited for the good there might be in it. However sterile from a purely economic standpoint, war could benefit Italy by giving her a greater sense of discipline, a greater seriousness of intent. Providing that no international complications ensued, it had its value. It was unjust morally, and damaging to the economy. But it could render Italy the service of giving Italians an awareness of their organizational abilities and discipline.[23] Napoleone Colajanni, who had also opposed the war, granted that it had a moral as well as political value. Morally it demonstrated the discipline and organization of the Italian people. Politically it was the "baptism and confirmation of Italian unity." Giustino Fortunato forgot his recent pessimism. It was clear to him that fifty years of the nation's existence had not passed in vain. If there was "something new, beautiful, and promising in Italy, then long live the war." He recalled his days in the army during Crispi's first ministry. There was the famous war scare, talk of a French invasion. Fortunato had feared for Italy's safety; but when he had talked to the other soldiers, they answered that Italy was Piedmont, and they were Neapolitans. Now all that was changed. He had seen the peasants of the Basilicata and Puglia give their common recognition to being Italians. This filled him with joy.[24]

The Socialist party's opposition to the war had little effect. Arturo Labriola had predicted as much. The party, he wrote, was a long way from manning the barricades to stop the embarkation of troops for Africa. He also noted a new longing for heroism [25] in the air. This did not take long to reveal itself. The literary reaction to the Libyan War produced effusions of D'Annunzian rhetoric that would not be seen again until the "Radiant May" of 1915. Lachrymose poetry such as Ada Negri's "The Mother," heroic dispatches from the front, volumes of letters from the troops, many written to order, flooded Italy [26] and suggested all too well the revolutionary character of war for an untried country. The poet Giovanni Pascoli, imbued with a humanitarian and romantic socialistic sentiment, coined the phrase that expressed this feeling: "The great proletariat has moved." As far as the socialist hierarchy was concerned, it failed to check the popular backing for the military venture that now invaded the party's own ranks. At the very top, two of its leaders, Leonida Bissolati and Ivanoe Bonomi, were expelled for having defended the war. Lesser figures such as Giuseppe De Felice, who had gone to prison in 1893 for his part in organizing the revolt of the Sicilian Fasci, spoke out at the Socialist Party Congress of Reggio Emilia that saw the expulsion of the old men of the party. He declared that he would call for revolution if the Government recognized the local independence of Tripoli, revolution not against war but against the Italian government. De Felice now spoke of the war as a means of solving the problems of the South.[27] Scipio Sighele, a federalist who had taken part in the earlier discussion of the southern problem, remarked that this was a new Italy, its people vibrant with enthusiasm, no longer skeptical of themselves, repossessed by the great passion that motivated the heroes of 1848, 1859, and 1866.[28] The romance that Sighele and De Felice had found in the bandit was transferred to war.

Salvemini gave his assent to this view of the moral values of the war. So great was his distaste for Giolitti's Italy, even with universal suffrage, that he wrote — or permitted to be included in his review — an editorial not unfavorable to the program of the Nationalists. Admitting that the Nationalists were antidemocratic and antiproletarian whatever they might claim to the contrary, even this reactionary movement would be an "opportune and beneficial revivifier of our national energies, if we could see in it a real cure for the insincerity and baseness of public life; if it truly instilled a sharper and more active sense of duty . . . ; if love of country and national sentiment meant for the Nationalists a serious awareness and examination of our great, frightening domestic problems and of the problem of foreign expansion and a desire for a profound reform of our character and institutions."[29] When Filippo Turati, titular head of the Italian Socialist party, expressed his hope that the war would not make the reclamation of the Mezzogiorno more difficult, Salvemini's journal editorially suggested that it was a bit late for the party to be worried about the South. Then followed a remark which in retrospect can only seem ironic, in the light of Salvemini's later opposition to Mussolini's Italy: "Let us hope that Turati and his followers grasp that Italy is not reduced to the cathedral square at Milan or to that great barracks, Montecitorio."[30]

The reception of the Libyan War by democratic and independent socialist advocates of southern redemption points up the bond between war and revolution. The libertarian solution to the problem of welding the nation together rested on the premise of a people's movement. War might furnish this. In focusing attention on the Southern Question and its political significance, one finds the best expression of the dilemma of real versus official Italy. In large measure, the critique of united Italy had originated in the South among the lower middle class intellectuals; there was no factory proletariat, while the peasantry was really apolitical. A new Italy was the goal, breaking the bonds of excessive administrative centrality, giving the nation that "baptism of social morality without which every revolution is a lie, and, after a certain period, is condemned to die." So wrote the editors of the Republican Neapolitan newspaper *Il Popolo d'Italia* in 1860. That the paper owed its ideas to Pisacane[31] illustrates the

significance of the failure of his "people's revolution" of 1857. The idea
that the revolution had been betrayed by a "royal conquest" persisted
among leftist critics of the Postrisorgimento. In 1911–12 the revolutionary
impetus was directed into the path of a redeeming war not only by the
extreme conservatives but by the southern populists. We shall see, however, that this war failed to satisfy the need for action and unity that was
shared by the political extremes; that it left Giolitti and the parliamentary
regime no less despised by their critics than before.

From Tripoli to Sarajevo

Between this sudden rash of enthusiastic reportage on the war and
the Government's extremely sober, rational aims there was an obvious
difference of outlook, which was not long in coming to the surface. Giolitti recognized the dangers inherent in undue expectations, and doubtless
appreciated that he could not really count for long on the sort of rhetoric
his modest venture had inspired. In October, 1911, speaking in Turin at
the banquet celebrating the fiftieth anniversary of the foundation of the
nation, he tried to promote a realistic awareness of Italy's prospects that
the war seemed to have obscured. His speech, by emphasizing domestic
problems, also endeavored to discourage a frantic search for answers to
domestic problems in foreign fields. Giolitti paid tribute to Italian progress
over a century, underlining the fact that material advances had been made
under regimes that respected political liberty. The Premier seemed to
pass over the events in Africa altogether. Italy, he said, was dedicated to
a policy of loyalty to her alliances and friendship with all countries. "We
consider peace and complete accord with all powers," he went on, "the
greatest benefit to Italy, which has many domestic problems to resolve.
But we cannot sacrifice, for love of a quiet life, either the country's vital
interests or its national dignity. The Government is certain that these aims
correspond not only to the interests but to the feelings of the Italian
people." As if in answer to the Nationalists, Giolitti defended the vitality
of democracy against those who would make it synonymous with weakness. On foreign policy, he made the following observations:

Foreign policy, unlike domestic policy, can not depend entirely on the will
of the government and of Parliament. Rather, of absolute necessity, it must
take into consideration events and situations which it is not in our power
to modify nor sometimes even to accelerate or retard. There are facts which
impose themselves as if truly fated by history from which a people can not
escape without compromising irreparably its future. In such moments, it is
the government's duty to assume complete responsibility, since hesitation or

delay can mark the beginning of political decadence, producing consequences which the people will deplore for many years, and sometimes for centuries.

The Ministry is conscious of all the responsibilities it has assumed, engaging the country in war. But it has faced them confidently, being convinced that in the face of persistent, systematic hostility which for years hindered our every economic action in Tripolitania, and [in the face] of continuous provocations by the Turkish Government, any hesitation or delay would have both compromised the country's honor and its political and economic position.

We will await calmly the judgment of Parliament and of the Country. In the meantime, we send to our army and navy a greeting which testifies to the complete confidence which the Italian people places in them.

Foreign policy can not give rise to party divisions because [it is] dominated by a single thought, which unites us all: that of the *patria*.

But strong peoples must never allow preoccupations over foreign policy to suspend or disturb in any way their march toward a higher degree of civility and their serene examination of questions of domestic policy. Foreign policy must not, in any way, either directly or indirectly, influence domestic policy, save from the point of view of constituting a spur to more rapid progress in order to assure Italy an ever higher place in accordance with the concepts of civilized nations.

Let us now examine what must be the direction of our domestic policy . . .[32]

The address was devoted to Italy's major internal problems. It was a stylistic as well as a political challenge to the rhetoricians of power.

The text, with its reference to diplomatic and historical forces over which Italy had no control, robbed the Government of the momentary support, if not affections, of the intellectuals. It signaled the beginning of a steady devaluation of the war's significance as an act of national fusion and revolutionary drive. Again, as in the occupation of Rome, it appeared that Italy had acted not willfully, dynamically, but in response to events set in motion by the Great Powers. Simultaneously with what became a studied attempt to label Tripoli an "official" war, the vitality and patriotism of the people, which would make the "real" war of the future, were exalted by the anti-Giolittian press. More sinister was the rise of lurid D'Annunzian prose, which prepared the cultural climate for the frenzies to come during the period of Italian neutrality.

The *Idea Nazionale*, commenting on the Turin speech, accused Giolitti of a studied attempt to reduce the war to the most modest proportions. "We do not believe," the paper editorialized, "that he has succeeded in deadening and suppressing all enthusiasm, in restoring to mind the pessimism of old; because at the same time that the Honorable Giolitti was reading his speech, the cannon's round mouth was speaking with quite another eloquence, an exciting eloquence." The speech was dubbed "the most remarkable document of political bad faith in recent Italian history." [33] Something must be said about the validity of the arguments of those who criticized Giolitti's management of the Tripoli War. Nationalists, as would be expected of them, quickly reverted to their old position of attacking the regime on principle. But the *Idea Nazionale* was still a small paper, of limited circulation. One of the chief sources of the anti-Giolittian crusade, however, was the very influential *Corriere della Sera* and its director, Luigi Albertini. Albertini years later was to write a detailed history of the period associated with Giolitti's political pre-eminence. It subjects the Libyan War to the same sort of criticism that was prevalent at the time in his paper as well as in the *Idea Nazionale*. According to Albertini the Government, in mounting the invasion, acted precipitously and failed particularly to take account of the degree of Arab resistance to Italy's forces. Giolitti has stated that the Government, according to information received from the Italian consul at Tripoli, did not calculate on a general or even partial Arab defection, which would have weakened the Turkish position. This has been questioned, not only by Albertini, but in more recent works [34] sharing Albertini's negative view of Giolitti's role in recent Italian history. But if it were true that the Government underestimated the difficulties that lay ahead, that optimism certainly does not square with Giolitti's Turin speech, which, to the contrary, tried to check any unrealistic expectations. Arab resistance proved tenacious, beginning at the battle of Sciara Sciat of October 23, 1911, which cost four hundred Italian casualties. The Turin speech, however, was delivered before that engagement, on October 7. It is not the speech of an overconfident statesman nor of one who wishes to capitalize on war's popularity to secure his own position. In the Chamber, defending himself against charges of having foreseen a cheap victory, Giolitti stated that he had always rejected the opinions of those who told him it would be an easy undertaking. To advisers who predicted a quick war he had replied that it would take at least 40,000 men to begin the campaign. [35]

The Arab campaign in the hinterland, after the fall of Tripoli and Tobruk, dragged on until 1916, by which date Giolitti had been out of office for two years. In the end, invasion and pacification required between 80,000 and 100,000 men. This was anything but a smashing victory of the sort the imperialists, and not Giolitti, had led the public to expect. Giolitti had explained the over-all strategy to the Chamber as one of pacification of the hinterland, rather than a coastal operation, in order to assure that the area could be held in the future without constant Italian military reinforcements. His observation that prolonged guerrilla resistance was a general feature of colonial wars, of which Tripoli was no exception,[36] was certainly well taken. Moreover, the diplomatic front was most unfavorable to rapid victory. The Powers had secured Italy's assurance that, to the best of her ability, operations would be localized in order to minimize the chance of wider disturbances in the Ottoman Empire. In keeping with this promise, the Italian government refused to give any aid to insurrectional movements in Albania, and cautioned King Nicholas of Montenegro against unsettling the Balkan situation. On September 29, however, the Italian navy attacked a nest of Turkish destroyers on the Albanian coast. However, Aerenthal, Austrian foreign minister, warned that a repetition of military action in that sphere could lead to grave consequences. Italy then agreed to abandon any action in the Adriatic in return for Austria's backing against third powers that might press for similar neutralization of critical areas.[37] But the Turkish destroyers, a menace to Italian communications with North Africa, had been put out of action.

Another target of anti-Giolittian writers was Italy's proclamation, by the royal decree of November 4, 1911, of absolute sovereignty over the new colony. The proclamation was made in order to cut short maneuvers by the Porte designed to preserve a nominal sovereignty for the Sultan. The Porte had offered to discuss a settlement even before military operations had begun. Germany and Austria-Hungary suggested a solution similar to that which had been applied to Bosnia in 1878. The Porte accepted this idea on principle. France, on the other side, tried to promote mediation by the Entente in the hope of beating the Central Powers to the punch. This was blocked by Sir Edward Grey, who felt that a basis for mediation did not yet exist. In substance, the chief European powers having interests in the Ottoman Empire did not wish their rivals to steal a march at Constantinople by putting themselves forward as mediators. At the same time, it was not desirable to lose Italy's friendship by appearing to take up the Turkish cause. Had the Powers been able at an early date to agree to mediation on the basis of nominal Turkish sovereignty, it is doubtful whether Italy could have avoided that solution. Apparently Berlin hoped to deceive Italy into believing that agreement did exist by informing Rome that London was ready to accept the principle of nominal sovereignty. Sir Edward Grey, however, when asked about this by

Imperiali, the Italian ambassador at London, said he had refused pressures for mediation that did not have as their basis Italy's absolute sovereignty.

Di San Giuliano, the Italian foreign minister, in reply to the suggestion of a settlement along the lines of 1878, answered that although he was not personally opposed, it was in the general interest to liquidate the Tripoli question once and for all, and that Italian public opinion was increasingly favorable to annexation pure and simple.[38] Albertini has made much of the fact that Di San Giuliano did not agree with Giolitti's decision to proclaim Italy's sovereignty, insinuating that the latter tried to conceal this difference of opinion in order to escape personal responsibility for a policy which, according to Albertini, proved a blunder. He cites as proof of Di San Giuliano's position a dispatch sent to Berlin by Gottlieb Jagow, German ambassador at Rome, in which the foreign minister is reported to have been agreeable to Turkish nominal sovereignty. Di San Giuliano had also said he felt Giolitti would share this view. Two days later, on October 5, 1911, it was clear that the Italian government was in fact opposed to such a proposal. Giolitti, in his memoirs, mentions no disagreement, saying no more than that he conferred with Di San Giuliano before Italy rejected the idea of nominal sovereignty.[39] Prior to the war, De San Giuliano, in unofficial talks, apparently did mention the possibility of a solution such as had been applied to Bosnia. Hence, it is possible that some disagreement existed, and that Giolitti overruled his foreign minister. It was Giolitti, in the opinion of Albertini, who cut the Gordian knot, placing the Powers before a *fait accompli*. According to the *Corriere*'s chief, he should have listened to his foreign minister. Giolitti later defended the decree of sovereignty, which he admits was much criticized at the time. But he makes no attempt to escape his full responsibility as head of the Government by sharing the burden of the decision with others.[40] Albertini's charge that a conflict within the Cabinet was concealed makes little sense in the light of Giolitti's frank acceptance of any possible blame. The accusation must be seen in the light of the noted journalist's hatred of Giolitti, which colors all his work.

Albertini's strained attempt to blacken Giolitti's reputation by harping on a minor as well as debatable[41] point is significant as a reflection of an attitude which was current at the time of these events, and which is related to the rapid collapse of the Italian government's prestige. The Premier, Albertini claims, not only made the wrong decision, but did so under pressure from rising public demand for annexation. Prominent among those who called for annexation was the *Corriere della Sera*'s foreign affairs analyst, Andrea Torre. Thus, Albertini takes credit for the decree of sovereignty, reducing the Government to the status of a supine follower of the war party rather than a great leader. How is it possible, however, for Albertini to claim the decree was a stupid move and at the same time admit that his own paper demanded annexation? This is done by affirming that Giolitti knew the terms of the Triple Alliance, especially Article Seven respecting the status quo in the Balkans, as well as Italy's secret commitments not to enlarge the theater of war. Under these circumstances the decree of sovereignty stiffened Turkish resistance, prolonging the war under the most adverse conditions .Had the public known the facts, Albertini implies, it would have seen the folly of the proclamation of sovereignty.

Giolitti's critics can have their cake and eat it too. The Tripoli War is shorn of any glory save that of the popular manifestations of patriotism — including, one must assume, D'Annunzio's poetry. This welling up of enthusiasm was supposedly wasted by the bungling of official Italy. Giolitti unquestionably took public opinion into consideration. Had he not, he would have been rash indeed. That he was correct in his assumption Italy was ready for the move is clear from the positive response at the outset of the war. As for Albertini's ex post facto critique of the diplomatic situation that cautioned against annexation, is it really sound? It took little imagination, and none whatever for a correspondent as knowledgeable as Torre, to recognize that Europe would not permit Italy to enlarge the scope of her military operations. Yet the *Corriere della Sera* was calling for wider action, into European Turkey.[42] As a matter of fact, the Italian government in the end was forced to threaten just that in order to get the Porte to come to terms, to compel the European diplomats to put pressure on Constantinople for fear of seeing the war spread to the Continent. But for the Milan paper to play up D'Annunzio's Canzoni with their anti-Austrian incitements was an act of journalistic folly. For Giolitti to harken to that "voice from the people" would have led to disaster. On the other hand, had the Italian government accepted anything less than absolute sovereignty, the uproar from the war party press is not hard to imagine. And Italy might well have been forced to accept less had there been an agreement among the Powers. On this score, it should be mentioned that Giolitti was induced to put an end to the Porte's maneuvering partly because of information received that the Kaiser had obtained European backing for the Turkish request that the whole affair be submitted to a Congress. As for native resistance, Giolitti defended the proclamation of sovereignty on the ground that any other solution would have diminished Italy's authority over the Arab population.[43]

The *Idea Nazionale* admitted that Italy's proclamation of sovereignty was proper, but at the same time sought to divest it of any heroic character, calling it wordy and excessively diplomatic. The nation should drive ahead and not limit her military action. On the eve of the reopening of Parliament, the Nationalists were at work undermining confidence in the institution, pointing out the great disparity between the national spirit and its legal representation. Compared to the popular will, the Chamber was a miserable affair.[44] Giolitti, presenting the decree of sovereignty for the Chamber's approval in February, 1912, explained the motives behind the war. He made it clear that he had little enthusiasm for it. The enterprise was decided in the cold light of reason, weighing the advantages against the disadvantages. Since Italy refused to allow others to occupy Tripoli, he said, it was better to do it herself rather than wait until possible infringements of her rights brought the country into conflict with another power.[45] The Chamber, with the exception of the Socialists, voted to make the decree law. But the *Idea Nazionale* refused to accept this as a sign that Parliament was in any way rejuvenated. In voting the decree of sovereignty, the Deputies had only bowed to the "invincible will of the nation." During the parliamentary recess, back in their constituencies "far from the petty milieu of Montecitorio, they felt that imperious will and came to Rome to vote yes in order to obey it. It was the provinces, inexorable fount of pure spiritual energies, which at Rome proclaimed the necessity of Italy's new greatness."[46]

On April 18, 1912, Italian destroyers penetrated the Dardanelles in what proved to be a fruitless attempt to cripple parts of the Turkish fleet at their base of operations. In May, Rhodes and nearby islands were occupied in the hope of establishing a point from which to cut Turkish shipping lanes to North Africa. Austria-Hungary had given her consent to a temporary occupation of these islands. Italy then extended the occupation to the whole Dodecanese. Vienna reacted promptly. Italy gave verbal assurances that the islands would be restored to Turkey, and Austria made it known that should they be kept, claims for compensation under the terms of the Triple Alliance could be put forth. In July and August, Italy and Turkey discussed peace terms. Giolitti insisted on nothing less than sovereignty over all of Libya — and here Di San Giuliano was not in agreement, as Giolitti's *Memoirs* make quite clear. The Foreign Minister would have accepted the Turkish suggestion that Italian claims be limited to the coast. The Turkish representatives, encouraged by the German ambassador at Constantinople, refused to accept the Italian position as a basis for negotiations. Giolitti had good reason to believe, however, that Turkey wanted peace, but that no government would assume the responsibility of losing Libya. In order to force concessions the Italian spokesmen were instructed to make additional demands in the hope that Turkey would then bargain on acceptable terms. This tack failed. Turkey refused to agree to full Italian sovereignty. Italy threatened to enlarge the war, into Asia Minor and Albania if necessary. Even this proved useless. Rome then warned the Powers that the talks would be broken off if Turkey continued to stall, and that Italy would carry the war to the most vital parts of the Ottoman Empire. Greater pressure from European capitals to induce the Turks to give in still failed to produce results. But when the First Balkan War broke out, Rome informed European capitals that precise plans for Italian action in European Turkey were being drawn up.[47] The outbreak of hostilities in the Balkans and increased diplomatic pressure finally induced the Turkish government to give way. The autonomy of Libya was recognized by Constantinople. Italy then proclaimed annexation, with amnesty for the Arabs and religious liberty for the inhabitants.

The Treaty of Lausanne was signed October 18, 1912. Italy allowed the Sultan to keep his spiritual authority and agreed to make a flat payment to cover that portion of the Turkish debt resulting from the loss of Libyan revenues. The *Idea Nazionale* called the treaty cold, joyless, and unworthy of the national spirit. News from the Balkans, on the other hand, inspired Futuristic raptures about the beauties of war, as well as demands that Italy now shift her attention to a defense of Italian rights in the Balkans against possible moves by Austria-Hungary.[48] No sooner was Libya won, if not pacified, than the African imperialists were looking for fresh fields of action. The *Corriere della Sera* took a more realistic view of the treaty. Albertini had covered the peace talks personally. He conceded that Turkish diplomatic maneuvers were insuperable. He later took pains to point out that his paper had defended the treaty and therefore had had no part in the socialist and chauvinist devaluation of the Tripoli expedition. This protestation is in itself an admission that the downgrading of the war was exploited as a political weapon by Italian extremists, and that Albertini recognized the dangers implicit in their attempt to deprive the Government of its laurels. But the full page the *Corriere* of November 28,

1912, devoted to the war certainly did nothing to counteract the Nationalists' attacks on the Government. The Milan paper insisted that the war
was a response to public demand, and that Italy's diplomatic isolation
was proof that the nation counted for little in the field of international
politics.[49]

Corradini made use of the *Corriere*'s negative view of the African
venture and of the Giolitti government's direction of it. He then went on
to deny that there had been a war at all! It was, he wrote, a "peaceful
war." Far more insidious than this absurdity was his comparison of Libya
with Adowa. The reasons for the moral failure of the 1911 expedition lay
in the spirit of Adowa that still hung over official Italy. Crispi's nephew
and biographer, T. Palamenghi-Crispi, whom we have met in the days
of the Bank Scandals, followed suit with a biography of Giolitti which,
besides raking up the Bank of Rome, assured the reader that Crispi's
successors had not fulfilled his African mission.[50] Federzoni made this
the theme of his maiden speech in the Chamber. "The Italo-Turkish
War," he said, "undeniably has left something unfulfilled as far as the
country's sense of satisfaction is concerned. . . . The material, concrete
result aimed at has been achieved. But spiritually the Nation remains
disappointed. Once again, we have felt ourselves persecuted by a name
and a memory, the name and memory of Adowa." During the period of
Italian neutrality, the Nationalists having become strenuous advocates
of intervention on the side of the Entente, the Libyan War, once so popular, but become simply "wretched." The same sort of parliamentary ineptitude that had been responsible for the disgraceful vilification of Crispi
after Adowa [51] had ruined the expedition of 1911.

That Tripoli should call forth Crispi's ghost was testimony to the intensity of dissatisfaction among intellectuals that the admitted material
progress of the Postrisorgimento could not appease. Other ghosts soon
appeared to challenge the Government, which by March, 1914, was in
the hands of Salandra. Imitating their grandfather's gesture of 1870,
Bruno and Costante Garibaldi served in France, in defiance of a Government order against volunteers. Both died in battle. In January, 1915,
Bruno's body was brought back to Rome. Memorial ceremonies served
as a platform from which to attack neutrality, the prolongation of which
was making the interventionists increasingly uneasy about the Salandra
regime. Federzoni, who had once cautioned Corradini not to play into
the hands of the radical interventionists, raised the specter of revolution
should Italy refuse to fight. According to Federzoni, the persistence of

revolutionary elements following 1860, the current of dissatisfaction with the monarchy, was small; but it did exist, and gave rise to a dangerous individualism, whereas Italy needed discipline. The Government must, therefore, possess a prestige greater than the revolutionary impetus that carried over into the nation's unitarian phase. "Italy," Federzoni wrote, "has awaited since 1866 her truly national war, in order to feel unified at last, renewed by the unanimous action and identical sacrifice of all her sons. Today, while Italy still wavers before the necessity imposed by history, the name of Garibaldi, resanctified by blood, rises again to warn her that she will not be able to defeat the revolution save by fighting and winning her national war."[52] This was essentially Oriani's version of Italian history, brought up to date.

The ultraconservative Nationalists, defenders of class solidarity, and the monarchy, having bid in vain for clerical support, took up the radical interventionists' cry of "war or revolution" in order to intimidate the King and his ministers. In Milan, Mussolini capitalized on the deaths of the Garibaldi brothers to proclaim the unity of France and Italy, joined by blood and the "test of fire." The *Corriere della Sera* saluted the fallen Italians with a similar reference to the "baptism of fire." Its correspondent in France, Luigi Barzini, sent back an overblown literary series of articles on the Italian voluntters entitled "Italian Blood in the Forest."[53] Jean Carrère, Rome correspondent of the *Temps*, saw the advantages of pro-French sentiment the deaths had stimulated. He wrote to Ricciotti Garibaldi, father of the fallen volunteers: "In the crucible where tomorrow's civilization is being made, Italian blood spilled on the battlefield of the Argonne will act as a mystical and irresistible ferment."[54] Coppola also used the by then hackneyed simile. Italy, he wrote, must finish the work of the Risorgimento by war, the "only fiery crucible in which the national psirit receives its temper . . . and is made sublime, purified by the suffering of sacrifice."[55] By May, 1915, during the brief crisis of the Salandra ministry when the threat of a new Giolittian cabinet appeared, the *Idea Nazionale* joined Mussolini's *Popolo d'Italia* in calling for intervention or revolution, inciting the public to violence against the neutralists, headed by Giolitti, "enemy of the patria," who had risen to power from the ruins of Adowa.[56]

The subversive temper of extreme Italian conservatism reappeared. The Nationalist party, which had lost its virtue by being drawn into the quagmire of politics, sought to recapture its old zest through a return to that populist pose, the concept of the revolutionary nation. What of the southern reformers? They, too, had conceded the advantages of Tripoli during the war's initial stages. This attitude, like that of the Nationalists, quickly gave way to the old opposition that was then inflamed by the Great War. De Felice soon lost his enthusiasm for Tripoli. He returned from a visit to Libya with tales of Italian atrocities committed against the Arab rebels. The former leader of the Sicilian Fasci accused the Government of allowing Italy's colony to be exploited by big business, headed by the Bank of Rome.[57] In the Chamber he reported on the mismanagement of Italian officials, their failure to win over the Arab population for whom Italian rule had become worse than that of the Turks. By February, 1915, De Felice was calling for radical steps to relieve the peasantry from the burdens imposed by neutrality, a reference to the rising cost of bread that had produced local riots in the South. Neutrality, he told the Chamber, is worse than war if the proletariat suffers privations at home. Reminding the Salandra government that a bread march had set off the French Revolution, the southern socialist threatened to lead the coming uprising if the situation were not rectified. In May, 1915, during the tumults that followed the announcement that Salandra had resigned, he took up the cry "war of revolution," inciting the Roman mobs against the parliamentary majority, which was known to approve of Giolitti's neutralist position. When Giolitti's friend and political backer, Camillo Peano, complained to the police that the buildings of Parliament had not been properly protected from the mob, De Felice was said to have retorted: "Who runs Italy, anyway? The Giolittians?"[58]

Salvemini, despite his opposition to colonialism, conceded that the display of national unity the war brought forth was not to be disparaged. He agreed with the Nationalists that the Government had been forced to act by public opinion. The imperialists, for their part, hoped to steal the Government's thunder. But Salvemini wished to show that they themselves were responsible for the country's illusion that Libya would be an economic benefit. When the peace was signed, however, he joined the ranks of the detractors, feeling, he wrote, that it would go down in history as a "diplomatic joke." Aware that these attitudes only fed the currents of reaction, Salvemini refused to be associated with those who attacked the ministry indiscriminately. He paid Giolitti the compliment of saying that another leader probably would have made even more mistakes. That cool and calculating manner, so damaging in his handling of domestic politics, was an advantage in foreign affairs. The real source of Italy's political ills, according to Salvemini, was not the man, but the entire ruling class.[59] Unlike the intellectual dandies who heaped abuse on official Italy and refused to be sullied by responsible political action, Salvemini in a series of documented articles defended universal suffrage. In 1913 he ran for the Chamber from his hown town of Molfetta. His defeat raised a howl of protest in anti-Giolittian circles. Carlo Altobelli, an independent Socialist Deputy and an interventionist by 1915, attacked in a noisy session the "Minister of Corruption" whose parliamentary dictatorship, personal dishonesty, and election rigging made universal suffrage a mockery.[60]

With the coming of war in Europe, Salvemini became an ardent interventionist. His ideals had nothing in common with those of the Nationalists. The latter shifted with ease from their long-standing defense of the Triple Alliance to the side of the Entente. Military action was at the heart of their program. Since the Socialists backed neutrality, as did the great majority of the Chamber of Deputies, the Nationalists saw the war as conservative and antiparliamentary.[61] Salvemini's championing of intervention was another matter. He had always been anti-Austrian although willing to accept the Triple Alliance as a purely defensive pact that would not involve Italy in defense of Vienna's opposition to the aspirations of the subject nationalities. When the war broke, it became, for Salvemini, a struggle for the liberation of the Balkan peoples and for the creation of a Yugoslav nation.[62] In this he was returning to the Mazzinian tradition. Unfortunately the crisis of May, 1915, found him in the company of many who were the enemies of all Mazzini stood for, and who would one day become Salvemini's enemies as well. Divergent as were their political philosophies, a common disgust for Giolitti united Salvemini and the authoritarians of the Left and the Right against the "system" that was associated with the Minister of Corruption. The fact was that although Salandra was premier, the majority of the Chamber was regarded as being loyal to Giolitti. Salvemini's deep loathing for what he considered the immorality of Italian politics can explain his actions in 1915, but not detract from their antiparliamentary nature. On May 14, haranguing the students of Rome, Salvemini attacked the disgraceful politicians and their leaders: "Don't be impressed," he is reported to have said, "by the fact that the very great majority of the five hundred men of Montecitorio approve of the infamous man. They don't constitute the country's representation, but are the product of election by the cudgels of his henchmen." [63]

For Salvemini, then, the momentary bond established between the

country's legal representatives and the people during the Libyan War
faded into the background with the World War. The brief moment of
Giolitti's partial absolution from the sins of the past was over. His reputation as the corrupting Minister returned, in the Chamber, through the
speeches of Altobelli and others, and in the streets through the incitements of the interventionists. There were others among the ranks of the
southern radicals, however, who were closer in spirit to the Nationalists
and to Mussolini's interventionist Fasci. Another figure from the 1890's,
Colajanni, is illustrative of this wing of the radical war faction. The noted
Sicilian Republican Deputy, anthropologist and statistician, had been
known for his opposition to colonial expenses. And yet when the first
flush of enthusiasm for the Tripoli invasion swept over Italy, he too had
been caught up in it, speaking of the Libyan War as the "baptism and
confirmation" of united Italy. The rhetoric of that statement informs
against the noted social scientist, and suggests that his satisfaction would
be short-lived. By February, 1914, writing in the *Rivista popolare*,
which he edited, Colajanni was retracting his praise of the African War.
Italy had gained greater self-confidence, but the gain was ruined by the
failures of the Government to pacify and exploit Tripoli. With the outbreak of the World War, Colajanni showed the same tendency to shift
rapidly from advocacy of armed neutrality, which he defended on August
15, citing the great expenses of Italy's participation, to intervention for
the winning of the Adriatic, *mare nostrum*, which he upheld on August
31! [64] This was hard to square with his long political campaign not only
against military expenses, but against irredentism. Again, however, the
link between Africa and the Adriatic was to be found in the longing for
action; this could be seen in the evolution of Colajanni's position during
the months of Italian neutrality. By November 15 the *Rivista popolare*
was speaking of neutrality as treason. He dug out Carducci's lament for
Oberdan as the anniversary of the young martyr's death rolled around in
December. In part, of course, Colajanni's republicanism was involved
here. In 1912 he had written a book attacking the role of the House of
Savoy in Italian unification, and in particular the Crown's betrayal of the
revolution. Victor Emmanual III was showing no signs of leading the
country to war. To fail to do so, according to Colajanni, would be to
repeat the national disaster of 1866 when the Trentino had been left to
Austria and Garibaldi forced to retreat from the Tyrol.[65] But more illustrative of the spiritual attraction of war as a unifying foce, a redemption

La Voce, ediz. politica

Anno VII ✎ 22 Maggio 1915 ✎ Numero 2
Numero straordinario: Abbasso Giolitti!

"Down with Giolitti," from *La Voce*'s special interventionist edition. The "Minister of corruption" is portrayed as a Central American dictator.

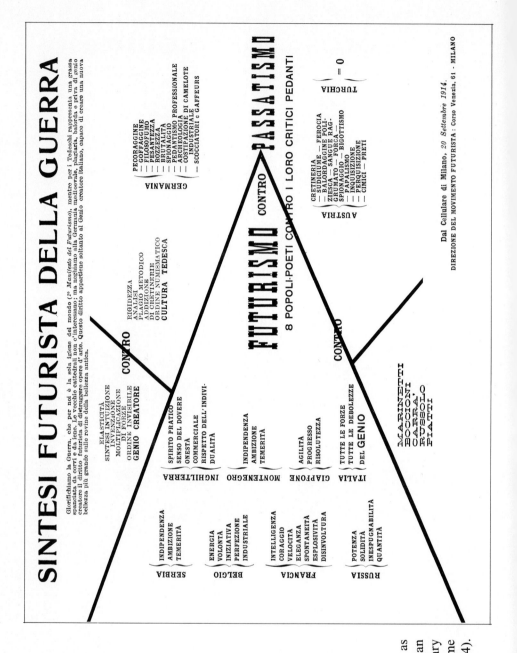

The aesthetics of war as represented by the Italian Futurists on the anniversary of the occupation of Rome (September 20, 1914).

Cartoon at left from *Popolo d'Italia*, March 18, 1915.

The "Spirit" of War and the "Belly" of Neutrality, from *Popolo d'Italia*, March 31, 1915.

This essentially anti-positivistic symbolism also recalled the era of the French Revolution. It was during the National Convention (1792–95) that the Mountain referred to the Plain as the "Marsh" or the "Belly." As in the 1870's, war was again the mainspring of Revolution.

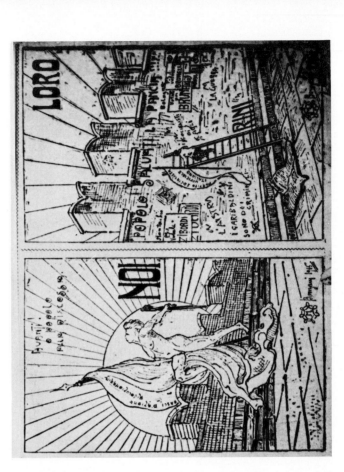

LA COMUNE

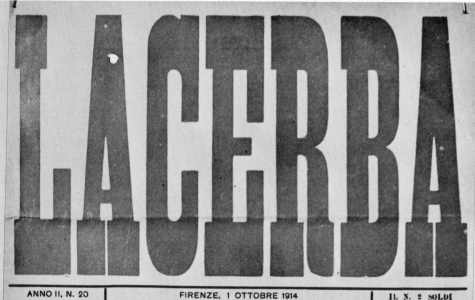

An interventionist appeal to "intelligent Italians" from *Lacerba*
(October 1, 1914). The title of the review is in red.

from the weakness of the Postrisorgimento, was his speech in the Chamber of December 14. The people had given too little blood for Italy.

Look at the ranks of the Thousand. You will find a great prevalence of bourgeoisie rather than workers. . . . I will even say that the lack of a truly popular contribution to the unitarian process has resulted in the fact that the national feeling which we would have liked to have seen completely developed has not yet sufficiently been achieved. And I should like to be able to predict that the war, which I hope is near, far better than that [war] preached by the Nationalists in the inauspicious year 1911, may . . . by means of the common blood solidly bind up the Italian nation." [66]

Prezzolini and the *Voce* followed a similar path. At first the *Voce's* chief seemed to have thrown over the bombast and literary irrationalism of his earlier days. As if tamed by official Italy's successes, Prezzolini wrote that one of the benefits of the Libyan campaign was the new luster that Giolitti derived from it. He was no longer the Ministro della malavita.[67] A more practical and responsible outlook apparently had replaced the sensationalism of the past. In association with Giovanni Gentile, Prezzolini was writing about militant idealism, a coming to grips with concrete problems, abandoning the ivory tower of pure speculation. There was, however, a Nietzschean air to much of this, a picaresque posturing that glorified the heroic criminal, the productive knave, at the expense of the stuffy bourgeoisie or the idle philosopher.[68] This attitude of romanticized individualism that looked with favor on the southern bandit was still felt by the purveyors of militant idealism. It came out clearly in Prezzolini's attitude toward the Libyan War, praised less as a conquest by Giolittian Italy than as a new and violent vista of human action. The Ottoman Empire was breaking up. Tripoli had revolutionized European diplomacy. Prezzolini reacted to the First Balkan War with the same effusions about the virtues of battle that characterized the response of the Futurists. His lauding of Giolitti was scarcely sincere. The statesman was still the cool, cunning bureaucrat, now admired on the cynical grounds that he was at least a cut above other politicans in his craft. Prezzolini saw Parliament as a transitory solution to Italian political problems, not as an institution that had won its place in the nation's history. He wrote vaguely about a "new State" of the future, to be arrived at through action and disorder in the coming crisis of his generation.[69]

In June, 1914, during the Red Week, the *Voce's* editor defended the action of the mob. It alone had been "sincere," cutting loose from the leadership of the decadent Socialist party, which was in league with the

Giolittian majority against the Salandra government. "Revolutions," Prezzolini wrote, borrowing from Giovanni Bovio, "are not made by scholars or by people in white gloves. A member of the mob is worth more than a university professor when there is a barricade to throw up or a bank door to be broken down." As for violence, Marx had called it the matrix of modern society, and Sorel had made it a cult. Even the Thousand were called a "mob" in their time by the "sensible people." No idealist, however, could look upon those "turbid forces of life which burst forth from the darkest recesses" in the same way as did the bourgeoisie, closed as they were in their narrow shell of self-interest. The most harmful disorder, according to Prezzolini, was not the rioting in the streets, which had lasted only three days; it was the less obvious disorder of the ministers, the bureaucracy, the politicians. Those responsible for the Red Week of June, 1914, were the men who had led Italy to Libya. By October, 1914, Prezzolini had written off the African War as a complete waste. Libya had not been the test of blood. The *Voce* denied that Pascoli had been right in saying that Italians were at last united. Tripoli was not a national war; rather it had been the "false national war." [70]

By that time the Great War had come to Europe. The *Voce* hailed it as a source of new vitality, a much needed invigorator after years of peace. From the war, Prezzolini wrote, Italy would have what many Italians had awaited from a revolution. "Italy is made but not finished." The nation must fight, and not wait until the enemy is weak nor bargain with the Powers. It was up to the statesmen to find *casus belli*. If they could not, they were good for nothing. The *Voce* backed intervention as a means of "making the Italians." Unity had been won by good fortune, by the imposition of the will of a valiant minority, and by the "royal conquest" of the Peninsula.[71] This was Oriani's analysis of the Risorgimento put to use by the intellectual warriors five years after the death of the "lonely genius."

Papini, Prezzolini's friend and collaborator since the days of the *Leonardo* at the outset of the Giolittian decade, showed the same tendency to revert to a literary idealization of politics of which the revival of Oriani was symptomatic. For a moment he too paid his back-handed respects to Giolitti who, if no Bismarck, was not an imbecile.[72] But the waves of rhetoric loosed by the Libyan War soon found Papini riding out the flood with relish. More and more, the waning of the Government's prestige could be charted by the waxing of morbid D'Annunzian prose. Themes of blood and sex, that erotic militarism which was one of the Poet's specialties, became fashionable among the intellectuals of Italian journalism. Corradini wrote of the "soldier's blood," which like "man's seed" was a regenerating force. Prezzolini, in keeping with his Gentilian militant idealism, was no different. That cultivated European of whom Nietzsche spoke might forego the marriage bed as well as the battlefield, if only he produced immortal works of genius in place of sons. "But for the great majority," according to the *Voce*'s editor, "there is no other immortality save that granted by a fertile seed, nor other heroism than that of the trenches."[73] But Papini was perhaps D'Annunzio's closest rival in the art of wordy violence. He scoffed at the *Canzoni*, the war songs, and called the Poet an "interior decorator of de luxe brothels."[74] It was still customary for the aspiring apprentices to belittle him, since they were unable to replace him as the master of the trade. By 1913 Papini had done his best to do just that; he had joined the Futurists in their review, the *Lacerba*, for which he furnished examples of the richest sort of self-adulation and theatrical pomposity. He exceeded his earlier efforts, particularly in the use of obscenity.[75] Political commentary was reduced largely to writing off the Risorgimento as a failure. The nation would have to be made anew, lacking as it did a truly revolutionary genius. In October, 1913, Papini made a frantic effort to outdo the rest of the field in the mystical veneration of blood.

The future needs blood. It needs human victims, butchery. Internal war, and foreign war, revolution and conquest: that is history. . . . Blood is the wine of strong peoples, and blood is the oil for the wheels of this great machine which flies from the past to the future.[76]

The beginnings of the D'Annunzian revival date from 1912–14, before the World War. The style that was to be put to use by the interventionists was being polished during the years of agitation over Tripoli and universal suffrage. The culmination of all this was D'Annunzio's return to Italy on May 5, 1915, for the celebration of the anniversary of Garibaldi's sailing from Quarto. As will be seen, the moment was crucial for the Salandra government, which had signed the London Treaty with the Entente on April 26 and broken the Triple Alliance on May 4. No one could doubt that the "exile's" return was planned. Few knew as much as Albertini, who had suggested the idea of inviting D'Annunzio to Salandra.[77] The *Corriere della Sera* had done a major part in keeping the Poet's name and works before the public, printing his romanticized vignettes on France in the war. The paper, printing an advance copy of the Quarto speech, even tried to capture a bit of his sensualism in its editorial for the occasion. "We know not yet whether our Spring as well is to be unripe. But we know that everything is in bud and that it is Spring."[78] After this feeble effort, it was up to the bard of Italy's war for redemption to do his part.

Although conceding that few of those present could hear the Poet, pro-inventionist witnesses have placed the crowd at 200,000, many of them students.[79] What rankled the war-makers, however, was the absence of the King. At the last moment, it was announced that affairs of state would prevent the attendance of His Majesty. Albertini, sensing something was up, sped to Rome, cancelling his appointment with D'Annunzio at Genoa. In his history of the period, the *Corriere*'s chief has criticized the Salandra government for not taking advantage of the Quarto celebration, giving it an official stature, and then announcing that the Triple Alliance had been finally ended. That it was ended Albertini learned when he reached Rome. There were few in Italy who knew as much at that time, despite the many rumors. Regarding the King's absence, the truth was that news from Libya was bad. A serious reverse was announced on May 3. The *Corriere* played it down. As will be seen, the situation in the mopping-up campaign in Africa was deteriorating as the date set for Italy's declaration of war approached.[80]

D'Annunzio's oration was a confusion of familiar similes, with a heavy dose of blasphemy reminiscent of the days of Pius IX thrown in for good measure, doubtless because of the Vatican's neutralist position. Speaking of the Garibaldi brothers who had died in France, he likened them to the "Spartan Twins from the midst of whose breast that fountain of blood suddenly spread the scent of Italic Spring upon the Argonne's embattled mire." As Garibaldi's statue at Quarto was fused in bronze, so would the Italian people be fused that night. He closed on a parody of the Sermon on the Mount, full of erotic appeal to the young audience. Part of it is worth repeating, if only as an example of the style of the poetry of life and war.

O, blessed be those who have the more, for more will they be able to give, more will they desire.
Blessed be those who are twenty, chaste of mind, temperate of body, whose mothers are brave.
Blessed be those who, waiting and trusting, waste not their strength but preserve it with a warrior's discipline.
Blessed be those who disdain sterile loves that they may be virgins for this first and final love. . . .
Blessed be the young who hunger and thirst for glory, for they will be sated.
Blessed be the pure of heart, blessed those victorious returning, for they will see the youthful face of Rome, the brow recrowned by Dante, Italy's triumphal beauty.[81]

D'Annunzio's Quarto speech was the culmination of a moment away from a disciplined, more responsible attitude toward the realities of the times among Italian intellectuals and uncommitted politicians. Between 1911 and 1914 the search for dramatic means of expressing cultivated man's frustration with the bourgeois, positivistic world went forward with a new boldness. Government was being challenged by a resurgence of irrationalism that reached its peak during the Radiant May of 1915. This new mood of violence also challenged the leadership of Italy's leading academician. The coming down to earth that Croce had been pleased to observe in the pages of the *Voce* during its first two years, 1909–11, had given way to a new cultural insight into the deeper meanings of existence, to a more immoderate attempt to view life in the light of artistic and philosophical values, making style and speculation the canons of political action. The earlier strenuous phase of the "philosopher wolves" that had characterized the *Regno* and the *Leonardo* came back full force, enhanced now by the excitement of war. In Papini's futurist writings for the *Lacerba*, and in Prezzolini's and Gentile's militant idealism, the old poetry of life was revived.

The vogue of the bandit type, the mob, and syndicalism was also very much a part of this revival. It was taken up by all those who stood in total opposition to society. When the *Idea Nazionale* praised Arturo Labriola's defense of mass action and war, it was expressing for the extremists of the right what many independent Socialists were also saying. The common target was not only Italy's neutrality, personified by Giolitti and the majority of the Chamber, known to be in favor of preserving peace, but the Socialist party leadership. This was logical. Because the party was neutralist and had become since 1901 a part of the constitutional system — that is, become Giolittian — its fortunes were linked fundamentally to those of the Government. If the Socialists had opposed the Tripoli invasion, it was also clear that Giolitti had no love of Africanism. From his Turin speech as from his statements on the floor of the Chamber it was known that he had gone to war reluctantly, basing his decisions on the cold light of diplomatic reason. He had stressed the domestic tasks that lay ahead and tried to counteract the enthusiasm of the rhetoricians of power. There was, therefore, no real schism between his Government and the Socialist hierarchy at the time of the Libyan War.

As in the 1890's, it was the fringe Socialists, men who described themselves variously as Republicans, Democrats, and Marxists, the same who had been the source of the myth of Giolittian corruption, who now turned on the official Socialist party, demanding that it answer for its failure to stand aloof in complete opposition to Rome. Altobelli, De Felice, Salvemini, and Colajanni were the most outspoken propagandists for war and for direct action against the politicians of Montecitorio, including the Socialist Deputies headed by Turati. All of them had spoken of the moral values of the Libyan War that the party had condemned as a betrayal of the interests of the proletariat. Much the same was true of the two most important converts to the African War from the ranks of the party's hierarchy, Ivanoe Bonomi and Bissolati. Both had been drummed out of the party for this apostacy. But their support for the imperialist move was marked by an enthusiasm akin to that of the independents that had little in common either with the party's platform or with Giolitti's empirical foreign policy. In 1914–15 they were among Giolitti's most determined opponents.

The situation was really not at all different for the man who led the attack on their betrayal of the party's anti-imperialist stand. Mussolini, by serving as the Socialist executioner in 1912, had conveniently rid himself of two rivals among the ancients of Italian Socialism. His rise to eminence followed hard upon, carrying him to the top of the ladder as editor of the *Avanti!* The outbreak of the Great War, however, found him in the uncomfortable position of being an ally of official Italy. No less than the Nationalists after 1911, he faced political strangulation and the loss of his individuality, something he cultivated with great care. His reaction to the trap of organized political collaboration in 1914 was to be quite consistent with his dramatic pronouncements against Libya in 1911–12. In both instances, moreover, he was capitalizing on the new mood of violence that thrived in the years from Tripoli to Sarajevo.

The Emergence of Benito Mussolini

D'Annunzio's return to Italy was played down by one important interventionist newspaper, Mussolini's *Popolo d'Italia*. Although it had printed the famous oration,[82] it had done nothing to enhance the Poet's prestige by giving him unnecessary publicity. The Socialist renegade had a fine nose for competitors. His paper studiously avoided mentioning D'Annunzio while playing up the Quarto celebration as a popular manifestation of the will to war as contrasted to the "mercantile delays of diplomacy." The King's absence, according to Mussolini, underlined the sharp division still existing between the people and the institutions. Oriani's demand that the House of Savoy fulfil the goals of the revolution was cited by Mussolini [83] as it had been by Prezzolini and most spokesmen of the radical interventionist camp.

This was scarcely in keeping with socialist theory. However, Mussolini's intellectual origins were not those of Marxist scientific socialism. His outspoken antipatriotism, vulgar anticlericalism, and romanticized view of individual action, as well as his early literary efforts, placed him in the company of the deracinated literati more than in the camp of socialist theoreticians. In an essay on aesthetics, written in 1903, the future editor of the *Avanti!* had likened poetry to the rumblings of the mob. When Andrea Costa, grand old man of Italian socialism, died in 1910, Mussolini compared his idealism to the narrow, materialistic, and positivistic socialism of the succeeding generation, quite forgetting Costa's role in the parliamentary debates of the 1890's. This was the same sort of artistic view of politics, and of the Postrisorgimento generally, that could be found in Oriani. Gaudens Megaro was quite right in relating Mussolini's revolutionary activity to an aestheticism.[84] There are few ideas in Mussolini's prewar writings that cannot be found in the pages of the *Leonardo*, the *Regno* and the *Idea Nazionale*. His first biographer, Torquato Nanni, also from the Romagna, rich in romantic memories of the Risorgimento, stressed the unsettled, turbulent, and altogether Bohemian life of the future Duce. He quoted Mussolini as declaiming that he would go through life playing the violin,[85] hardly the approach of a scientific socialist to bourgeois society.

Scholarly attempts have been made to square Mussolini's Nietzschean attitudes with his Marxist background. Nietzsche gave his life its rhythm, Marx contributed the tone. According to this version, Mussolini was a left-wing Marxist, along with Trotski and Lenin, working for the triumph of European communism. The difference was that he accentuated *Lebensphilosophie* to an extent unusual for a Marxist. His stand for war, it has been said, was consistent with Marxism once the International had failed to prevent the capitalist explosion. Had it done so, Mussolini would have been a leader of the antiwar socialist revolution.[86] No one can doubt this. He would have used peace with the same agility that he used war, which he portrayed as a revolution. But one should not try to explain away the paradoxical confusions of Mussolini's ideas by logical subtleties. In keeping with unconventional intellectuals of his generation, he hated systems, and despised positivistic, mechanical, and lifeless forms, political as well as cultural. In this flight from formalisms, Papini was no better, nor worse. Nor was Italy unique in giving birth to mercurial political dodgers. The similarities between Mussolini's career and that of Georges Valois, Sorel's disciple, have been pointed out. Valois also began life as a vagabond intellectual, a self-styled Nietzschean, ony to be attracted to syndicalism and later to the *Action française*. In the case of Valois, Sorel is seen as the link between Marx and Nietzsche.[87] Whatever may be said of Sorel's influence on Valois, Mussolini really had little need for his ideas. When asked in 1921 about his supposed influence on Mussolini, Sorel was more historical than many founders of political theories: the idea of violence was in the air for anyone to use, including the French syndicalist himself.[88]

Mussolini's literary associations with the Florentine group headed by Papini and Prezzolini are well known. He had been attracted to the *Voce*, which he advised all Italians interested in Italy's spiritual renewal to read. The *Voce* printed part of Mussolini's study of irredentist sentiment in the Trentino.[89] As a Socialist he was opposed to irredentism. But his slim volume of 1910 on the subject had faint traces of the proletariat-nation theme we have met with in the *Idea Nazionale*. The workers in the Trentino were the only ones keeping Italian feeling alive; the bourgeoisie were pro-Austrian. After his conversion to intervention, his biographer, Nanni, singled out this passing remark as proof of Mussolini's patriotism. The *Voce* in 1914 also recalled Mussolini's stay in the Trentino, citing it as proof of his national interest. This showed that not all Socialists were against the war.[90] More interesting were the spiritual affinities between the Florentine group and Mussolini that had come to the surface even before the war began. Prezzolini had singled him out as the one party leader who had preserved his vitality, who was still untouched by the corruption of that base parliamentarianism that had infected the rest of the Socialist party's high command. As late as September 18, 1915, when Mussolini was wavering between neutralism and war, the *Voce* suggested — and may well have known — that Mussolini would not remain a neutralist.[91]

On October 3 an interventionist Socialist, Professor Lombardo Radice, revealed to the press that a prominent socialist leader, soon identified as Mussolini, had confided his belief that if war came the party would back it.[92] This placed the *Avanti!*'s editor on the spot. By October 18 Mussolini had clarified his neutralism to the extent of admitting that if Italy went to war against Austria-Hungary, the Socialists would not take active measures to prevent mobilization. A general strike would fail unless it had the backing of Europe's proletariat. Should the Italian Socialist party go it alone, the strike would either be crushed, or, if successful, the party would be saddled with power when Italy's enemies were at the frontier. This was not as radical a departure as might be thought. Most Italian Socialists were aware that a general strike was out of the question. And if the party was officially neutralist, its pro-Entente leanings were obvious. The *Voce*, however, demanded that Mussolini make up his mind to be a "sheep or a goat."[93] Mussolini then went beyond acceptable party theory by admitting the existence of a legitimate national problem in the Trentino. He claimed that Italians there were in full revolt against Austria — a pure fabrication made for the occasion. He now called for a new concept of neutralism, one that would be "active." The party directorate met on October 20. Mussolini offered a resolution that would attenuate the party's dogmatic neutralist position.[94] It was voted down; Mussolini then left the editorship of the *Avanti!*, which then passed to the hands of Claudio Treves. Lombardo Radice suggested that Mussolini might be the man to organize a national-socialist movement in Italy.[95] Treves, reflecting the party position, accused Mussolini of confusing war's violence with revolution, and seeing neutralism as conservative.[96] Unquestionably, he did just that; but the confusion was quite intentional. War's mass character, plus the fact that the majority of the Chamber, the Vatican, and the old guard of the Socialist party backed neutralism, were sufficient reasons for Mussolini to become an interventionist. An admirer, the ultramontane Missiroli, was later to write that the reason for his opposition to the Libyan War, which cost Mussolini a few months in jail, was that it had not been revolutionary.[97] It would have been more accurate to say that Libya was an official war, planned and executed by the parliamentary regime. In that sense, it lacked any aura of voluntarism. As far as the Great War was concerned, Mussolini accepted Treves' challenge, insisting that the conflict was in fact revolutionary.[98]

During the months of Italian neutrality, the Socialist party had become a bulwark of constitutionalism and political legality. This was the logical outcome of the crisis of the 1890's. Bonomi, who became an interventionist, later criticized the party's failure to re-evaluate its neutralist stand in the light of the war's larger significance. By refusing to do so, the party lost any heroic, dynamic quality and was reduced to a "gray mass."[99] That was something absolutely unsuited to the romantic pose Mussolini affected along with many other intellectual journalists. It offered him no platform for self-glorification. On the other hand, when he was expelled from the party he was able to milk the situation of all its drama. With show of great emotion, including the breaking of a water glass on the rostrum from which he addressed the assembled Socialists, he spoke of the antimonarchical possibilities of the war, and finished by affirming that his old comrades hated him only because they really loved him still. To a newspaperman afterward, he remarked that he was afraid of no one as long as he had a pen in his hand and a revolver in his pocket. "I am strong, even though I am almost alone. In fact, I would say that I am strong just because of that."[100] Italy had another "great solitary figure." The Nietzschean posturing of strength through solitude, so much a part of the neoromantic intellectual revolt, became a political platform for Mussolini as it had for Corradini and Papini. The difference was that Mussolini was an effective political organizer, whereas the latter two always smelled of the study.

Concerning the financing of Mussolini's paper, there can be little serious doubt that he did receive money from France, and probably through agents of the French government. There is too much evidence to admit of any other reasonable conclusion.[101] The press commission that investigated his conversion from neutrality to intervention entered a verdict that absolved him of any moral turpitude.[102] However, it never went deeply into the question of foreign backing. Friends who saw him at the time noted that his life had taken a turn for the better once the *Popolo d'Italia* was established. He seemed to be enjoying his new prosperity, cutting loose from the Bohemian existence of a young but poor intellectual. It is unlikely that Mussolini was motivated by veniality alone. It cannot be proved that the offer of money came before his break with the party.[103] Besides, his conversion was not really sudden any more than it was unique. Many other journalists, from the Republican-Socialist Colajanni to the Nationalist Corradini, had shifted ground when the war came.

Mussolini was essentially responding to the wave of rhetorical idealism set off by the war, which was portrayed by men in all political camps as a regenerating force, a great romance recalling the heroism of the Risorgimento, following fifty years of prosaic bureaucracy. He hoped to capture a personal following among the so-called better sort of Socialists, Republicans, and Democrats who had gone over to the cause of intervention. Staying within the Socialist party, still dominated by the older hands, his chances of achieving a commanding position were limited. He was already at odds with the party chiefs before the war began. His attempt to turn back to the anarchic, violent tactics of the nineteenth century when socialism had still been illegal was itself out of keeping with the legalitarian methods advocated by Turati which, with lapses, had represented the overall policy of the Socialist party since the days of Pelloux. Of course the purely dramatic, even theatrical quality of his grand gesture was not lost on Mussolini. Like D'Annunzio, who in 1899 suddenly rose from his seat among the Deputies of the extreme Right and went over to the extreme Left, which was leading the fight against Pelloux — remarking as he went that he was "going toward life" — Mussolini was joining the "vital forces" represented by the radical interventionists. The appeal of apostasy and the drama of war conceived as pure action were the means by which one might tap the flamboyant Young Turks of Giolittian Italy. On these Mussolini hoped to build a power for himself.

His expectations of success in the bold venture of breaking with the hierarchy of the Socialist party were encouraged by the proddings of men like Prezzolini who mentioned him as a singular exception to the drabness of the old guard Socialists' neutralism. More important was the possibility of picking up followers from the democratic and liberal wings of the Nationalist Association, young men who still clung to the proletariat nation concept that the Nationalists had abandoned when they went into politics. As has been seen, the chauvinistic Italian Right tended to be somewhat tolerant of the anarchic and syndicalist breed of socialism, reserving their sharpest criticism for the collaborationists. When the liberal Nationalists broke with the Corradini faction, they became a plausible and as yet uncoordinated group from which to draw converts to the Mussolinian creed of war as revolution. One of them, Tomaso Borelli, writing in May, 1914, when Mussolini still seemed fully committed to the Socialist party, pointed out that the *Avanti's* editor personified a return to the heroic origins of Italian socialism. On the other side of the fence, Colajanni's journal, in November, 1914, when Mussolini had already gone over to the interventionist cause, insisted that he had not become an antisocialist, but was in fact true to the fighting tradition of the movement. Prezzolini, for his part, publicized the foundation of the *Popolo d'Italia*,[104] whose staff he joined along with Papini.

There was also the historical ambivalence of Italian socialism at work here, its own heroic memory of a less restrained, more dashing era. Turiello's observation that the Socialist party would lose its hold on the masses once it had entered Parliament, giving way to the anarchic and artistic individualism of the Risorgimento, seemed to be confirmed by the emergence of this youthful firebrand from the Romagna. Mussolini sensed that the moment was right for exploiting the dissident urge for old-style subversion in the manner of Pisacane and Cafiero. Men like Turati were, because of their official stature, deprived of the glamour which attracted restless young radicals. It was always easy to taunt the Socialists for their lack of flourish, their bureaucratic decadence. In 1911–12 it was partly fear of governmental contamination that had led the party to expel Bonomi and Bissolati. Mussolini, hitherto a nonentity, had been the hatchet man at the party Congress that condemned them. But the *Voce* twitted the party for this belated emphasis on noncollaboration with Giolitti's majority. The Socialists, it wrote, were seeking their virginity which had been lost in the halls of Montecitorio.[105] In 1914 Mussolini was essentially saying the same thing of the neutralist position taken by the directorate of the party. There is no fundamental inconsistency, given his political personality, between Mussolini's violent opposition to the Libyan War, his excessive antipatriotism, and his equally violent preaching of revolutionary war in 1914–15.

Indicative of the current of revolutionary action promoted by the war was the fact that the collaborationist Socialists of 1911–12 also felt the tug of great ideals. At the time of Tripoli, Bonomi had answered the anti-collaborationists by warning the party that it was condemning itself to sterility if it refused to share political responsibility.[106] The same Bonomi, however, at an interventionist rally in February, 1915, sharing the platform with the imperialist Corradini and the irredentist Barzilai, spoke a different language. "We firmly believe," he said, "that a great movement of ideas loses all its expansive force when it refuses to harken to the voices of sentiment, the warnings of history, and the necessities of the future." To the claim that the people opposed the war and were unwilling to make the sacrifices it required, Bonomi objected that even were it true — which he denied — he had faith that

Italy's intellectual forces, the forces of culture and thought . . . will have in themselves enough energy to drag along the uniformed and indifferent elements which have never been the propellents of a people's destinies. . . . I hope, moreover I am certain, that the glorious memories of our national Risorgimento will be sufficient for the spiritual preparation of the country. It is our fortune that Italy's interests in this great world crisis coincide with the history, the traditions, the glories of our past, and are in harmony with the as yet unfulfilled aspirations of our unitarian revolution; for when a people walks in the tracks of its history, it always rediscovers the deep faith in its future. . . . To those who still have doubts, I say: let us raise on high the unforgotten and unforgettable words of Garibaldi and Mazzini, let us raise on high a half century of martyrdom, sacrifice, heroism, battles and struggles; and Italy's soul will find again its unanimous will for the necessary completion of national unity.[107]

The steps of Italy's manifest destiny, tracked through the pages of history, became the key to the nation's future for the moderate socialist parliamentarian as well as for his old enemy, Mussolini. The Great War's significance, as explained by men of the most divergent political convictions, was to bind up the nation, to erase the Postrisorgimento save as a necessary evil, an inevitable pause in the unfolding of the grand design of national resurrection that Oriani had preached. The brief but significant moment during the Libyan War when the shade of the lonely prophet seemed obscured by the light of real achievements of a half-century of unity was forgotten. The attraction of war for men who were raised on tales of noble sacrifice made war in itself justifiable as a historical necessity. Had not Trevelyan written, in 1911, that Italy's house was as sound as any in Europe? When the country of Garibaldi went to war, Trevelyan served in the Red Cross at the Italian front. Now it was a different story. If the parliamentary government created by Cavour had given Italy an enviable stability, it "lacked the breath of vital air." If prosperity had come to Italy, it was tainted by German financial and intellectual influences, by German investments and materialistic philosophy. Meanwhile, signs of an "incomplete nationality" remained. The period of Italian neutrality, Trevelyan wrote, "was memorable, not only because of the obvious consequences involved, but because it was a contest between two conceptions of the life of man and of nations — a moral and spiritual against a non-moral and material. . . . In moments of great crisis that higher conception, the poetized, almost religious anthropomorphic vision of the sad, drowned lady, mother of heroes and martyrs, would carry away a people who are only materialists part of the time." It was for this reason, he concluded, that Italy's idealists, almost without exception, were interventionists.[108]

We will see that this was not at all the case. The people were not carried away, and many Italian representatives of philosophical idealism, including the most notable, Croce, were neutralists. Nothing, however, even from Italian sources, better describes the spiritualization of power and military struggle than these words of a great liberal historian. War was a victory over positivism; it was also a victory for that mentality which, from the beginning of Italian unity, looked to the past for answers to the frustrations and ills of the present. Trevelyan was speaking for a great and heroic tradition, and for Italian liberalism. But his view of war in particular, of the Postrisorgimento in general, was expressed in words common to the irrational vocabulary of Mussolini and all those who would accept the destruction of liberalism.

Italy, united in 1911, was suddenly "incomplete." All the fundamental problems of a new nation were revived and given a new force during the months from the invasion of Tripoli to the proclamation of neutrality. During the succeeding nine months they grew to such proportions in the interventionist press that it seemed true that the regime, which Giolitti guided, was a miserable travesty of the Italy dreamed of by its creators. Against the policies of that regime, the nation went to war in May, 1915. The war, therefore, has the greatest significance for the historian's assessment of the viability of the half-century of Italian unity as well as for his understanding of postwar events. Let us examine the Great War as a response to the desire to right past wrongs, to rediscover lost ideals, and to harmonize political action with the predestined course of the nation's evolution.

.9.

THE HISTORICAL SIGNIFICANCE
OF THE GREAT WAR

The importance of the War for recent Italian history is best seen by examining those same issues that had been the source of so much dissatisfaction among Italian intellectuals during the years from the occupation of Rome to the fall of Pelloux. How were these treated in 1914–15 by the interventionists? Something of the link between war propaganda and long-standing grievances is already apparent in Mussolini's journalistic revival of the romance associated with Pisacane, a tradition that had never been completely rooted out of Italian socialism by Marxist teachings. On the right, the anarchic strain of Italian conservatism comes to the surface in the *Idea Nazionale*'s subversive editorials. It remains to discuss the other outstanding issues of the Postrisorgimento in relationship to the war: regionalism and the Southern Question; parliamentarianism; irredentism and the Triple Alliance; and the Church-State quarrel. Interventionists insisted that war was the balm that would heal all sores. The nature of their arguments, however, brings to light with particular clarity the ambiguous legacy of those men who claimed to possess a deeper understanding of culture and society, giving rise in Italy to the central paradox associated with the return of romanticism.

As for Mussolini, his later role as the leader of fascism gives his activities in 1914–15 a historical significance quite out of proportion with his influence at the time. He was by no means a leader of the war camp. In fact, there is much to suggest that he was faced with political extinction, having betrayed his party and having been unable to capture any personal following. But the future Duce showed signs of the political elasticity that was to carry him through many a postwar crisis. He was far too clever to risk his career in 1914 without leaving a loophole by which he might get back into the good graces of the Socialist party should the war campaign fail to move the Salandra government to action. At first the *Popolo d'Italia* played it safe. Mussolini announced that he had no intention of deserting or attacking the party. By equating war with revolution,

271

he hoped to obscure the logical contradiction between an obvious breach of discipline and his insistence that he remained a believer in the cause of the proletariat revolution. Using the familiar theme of the revolution that failed, the bourgeois and diplomatic rather than popular process of Italian unification, he described intervention as a people's movement, the first mass participation of the Italian proletariat in any political action, giving the workers that sense of discipline essential for all social revolutions. In order to square military nationalism with Marxist theory, the *Popolo d'Italia* claimed that by leading the drive for war the working class would replace the discredited bourgeoisie, which had failed in its mission. Class struggle would be set aside for the duration of hostilities, it was true. But this was defended by the contrived argument that national solidarity would benefit the International. A united front would shorten the war and bring down the Hohenzollern dynasty, enemy of all European workers.[1] Mussolini was doing no more than taking up Corradini's concept of Italy as a proletariat nation. Whereas the Nationalist used it to counteract the suspicion that he was an enemy of the masses, Mussolini used it to prove that he was not an enemy of the nation.

Makeshift as they were, these arguments at least tried to give a theoretical justification for intervention. But it was soon apparent that the Socialist party's rank and file, as well as the great majority of its leaders, were not prepared to accept Mussolini's amalgam of nationalism and socialism. Even his old paper, the *Lotta di classe* of Forlì, which he had edited before rising to prominence, came out against him.[2] At this point the *Popolo d'Italia* shifted from a theoretical to a romanticized and historical defense of intervention. More and more the paper played upon the theme of a return to the heroic period of Italian socialism, to the days of Amilcare Cipriani, Pisacane, and Costa. Garibaldi was thrown in as well. That Costa was the first Socialist elected to the Chamber of Deputies was conveniently forgotten. And Garibaldi's adherence to socialism rested at best on a few generic remarks in praise of the movement in its infancy. The Hero certainly had not understood socialism in terms of Marxist theory. But he represented the idealism of the Risorgimento and was Italy's greatest popular revolutionary leader. The *Popolo d'Italia* now proclaimed the International dead. It had failed to face the historical problem of the nation. Mussolini charged the German Socialists with the crime of having killed it.[3]

When all else failed, Mussolini used the death of Costante Garibaldi to attack the Socialist party on the grounds that its program lacked any grandeur, any sense of sacrifice. The "infallible intuition" of the people grasped the war's significance, understood the glory of death in battle. The party leaders had corrupted socialism by converting it from a "mystique" to "politics." Worse, the party was a force of conservatism. Its neutralist position tallied with that of the Crown and the Vatican. Mussolini's hopes lay instead in the *Fasci d'azione rivoluzionaria*, which had been formed prior to his split from the party, and into which he entered hoping to bring the radical interventionist group under his own leadership. The Fasci appealed to the workers against the "dynastic" policy of the party. Typically, it made clear that it was not itself a "party." The word was too suggestive of a formal sort of organization, something that must be avoided in order to preserve the dynamic character of intervention. By leaving membership open to all subversives,[4] whether of the Right or the Left, the chances of success were better.

It was impossible, however, to claim any great following for the group. Mussolini was forced by the facts to admit that only the thinking minority of the Socialist party, the farsighted elite, had accepted the war platform. The more this became apparent, the more Mussolini's paper gave up any pretense of logical argument in favor of blatant mysticism. It was the only way one could avoid the harsh truth that the great majority of Italians, and particularly of the lower classes, were opposed to war. Poor Pisacane, Garibaldi, and Cipriani, he wrote. Italian socialism had not always been so degenerate. Once it had had its "springs of ideals and enthusiasms." "The *civitas solis* — the divine and human City of the Sun prophesied by Tommaso Campanella — cannot be made of mud. . . . It will take stones, hard and smooth stones, polished by muscle, and even more by the soul, cemented with blood." [5]

The same obscurantism was put to work in the veneration of the Commune as a testimonial of the people's defense of a national ideal which was being betrayed by bureaucrats and diplomats.[6] Here as well the appeal was to a lingering problem that arose early in the Postrisorgimento. Just as the old heroes of socialism were recalled to life to challenge the party platform, so the Commune was meant to summon forth old regional resentments. Bakunin had used it in a similar fashion in the 1870's, hoping to channel local hostility to Piedmontese unification into the anarchist movement. The image of the Commune served Mussolini in much the same way in 1915. It became the symbol of the spontaneity of popular forces as distinct from diplomatic caution and parliamentary neutralism with their focal point at Rome, center as well of the administrative system.

In this Mussolini was tapping an old vein. Cattaneo's works on the Five Days of Milan, his stress on the power of spontaneous uprisings, betrayed in 1848 by the monarchy, were in the background. The Commune also reminded Italians of Prussia's methodical humiliation of the gay France in 1870, an act that had wounded Burckhardt's artistic and federalist sensitivity.

Mussolini was not the only interventionist to use regionalism as an argument for war. The noted Republican, federalist, and critic of parliamentarianism, Arcangelo Ghisleri, in August, 1914, issued his own "Manifesto for the Last War of Independence." But Mussolini's background helped him pose as the man best suited to understand and direct the ferment that was said to be working through the towns and countryside. He came from the Romagna which, in the words of Merlino long ago, was one of Italy's "two Irelands." Unfortunately, that traditional land of republicanism and anticlericalism showed no more inclination for war than did Piedmont. However, the most plausible area in which to seek out regionalist resentments, converting them into popular demonstrations for war, proved even less promising. The Mezzogiorno seemed especially suited to Mussolini's propaganda. Not only was there increased unrest as a result of the growing grain shortage, a possible spark that might produce a remanifestation of the Sicilian Fasci; the fact that the Socialist party had never made great inroads among the contadini allowed Mussolini to claim that southern urban and rural labor was interventionist as opposed to the Socialist party, which was neutralist and based in the North. It was, Mussolini wrote, those Prussians of Piedmont who opposed war. From Palermo, in the other of Italy's "two Irelands," the *Popolo d'Italia*'s man, Cesare Rossi, reported that the Sicilians had a greater sense of sacrifice and were behind the war as a great national goal. He claimed that if war did not come, the Island would return to the days of the Vespers.[7]

War conceived as a vehicle for the resurrection of the Mezzogiorno, which, in turn, was supposed to embody the vitality of the simple people, was not a very profitable motif. There were several reasons for this. In the first place, it was an admission that Italian Socialists, whether mostly northern or not, were neutralist. Secondly, the idea that the economic privations, particularly the shortage of grain caused by the war's effect on trade, were worse than the sacrifices that war would demand, was too specious. Nonetheless, Mussolini's propaganda was helped by southern radicals. De Felice, speaking in the Chamber as late as February, 1915, when the slaughter on the Western front had already shown the horrors of trench warfare, claimed that unemployment and food shortages took more lives than war.[8] This can only be understood as an example of interventionist madness. Saner men, among them Pietro Bertolini, Giolitti's minister for colonies, long an advocate of federalism, were privately warning Salandra that the First Battle of the Marne suggested a long war; that the Mezzogiorno's material progress would be set back by Italy's participation; and that neutrality offered important economic possibilities through trade with the belligerents.[9]

The weakest part of the attempt to put the Southern Question to use as a justification of intervention, however, was the obvious falseness of the claim that southern Italians were behind the war party. The *Popolo d'Italia*'s principal correspondent from the Mezzogiorno, Guido Dorso, in his own articles on the situation in Naples only proved that the great southern city was overwhelmingly neutralist. The one Neapolitan interventionist paper, Arturo Labriola's *Roma*, was a "voice crying out in the desert." Dorso's plans for a "southern revolution" — a mass uprising that would release those treasures of energy latent in the people, freeing the lower classes from the corrupting influence of the *galantuomini* and breaking the excessive centralization resulting from Piedmontese unification — proved a miserable failure. He also regretted that no one had taken up the idea of war as the panacea for the ills of the southern proletariat.[10] De Felice had, it is true. But Salvemini was more important by 1915, and he did not make that an argument for war. Rather, by promoting the Mazzinian ideal of national self-determination, Salvemini had tacitly recognized that Italy was sufficiently united to take her place in the European struggle for the rights of all peoples. If additional proof were needed that the historic southern problem could not effectively be exploited, one could cite the *Idea Nazionale*. The imperialists had always elevated foreign above domestic policy. It was through colonial expansion that all the nation's internal problems were to be solved. Yet the nationalist paper devoted only one article of any significance to the topic of intervention as a benefit to the Mezzogiorno.[11]

Assisted by Papini and Prezzolini, Mussolini's paper placed increasing stress on the spiritual and moral content of Italian intervention. Italy's entry into the fray was described as a victory of the human spirit over the narrow, materialistic views of men who were dominated by the "belly." The pun "paunchafist" for "pacifist" became popular in this sort of cultural realpolitik. Salandra's *sacro egoismo*, like Giolitti's parecchio, was likened to a mercantile, positivistic diplomacy. The transference of the language of philosophy to the realm of power politics, something that had begun with De Meis and his friend Oriani, was a favorite device with much of the war press. It was a convenient escape from the truth. It was even used to cover up the deep-rooted neutralism of the Mezzogiorno. Those "flashes of synthetic genius" that Marselli had singled out as a peculiar characteristic of the South, where the idealist school of philosophy and history still flourished at Naples, were brought up again as proof that the Southerners were ready for war, unlike the utilitarian Northerners.[12] Antonia Renda, whose study of the Southern Question fifteen years earlier had done much to focus attention on the very real material deficiencies of the region, was writing in 1915 of the war as a means of freeing Italy from her spiritual torpor. As would be expected, Papini's *Lacerba* made this sort of political wisdom a specialty. The futurist review shifted from being an outlet for shocking literature to a sounding board for interventionist rhetoric as soon as the war began in Europe. It was occasionally censored by the Salandra government.[13] But the same type of intellectualized pro-Entente pieces were carried daily by the major organs of the interventionists without apparent interference from the regime.

Besides its value as a cultural mask for the concealment of facts, this idealization of war also served the necessary purpose of explaining away much of the artful dodging of men who had been pro-German until the proclamation of Italian neutrality. An example of this was Giuseppe Borgese, literary critic of the *Corriere della Sera*. In 1909 Borgese had written a work on Germany that was full of praise for the sense of discipline, order, and political stability of Italy's ally. It is true that he had criticized the excessive materialism of Wilhelmian Germany, the decline in art and philosophy, all of which Borgese referred to as the Americanization of the country. Nonetheless, it was an altogether flattering study of the leader of the Triple Alliance. In December, 1914, the same Borgese was speaking of war as a spiritual necessity. Italy had been made not by sensible men but by men of rashness and daring. Two months before Italy's entry into the war, he wrote an article labeling Germany the home of materialism and of a new paganism. On the very eve of intervention he published a slim volume that attacked positivistic Germany. Like most warriors of the pen, Borgese described his approach as coolly rational. The choice to fight or not to fight had to be made solely on the basis of real interests, without rhetorical flourishes. He then went on to speak of war as having rebeautified the world, as being always revolutionary, whereas too few

Italians had died for the Risorgimento. All of this was suspiciously D'Annunzian. The same treatment of Germany was served up by Papini in the *Lacerba*.[14]

The danger in all this was that it placed the nation's choice on a mystical level where nothing save war could ever be accepted. At the same time it glossed over diplomatic, economic, and political realities that could not be ignored without jeopardizing the nation's existence. To urge war at all costs when it was well known that the South was neutralist in the great majority, that Tuscany as well showed lack of enthusiasm for war[15] in central Italy, and that those "positivistic Prussians" of the North, the commercially-minded Piedmontese, without whom war was inconceivable, wanted to preserve neutrality if posible, was to court disaster. There is no doubt, despite interventionist disclaimers, that it was to be war at all costs. This is obvious by the manner in which another of the sore points of the Postrisorgimento was utilized by the war press: irredentism and the Triple Alliance.

Irredentism was always a source of friction between Rome and Vienna. Even those who, like Robilant, had played a prominent role in consolidating the Triple Alliance conceded that in the event of European war Italy would have to be satisfied. But we have also seen what the limits of Italy's demands were in the period from 1866 to 1900. They centered on the Trentino. Trieste was not the real concern, save that better treatment of its Italian population, in particular the granting of an Italian university, and municipal autonomy if possible, were demands that most interested Italians would have considered reasonable. Franz Joseph's refusal to visit Rome also rankled. Even the *Idea Nazionale*, which backed the Triple Alliance as consistently as any Italian paper, was always touchy about Italy's relations with Austria-Hungary. As has been seen, the Nationalists had begun to shift their attention from the Mediterranean to the Adriatic before Sarajevo. This in itself suggested that chauvinistic Italian groups were prone to seek out fields for war at all costs. Once Libya was invaded there began that steady devaluation of its significance that prepared the climate of opinion for the interventionist campaign. In April, 1914, the *Idea Nazionale* was taking a stiffer stand toward Austria-Hungary. In general, however, it still attacked "noisy irredentism," always associated with Freemasonry, Republicanism, and the Italian Left. The Triple Alliance was defended as a necessity. Franz Ferdinand's death was considered a promising indication of better relations with Vienna since he had been known to be a backer of Trialism. In mid-July the *Idea Nazionale* was still taking a dim view of irredentist literature such as that of Virginio Gayda. On July 25 Davanzati, the leading foreign policy analyst of the paper, was talking in terms of Italian intervention on the side of the Central Powers should France go to war. He also attacked what he called "Austrophobe sentimentalism."[16]

On August 13 the same Davanzati was calling for war to solve Italy's Adriatic problem. In September, Corradini demanded the liberation of Trent, Trieste, and Dalmatia! He had to admit himself that such a program would have seemed absurd a month before. In October, Di San Giuliano died. Salandra assumed temporary charge of foreign affairs. Even before Di San Giuliano's death, however, Salandra had been in close touch with Sonnino, whom he now begged to enter the Cabinet as foreign minister. Sonnino accepted on October 30.[17] Then, in early December, it was announced that Bülow would be the new German ambassador to Rome. There is no question but that this threw a scare into the interventionist camp. Bülow's prestige as a former chancellor was great. Moreover, he was well connected in Italy through his wife's family. His brother-in-law, Prince Paolo Camporeale, was a member of Parliament. Bülow chose to live in his own Roman Villa Malta, soon to become, according to the interventionists, the site of treacherous intrigues between the Giolittian majority in the Chamber and the German ambassador.

The announcement that the illustrious German was coming to Rome gave rise to rumors of compensations. It seemed that the suggestion Solms had put forth in 1889, that Vienna could cede the Trentino, was now being reconsidered following the First Battle of the Marne. The *Idea Nazionale* on December 12 went so far as to preclude the acceptance of any compensations. Bülow arrived in Rome on December 17. On February 19 the Nationalists, perhaps sensing that a flat refusal to dicker at all was too close to a war-for-war's-sake position, set the minimum Italian demands so as to include Fiume.[18] On March 8 the Austro-Hungarian government relented to the important extent of admitting discussions for compensations on the basis of Article VII of the Triple Alliance.[19] Talk of an offer of the Trentino and a rectification of the Isonzo frontier was in the air. This was written off by the *Idea Nazionale* as a bad joke. According to the once anti-irredentist paper, such an offer left out Trieste, Istria, Dalmatia, Pola, and the Dalmatian archipelago and said nothing about Italy's "world position"! Coppola wrote of the absolupte necessity of fighting for the Entente regardless of any concessions Austria-Hungary might be forced to give.[20]

Since the Nationalists affected, as did most interventionist journalists, a Machiavellian pose, it was necessary to offer rational diplomatic support for this position. But when one examines what Coppola offered in the way of arguments based on realpolitik it can be seen that he was only paying lip service to reasonableness. His analysis of foreign policy was really quite spurious. Again, what was at the heart of his position was the moral necessity of war. A dangerous tendency to cloak brute power and territorial greed in the garb of idealism showed up in the field of diplomacy as it had in relation to the Southern Question and the Socialist party's neutralism. What served as a concrete basis for this approach was the historical failure of the Risorgimento. Italy did not possess a truly national spirit because she had not had a great national war. The Risorgimento, according to Coppola, was the work of a small, aristocratic, and mystical minority of heroic men. When those heroes died, there followed a period in which the country's spiritual existence was depressed. During the decades following the occupation of Rome, the "most cynical materialism" prevailed, beneath which the "national consciousness was obscured, disintegrated and submerged. . . . Today, the question is whether our Risorgimento must remain, and perhaps due to neutrality end up as, simply a political and geographical fact; or whether, through a great war, it may be enriched and animated by a moral content, meaning and value."[21]

The same idealization of power and lighthearted disregard for realities showed up in the pages of Mussolini's radical interventionist *Popolo d'Italia*. As for consistency, its shift toward irredentism was just as startling as that of the chauvinistic Nationalists. Prezzolini had written, in 1910, that irredentism played into the hands of the parasitic, cosmopolitan Freemasons. But as a member of the *Popolo d'Italia*'s staff, he was writing, in November, 1914, "enough of Libya, and on to Trent and Trieste."[22] For Mussolini the cause of the unredeemed lands was harder to square with his own 1911 study of the Trentino. Nothing was impossible for that supple mind, however. Those casual references to the patriotism of the proletariat in the Trentino were dredged up as proof that he had always defended Italy's rights. When Bülow came to Rome, the radicals, like the ultraconservative Nationalists, began to up the ante. Prezzolini had thrown in Fiume by January, 1914. It is interesting to note that Mussolini wavered at this point. He squirmed, as well he might; for he was still trying to leave open an escape hatch that might save him should the war campaign fail. Finally he seemed to give way[23] before Prezzolini's insistence. In many ways the future Duce was a follower rather than a leader in the months of Italian neutrality.

Once Mussolini had made his stand, with customary enthusiasm he went all the way. Not even Fiume, he wrote in early March, would keep Italy out of the war. On March 21 he increased the pressure: should Austria cede all the lands needed to complete Italy's geographical unification, war would still be unavoidable. The nation needed a victory that would give her a sense of internal cohesiveness. Only parts of Italy had fought for unification. The Piedmontese fought at Novara and in the Crimea; Garibaldi had won the Two Sicilies; 1866 was not a national war since it was fought before Rome and Venice were absorbed; as for the occupation of Rome, it was a mere walkover; and the colonial wars that came in the Postrisorgimento were "parliamentary" in their scope and planning.[24] What if Italy should lose? Mussolini covered that eventuality with ease. Even defeat was better than peace, he wrote in mid-February. "One must win," he admitted, "but it is even more necessary that one fight."

There are defeats which do not humiliate people. But that which debases and degrades . . . is the fleeing from all risks . . . staying 'neutral', almost like plunderers or jackals, while everyone else is fighting. The war must reveal Italy to the Italians. Above all, it must discredit the ignoble legend that Italians don't fight; it must erase the shame of Lissa and Custoza; it must show the world that Italy is capable of fighting a war, a great war. This must be repeated: *A Great War!* Not a parliamentary, diplomatic war, but a war made by soldiers who stop only when they have reduced the enemy to impotence. . . . Only this can give Italians the awareness and pride of their Italianness. Only war can make the "Italians" of whom D'Azeglio spoke. Or a REVOLUTION.[25]

The "revolution," of course, was his escape hatch through which he might slip back into the ranks of the Socialist party if all else failed. That the Machiavellians of Italian intervention wanted war at any cost is apparent from their own defense of the necessity for Italy's participation. The *Corriere della Sera* on April 8 said essentially the same thing as Mussolini: no compensations would suffice.[26] It is difficult to escape the conclusion that, incredible though it may sound, the weakest link in the Triple Alliance was that it would have permitted Italy to stay neutral. When Mussolini wrote that neutrality was worse than defeat and that the fleeing of all risks would depress the nation spiritually, he was paraphrasing, without knowing it, the note of March, 1882, in which the Italian government rejected a simple neutrality pact with the Central Powers on the ground that, given the conditions in which Italy's past placed her, such a treaty would have the appearance of reluctance to run any risks at all. This would entail a "serious, irreparable moral injury for a Power not yet surrounded by that halo of military glory." If in 1882 the Italians insisted on an alliance obligating them to a possible, although unlikely, military contribution, it was the same moral reasons that gnawed at the consciences of the war party of 1914–15.

During the negotiations with the Central Powers for compensations, the Austro-Hungarian government stalled. This we know from Baron Burian's postwar admissions. Bülow and Erzberger have made public their own criticisms of Vienna's folly in not coming through with territorial amputations of Hapsburg lands in time to keep Italy neutral. Count Tisza was equally loath to be pressured into excessive concessions. At the last minute Bülow forced von Macchio, the Austro-Hungarian ambassador at Rome, to write down at Bülow's dictation the following concessions: the Tyrol, Gradisca and the west bank of the Isonzo in so far as the population was Italian would go to Italy; Trieste was to become a free city within the cadre of the Dual Monarchy, but with an Italian municipal council and an Italian university; Austria recognized Italian sovereignty over Valona (which Italy had occupied between October and December, 1914); Austria also declared her disinterestedness in Albania. In fact the final offers to Italy were even larger, as Erzberger's account makes clear. Trieste would be made a free city with municipal autonomy and a free port. Furthermore, Italy's requests for Gorizia and the islands of the Curzolian archipelago would be given benevolent consideration. Protection of the national interests of Italian subjects of the Dual Monarchy and a German guarantee of the execution of the accord between Italy and Austria-Hungary rounded out these offers. Bülow officially informed Salandra that the German Empire would back this up and that a mixed commission would be authorized to settle the transfer, thus beginning the actual putting into effect of the agreement. Finally, soldiers of Italian origin would be released from service with the Austro-Hungarian armies.[27]

There is no doubt that these offers, late as they were, went beyond the traditional demands of all but the purely rabble-rousing Irredentists of the 1866–1914 period. As Giolitti noted in his memoirs, they also closely approached Italy's own demands as set down in the first week of April, 1915. Salandra himself has admitted that the April demands would have more than satisfied many Italians.[28] The question of whether the final Austrian concessions, which Salandra received officially only on May

11, could have been accepted by that date is another matter to be considered later. But as far as the war press was concerned, the possibility of Vienna's belatedly giving way was prepared for by an a priori refusal to accept neutrality at any price. The problem was to play down the news of Vienna's concessions once it was released. The neutralist *Stampa* of Turin had publicized the Austrian offers on May 11. They were therefore public knowledge, although the Government never confirmed them; in fact the *Giornale d'Italia*, which was known to represent Sonnino's views, tried to convince its readers that they were meaningless. The *Corriere della Sera* called them laughable. Nor did it mention the fact that a commission would be established to begin work on the transfer of the lands. That is, it did not mention this until May 20,[29] the day when the Chamber was to reconvene. By that date, it was falsely assumed even by those who had worked for peace [30] that the Salandra government and the King were bound by inescapable obligations to fight.

What probably forced this tardy information out of the Milan paper was Bethmann-Hollweg's speech in the Reichstag on May 19, in which the formation of the mixed commission to effect the cession of the territories was mentioned. The surmise that it was forced out by the Chancellor's speech rests on the fact that Albertini was privy to other state secrets and may well have known how far Germany was willing to go to keep Italy neutral. He was closer than any other Italian journalist to the Salandra-Sonnino regime. It was his paper that informed the public, on May 14, that the Triple Alliance had been denounced.[31] When precisely Albertini learned this we do not know. He tells us only that he found out about it at Rome, where he went on May 4, breaking his appointment to meet D'Annunzio at Genoa. On May 15 the *Corriere della Sera* leaked the news, already widely rumored, that definite accords with the Entente had been signed. According to the *Popolo d'Italia*'s Rome correspondent, D'Annunzio and Albertini were the sources by which this information reached the public. In the case of Albertini this is probably correct. As for D'Annunzio, there is no doubt that he knew. The Minister for Colonies, Ferdinando Martini, told the Poet all, over Sonnino's objections.[32] The result was the inciting of mobs against the Chamber and against Giolitti, who was portrayed as the blackest sort of traitor. That the Triple Alliance had been ended a week after the London Pact with the Entente was formed was not mentioned. The *Corriere* merely stated that any belated Austrian offers were unacceptable because the thirty-year-old pact with the Central Powers was no more.[33] Unquestionably, the extent of the final offers was such that it was indispensable to the war press to convince the public and the Deputies that there was no possibility of accepting them. Journalistic sleight of hand was one device. Albertini's paper also took up the same arguments used by the anarchic and radical interventionists. Italians must demonstrate their willingness to fight. Opposed to that willingness, Giolitti's "mentality" was described as being given over to the day-by-day search for material advantages.[34] In a more subtle fashion, the respectable Milan daily made the literati's cultural cliché of idealism versus positivism part of its own rhetorical war arsenal.

Albertini's paper, if not prone to Mussolinian haranguing, certainly showed signs of that subversive temper of Italian conservatism already remarked upon. This became clearer in the *Corriere*'s attitude toward the Chamber of Deputies. The war brought to the surface that other "great historical problem" whose solution was to be effected by intervention. In the background there was the mass of antiparliamentary literature that has been discussed. During the critical period between Tripoli and the Great War, mounting tensions served to give a boost to the enemies of parliament. That men of the extremes should use the passions engendered by neutrality to ride roughshod over the Chamber, viewed as a Giolittian bailiwick, was to be expected. The *Corriere*'s views, however, are more illuminating precisely because of the paper's staid tradition as a defender of social order and of the constitutional monarchy.

In September, 1914, the *Corriere* stated that its mission was to inform the Government of the people's attitude toward the war. The paper would back the ministry if it showed itself in agreement with the popular will, oppose it if it went against the national interest, and prod it should it seem uncertain of its direction. Salandra's slowness soon began to test the paper's confidence in the Government. In early October it repeated its belief that he would take the nation into the war. But it dropped a hint, which was a warning to Salandra, that there were limits of patience. The *Corriere* had no intention of substituting "something else" for governmental authority, that is until it found something better. In the meantime, it would have to be content, and vigilant. The death of Di San Giuliano and Salandra's assuming the post of foreign minister seemed to restore the paper's faith in the system. Parliamentarianism, which had always stifled action, had been transformed by war. Party squabbles and petty considerations, Albertini's paper wrote, had melted into a gray background against which the vision of Italy's destiny stood out. It was easy to criticize government for those who were not a part of it, the *Corriere* admitted. Nonetheless, public opinion had a superior value because it was free from any calculation save love of country. The greatness of events, amplifying the vision, had made it apparent that "the history of the Third Italy is not in fact finished, bound in books, and represented in monuments. We have been a nation for forty-four years; we are still living our origins. The future historian . . . will assign this opening part of the century as well to the period of the Italian Risorgimento. . . . This is not the time to commit a chronological error which could suffocate us." [35]

The Chamber recessed from December 12, 1914, until the following February 18. Parliamentary politics was in abeyance. In its stead, coverage of the Garibaldian volunteers on the western front held a prominent spot in the war press. Giolitti's parecchio letter then appeared to refocus attention on the "petty considerations" of party strife. The *Corriere*'s commentary was interesting, in part because it was an admission of the positive achievements of the former Premier. Giolitti's domestic policy, the paper conceded, had given the Italian masses a political power unknown in any other European constitutional regime, including the French. And yet his foreign policy was the antithesis of popular sentiment. "Giolitti knows the Chamber well, but he does not know the country." How Giolitti, so successful as an interpreter of popular political aspirations on the home front, could be out of touch with Italian opinion regarding the war is hard to imagine. Of course, he was not. The *Corriere*, however, constantly skirted the topic of Italy's obvious opposition to war. Instead it turned to the old chestnut of the disparity between the Chamber and the people. By March this approach had become more pronounced, with traces of Mussolini's threat of "war or revolution" thrown in. Ugo Ojetti, one of Italy's more prominent cultural-political pundits, wrote that in 1915 the Italian "anonymous masses" felt the same shame Italians had felt in 1866 when Venice was received through the charity of the French. After forty years of trasformismo under mediocre statesmen like Giolitti, duing which time Italy was told to "sleep quietly between German and Austrian pillows," the real Italy was awakening. The country, Ojetti noted, was beginning to move, and "the country must be followed before the point is reached at which war will have to be given it because nothing else will calm it down." [36]

The Chamber's spring session was short, running from February 18 to March 22. The Deputies were anxious to go home. Only 265 out of the total of 508 were present at the final sitting. Salandra requested that the Easter vacation begin early and run until May 12. In what turned out to be a prophetic speech, Turati asked that the Chamber be opened by April 15, citing the many pressing domestic problems remaining to be discussed, as well as the whole international situation. He noted that the confidence placed in the Government was equivocal, that men understood neutrality in different ways. What would happen if, with the Chamber closed, that confidence had to be manifested on concrete issues? But Salandra had his way. He referred to the exceptional situation, and the fact that he had obtained an overwhelming mandate for the Ministry's full powers to handle diplomatic talks. That vote of confidence, he said, meant that the Government possessed freedom of action. By a standing vote the Chamber was prorogued until May 12. How right Turati was in pointing out the vagueness of Salandra's position was reflected in the *Corriere*'s editorial. The Premier's words were "generic," true. Yet they were "significant and transparent" in their meaning. Salandra was free to act; but he had the obligation to prove worthy of the country.[37] For the interventionist paper, Salandra was headed toward war, or so it persisted in claiming. The majority of the Chamber, however, was neutralist. Hence the Government's freedom of action was not only "generic" but dangerously ambiguous.

During the long Easter recess Salandra and Sonnino secretly came to terms with the Entente. For its part, the war press tried to create the mood for battle, and for popular pressure on the Ministry should it not be worthy of the nation. The *Corriere*, too respectable to indulge in futuristic chanting or openly incite to riot against the Chamber, managed all the same to devote considerable space to public rallies of less moderate elements who did call for "resolute action" against the Giolittian majority. Far too much free publicity was given to the more turbulent interventionist groups to absolve Albertini's paper of its share of responsibility in the fomenting of mob hysteria. Something of this has been seen in the role of the *Corriere* in preparing for D'Annunzio's return on May 4. On May 7 the royal decree postponing the reconvening of the Chamber to May 20 was announced. The *Corriere* took this as a sign that war was to be declared when the Deputies returned to Rome. It also took the occasion to report on rumors of clandestine contacts between Austrian and German agents, particularly Erzberger, and those Italian politicians who viewed Italy's interests in "mean proportions,"[38] an obvious allusion to the backers of Giolitti. A campaign to discredit the parliamentary majority in the eyes of the people before the Chamber reopened was under way.

No protests were made, however, about the activities of the propaganda agents of the Entente. Since October, 1914, the Belgian Socialist Jules Destrée,[39] with the help of Maeterlinck and occasionally Paul Claudel, had been carrying on an incredibly strenuous speaking tour that was publicized by all interventionist papers and unhampered by the Government. To counteract such pro-Entente propaganda was extremely difficult, since very, very few Italians would have supported a war on the side of the Central Powers. Those who would have backed Italy's allies at the beginning of the war — and Sonnino had been one of these — soon recognized that it was out of the question. The Italian ambassadors at Vienna and Berlin, Avarna and Bollati, are another case in point. Once the allies had accepted Italian neutrality, the opponents of war could not effectively summon up those romanticized arguments of the need for action to fulfill Italy's destiny. Nor could the neutralists exploit the rape of Belgium, the destruction of the Cathedral of Rheims. Books defending Italy's duty toward her allies are very rare items.[40] German propaganda was competing with the poetry of Italy's Great War. The best neutralist jounal, the *Italia Nostra*, was aware of the difficulties in gaining sympathy for a negative policy.[41] Although it represented the wishes of the majority of Italians, it was fighting a losing battle against the intellectual petty bourgeoisie. Its arguments, put forth by men of great scholarly distinction — foremost among them Luigi Salvatorelli and Croce — were for the most part characterized by sensible reasoning and diplomatic analysis of the European balance of power. Against the irrational temper of the interventionists, the language of calm reflection made little headway.

This was the situation when, on May 9, Giolitti returned to Rome to await the opening of the Chamber and to visit his wife, who was recuperating at nearby Frascati from a recent illness. He had been told, quite unofficially, that the Triple Alliance had been broken. The news of his coming had been spread in the press. Met at the station by crowds of interventionists, he walked unperturbed, and unescorted save by a few friends, to his Rome residence. With habitual self-control, developed over four decades of public service, he moved unscathed through the streets of Rome to cries of "Down with Austria," "Down with Germany," "Down with Giolitti." To one noisy demonstrator, he remarked: "At least cry long live Italy." This was met with the rejoinder that "Down with Giolitti" meant the same thing. It also meant, given his stature as the leading Italian parliamentarian, down with the Chamber of Deputies. This was made clear that evening when there began a voluntary trek to his door by at least three hundred Deputies and some one hundred Senators who left their calling cards between the afternoon of May 9 and noon of May 10. It was a clear manifestation of the majority's opposition to a war that was rumored to be coming and that the politicians could not prevent as long as the Chamber was in recess. The *Corriere*'s reporter in Rome mentioned that quite a few such cards had been dropped off at his house. On the 12th the paper wrote off the calling-card demonstration as the work of a faction of Deputies who represented no particular political program but lived instead off the "nostalgic memory of its parliamentary omnipotence." In poetic retaliation, one hundred similar tokens were deposited at the lodgings of D'Annunzio [42] when he arrived in Rome on May 12. These, one may assume, represented the "real country" rising in wrath against the master of parliamentary corruption.

In response to the supposed maneuvers by the notorious ex-minister, Mussolini called for his lynching and the summary execution of a few dozen Deputies. Prezzolini suggested assassination. The conservative press, to be sure, did not go to such violent extremes. The *Giornale d'Italia*, which in the public's mind represented Sonnino's views, spoke only of sabotage of the nation's true and proper interests. The *Corriere* spoke of an insurrection, an attempt at violence on the part of the Giolittians who had given their vote of confidence to Salandra.[43] On May 13 Salandra's resignation was announced on the ground that the Ministry did not possess the support of a majority of the constitutional elements in the Chamber. This suggested, as Turati was to emphasize,[44] that Salandra did not even include the votes of the official Socialists, estimated at fifty-two, in calculating the neutralist bloc in the Chamber. These Socialists would not have been referred to as "constitutional" by Salandra, although they had in fact become, as in the days of Pelloux, an important bulwark in the defense of Italy's parliamentary institutions. The Cabinet's resignation provoked an incredible wave of linguistic violence from the war press. The *Idea Nazionale* called for a purge of Giolitti and his brood who "in their fat bellies, thick skulls, and filthy beards contain all the condensed vileness which any people would hide in their slums and in their Parliament."[45] Taking a sampling from the moderate papers — the reader can imagine the tenor of similar Papinian-Mussolinian diatribes — the *Corriere* claimed that foreign and domestic elements opposed to Italy's progress had triumphed. "We deplore violence," the editorial went on, "but even more we deplore the irregularities which engender it." The Milan paper tipped off its readers that the Triple Alliance had been broken, adding that it had been assured Giolitti knew the full truth of Italy's diplomatic position. Were this the case, there would be no word sufficiently "burning" to describe his action. Thus began a legend concerning Giolitti's perfidy that has persisted down to this day. As to what Salandra should do, the *Corriere* advised him to proceed along his glorious path even without the Chamber's backing. On May 15 the paper still was deploring violence, but deploring more the fact that men who would treat Italy as if it were a Giolittian majority would lead the nation to humiliation. It was at this point that the *Corriere* announced that a pact with the Entente had been signed. Italy was rising to show the world that the many years of Giolitti's dictatorship might have compromised the dignity of the Chamber, but had not blemished the national conscience.[46] The *Giornale d'Italia* also accused Giolitti of knowing all, and concluded: "Italy is drowning in a parliamentary swamp." [47]

On the afternoon of May 16 the announcement that the King had refused Salandra's resignation was released. At 2:00 P.M., May 20, the Chamber opened its last prewar session. Salandra presented the Government's request for extraordinary power in case of war. He cited the "supreme law which is the welfare of the State." A commission of eighteen Deputies, representing all factions of the Chamber, was selected by Giuseppe Marcora, the President of the Chamber. Sonnino then presented the Green Book covering diplomatic talks from December 9, 1914, to May 4, 1915. Thus the Deputies did not have access either to the documents relating to Di Dan Giuliano's negotiations or to the final Austrian offers.[48] Later editions of the Green Book did, however, contain the Austro-Hungarian note, dated May 23, in reply to Italy's breaking of the Alliance. That note, while not listing concessions, affirmed Vienna's willingness to keep the Alliance alive by making concessions so large that they could only be justified by that desire. The note also refused to recognize Italy's declaration of freedom of action and nullification of the Alliance, since one year's notice was required. Further, Vienna stated that if immediate cession of the territories was materially impossible, the Imperial Government was perfectly prepared to offer all necessary guarantees to prepare and assure consignment of the lands within a very short time.[49] This document came too late to have had any influence on the Chamber's vote.

After the presentation of the Green Book a secret vote was taken, in accordance with the rules, to decide whether to discuss the bill for extraordinary powers immediately. This was passed 367 to 54. Marcora then announced that since the ministers had to go to the Senate, and since the Commission must have time to examine the law, the Chamber would recess until 5:00 P.M. That was at 3 P.M. The Chamber had two hours to decide. When the Deputies reassembled, Paolo Boselli, head of the Commission appointed to consider the Government's request for extraordinary powers, spoke of the days of Garibaldi, of the great shades of Italy's creators who seemed returned to life. He referred to "happy Italian youth risen again to impassioned ideals," in a style that must have sounded familiar to D'Annunzio, who was sitting in the gallery. There were few speeches on the bill, and these were mostly pleas for war. Barzilai spoke of the "lands which were in the vision of Dante." "Only now, when Italy in their name takes up the torch of life which had fallen from her hands," were they to be "gathered up in the religion of the *patria*."

It was Turati who spoke in defense of neutrality and of Italy's parliamentary institutions. He was thereby defending the regime that Giolitti symbolized. Giolitti himself was absent: he had returned to his home on May 17. In his long speech, by far the longest of the session, the socialist leader insisted, correctly, that the great majority of both houses opposed the war unless it were prescribed by a "necessary defense . . . in the most literal sense: by absolute, material, brutal necessity." This was an answer to the sophistical argument, frequently employed by the war press, that by voluntarily going into the war Italy was really defending herself from the inevitable *revanche* of Austria-Hungary and Germany. Indicative of the split in socialist ranks, this very argument was presented in rebuttal by Ettore Ciccotti, formerly a neutralist Socialist. After Ciccotti's speech, by which the Deputies were reassured — although it was obvious to all by that time — that the Socialists would never sabotage the war, the Government's request for full powers was passed by a secret vote of 407 to 74. The Chamber then closed.[50] Italy had her Great War.

Outside, among the intellectuals, it had been predicted that the Chamber, by accepting war, would give the final proof of its degeneracy, canceling itself out as a force in the country. "The Deputies," the *Voce* wrote, "so base that they did not want war, will be even more base in accepting it without wanting it."[51] It was partly to disprove this prediction that Turati had spoken, to refute the interventionists claim that Parliament had retreated before their demands. There is no serious doubt about the antiparliamentary character of the Radiant May. Salandra's government still has its defenders who persist in denying that the events of 1915 were anything but constitutional. But their arguments are very strained, as well as being interesting precisely because of their dredging up of familiar nationalist casuistry. It is claimed that in all the demonstrations for war the crowds never attacked Parliament as an institution, as a "characteristic organ of the political regime." Proof of this is found in no less an example than D'Annunzio's theatrical speeches of 1915. His well known gibe at the Chamber of Deputies as a "third rate club," and his famous appearance at the Costanzi Theatre in Rome in May, 1915, during which he accused Giolitti and the neutralist Deputies of treason, were not attacks on Parliament. Indeed, D'Annunzio was appealing to Parliament, to a "free Parliament," according to one historian, to save Italy from Giolitti.[52]

By a free Parliament one can only mean a Chamber liberated from its constitutional majority. What we have here is a latter-day use of that idealized Parliament which we encountered in the 1890's, and of which Corradini and his nationalist colleagues spoke. Since Parliament was a common heritage of the Risorgimento, it could not be attacked but only subverted. It was national and unitarian in its roots. In the *Idea Nazionale*, as we have seen, the appeal was made to a "pure" parliamentary system. D'Annunzio was doing the same in 1915, and Mussolini would continue this tradition in the postwar period.[53] As for the Chamber of Deputies considered as a concrete, historical body, committed in the great majority to the preservation of neutrality, it became a sort of anti-Parliament. Its leading personality, Giolitti, was pictured as thoroughly un-Italian, a positivistic bureaucrat incapable of intuiting the voice of the people or of sensing the mysterious redeeming power of war.

The attempt to deprive the Radiant May of its antiparliamentary coloring has been justly criticized as contrary to the logic of things.[54] Perhaps the best support for this judgment is the description left by a noted historian who was an interventionist in 1915. Giolitti's realm, Gioacchino Volpe wrote, was the Parliament. He thought he could harness that "machine" and with it dominate the country. "But less than ever was Parliament the country." Giolitti fell midst violence akin to civil war.[55] Volpe's remarks have the virtue of honesty, and are certainly more factual in accepting the revolutionary responsibility of the war party.

Intervention was the cure for every conceivable national deficiency, domestic or diplomatic. It was also, therefore, a refutation of the whole work of the Postrisorgimento. Because of this, the Great War was the outstanding turning point of modern Italian history. The magnitude of the shock that awaited Italy is obvious from any realistic examination of the situation in which Italy found itself in 1914–15. In the face of historical realities, much interventionist propaganda is simply insane. Bloodshed would help solve the Southern Question, restore the heroic character of Italian foreign policy, revive the vigor of political radicalism, and create a new regime that would integrate governed and government. When the list of war's magical benefits was drawn up, the issue of Church and State was not forgotten. Here was another old problem, a product of Italian unification itself, brought back to life by the crisis of neutrality.

There is no need to question the fact that the Vatican opposed Italy's joining the belligerents. The Nationalist party had made its bid for Catholic support, and managed to get some, only to be forced to recognize the barrier the war had erected between their embryonic organization and the Church's hierarchy. Despite this rebuff, Nationalists and other interventionist groups continued to claim that war would help heal the breach opened at Porta Pia in 1870. Their argument had two main parts, both of which were fundamentally hostile to the relationship that had emerged, for good or evil, between Church and State over the past fifty years: the creation of a patriotic clergy and a national Catholicism; and the alteration of the Laws of the Guarantee in order to prevent papal diplomacy from exploiting the Roman Question in wartime.

Regarding the first of these two points, we come again upon a theme reminiscent of Luigi Tosti's attempt to end the struggle between the Vatican and the Quirinal. If the patriotic abbot of Monte Cassino personified the outlook of an older generation of clerics, men who had labored for the faith and the nation during the saga of the Risorgimento, the futility of his enterprise revealed that the conflict of Church and State was stronger than the passions of patriotic priests. The cleavage of nation and clergy, of citizen and Catholic, became a significant feature of that feeling of national incompleteness which Crispi had hoped to remove. This was true as well in 1914–15. Since many who hoped for clerical collaboration also feared the power of the Blacks, just as Bonghi had in the late nineteenth century, it will not be surprising to see the Vatican come under attack from its former friends once the Papacy had taken a stand on the war. What will emerge at this point, at the point when there could be no more glossing over the Pope's explicit condemnation of war, is the revival of the figure of the patriot-priest, the heroic cleric. Interventionists, frustrated by the Church's pacifist position, would play up the examples of courageous martyrdom in contrast to the cold, formal pronouncements of the Holy See. In this, as in so many other aspects of national insecurity, the way was prepared for by Oriani and his literary tribute to Don Giovanni Verità, Garibaldi's benefactor.

The difficulty of finding the counterpart for Don Giovanni Verità in 1914 soon became obvious. However much the interventionist press exaggerated the extent of popular enthusiasm for war, only rarely does one find a report of rallies in which priests took part, while there are significant examples of open clerical antiwar demonstrations.[56] Clerical opposition to Benedict XV's plea for peace was rare, so rare that a prominent Socialist Deputy, Claudio Treves, speaking in the Chamber against entry into the war, insisted that all those Italian organizations that reflected the wishes of the people, who were close to the masses, were for peace.[57] This was a transparent allusion to the Vatican and the Socialist party, a surprising linking of interests from a leader of a traditionally anticlerical party. Mussolini's paper jumped at the chance to use the tacit alliance of Socialist and Catholic as a basis for his own revival of old-style Garibaldian Church-baiting as well as for trimming up his image as a true revolutionary Socialist. War was a school of discipline and heroism demanding of men the same courage that went into the making of class warfare. Socialist neutralism, however, was akin to Catholic humanitarianism. The party's platform "stank of the sacristy." The *Popolo d'Italia* compared Socialist dogmatism to that of the Vatican. Mussolini's expulsion from the party was explained as a purge of the heretic. The paper did its best to remind its readers that the official Socialists were bosom brothers of the Jesuits. Benedict's first encyclical, *Ad beatissimi*, which taught that the roots of war lay in secular, anti-Christian society, was answered for Mussolini's journal by Papini. Putting on the old toga of modern paganism, a bit faded since the days of the *Leonardo* back at the turn of the century, Papini attacked Christianity as a source of femininity and cowardice, whereas war and deeds were masculine.[58]

Nationalists were just as incensed by the Pope's pacifism as were the writers of the *Popolo d'Italia*. But they could not lapse into anticlericalism without throwing themselves into the radical camp. Their insistence on traditional social unities and their theory of the integrated nation, especially as elaborated by Coppola, forbade out-and-out attacks on the clergy. There was also some reason to hope at the outset of his pontificate that the new Pope would turn out to be pro-French. Cardinal Della Chiesa, who became Benedict XV in August, 1914, was known to be an admirer of Cardinal Rampolla, Leo XIII's Secretary of State. This would suggest that he might prove to be a friend of France and of the Entente. It was said that he had voted for Cardinal Ferrata, formerly nuncio to Paris, whom Poincaré described as the "French Candidate."[59] The *Corriere della Sera* looked upon Benedict's election as a victory for the politically inclined members of the Curia, those churchmen who wished to have a trained diplomat on the throne during war. The Milan paper picked up *Figaro*'s conclusion that the election was France's answer to the Austrian veto of Rampolla during the conclave that elected Pius X. When Cardinal Ferrata, whom Benedict had chosen as his Secretary of State, died a month later, he was replaced by Pietro Gasparri, also considered inclined to work for an end of the clash with the Third Republic.[60]

In the light of these hypotheses, the *Idea Nazionale* hopefully suspended judgment as to which stand the new ruler of the Church would take regarding the war. The paper played down the papal references to the abnormal conditions of the Holy See in the first encyclical.[61] It was impossible, however, to avoid the overwhelming evidence that the Catholic press, with few exceptions, was neutralist, and that the Pope was opposed to any extension of the war, whatever success his efforts for restoring peace might have. There was also a leaning towards the Dual Monarchy in certain Catholic quarters. This was not necessarily a reflection of a national favoritism. For many, especially the Jesuits, war was the result of a universal collapse of authority. De Maistre's concept of the papacy seemed especially appropriate in times of widespread chaos among secular states. The Hapsburg cause could be regarded as the cause of all earthly authority, not just that of a specific power. There were, of course, those laymen who favored Austria for narrower reasons, just as there were clerics whose position was motivated by hatred for Masonic France.[62] In any event, the Nationalists had little hope that the Catholic press would come out against the Central Powers. The *Civiltà Cattolica*, which had shown an interest in the nationalist movement, editorialized that the spread of war and disorder was such that it was useless to indulge in sterile recriminations as to which party was to blame. The root of the evil was to be found in the anarchic and anti-Christian nature of liberalism.[63]

Nationalist theoreticians were in complete agreement when it came to the social insufficiencies of liberalism. It was all the more galling to see their dream of a national-clerical political union ruined by the Vatican's universalist attitude. The *Idea Nazionale* grasped at every straw that might weigh in the balance against the Pope's clear pronouncements. An interview with a Catholic Deputy, Luigi Montresor, in which the politician denied that Catholics were all neutralists and affirmed the inevitability of war with Austria, was picked up by Coppola as proof that the Vatican's position did not reflect the patriotic feelings of the Catholic masses. Montresor's interview, however, was immediately challenged by the *Unità Cattolica,* whose director, Alessandro Cavallanti, was decidedly pro-Austrian. Other speeches by prominent laymen were given publicity whenever they suggested the possibility of war.[64] The *Idea Nazionale* persisted in maintaining that the view of such journals as the *Unità Cattolica* did not express more than a minority sentiment. In desperation, the Turks' intervention was made into a "holy war."

Nothing could obscure the truth that Corradini, far less ultramontane than Coppola, recognized along with Mussolini: the Church and the Socialist party were on the same side. The split between Nationalists and the Catholic hierarchy was out in the open by the fall of 1914. Yet the Nationalists still tried to woo patriotic clergy and laity. This forced the Nationalists to take a stand against the Vatican that was more hostile to the Church's authority than was Mussolini's anachronistic anticlericalism. Appealing to the faithful against the teachings of the Pope became a common feature in the *Idea Nazionale.* By February, 1915, the paper was threatening a rise of Gallicanism in Italy as a reaction to the Vatican's neutralism. On its side, the *Civiltà Cattolica* examined the question of the Nationalists and religious obedience in such a way as to distinguish between legitimate patriotism and excessive nationalism.[65]

If war were to heal the nation's wounds, unite Italy as never before, some answer to Catholic neutralism would have to be found. It was not possible to pretend that the Catholic churchmen were at all moved by interventionist literature. The answer to this dilemma, therefore, had to be sought outside of Italy, in the battlefields of France and Belgium. Here the figure of the "priest in knapsack" attested to the power of war to end the historic conflict between Church and State. The first Catholic hero of the war press in Italy was Cardinal Mercier, Archbishop of Malines, the Primate of Belgium. He had been in Rome when the Germans swept into Belgium. The *Corriere della Sera* described his grief as he wept for the destruction of his church and homeland. Once back in Belgium, Mercier sent appeals to Benedict XV protesting German atrocities. These were answered by the Cardinal Secretary of State. The Pope shared the anguish of a sorely tried people.[66] But there was not, nor could there be, a specific condemnation of any one nation.

The high point of the press campaign to convince Italians of the advantages of war for the question of Church and State came at Christmas, 1914. Cardinal Mercier's pastoral letter was taken as an example of war's redeeming qualities. The prelate had described German atrocities, but more important were his descriptions of the increased nobility of the Belgian people during war. There had been a simultaneous rise of patriotism and Christian virtue. "The religion of Christ," he wrote, "makes patriotism a virtue. No one who is not a perfect patriot is a perfect Christian."[67] Borgese, writing in the *Corriere della Sera*, called the message the masterpiece of the war. Belgium was being consecrated through suffering attended by the rise of a heroic belief. French cardinals backed up their Belgian brother with similar appeals to Rome. One of them, Cardinal Amette, Archbishop of Paris, prefixed a sermon on the responsibility for the war to a papal plea for peace he had been obliged to deliver. The *Popolo d'Italia* capitalized on this, and on reports of strong criticism of the Pope coming from Belgian churchmen.[68]

In reply, the allocution of January 22, 1915, stated that while no one was permitted to injure justice, the Pope found it neither suitable nor useful to involve the pontifical authority in the debates of the contesting parties. All combatants were equally embraced. According to the interventionists, the allocution was a cold and lifeless message, lacking in Christian spirit.[69] This reaction to the papal pronouncement hinted at a new use for antipositivist attitudes: to attack the official position of the Church on the war. These bureaucratic formulas, whether of Church or State, so the argument went, were contradicted by the spontaneous idealism of the people both as Christians and as patriots.

The focal point for this appeal to the cultural revival associated with antipositivism was France. Nowhere were the mystical powers of battle more apparent, according to Italian interventionists, than in the sister Latin nation. A new morality, a new toughness, the fading away of effete cosmopolitanism supposedly revitalized the once decadent Third Republic. French agents in Italy were pleased to note that this was a much-talked-of aspect of the war, suggesting growing sympathy for the French cause.[70] We have seen that the Nationalists used this theme in order to justify their switch from the old virile Germany, home of order and civility, to the once foppish France. In war, Frenchmen had drawn together and closed ranks even around the clergy. Catholic enthusiasm for defense of the fatherland could be seen in those criticisms of Benedict XV by high French clergy. It was the death of Charles Péguy, however, that best testified to the birth of a new France. Coppola had always enjoyed raking over the Third Republic, which he pictured as a cesspool of dandies, Freemasons, and democratic idiocy. War, however, had restored France's ancient virtues. The death of Péguy at the front was a sign of this.[71] Prezzolini, in the *Voce*, wrote of Péguy's martial literary style, of his realization that behind all party squabbles there were only two categories of men: the mystics and the politicians. Péguy was the former, a Bergsonian who stood for "life against intellect; movement against stability." A Republican interventionist, Eugenio Vajna, who, like Fazzari long before him, hoped to fuse the Mazzinian tradition with Catholicism, also made Péguy his ideal. Péguy's was an active Catholicism whereas neutrality was cowardice.[72]

This confusion of religious sentiment with Bergsonian activism was in keeping with neither the diplomacy nor the theology of the Vatican. But it was a very convenient weapon for the Italian interventionist elite precisely because it fit in so well with the running attack on positivism. It was indicative of the cool reception this ploy was to have among orthodox churchmen in Italy that the defrocked priest and founder of the National Democratic League, Romolo Murri, took up the appeal to war as a vital experience resulting in religious awakening. The *Civiltà Cattolica* warned its readers that press releases from France claiming that war was producing a religious revival were based on the personal opinions of the correspondents.[73]

Save for the interventionists, the months of Italian neutrality seemed to bring Church and State closer together than ever before. Giolitti had remarked in 1904, at the time of Loubet's visit to Rome, that the Roman Question was dead. It certainly appeared to be in 1914, for the simple reason that the majority of the Chamber, the Vatican, the Socialist party membership, and the party's parliamentary spokesmen were agreed that war should be avoided unless forced upon Italy. This common ground was reflected in the similar treatment given all neutralist advocates by the war camp. Praise for Belgian and French clerics, and for Catholic citizens like Péguy, was coupled with downgrading of the Pope's bureaucratic encyclicals. From the Marne there arose the voice of the Catholic masses, source of true piety and patriotism, speaking out against the sterile universalism of the Vatican. The contrast between Cardinal Mercier and Benedict XV was the interventionists' equivalent of the cliché that there were two Italies, one real and one official, or that there was a heroic and a "paunchafistic" socialism. This does not mean that unity of interests existed. Papal condemnation of liberalism, source of all disorder, was a repetition of the teachings of Leo XIII. Between the Church hierarchy and the Socialist party fundamental doctrinal differences were obvious. Nonetheless, the stable, moderate, and practical outlook that shunned facile solutions to the insoluble problem created by Porta Pia had led a modus vivendi, the result of a half century of political experience. Church and State were brought together in 1914–15 by the mutual recognition that, great as might be the ideal differences which separated them, they were united on a momentous issue.

To deny this is to question the viability of the Postrisorgimento as a whole. As in every other branch of war propaganda, the necessity of intervention was linked to the belief that the fifty years since 1870 had not solved the nation's most pressing problems, in this case the Roman Question. In order to dramatize the persistence of the Church-State dilemma, however, the war press was forced, by the logic of things, to resort to the specious appeal to Catholics against the Vatican. This was too labored to be convincing. There was the other edge to the sword, which remains to be considered: the charge that the Pope planned to use his universal position to secure a place at the peace conference with the intention of effecting an internationalization of the Guarantees. This argument was more successful, having a long history behind it and being given immediacy by the attitudes of prominent Catholic journalists.

For background it must be recalled that once the offer to allow the Powers to mediate the dispute between the Vatican and the Italian government was rejected, future Italian ministries forbade any interference in what was considered a purely domestic problem. The Laws of the Guarantees were part of Italian statute law. Stefano Jacini, a moderate Catholic federalist, was himself forced to admit that the idea of an international settlement of the Roman Question appealed to none but the French. At the time, during the pontificate of Leo XIII, this was tantamount to killing the idea even for conservatives who dreamed of ending the Roman Question. Fear of papal machinations in this direction frightened Sonnino, among others, and prompted Italy's veto of papal attendance at the Hague Peace Conference.

When Benedict XV came to the papal throne, it appeared that the Church might be moving toward a policy of securing an international guarantee of the Holy See's territorial and juridical position. In the encyclical of November 1, 1914, the prayer for peace was followed by the Pope's wishes for an end to the "abnormal state in which the Head of the Church finds himself." Commenting on the encyclical, the *Civiltà Catto-*

lica stressed the over-all effects of war on Catholics and Italian citizens. The Church and the Italian public were closer together than before the war, the Jesuit review wrote. The mood was right for conciliation. Moreover, had not the war demonstrated that the Pope's position was abnormal and that the Laws of the Guarantees were a miserable illusion? The *Corriere della Sera* perceived a new direction in papal diplomacy, or rather the revival of an older policy that had lapsed. While not wishing to exaggerate the portent of the encyclical, the Milan daily had reason to think that Benedict might be hoping to vindicate the Church's claims by exploiting the international situation. The traditional protest against the Church's abnormal conditions seemed more detailed than usual. This was also the topic of conversation in Rome. The American ambassador, Thomas Nelson Page, informed Lansing in December of feeling in Roman circles that the Vatican was trying to strengthen its position abroad in order to get to the peace conference.[74]

There was unquestionably fear of papal diplomacy in many quarters. And it must be said that this fear was fed by editorials in prominent Catholic papers, which helped to excite nervous statesmen and to incite ardent interventionists. When the conclave met to choose Pius' successor, neutrality had already been proclaimed. It was rumored that Italy had stayed out of the war in order to prevent any interruption of the conclave's work. Italian news agency *Stefani* carried an official bulletin on August 25 denying this. Italy would defend the nation's best interests as it thought fit, regardless of secondary considerations. The declaration of neutrality had no relation to the death of Pius X. The *Civiltà Cattolica* unwisely chose this moment to raise the question of the Papacy's diplomatic immunities in time of war as these were protected by the Laws of the Guarantees, insisting that the Government's bulletin proved that the Guarantees were insufficient. Were Italy in the war, it was clear that national interests would triumph over papal rights. It was obvious, the journal concluded, that the Roman Question, said to be dead and buried, was alive and flourishing. Had the interests of state demanded it, the conclave would have had no freedom whatsoever. Had not Ruggero Bonghi, who drafted the Guarantees, admitted that a day could come when they would go up in smoke? Had not Visconti Venosta once offered to place them before the Powers? This proved them both insufficient and juridically an international problem.[75]

The crux of the matter was Article XI of the Guarantees, which assured the Vatican's diplomatic rights. At the time the laws were drawn, the suggestion of an amendment suspending this article in time of war was made by Count Corte. Bonghi, whatever his later qualms, had rejected this rider as being too hypothetical. But the idea Corte had raised did not die. It was taken up in 1889 by a noted student of the Roman Question, Francesco Scaduto. Scaduto also proposed suspending diplomatic immunity in case of war. He insisted that this had always been the understanding of the law's framers. Scaduto was also an advocate of what he called a democratization of the Church's structure that would end the authoritarian spirit associated with the closed priesthood.[76] This was not entirely at variance with interventionist incitement of the Catholic masses against the Vatican's authority.

There were calmer observers who refused to be panicked into a break with past policy by the *Civiltà Cattolica*'s inopportune articles — inopportune because they played into the hands of the enemies of Church as well as State. Foremost among these was Luigi Luzzatti, statesman and economist, one of the "responsibles" in the days of the Bank Scandals. Writing in the *Corriere della Sera*, Luzzatti praised the Italian government for having in no way hindered the meetings of the conclave, for having upheld the great tradition of the Guarantees — described as a monument to Latin wisdom. Luzzatti rejected the idea of an internationalization of the laws or of any tampering with Article XI. The rashness of those Catholic papers that demanded internationalization is seen by the fact that they were demanding more than would be agreed to by liberals, who upheld Cavour's interpretation and who would grant the maximum liberty to the Church in all circumstances. Considered in connection with the interventionists generally, however, the significance of Luzzatti's point of view was that he implicitly defended the work of the statesmen of the Postrisorgimento by shunning any drastic reversal of their policies. Italy should stick to these policies. Despite the delicacy of the situation, the nation could survive the test.[77] By pressing for a reversal of the older liberal viewpoint, the Catholic press furnished the extremists in the interventionist camp with welcomed ammunition. Napoleone Colajanni, speaking in the Chamber, referred to the Vatican's intentions to get to the peace table in order to obtain an international settlement of the Roman Question. De Felice warned that the Powers would never listen to the claims of any nation, faced with the Vatican's intrigues, if that nation was absent from the list of belligerents.[78] Francesco Ruffini, rector of the University of Turin and a close friend of Orlando, minister of justice in the Salandra cabinet, insisted that there was nothing binding on

Italian policy in respect to Article XI should the nation be involved in war. On the eve of Italy's intervention, Scaduto wrote a preface for a historical study of the vexing topic. This book was a summary of all the interventionist arguments relating to the Roman Question, from Benedict's first encyclical to Cardinal Mercier's pastoral letter and the Central Powers' intention to use the Church-State problem to blackmail Italy, just as Bismarck was said to have done in 1881.[79]

Bismarck, of course, had not tried to blackmail Italy. But the claim that he had, which Ruffini put forth after the war, ties in with interventionist propaganda in 1914–15. To say that the fate which would have been reserved for Italy had she stayed out "freezes the soul of every Italian"[80] is no more than a historical defense of the decision to go to war. And it is a very weak defense as far as the Roman Question is concerned. However much German and Austrian diplomacy may have lost its edge since the days of Bismarck and the elder Andrássy, it was absurd to imagine that any power would risk throwing Italy into the opposing camp in 1915 by seriously taking up the demands of immoderate clerical groups against the existing Laws of the Guarantees, much less by promoting the Vatican's temporal claims.

By demanding the inclusion of Article XV in the London Treaty of 1915, thereby barring the Pope from the peace conference at war's end — assuming a clear victory for the Entente, which was very debatable at the time — the Salandra government was turning away from the spirit of slow accommodation and political pragmatism that had motivated the clearer minds of the Postrisorgimento. It may be argued that Article XV was in keeping with the veto imposed by Italy at the time of the Hague Peace Conference. But there is really little similarity between a diplomatic move that cost Italy nothing and the gigantic sacrifice war would entail. Whatever the Vatican's hopes of removing the Guarantees from Italy's unilateral keeping, it was Italy itself that succeeded in making them an international question in 1915, having failed to believe that the nation was strong enough to secure its own house. It is revealing that Orlando, who as Salandra's minister of justice was involved in securing Article XV, and who prided himself on having always worked to bridge the gap between the Vatican and Quirinal, carefully avoided mentioning the clause in his memoirs. One could not claim to be a partisan of smoothing out relationships between Church and State and at the same time make much of the London Treaty. Even more revealing is Orlando's insistence that the Lateran Pact was consistent with the spirit of the Guarantees.[81] Involved here is the larger question of the continuity between the period 1870–1915 and fascism. For those who see the latter emerging naturally from the first half century of Italian unity, it is essential to distort the reality, as well as to minimize the tangible accomplishments of the earlier period. Few greater distortions are imaginable than Orlando's juxtaposition of the Guarantees and the Lateran Pact. The Concordat was arranged with a government that had destroyed constitutional rule. Failure to end the quarrel between Church and State would have benefited liberalism in the 1920's as it had in the late nineteenth century.

In assessing the Government's reasons for going to war, the re-emergence of the Roman Question must be kept in mind. The Salandra government was certainly influenced by interventionist claims that war alone would parry the thrust of the internal enemy. Overtures to members of the Cabinet by prominent neutralist prelates [82] backfired by strengthening the arguments of the minority war faction. Erzberger's presence in Rome and his real and imagined visits to the Vatican were given constant publicity in the war press. German diplomacy was heavy-footed in neutral Italy as in neutral America. A skillful French agent, Charles Benoist, whose own contacts in high ecclesiastical places were excellent, shrewdly advised Paris to avoid any semblance of meddling in a domestic issue about which Italians were very sensitive. He knew that there was insufficient popular enthusiasm for war. Nothing would have been more likely to dampen what pro-French feeling there was than an attempt to capitalize on the Roman Question. The American ambassador, partial toward the Entente, urged Lansing not to appoint a representative to the Holy See for fear of antagonizing the Quirinal.[83] The tragic Erzberger, sincere as were his desires to preserve Italian neutrality, solve the Roman Question, and satisfy legitimate irredentist demands was only serving the friends of war by his actions.

German clumsiness, however, neither explained nor necessitated Italy's final decision. There was no real reason to believe that the State would suffer from the intrigues of the Blacks. Luzzatti as late as April 25, 1915, pointed out that there were indications of the Vatican's willingness to be conciliatory regarding its diplomatic immunities in the event Italy should go to war. Those who wished to strengthen the Guarantees by means of international ties harmful to Italy's position, he wrote, and those who wished to weaken them — that is, by restricting Article XI — were a minority that would gladly drive both Pope and King out of Rome.[84] This was a very perceptive analysis. It meant that Church and

State, King and Pope, had mutual interests to preserve against the assaults of both sets of extremists.

Luzzatti was correct in his appraisal of Vatican policy. Whatever intransigent clerical organs might say, it was quite clear that they did not speak for Benedict XV. The prestige of such journals as the openly pro-Austrian *Unità Cattolica* was in fact diminished by the statements of the Pope's new Secretary of State. In one of his first acts, Cardinal Gasparri reversed, rather audaciously, a journalistic trend that had its roots in a noted "Warning" of 1912, put forth by Pius X in order to check the ardor of Catholic papers, which were too prone to listen to the modernists and too enthusiastic about the Libyan War. Ever since the publication of Pius's message, the *Unità Cattolica* had tried to establish itself as the paper most closely reflecting the Vatican's position. By denying that any one paper could put itself forward as the true interpreter of the Vatican's wishes and attitudes, Gasparri's letter threw cold water on the *Unità's* pro-Austrian campaign.[85]

After Italy had declared war the ministers of Bavaria, Prussia, and Austria accredited to the Holy See left Rome. Now that the former ally had made its choice, Germany was free to speak out against "unjust pressures" being exerted on the Pope and to predict that Benedict would be forced to leave Italy. To put an end to the press campaign from across the Alps, Cardinal Gasparri issued a statement that cut the ground from under this opportunistic use of the Roman Question by the Central Powers. The Holy See, out of respect for its neutrality, had no intention at all of causing embarrassment for the Italian government. It placed its faith in God, awaiting a suitable systematization of its position "not from foreign arms, but from the triumph of those sentiments of justice which it is hoped are ever more widespread among the Italian people, in keeping with their true interests."[86]

Orlando later claimed that this renunciation of the policy of Pius IX removed another obstacle from the path toward pacification between Church and State.[87] The Italian government, however, had already created a new obstacle, damaging the liberal pattern of agreeing to disagree, of working out the problem without recourse to foreign backing or to concordats. It was Italy, not the Vatican, which turned to foreign arms in 1915. The diplomacy of the Salandra regime, in this as in other questions, was a decided departure from the practices of his predecessors, the more unfortunate as it was unnecessary, the more suggestive of im-

pending disaster as it was founded on feelings of internal insecurity conjoined with diplomatic and military carelessness.

In conclusion, what can we say of the significance of the war and of
the crisis of May, 1915? Not only did the events and decisions of that
month represent a reversal of the policies of a generation of Italian
statesmen; they seemed to refute the very existence of a united Italy. And
yet, contrasted with the frequently specious and twisted arguments of
the war press, there is a great accumulation of evidence to prove that
Italy was far more united than ever before. When E. J. Dillon arrived
in Milan sometime in February, 1915, three months before Italy marched,
his first dispatches caught the essence of this truth. "Nowhere in Europe,"
he wrote back to the *Daily Telegraph*, "is there a people more averse to
war than the subjects of Victor Emmanuel." Italy, by virtue of its "thrift
and sobriety," had made much more progress than the average European
realized. The Government could not, therefore, make a decision without
"an overpowering sense of responsibility." Since the Salandra government was trusted by all, Dillon concluded that "unless the motives for
departing from her attitude of vigilant neutrality were rendered irresistible by advantages to be secured or disaster to be avoided, it is hard to see
how any government could take upon itself the responsibility for war." [88]

Despite this accurate description of the situation as it existed in March,
May produced that "cyclone of hatred," as Ferrero called it,[89] which
welled up against the man who had directed Italy's fortunes for fifteen
years, Giovanni Giolitti, and against the Parliament that supported him.
Had the deeper understanding of the interventionists, then, prevailed
against the feeble resistance of the great majority of Deputies? Was the
Chamber in truth a swamp where all national ideals were suffocated?
Was the regime founded by Cavour based on sand, and was it what Bonomi later called the "vital and incoercible currents" among the "cultivated elite"[90] which alone intuited the inner laws of Italian history, laws
which were too powerful to be thwarted by human choice? For all the
material accomplishments of Italian politicians from Lanza and Sella to
Giolitti, had the Postrisorgimento failed to produce that synthetic nation
without which mere government could not endure?

It would be convenient to agree that the intervention, by its very hap-
pening, proved the irresistible need for satisfying unfulfilled Italian aspirations; that the whole edifice, whatever its superficial achievements,
was undermined by the historical failure to complete the Risorgimento;

and that, as Oriani had prophesied, it would give way before the predestined crisis that brought to the surface all the tensions held in check, but never resolved, over half a century of artificial unity. The wish to discover some great design, a pattern of history, is particularly strong in the case of a country that chose to risk its very existence in the face of the reluctance of its people, its institutions, the Socialist party, the Church, and its leading politician.

Leaving aside the imponderable as to just what a "synthetic" nation should be, there is the verifiable historical fact that Italy was never so unified as during the months of neutrality. The nation had by no means lapsed into anarchic individualism, embittered regionalism, and apoliticism. Indeed, the essential agreement of North and South, Church and State, Chamber and people on the advisability of maintaining neutrality unless war were forced upon them is in itself indicative of the over-all success of the Postrisorgimento. Unless one could accept the mystical arguments of the intellectual interventionists that war was predestined, there must be some logical explanation for the collapse of the neutralist position, and with it of the structure built by Cavour's successors. The explanation is crucial for later Italian history. Fascist apologists would claim that war was the beginning of the new era that opened with the triumph of the minority of visionaries who represented Italy's true interests, charismatic leaders who felt the unconscious longing of the masses.

Certainly the Radiant May was the prelude to the March on Rome, if only because it represented the apparent triumph of intellectual anarchy, of D'Annunzian journalism, while teaching Mussolini the methods of subversion. The passivity of the Chamber before the assaults of the war party dangerously weakened the fiber of constitutional government. The disasters of war then came, creating immense economic and social problems. Looking back on the propaganda of the war press, however, one cannot fail to be struck by the absence of any utilitarian, rational defense of intervention. It is the completely nonsensical nature of the arguments that is so amazing. If fascism was to identify itself with the Great War, it had as its foundation an act of political and diplomatic insanity, the triumph of irrationalism. According to Fascists, this was an inevitable triumph of the farsighted. But the same articles in the war press show that the interventionist minority was losing out in its battle to force the issue on the Government. The hatred of the parliamentary regime, which became more and more pronounced as neutrality dragged on, only reveals a sense of impotency turned into the most vulgar sort of journalism.

The same may be said for a shift that took place in political theory. When Papini, Corradini, Mussolini, and others appealed to an elite of intelligent Italians, they were conceding their own defeat, abandoning the older claim to leadership over a mass movement. The charismatic concept of leadership, the use of intuition with its emphasis on the unconscious will of the people, was a means of avoiding the confession that few Italians wanted to go to war, or the admission that the interventionists were no more than a narrow oligarchy recruited from the petty humanistic bourgeoisie.

This suggests that had Italy stayed out of the war in 1915, entering if at all very late in the day when the outcome was certain and the full weight of her contribution in the balance of the struggle could have been measured, the interventionist minority would have been discredited. Protracted or permanent neutrality would have been a victory for the parliamentary system, for the constitutional monarchy, and for those materialistic bourgeois values so bitterly assailed by the prophets of action. Had the minority failed in its frantic efforts to drive the nation to war, its failure would have implied as well preservation of the balance between the material needs of society, not intuited but known from ledgers and empirical studies, and the claims of men of letters to be allowed freely to speculate and to create, bringing to the realm of culture the fruits of their labors. When, however, in defiance of facts, the Italian government took up the sword forged by the rhetoric of poets and with it struck out against the hard stuff of real war, the cause of human reason was shocked and offended, leaving a void in man's confidence in himself and in a society that was supposed to protect him against such disasters. The very meaninglessness of the Government's decision also seemed to give substance to the claims of the few who preached the superior wisdom of laws of politics and human conduct learned from the study of the past and from an appreciation of the culture of the present. The ambiguous legacy of the intellectual renaissance of the late nineteenth century became quite clear in 1915.

The explanation of this ambiguous legacy does not lie in the movement of ideas alone. Unless one accepts the determinism imposed by ideas, there must be an explanation for this catastrophe in Italian politics and foreign policy that was a part of the larger crisis in Western Europe. To find the answer, however, one must leave the high road of intellectual history and descend to the level of politics, seeking there to uncover errors of judgment, the responsibility of individuals. However valuable for an understanding of the times the history of ideas may be, the decisions of men, when these are momentous for generations to come, affect the course of ideas themselves, giving force to concepts that might have gone the way of other museum pieces, becoming in time of no more than scholarly interest. This is not to pose a conflict between schools of history, to give primacy to one or the other approach. All roads may prove fruitful. Now that we have examined the nature and political implications of the climate of opinion at the time of the Great War, it is necessary to turn to more traditional materials, looking at the decisions of 1915 in the light of domestic politics and diplomacy.

·10·

SALANDRA AND ITALY'S INTERVENTION

Before taking up the question of how Italy got into the war, one thing must be made quite clear. This regards the state of public opinion. From the pages of the war press itself, the lack of mass support for the war is evident. However much those papers tried to maximize the size, fervor, and geographical distribution of popular rallies against neutrality, the discouraging reports of Guido Dorso from Naples and Arcangelo di Staso from Tuscany, plus the prevalence of students and intellectuals among the demonstrators, show that the war party was very much an elite. When war had come, the romantic Nationalist claim that the people had saved Italy from the politicians was still used.[1] Not even the propagandists of war believed this. Mussolini confessed on more than one occasion that there was insufficient popular support for his movement,[2] which was to be both the equivalent of and the substitute for war. Those historians who maintain the contrary are few, and they are obviously partisans of the interventionist cause. The usual explanation is that the better sort of Italians appreciated the great historical significance of Italy's entry into the Great War, and that they had triumphed over less farsighted neutralists.[3]

This in turn raises the question of Salandra's awareness of the situation. He has been described as a "modest burgher from the South of Italy," who with indomitable courage took upon himself the great task after having been called to power only as a stopgap until the "dictator" returned. "With profound insight and trust in the better self of the Italian people," the historian Thomas Okey wrote in 1916, "he appealed from the Chambers of the timid politicians to the market place."[4] The anti-Giolittian bias of this assessment of Salandra's heroism is not unusual. It is not possible to defend his actions without at the same time demeaning the work of Giolitti and thereby of the regime he represented. However, did the "modest burgher" realize the narrowness of the "market place" he used as a counterweight to the Chamber of Deputies? He was, after

307

all, a professor. One could conceive of his being led astray by the artful persuasions of the war party, which included men of undoubted cultural prestige and literary skill.

In his account of the intervention, written in 1930, Salandra speaks of the interventionists as those "who spoke or wrote — that is the active minorities which, in every great nation, draw the mentally inert majorities after them." [5] That statement, besides revealing something of Salandra's personality, is a recognition of widespread disinterest in the war. But it is ambiguous. It avoids getting down to details of the degree and distribution of the inert majority. Had he known that the great bulk of Italians were for neutrality, it would have taken more than indomitable courage to risk the nation's future in a conflict that had already opened a new page in military history by its immense wastage of lives and resources. It would have taken incredible foolhardiness.

Thanks to the work of Alberto Monticone [6] in the Italian National Archives, it is now known, without possibility of equivocation, that the Premier was in full possession of the facts. Indeed, Salandra himself set out to get them. By mid-April, 1915, an important stage in the talks with the Entente at London had been reached, making accord possible. The principal stumbling block in the path of any agreement had been the Russian Foreign Minister Sazonoff, who was unwilling to sacrifice Slavic lands to the Italians. His resistance was finally broken by strong pressure from the British government. [7] Seeing a treaty in the offing, Salandra on April 12 ordered the Prefects to carry out a survey of public opinion. He explicitly directed them to get a "precise and succinct" report, to find out the true feelings of the people concerning an eventual entry into the war. He cautioned the Prefects against being swayed in their analysis by attitudes that might reflect local feuds between interventionist and neutralist groups. Of sixty-nine Prefects, fifty-five had time to reply before the survey was called off on April 21, at which date the Treaty of London was in the final stages. Not all the reports are objective. Signs of extreme patriotism, testimonials of confidence in Salandra appear in some of them. There are assurances from Prefects that they will guarantee the conduct of the people in case of war. [8] That alone suggests an expected popular resistance.

On the whole, however, the replies showed clearly the prevalence of the neutralist current. More significantly, it was not so much a matter of the organized neutralism of the official Socialist party, but of the spontaneous, uncoordinated sentiments of the contadini, whose outlook was characterized by apathy toward the great issue. This was especially noticeable in the Mezzogiorno. In the North, neutralists often attached themselves to political groups which held that war would be justified only in defense of the nation against armed invasion. In either region, there was no question which view prevailed. A few salient details will suffice to complete the picture. In Sicily, neutralist opinion was not limited to the workers but was shared by the landowners. In Puglia, Salandra's own region, a war party existed only where the urban bourgeoisie was strong. In the Abruzzi, even the educated classes were neutralist. In Naples, 90 per cent of the population was estimated as being opposed to war. The Prefect added the sobering comment that the people were resigned to the possibility of war and would see the troops off with enthusiasm. He had doubts, however, how long that enthusiasm would last. Taking the South as a whole, only the intellectuals were to be considered interventionists.

Set against the background of old North-South animosities, resentment of Piedmontese unification on the one side and lingering strains of nothern contempt for the South on the other, a very practical and immediate agreement existed between the two major Italian regions where the problem of war was concerned. If Naples and the agricultural South were 90 per cent neutralist, the report from Turin, a city crucial to any military effort, showed that the northern urban population also wished to stick to neutrality. Piedmontese generally opposed war. Venice was the same. There the Prefect was upset by what he called "fictitious agitations" provoked by refugees from Trieste. Irredentism was not so widespread as its vociferous champions would have one believe if the great Adriatic city itself was unwilling to fight for Trieste.

The place where one might expect to find a decisive interventionist current would be Rome. As capital, symbol of the Risorgimento, with an active political and journalistic life and those visible testimonials of the "Roman mission" that the Nationalists preached, it could understandably have been a notable exception to the rule. The report of the Prefect to Salandra is, therefore, particularly interesting. He wrote that after having conferred daily with the mayors and other influential figures in the city and the surrounding area, he could say with complete assurance that the "great majority of the population of this province is opposed to an eventual entry into the war due to the derangement and disturbance which the great test would produce in the nation's life." This feeling was shared by the farmers of Latium, the city workers, the clerks, the businessmen, and by the "most educated and calmest sort of persons" who feared that "Italy is not sufficiently prepared nor mature to be able to face, without frightening domestic and foreign consequences, a long and difficult war against strong and battle-tested enemies." In reference to the clique of interventionists, among which the staff of the *Idea Nazionale* must have been included, he added: "There is, it is true, a notable minority, both loud and bold, which calls for war against Austria; but, formed as it is of the most disparate parties with goals that are discordant, contradictory and not always patriotic, it has not been effective in altering the state of public opinion."[9]

This report was dated April 17. A week later, Italy joined the Entente by the secret Treaty of London. The "modest burgher" in appealing to the "market place" was counting on little real backing from the hundreds of thousands of Italians from Palermo to Turin who would have to go into the trenches. And the "timid politicians," many of whom were probably included in the group of "educated and calm" men whom the Prefect of Rome questioned, were justified in their fears. This leaves one with the outlandish conclusion that a head of state was willing to take his nation into a conflict that had already demonstrated its fury without having any positive popular support. Of course, it may be suspected that Salandra hoped to make war "on the cheap," counting on the apathy of the contadini and the initial enthusiasm of the Neapolitans to tide things over until the war was won. The Prefect of Rome, however, had it as the opinion of experienced and responsible men that the country could not face up to a long and difficult campaign. In assessing the Premier's motivations, it is important to see whether he had any reasonable expectation that the war would be short. In his memoirs Salandra states that no one could have foreseen a war of forty months when Italy went in.[10] To this one might counter that, given what he knew from the prefectural reports, even twenty months would have been too long. But there is more to the story than that surmise.

Vilfredo Pareto, writing in Sonnino's own paper as early as September, 1914, predicted that the war would be long. To those who, like Sir Norman Angell, felt this to be impossible because of the immense financial drain and the slaughter wrought by modern weapons, he offered his professional advice to the contrary. Public indebtedness would not stop production, he wrote. And the people, although feeling the pinch, would not experience economic destruction at home. The World War, according to Pareto, was the beginning of a new era.[11] In the same month, an unidentified "Former Diplomat," writing in the *Nuova Antologia*, pointed out that the signing of the London Pact by the members of the Entente, by which the allies bound themselves not to conclude a separate peace, suggested a long struggle. Italy's economy, he went on, was already benefiting from the country's neutralist position. Nothing had changed on the international front since August, when Italians had almost unanimously been in favor of the declaration of neutrality. The same journal carried three important articles by the noted economist Maggiorino Ferraris in November, 1914, and in January and March, 1915, all of which cautioned against staking the nation's very unity, as yet imperfectly developed, on a costly war. Ferraris' opinion, that Italy, weakest of the Great Powers, had to consider its own interests and not play the role of vindicator of international law,[12] was essentially that of Giolitti as expressed in his notorious parecchio letter of February, 1915. *La Stampa* of Turin, a target of the warmongers, said the same thing in its editorial of April 10, 1915.

Similar cautions were given by men close to the Government. Salandra's own Foreign Minister, Di San Giuliano, was reported to have said on September 26, 1914, that the war would take at least fifteen more months. Italy would have to consider whether her economy could take such a long conflict. Any intervention would have to come in the last stages. It is true that Di San Giuliano was quoted as affirming his belief that Italy would get in eventually. But this does not remove his own grave worries about the country's readiness. Furthermore, the interview was released only after the Foreign Minister was dead, and the journalist who had taken it down, Arturo Labriola,[13] was an interventionist. It must also be remembered that at the time of the interview a fifteen-month war was not as unlikely as it would be by the following April. It was in April that Alfredo Frassati, director of *La Stampa*, went to see his good friend Sonnino to tell him of the general concern caused by the rumors of coming war. At the time the two men were discussing the matter, the London Treaty was all but settled. Frassati told the Foreign Minister of his forebodings. The war had settled down after the Battle of the Marne. Sonnino was apparently unimpressed. E. J. Dillon, as late as March, 1915, estimated that Italy would be drained dry by a war of eight months.[14]

As for Giolitti, when he came to Rome for the opening of the Chamber in March, 1915, he expressed the same thought to his political friends. The end of the war could not be foreseen.[15] There is no reason to believe that this sage advice was included in his memoirs merely to justify his wisdom after the fact. From the recollections of Marcello Soleri, as well as from Giolitti's remarks in the Chamber, we know that Giolitti felt this way at the time the events were shaping up. Elaborating on his views of Italy's proper policy, the ex-Premier stressed the advantages of neutrality — the saving of lives and money — and the country's lack of political, social, and economic preparation for a long war. Giolitti made clear his willingness to fight if adequate concessions could not be obtained through bargaining, according to Soleri's account. Again, this is consistent with the parecchio letter in which Giolitti said that war was to be faced "only when it is necessary for the honor and great interests of the country." It is very important to note, however, that if war had to be, Giolitti would have delayed Italy's entry until late in the war, and then entered by a prearranged agreement with Rumania and the United States. Di San Giuliano had in fact laid the basis for Rumanian-Italian joint action, something the Salandra-Sonnino government failed to follow up.[16] As for the United States, the Ministry apparently did not take that country into consideration at all.

Added to this there was the question of Libya. Whatever suspicion and resentment Salandra may have felt about words of caution coming from neutralist, and therefore Giolittian, sources [17] — and this is a factor always to be considered in judging his motives — as chief of state he could have had no doubts about the situation in Africa. His Colonial Minister, Ferdinando Martini, replying to criticism of the Government's African policy by the interventionists De Felice and Bevione, could not conceal the military problems still to be solved in the new colony. In effect, a reverse had been suffered after a difficult campaign to penetrate the hinterland Fezzan region of Libya. Salandra himself, in his inaugural address as Premier in April, 1914, had mentioned that considerable forces were still involved in the Libyan campaign. Giolitti's Colonial Minister, Bertolini, took the floor after Martini to explain the reasons that had necessitated penetration into the interior. His speech was really an attempt to recapture the momentary pride of accomplishment that Mosca and many others had exhibited a few years before. He mentioned the country's "spiritual renewal," the lifting of the "moral fog" that had attended the African venture in its initial stages. That sense of unity was slipping away under the impact of the debate over intervention. Bertolini ended with a plea for continued neutrality.[18] His use of the language of the war party, however, was both a dangerous concession to the false idealism that obscured the lust for power and an example of the contagion of rhetoric that Tripoli had stimulated. Nonetheless, his words were another warning to the Government. As if aware that events were moving against the diplomacy of caution, he reiterated his advice in private to the heads of the Government, stressing the length of war and the strain it would place on Italy's economy, particularly in the Mezzogiorno. He did this repeatedly from the beginning of the war down to the last minute. Moreover, he told Martini in September, 1914, that he had word that the chief of the artillery was worried about the lack of munitions on hand as revealed by the enormous consumption on the French front. Martini, according to Bertolini, had been unaware of this, and went to see Salandra. But when Bertolini asked Salandra personally about it, the Premier cut him short by saying the concern was completely unjustified, and that such talk could have a bad effect at home and abroad if known.[19]

Despite all this, the Ministry was banking on a short war. When Frassati visited Sonnino on April 25, he tried to impress him by relating something he had witnessed as a student in Germany. At a meeting of the Reichstag, Chancellor Caprivi was presenting a bill for increasing the military budget. General von Moltke spoke in defense of it. The victor of the Franco-Prussian War told the Deputies that they must vote it through because "it is not an easy undertaking to defeat France, and the next war won't be one of armies, but of peoples. It won't last six months like the one in 1870, but five or six years." Frassati then asked where the money was coming from, and Sonnino replied that there would be plenty of it, by which the journalist understood that Italy's new allies would furnish it. As it turned out, the loan stipulated under the terms of the Treaty of London was enough to cover three months of war, according to the then current calculations of the expenses borne by the belligerents. In August, 1915, Salandra felt that the war would not go beyond the next winter.[20]

One must assume that Salandra was heeding the advice of the war press when he made his plans; for it is there, and only there, that the short-war concept appears. Literati turned military specialists were listened to in preference to neutralists turned Giolittian. In November, 1914, after the Turkish intervention, the *Idea Nazionale* began suggesting that war by the next spring could be too late for Italy to reap any benefits. When Ferraris wrote of the material facts, he was criticized by Corradini for debilitating the nation with talk of the horrors of combat. If there was to be "suffering, death, mutilation, illness, slaughter and destruction," the paper intoned, "these are also a thing of moral beauty;

they represent the human spirit which triumphs over them." Coppola insisted in April that Italy had to enter immediately. Austria-Hungary might pull out soon.[21] Borgese, who five years earlier had written in praise of German organization and discipline, now came forth with the historical proof that Germany's past did not show its ability to resist after having met with a defeat. Therefore he guessed that the war might be finished soon. The Corriere objected to Bertolini's speech on the Libyan campaign on the ground that it could raise doubts about Italy's readiness. The setback in Africa of early May, which may have been an important consideration in canceling the King's trip to Genoa for the Quarto celebrations, was described by Albertini's paper as an insignificant event when viewed in the light of the total European problem.[22]

Expectedly, Mussolini's Popolo d'Italia preached a short war. The many references [23] to this need not be gone over in detail, since they follow essentially the same line of argumentation found in the interventionist press generally. There was also a tendency in the coverage of the military scene to play up allied victories and to capitalize on reports of food shortages in Germany. In view of Giolitti's interest in the future course of American diplomacy, it is interesting to note that the Popolo d'Italia seemed to regard the United States' opinion as leaning toward Germany. Prezzolini, in January, 1915, wrote that it would be unwise to accept an American offer of earthquake relief assistance, because Italy should not be obligated to a nation that might prove to be an enemy. A report to the Popolo d'Italia from the United States in February emphasized the strength of German-American public opinion.[24] To urge intervention while at the same time suggesting that the United States might back the Central Powers was simply irrational.

Equally illogical was the journalistic campaign against the Giolitti government for having left the military in poor shape. From the outbreak of war in Europe down to the winter of 1915, the war press was calling for intervention as soon as possible and at the same time using military unpreparedness as proof of incompetence of the previous ministry.[25] This was a continuation, in effect, of the downgrading of the Libyan venture. More and more Giolitti's African campaign was made responsible for the depletion of arms and ammunition. The absurdity of this contradiction was apparent even to some interventionists. The Corriere, in April, 1915, had to admit that to have demanded war in the fall of 1914 was excessive. But, it added, the interventionists were not to blame if Giolitti had been irresponsible in his direction of the Government. Besides, the exponents of war were intellectuals, not politicians. Hence they were unaware of the facts of Italy's military unpreparedness.[26] What made the Milan paper think that an army unprepared in the fall of 1914 could have become sufficiently organized and provisioned by April, 1915, to stand up to the crushing expenditures in lives and material of the Western Front, is impossible to imagine. There was always that mystical solution to such mundane problems upon which one could fall back, avoiding harsh realities. The *Idea Nazionale*, in October, 1914, advised Italians not to discuss a problem that only helped the subversives. Coppola followed this up with the suitable explanation. France, he wrote, had been morally and militarily worse prepared in August, 1914, than Italy was. But war had automatically cured all that, renovating the French and freeing them from that positivistic outlook that suffocated moral values.

According to this mystical concept of war, struggle was in itself elevating. And the bigger the battle the better. It must be a total war, as Mussolini wrote, not a diplomatic, parliamentary war like that of Africa. Italy, Borgese insisted, had been made too easily.[27] A literary substitute for diplomatic and military competence, the use of the blood bath as the answer to Italy's domestic ills, ending that scioltezza which Turiello considered one of the nation's fundamental weaknesses — these ideas were commonplace in the propaganda of the interventionist elite. That did not oblige Salandra to turn his back on responsible opinion, however. True, he felt pressed by events in Europe. He told Bertolini on April 16 of his fears for a separate peace between Austria and Russia that would leave Italy in the cold. The fall of Przemysl on March 21 to the Russians opened up the possibility of an invasion of Bulgaria. Bertolini tried to dissuade both Salandra and Sonnino from believing that Russia's successes would turn out to be permanent. After Przemysl, Salandra refused to listen. Sazonoff was able to take a stiffer line in resisting Italian claims in Dalmatia. This obliged the Government at Rome to drop its demands for Spalato, much as Salandra regretted abandoning that "site of glorious Latin civilization and of fervid Italian patriotism."[28]

It could be argued that at the very worst Salandra was a stupid man, ill-informed and apparently unwilling to take any advice that seemed to come from neutralist sources. But the real issue of intervention is not Salandra's and Sonnino's stubbornness in the face of respectable pleas for caution. The major significance of Italy's entry into the war lies in the implications it had for the parliamentary regime, which, despite momentary variations such as that of Pelloux (incidentally, a neutralist in

1914–15), had preserved liberty in the Postrisorgimento, giving Italians, by the *Corriere*'s own admission, a degree of domestic political power unsurpassed in Europe. If the public and its political representatives opposed war in the great majority, either something must have gone wrong, or else the Chamber itself was unworthy of its trust, too cowardly to fulfill its obligations to the electorate and hence fated to extinction. The failure of official Italy to prevent the war would weigh heavily on the reputation of representative government in Italy. For the Fascists the system was too rotten to meet the challenge of Italy's destiny. For many anti-Fascists, it had, by giving way in 1915, prepared the way for fascism.

Again Salandra's views are critical. Knowing the facts as he did, how did he suppose that the Chamber's will could be brought around to the cause of intervention? To Bertolini, he stressed the prestige of the Crown. He and Sonnino feared for the monarchy should Italy not come out of the World War enlarged territorially.[29] In saying that, Salandra was really exploiting the "war or revolution" threat of the radical interventionists, led by Mussolini. It was a very doubtful argument for the simple reason that the state of public opinion, and the Socialist party's support of neutrality, made an antimonarchical insurrection extremely improbable, as Salandra well knew. Yet Salandra was a spokesman for a revived conservative party. He might have been unduly swayed by revolutionary talk which even the supposedly monarchist *Idea Nazionale* succumbed to when it saw, or thought it saw, that there would be no war. Sonnino had written in the 1890's of a return to the *statuto*, a restoration of royal prerogatives. Recalling Mosca's observation, however, that monarchist sentiment in Italy was not sincere, but represented instead disillusionment with the parliamentary system, and having discussed the reasons that made legitimist theory untenable in Italy, there is an alternative explanation of Salandra's motives: that he shared in the subversive character of much of Italian rightist thought. If this suspicion were well founded, the Premier's willingness not only to bypass the Chamber but to disregard the King, whose fortunes were tied to the Parliament, would be understandable. This suspicion has been confirmed by a letter Salandra wrote to Sonnino, which deserves to be given in full.

Rome: March 16, 1915

8 A.M.

Dear Friend,

I must tell you about the outcome of my long reflections of last night.
From the whole assemblage of the facts, and more from the state of mind

that they produce, I have the impression that we are rapidly moving toward a complete rupture with the Central Powers; and this:

1. Without the King's explicit assent;
2. Without being sure that the Country and through it the Chamber, wish it;
3. Without the army being ready, unless by the end of April — according to the military — which means at least a month later, not certainly before;
4. Without having any assurance, or indications of assurance, on the part of the Entente.

As to numbers 1) and 2) we could do without them — because the King will never speak out clearly and the Chamber even less — if we had the army ready and the pacts concluded, or almost so, with the Entente. But as things stand now, *we two alone* absolutely cannot play the terrible card.

The conclusion is that we must continue to deal with the Empires, pretending to believe a favorable solution possible, even if the question has to be shifted, as Bülow has proposed to you, to the ground of the extent of territorial concessions, while keeping back for the moment the demand for immediate execution.

Your arguments against such a procedure are doubtless serious and well founded. But they do not destroy my very grave anxieties.

It seems to me that for now, whatever the cost, we must slow down rather than rush the course of events until we are sure of at least those points which I have indicated with the numbers 3) and 4).

I wanted to write to you in order to be precise, and because between the Ministry and the Chamber I would not have found an hour free to come to you today.

Ti stringo la mano.

Affectionately,
A[ntonio] S[alandra] [30]

Salandra was prepared to go to war as long as two conditions were met: that the army be ready, and that the alliance with the Entente be sealed. The Chamber, which he recognizes as expressing the will of the country, and the Crown, which he told Bertolini he had to save, could be bypassed. One week after this letter was written Salandra went to the Chamber to request the long Easter recess. Turati's speech in favor of a shorter vacation was not only prophetic; Turati put his finger on the factor that allowed Salandra to smother the majority's opposition to war.

It was Salandra's ambiguous relationship to the Giolittian majority [31] that permitted him to subvert the nation and the Chamber of Deputies, entering an alliance that was contrary to the wishes of both real and official Italy. The beginnings of this go back to the last months of the Giolitti government. In November and December, 1913, Giolitti was being subjected to a revival of polemical anti-Giolittian speeches, with Altobelli, his perennial critic, leading the way. The errors of Libya, electoral cor-

ruption, and the Gentiloni Pact were the principal targets. Salandra, although a recognized spokesman of the conservative viewpoint, backed
the Government. For this apparent change of heart he was chided by one
Deputy, Ludovico Calda who said it was a poor time to become a convert
to Giolittism. Calda said he could have respect for men like Sonnino who
had maintained their political independence, but Salandra's sudden shift
looked insincere. Salandra was given to standing on his dignity. The barbs
went deep, wounding his pride and making him look like a lackey for the
"Great Minister" — another flunkey who had lost his purity. In rebuttal
he tried to point out that he was not going over for any advantage to
himself, as could be seen by the fact that it was a difficult moment for
Giolitti.[32] By this Salandra hoped to protect his reputation as an "incor-
ruptible." The incident should not be forgotten. It tells us something of
the personality of the man, of the sensibility that must have been a factor
in his final decision.

When Giolitti resigned, after a defection of the Radicals, he and others
suggested Salandra as successor. Giolitti felt that the Government, after
losing its grip on the radical faction — although it still had a majority
— should give way to a conservative leader, and Salandra was the man
most in view. Salandra asked Giolitti's advice in forming his cabinet; the
ex-Premier's help was solicited especially to induce Di San Giuliano to
remain as foreign minister.[33] The new Government was stamped as carrying over the previous administration's foreign policy even before the
World War began. Salandra's maiden speech to the Chamber of April 2,
1914, did nothing to dispel this general conviction; it was a defense of
his predecessor's work. On the burning issue of Italy's military stature,
a source of much acrimonious debate and comment, Salandra corroborated the previous Government's assurances that any deficiencies in military stores caused by the African campaign had been made up.

Despite this, the fact that an anomalous relationship between the Government and the parliamentary majority existed was recognized from the
very outset. One Deputy put it succinctly when he said that Salandra's
majority was not his own.[34] That did not help assuage the new Premier's
ego. Worse, Salandra was treated to a long speech in which his own conservatism was compared with the positive achievements of Giolitti in the
field of domestic reform. This speech is notable for several reasons. In
the first place, it must have piqued Salandra. Secondly, it hit the nail on
the head when it contrasted Giolitti's liberal methods with Salandra's

extreme conservatism. But it is also interesting in the light of the historian's assessment of Giolitti. There are still those who maintain that Giolitti's Italy "had something of the police state about it."[35] Since the speaker, Arturo Labriola, later an interventionist, was not only an independent Socialist but one of Italy's earliest students of Marxist theory, his words have some bearing on the justness of that verdict. Labriola admitted that he would not care to be suspected of being favorable to Giolitti. But he conceded that as far as parliamentary government was concerned,

it must be recognized that the honorable Giolitti understood the necessity of governing if not with the Left, at least in its name. However one may appraise his attempt to have Catholics enter within the orbit of constitutional parties, which were to be part of his majority, one cannot deny that he was able to utilize their votes to the advantage of a system of government which, in domestic affairs, was rather respectful of public liberties. Taking into account the great difficulties which the police state traditions and very antiquated attitudes of the official ruling classes pose, one can admit that the Honorable Giolitti in his own way saw to it that Italians were accustomed to the most regular possible exercize of political liberties.

Salandra, to whom Labriola referred as a "place holder," was essentially conservative, even authoritarian. He could not pretend to be following Giolitti's tradition.[36]

Salandra's troubles in the Chamber, however, were only beginning. In June, 1914, the riots of the Red Week seemed to indicate a return to anarchic socialist tactics. Almost as if in response to a new ministry that lacked the prestige of Giolitti among the Left, tumults broke out. Salandra's prohibition of public meetings added fuel to the fire. He was accused of trying to return to the days of General Pelloux. The Socialist Deputies led the attack on the new Government, but they were not alone. Salandra was cross-examined as well by Carlo Schanzer, a young minister in Giolitti's 1906–9 government. Although Schanzer was disturbed by this departure from Giolitti's methods, he stated his willingness to vote with the majority thereby maintaining a united front in the face of domestic problems occasioned by the Red Week. Salandra showed his lack of tact, and his parliamentary ineptitude, by inviting trouble. With mock courtesy and pompous disregard for the political needs of the moment, he patronizingly referred to Schanzer as a young man who had come up fast and would undoubtedly go far. To this Salandra compared his own status in the Chamber as head of state, a post he held because of that "political sincerity" which he had made a "rule of life." Offended by the insinuation that his success had been bought at the price of fawning on Giolitti, Schanzer defected from the majority and voted against Salandra.

Calda's remarks in the winter of 1913, his suggestion that Salandra was insincere, had sunk in. Meanwhile, the Socialists continued to brand Salandra as a new Pelloux. Labriola spoke of the carabinieri as a band of assassins, and claimed, without proof, that he had seen children brutally assaulted. This was obviously a bit of parliamentary rabble-rousing. Having inherited Giolitti's power, Salandra was getting a taste of the myth of governmental brutality that had gone with it ever since the days of the Bank Scandals. Giolitti, quite fairly one feels considering what must have been his private opinion of Salandra, defends the Government in his memoirs from the charge of authoritarianism.[37] However, even with the opposition of Schanzer and the Socialists, Salandra maintained clear majorities in the first tests of his strength. On June 10, 1914, he won a 254 to 112 vote of confidence. But the insecurity of his situation was shown by the fact that his votes came not only from the old majority of Giolitti, but included such anti-Giolittian Deputies as the Nationalist Federzoni. This pattern continued throughout the summer sittings of the Chamber. Usually his opposition was limited to about thirty votes. This was due in part to the obstructionist tactics of the Socialists, who momentarily seemed to be out to recapture some of the anarchic flavor of their own heroic past with the memories of 1898. The heat of July also cut down attendance, which was running at about 60 per cent of the Chamber's full capacity. But the last vote before the summer recess indicated that had the war not come, Salandra's government would have been short-lived. On this occasion a conspicuous bloc of seventy-two Deputies abstained entirely.[38]

This, in brief, was the history of Salandra's management of the Government's majority prior to the coming of the Great War. When the Chamber met in December, Italy had been neutral for four months, and the neutralist-interventionist debate in the press had already created an entirely new political atmosphere. In October the cabinet had been reshuffled following the death of Di San Giuliano. Salandra had been criticized for failing to take adequate measures to beef up the military. The chief source of this criticism was General Porro. But within his Cabinet, confusion reigned. His Minister of War, Grandi, was not in agreement with the high command. And the Finance Minister, Rubini, refused to agree to mobilization unless Italy were attacked. Rubini cited the grave economic situation, and Salandra agreed with him. Salandra also had wanted to dump Di San Giuliano, and was in fact closer to Sonnino through their correspondence, from August to December, 1914, than he was to his own ministers. Sonnino pressed for an occupation of Valona, and suggested that Salandra take advantage of Di San Giuliano's illness to carry it off. This was to give the war party some slight satisfaction. As for Giolitti, Salandra was in touch with him, too. Giolitti had informed Salandra that he was always at his disposition. From Salandra's remarks to Sonnino, part of the sinister and dubious misunderstanding of the Premier and his predecessor appears. Salandra stated that Giolitti was in complete agreement with him. At the same time, he was privately blaming all his woes on "ten years of an ill-omened policy" that had preceded his taking office. Here he was "entering history" only to find the state weakened by Giolitti's incompetence.[39] With the death of the foreign minister, the Cabinet was reformed. The *Corriere della Sera* found this a bit tardy, and was showing its dissatisfaction with Salandra.[40] Salandra, in turn, seems to have been chafing under the attacks of the interventionists, whose press he could not control. He did not look forward to going back to face the Chamber in December. He made a passing remark to the effect that this was a sort of unavoidable necessity that should be cut as short as possible.[41]

The opening meetings of the Chamber in December are of fundamental importance in explaining the future course of events leading to the intervention of May, 1915. Addressing the Deputies on December 3, Salandra defended Italy's proclamation of neutrality. He spoke of the war as having "no foreseeable end." In all, it was a Giolittian outlook, the response to which was a new, more positive support for the Ministry. The key phrases of his speech were these: "On the lands and seas of the Ancient Continent, whose political configuration is perhaps being transformed, Italy has vital interests to protect and sustain —" Here Salandra was interrupted by a long round of applause as the Deputies rose to their feet. He then continued, "— not only to maintain itself intact as a great power; but that it may not be relatively diminished by possible aggrandizements by other states." Again there were cheers. He concluded with a plea for armed neutrality. According to the reporters at Montecitorio, Giolitti was the first to go forward to congratulate the Premier.[42]

The day after this spontaneous demonstration of support for Salandra, representatives of the opposing factions took the floor to uphold or condemn neutrality. Treves spoke for the Socialist party and against war.

In the course of his speech, he defended the patriotism of all Italians who would fight for the country were it invaded. While not renouncing a possible rising of the workers to block Italian mobilization for any reason other than national defense, it hinted at the dilemma of the party that was to prevent it from embracing a policy of out-and-out subversion in case of war. This must be considered in weighing Salandra's motives. He would have been far more reluctant had he not been able to count on the essential patriotism of socialist leadership. Following Treves, Colajanni made his speech for war in which he pleaded the cause of intervention on the ground that too little blood had been shed for the making of Italian unity. At one point he alluded to the common neutralist stand of the Socialists and the clericals. Treves here interjected the remark that "all those who were close to the people" stood for the prevention of war.[43] The Reds and the Blacks were again linked by that momentary and circumstantial alliance that Sonnino, defending a return to the Statuto, had seen as a two-pronged attack on the regime. Unlike the 1890's, however, those inimical allies were joined not in subversion of the regime, but in support of a policy shared by the people and the Chamber.

It was this apparent agreement that helped to create a false sense of trust on the part of the neutralists. That trust was given added force by the remarks of the avowed interventionists. It was they who took Salandra to task for his vague references to Italy's "vital interests." Ciccotti called the speech "ambiguous," and demanded open discussion of Italy's diplomatic policy. This defense of the rights of the Chamber to survey all aspects of the nation's planning, which became a recurring idea in Ciccotti's speeches, sounded odd in the mouth of a man who had six years before written a snide anonymous pamphlet ridiculing the Italian Parliament. Altobelli, Giolitti's old nemesis, also called Salandra to task for not speaking out clearly. Italy, he said, could not prevent the triumph of German militarism. Barzilai, the irredentist leader, was of a similar mind.[44] The same confusion of evaluation existed in the great press. The *Corriere della Sera* professed to be pleased by Salandra's speech. The *Giornale d'Italia* saw war as coming sooner or later. The *Idea Nazionale* said the "meaning was clear," that neutrality was not sufficient protection for Italy's interests. But the neutralist *Tribuna* regarded the first sessions of the Chamber as an indication of solid backing for the Government. The country had confidence in its "vigilant and prudent" action, its intention to avoid intemperate moves.[45]

Giolitti's speech was the most important of all. In that it overshadowed

Salandra's, it must have been another bitter pill. Giolitti made public for the first time an Austrian move to attack Serbia in 1913. He related how Di San Giuliano had contacted Berlin to check Vienna's avowed plans to move into the Balkans. For his part, as Premier, Giolitti had instructed the late Foreign Minister to make it plain to Austria that such action would in no way obligate Italy under the terms of the Triple Alliance. This, he said, was proof that Italy's proclamation of neutrality in 1914 was entirely justified. Privately Giolitti explained his revelations, which were understandably embarrassing for the neutralists, on the ground that he wished to counteract certain "English circles" which had suggested that Italy had not backed her treaty obligations. But what he had to say about the Government's policy was more significant, and also should have been sufficient to set to rest Salandra's later claims that no one could have predicted so long a war: "The Honorable President of the Council said with reason that the gigantic disturbance grows larger every day and that no one can foresee its end. The military and financial forces which the combatant Powers possess exclude the possibility of a not distant end to the conflict. Until the necessity of entering the field for the protection of our vital interests may arise, we must all loyally observe neutrality; because only this loyal observance will leave intact that great strength which is [our] freedom of action." Giolitti concluded his brief address with a plea for prudence, not only on the part of the Government and the Chamber, but on the part of the press. He received a standing ovation, after which the Ministry won an overwhelming vote of confidence, 413 to 49. But Turati, even before Giolitti's speech, had spoken of the equivocal nature of the majority, the contradictory tendencies that were joined in support of the Government. He was quite right; in the vote, Giolittians were joined by Federzoni, Barzilai, Labriola, De Felice and others of the war party. The official Socialists voted no confidence.[46]

This unholy coalition continued to vote for the Government throughout the period of Italian neutrality. To all outward appearances, the minority of interventionist Deputies was impotent. As weeks dragged on without any visible token of dynamic action, the war party became impatient. More vigorous antineutralist Deputies began to express their distrust for Salandra. As late as March 13 Ciccotti linked the Premier's name with what he called pro-German Italian newspapers, a reference to the Neapolitan *Il Mattino*, notoriously neutralist. This sort of polemic was bound to be taken by the neutralists as a negative justification of their confidence in the Ministry. The Ministry itself offered positive signs of its Giolittian direction. Salandra's Finance Minister, speaking in the Chamber on March 14, mentioned the economic benefits of Italian neutrality.[47] This, in essence, was the parecchio mentality, that positivistic, jackal-like view of diplomacy the intellectual journalists decried.

The Young Turks exhibited the same frustration with the Ministry's do-nothing policy in the pages of the press. Reading the *Popolo d'Italia* and the *Idea Nazionale* makes it easier to understand why the Italian people and their legal representation were led astray. These and other war party papers were very hostile to Salandra until the spring of 1915. Sacro egoismo, according to Mussolini's organ, was no better than Giolitti's "historical inevitability," which had sapped the Tripoli venture of all its grandeur. Papini's *Lacerba* attacked Salandra from the outset of his administration. Pietro Nenni, then a Republican, and a contributor to the *Popolo d'Italia*, accused Salandra of plotting with Bülow against Italy's interests — an accusation that would be aimed exclusively at Giolitti later on. Federzoni pointed out that since Salandra had confirmed the former Ministry's statements that the military depots had been restocked, his Government could have no more than the relative confidence of the Nationalists. Coppola wrote of sacro egoismo as a betrayal of ideals. The death of Di San Giuliano and the entry of Sonnino as Foreign Minister was a shock to the chauvinists who had switched sides late in the day only to see Italy's foreign policy directed by an ardent champion of the Triple Alliance. Coppola became incensed by mid-November. Corradini called Sonnino the "incarnation of the antithesis of a Foreign Minister."[48]

In the months of January and February a momentary shift in the tenor of interventionist commentary on Salandra took place. There were two reasons for this: a severe earthquake in January, and the publication of Giolitti's parecchio letter on February 1. On January 13 Latium and the Abruzzi were struck by a quake of considerable force. Evidently the Government did not at first appreciate the severity of the disaster. Salandra admits that relief work was not as efficient as it might have been. Twenty thousand died, and 100,000 were estimated to have been left homeless. The idolators of bloodshed, as in the days of the Messina quake, came out with mystical pieces on the ennobling effects of human suffering, quite as if natural disasters were substitutes for war. But the Government's obvious lack of dispatch was severely criticized by the interventionists. The *Popolo d'Italia* was hard on Salandra.[49] That tough line was only a continuation of the general dissatisfaction thus far shown by the radical antineutralist factions.

The quake gave rise to a political incident that frightened the interventionists. Soleri tells us that he and Bissolati visited the scene of the disaster, saw the full extent of the damage, and hurried back to Rome to advise Salandra. Salandra at first interpreted this move as a device by which an incident could be manufactured to bring down his Government when the Chamber opened. He referred to it as "stage coach holdup," and made a remark, widely quoted, that the authors of the political maneuver wouldn't get away with it.[50] At this point the war press realized the folly of their attacks on the way Salandra had handled the emergency, for if it were made too much of, he might be defeated in the Chamber. Dissatisfied as they had been with his policy toward the war, he was their only hope. Prezzolini began to shift ground, warning his readers that the Giolittians would use the quake as a political weapon. The *Corriere* played down Salandra's reference to a "stage coach holdup."[51]

Then came the Giolitti letter. This may have proved a grave error on Giolitti's part, as will be seen. The *Corriere d'Italia*, a clerical neutralist paper, saw no difference between Salandra's views and those of Giolitti's letter.[52] Again it was Prezzolini who grasped the need to defend Salandra. By February 9 he was backtracking, letting Salandra off the hook as far as the recent disaster was concerned. Guido Dorso, still writing from the Mezzogiorno, sent some strong anti-Salandra articles to the *Popolo d'Italia* only to have them killed by Mussolini. Mussolini wrote Dorso on February 25 that while he was not indulgent toward the Premier, or toward any Ministry that would not go to war, the articles had to be quashed for reasons which he did not care to elaborate.[53] The reasons, of course, were so patent that no comment was needed. Now that Giolitti had come out for a neutralist position that upheld avoidance of war and diplomatic bargaining, he was publicly committed to that policy. He had to be kept out of office at all costs, even if this meant backing Salandra despite the latter's manifest signs of ineptitude and, so it seemed, of naturalist sentiment. Davanzati, writing in the *Idea Nazionale* on February 12, emphasized this very point.[54] Neither the Nationalists nor the anarchic interventionists of the *Popolo d'Italia* were happy with Salandra; but they had no other man to turn to.

All of this attests to the extremely insecure spot in which the interventionist minority found itself. They were powerless without Salandra's assistance from within the Government. There was never any real threat of a revolutionary move from forces existing outside the Chamber. It was now simply a matter of stopping Giolitti's return. The question is whether

Giolitti did not inadvertently help the war party by having his letter published. In assessing the wisdom of that move, it must be remembered that he had advertised his neutralist attitude in the Chamber as early as December 5. Furthermore, the letter was intended, in part, to show that he still backed Salandra. Since the Chamber was closed, he may have wished to keep that fact before the public eye. However, the parecchio letter was far more explicit in advocating bargaining for territorial gains. By saying this, Giolitti made it very difficult for himself to take back power should his confidence in Salandra prove unjustified. Since he was in favor of the talks with the Central Powers, he would have been expected to continue them, if possible, should he step back into his old post as Premier. But having made this known to all the chancelleries, his effectiveness as a negotiator was badly undermined. This is of the utmost importance in explaining why Giolitti did not return to power in May when his backers needed his leadership. It is possible that he overlooked the implications of his remarks. Giolitti released the letter for publication in order to quash reports, put forth by interventionist Socialists, that he was plotting with the Socialists to unseat Salandra. His intentions were clearly domestic in scope,[55] not diplomatic. Hence it is quite plausible that he missed the full impact of the parecchio letter.

Whether the letter was a profound miscalculation depends not so much on Giolitti's failure to perceive, as on Salandra's willingness to deceive. The possibility of deception was enhanced by all the outward signs that Salandra would follow a Giolittian line. With the war press attacking Salandra from without the Chamber and the interventionist Deputies from within, and the neutralist Deputies voting him repeated majorities, there was little reason to wish a change in Government. When Giolitti returned to Rome for the February-March session of the Chamber he had a talk with Salandra, following which he continued to advise support for the Ministry. In April, by which time Salandra had told Sonnino of his plans, Giolitti wrote Count Giacomo Rattazzi — a contributor to the neutralist *Italia Nostra* — that it would be very dangerous to weaken the Government in any way. It needed backing at home in order to carry out talks abroad. Giolitti also felt that a strong majority would help the Salandra government keep a check on the frenzies of the interventionists in Italy.[56] How wrong he was would be seen during the critical week from May 12 to May 20, when the interventionists were allowed to run wild in the streets of Rome, to fan the fires of antiparliamentary revolution, and to incite the mob against Giolitti and his pack of traitors.

When the Chamber of Deputies met on February 18, the policies of the Salandra ministry soon weakened the tenuous and conditional willingness of the radical war party to uphold his Government. Ciccotti again took up his charges against the Premier, whom he described as the manager of a bankrupt firm. While the country was confused, disoriented, and unable to discuss fundamental issues of foreign policy, Salandra was doing business with clerical groups. Ciccotti despaired that war would ever come.[57] On February 26 an important debate began on a decree forbidding private as well as public meetings. This measure was designed to prevent outbursts of popular violence, which had claimed one life in Reggio Emilia. By an earlier decree, of August 6, 1914, public rallies had been suspended. In truth, the Government had been very lax in enforcing this ban.[58] Interventionists had been given far too much leeway. Furthermore, private meetings had not been covered. The activities of such propagandists as Destrée had gone on without any effective governmental control. The new decree, it seemed, would limit even scheduled speaking engagements of that sort.

The opposition to this decree illustrated the confused and dangerously uncertain political mood of the country. In the Chamber, speaking for the Socialists, Turati condemned the decree as a suppression of civil liberties worse than in the days of Pelloux. Let the people manifest their opinions, he said, and they will prove that the call for war was only a literary bluff of a few newspapers.[59] Undoubtedly Turati was following his principles in attacking the measure. Knowing that the people were for neutrality, to shut off public debate suggested as well a plot to gag the majority and to prepare for a coup by the interventionist elite. The loudest protests, however, came from the interventionists themselves. Their only hope was to have access to the squares and meeting halls, to stir up interest in war or in revolution. Salandra's belated effort to enforce the ban on neutralist-interventionist meetings and rallies threatened to ruin them. The neutralist Turati likened this to Pelloux's reaction, and the radical interventionist Labriola drew up the same parallel. The *Popolo d'Italia* lifted its censorship on anti-Salandra editorials. It accused him of being an ally of Giolitti and a confirmed reactionary. Mussolini insisted the decree was forced on the Government by the Central Powers. Ironically, Turati had insinuated the same thing in the Chamber.[60] By March 1 the *Popolo d'Italia* dropped its mask and came out openly for the ruination of the Salandra ministry. Then, in early March, Giolitti and Salandra held their private talks, from which Giolitti emerged more confirmed than ever in his belief that his successor was following the path of sanity and rational diplomacy. This meeting was given considerable publicity in the war press, all of it unfavorable to Salandra.[61] The fact that Salandra, although chief of state, had gone to Giolitti's Rome residence for the talks was another testimony of the continuity of Giolitti's policy. It also made Salandra seem the lesser power, the "lieutenant" of the great Minister. This, along with other pricks at his ego, was to be on Salandra's mind when the critical moment came for the formation of the Cabinet that was to decide the issue of war.

Mussolini was the most exasperated of all the interventionists. He found himself in an impossible position. Unable to capture a sufficient following among the rank and file of Italian socialism, staking all on his chances of fomenting violence from the passions generated by the great debate, the Government's decree meant personal disaster. By March 6 he showed signs of frantic impotence. His editorial was strikingly erratic, confused, and repetitious. Salandra, he wrote, had failed to see war's moral factor. Italy's leaders thought only of "material needs; all the rest was but romantic and idealistic excess. However," he went on, "if the honorable Sonnino and Salandra had concerns of a superior, that is, moral nature . . . they would see in the war against the Central Powers a necessity above all of a moral nature." Neutralism threatened to "decompose the national organism," bring all the worst defects of the Italian character to the surface where they "festered like great pestiferous boils." Farsighted men considered not only the physical but the moral health of nations. "Governments capable of seeing beyond the present . . . sense, or should sense, that war quickly and radically cauterizes 'ills' of a moral nature." By April 7 he had conceded the weakness of the Fasci, their inability to carry off revolution. He had little left save the old pose of the solitary figure who would give in only if neutrality became permanent, unless someone would "come forth from the anonymous throng to punish those responsible with a Browning or with dynamite."

The future Duce tried to slip out of the corner into which his apostacy and Salandra's apparent Giolittism had forced him. With typical disregard of principles he now took up the revolutionary half of his battle cry. There is evidence that he had abandoned hope in the anarchic possibilities of intervention, and sought to reverse ground by taking up the cause of militant socialism. On April 11 he wrote in praise of the Socialists. Neutralists though they were, the party, even the "official" party, had shown more patriotism by its display of discipline than the bourgeoisie, who waxed fat off neutrality.[62] On April 11 interventionist rallies at Milan and Rome were broken up by the police. Mussolini and the Futurist Marinetti were arrested and held briefly. The next day the *Popolo d'Italia's* editorial talked more about the sins of the Italian monarchy and of police brutality than it did of war. The *Idea Nazionale* said Mussolini was trying to recover his "revolutionary virginity." This was correct. On April 14 the *Popolo d'Italia* came out in support of a socialist strike[63] called to protest the death of a man at the Milan rally of a few days before.

Turati, however, wisely refused to give the anarchic elements within the party a chance to exploit this incident. Speaking at the funeral for the dead man, he attacked the Government's policy but called off the scheduled protest demonstration. He was quite aware, and had so stated publicly,[64] that violence only played into Mussolini's hands. This raises the question of the Socialist party's tactics regarding war. What stand the party should take was a source of much soul-searching debate. In general, Socialists who would have sabotaged any war effort were in the distinct minority. In the light of Mussolini's hopes and of his own regionalist background, it is interesting to note that one socialist local which did insist on mass undermining of mobilization was that of Forlì, Mussolini's own stamping ground. While the *Lotta di classe* had come out against Mussolini's desertion of party theory, the common link of individualistic, romanticized action, that undercurrent within the party that recalled the days of the Risorgimento, came into play again in 1915. Mussolini doubtless hoped to use this to save himself from political extinction. His over-all elasticity, a serpentine talent for avoiding being trapped by any middle ground necessitating compromise, was demonstrated in the month preceding Italy's intervention.

For the bulk of the party leadership, and for the General Confederation of Labor, what platform to adopt posed great difficulties. As confirmed neutralists, the thought of publicly abandoning popular agitation against mobilization was impossible. And yet a flat proclamation against a war that might be necessary to defend Italy from attack was equally untenable. For, as Treves had said in the Chamber, all Italians were patriots where the defense of the nation was at stake. Hence the manifestos of the party and of the General Confederation of Labor became increasingly unclear as to just what steps should be taken by the workers in response to a declaration of war.[65] As with all neutralists, the uncertainty of the situation, the blackout of information relating to the progress of diplomatic talks, and the negative aspect of a policy for the prevention of war deprived the party of a dynamic policy. But it also prevented the extremists and opportunists from making use of violence, be it for or against war, to wreck the party and, in the process, to strike at the constitutional regime. Mussolini later, as Duce, would claim that the turning point in his career came in 1903, when the Socialists refused to enter the Giolitti cabinet.[66] That was no more than prophetic hindsight. The real turning point came when Salandra, who knew he could count on the loyalty of the party as a whole, went to war, creating the conditions that Mussolini would later feed upon. Turati's position in 1914–15, one feels, was sound. If the party feared the taint of official responsibility, and at times looked the other way when those romantic roots from the past sprouted up to challenge its official status, the Italian Socialist leaders had, in effect, become part of the legally constituted government since the days of Pelloux and Rudinì.

At first glance it may seem unfortunate that the Socialist party did not come out in support of Giolitti's policy. Labriola, an ardent interventionist, had been lavish in his praise for the old Premier, but only when he was out of office and before the outbreak of war. It was clear that his generous recognition of Giolitti's services to liberty was prompted by a desire to hurt Salandra, a recognized conservative. Turati, however, did not approve of the parecchio concept. He pleaded instead for a moral defense-of-the-peace movement, in cooperation with other neutral states, along what were at the time Wilsonian lines.[67] He rejected the idea of a Machiavellian plucking of territories by using neutrality as a weight in the balance of power. This idealism, certainly laudable compared to the rank opportunism of many interventionists, forbade a more explicit defense of the parliamentary majority's neutralist stand. Too much should not be made of this, however. It is quite incorrect to speak of a dogmatic self-paralysis of the Socialists, or to affirm that they preferred to hope for the catastrophe of capitalism rather than actively opposing interventionists.[68] In every real sense the Socialist Deputies were behind the regime. Everyone knew this, including Salandra. To go into the streets with clubs would only have enhanced the very slim possibilities of the Mussolinian renegades. Turati saw this and wisely refrained from playing Mussolini's game. The tragedy was that the Government betrayed him, not that the party betrayed the parliamentary regime. But the Government also betrayed Giolitti and the majority of the Chamber.

The moderation of the Socialist party and the obvious feebleness of the revolutionary interventionists, whose threat to topple the Throne was meaningless, must be kept in mind when considering Salandra's motives and responsibility for the events of May. His letter to Sonnino of March 16 proposed a clearly unconstitutional *fait accompli*, forcing war upon the nation. There can be no excuse for this plot on the ground that he had legitimate fears that neutrality would produce a revolution, however much this was referred to by his ministers in their talks with foreign observers. That he was ready to go ahead without the King's assent is sufficient proof that he was not moved by a desire to protect the Crown even had he sincerely feared the strength of the mobs.

Yet all these facts — the unmistakable readiness of the Ministry to take advantage of a trust obviously predicated on a desire for peace, the false confidence of the neutralists, the virtual impotence of the radical interventionists — do not explain how it came to pass that the Parliament on May 20 voted for a war it did not want. Nor do they explain why Giolitti, famed as a master practitioner of parliamentary wiles, permitted the disaster to occur. Those students of the intervention who still hope to prove that it was a responsible action in which the nation concurred emphasize as proof of their thesis the failure of the neutralists throughout Italy to take action.[69] As for the Chamber, even Salandra had to reckon with it at last. The fact that he could not avoid this, as he would have liked, is in itself a sign that Parliament was indispensable in Italy. It had to be subverted. But when it failed to protect the will of the people on May 20, it opened the path for new and more pernicious attacks on representative government in the postwar years. If the regimes of the Postrisorgimento were viable, the causes of the failure of the neutralist majority must be explained.

·11·

THE COLLAPSE OF THE
NEUTRALIST MAJORITY

There is no doubt that Giolitti trusted Salandra even after the date on which the London Treaty was signed. It was this drawn-out confidence by the one man who could easily have returned to power that was to make Salandra's victory possible. Giolitti's letter to Count Rattazzi in support of the Ministry is dated April 27. He speaks of his incurable optimism and his belief that all would turn out well, indicating only that he had suspicions that all was not actually going as it should. Still, he had no proof. Nothing but rumors and words of caution came to him at Cavour, where he intended to stay until the Chamber reconvened on May 12. In a letter of April 3 he mentioned his wish to avoid the petty political squabbles that always infested the air when the Parliament was shut down.[1] For Giolitti, Montecitorio was the vital and only center of Italian politics.

On May 4, however, we are told that Rattazzi appeared at Cavour to tell Giolitti the Triple Alliance had been ended. Our source for this, Ansaldo's biography of Giolitti, gives no documentation. Talk to this effect was soon widespread. Ansaldo has hypothesized that Giolitti suspected there must be a pact with the Entente the minute he heard the old alliance was dead. He delayed action because he did not wish to be told of the new treaty. The reason for this, following Ansaldo's surmise, was that if he were told his hands would be tied. This theory — and it is only a theory — is, as Salvatorelli notes,[2] far too ingenious. It is intended to explain away Giolitti's apparent slowness to move to Rome in the face of a gathering storm. Assuming that Ansaldo's version of Rattazzi's visit is correct, however, there is a better explanation of why Giolitti waited before going to the capital.

On the same day Rattazzi visited Cavour, the papers carried the announcement that the King would not go to Quarto. There was also the news of the uprising in Tripoli, the outbreak of native warfare at Sirte. The bulletin also stated that the Ministers would stay at Rome; they also would miss the national festival. Knowing the military situation as he did, and hearing of the cancellation of the royal trip to Genoa, what was Giolitti to think? The sudden change of plans pointed to a cautious and studied attempt to deprive the Quarto celebration of any diplomatic overtones. In his memoirs this announcement is given some importance. Giolitti says that throughout April he had letters from friends and others unknown to him expressing alarm that the country might be dragged into war without knowing it. However, these warnings were supported by no facts. "One fact alone was noted by me which could have been quite significant; and that was that at the Quarto ceremonies, to which D'Annunzio, who had already expressed heatedly his conviction that Italy would take part in the war, had been called as speaker, the King would attend. But then that did not happen." [3]

Even were Ansaldo correct about the Rattazzi visit, and his knowledge of the events is intimate, Giolitti would have been reassured. But on May 7 the news that the Chamber would not reopen until May 20 was released. It has been suggested that this was the moment at which Giolitti made his plans to go to Rome. The postponing of the session alarmed him.[4] While this is possible, it is more likely that he retained his confidence in Salandra's essential honesty. The prorogation was taken by the neutralists as a hopeful sign that talks with Vienna were to continue. It was also announced that Giolitti's plans to come to Rome to visit his wife, who was ill, had been made well in advance.[5] The continued trust he placed in Salandra after May 9 is hard to explain in view of the warnings he was to receive from friends, unless we assume that his coming to Rome was a matter of course.

On May 9 and 10 the calling-card demonstration took place. This attests to the fact that the Deputies were not as slavishly dependent on Giolitti as anti-Giolittian writers would have us believe. In fact, the neutralists took the initiative and would have welcomed Giolitti's leadership, his return to power. It was Giolitti who refused to move. The calling-card affair was a voluntary expression of the Chamber's continued support of the neutralist position. Historians favorable to Salandra have tried to twist it into an antiparliamentary, unconstitutional uprising. That is simply absurd. With the Chamber closed, it was the logical way of showing their sentiments. In his memoirs Giolitti refutes the charge that the Deputies were rising up against the King's prerogatives by citing the English declaration of war, which was sufficient only after the House of Commons had voted the funds.[6]

Beginning on May 9 and continuing for a week, a series of talks between the principals of the drama of intervention held the attention of the Italian press. In journalistic circles the advocates of war claimed that Giolitti and his minions were attempting to sabotage the naton's destiny, wreck the Salandra government, and degrade Italy in the eyes of the world. As has been described, Giolitti was accused by the war press of knowing the full truth of Italy's diplomatic commitments. Therefore his actions in Rome were treasonous. The question whether he did know of the London Treaty was to become a subject of wide historical speculation and investigation, much of it polemical in nature. Frassati and Salvatorelli have written that the matter has been settled once and for all: he did not know. But very recent studies persist in casting serious doubts on this and on Giolitti's honesty,[7] showing that there are some for whom it is still an issue. Far more than the reputation of the man Giolitti is involved in the answer to the riddle of his behavior in May, 1915. The vitality of Italy's constitutional regime is at stake. Because of this, it will be worth our while to follow the course of events as closely as possible from the available sources, drawing on the memoirs of the personalities involved, including some which have come to light quite recently. In this way part of the riddle may be unraveled. In the process, the lesser but certainly important problem of Giolitti's personal morality will also be clarified.

One of the first to rush to Giolitti's Rome residence was Bertolini. The former Colonial Minister, together with Luigi Facta, saw Giolitti on May 9 at about 11 A.M. They brought Giolitti up to date on the over-all situation, and then tried to persuade him to see Salandra. Giolitti was very reluctant. He told Bertolini that since Salandra knew he was in Rome, the Premier could invite him to confer if he saw fit. According to Bertolini, Giolitti gave way before their entreaties and agreed that Bertolini should go quickly to Salandra to arrange for a personal meeting. Bertolini suggested it should take place at Salandra's home. He recalled that the last such talk was held at Giolitti's house. This was, of course, proper. Moreover, although Bertolini does not mention it, he must have remembered that the interventionist press reacted strongly when Salandra went to see Giolitti in early March. A similar affront to his dignity was to be avoided. Just as the two were leaving, a note arrived from Paolo Carcano, Salandra's Minister of the Treasury, asking Giolitti for an appointment. Carcano, an ex-Garibaldian, was an intimate of Giolitti's. Bertolini assumed he was coming to speak to his friend on behalf of the Government. Nonetheless he persisted in advising a personal confrontation with Salandra. He then left to arrange it.[8]

Carcano saw Giolitti at 4:30 P.M. the same day. Giolitti's memoirs, anything but prolix, describe the encounter with the utmost brevity. It was a long conversation, in which Carcano explained at length the reasons the Government considered entry into the war necessary. Giolitti opposed these arguments with a detailed explanation of the risks Italy would be facing. According to Giolitti, Carcano was very moved, and tears came to his eyes. But he ended by saying that the decision was definite. "He did not speak to me in any way, however, nor made the least allusion to a treaty which had been signed." This, Giolitti says, he later explained to himself on the basis of Carcano's own ignorance of the London Treaty. But when the document was published following the Bolshevik Revolution, Giolitti then saw that the reason his old friend, who had been Secretary of his Cabinet in 1893, had not spoken was that the secrecy clause forbade it. Here, one feels, Giolitti was being very generous. For despite that clause it would have been quite ethical, as Salvatorelli had pointed out,[9] to mention the existence of a formal treaty. One would go even farther: given Giolitti's stature, his forty years of state service, his unparalleled experience and knowledge of the nation, to have kept him in the dark was a grave error, whatever the clauses of the Treaty.

When Bertolini saw Salandra on May 9, after he had seen Giolitti and prior to the Carcano-Giolitti talk, Salandra told him that Carcano already had been instructed to inform Giolitti of the international situation. But, writes Bertolini, Salandra gladly agreed to a personal exchange of views. It was understood that this would take place the next day, May 10, at Salandra's residence at 4 P.M. Returning to Giolitti's home after seeing Salandra and arranging for the meeting, Bertolini was told that on the basis of Carcano's remarks Giolitti did not have a very clear concept of the situation. But Bertolini was assured that Giolitti would see Salandra the next day.[10]

Turning now to Salandra's memoirs covering the intervention, we may fill in the details lacking in the recollections of Bertolini and Giolitti. It will then be instructive to compare Salandra's memoirs, published in 1930, with another document first made public in 1957. This latter is a diary that Salandra kept in order to recall the salient events of the week from May 9 to May 16. It was, he tells us, on the basis of these notes that he was able to write with such "exactness"[11] about the happenings of that critical week when he set about to record his own story of the intervention.

On the morning of May 9, we read in the memoirs, Salandra saw the King. They spoke of the parliamentary situation and of Giolitti. The King, who had been kept abreast of the international situation and of the latest offers from Bülow and Baron von Macchio, was "always calm and confident," if justly concerned about the domestic front. He suggested the advisability of seeing Giolitti and coming to an agreement with the former Premier so that he would help rather than hinder the Government's plans. "I stated very frankly," Salandra wrote in his memoirs, "that Giolitti was now considered a power *sui generis*, outside the King, the Government and the Institutions; that, however little I might think of myself, I would not, like Luzzatti and Fortis, be President of the Council under his protectorate; that in March, I had gone to see him at his house in a friendly way, but his friends and his paper[12] had spoken of my visit with a great lack of delicacy; and that therefore I would receive him when he asked me, but I would not go to him. The King, kindly admonishing me, said that he and I must act 'like two brave persons, ready to sacrifice ourselves in the interest only of the country.' To these noble and simple words I consider it my duty," Salandra continues, "not to add other references to comments and expressions of his Majesty. I told him, however, that Sonnino and I had thought of asking Carcano . . . to contact him [i.e. Giolitti], and to put him abreast of the entire situation, without withholding anything from him. He approved and accepted my suggestion to invite Giolitti immediately to confer, but after the Carcano talk about which he wished to be informed." [13]

Following the royal audience, Sonnino, Salandra, and Carcano met at the foreign office. There — still drawing on Salandra's memoirs — Carcano read some notes he had made from memory on a recent letter Giolitti had written to a Deputy, in which Giolitti's opposition to war was reaffirmed on the basis of the country's lack of endurance, the opinion of the great majority of the nation, and the economic disaster that would follow the war. Despite this new confirmation of the statesman's views, Carcano had agreed to undertake the difficult mission of seeing Giolitti. From Sonnino he took precise notes on the international events "which were to be referred" to Giolitti. At this point, around noon of May 9, Bertolini arrived. Carcano had left. "He told me," Salandra writes, "that Giolitti wished to see me." Salandra said he was quite willing to receive him at any hour Giolitti might select. To avoid misunderstandings, he told Bertolini of the Carcano visit, and found that Bertolini already knew about it. It was agreed, Salandra notes, that if Giolitti still wanted to see him after he had spoken with Carcano, Bertolini should telephone telling Salandra the place and the time.

On the evening of the same day, Carcano came to report to Salandra on the talk with Giolitti. Salandra quotes him as saying that Giolitti was very "gloomy." He had listened calmly to Carcano's description of the talks with the Central Powers but had "sprung up" when he heard of the denouncing of the Triple Alliance and of the telegrams exchanged between the King and the heads of the Entente. "Then the King is obligated," Giolitti is said to have exclaimed. "One can understand," Salandra inserts, "how that must have bothered him, it no longer being sufficient to disavow the Government." After this, he had expressed the gloomiest forecasts for the future: no confidence in the troops, after the experience with them in Libya; nor in the organization of the army, in which generals who had spoken with him lacked confidence; nor in the country's endurance, the war continuing, as was probable, into the winter. He foresaw invasion, the Austrians and Germans at Verona, revolution at home. He insisted at length that Piedmont was opposed to war and held not only the Ministers but the King responsible. "Carcano came away with a heavy heart," Salandra continues, "but with the unshaken confidence of an old Garibaldian." Salandra reassured him, took note of what he had recounted, and went to the King to report on the outcome of the Carcano-Giolitti discussion, "omitting only the part which concerned the assertion of his own [i.e. the King's] responsibility."

"I have an indelible memory of the long and confident conversation with his Majesty which went as far as the worst hypotheses," Salandra writes. "Since his Majesty insisted in his wish, fully justified and in keeping with his office, to have the constitutional parties in agreement in facing the events, I declared that the Ministry was ready to leave the field if the King considered that advisable for the country's interest, either by letting it be defeated in the Chamber, or else departing beforehand. But it was not enough to turn back to the parecchio, even if somewhat enlarged by the latest offers communicated to his Majesty the evening before by Bülow by the means I have mentioned. Leaving out his personal obligation — which he had not the slightest intention of backing down on — I could not help pointing out to him the situation in which the country would find itself, discredited by both sides, exposed to the reprisals of the Entente, perhaps losing its colonies, torn by internal factions, and what a blow such a crisis would have meant for the Institutions."

Salandra tells us that the only conclusion to his talk with the King was that Giolitti would be summoned to the palace the next morning, May 10. Salandra then returned to his office, where he found a note saying that Bertolini had telephoned to say that despite the meeting with Carcano, Giolitti still wanted to see him. The appointment was set for 4 P.M. on May 10. Salandra then wrote the King about this and in his letter repeated his willingness to bow out, by a vote of the Chamber or before. If the King felt it in the interests of the country, he would come to an understanding with Giolitti on how best to handle this.[14]

Giolitti saw the King on the morning of May 10. His memoirs, published in 1922, devote only a few lines to the meeting. He expressed to the King his reasons for not going to war. The King, he writes, obligated by the written clause regarding its secrecy, did not mention the London Pact. Bertolini then came to Giolitti, saying that Salandra wanted to see him. Giolitti agreed, and was to go at 4 P.M. that same day.[15] Salandra has denied that he ever told Bertolini, whom he calls even more neutralist than Giolitti, that he wanted to see the ex-Premier. Bertolini claims that at about 1 P.M. on May 10, that is after Giolitti had seen the King, Salandra telephoned to inform him that the King, having suggested Giolitti see Salandra, had the impression that Giolitti was uncertain whether he had as yet a precise appointment. Bertolini told Salandra that Giolitti had certainly understood that he had, but in any case he would see him at 3 P.M. and remove any doubt.[16] Here a discrepancy exists, for Bertolini claims that an appointment had been fixed when he saw Salandra on May 9, while Salandra says that he was willing to see Giolitti, described as wishing to see him, *if* Giolitti still felt that way after talking to Carcano. Giolitti says nothing about seeing Bertolini on May 9. He refers only to Bertolini's telling him on the afternoon of May 10 that Salandra wanted to see him.[17] The real discrepancy between Giolitti's account and Salandra's hinges on who asked to see whom. Salandra quite clearly denies that he asked to see Giolitti. This confusion is of no great significance save as an illustration of Salandra's personality. He did not wish to appear to posterity as beholden to the leader of Parliament, to be characterized as the lieutenant of the "Great Minister." Furthermore, the implication is that Giolitti, a Deputy and no more, was interfering intentionally in the operation of the Government, intruding himself as it were. It is obvious that he was not. Bertolini had no reason to dissemble when he wrote of Giolitti's reluctance to see Salandra unless asked. Besides, by Salandra's own admission, the King approved of consulting Giolitti. The insinuation, one of many, is typical of Salandra's style, as well as revealing of his sensitivity. He had been cut to the quick more than once since taking office by implications that he was, like Fortis and Luzzatti, only a stopgap Premier.

Returning to Salandra's memoirs, what does he tell us about Giolitti's visit to Victor Emmanuel III? He writes that Giolitti told the King of his grave forebodings and advised acceptance of the latest Austrian offers, which he had learned of from Senator Chimirri, described by Salandra as a frequent visitor at Bülow's Roman villa. Giolitti maintained that the Government could be released from its obligations to the Entente by means of a vote of confidence in the Chamber. But he absolutely excluded his own return to office on the ground that he would be tagged pro-Austrian and "for other reasons," unspecified by Salandra. Giolitti said he would see Salandra and place himself at his service in order to avoid war and to back up the Ministry. "He tried," Salandra writes, "to dissuade the King from the emphasis he placed on his personal obligations, holding that they were a matter merely of political commitments between the Chancelleries." The King informed Salandra of what transpired soon after he had seen Giolitti. Salandra quotes the King as being impressed by Salandra's calmness in the midst of such difficulties. The Premier replied that he could always maintain his serenity when accusations against him were unjustified, but were he to feel in his conscience that they were justified because of his staying on without following out the accords with the Entente, that calmness and strength would vanish immediately.[18]

Thus far the memoirs have carried us down to the afternoon of May 10, when the most important and most violently debated conversation took place. Giolitti went to Salandra at 4 P.M. As usual, Giolitti's written account is as bare as bones. He limits his description to less than a page.

Salandra told me he knew of my conversation with the King; I repeated to him all the reasons for which I believed that Italy would have committed an error entering the war in the conditions which the war then presented. No one even imagined then that the United States would come in. Salandra answered that the government had by this time made the decision to enter the war; that it was impossible to turn back; and that if he were unable to declare war due to the obstacles on the part of the Parliament, he would have had to resign. He was informed of the degree of support which the Deputies had expressed for my point of view, from which he deduced that Parliament would vote against him. These same declarations by the Honorable Salandra exclude my having been informed of the Treaty of London, because otherwise the conversation and the discussion would have turned to other points and would have taken another course.[19]

From this last remark, we may conclude that if Giolitti felt a binding pact had been signed, he would not have spoken as he did. But let us see what Salandra's memoirs have to say on this important conversation. The talk was long, calm, courteous, "if not cordial," and circumspect on both sides. Giolitti repeated his reasons against war, even making them more emphatic. He foresaw the occupation of Verona, conquest of Milan, and revolution in the country. Salandra recalls that Giolitti praised him for having extracted the latest Austrian proposals from the diplomatic talks. He said he had seen, in Bertolini's possession, the list of Vienna's offers. These, Salandra adds, were on a sheet of paper destined for the Vatican. "He did not tell me he had them from Chimirri in order not to admit having had dealings with Bülow, even were it by way of a most worthy person." Salandra objected that the signed list of concessions, which he informs his reader was destined for the Vatican, had not yet reached the Government. Giolitti agreed and said he would tell Chimirri, their mutual friend, about this.

On the parliamentary situation, Giolitti, as reported by Salandra, began by refusing absolutely to take the reigns of government. He sustained the same idea he put to the King: that the Ministry could free itself from its obligations to the Entente with the help of the Chamber. Giolitti suggested a motion implying confidence in the Ministry, to be signed by many Deputies of the constitutional parties excluding himself.

I flatly disagreed. Even admitting that the ministry had erred thus far and were disowned by the Chamber, the consequence [of this] was to leave, a discredited government being forbidden by the domestic and international situation. The strange thesis left me doubtful as to the good faith of him who was proposing it. How could a ministry reduced to the status of a dirty rag stand up? In order to accept such an idea one would have to suppose us to be men without intelligence and incapable of shame. As for the rest, Giolitti's aversion to war was certainly sincere; nor were his reasons of little value. I had the impression, also because of this, contrary to the suspicions of my friends and the desires of his followers, that for the time being he really did not wish to take power again. He had preferred on other occasions to consign power to others in more difficult moments. Only it must be admitted that he must have been in a singular state of excitement to have believed it possible to get out of the situation which we were in through one of the usual parliamentary maneuvers.[20]

Salandra states that there was no definite conclusion to this talk, save that they agreed to see each other again if it were necessary. "In substance," he writes, "I was convinced, and I maintain Giolitti was convinced, of the impossibility of agreement. I wish only to point out that from Carcano, from the King, from me, and, I may add, from Bülow, Giolitti had in those two days full information on the international situation. To clear himself of the accusation, fiercely brought against him, of having come to foment discord, to disturb the public mind, to enervate the country when the King and the government were irrevocably obligated, he maintained and repeated in his *Memoirs* that he had not been informed of the London Pact; which, as usual, is exact only in the letter, in the sense that he was not given a copy or perusal of it, not that the contents of it were not spoken of to him, if the later telegrams to the King were even mentioned to him."[21]

Giolitti left Salandra the evening of May 10 and returned home for dinner. At 8 P.M. Bertolini stopped by to get a report on his talk with the Premier. In his diary, Bertolini noted that Giolitti described the talks as long, about an hour and a half, and very cordial. Giolitti said he gave all his reasons against war, insisting on the serious harm it would do to the Mezzogiorno in arresting its progress. "Giolitti assured me that Salandra had declared himself to be very impressed by these and other considerations of Giolitti's." Giolitti expressed his confidence that the war would be avoided. After having left Giolitti, however, Bertolini writes that he reflected a moment and decided that the outcome of the conversations was not at all reassuring.[22]

Here, certainly, is a contradiction of fundamental significance. Salandra's description of the meeting simply does not tally with Giolitti's remarks to Bertolini, not only on such small points as to whether it was "very cordial," but on the central issue of whether the two agreed. On the basis of Salandra's memoirs, Giolitti could never have felt confident that war was going to be avoided. Before delving into the truth, it is worth while pointing out what does emerge even from Salandra's description. He admits Giolitti never actually saw or read the London Pact. As for the telegrams, on which he is counting very heavily to sway the reader, they were not as yet published. In his memoirs, Salandra refers to them very vaguely in passing. Giolitti never mentions them. The King was still living when he was writing, of course. It is true that the Government got the final Austrian offers, signed by the ambassadors, only after Giolitti and others had copies of them. Salandra thought Giolitti got Erzberger to send them, which is quite possible. Erzberger tells us of running frantically about Rome trying to find Macchio, whom he did not locate until midnight of May 10. Hence, Salandra was officially informed on May 11. Undoubtedly Erzberger was heavy-handed in his spreading of the offers. This was bound to be offensive to Salandra, and Giolitti quite properly admitted the Government should have had them first. But that is not enough to go to war about. The attempt to link Giolitti to the Vatican is obvious. He infers that the list Giolitti saw was the same that was to be carried to the Vatican. In fact, a copy was sent,[23] but Giolitti had no part in that.

The most glaring contradiction that emerges from Salandra's own accounts relates to the nature of the Treaty of London. He concedes that he was ready to resign for the good of the country if the King wished it. He also insists that the King and the Government were irrevocably obligated. They could not go back. And yet, vague as his remarks on his talk with Giolitti are, it is obvious that they were discussing the possibility of a new vote of confidence in the Chamber, which Salandra says would be possible only for men without a sense of shame. How could they have even discussed it if the Treaty had been unconditional? It is impossible to be both ready to leave office, which would mean inevitably a collapse of the war policy, and to assert that there could be no turning back. It was this internal evidence from the memoirs themselves that prompted Salvatorelli, the leading authority on the subject, to reverse an earlier judgment. Salvatorelli once held that since Giolitti did not know that a state commitment, as opposed to a Cabinet commitment, existed, the only explanation for his ignorance was that Salandra and the King had laid a trap for him. By keeping him uninformed, they placed him in the position of appearing to sabotage the nation's honor. The intervention became a *coup d'état* that stripped the parliamentary majority of its power.[24]

It seems that Giolitti himself in later years believed the Treaty to be absolutely binding. He writes in his memoirs of not having known of a "signed" treaty. In later years he told Frassati that had he known of the Treaty he would have either gone to war, which he was not willing to do, or retired to his home in the country. Any other course, he said, would have degraded the nation.[25] But Giolitti ascribes his ignorance to the secrecy clause, although he certainly must have felt that he had been ambushed. However, Baron Burian and Erzberger [26] speak of a "conditional" pact. And it must have been from Salandra's own words. This finally led Salvatorelli to the theory that Salandra did not himself consider the pact binding. Hence his actions were less consciously reprehensible than had been thought.[27] The publication in 1957 of part of the notes Salandra used when he wrote his "exact" description of the events confirmed Salvatorelli's analysis. This document proves much more. It shows why Giolitti was able to tell Bertolini that he had confidence the war would be avoided. It also reveals the depth of duplicity on Salandra's part that is the logical conclusion to the ambiguous parliamentary arrangement he had decided to exploit as early as March 16.

We will summarize the essentials of the diary's day-by-day notations, with parallel references from the memoirs.

Sunday, May 9, 1915: 9–10 A.M.

Salandra went to the King at 9 A.M. He had last seen the monarch on Friday, May 7, in the company of Sonnino. At that time, the decree extending the parliamentary recess to May 20 had been signed by the King. Also on May 7, the latest Austrian offers were explained to the King. The King on that day had been very calm and confident, "not at all repentant of what had been done. This morning he was very worried, above all about what was supposed to have happened at the Chamber and concerning which Giolitti's coming, announced for this morning, was an indication." The King advised seeing Giolitti, and — as in the memoirs — Salandra spoke of not wishing to be Premier under his protectorate. The King then said they should behave like "brave fellows" for the good of the country.

To these "noble and simple words," according to the memoirs, Salandra wished to add nothing further relative to "comments and expressions of his Majesty."[28]

In fact, the King repeated an "allusion already made a few times before without dwelling on it, but this time dwelling on it, that he is ready to leave." Together with his son, Victor Emmanuel III would yield the throne to the Duke of Aosta. "He told me for the first time," the diary continues, " 'Perhaps I would never have come here and I wished to speak about it to my father but he died in that way and I was forced to come.' " As in the memoirs, the diary relates telling the King that Giolitti was to be contacted by Carcano. The King "approves warmly," unlike the simple "approved" of the memoirs. It was decided to inform Giolitti he would be summoned, but to set the time after the talk with Carcano. "The King was plainly confused and worried," quite unlike the "always calm"[29] monarch of the memoirs.

10–11 A.M.

The diary notes the meeting of Salandra, Sonnino, and Carcano at which the latter was instructed to see Giolitti. As to the points on which Giolitti was to be informed, it was not a matter of "concealing nothing from him," but to tell him only of the denunciation of the Triple Alliance, of the "true" Austrian offers and of the telegrams.[30]

12 P.M.

The diary says nothing about the talk with Bertolini save that Salandra would see Giolitti if the latter still wanted to come after having talked with Carcano.[31]

5:15 P.M.

Carcano arrives. Giolitti is very "gloomy" and "sprang up" when he heard of the ending of the Triple Alliance and of the telegrams. As in the memoirs, he is quoted as saying "Then the King is obligated." Then came those dark forecasts, much the same as in the memoirs save that Giolitti is supposed to have referred to desertions during the Libyan campaign, and to have said that he had little confidence in the generals. He also had little confidence in the country's endurance especially in a war that would probably be long, a bit different from a war that would drag on "into the winter," as the memoirs have it. Piedmont was against the war and held both King and Ministers responsible,[32] this last in keeping with the memoirs.

6:15 P.M.

Salandra saw the King again, reporting of the Carcano talks. The King was told everything save Giolitti's remarks relative to Piedmont's opposition and the fact that the Piedmontese held the King as well as the Ministers responsible. It will be recalled that in the memoirs Salandra omitted only the part about the royal responsibility. Hence Piedmontese opinion, on which Giolitti was an authority, was not mentioned. "The King is even more confused, worried and hesitant than this morning," the entry reads, whereas it was a "long and confident" talk in the memoirs. In fact, so confused was the King that Salandra had a hard time summarizing their talk. The King then read a two-page report given him by General Brusati, his aide-de-camp, which summarized the General's exchange with Bülow that had taken place at Bülow's request and with the King's permission. Bülow blamed everything on Sonnino, who had stalled the talks in order to go to war. Salandra said that was not true since in the early months Sonnino had felt quite the opposite. Bülow was also to have mentioned the end of the Triple Alliance, and Sonnino, when asked, had denied it.[!] Salandra answered that this was absurd since Sonnino knew Bülow had been told about it by either Vienna or Berlin. Bülow then gave the concessions, essentially those of the ultimate offer, but without saying anything, according to the diary, about the manner of execution of the agreement — an important concession added at the last minute. Brusati then expressed to the King his own neutralist sentiment and his lack of confidence in the generals. At this point Salandra offered to resign. The King suggested it would be better to do so in the Chamber by a vote, which is not recorded in the memoirs. Salandra replied that he did not foresee being defeated, but even if the majority held, the situation would be very serious if the constitutional parties split on the war issue. But if it pleased the King, Salandra would "arrange" for a collapse of the Ministry. The King praised Salandra's character, and then interjected a few observations on the "dirty" things he had seen in politics. Zanardelli was a "liar." The King said of Giolitti that he "never lied" but was "reticent." [33]

We now come to the question of the King's personal obligations resulting from the famous telegrams. Salandra made a point of the monarch's intention of sticking to these, as has been seen. But in the diary, the King again insisted he would abdicate, and when Salandra himself pressed home the fact that the King was bound by his commitments, Victor Emmanuel said he didn't care about them, that they were simply political, an affair of the Chancelleries. However, as he could foresee publication of the telegrams, and didn't wish to be considered faithless to his word or an imbecile, he would retire. Salandra tried to discourage him from taking this course. He spoke of Italy's exposed position, open to reprisals from the Entente, perhaps in danger of losing the colonies. The King, the next entry in the diary records, said he would see Giolitti the next day. Salandra was instructed to put off his talks with Giolitti until after the King had seen him, if those talks had been arranged by Bertolini.

After leaving the King, Salandra heard from Bertolini that Giolitti was coming at 4 P.M. on May 10.[34]

It might be remarked here that General Brusati was a prime target of the interventionist press. Salandra alludes to him in the memoirs in a rather scurrilous manner, describing the "unnamed officer of the court" as a frequenter of salons patronized by foreigners. While he admits that the King authorized the General's talk with Bülow, the claim that nothing new was learned from it is wrong.[35] The King's increased anxiety must have been in part caused by the extent of those concessions, even without the final agreement to appoint the commission that would put them into effect. One also has the impression that Salandra's attempt to dissuade the King from abdicating was not without some consideration of his own position. Further, on his telling the King that he could get a majority, that he did not foresee defeat in the Chamber, what are we to think? Salandra was willing either to continue the ambiguous parliamentary game, or else stay in office as a neutralist leader. There is no doubt from this section of the diary, however, that the latter course was possible. Neither the King nor Salandra considered the London Treaty binding on the Italian government understood in its constitutional sense. Victor Emmanuel was in fact in favor of letting the Chamber decide the issue.

Monday, May 10: 11:30–12 A.M.

Salandra went to the King and was told of Giolitti's conversation that morning with the monarch. The veteran politican had advised against war, repeated his dire predictions, and counseled acceptance of the improved Austrian offers. He listed these. They were, according to the diary, essentially those Brusati had spoken of with the addition of a possible immediate cession of the Trentino. Giolitti's source, the King told Salandra, was Chimirri, who got them from Bülow. Salandra was asked not to mention Chimirri to anyone.

On the future of the Ministry, Giolitti stated that Salandra could get a vote of confidence and stay on; four-fifths of the Deputies would agree to this. But he absolutely excluded his own return on the ground that he would be called pro-Austrian. However, he did not insist on Salandra. As an alternative he suggested Tittoni, ambassador to Paris. He seems to have preferred another Salandra ministry, for he told the King that Salandra was very popular and could do what he wanted. Giolitti felt that there was no need for the King to abdicate. We know, therefore, that this significant point was discussed by the King with Giolitti as it had been with Salandra.

Salandra stated, as did the memoirs, that he could stay with clear conscience and calmness by keeping his promises to the Entente. The King then told Salandra that if he decided to abdicate no one could stop him. He was still prepared to go through with it. "I answered," Salandra noted in the diary, "as I should, agreeing with Giolitti." [36] There would be no abdication, then, according to either Giolitti or Salandra.

12–1:00 P.M.

Salandra saw Sonnino and related what the King had said, leaving out the remarks that could be personally offensive to Sonnino. These must have included Bülow's attack on the Foreign Minister, and probably the interesting claim that Sonnino had lied about the denunciation of the Triple Alliance.

The next entries in the diary concern the critical Salandra-Giolitti talks. Before outlining the diary's version of these, it is important to take note of certain facts that appear from the King's exchanges with Giolitti and Salandra. Giolitti had been accused of "supreme cowardice" in recommending a Premier who would support the war policy of the Court.[37] Obviously, that is not at all the case. In the first place, Giolitti suggested alternatives. Tittoni was thought to be inclined to neutrality. Secondly, Giolitti was backing Salandra on the assumption that a four-fifths neutralist majority could be scraped together. Thirdly, the whole pattern of parliamentary action since the declaration of neutrality, plus the fact that the Ministry had not only followed the parecchio theory but had done so with considerable success, led Giolitti to believe that reconstituting the Salandra government was the best solution. He obviously wanted the Government that had squeezed the concessions out of Austria to finish off the diplomacy it had begun. For himself, there is no doubt that the parecchio letter ruled him out as successor. However, the fatal error Giolitti was making was in assuming that Salandra was capable of swallowing his pride for the good of the nation. Had Giolitti known of Salandra's letter to Sonnino of March 16, which revealed a willingness to subvert the proper functioning of the constitution, he would never have placed such trust in the man.

4–5:30 P.M.

Giolitti came to see Salandra. He repeated, in almost the same words he had used with the King and Carcano, his reasons against war. He feared the troops wouldn't hold up under the strain of long trench warfare. According to Salandra, Giolitti admitted "falsifying" dispatches from Libya which showed that the soldiers won only when they outnumbered the enemy ten to one. He repeated his dire predictions of revolution and invasion. Giolitti praised Salandra for getting the latest Austrian concessions. He was very friendly generally. He told Salandra that he had been shown the list signed by Macchio and Bülow by Bertolini. In his diary Salandra jotted down his suspicions. Giolitti wasn't telling the truth, because the list was almost the same one which the King had obtained through Chimirri, known to be a notorious neutralist. When Salandra pointed out the danger of letting the Vatican get mixed up in the affair, Giolitti is described as becoming "confused." This gave Salandra the impression that Giolitti didn't wish to name Chimirri for fear of revealing his own contacts with Bülow, through intermediaries, or directly, and "perhaps also with Erzberger (Vatican)." Giolitti agreed that the concessions should be made to the Government, and said he would let this be known, alluding to — but not naming — Chimirri as the go-between. Then, "anticipating my proposal," Giolitti declared firmly against his own return to power. Salandra records that he felt Giolitti's reasons insincere. He had suggested releasing the Government from its obligation through a vote in the Chamber attesting to its desire for peace with the acceptance of the Austrian concessions. "I did not agree on this point," Salandra writes. "I admit that the Ministry may have erred in obligating itself and that it may even recognize this itself, due to the changed circumstances; but precisely because of that, it must go, the domestic and international situation not permitting a government which would be discredited. Giolitti still insists (it is the thesis most expedient for him) on the necessity that the Ministry stay, also to better cover the king. The question remains undecided."

"On the means of provoking the parliamentary manifestation in favor of peace, subordinated to the improved Austrian proposals," the diary goes on, "various ideas were suggested. We stopped at the one for a motion which would be signed by numerous constitutional Deputies from various sectors (Giolitti excludes himself) and presented in the coming days to the President of the Chamber. But Giolitti wants it to have the sound of confidence in the Ministry, on which I have doubts. We parted with the understanding to continue to think about it and with the mutual promise not to let anything leak out about our talk." Giolitti, on leaving, told Salandra he would be at his disposition, that he was staying in Rome save for trips to nearby Frascati.

What were Salandra's reflections after this meeting? Here the man's character is laid bare, and his personal motivations made clearer. "My impression is that he is sincere and convinced about the catastrophic prediction of the war's effects — but not equally so in his suggestions of parliamentary policy. Naturally he wishes to leave us in the messy situation from which we would come out certainly badly shattered. He is certainly sincere in his refusal for himself: it isn't expedient for him. He would lose popularity which he recognizes I have (and perhaps envies me for it)."[38]

Quite the contrary of the memoirs, this talk ended with an essential agreement on the parliamentary maneuver that would free the Government from its diplomatic obligations. The disagreement involves the procedure to be adopted, and the question of whether Salandra will stay on. Salvatorelli, with scholarly generosity, calls it a "psychological mystery"[39] how, with the diary in his hand, Salandra could have written in 1930 that Giolitti must have been in a singular state of excitement to believe such a maneuver possible. Also, the diary leaves no doubt about the nature of Italy's obligations. The Government is bound, not the state in its constitutional sense. The memoirs state, "Even admitting that the Ministry might have erred thus far,"[40] leaving off the "in obligating itself." Salandra was on the verge of saving his own reputation rather than letting Giolitti avoid his responsibility. That he ascribes Giolitti's unwillingness to take over to the fear of losing popularity, suggesting that Giolitti envies his own, is most revealing. That is a psychological mystery, if Salandra really believed it, because the Chamber and the public were back of the parecchio and Giolitti had made his position widely known. Above all, no one who had seen Giolitti in action for many years could ever have arrived at such a conclusion, unless, of course — and this appears to be probable — he had swallowed whole the legend of the Ministro della malavita and the hallucinations of the interventionist press, particularly those linking Giolitti to foreign agents.

That is where Chimirri comes in. Giolitti did not mention him to Salandra by name for the same reason the King told Salandra not to. His name was left out by request. Giolitti does not name him in his memoirs, but refers only to getting a list of concessions from Bertolini. The reason he named Bertolini to Salandra was that he had asked the man's permission to do so.[41] This led Salandra to assume, with evil consequences, that Giolitti was lying. In fact, Giolitti received two lists, one the morning of May 10, as Erzberger makes clear, and the final offers later from Bertolini. Salandra, in his memoirs, manages to get Chimirri's name into the text in order to keep alive the myth of Giolitti's lack of patriotism,[42] a myth very essential to cover up his own folly. The diary also assumes that Giolitti might have been in touch with the Vatican. Here the old fear of the Blacks comes in. It is all intimately bound up with Article XV of the London Treaty. That clause, from Salandra's own statements, was put through by himself and Sonnino independently of the Cabinet. Sonnino's old fear of the Vatican, dating back to the years before the formation of the Triple Alliance (which he backed partly because of the supposed guarantee of Rome), was at work here. Salandra denies this.[43] But it is an unavoidable conclusion.

It might be added that Salandra must have sweated at the thought that the Entente would publish the Treaty of London in retaliation for Italy's staying neutral. That clause would certainly not help him, particularly since his own election to the Chamber was known to have rested in part on clerical backing. Also, the very damaging blow to his reputation that would have followed public knowledge of Article II, by which Italy was obliged to fight all the enemies of the Entente, is easily imaginable. Giolitti writes, quite correctly, that the talk of war was directed against Austria-Hungary. Salandra himself told Erzberger Italy would never fight against Germany, if we can believe the German Deputy. That, it turned out, was what Salandra foolishly tried to avoid, despite Article II; he declared war only on Austria. The possibility that these facts would come out through neutrality is suggested by a letter Sonnino wrote Salandra on or about May 12 in which he speaks of the possibility that the Entente might try, by some action, to compromise Italy irrevocably, knowing the Chamber was opposed to war.[44]

When Giolitti left Salandra he was confident that the means of arranging the parliamentary expression of neutralist opinion would be soon found. Bound to secrecy by Salandra, he said little or nothing to his good friend Bertolini, save that he was hopeful. The word must have spread among the neutralist Deputies. Labriola, reporting on the political scene in Rome on May 12, noted that the neutralist faction seemed to be losing ground.[45] More likely they were waiting for the word to go to the Chamber to vote for peace and acceptance of the last offers.

Having summarized the talk with Giolitti, we will go back to the diary on the evening of May 10 for the concluding annotations.

5:30–6:30 P.M.

Sonnino felt that the Ministry could give way, but only before a show of no confidence in the Chamber, or at least before a motion backed by a large number of constitutional Deputies. He wanted Giolitti to provoke it. Salandra, at that point, noted that he could not force Giolitti to do this, and that Giolitti wouldn't because it wasn't to his advantage. This talk left Sonnino with the impression that Salandra wanted to quit and that the Austrian offers were acceptable, but by another Ministry. Deception on Salandra's part is apparent, because he led Sonnino into believing that Giolitti was working to escape his own responsibility, when in fact Giolitti would have *preferred* a Salandra ministry. By now, however, Salandra must have come to the point where he was ready to choose between his prestige and peace. He could not have both, because of the folly of the London Treaty.

6:30 P.M.

General Cadorna came to ask "several serious questions," especially about how many troops to send to Libya, where matters had gone from bad to worse. Salandra told him to make no hostile move, even if it were advantageous from a military standpoint, until May 20 and the Chamber's discussions. He stated that the King, Sonnino, and Giolitti agreed on this.[46] There is no proof that it was ever discussed with Giolitti, although he too would have wished to move cautiously.

Tuesday, May 11: 9 A.M.

Salandra went to the King, a meeting not discussed in the memoirs. The King seemed calmer, as if he had found a solution. He asked Salandra to stay on as Premier if the Ministry were reconstituted. Salandra objected that he lost all strength when he didn't feel "in agreement with my conscience." But the King insisted. Salandra suggested Bertolini [!] instead. The King objected on the ground that he didn't trust the man, and Salandra, although he had brought his name up, agreed that Bertolini lacked ability and was associated with Bülow and Austria. Salandra also put forth Carcano as an alternative. The King's response to this is not recorded. But Salandra does include a most significant reference to Sonnino. Victor Emmanuel professed to be worried about the Foreign Minister's "stiffness" (*raideur*). Apparently the King and Sonnino were not on the best of terms. The reason for this, Salandra jotted down, arose from the "necessity which the King has recognized of wresting every possible concession from Austria even if there were not to be war. This can be done only by holding up the Ministry for a few days. I promise the King to go quickly to Sonnino in order to predispose him to act with *souplesse* in the talks which Bülow had requested for this morning."[47]

10 A.M.

At the foreign office. Sonnino has the latest offers, signed by Bülow and Macchio. They are the same as those that were circulating on May 10. Salandra advises Sonnino to rush a copy to the King. It is agreed that Sonnino will press Bülow to be less vague, particularly about Gorizia. Sonnino thinks that a "true and proper parliamentary manifestation can free the King and us, as in the case of a *force majeur*, from the assumed obligations." He would accept a motion from a large number of constitutional Deputies. "Even Sonnino has the impression that the country, placed before the approaching reality of war, will declare itself opposed."

11:30–12 A.M.

Carcano arrives with Ferdinando Martini, Minister for Colonies. Salandra tells them "in part" of his talks with Giolitti. They are very "downcast," Martini even more than Carcano, because of the terrible figure the country is making, especially the ruling classes. But they believe the Government must face the Chamber and not dissemble the gravity of the situation. They almost wept. Salandra showed them the latest offers, a copy of which, he said, had "also" been sent him. It is impossible to tell from the diary whether he made clear that Giolitti was informed first. This entry suggests he was.

12:30 P.M.

Admiral Thaon di Revel wired from Paris. The naval accords, supplementary to the London Treaty, had been signed. There follows a notation, not at all clear, mentioning that Tittoni, the Italian ambassador, felt his instructions were not followed. The naval accords were sent to Sonnino so that he "may take care of this, if possible." The Admiral was very concerned — Salandra notes, "too much so" — by news from an officer who claimed that the French and English fleets, after ten months at sea, would not be of much help to Italy. Salandra considered Thaon di Revel "defeatist and excited. His lack of confidence in the outcome makes a rather sad impression on me." The diary records the criticism that the Admiral should have found out about such matters before.[48]

Tittoni, it may be noted, had insisted from the beginning of the talks with the Entente that Italy enter the war only by agreement with Rumania. With the death of Di San Giuliano the Italo-Rumanian secret agreement of September, 1914, had died. On the naval accord of May 10, 1915, the Admiral had cause for alarm. Articles II and VI provided for a special allied fleet to back up the Italians, and to assure naval primacy in the Adriatic.[49]

May 12.

The Pope, Salandra recorded in his diary, knew of the concessions before the Government did. According to Orlando, the Minister of Justice, it was Baron Monti who furnished them to the Vatican. The Pope is reported as having said, "Insist with Austria and you will have Gorizia and the islands." There then follows the last entry in the diary prior to the final decision to go to war.

"Remember that piece of paper signed Bülow-Macchio, Giolitti told me he had seen it when it was taken to the Vatican.

"Enervation of the country: every day more so. This is the really bad thing." [50]

There the diary stops. The next entry, and last, is for May 20, the day of the Chamber's session, so long delayed. What happened between noon on May 12 and the next few days when the die was cast must be gleaned from other sources. However, there is excellent reason for believing that the published version of the diary is not complete. Salandra's notes for the decisive days did exist, and have been withheld.[51] But it is unmistakably clear from the discussions of May 11 and 12 that the King wished to follow Giolitti's plan, to hold up the Salandra government, if only for a few days, hoping to get the most out of Austria. The most would have been the final offers, guaranteed by Germany, with a promise to set up a commission to put the transfer into effect. Little more, save possibly in the islands, could be had in a few days. Since the London Treaty went into effect on May 26, there was no time to face a political crisis. The Salandra ministry had the best chance of concluding the affair speedily since it had carried out the policy that forced Vienna to give way. Salandra's hasty entry for noon, May 12, is illuminating. The fear of enervation, described as the real evil, is no more than an echo of a constant wail of the war press. And the press was by that time at its wit's end. Even the *Corriere della Sera* showed its frustration, as has been seen. If Albertini's journal was less strident than the blood-bath journalism of Mussolini and Papini, one reason was its respectability — although even that gave way to erotic militarism at times. More important, Salandra had told the *Corriere*'s chief diplomatic analyst, Torre, about the London Treaty, and Italy's obligation to enter the war by the end of May. In this connection, it is interesting that the name of Albertini figures somehow in the missing pages of the diary covering the period after noon on May 12.[52]

Salandra's linking Giolitti to the Vatican is important. While one has the impression he was grasping at any straw that would help justify a decision he wished to make, it is true that the question of the Vatican's position in wartime was given great play in the press. The bogey of an internationalization of the Guarantees was raised, particularly in a work published on the eve of the war. In it the old theme of Bismarck's blackmail returned as well.[53] Diplomatic immunity accorded the Vatican under the terms of the Guarantees was also an issue. As has been shown, not all men lost their heads. Luigi Luzzatti, in the *Corriere*, maintained that the Guarantees should not be touched.[54] But others were less secure. Orlando was one of them. He had stated, as early as 1908, that had he a choice between a settlement granting territory to the Vatican and internationalization, he would have preferred the former. His postwar study of the Roman Question is in effect an attempt to justify the Lateran Pact as a logical continuation of the spirit of the Guarantees. It also defends, but manages to avoid discussing, Article XV of the London Treaty, of which he, Salandra, and Sonnino were the chief authors. Orlando uses the idea of a German threat to exploit the Roman Question to Italy's disadvantage, once the Central Powers won.[55] In the postwar period, as has been noted, a significant body of literature attempted to show that the Triple Alliance was the result of German blackmail. Such studies are polemical in that they all tend to be scholarly defenses of Italy's intervention. Salandra's remark in his memoirs, that the priests had again become political in the changed atmosphere[56] — by which he means the Gentiloni Pact — is of the same order. The necessity of showing Giolitti's handling of the Church-State issue as detrimental to Italian sovereignty is tied to the whole question of war. But no one can seriously say that the independence of the lay state was weakened by his approach, which was essentially one of avoiding unnecessary exasperation of an insoluble problem. Labriola's speech in the Chamber is a rather vivid contemporary proof, coming as it does from a socialist source, of the over-all benefits of Giolitti's policy.

On May 12 Salandra made up his mind. Picking up his memoirs where the diary stops, we read that there was no turning back. The Ministers, summoned the afternoon of May 12, agreed, he asserts. But serious problems were discussed. The Germans had won a victory at Görlice, the Entente's Dardanelles campaign was not going well; the Chamber seemed more opposed to war than ever. Bissolati, an interventionist right-wing Socialist, calculated only about seventy votes for war among the Deputies. It was "an anguishing moment," Salandra writes,

but it had to be resolved. Useless to lose one's way in discussions and consultations. I spent a sleepless night going over in my mind hypotheses and solutions. I reached a conclusion which I did not communicate in advance either to his Majesty or to my colleagues. The next day, Thursday the 13th, at the meeting for the royal signature [of decrees], I called the Council of Ministers for that afternoon. It ended with the unanimous deliberation for resignation. . . . Great efforts were not needed to persuade the colleagues, some of whom were downcast and perplexed. I indicated that I, for my part, in any event, was decided. Sonnino raised some doubts, then agreed, indeed he wrote the note on our decision with his own hand.

The note was given the King, but the news was withheld from the public until midnight on May 13. Salandra says this was because of fear of popular agitation.[57] That is a transparent excuse, because most of the agitators were from the minority war factions, many of them school-age children, and they were growing more frustrated by the hour.

Salandra's motives, as he describes them, were that a decision had to be made; that the Ministry could not turn back from its obligations; that he would never have consented to exist, "small and mean," under Giolitti's protection. It was up to the King to decide. The responsibility, he writes, was thereby placed where it belonged, on Giolitti and his followers. The war press was up in arms, for it failed to see that the resignations were its victory since they destroyed the plan for carrying out the peace program through a parliamentary vote, a plan that the King obviously wanted to follow as late as May 12. Salandra writes that he was attacked by the interventionists. "But they understood. The Honorable Salandra had not surrendered, nor had he given in. He had placed the question frankly before the country and the King, the only legitimate interpreter of the present will and the future interests of the country, even against the majority of Parliament." [58]

The King, whom Salandra knew to be so anxious to relieve himself of the annoyances of politics and of the throne itself, was forced to choose. Giolitti saw him on May 14 and repeated that a man who had opposed war could not take over. He suggested Carcano and Marcora, both of whom were known to be willing, if necessary, to go to war. They were, therefore, in a position to get the increased concessions from Austria. Marcora came to tell Giolitti that he believed in immediate entry into war. Giolitti never saw Carcano. Paolo Boselli, oldest of the Deputies and President of the irredentist Dante Alighieri Society, was suggested by Salandra. He rushed to Rome on May 16 and agreed to do it, but told the King he saw no reason for not keeping Salandra.[59] The King then summoned Salandra, in the early afternoon of May 16, and rejected his resignation. On May 17 Giolitti left Rome for his home at Cavour.

From May 12 to 16, while the King was being forced to decide, the city of Rome became a stage for a rhetorical orgy. On May 12 D'Annunzio arrived in Rome. He had been summoned by an unnamed interventionist in order to counteract the Bülow-Giolitti plot.[60] The poet's arrival was prepared for. He was met by crowds at the station. The *Corriere* spoke of 100,000 from all classes, showing that "Italy exists even outside of the halls of Montecitorio." [61] D'Annunzio brought the Romans the message of Quarto, which is nothing if not a Roman message. . . . Is it possible that we will allow enemies within and without, enemies domestic and intrusive, to impose this sort of death on the nation that yesterday, with a violent shudder of force, raised above its sea the image of its proudest myth, the statue of its true will which is a Roman will, oh citizens? As yesterday Italy's pride was all directed to Rome, so today Italy's anguish is turned to Rome, suffocated these last three days by I know not what stench of treason. No! We are not, we don't want to be a museum, a hotel, a country inn, a horizon painted with Prussian blue for international honeymoons, a charming market place for buying and selling. . . . Let the power and anger of Rome upset at last the benches of barterers and counterfeiters. . . . As it is Roman great things to do and to suffer, so it is Roman to win and live in the eternal life of the Patria. Sweep out, then, sweep out all the filth, push back all the putridness into the sewers.[62]

Following the speech, he threw roses to the crowd from his hotel balcony. Salandra, meanwhile, was passing a sleepless night pondering the "anguishing" decision. The next day, D'Annunzio stepped up the pace.

Companions, it is no more the time to talk but to act, no longer the time for speeches but for actions, for Roman acts. If it is considered a crime to incite to violence, oh citizens, I will boast of this crime, I will take it on myself alone. If instead of warnings I could cast weapons to the resolute, I would not hesitate, nor would I need have pricks of conscience for it. Every excess of force is licit, if it works to prevent the Patria's being lost. You must prevent a handful of ruffians and defrauders from succeeding in dirtying and losing the Patria. The law of Rome absolves every necessary action. Understand me. Treason is now manifest. . . . Treason is done in Rome, in the city of the spirit, in the city of life. In your Rome they are trying to strangle the Patria with a Prussian rope in the hands of that thick-lipped old hangman whose fleeing heels know the path to Berlin. . . . Listen to me. We are about to be sold like an infected flock. Over our human dignity, over the dignity of each one of you, over everyone's forehead, over mine, over yours, over that of your children, over that of those yet to be born, there hangs the threat of a servile brand. Italian will be a name to blush for, to hide, a name to burn the lips. Do you understand? Have you understood? The intriguer from Dronero would do this to us. . . . Swear, let us swear that they will not prevail. . . . Tonight the Roman fate hangs over us, tonight the Roman law hangs over us. We accept the fate, we accept the law. We will make good that fate, we will make good the Roman law.[63]

Such speeches went on until the Salandra ministry had been recalled. On May 14, when the resignations were known, D'Annunzio, speaking at the Costanzi Theatre near Giolitti's home, after reading the censored *Canzoni della gesta d'Oltremare* called on the audience to kill the old intriguer. A crowd later managed to get a fire ladder and was set to reach his window when stopped by the troops.. It has been suggested that a serious move to assassinate Giolitti was under way that evening, and that when Salandra was warned by a police official, he was impressed by the official's remark that if Giolitti died they would say Salandra had killed him. It is possible.[64] But that there were truly revolutionary mobs is quite false. Bertolini tells us he was followed and hooted at, but never really harmed. The descriptions in the interventionist press speak of massive crowds crying "burn the Parliament," and moving on Montecitorio where they did much superficial damage like breaking windows. And yet they never managed to get inside. The door to the Chamber proper was blocked for repairs. The *Idea Nazionale* wrote of the assault as a new Bastille.[65] It was only a mock revolution.

However, close at hand, its size doubtless appeared greater than it was. The King might well have been frightened into believing that the Mussolinian cry of war or revolution had to be taken seriously. We know, for instance, that an interventionist Deputy, Luigi Gasparotto, saw Salandra on May 14, when the King's decision was in the balance. Gasparotto told Salandra the interventionist crowds were threatening revolution, and Salandra "authorized" him to inform the King.[66] There is an interesting confirmation of this in Jacques Bainville's study of the significance for Italy of the war. He writes, after coming to Rome in June, that the Radiant May was above all an appeal to the King to carry out his mission. Bainville, whose book is heavily dosed with Oriani's concepts, saw the war as giving Italy her real synthesis, uniting the monarchical and republican roots of the Risorgimento. He was not the first of his countrymen to insist upon the artificial nature of Italian unity. However, he also saw many signs reading "down with the war" still present on the walls of the city; and he admits that there was no bloodshed, nor was the Parliament sacked. In the end, had the King said "no," Bainville concedes that the mobs would have quieted down.[67]

If this were true, what prevented the master of Parliament from taking over? Since the was was unwanted, Giolitti's failure to stop it casts discredit on the whole regime. Frassati, Giolitti's friend and journalistic voice, wanted him to go back into office as early as August, 1914. In trying to explain why he did not, Frassati offers the opinion that the King was not favorable, and that Giolitti would not have started a crisis unless he could have foreseen the end. Hence he stayed out.[68] We know now, through the Salandra diary, just how ambiguous and deceptive the political situation was. Until the time of the Salandra resignation, which was announced May 14, Giolitti had had confidence in a continuation of his policy, a confidence buttressed by the King's own willingness to go along. If and when the rest of the diary is found, more of the crosscurrents that worked against Giolitti's return may be revealed. When he suggested Marcora and Carcano, however, we must assume that he realized the error of sticking with Salandra. As for his own refusal, it was repeated too often to be considered merely a maneuver. Giolitti was far more straightforward than his critics, and even some admirers, allow. On a fundamental issue such as the war, he would never have equivocated. He was against it. In 1916, Nitti, also a neutralist, made a speech in which he said that Giolitti would also have gone to war. It stung the old Premier, and he wrote a letter that shows how definitely he was committed to the path of peace short of absolute necessity.[69] Knowing the truth about Italy's financial, military, and social assets, he would not have gone in unless toward the end and, as he wrote, in conjunction with a winning team. This was Machiavellian. It was also highly patriotic. The parecchio letter certainly was a factor. Perhaps, however, had he known the terms of the London Treaty, particularly those binding Italy to fight Germany as well and the totally unrealistic territorial gains involved, he might have been disposed to ruin Salandra. Undoubtedly he would not have trusted him as long as he did. As for the theory of his cowardice, his fear of losing popularity, no one who has studied the documents relating to the period in which Giolitti stands out as Italy's great statesman can take it seriously.

And the Chamber of Deputies? They were the last stumbling block in Salandra's path. The radical interventionists gloated at the vote for war, 407 to 74, because it was known that the great majority wanted neutrality. The Deputies' failure, as well as Giolitti's, would be another club in the hands of the Fascists and their cohorts. Under the circumstances, however, faced with the fait accompli and the King's weakness — for that was a decisive factor — how many representative institutions would have cast even seventy-four votes against the war? In ignorance of the terms of the treaty, and uncertain to the end, thanks to the war press, as to the acceptability of the Austrian offers, there was little to be done save to leap into the dark with a last-minute vote against the Ministry. Bertolini wrote in his diary on May 18 that there was no way out, short of a coup d'état; the treaty, he felt, was irrevocable; the King had exercised his prerogatives under the Statuto; all that was left was to defend the nation, and keep his intimate convictions to himself.[70]

It is essential to point out that not supine obedience but a high sense of reasonable patriotism, as expressed by Bertolini, dominated Italy's neutralist politicians. Even the official Socialists, whose votes counted for half of the seventy-four cast against the war, did their duty. Turati went to Salandra and pledged the party's willingness to prepare for a new direction, a new attitude during the war, clearly setting aside any attempt to sabotage the nation's security.[71] The Catholic press had written during the long and tortuous period of neutrality that the faithful would go to war only if forced to, like sheep led to the slaughter. When it came, the Church did nothing to weaken the nation. Cardinal Gasparri released the announcement that the Holy See, out of respect for its neutral position, "has no intention whatsoever of creating embarrassments for the government and places its faith in God, awaiting the suitable systemization of its position not from foreign arms, but from the triumph of those sentiments of justice which it is hoped may be diffused ever more among the Italian people, in keeping with their true interests."[72] Article XV of the London Treaty would not help, when it became known, to further the sane and realistic policy begun with the Guarantees and ended with the Lateran Pact.

That the Deputies, uninformed of the nature of Italy's diplomatic agreements, could be forced to choose between their convictions, which represented the will of the Italian people, and their legitimate fears for their country's security, demonstrates the weakness of parliamentary government in times of international crisis. Government by assembly offers no assurance against the wiles of irresponsible statesmen in foreign policy. In his Turin speech at the time of the Libyan War, Giolitti had insisted that affairs of state and domestic policy were separate entities. In 1915, holding to the same principle, he sought to avoid any impression that he was interfering with the policy decisions of the Salandra government. His *parecchio* letter underlined his belief that men who were not privy to state secrets were not in a position to form clear judgments as to the country's proper conduct of diplomatic negotiations. These should be left to the legally empowered government. But at Turin he had also stressed the Government's duty to await the final judgment of the Chamber. Knowing he could depend on Giolitti's constitutional scruples, Salandra was able to lull him into impotent silence through private talking in the spring of 1915 and then confront the Chamber with the horns of the dilemma.

However, one last prop of the neutralist majority that gave way in 1915 remains to be explained. What of the Cabinet? Were Salandra's colleagues behind his plans to force war on the Parliament and its acknowledged leader, or were they as well presented with a fait accompli after months of anxiety and ignorance? In one important respect, we know from Salan-

dra's own memoirs that the latter was the case. He admits that his decision
to resign was made without consulting the Cabinet. It was useless, he later
wrote, to get lost in discussions and idle consultations. After that sleepless
night of May 12, while D'Annunzio was entertaining Rome, he unex-
pectedly called the ministers together and told them of his determination
to resign.[73] That bold move, which shocked those who wanted war, was
in fact the means by which he unburdened himself of Giolitti's support and
confidence.

Aside from this admission, there is evidence that the Cabinet was not
only ignorant of the true nature of the agreement that had been arrived
at between the King, Giolitti, and the Premier; but that they had no precise
information on the nature of Italy's diplomatic ties with the Entente. This
was made possible by several factors, over and beyond Salandra's willingness to obscure the issues. One was Giolitti's discretion. He never revealed
what went on in his confidential talks with the head of the Government
and the King, not even to his closest friends. He kept his promise of silence,
trusting in Salandra until it was too late. On the course of Italy's talks with
foreign governments, it must be borne in mind that negotiations were
handled in such a way as to prevent any concrete details from leaking out
in Rome. Even in the days of Di San Giuliano's control of the Consulta it
had been decided to carry out negotiations only in foreign capitals. Because of this, the existence of the London Treaty and Italy's drift toward
war were known abroad while Italy was flooded with contrary rumors,
many of them equally plausible. Avarna, the Italian ambassador at Vienna,
saw quite clearly which way things were going, as did his friend Bollati,
stationed at Berlin, long before anyone in Rome not trusted by Salandra
and Sonnino had any accurate information. The London Treaty was an
open secret in Paris within a few days after its signing. The foreign editor
of the *Times* of London, Wickham Steed, knew its essential clauses by
May 1. Distressed by the surrender of Serbian lands to Italy, a violation
of self-determination in his mind, he made sure that the American ambassador Walter Hines Page knew of it. He also informed the Rome correspondent of the *Times*.

But very few Italians knew as much as Steed. Not only did he know
that a document existed; he knew that it was not a treaty but a conditional
pact, or a "convention," as he called it. All depended on Italy's going into
the field by May 26. Lansing has the same description of the agreement in
his papers.[74] The Italian war press, however, insisted that Italy was
already committed to war. Giolitti and the King knew this was not true,

as is evident from Salandra's diary. But they were silent, and had every reason to be since they wished to effect a change in policy without exposing Italy to the danger of diplomatic isolation. What of the Cabinet? According to Baron Macchio, Salandra's colleagues were not being told the true nature of Austria's offers. On May 10 he wired Burian that there was a game afoot to conceal the truth from the Government. Macchio singled out Salandra, Sonnino, and Ferdinando Martini as the partners in this deception. It was because of this that he wanted to have the list of Austrian concessions spread around Rome as quickly as possible. When this accusation appeared in the Austrian *Red Book*, issued after Italy's declaration of war, Salandra denied it in a characteristic fashion, attributing such an absurdity to an Italian source. This statement in the press was calculated to keep the finger of suspicion on Giolitti, by that time in self-imposed retirement at Cavour.[75]

Macchio was in fact partially correct about the Austrian offers and exactly so about the existence of an inner group within the Salandra regime. In January, 1915, the French government sent Charles Benoist to Rome in order to counter the influence of Bülow's missions. Benoist, editor of the *Revue des Deux Mondes*, had been at home in Roman society since the days of Crispi. He soon discovered that there was no way of predicting which way Italy would go in the conflict, and advised Paris to act with discretion, allowing the German and Austrian diplomats to overplay their hand. By the middle of February, however, he had become aware of the existence of a clique within the Cabinet that was decided on war. Martini, if we can trust Benoist's memoirs, told him that Italy would march. The Colonial Minister made clear that war would have to bring Italy gains in Africa, his own primary interest. More important, a certain Signorina Melagari, a lady close to Martini and active in Belgian war relief, told the French journalist that there were only three members of the Cabinet in on the secret of Italy's plans to join the Entente. Martini was one, and the other two were just as firmly decided on war as he. Benoist reflected that this information tallied with what he had been able to find out on his own.

The most significant confirmation of the existence of Salandra's privy council, comprising Martini and Sonnino and himself, came from a talk Benoist had with a noted Italian journalist, Vincenzo Morello. Morello was an imperialist as well as a writer. Under the name of "Rastignac," he specialized in pushing the cause of Italian overseas expansion and poking fun at the mediocrity, political and cultural, of Italian society. Morello told Benoist quite openly that a plot existed within the Government to bring Italy into the war. All was ready, at least as far as the inner three were concerned. Benoist asked whether this had come up for debate within the Cabinet as a whole; and Morello is reported to have said it had not. Nonetheless, war was certain. But he warned Benoist that Italy's hand could not be forced. Precautions were necessary, chiefly that of allowing the war faction within the Cabinet the moment of choice. While there was no formal or official decision, the "principals" were in agreement. Italy, Morello concluded, needed the war not only to expand abroad and be strengthened at home, but to be "purified politically." Looking back on this conversation years later, Benoist asked whether these ideas were not the germ of fascism.[76]

What of the other members of the Government? Salandra had reshuffled his Cabinet in early November following the death of Di San Giuliano. Its composition reflected the obvious truth that Salandra's grasp on the Giolittian majority in the Chamber was slipping. To all outward appearances, the new Cabinet was an attempt to bring in men who, if not part of the ex-Premier's faction, were not hostile to him. Chief among the additions was Paolo Carcano, who became Minister of the Treasury. Carcano, from the Left, was reluctant to join the Government of a noted conservative. Salandra admits that it took the urging of Giuseppe Marcora, President of the Chamber and an old patriot, to induce him to accept the post. Orlando became Minister of Justice. Both had served in Giolitti's past governments, Orlando twice, while Carcano was one of Giolitti's oldest political cronies. Gian Carlo Daneo, a member of the original Government formed in March, 1914, was shifted from Education to Finance. Salandra tells us candidly that he had to be kept on because he was a Piedmontese and not considered one of Giolitti's enemies; in fact Giolitti had suggested him to Salandra when the original Government was constituted. To fill the vacancy at Education, Salandra chose Pasquale Grippo. Grippo was not one of Giolitti's active supporters in the Chamber. On the other hand, he was a close personal friend.[77]

This new group was nothing if not reassuring to the neutralists. Sonnino, for decades a defender of the Triple Alliance and an anti-irredentist, was not likely to depart drastically from Di San Giuliano's cautious policy of military preparations at home and diplomatic soundings abroad. Added to this was the fact that Martini, who stayed on as Colonial Minister, was a concession to the progressives in the Chamber when he took the post in March. Moreover, he had served as Minister of Education in Giolitti's first Cabinet of 1892. He had stood by Giolitti in the months of the Bank Scandals. When the Government fell in 1893, Martini continued to vote against the reactionary domestic policies of Crispi and Pelloux.

The same could not be said for Grippo. In 1899 he had voted, following Sonnino's leadership, for Pelloux's public security laws. On foreign policy, however, there was every reason to believe that he would prove circumspect. A month before taking his portfolio, during a meeting of the Rome section of the Liberal party, Grippo offered a motion expressing continued confidence in the Salandra government with the qualification that Italy never permit any part of the Dalmatian Coast to become Slavic. The fear of Panslavism, which had inhibited much conservative support of irredentism in the nineteenth century, was still alive; and it was obviously an argument against any alliance with Russia. The *Corriere della Sera* jumped on Grippo for his allusions to Dalmatia. Such talk only helped the neutralists.[78]

There is one last figure to consider. This was Vincenzo Riccio, who held the relatively unimportant Ministry of Post and Telegraph. Like Grippo, Riccio was a convinced conservative, having voted for Pelloux in the days when Giolitti and the Socialists were allied against the General. In his memoirs Giolitti refers to Riccio as a sincere spokesman for the principles of the old Destra. Riccio was an admirer of Silvio Spaventa, whose seat in the Chamber he inherited in 1897 and for whose collected speeches he wrote the preface. For his honest convictions, Giolitti respected him. When the original Salandra cabinet was formed, Riccio was a member. Salandra speaks of him as a close collaborator who was influential in getting Sonnino to take over at Foreign Affairs when Di San Giuliano died.[79]

For the historian, Riccio's importance rests on the diary he left, the only account of the Cabinet meetings from the hand of one who was not in the inner group. Unfortunately these papers were edited by a hand that is clearly unsympathetic to Giolitti and to the neutralist positions. There is evidence that the published version was not, as it claimed to be, a faithful account written hastily at the time of the events. There are indications that Riccio retouched his notes in order to make them coincide on certain points with Salandra's postwar claims.[80] What Riccio does tell us, therefore, is all the more illuminating. It is clear that Riccio and his colleagues, with the exception of Martini, were not given an accurate picture of Italy's diplomatic negotiations. At the important meeting of May 7 Sonnino reported on the progress with the Austrian talks, playing down the significance of the concessions thus far made. They were prompted,

Riccio has Sonnino say, by Austria's desire to embarrass Italy, knowing the Treaty of London made them unacceptable. The conditional nature of that pact is not mentioned, nor any of its specific clauses, certainly not the one that would involve Italy in war against Germany. Riccio's diary also makes it apparent that while the King, Giolitti, and Salandra planned to keep the talks with Vienna open in order to avoid war, the Cabinet was told by Sonnino that the aim was only to stall in order to ready Italy's armed forces. On the important meeting of May 12, Salandra, who briefed his colleagues on his talks with Giolitti, allowed them to think that Giolitti knew of a binding, irrevocable treaty with the Entente; that he had agreed that the Austrian offers were not yet official; and that he was interfering with the foreign policy of the constitutional Government while refusing to return to power himself.

Riccio emerges as an innocent tool of Salandra's duplicity. But on other details his notes are even more interesting, for they tell us much of the incredible folly of the inner group's policy while helping to explain how many of the interventionists were themselves deceived. For example, on the invitation to D'Annunzio to address the crowds on May 5, we discover that when the Cabinet was given an advance copy of the Quarto speech it was shocked to find that the aggressive tone threatened to precipitate hostilities. Riccio calls it a trumpet call to war. The King had agreed to attend, although he made it clear that he would not speak to the crowds. Riccio was worried because he knew the Poet would never consent to alterations in his address. Something had to be done. After long deliberations, it was decided to issue the bulletin, which Giolitti carefully read at Cavour, to the effect that affairs of state demanded the royal presence at Rome. Riccio admits this was a gaffe that badly compromised the Government's prestige.

On May 6 Riccio was besieged by prominent Italians, many of them Deputies, who advised accepting the Austrian offers being circulated in the press. Riccio was worried, for he recognized that many of his visitors were loyal patriots. Visits from prominent churchmen are also noted in his diary, and these approaches certainly did not help the cause of neutrality, especially when one considers Riccio's attachment to the ideas of Silvio Spaventa. Nonetheless, Riccio was shaken by the uniformity of views expressed by the neutralists. At this point, there appears in the diary an entry which if not an afterthought of the postwar reflects the ideas Salandra was to put down in his own diary. Riccio speaks of himself as part of a tired generation, the offspring of the men who made Italy. Could he betray that generation to come by allowing a chance to complete Italian unity to slip by?

By May 10, however, things were even worse. Riccio received four interventionist Deputies who came to him in despair. News of the new Austrian concessions and the claim that they were still acceptable placed them in an impossible position. Protesting that they still wanted war, they admitted it was difficult to answer the neutralist press. What they needed was information. Riccio pointed out that he was unable to reveal state secrets, but added knowingly that they need not worry. Decisions had been taken that represented the unanimous opinion of a Cabinet which in turn reflected the political divisions of the Chamber.[81] Since the Government formed in November was split between Salandra conservatives and old allies of Giolitti, the war party was allowed to go on believing that war was unavoidable and had been agreed upon in an entirely constitutional manner, and that Giolitti was plotting treason. All this they were ready to believe without these official hints. But after such interviews, the Radiant Days of May, including attempts on Giolitti's life, become more understandable. One last observation on the Riccio diary. Although it does not exclude the possibility, it nowhere suggests that the Cabinet was given a true picture of Salandra's talks with Giolitti and with the King. The plan to go before the Chamber in order to relieve the Government of its conditional agreements is never mentioned. The distinct impression is left that Salandra and Giolitti were at odds on the solution to the crisis.

One other source for the meetings of the Cabinet remains to be discussed. Martini himself left a diary. From it we see that his job was to act as the roving spokesman for the inner group, contacting journalists, diplomats, and leaders of society. We know from Benoist that he spread the word Italy would fight for France. His diary tells us he tipped off D'Annunzio about the London Pact when he saw him in Rome, although D'Annunzio had already had the word while still in Paris. Martini was especially valuable as the go-between for Salandra with the literary world. By the 1870's he had won a reputation as a rising journalist through his frequent contributions to the popular *Fanfulla della Domenica*, which he later edited. His writings were witty and conversational, with decided traces of serious critical ability. He early recognized Verga's talent, and in his numerous articles sought to bring Italian prose writing down from the artificial clouds where, as he said, it lived off the scraps of literary banquets of long ago. Martini as critic, playwright, and commentator on the foibles of his time stood somewhere in the misty zone between journalism and serious artistic endeavor. He was the ideal man to contact Maeterlinck, Claudel, and other foreign visitors, including Barrère, whom he knew personally. He also served as the scribe of the Cabinet. When Italy finally broke the Triple Alliance, he was given the job, as he put it, of breathing some life into Sonnino's arid prose. And when the announcement that the King would not go to Quarto had to be drafted, Martini again put his facile pen to work. This was necessary, according to Salandra, in order to satisfy the tastes of cultivated Italians.[82]

Martini's talents and position in the world of letters made him a reasonable choice for the post of Minister of Education under Giolitti. Since he was from the Sinistra, his politics also fit in with the attempt of 1892 to reconstitute a cabinet of one party. But Martini had become a convert to Africanism. As Colonial Minister in 1914–15, he was most anxious to see Italy's Libyan and Red Sea possessions enlarged. In the field of foreign affairs, however, his literary skills were insufficient credentials. He was tragically inept. Not only was he far too frank in making his pro-French sympathies known to Barrère; in his talks with Bülow he seems to have gotten the impression, thanks to the German's bitter remarks about maladroit Austrian diplomacy, that a war was possible against the Hapsburg Empire, sparing Italy the expense of facing Germany as well. It may be that the talkative Martini was responsible for putting this idea into Salandra's mind, for that is exactly what the Government tried to do in May. Martini may also have helped encourage Salandra in his delusion that the war would be short. The source of this estimate was another journalist, Ugo Ojetti, whom he met on March 22 shortly after Ojetti's return from Paris. Ojetti reported on statements made to him by French leaders to the effect that the war would be over in two months if Italy entered. These were coupled with assurances that Italy's African boundaries would be rectified.

With his eyes glued on Africa, Martini seems to have known very little about the western front. Even if he could have been so naive as to accept Ojetti's report as anything but well planted French propaganda, he might well have had some qualms about engaging in the war in Europe. On March 8 his diary has a pessimistic entry concerning the Italian infantry. The required two rifles for each man were not on hand. There were not even enough of the preferred 1891 model to supply all the front-line troops, while other available models lacked ammunition.

That he was indeed a member of the inner three is also proved by the diary. It was not until April 21 that Sonnino finally briefed his colleagues on the talks with Vienna. Martini noted that the information they then received he had already obtained. On the D'Annunzio spectacle at Genoa he gives us the very important information that it was planned to offset expected socialist agitation on May Day. When May Day passed without violence, the inner group was obviously encouraged to go ahead, proving again that socialist moderation, like neutralist restraint generally, was serving the cause of the plotters. On the question of whether his colleagues knew about the conditional nature of the London Pact, Martini's account reinforces the Riccio diary. At the May 7 meeting Sonnino permitted the Ministers to believe there was no retreat. From Martini, however, we have the added information that Grippo, as would be expected, argued against war on the ground that the Vatican, the Socialist party, and the great majority of the middle class were opposed.

Following this entry there is Martini's own opinion that Grippo's arguments might have had some force two months before, but that when they were made it was too late. Does this mean that he as well as the rest thought the Pact was unbreakable? It cannot, for he also briefly records the tenor of a private conversation he had with Salandra sometime between the sessions of May 7 and May 9. He told Salandra in this conversation that the Libyan situation was not at all encouraging, but assured the Premier that steps had been taken to cope with it. Salandra then began to complain about France and England. They were evidently trying to pare down their naval and financial obligations under the terms of the London Treaty. Salandra's advice was that since this aid was part of the "convention," Italy should get tough, even threatening to "turn back and if necessary to make war as it pleases us."

It is conceivable that this only meant to make war against Austria in disregard of the clause binding Italy to fight both Central Powers. But it is more likely that Martini understood it as allowing Italy to pull out of the agreement if she chose. But what is certain is that others did not know this was an alternative to war. In particular, the crucial figure of Carcano and his failure to trust Giolitti is clarified. On May 11 Salandra, Martini, and Carcano had a long talk regarding Giolitti's attitude. From the diary it is clear that whatever Martini may have known about Italian commitments, Carcano thought war was inevitable. He was another of Salandra's tools.

Martini was soon to pay the price of his folly. Drawn from the ranks of the literati, he had sought war in utter disregard of Giolitti's warning about the domestic front, Libya, and the probable duration of hostilities. Who was Giolitti, after all, but a narrow-minded politician? When the war press reported that Bülow had gone to Frascati and there held treasonous talks with Giolitti in the latter's library, Martini jotted down his own disbelief. He was sure Giolitti didn't have a library, at Frascati or anywhere else for that matter. When the war was on, the truth of Giolitti's predictions became a nightmare. On May 22 General Tassoni wired from Libya for more troops. Martini had to deny the request; the Minister of War and the Chief of Staff couldn't spare them. A clash between the Africanists and those in charge of the war in Europe soon threatened to wreck the Cabinet. These were the worst days of his life, Martini noted in the diary. He had insomnia. His whole being was shaken by nervous exhaustion. The decision was taken to evacuate the interior of Libya and hold the coast. This, he admitted, meant the loss of the colony. In despair, Martini went to nearby Frascati to rent a room for the August holidays. The diary concludes with the terse understatement, "What terrible days!" [83]

Over Sonnino's role in the inner Cabinet mystery still hangs, generated largely by his own silence. The taciturn Tuscan carried his secrets to the grave. It is clear that he was not wholeheartedly behind the plan to avoid the neutralist majority in the Chamber. He was also opposed to Martini's telling D'Annunzio about the London Pact. Yet he gave way. There is no other conclusion. In the absence of documents that might explain his motives, we can only posit certain probabilities. One was his own career in the Chamber. In the 1890's no one was more responsible for the abortive Pelloux dictatorship than Sonnino. By 1904 he had relented, telling Giolitti that his faith in Parliament was restored. But in 1915 it is impossible to absolve him from grave responsibility in the antiparliamentary events of May.

There was also something about Sonnino's personality that strikes a familiar note. He was the great puritan of the Chamber, the last uncorrupted man. To this reputation he always clung, as if he stood for that superior wisdom that only the cultivated elite possessed. Like other solitary heroes, he liked to stand against the crowd, avoiding the confining ties of political compromise. When war broke, he had been one of the very few Italian statesmen who wanted to fight for Germany and Austria. It was reported that when he heard of Italy's proclamation of neutrality he was furious. He later wrote Bertolini that Italy should have stuck by the Triple Alliance.[84] When the war was over, Bertolini and Count Sforza tried to fathom the case of a man who could shift his position so dramatically. Bertolini explained it by Sonnino's naive pride in going against the country's unanimous opinion when he stood for war in August, 1914, against the King, Giolitti, and the Socialists. For Sforza, who had served his apprenticeship under Visconti Venosta, a man who blended warm sympathies for France with a stern realization of Italy's best interests, Sonnino was obsessed by the pharisaical mania for thanking God that he was not like other men. The sort of official honesty that enabled Cavour to act in ways he would have shunned in private life on principle was something Sonnino held suspect. And Sforza then recalled that before the war, as a young diplomat, he had visited Sonnino's house in the center of ancient Rome. Above his library, of which Sonnino was very proud, was carved the motto, *Quod aliis licet non tibi.*[85] For such a man, who had also lived through the years when the myth of Giolitti's dishonesty was being formed, it was possible to come about-face and join in a plot to drive the nation into war against its will once the Minister of Corruption had spoken the language of Machiavelli, which was also the language of diplomatic sanity.

One last hypothesis remains that may explain Sonnino's otherwise indefensible actions. We know that Victor Emmanuel did not care for his Foreign Minister, and that Salandra was the link between the Crown and the Cabinet. Given Sonnino's ardent defense of the monarchy in the days of Pelloux, it is possible that he, too, was deceived as to the King's attitude. This holds as well for Martini, who, although he had no such monarchical past, does plead the sanctity of the Throne in his memoirs. The King must be protected. That revolution was likely is an idea that has already been discarded. Salandra may have distorted the royal position on the war when confiding his plans to his two intimates, telling them that the King insisted on holding to the Treaty. As for Salandra's own protestations of loyalty to his King, too much is now known of his real designs to view them with anything but contempt. The reluctant monarch of 1900 who had been happy to reign and not to govern, observing at all times his constitutional limitations, was but another of Salandra's unwitting henchmen.

It was the basic unity of the nation, the sober patriotism of the vast majority of neutralists, rather than any mystical fusion through war, upon which Salandra counted. That a man of his character — vain, reckless, politically inept yet cunning — should have been so largely responsible for a catastrophe that virtually wrecked a regime that had survived a half-century of grave problems without abandoning liberty is not the least tragic aspect of the Great War. Italy by 1915 had many outstanding problems to solve; and Giolitti's arguments against war are proof of this. But it was not the gâchis that had been predicted in 1870, nor had it lapsed into despotism. Those who still speak of a "parliamentary dictatorship" might recall that, from the vantage point of another fifty years, one could wish Giolitti had been the cynical politician his enemies made him out to be. The Italian nation was not as strong as any in Europe. That is clear. But Giolitti's dire prophecies fell short of the mark. The Turin riots of 1917 did not become revolution; after Caporetto the line was held at the Piave; Northerners and Southerners, over half a million of them, died for their country in a war that could have been avoided. That the results were not worse is itself testimony to the work of the leading men of the Postrisorgimento.

·12·

CONCLUSION: THE WAR AS A CULTURAL CRISIS

In January, 1915, the faculty of the University of Leiden assembled for a lecture by the newly-appointed professor of European history, Johan Huizinga. In Italy where neutrality had not given way to the fanciful arguments of the interventionists the shock of war to the nation's cultural as well as political life was not yet felt. But in northern Europe the war was six months old and had already left its mark on the historian's consciousness. The subject of Huizinga's lecture was a figure from the past, Charles the Bold, Duke of Burgundy. In effect, however, the Dutch historian was trying to understand why Europe was being destroyed and what part ideas might have played in the catastrophe of his times.

Huizinga wished to illustrate how historical concepts, ideals of life, could influence and sometimes perhaps dominate the evolution of a culture, a state, or even an individual. In reply to the objections of the historical materialists who denied that ideas, mere cultural arabesques, could be active factors in history, Huizinga argued that although these life-ideals did emerge within an existing society they could become active forces in their own right. Not all recollections of the past would acquire value as life-ideals. Which ones did so would be determined, he said, by the direction in which contemporary objectives were sought. Huizinga believed that with the aid of specific cases he could demonstrate how a historical concept could very directly influence a person's or a government's conscious acts. Charles the Bold was a good example because he had an unbridled craving for glory that was stimulated by his vast admiration for ancient heroes.

After having examined traditional life-ideals — the classical belief in a gold age, the ideal of poverty, and the pastoral life in the Middle Ages — Huizinga came down to his own historical era. Here he noted a profound change. The nineteenth century with its great interest in history had banished older life-ideals showing them to have been illusions. Man was taught to look forward for his happiness, not to the past. Yet the need for

371

the ideal remained. Hence there had arisen in Europe a historical concept of a more limited value, the national ideal. Huizinga was disturbed not only by the role his fellow historians had played in the formation of this modern ideal, but also by the fact that it was less an ideal of happiness which could embrace all Europe than one of power and honor which would divide the continent. However just as life-ideals in the past had been conditioned by the historical context in which they emerged, so Huizinga thought he saw a disparity in the influence the national ideal exerted on the actions of European states. The role of the national concept depended on whether nations had already attained their full development or were still struggling toward it. It was the lack of full development that explained the extraordinary place of national ideals in the Balkan states whose irredentism and cult of heroes served as necessary historical stimuli. This also explained why history played such a prominent role in German nationalism, why the English and French, although proud enough of their noble history, invoked it less often.[1]

Huizinga's patriotic feelings certainly entered into his explanation of the origins of the forces that were destroying Europe. Compared to France and England, old and stable powers, Germany emerged from his analysis as a restless, historically minded, and hence aggressive factor in modern European history. One can quarrel with this judgment, pointing out examples of Anglo-French bellicosity and the same use of the past to support imperial claims that Huizinga found so prominent in the new nations. But what is interesting was Huizinga's omission of Italy from the list of states in which narrow ideals of power had become active forces in history. No country was more appropriate to his discussion of the crisis of his times. What better instance of a new nation seeking historical stimuli and finding them in an idealized past which became a guide to present action? Irredentism; the glorification of the Risorgimento, an era not of attainment but of struggle for unity; Crispi and the solitary heroes; Giolitti, trasformismo and the problem of the Postrisorgimento, symbols not of life but of the antilife that supposedly came after 1870 — all these facts of Italian history answered Huizinga's description of a country in which historical concepts should have weighed heavily on political decisions.

If Italy was never mentioned the reason was not Huizinga's ignorance of her history, nor may we seriously suppose that it was an oversight. Given the European situation in January, 1915, it was impossible to illustrate his thesis by citing a nation which refused to allow ideas to become political forces. Peace meant the rejection of the life-ideals used by the interventionists to conceal their love of power. As long as war was avoided, their arguments could not have been said to have become active factors in history, nor could the direction in which Italy sought contemporary objectives have given them the appearance of such. Intervention, on the other hand, was a victory for the uncritical and often absurd claims of the war party, for ideas which might otherwise have become no more than the arabesques of cultural history, curious examples of a desire to escape from the present that time and peace had repudiated.

That this is not merely a hypothesis is amply demonstrated by the political and cultural history of modern Italy. The irrational currents which sought to control Italian domestic and foreign policy were dying down between 1900 and 1911. The Tripoli war revived them. They then reached their maximum intensity in 1914–15. But as the months of neutrality passed interventionist propaganda revealed its impotence by an almost hysterical, even incoherent demand for war under any circumstances. The Government's decision was a godsend to men like Mussolini, Papini, and Corradini whose backgrounds have as much to do with the history of ideas as with the history of politics. Mussolini was on the verge of going back to the socialist camp. War allowed him to escape abject surrender to the party leaders. Italy's armies were not yet in the field when he turned on the Government and on the very war he had helped incite. The June 1 editorial of the *Popolo d'Italia* was completely censored; but the headline remained and told the story. Italy must declare war on Germany as well as on Austria or lose her honor and betray her destiny. Total war was Mussolini's new cry. The spiritual and political vacuum of the Postrisorgimento that war was to have filled was still there to remind those Italians who were sensitive to the message of the past of their nation's fundamental problem. More would be needed to return Italy to her origins. Even war on Germany did not prove enough. Fascism became the answer in the postwar.

This does not mean that in May, 1915, some mystical force controlling Italy's future came into being. What can be said, however, is that the war seemed to justify the historical concepts of the interventionists whereas peace surely was working to discredit them. It makes no difference whether the war party's outlook reflected historical truth. The fact that the Government decided to throw peace away in the face of the facts would become for many Italians proof that the myth of the Postrisorgimento and of Giolitti was correct. In terms of the interrelationship between politics and culture, the war also revealed something else which

was hitherto unsuspected. If intervention was a disaster for Giolitti's policy of avoiding war in Europe while making Parliament the center of
political life at home, it was also a defeat for those intellectuals who
thought and wrote of their country's history in reasonable terms rather
than in the vocabulary of an extravagantly rhetorical idealism. Such men,
by the example of their own lives and through their sober criticism of prevailing thought, acted as Giolitti's partners, however far removed from
his bureaucratic world they seemed to be. By decrying the corruption of
politics and culture that resulted from a facile blending of the two, such
men served not only the cause of the critical spirit but of political sanity.

The confusion between cultural movements and politics had been going
on since 1870 when the concept of the Postrisorgimento first took shape.
The habit of linking ideas to existing political trends had, therefore, an
old and established tradition. This made the task of the serene intellectual
and political guides the more difficult. It was also true that a country with
severe foreign and domestic problems, which lacked an acceptable overseas outlet for frustrated talents, was particularly well adapted to the
genial search for solutions to real problems in the realm of culture. The
reverse was equally true. Political deeds were easily portrayed as being in
harmony with a new awakening of creativity. Even when they insisted
that their writings were strictly limited to the world of ideas, it was
clear that the dissatisfied intellectuals were thinking in political terms. In
their small journals, their newspapers and books, even in the debates in
the Chamber, specific aspects of Italian politics were used to demonstrate
a corresponding decline of culture. A lack of creative spontaneity became
at the same time a sign of political decay. Too often these attitudes enabled imaginative thinkers to avoid the obvious truth that Italy was not
going to have great material power while cultivating a taste for power that
was never to be satisfied by any action that bore the mark of government.

It was this contrast between politics and culture that seems at first
glance to have produced in Italy the same paradox noted for Europe as
a whole. The "deeper understanding" associated with German thought
came to be tied to a growing worship of naked power while failing to
produce a social equilibrium. French and English utilitarianism, in contrast, however starved artistically, were more compatible with democracy.
It was because of this, we are told, that idealism left an ambiguous legacy.[2]

The course of Italian history since 1870 would appear on the surface
to confirm this judgment. When one examines much Italian idealism, however, in particular when one relates it to the political and social context

in which it emerged, it is soon clear that such ideas amounted to little more than materialism, social Darwinism, and aggressive nationalism in disguise. Gentile's and Prezzolini's militant sort of idealism is an example of this masquerade. The use of the vocabulary associated with the deeper currents gave intellectual respectability to brute power.

A distinction must be drawn, therefore, between a productive intellectual perception and the sort of mysticism that resulted from utilizing culture as a veneer for political programs of a most destructive sort. This distinction has been explained in terms of a friendly rivalry between different generations, between the lesser thinkers who came to maturity around 1905 and their elders. It was the younger intellectuals, according to this interpretation, who respected their elders but departed from their ideas. No longer did men of the generation of 1905 limit themselves to questioning the potentialities of reason; they became frank irrationalists or even antirationalists.[3]

The explanation of historical developments by means of a contrast of attitudes between succeeding generations seems appropriate to the Italian case. Papini was born in 1881, Prezzolini in 1882, and Mussolini in 1883, making them ideal types for the generation of 1905. But the contrast was never really a function of chronology. The same tension, as we have seen, can be observed throughout the political and cultural history of united Italy. It can be found in the days of Cavallotti and De Sanctis, Jacini and Turiello just as much as during the early twentieth century. It was a continuing problem and cannot, therefore, be centered in the decade that saw the fight between the positivists and antipositivists however much that debate heightened the tension. Furthermore the historian cannot ignore statistics which show that Colajanni was born in 1847, Ciccotti and D'Annunzio in 1863, Corradini in 1868, and Gentile in 1875, to mention a few interventionists whose war propaganda can fairly be described as frankly irrational.

Attractive as it is, the generation theory must not be made too much of. This is particularly advisable since fascist apologists like Gentile were the first to insist that the nation's youth, as opposed to Italy's elders — that is the generation of Giolitti — burned with a desire to return to an ideal past, and that in the Postrisorgimento those of the older generation who shared this youthful enthusiasm were lonely heroes. To pose a conflict of generations is to accept a portion of fascist historiography. But there is a much more serious issue involved here. Can one speak of a paradox or imply that utilitarian ways of thinking were somehow safer for democracy? To suggest this is to suggest as well that men who were part of the revival of deeper currents were associated despite themselves in the crude corruptions of their own ideas and, consequently, with a tradition that produced a demon in the political world. Is there not hidden in this view of history the makings of a determinism of ideas that is no less questionable than its materialistic twin? And as in the case of the generation theory the historian who would tie political developments to the revival of idealism risks agreement with another canon of fascist historiography. It was the interventionists and later the Fascists who looked upon the war and their political movement as proof that a deeper vision, a life-ideal, had won out despite the moderate counsel of reasonable men.

In order to establish more clearly the interrelationships between culture and politics, it is useful to consider the career of the most important Italian thinker to be associated with the revival of the historical consciousness and the attack of positivism. When one looks at the life and work of Benedetto Croce within the political context of his times, it becomes apparent that we are not dealing with a necessary outgrowth of political irrationalism from a body of literature. Had Croce been unaware that antipositivism was being made to serve illicit ends, had he not seen the trend away from serious speculation and toward decadence and a love of power, a case might be made for the historian's suspicion of idealism. But by 1915 Croce was aware, indeed had been since the turn of the century, not merely of the dangers of antipositivism; he saw that his own work was being exploited by men who, far from respecting him as an elder, were his enemies, even if they posed as disciples. He also saw that a legend was taking shape according to which he was partially responsible for the dangerous course Italian culture and politics seemed to be taking. This legend, which is not yet dead, is the parallel to the political myths concerning Giolitti. Frequently men who believe the untruths concerning the scholar also accept the distortions about the politician. Both have been accused of contributing to Italian totalitarianism. However false this may be, it is quite natural that Croce and Giolitti should be linked, for they pursued similar goals. Where the politician sought to confine Italian expectations within reasonable limits, the philosopher worked to prevent the uncritical spirit from converting ideas into political rhetoric.

The beginning of eventual misconceptions among historians regarding Croce's place in Italian thought and politics dates from the days of the *Leonardo*, Papini's and Prezzolini's journal that appeared in 1903. Papini was twenty-two, Prezzolini a year younger. The two made their distastes for the modern work evident by writing under Renaissance pseudonyms. In its physical appearance the *Leonardo* was also designed to recall the quattrocento. Printed on richly textured rag paper, with hand blocked prints of jousting knights and Pre-Raphaelite drawings by Adolfo de Carolis, D'Annunzio's illustrator, the slim journal of ideas was the antithesis of the industrial age that had witnessed Italy's loss of power. Italy had sunk so low under the leadership of a materialistic ruling class, according to the *Leonardo*, that a mere inventor like Marconi was considered a genius. The journal specialized in this sort of polemic; it was always delighted to shock the bourgeoisie, to attack positivism, and to flaunt all academic conventions. Philosophy, Papini wrote, was no more than a man's way of life. Only ordinary men worried about logic and consistency. The *Leonardo* was extraordinary because it was an intellectual amusement. Its creators were extraordinary because they loved the sport of the mad paradox.[4]

1903 was also the year in which Croce founded his own review, the *Critica*. In it he took stock of the *Leonardo*. He noted the idealistic basis of the Florentine journal and especially its debt to Henri Bergson. Croce was pleased, however, that the Leonardists were more than slavish imitators of the Frenchman's ideas. They did possess originality. The style was lively and the literary criticism of Giuseppe Borgese was especially noteworthy. All in all, Croce found the youthful group a refreshing spectacle and a possible antidote to the extremes of empiricism and pseudoscience. He welcomed the attack on positivism. But Croce also sounded a very distinct warning. He stressed the fact that there was a danger to guard against in this sort of idealism. In the limitations which the young writers of the *Leonardo* imposed on deterministic and materialistic science they had gone too far. In rising above empiricism and naturalism, idealism could not pretend to abolish them, for in so doing idealism would logically abolish itself. Idealism, and those who professed it, Croce wrote, must understand life and not merely try to formulate an existence different from the real one in which men live. Croce also noted a certain romantic exaltation and a love of shocking society of which he could not approve. Such traits had led the Leonardists to pose as men who stood removed from the here-and-now. Their intellectual game and their refusal to grant the validity of logic in its proper sphere, that of the natural sciences, were examples of a denial of reality. Idealism, in short, must recognize that logic becomes false only when it makes claims to universality. Idealists must not, therefore, belittle the value of the natural sciences. As for technology, Marconi's inventions should be praised, not ridiculed. Croce concluded his first assessment of the *Leonardo* on a hopeful note. He looked forward to a more balanced attitude toward idealism and positivism once the Florentine group had matured.[5]

This exchange between Croce and the Florentine iconoclasts was the opening of an intense rivalry that continued throughout the lifetimes of the men involved. At the outset Croce was pleased by the originality he saw in the Leonardists and approved of their defense of idealism. He went so far as to ponder whether the theory of the contingency of language, a decadent aesthetic that Prezzolini had taken up, was not, for all its faults, superior to the rage for positivistic interpretations. But he never approved of decadence nor did he fail to point out the excesses that he found in the writings of the Florentine group. At the same time Croce tried to encourage them to do more serious work. He induced Papini to write a translation of Berkeley for a collection of philosophical classics, hoping that the effort would teach discipline. Papini never forgot the painful lesson. He later referred to Croce as an academic beast of burden.[6]

As for Croce's hopes that experience would tame the Florentine firebrands he was to be badly disappointed. One of the causes of this disappointment is interesting because it illustrates the relationship between ideas and the political context in which they exist. In 1904 the Italian translation of William James' *The Varieties of Religious Experience* appeared. The book sent the *Leonardo* into ecstasies. Prezzolini found James the greatest, most original, living philosopher. His only objection to the American's outlook was what he called a certain psychological ballast that held James back from greater flights.[7] The Italian response to pragmatism would take care of this deficiency, cutting it free from any anchor and sending it out in search of the sources of power. Whatever practical results may be ascribed to pragmatism in the United States, it operated in Italy to encourage the trend toward mysticism already apparent; and, in the political realm, it became one more argument against any sort of contamination by the existing political system.

It was pragmatism's indeterminate richness, as one student has written, that allowed it to develop either into the positivistic instrumentalism of John Dewey or into the mysticism of Bergson or Papini. The Florentine group was well aware of this ambivalent characteristic. They insisted that their adoption of pragmatism implied no taint whatsoever of utilitarianism. The value of the American philosophy, they argued, was precisely in its return to the supernatural values that had been cast off by traditional philosophies. James' work was defended as a doctrine of power and of the irrational nature of human motivation.[8]

But the Leonardists seized on pragmatism for another reason besides its irrational possibilities. Its lack of any formal system permitted them to favor the new concept without giving themselves the appearance of being organized. When the Florentine Pragmatist Club was founded in 1904, it avoided the stigma of belonging to any formal school. After all, if philosophy were only a joke it didn't make sense to take any idea too seriously. It was just that sort of bourgeois love of formalities, typified by party platforms as well as by systems of thought, that had robbed Italian life of its vitality. This hostility to organized, methodical thinking was soon to be transferred, as has been seen, to politics. The word *party* became the incubus of the nationalist movement that had its origins in the Florentine coterie.

The Leonardists now began expounding a frankly irrational theory of power that soon had political undertones. Papini proclaimed grandly that he and his fellow pragmatists sought no less than the quickest and most potent means of ruling the world. The means offered by science were insufficient to man's inherent desire for power. What was needed was a suppression of the intermediaries which stood between the mind and matter. Papini cited James as proof of the use of will to affect the material universe. Man's task, he wrote, was to harness the subconscious in order to conquer the world. Papini also lauded Romanticism as an explosion of the European mind against the classical hegemony over man that had begun with the Greeks. Romanticism had returned man to his natural form. Now man must go beyond into what Papini called the empire of the spirit. The *Leonardo* spoke ominously about great changes that were impending in which man would become godlike, making it quite clear that this spiritual reawakening was directed against the cultural and political nullity of the Postrisorgimento.[9]

Croce's reaction to this phase of the Florentine movement was to sound a stern warning. He found pragmatism alarming for anyone who considered the search for truth sacred. As for Papini's attack on all previous philosophers — his *Twilight of the Philosophers*, a book that James had much admired — it was simply a joke and a stale one at that, having been worn thin in the nineteenth century. For another young Italian pragmatist, Mario Calderoni, who had referred to Kant as a cretin, Croce had nothing but contempt. In regard to the clash between the idealists and the positivists, Croce wrote in 1905 that much as he detested the arrogance of the positivists, their contempt for all other philosophies, he felt that the job of attacking their extreme claims to wisdom had had its effect. There was no need to go on with the campaign now that the battle had been won. In addition Croce reminded his readers that since idealism could never pretend to escape from reality, idealists should recognize that empiricism had a value of its own and so did even positivism. On the subject of Italy's political decline since the end of the Risorgimento which the *Leonardo* harped upon, Croce wrote in defense of the accomplishments made during the period of national unity.[10]

The *Leonardo* toned down its mystical utterances, partially in response to Croce's criticisms but also because progress in the Giolittian era tended to narrow the audience for this sort of escapism. In 1907 the journal went out of existence. The next phase for the Florentine rebels was the *Voce* which came out in 1908. It marked a decided victory for Croce's campaign to prevent a healthy and creative trend from going astray. While the old love of carelessness and journalistic bohemianism was by no means gone the *Voce*'s fight to focus attention on the plight of the Mezzogiorno attested to a new sense of responsibility. Croce wrote that the *Voce* was a sign that the men of the *Leonardo* were coming down to earth. He praised Papini's articles in defense of Italian literature which many Italians ignored for foreign products. He was happy to see that Papini showed no traces of chauvinism but rather a sound appreciation of the worth of Italian artists. Croce was especially pleased by a series of articles devoted to the corrupting influences of journalism on Italian thought. In recognition of this shift away from the dilettantism of the *Leonardo*, Croce himself contributed to the new review.[11]

Croce's influence over the *Voce*'s staff was short lived. In 1911 events on the political front encouraged a new flight from reality. The Tripoli war and the excitement it caused cannot be disassociated from a new outbreak of irrationalism that culminated in Gentile's and Prezzolini's militant idealism. This was little more than the old *Leonardo* fare warmed over and served to a wartime public. But it was decidedly political in tone and therefore marked a setback for Croce's attempt to keep the cultural revival within the bounds of legitimate speculation. As for Papini, he came out with his *Lacerba* in which futurism and vulgar diatribes against Italian society were the outstanding features. Both *Lacerba* and the *Voce*, joined by the recently founded *Idea Nazionale*, attacked government as the source of all contagion. This assault was carried on into the revolutionary period of Italian neutrality. In response, Croce published some uncollected speeches by De Sanctis made when the patriot and scholar was Minister of Education in the heyday of trasformismo. In them De Sanctis rejected the negative view of politics that was fashionable among the artistically sensitive.[12]

Seeing his warnings go unheeded Croce in 1912 wrote a very significant article in which he tried to pin down the cause of the political and cultural distemper of his times. He noted a tendency in recent political movements toward extremism. One faction embraced an absolute moralism; another, the so-called new Machiavellians, called for absolute politicism. According to Croce both were in error. The camp that demanded absolute justice was seraphic, hence too little human. The belief in struggle without justice, however, was actually inhuman. In either camp Croce found the real flaw to be pessimism, a passive pessimism among the moralists and an active pessimism among the advocates of war.[13] This telling criticism obviously reflected Croce's study of contemporary Italian literature, for it was largely from a literary base that many political factions exhibiting just these extremes had arisen. We have seen how the morbid, neurasthenic strain typical of the early works of Corradini and Papini gave way in the period of the *Regno* and the *Leonardo* to a sudden exaltation of life. They called themselves philosopher wolves and professors of energy after a decade of pale lost lilies and suicides. When these literary devices became politically directed, they had the effect of uniting the extremities. Syndicalism, which demanded a purification of the world, and national imperialism which called for war, were the poles between which men like Papini, Mussolini, and Corradini moved. It is very likely that Croce's early judgment of this phenomenon was in his mind at a later time when he wrote about Jacob Burckhardt. Burckhardt's loathing for the modern world had driven him into his Swiss retreat from which he watched the fall of gay and cultured France before the material forces of Prussia. In Burckhardt's attitude Croce also saw a pessimism that gave rise to hedonism and withall to a decided scorn for democracy.[14]

By 1914 Croce's influence over Italian intellectuals was already weakened. How wide the cleavage between his painstaking, disciplined view of the academic life and that of his contemporaries had become was painfully evident in Giovanni Gentile, who had helped Croce found the *Critica*. Like Bergson, Gentile was now lecturing on the philosophical meaning of war.[15] Once more, however, Croce tried to stop this political distortion of ideas. When D'Annunzio came to Quarto to deliver his erotic appeal to Italian youth, the *Critica* carried a note on Carducci in which the late poet's patriotism was compared to D'Annunzio's love of war for its own sake. When the Cathedral of Rheims was shelled by the Germans and Italian interventionists used the act to incite their people to war, Croce joined other academicians in addressing a letter to a German professor then in Italy who had asked that Italians await proof before condemning his country. For this act of academic honesty and courtesy Croce was attacked severely. The *Idea Nazionale* purported to find a philosophical motive — his admiration for German thought — behind the letter. Croce was amazed at this subtle search for intellectual roots of his opinions. He asked again that his critics try to distinguish between philosophy and the practical world of politics.[16]

It is important to see how Croce responded to the war. Not only does his position illustrate the significance of the war as a crisis in the cultural life of Europe; it is also necessary to clarify his stand in order to correct some false notions regarding his activities that still may be found in the works of knowledgeable scholars. There are still those who see him as a portly Brahmin, locked in his Neapolitan library while the world was falling to pieces. Croce's response to the war has been described as not unlike that of the Pope whose bishops blessed the arms of Germans and French alike.[17] This is quite wrong. That Croce could assume such a universalist attitude toward a war in which Italy became involved runs completely counter to the strong sense of patriotism to be found in his writings. He had a very deep concern for the political fortunes of Italy. The misconception that he stood apart in lofty academic seclusion is tied as well to another myth concerning his passive attitude toward fascism. In both cases Croce made his position quite clear.

When the war came to Europe, Croce was distressed by the thought that Italy might become involved unnecessarily. He was equally upset by evidence of a mounting disregard for the spirit of critical inquiry. Like Huizinga he saw that the war had produced a fearful corruption in academic circles. Croce's statements on the war reveal his anxiety for the political and cultural balance of modern Italy. They are to be found chiefly in the neutralist journal, *Italia nostra*, which Croce helped found in December, 1914. He wished to keep his own philosophical and literary review as free from political intrusions as possible.[18] This was to set an example for others whose scholarly writings threatened to degenerate into little more than propaganda.

The advisability of keeping the worlds of thought and political action as separate as possible in order to prevent a mutual corruption was stressed in the first editorial of the *Italia nostra*, an unsigned appeal to its readers which if not actually written by Croce certainly shows the imprint of his ideas. The contributors stated that if as scholars they had become politically involved it was precisely because they saw that the arguments in favor of war constituted an appalling loss of balance among intellectuals. Not only were the demands of those who wanted Italy to fight on the side of the Entente contrary to the manifest will of the majority of Italians, they were contrary to the traditional good sense of the Italian people. The journal also underscored the fact that the political extremes in Italy seemed united by a common purpose, that of domestic revolution. In the war press, moreover, sentimentality had won out over a regard for Italy's real interests. But the *Italia nostra* also emphasized that if war did come, whether for or against the Entente, the decision would rest with the legally constituted government. Above all, what the neutralist scholars wanted was Italy's welfare.[19]

There was no question of sabotaging the war. The *Italia nostra* represented the same sort of responsible patriotic neutralism found in the Chamber of Deputies upon which Salandra knew he could count. As to the claims that war was needed to complete the work of Italian unification, such a concept struck Croce as simply a misuse of history. He very neatly pointed out the absurdity of calling for war on one hand while insisting that the national bonds were weak and that severe domestic problems remained to be solved. Croce's own advice to those who were worried about Italy's strength was that they get to work on whatever job they might have, whether they were government clerks or teachers of history. He observed that the war had a strong appeal to students who preferred to jeer at their professors of German than to study. War and academic sloth, he wrote, were often related. Above all Croce raised his voice in defense of clarity of expression and thought. Against the rhetoricians he called for sanity. He had met these men before, he wrote. He had watched them at work developing new religions, new philosophies, new socialisms, art, and music. Now they had turned their talents to a crusade for war with the resulting danger that whereas all that had been wasted thus far was much ink and paper, in 1915 Italy was at stake.[20] The vicious attacks on Croce's position may easily be found in Papini's *Lacerba* or Mussolini's *Popolo d'Italia*, to mention only two extreme sources.

By April, 1915, Croce feared that the wave of emotionalism would sweep the Italian government into the war despite the country's lack of preparation and will. He was also struck by a sinister attempt to cut the ground from under his reasonable arguments by insinuating that he himself was responsible for the cultural crisis of his times. In order to set the record straight, to leave an accurate account for anyone who might be interested in his ideas, Croce sketched out a history of his intellectual development. He call it a *Contribution to Criticism of Myself*. When he had finished it he put it aside. It was not meant for publication. Not until 1926, by which time he had given copies of it to interested students, did he allow it to be published commercially.

The slim booklet was not intended as an autobiography. Croce disliked that genre and had good reason to, recalling such outpourings as Papini's *Un uomo finito*. He was, therefore, very thrifty in relating details of his life, limiting himself to those incidents which had a bearing to his intellectual development. He neglects to tell us of his birth — which occurred in 1866 — of his marriage in 1914 or of his being named senator in 1910. His boyhood love of books and bookstores; his struggle with his faith and his break with Catholicism; the influence on his literary style of popular literature, especially of the *Fanfulla della domenica* which tried to free Italian literature from classical embellishments — these moments in his life Croce mentions because they were connected to his philosophical development. Of the monstrous tragedy of his childhood, the earthquake of 1883 that killed his mother, father, and only sister, while leaving him badly hurt, very little is said. What was obviously important about it was that Croce entered a period of deep pessimism. He thought of suicide and turned away from all worldly pleasures. It was in these years that he began to bury himself in libraries and there to seek some new meaning to his existence. By 1902, however, he felt that he had triumphed over his weakness. He was able to start afresh, to put his scholarly abilities to some productive use. No wonder Croce developed such a distaste for pessimism and saw so clearly its political possibilities.

It is in regard to his attitude toward politics that the *Contribution* is most significant. Croce makes it clear that he was raised in an apolitical household by parents who were attached to the Church and to the memory of the old Bourbon regime under which Croce's grandfather had served as a judge. The heroes of the Risorgimento were rarely mentioned in his home, and then with sarcasm. By his own admission his was a tardy political development. He attributed this youthful disinterest in politics to his being immersed in literary and scholarly work from a very early age. This, Croce concedes, was a defect of his adolescence. But it did have, as he looked back on it from the year 1915, a decided compensation in that he learned to be suspicious of political myths and also developed an early aversion to political rhetoric, while on the other hand he learned to value useful work no matter from which side of the political fence it came.

In the years 1884–85, when Croce was eighteen, he lived in Rome with his father's cousin, the noted leader of the Destra, Silvio Spaventa. Spaventa's house was next door to the parliament building and was always being visited by politicians and journalists. The Sinistra was in power, trasformismo was firmly installed. Croce recalled his dislike of the constant biased criticism he heard about Depretis during his stay in Rome. These facts are helpful in explaining why Croce's writings showed no trace of the scandals of the Bank of Rome or of the myth of Giolitti's corruption But this does not mean that he intentionally avoided political life. Croce took pains in 1915 to stress the fact that he had never shirked any call for service to the community unless he had found someone who was better equipped than himself. He recognized that his philosophic training and academic scrupulousness did not really fit him for the life of a party leader. But he never scorned those who did choose that career as a productive outlet for their talents.

In looking back over his thirteen years as editor and chief contributor to the *Critica* Croce remarked that the journal represented his very best work precisely because it was a political effort in the broad sense of the word. In it he had done, he wrote, the work of the scholar and of the citizen. Therefore he need not blush, as in his youth, when he found himself in the company of men who were active in society. By this Croce did not mean that the *Critica* indulged in political commentary. It was just that of which he disapproved. What he meant, obviously, was that by fighting for academic discipline and the voice of reason he was serving his country's real interests. By 1915, however, Croce saw that the war mania had become a crisis. It meant the overthrow of reason. At the same time he saw that a legend was growing concerning his own contribution to political and intellectual dilettantism. He was annoyed, he wrote, at being referred to as the guide of young Italian intellectuals, particularly after a decade of attacking their slipshod work. Even if he had been impressed by the talent displayed in some of D'Annunzio's poetry, Croce wanted it to be known that he totally rejected the ethics embodied in the poet's message. Mine, he wrote, was the generation of Carducci, not of D'Annunzio,[21] by which he meant the intellectual generation; for in fact Croce and D'Annunzio were born three years apart.

On May 20, 1915, Croce went to the senate and voted for war. He did this not because he was unconcerned, but because, like the great majority of neutralists, he was trapped by Salandra's machinations. During the war Croce took his own advice. He settled down to hard work. Far from showing a flagging of his creative energies, as has been written, he began to work on his *History of Italian Historiography in the Nineteenth Century*. He continued to steer imaginative young men away from the genial sort of literary dabbling that had already done so much damage and into serious studies. He had failed with Papini who, according to Prezzolini, never was consistent about anything save his dislike of Croce. But others were unquestionably influenced in the direction of serious work by Croce.[22]

After the war Giolitti returned to public life. In 1920 he formed what was to be his last cabinet. His friend Alfredo Frassati, editor of the neutralist *Stampa* of Turin, suggested Croce for the post of Minister of Education. Giolitti was at first dubious. "But he's only a philosopher," he remarked.[23] Croce himself was not at all sure he had the ability to handle the job. He ended by accepting the offer and served until the cabinet fell in 1921. When fascism arose and Giolitti in keeping with his lifelong practice tried to draw the movement into the Chamber and thereby tame it, Croce gave his support to this policy. There were signs that by making Mussolini a legal political leader he could be forced into opposition to his more violent followers. When Mussolini became premier in 1922, the most intransigent Fascists began to turn on him.[24] But by 1925 it was clear that Giolitti's tactics had failed, in part because the Chamber that was to serve as the moderating force and as the center of Italian political life was weakened by a boycott of important antifascist groups. A deeper cause of the failure to contain fascism was the effect on the Chamber's prestige of the antiparliamentary revolution of 1915.

Giolitti was eighty-three in 1925. He spent the last four years of his life holding on to the seat in the Chamber that he had occupied since 1882. From it he continued to defend the Constitution. In the academic world outside Parliament, 1925 witnessed the clash between the fascist and antifascist intellectuals. To the *Manifesto of Fascist Intellectuals* drawn up by Gentile, Croce answered for himself and other prominent scholars and politicians. In his attack on the *Manifesto* Croce repeated many of the same criticisms he had been raising against the dilettantes since 1903.[25]

Soon after Giolitti's death the legend of his contribution to the failure of liberty in Italy became widespread. Among Fascists as well as among antifascists he was regarded as essential to the evolution of tyranny. The

Fascists explained their triumph as the inevitable liquidation of Giolittian corruption. Many antifascists insisted that Giolitti paved the way for totalitarianism by debasing Italian politics. When students of recent Italian history began to restore the historical balance, freeing history from the prejudices and emotions of a troubled era, Croce helped by lending his name to studies in which the myths about Giolitti were rejected. Croce was also responsible for the publication of a perceptive comparison of Salandra's and Giolitti's political practices by a young man who had been an ardent interventionist only to discover that he had been betrayed.[26] Croce's most important contribution to historical objectivity, however, was his *History of Italy from 1871 to 1915* in which he attacked the concept of the Postrisorgimento that had been used by the enemies of freedom.

Despite the historical record, Croce is still being associated in historical literature with the collapse of political liberty in Italy. It has been written quite recently that he was curiously slow to sense the dangers of decadentism; that it was not until 1925 when the alliance between those turbid currents and politics was revealed that he threw down the gauntlet.[27] Croce's attitude toward fascism had been likened to that of the artist who becomes alarmed only when his personal freedom to create is involved. According to this view Croce lacked a primary concern for social justice or even for political freedom. Fascism he saw as a direct menace to true aesthetic expression; hence he did no more than advise Italians to oppose fascism by working for culture.[28]

Such judgments are interesting not merely because they distort Croce's position but because they make him out to be the opposite of what he was. It is clear from what has been said here and from what scholars who are specialists in Croce's thought have written [29] that he recognized the corruption going on in Italian literature and philosophy at a very early date. It is also apparent that his attitude toward society was never that of the aesthete whose overriding concern was for his and his colleagues' freedom regardless of the fate of their countrymen. By defending culture Croce was continuing his long struggle to prevent the world of letters from becoming a grab-bag of political rhetoric or the world of politics from becoming the stage for disgruntled artists. In 1925 as in 1915 he felt he was doing his duty as a scholar and a citizen and doing it in a way for which his training best equipped him.

What is more interesting regarding these confusions about Croce that have maintained a hold over histories of Italy is their ultimate source. When Croce is portrayed as a socially disinterested artist, one is struck by the fact that it was precisely that sort of attitude that he disliked in the escapist, decadent trend he watched emerging in the prewar decade. Apparently some historians have taken up Croce's old attack on the dilettantes and have used it against him. But this phenomenon is by no means a recent development. Croce realized by 1915 that his enemies were trying to involve him in their crimes against the critical spirit. In his autobiographical sketch he tried to defend himself against this strategy. That he did not entirely succeed represents a victory for the irrationalists. These men did not respect Croce. They feared him. The best way to attack the man, since he could not be ignored, was to insist that he himself was responsible for the very decadence he opposed. In 1912, stung by Croce's criticism of his journalistic approach to literature, Borgese sought to involve Croce in the flowering of irrationalism then going on among young writers. Prezzolini and others spoke of themselves as Croce's admirers. The end in mind, however, was to undermine Croce's demand for discipline by showering him with compliments. What Prezzolini didn't like in Croce was his "Olympian air," his "good sense." Croce was simply too bourgeois. The weakness of the *Critica,* Prezzolini wrote, was that it was not sufficiently irrational and passionate. But Prezzolini insisted that the irrational elements were there.[30]

This attempt to draw Croce into the opposing camp has a long history behind it. The pattern continued in the fascist period. Again the intent was to reduce Croce's opposition to impotence being unable to dispense with his presence. When his *History of Italy* appeared in which Croce defended the Postrisorgimento, the fascist historian Gioacchino Volpe called it a polemical work. He accused Croce of turning his back on a movement he had helped create. Had not Croce praised Oriani, the idol of the Fascists? Had he not helped introduce Sorel into Italy? Volpe might also have cited Mussolini's youthful debt to Croce. In 1911 when he was on trial for his attempt to sabotage the Tripoli invasion, Mussolini based part of his defense on the claim that Croce, then a senator, had exalted the moral value of sabotage in his preface to the Italian translation of Sorel's *Réflexions sur la violence.*[31]

Obscuring of Croce's ideas began before the war, was taken up again by the Fascists, and seems ironically to have found a place in the work of intellectual historians who are decidedly antifascist. In each stage of this process of distortion, however, the scholar who links Croce somehow to fascism as a precursor or a passive accomplice must overlook his constant hostility to a specious use of literature, philosophy, and aesthetics as justifications for political programs. He must disregard what Croce wrote about Oriani, that his early work showed signs of a convulsive nature, that only later did he reveal a potential for serious work, and that the weakest part of Oriani's attitude toward history was his attempt to find a plan for Italy's future in the past. As for Croce's appreciation of Sorel, Mussolini was no more precise than was his custom. Croce did not write that sabotage had a moral value. What he saw in Sorel was a return to Vico's concept of history and a dislike of political rhetoricians. Croce made it very clear that his remarks were not in any way concerned with Sorel's political theories.[32]

It is true that Croce later regretted that he had been so generous to Oriani.[33] It is also true that in his *History of Italy* Croce underrated Italian sources of irrationalism and chauvinism, ascribing the nationalists' ideas to French political theory. Despite this defect Croce's general picture of the years 1871–1914 as a period of progress was fundamentally sound. The war, however, brought a decided change in the manner in which Italy sought to achieve progress. It also reinforced waning ideological trends. Because of this it was to have a deep effect on Croce's remaining life and work. By trying to rid his country's past of irrationalism he hoped to free it from the taint of being involved with the cultural crisis of the modern world. He wished as well to reaffirm his own belief in that sense of balance that he considered to be a fundamental characteristic of the Italian people.

Perhaps the greatest crisis for Croce was his fear that he should have done more. It was probably his patriotic sense of responsibility and his social consciousness that led to a noticeable change in his theories of aesthetics and in his later histories. In the postwar Croce moved more and more toward a moralistic view of art. Whereas in his prewar criticism he had held that nothing could be inferred as to the quality of a work of art from its moral content, he began to move toward an aesthetics that excluded immoral works from the category of true art. Literature he had once defended against the moralists, not because he approved of its ethical or unethical content but because he wished to free the artist from narrowness of mind, he now opposed. The point at which this change begins was the war. In his reflections on his life written in 1915 Croce noted in passing that even before his *Aesthetics* was published in 1902 he had recognized that it needed more work.[34] Too many dilettantes had by 1915 claimed it as their own and used it as an excuse for uncontrolled fancies for Croce to allow it to stand.

A similar change has been pointed out in Croce's later historical works.

The love of the concrete in history that he first acquired from his boyhood walks through the streets of Naples gave way to a greater emphasis on ideas. His earlier insistence that the historian avoid the abstractions involved in pure intellectual history, considering instead all forms of human activity as interrelated, was partially forgotten in his later years. This was especially the case with his *History of Europe* in which the nineteenth century was portrayed as under the sway of ideas that seemed to have overwhelmed the world of politics and diplomacy.[35] No doubt the cause of this change in Croce's outlook was the war and later fascism, for they did seem indeed to be triumphs for some disembodied force.

The impact of the war and totalitarianism was to be felt by historians everywhere. Increasingly the tendency would be to review the nineteenth century in a search for the origins of disaster, finding these primarily in the world of ideas. So unlikely was the nature of modern tyranny, so utterly foreign to the prewar scholar's optimistic, rational attitude that the demons must surely reside in ideas themselves.

While this trend has given rise to significant historical works, it has also led to misconceptions, doubts, and paradoxes. Nor can these be avoided by taking the high road of intellectual history, treating only the ideas of significant men and leaving the world of politics below. No matter how much the scholar seeks to keep to that lofty perch, his historical curiosity, his desire to find the cause of events, inclines him to look down at the lower level of history and to suggest the causes of its successes or failures. In drawing his conclusions, hesitant as he may be, the intellectual historian is conceding that for all the pitfalls involved he must examine ideas and politics as constantly interrelated aspects of human activity. That is what we have tried to do in this study of ideas within the context of a national history.

REFERENCE MATTER

NOTES

PREFACE

1 B. Croce, *Storia d'Italia dal 1871 al 1915* (10th ed. Bari, 1953), p. 2.
2 L. Salvatorelli, *Pensiero e azione del Risorgimento* (3rd ed. revised, Turin, 1950), p. 174.
3 *Atti del parlamento italiano. Camera dei deputati. Sessione 1913–15. Discussioni*, VII, 7911–12.
4 *Divina commedia*, Inf., IX, 113, a passage frequently cited by Irredentists.
5 *Atti. Camera. Sessione 1913–15. Discussioni*, VII, 7913–14.
6 For an example, see L. Gasparotto, *Diario di un deputato* (Milan, 1945), pp. 17 ff.
7 F. Chabod, "Croce storico," *Rivista storica italiana*, LXIV, Fasc. 4 (1952), 521, n.1.
8 D. Mack Smith, *Italy. A Modern History* (Ann Arbor, 1959). Although Chabod did not live to discuss this interpretation of the Postrisorgimento, his observations on the debate among scholars over this period and his warning not to view the years 1860–1915 in the shadow of fascism suggest the position he might have taken ("Croce storico," pp. 516–20).
9 G. Ferrero, "La crisi di maggio e la guerra," *La Guerra europea. Studi e discorsi* (Milan, 1915), pp. 222–23.
10 H. Stuart Hughes, *Consciousness and Society. The Reorientation of European Social Thought 1890–1930* (New York, 1958).
11 *Ibid.*, pp. 8–11, 184–85.

CHAPTER ONE

1 A. Dru, ed., *The Letters of Jacob Burckhardt* (London, 1955), pp. 140, 144, 145–46, 205.
2 F. Chabod, *Storia della politica estera italiana dal 1870 al 1896*, Vol. I, *Le premesse* (Bari, 1951), p. 308.
3 V. Gorresio, *Risorgimento scomunicato* (Florence, 1958), pp. 231 ff.
4 Chabod, *Storia della politica estera*, pp. 654 ff.
5 S. W. Halperin, *Italy and the Vatican at War* (Chicago, 1939), pp. 40–46 and n. 79.
6 A. M. Ghisalberti, "Il problema del potere temporale," *Ricerche religiose*, XX (1949), 128–61.
7 L. Salvatorelli, "De la brèche de Porta Pia aux accords du Latran," *L'Esprit international* (July, 1929), 350–51; G. Spadolini, *L'opposizione cattolica da Porta Pia al '98* (Florence, 1954), pp. 617 ff.
8 E. L. Woodward, "The Diplomacy of the Vatican under Popes Pius IX and Leo XIII," *Journal of the British Institute of International Affairs*, III, No. 3 (May, 1924), 135–36.

9 F. Quintavalle, *La conciliazione fra l'Italia ed il Papato nelle lettere di P. Luigi Tosti e del Sen. Gabrio Casati* (Milan, 1907), pp. 313–15, 329–33.

10 Count Charles de Moüy, *Souvenirs et causeries d'un diplomate* (2nd ed. Paris, 1909), pp. 33–34.

11 Ministero degli Affari Esteri, Commissione per la pubblicazione dei documenti diplomatici, *I documenti diplomatici italiani*, 2nd series: 1870–96 (Rome, 1960), I, Nos. 3, 13; Chabod, *Storia della politica estera*, pp. 569–71.

12 Halperin, *Italy and the Vatican at War*, p. 65; Chabod, *Storia della politica estera*, p. 572 and nn. 2, 3.

13 G. Giolitti, *Discorsi extraparlamentari* (Turin, 1952), pp. 259–73.

14 Halperin, *Italy and the Vatican at War*, pp. 104–06; D. Pantaleoni, *L'idea italiana nella soppressione del potere temporale* (Turin, 1884), p. 105.

15 *Documenti diplomatici*, 2nd series, I, Nos. 16, 17, 61, 62, 63, 64, 100, 102, 114.

16 Woodward, "The Diplomacy of the Vatican," p. 127; A. C. Jemolo, *Chiesa e Stato in Italia negli ultimi cento anni* (3rd ed. Turin, 1952), p. 246.

17 *Documenti diplomatici*, 2nd series, I, No. 62.

18 Jemolo, *Chiesa e Stato*, pp. 558–60.

19 Halperin, *Italy and the Vatican at War*, pp. 136 ff.

20 G. M. Trevelyan, *Garibaldi and the Making of Italy* (3rd ed. London, 1911), pp. 3–4.

21 Chabod, *Storia della politica estera*, pp. 315–23.

22 *Ibid.*, p. 307 and n. 1.

23 *Documenti diplomatici*, 2nd series, I, No. 773, and nn. 2, 3.

24 F. Gregorovius, *The Roman Journals of Ferdinand Gregorovius, 1852–1874*, trans. Mrs. Gustavus W. Hamilton (London, 1907), p. 394.

25 Oriani's significance in the history of the Postrisorgimento will be discussed in detail. It is sufficient here to indicate important examples of the Oriani revival. For the fascist adoption of Oriani, see Mussolini's preface to *La rivolta ideale. Opera omnia* (30 vols. Bologna, 1942), XIII, iii–v. For the anti-Giolittian revival, cf. G. A. Borgese, "Il ritorno di Oriani," *Studi di letterature moderne* (Milan, 1915), pp. 63–71, and *La vita e il libro* (3 vols. Bologna, 1923), I, 322–23; M. Missiroli, *L'Italia d'oggi* (3rd ed. Bologna, 1943), p. 24, and *La monarchia socialista. Estrema destra* (Bari, 1914), passim; G. de Frenzi (Luigi Federzoni), *Un eroe. Alfredo Oriani* (Rome, 1910); G. Papini, "Alfredo Oriani," in *Testimonianze* (Milan, 1908), pp. 135–48, and *Ritratti italiani, 1904–31* (Florence, 1932), Vol. XII, pp. 211–37 of *Opere di Giovanni Papini*. Croce's article in *La Critica*, VII (1909), 1–28, should also be mentioned but not as part of the anti-Giolittian campaign, as will be made clear.

26 A. Oriani, *La lotta politica in Italia: origini della lotta attuale (476–1887)* (2nd ed. Milan, 1895), p. 812.

27 "Donato un regno al sopraggiunto re . . . ," from *La notte di Caprera*. For a description of D'Annunzio's reading of his poem in March, 1901, see L. Gasparotto, *Diario di un deputato* (Milan, 1945), pp. 44–47.

28 G. Mazzini, *Scritti scelti* (Verona, 1941), pp. 204 ff., in N. Valeri, *La lotta politica in Italia* (2nd ed. revised, Florence, 1958), pp. 3–6; G. Megaro, *Mussolini dal mito alla realtà* (Milan, 1947), p. 35.

29 G. Carducci, *Edizione nazionale delle opere di Giosuè Carducci* (30 vols. Bologna, 1935–40), II, 377–85. Carducci later called the poem "ugly" though a useful excess at the time ("Levia Gravia," in the preface to *Opere*, XXIV, 142–43). On Carducci's anticlericalism, see L. Russo, "Incontri e scontri del giovane Carducci," *Belfagor* (1949), reprinted in his *Carducci senza retorica* (Bari, 1957), pp. 39–81.

30 B. Croce, *Storia d'Italia dal 1871 al 1915* (10th ed. Bari, 1953), p. 72.

31 D'Annunzio, *L'orazione e la canzone in morte di Giosuè Carducci* (Milan, 1907), p. 48.

32 Carducci, "Canto dell'Italia che va in Campidoglio" (November, 1871); see also I. Bonomi, *La politica italiana da Porta Pia a Vittorio Veneto* (Rome, 1944), p. 7.

33 Carducci, speech at the Brunetti Theater, Bologna (June 4, 1882), *Opere*, VII, 445–57. The Marseilles riots between French and Italian workers took place June 17, 1881. The King's trip to Vienna, opposed by Republicans and Irredentists, took place October 27–31, 1881, and was a prelude to the signing of the Triple Alliance. Carducci refers here to Garibaldi's service with the French army in 1870.

34 Carducci, speech at the Teatro Nuovo, Pisa (May 19, 1886), *Opere*, XXV, 25–38.

35 On Corradini, founder of the Italian Nationalist party, the flattering biography by P. L. Occhini, *Enrico Corradini e la nuova coscienza nazionale* (2nd ed. Florence, 1925) is useful, particularly for its bibliography. The evolution of Nationalist political theory will be examined below. D'Annunzio's famous motto, "Arm the prow and set sail toward the world," from the Prologue of *La Nave* (1908), became a popular literary expression of Italian imperialism.

36 R. Williams, *Culture and Society, 1780–1950* (New York, 1958); G. Orwell, "Rudyard Kipling," in *A Collection of Essays* (New York, 1954), pp. 138–39. On Carlyle, see G. L. Mosse, *The Culture of Western Europe. The Nineteenth and Twentieth Centuries* (Chicago, 1961), p. 29.

37 M. Missiroli, "Le Nationalisme italien," *L'Indépendance*, I (1911), 433.

38 J. W. Meisel, *The Genesis of Georges Sorel* (Ann Arbor, 1951), pp. 216, 221. For early Italian editions of Sorel's works, see *International Review for Social History*, IV (Leiden, 1939), 463–78.

39 A. P. d'Entrèves, *Italy in Europe*, Montague Burton International Relations Lecture, 1952–53 (Nottingham, 1953), p. 13.

40 N. W. Senior, *Journal Kept in France and Italy from 1848 to 1852* (2 vols. London, 1871), I, 316; R. Michels, "Quelques aperçus sur l'histoire de la bourgeoisie italienne au XIXᵉ siècle," *Revue historique*, CLXX (1932), 424–25.

41 B. Croce, "Dai 'Discorsi politici' non mai raccolti, di Francesco de Sanctis," *La Critica*, XI (1913), 395–405; F. S. Nitti, *L'Italia all'alba del secolo XX* (Turin and Rome, 1901), p. 77.

42 L. Salvatorelli, *Nazionalfascismo* (Turin, 1923), pp. 20–23 and passim.

CHAPTER TWO

1 N. W. Senior, *Conversations with Distinguished Persons during the Second Empire* (2 vols. London, 1880), I, 213–16, 256–58; II, 176–79.

2 F. Crispi, *The Memoirs of Francesco Crispi*, trans. Mary Prichard-Agnetti (3 vols. London, 1912), I, 390–91.

3 F. Chabod, *Storia della politica estera italiana dal 1870 al 1896*, Vol. I, *Le premesse* (Bari, 1951), p. 491 and n. 1.

4 G. M. Trevelyan, *Garibaldi and the Making of Italy* (3rd ed. London, 1912), pp. 305–15.

5 Senior, *Conversations*, I, 332–36; E. Artom, "Il Conte di Cavour e la questione napoletana," *Nuova Antologia*, CLXXX, Fasc. 717 (November 1, 1901), 145.

6 B. Croce, *Storia d'Italia dal 1871 al 1915* (10th ed. Bari, 1953), pp. 406–08.

7 A. Plebano, *Storia della finanza italiana nei primi quarant'anni dell'unificazione* (3 vols. 2nd ed. Padua, 1960), I, 63, 68, 102–08, 140–42; A. Fossati, "Problemi economici e finanziari del Risorgimento e dell'unità d'Italia," in E. Rota, *Questioni di storia del Risorgimento e dell'unità d'Italia* (Milan, 1951), pp. 740, 743.

8 E. Sereni, *Il capitalismo nelle campagne* (Turin, 1949), p. 111; R. Hostetter, *The Italian Socialist Movement*, Vol. I, *Origins (1860–1882)* (Princeton, 1958), pp. 128–30, 326–29.

9 Chabod, *Storia della politica estera*, p. 499 and n. 4.

10 G. Giolitti, *Memorie della mia vita* (Milan, 1922), pp. 15–20.

11 M. Ferraris, "Il problema della scuola popolare in Italia," *Nuova Antologia*, CXCV, Fasc. 778 (May 16, 1904), 193–227; Chabod, *Storia della politica estera*, p. 486 and n. 1.

12 A. W. Salomone, *L'età giolittiana* (Turin, 1949), p. 16.

13 Croce, *Storia d'Italia*, pp. 47–63; F. S. Nitti, *L'Italia all'alba del secolo XX* (Turin and Rome, 1901), pp. 34–54; A. Pingaud, *L'Italie depuis 1870* (Paris, 1915), pp. 237–84; Fossati, "Problemi economici," pp. 739–53.

14 Croce, *Storia d'Italia*, pp. 62, 315; Norman Douglas, *In Old Calabria* (New York, The Modern Library, 1928), passim.

15 G. Goyau, *Lendemains d'unité* (Paris, 1900), Preface, "If we were fond of more spectacular titles . . . we would have entitled this collection of articles, 'Why Italian unity is not yet made.'" The French Church historian was editor of the *Revue des deux mondes*.

16 Chabod, *Storia della politica estera*, pp. 501 and n. 2, 504 and n. 3, 507 and n. 1; Plebano, *Storia della finanza italiana*, I, 280–81.

17 Giolitti, *Memorie*, pp. 18–20.

18 *Nuova Antologia*, LXXV, Fasc. 9 (May 1, 1884), 155–62.

19 W. R. Thayer, *The Life and Times of Cavour* (2 vols. Boston and New York, 1911), I, 401, II, 428; G. Dorso, *La rivoluzione meridionale* (2nd ed. Turin, 1955; first published in 1915); C. Scarfoglio, *Il Mezzogiorno e l'unità d'Italia* (Florence, 1953).

20 Senior, *Conversations*, I, 164–66; D. Mack Smith, *Cavour and Garibaldi 1860* (Cambridge, 1954), pp. 68–69.

21 Trevelyan, *Garibaldi and the Making of Italy*, pp. 3, 115, 268.

22 F. Cataluccio, "Linee politiche della vita interna italiana (1861–1922)," in Rota, *Questioni di storia*, pp. 444–46.

23 V. Titone, "Una rivoluzione mancata. Palermo nel 1866," *L'Osservatore*, I, Fasc. 1 (October, 1954), 4; V. Gorresio, *Risorgimento scomunicato* (Florence, 1958), pp. 160, 162; G. Pagano, *Avvenimenti del 1866. Sette giorni d'insurrezione a Palermo* (Palermo, 1867), pp. 64, 68, 70–71; P. Silva, *Il sessantasei* (Milan, 1938), pp. 134–37.

24 F. Quintavalle, *La conciliazione fra l'Italia ed il Papato nelle lettere di P. Luigi Tosti e del Sen. Gabrio Casati* (Milan, 1907), pp. 216–17, 305–06.

25 Titone, "Una rivoluzione mancata," pp. 18–19, 26.

26 Mack Smith, *Cavour and Garibaldi*, pp. 411–32.

27 For Minghetti's plan, see E. Artom, "L'antico disegno delle regioni," *Nuova Antologia*, CCC, Fasc. 1195 (January 1, 1922), 37–49.

28 E. Ragionieri, "Politica e amministrazione nello stato unitario," *Studi storici*, I, No. 3 (April–June, 1960), 472–512. For Cavour's sentiments regarding the South and its inhabitants, see Artom, "Il Conte di Cavour e la questione napoletana."

29 R. Moscati, "Il Mezzogiorno nel Risorgimento italiano," in Rota, *Questioni di storia*, pp. 276–86; Croce, "Dai 'Discorsi politici' non mai raccolti, di Francesco de Sanctis," *La Critica*, XI (1913), 141–60.

30 M. D'Azeglio, *La politica e il diritto cristiano considerati riguardo alla questione italiana* (Florence, 1860), translated from the French edition (Paris, 1859). See also his *Questioni urgenti* (Florence, 1861); and his *L'Italie de 1847 à 1865. Correspondance politique* (Paris, 1867), pp. 259–64, cited in Quintavalle, *La conciliazione*, p. 82 and n. 2. Cavour himself described Naples as "rotten to the core": Mack Smith, *Cavour and Garibaldi*, p. 412.

31 S. Jacini, *La questione di Roma al principio del 1863* (Turin, 1863).

32 Crispi, *Memoirs*, I, 432–34.

33 A. C. Jemolo, *Chiesa e Stato in Italia negli ultimi cento anni* (3rd ed. Turin, 1952), pp. 244–45; Plebano, *Storia della finanza italiana*, I, 103.

34 For a bibliography of some of these works, see Quintavalle, *La conciliazione*, pp. 92–98.

35 S. Jacini, *Due anni di politica interna. Dalla Convenzione del 15 settembre alla liberazione del Veneto* (Milan, 1866); see also his *Sulle condizioni della cosa pubblica in Italia* dopo il 1866 (2nd ed. Florence, 1870), pp. 26–28, 39–42, 47–48, 85–87. For his later arguments on the same question, see "Pensieri sulla politica italiana. Parte prima," *Nuova Antologia*, CV, Fasc. 10 (May 16, 1889), 201–36. On northern resistance to the move southward, see Chabod, *Storia della politica estera*, pp. 181 ff.

36 A. M. Ghisalberti, "Il problema del potere temporale," *Ricerche religiose*, XX (1949), 158.

37 A. De La Gueronnière, *L'Empereur Napoléon III et l'Italie* (Paris, 1859); also the anonymous *Le Pape et le Congrès* (Paris, 1860). See also Jemolo, *Chiesa e Stato*, p. 236.

38 G. Gentile, *Il tramonto della cultura siciliana* (Bologna, 1919), pp. 20 ff., in N. Valeri, *La lotta politica in Italia* (2nd ed. revised, Florence, 1958), pp. 67–72.

39 Titone, "Una rivoluzione mancata," pp. 14–15, 20–26. Sicilian draft evasion was evident from the beginning of the movement for unification. Garibaldi was forced to water down his decrees relating to military service during the early days of his dictatorship in the Island. Crispi, *Memoirs*, I, 225–29.

40 Nitti, *L'Italia all'alba del secolo XX*, pp. 83–101, 107–49. For a later survey of the question, see G. Carano-Donvito, *L'economia meridionale prima e dopo il Risorgimento* (Florence, 1928).

41 Ferraris, "Il problema della scuola," pp. 193–227.

42	L. Franchetti, *Sulle condizioni economiche e amministrative delle provincie napoletane, Abruzzi e Molise, Calabria e Basilicata. Appunti di viaggio* (Florence, 1875), pp. 24 ff.

43	P. Turiello, *Governo e governati in Italia* (2 vols. Bologna, 1882), I, 351–78.

44	Mack Smith, *Cavour and Garibaldi*, pp. 424–25.

45	Moscati, "Il Mezzogiorno nel Risorgimento italiano," pp. 274–76; Nitti, *L'Italia all'alba del secolo XX*, pp. 83–101.

46	L. Franchetti, *La Sicilia nel 1876. Condizioni politiche e amministrative* (Florence, 1877), pp. 58–64, 145, 152–60, 235–41, 241–430; Artom, "Il Conte di Cavour e la questione napoletana," pp. 150–52.

47	*Atti del parlamento italiano. Camera dei deputati. Sessione 1890–92 (1ª della XVII Legislatura). Discussioni*, VI, 7816–20, 8437–45; *Sessione 1892 (1ª della XVIII Legislatura). Discussioni*, I, 129–31; III, 3847–49.

48	*Atti. Camera. Sessione 1892. Discussioni*, I, 132; III, 3849–53; IV, 4347–52, 4282–89.

49	*Atti. Camera. Sessione 1892–94. Discussioni*, V, 6391–92, 6407–08, 6551–59, 6626–41, 6702–05, 6783–90, 6882–89, 6902–07, 7965–66.

50	*Ibid.*, 6559, 6621–27, 6626–41, 6676–90, 6735–50, 6817–22, 6829–33, 7292–95.

51	*Atti. Camera. Sessione 1895–96 (1ª della XIX Legislatura). Discussioni*, III, 3428–30; Bertolini, "Note parlamentari intorno al problema regionale," *Nuova Antologia*, CXLIX, Fasc. 19 (October 1, 1896), in Valeri, *La lotta politica in Italia*, pp. 75–86.

52	*Atti. Camera. Sessione 1898–99 (2ª della XX Legislatura). Discussioni*, IV, 4770–74.

53	*Atti. Camera. Sessione 1892–93. Discussioni*, IV, 5347–57; Giolitti, *Discorsi extraparlamentari* (Turin, 1952), pp. 124–37, 138–59.

54	F. Nitti, *Nord e Sud. Prime linee di una inchiesta sulla ripartizione territoriale delle entrate e delle spese* (Turin, 1900), preface.

55	Moscati, "Il Mezzogiorno nel Risorgimento italiano," pp. 282–84; Plebano, *Storia della finanza italiana*, I, 96–97.

56	For an account of a lingering regionalism that is pro-Bourbon, and almost secessionist, see C. Scarfoglio, *Il Mezzogiorno e l'unità d'Italia*; Jacini, "Pensieri, Parte prima," pp. 218–36; and G. Salvemini, "Risposta ad un'inchiesta," in the *Pensiero contemporaneo* (April 15, 1899), reprinted in *Opere di Gaetano Salvemini*, Vol. I, *Scritti sulla questione meridionale (1896–1955)* (Turin, 1955), pp. 60–63. Salvemini had no use for the regionalism that was represented in the late 19th and early 20th centuries by the elder Scarfoglio, editor of the Neapolitan *Il Mattino*: see Salvemini, "La Questione Meridionale e il federalismo," *Critica sociale* (July 1, August 1 and 16, 1900), reprinted in *Opere*, I, 67–107. The most outspoken attack on parliamentary corruption, and on Giolitti, is still his *Il ministro della malavita* (Florence, 1910). Ghisleri also saw a bond between the failure of local autonomies and political corruption: see *Lo stato italiano e il problema del decentramento* (Rome, 1943) and *Il fallimento del parlamentarismo in Italia* (Rome, 1943).

57	Turiello, *Governo e governati in Italia*; see also his *Politica contemporanea. Saggi* (Naples, 1894). Mosca's debt to Turiello, as well as to other now obscure critics of parliamentarianism, may be seen in his

Teorica dei governi e governo parlamentare (2nd ed. Milan, 1925), pp. 258–59 and n.

58 *Atti. Camera. Sessione 1892–94. Discussioni*, V, 6705–10.
59 Thayer, *Cavour*, II, 459–75; Trevelyan, *Garibaldi and the Making of Italy*, p. 272.
60 Trevelyan, *Garibaldi and the Making of Italy*, Appendix B; R. Michels, "Quelques aperçus sur l'histoire de la bourgeoisie italienne aux XIXe siècle," *Revue historique*, CLXX (1932), 402; Crispi, *Memoirs*, I, 128.
61 Hostetter, *Italian Socialist Movement*, pp. 50–67, 198–99; A. Tasca (A. Rossi), *Nascita e avvento del Fascismo* (Florence, 1950), preface, xli.
62 C. Sforza, *Contemporary Italy*, trans. Drake and Denise De Kay (New York, 1944), pp. 88–89, 149–50, 159.
63 G. Salvemini, "Fu l'Italia prefascista una democrazia? I," *Il Ponte*, VIII (January, 1952), 13, 17; Chabod, "Croce storico," *Rivista storica italiana*, LXIV, No. 4 (1952), 520–21.
64 A. Monti, "Guerra regia e guerra di popolo nel Risorgimento," in Rota, *Questioni di storia*, pp. 183–216; Hostetter, *Italian Socialist Movement*, pp. 23–24 and n. 58; G. Berti, "La dottrina pisacaniana della rivoluzione sociale," *Studi storici*, I, No. 1 (October–December, 1959), 24–61.
65 Berti, "La dottrina pisacaniana," passim; Thayer, *Cavour*, 446–54.
66 [Un amico del D'Azeglio], "I nuovi casi di Romagna. A proposito del pellegrinaggio nazionale," *Nuova Antologia*, LXXIII, Fasc. 3 (February 1, 1884), 514–28; Hostetter, *Italian Socialist Movement*, p. 211 and n. 85.
67 Hostetter, *Italian Socialist Movement*, pp. 4–6.
68 A. Sandonà, *L'irredentismo nelle lotte politiche e nelle contese diplomatiche italo-austriache* (3 vols. Bologna, 1938), III, 151–52.
69 F. Crispi, *Scritti e discorsi di Francesco Crispi (1849–1890)* (Turin, n.d.), pp. 309 ff.; *Memoirs*, I, 441–49; III, 7–10.
70 Chabod, *Storia della politica estera*, pp. 13–15: V. Riccio, *Francesco Crispi* (Turin, 1887), p. 49. D'Annunzio's "La canzone d'oltremare," first of *Merope*, Book IV of the *Laudi* (1911), achieves better effect by having the head of a drowned sailor emerge from the "sacred waters of Lissa," to hurl a challenge through bloodless lips that Italy remember the defeats.
71 L. Russo, *Francesco de Sanctis e la cultura napoletana (1860–1885)* (Venice, 1928), p. 228.
72 S. Jacini, "Pensieri sulla politica italiana. Parte seconda," *Nuova Antologia*, XXI, Fasc. 11 (June 1, 1889), 417–45; *Sulla condizione della cosa pubblica*, pp. 1–15, 37–38, 56–58.
73 G. Gentile, *Origini e dottrina del Fascismo* (Rome, 1929), p. 20.

CHAPTER THREE

1 R. De Mattei, "La critica antiparlamentaristica in Italia dopo l'unificazione," *Educazione Fascista*, VI, No. 4 (April, 1928), 193–210. See also A. W. Salomone, *L'età giolittiana* (Turin, 1949), pp. 24–35, for a brief analysis of some outstanding antiparliamentary works.
2 B. Croce, *Storia d'Italia dal 1871 al 1915* (10th ed. Bari, 1953), pp. 21–22.
3 G. Salvemini, introduction to Salomone, *L'età giolittiana*, pp. xvi–xvii.

4 E. de Laveleye, "Le Régime parlementaire et les partis en Italie," *Revue des deux mondes*, XCIII (1871), 88–92.

5 *Ibid.*, pp. 88–89.

6 G. Salvemini, *Mussolini diplomatico* (Bari, 1952), p. 24. On the noted anti-Fascist historian's change of view, see below, n. 11.

7 S. Jacini, *Sulle condizioni della cosa pubblica in Italia dopo il 1866* (2nd ed. Florence, 1870), pp. 14–15, 22–24, 26–28, 39–41, 50–56, 79–94.

8 S. Jacini, "Pensieri sulla politica italiana. Parta prima," *Nuova Antologia*, CV, Fasc. 10 (May 16, 1889), 201–36.

9 *Ibid.*, pp. 232–33.

10 G. Salvemini's *Il Ministro della malavita* (Florence, 1910) falls in this category, as does E. Ciccotti's *Montecitorio. Noterelle di uno che c'è stato* (Rome, 1908).

11 F. Chabod, *Storia della politica estera italiana dal 1870 al 1896*, Vol. 1, *Le premesse* (Bari, 1951), pp. 509–14; Salvemini, introduction to Salomone, *L'età giolittiana*, pp. xiii, xvii–xxix. Salvemini recognized that wider experience with politics outside Italy had a decided effect on his opinion of the political history of his homeland.

12 Chabod, *Storia della politica estera*, pp. 525–26; H. Stuart Hughes, *Consciousness and Society* (New York, 1958), p. 78; G. Carducci, "Per la poesia e per la libertà," *Giornale per gli interessi del popolo* (November 26, 1876), in *Edizione nazionale delle opere di Giosuè Carducci* (30 vols. Bologna, 1935–40), XXV, 7–17; Carducci, "Rifiuto di candidatura politica," *Don Chisciotte* (January 4, 1883), *Opere*, XXV, 178–79.

13 Speech given at the *Teatro Nuovo*, Pisa (May 19, 1886), *Opere*, XXV, p. 34. He had first used the expression in 1883. By 1886, it was widely repeated.

14 Luigi Russo writes of Italy as being "drunk with positivism and *trasformismo*" and having forgotten the Risorgimento's feeling for life: *Francesco de Sanctis e la cultura napoletana (1860–1885)* (Venice, 1928), p. 198. Villari refers to the era as one of moral depression, of "soulless positivistic materialism" and parliamentarianism: *Italy* (New York, 1929, pp. 88–89). Similar references to parliamentarianism and moral decay can be found in G. Volpe, *L'Italia in cammino* (Milan, 1931), pp. 36–37. Mack Smith considers Depretis' primary intention that of creating a "benevolent parliamentary dictatorship," with the result that in his effort to stifle discord politically he sometimes stifled all idealism: *Italy. A Modern History* (Ann Arbor, 1959), p. 112. Similar judgments may be found in C. J. S. Sprigge, *The Development of Modern Italy* (New Haven, 1944). G. B. McClellan, *Modern Italy. A Short History* (Princeton, 1933) relies very heavily on Villari for his evaluation of Depretis, *trasformismo*, and Giolitti, with similar results.

15 Chabod, *Storia della politica estera*, p. 523, n. 2; Bonomi, *La politica italiana da Porta Pia a Vittorio Veneto* (Rome, 1944), p. 58; F. Crispi, *Politica interna. Diario e documenti*, T. Palamenghi-Crispi, ed. (2nd ed. Milan, 1924), p. 58; G. Giolitti, *Memorie della mia vita* (Milan, 1922), pp. 34–35.

16 Chabod, *Storia della politica estera*, p. 514, n. 3; Hostetter, *The Italian Socialist Movement*, Vol. I, *Origins (1860–1882)* (Princeton, 1958), p. 335.

17 For a handy survey of Italian elections and election laws, see L. Luzzatti, *Elezioni politiche e leggi elettorali in Italia* (Rome, 1958). Jacini, *Sulle condizioni della cosa pubblica,* p. 22.

18 Chabod, *Storia della politica estera,* p. 514, n. 3.

19 Croce, *Storia d'Italia,* pp. 86–87; Bonomi, *La politica italiana,* pp. 66–67; Volpe, *L'Italia in cammino,* p. 37.

20 Croce, "Dai 'Discorsi politici' non mai raccolti, di Francesco de Sanctis," *La Critica,* XI (1913), 323–37.

21 Hughes, *Consciousness and Society,* pp. 62–63.

22 See L. Einaudi, *Lettere politiche di Junius* (Bari, 1917), for examples of this.

23 Giolitti, *Memorie,* p. 35; V. Gorresio, *Risorgimento scomunicato* (Florence, 1958), pp. 52–58, 64, 72, 77. For Mancini's view of Church-State relations, see A. C. Jemolo, *Chiesa e Stato in Italia negli ultimi cento anni* (3rd ed. Turin, 1952), pp. 304–17.

24 Bonomi, *La politica italiana,* pp. 48–49; Jemolo, *Chiesa e Stato,* p. 444; S. W. Halperin, *Italy and the Vatican at War* (Chicago, 1939), pp. 51, 305, 403.

25 S. Spaventa, speech given at Bergamo, September 20, 1886, during celebration of the anniversary of Porta Pia, in *La politica della Destra. Scritti e discorsi raccolti da B. Croce* (Bari, 1910), pp. 181 ff. For the Vatican's attitude toward the Destra, see G. Spadolini, *L'opposizione cattolica da Porta Pia al '98* (Florence, 1954), pp. 124–26.

26 Chabod, *Storia della politica estera,* pp. 159, 308, n. 2, 503–04, 669–70, 674; Bonomi, *La politica italiana,* p. 43; Giolitti, *Memorie,* pp. 37–38

27 Chabod, *Storia della politica estera,* pp. 682–88; Bonomi, *La politica italiana,* pp. 71–72; A. Sandonà, *L'irredentismo nelle lotte politiche e nelle contese diplomatiche italo-austriache* (3 vols. Bologna, 1938), I, 174, 177. It is true that the King was miffed by Vienna's refusal to accept his personal guarantee that Italian irredentist movements would not be encouraged. That he would have carried out the menacing statements Crispi attributed to him is most unlikely. For the Crispi version, see *The Memoirs of Francesco Crispi,* trans. Mary Prichard-Agnetti (3 vols. London, 1912), II, 1–11.

28 Sandonà, *L'irredentismo,* I, 130–34.

29 A. Fossati, "Problemi economici e finanziari del Risorgimento e dell'unità d'Italia," and F. Cataluccio, "Linee politiche della vita interna italiana (1861–1922)," in E. Rota, *Questioni di storia del Risorgimento e dell'unità d'Italia* (Milan, 1951), pp. 450, 744; A. Plebano, *Storia della finanza italiana nei primi quarant'anni dell'unificazione* (3 vols. 2nd ed. Padua, 1960), II, 421.

30 Chabod, *Storia della politica estera,* p. 358; Bonomi, *La politica italiana,* pp. 51–53.

31 Cataluccio, "Linee politiche," p. 454; G. Dorso, *La rivoluzione meridionale* (2nd ed. Turin, 1955), pp. 7–10, 82–83.

32 A. Labriola, *Storia di dieci anni (1899–1909)* (Milan, 1910), Chap. IV; Bonomi, *La politica italiana,* pp. 35, 60–61.

33 A. Tasca (A. Rossi) sees *trasformismo* as part and parcel of an attempt to restrain democracy, and lumps it together with Pelloux's reactionary government, Giolitti's later "collaborationism," and the conservative dictatorship of the war years: *Nascita e avvento del Fascismo* (Florence,

1950), pp. 6–7. The theme of fascism as a continuation of *trasformismo* is quite common: Dorso, *La rivoluzione meridionale*; G. Spadolini, *Ritratto dell'italia moderna* (Florence, 1948); G. Colamarino, *Il fantasma liberale* (Milan, 1945); F. Cusin, *Antistoria d'Italia* (Turin, 1948). While admitting that economic advances were made under the "oligarchic" governments of parliamentary Italy, Salvemini condemned, even in post-Fascist writings, the electoral manipulations he associated with Giolittism in particular and Italian politics in general. "The difference between Mussolini and Giolitti was one of quantity and not of quality. Giolitti was for Mussolini what John the Baptist was for Christ: he prepared the way for him. Gobetti rightly said that Mussolini did no more than extend Giolitti's 'henchmen' to all Italy." "Fu l'Italia prefascista una democrazia? III," *Il Ponte*, VIII, No. 3 (March, 1952), 285.

34 De Mattei, "La critica antiparlamentaristica," p. 196.

35 G. Giolitti, *Discorsi parlamentari* (4 vols. Rome, 1953–56), II, 544; G. Natale, "Scandali e corruzione parlamentare," *Il Ponte*, III (1948), 223–27; Villari, *Italy*, pp. 85–89, 109.

36 A. Oriani, *La rivolta ideale* (2nd ed. Naples, 1908), pp. 70–84.

37 *Ibid.*, pp. 52–84.

38 Villari, *Italy*, pp. 88–89; Mario Missiroli, *L'Italia d'oggi* (3rd ed. Bologna, 1943), pp. 24, 32–33, and passim. See also his *La monarchia socialista. Estrema destra* (Bari, 1914).

39 Oriani, *La rivolta ideale*, pp. 10, 22, 105–13, 251–52, 385–88.

40 *Atti del parlamento italiano. Camera dei deputati, Sessione 1890–91–92 (1ª della XVII Legislatura). Discussioni*, VI, 7866–69, 7869–73; *Sessione 1892–93 (1ª della XVIII Legislatura). Discussioni*, II, 1686.

41 *Atti. Camera. Sessione 1898–99 (2ª della XX Legislatura). Discussioni*, IV, 1979–80.

42 *Atti. Camera. Sessione 1890–91–92. Discussioni*, VI, 7863–65, 7899–7902, 7921–24.

43 *Ibid.*, 7816–20, 7926.

44 Nello Quilici, *Banca Romana. Note e appunti* (Verona, 1935), p. 36, n. 1.

45 *Atti. Camera. Sessione 1890–91–92. Discussioni*, VI, 8386–88, 8526; *Sessione 1892. Discussioni*, I, 93–95, 545–57, 556–70.

46 *Atti. Camera. Sessione 1892. Discussioni*, I, 646–47, 708–15, 717–19.

47 *Ibid.*, 716–17, 720–21, 721–23.

48 *Atti. Camera. Sessione 1892. Discussioni*, I, 721–23; II, 872–78, 920–28, 953–65, 1620–21.

49 *Atti del parlamento italiano. Camera dei senatori. Discussioni. Legislatura XVIIª. Sessione 1890–91*, 1290–97. Colajanni, *Banche e Parlamento* (Milan, 1893), pp. 4–10.

50 V. Pareto, *Lettere a Maffeo Pantaleoni, 1890–1923* (3 vols. Rome, 1960), I, 144–45, 178, 185, 208–09, 232–36, 240, 243–45, 262, 310–11, 327–28, 336–37, 383–84.

51 *Atti. Camera. Sessione 1892–93. Discussioni*, II, 872–77.

52 *Ibid.*, 877–79, 886–87, 889–91, 911–18, 920–33, 973–74.

53 *Ibid.*, 1023–25, 1616–17, 1620–22.

54 *Ibid.*, 2506–07, 2509–12, 2561–62, 2574, 2582–86; IV, 4766–68.

55 *Atti. Camera. Sessione 1892–93. Discussioni*, IV, 5354–75, 5386–87.

56 *Ibid.*, 5429–53, 5514–29, 5583–87, 5725–44, 5807–16, 5919–23, 5945, 6086–87.

57 *Ibid.*, 5420–29, 5587–98, 5757–59, 5792–96, 5862–66, 5871–72, 5892–93. See also M. Ferraris, "La nuova Banca d'Italia," *Nuova Antologia*, CXXIX, Fasc. 9 (May 1, 1893), 41–79.

58 *Atti. Camera. Sessione 1892–93. Discussioni*, IV, 6269–70, 6278–82, 6285–87.

59 *Nuova Antologia*, CXXXI, Fasc. 19 (October 1, 1893), 533.

60 *Atti. Camera. Sessione 1892–94. Discussioni*, V, 6349–83, 6387–88.

61 *Ibid.*, 6391–92, 6626–41, 6676–90, 6702–10, 6882–89; VI, 7965–66. T. Palamenghi-Crispi, ed., *Carteggi inediti di Francesco Crispi (1860–1900)* (Rome, 1912), pp. 484–86.

62 *Atti. Camera. Sessione 1892–94. Discussioni*, V, 6500–05 6551–59, 6559–80; VI, 8471–96.

63 *Atti. Camera. Sessione 1892–94. Discussioni*, VIII–IX, 10239–40, 11530, 11542; *Sessione 1895–96 (1ᵃ della XIX Legislatura). Discussioni*, III, 2597–2602.

64 *Atti. Camera. Sessione 1892–94. Discussioni*, V, 6408–22.

65 *Camera dei deputati. Legislatura XVIII. Sessione 1892–94. Raccolta degli Atti Stampati per ordine della camera*, V: No. 169 (*Allegato* B), 7–13, 25–35, 100–101, 115–17, 141–46, 157–58, 341–42; VI; (*Allegato* I and I *bis*), 230–31, 85–133.

66 *Atti. Camera. Sessione 1894–95 (2ᵃ della XVIII Legislatura). Discussioni, Volume unico*, 21–25, 37–39, 104–22.

67 *Ibid.*, 160–64, 192, 204–07, 219–25 and Appendix, p. 5.

68 *Camera dei deputati. Legislatura XVIII. Seconda sessione 1894–95. Raccolta degli Atti Stampati*, II: No. 76–A, 1–30. For a recent example that the myth still lives, see Margot Hentze, *Pre-Fascist Italy. The Rise and Fall of the Parliamentary Regime* (London, 1939), p. 240.

69 F. Cavallotti, *La questione morale su Francesco Crispi nel 1894–1895, esaminata da Felice Cavallotti* (4th ed. Milan, 1895), pp. 117–210 and passim.

70 *Atti. Camera. Sessione 1895. Discussioni*, I, 205–07, 241–47, 451–52; II, 1619–23, 1670–71, 2374–75.

71 *Atti. Camera. Sessione 1895–96. Discussioni*, III, 2508–20, 2696–2704, 2763–67.

72 *Ibid.*, 2934–36, 3031–34, 3073–74. *Camera. Unica Sessione 1895–97. Raccolta degli Atti Stampati*, III, No. 120.

73 *Atti. Camera. Sessione 1895–96. Discussioni*, III, 3075–78, 3082–95, 3095–97, 3099–3109, 3124–25; Giolitti, *Memorie*, pp. 46–47.

74 Quilici, *Banca Romana*, pp. 28–29, 74–75, and passim.

75 *Atti. Camera. Sessione 1895–96. Discussioni*, III, 3385–89, 3392–3421.

76 Sonnino, "L'Africa italiana. Appunti di viaggio," *Nuova Antologia*, CIX, Fasc. 3 (February 1, 1890), 425–65.

77 *Atti. Camera. Sessione 1895–96. Discussioni*, III, 3428–39.

78 *Atti. Camera. Sessione 1890–92. Discussioni*, VI, 8386–88; *Sessione 1892*, I, 93–97.

79 *Atti. Camera. Sessione 1892–93. Discussioni*, II, 966–68; III, 2596–2612. For other reports of the Committee, see III, 2887–92, 3996–4009; IV, 4771–81.

80 *Atti. Camera. Sessione 1892–93. Discussioni*, IV, 4334–42, 4388–4400, 4471–72.

81 *Atti. Camera. Sessione 1892–93. Discussioni*, III, 2850–52, 3996–4009, 4036; IV, 4384–86, 4622–26.
82 *Atti. Camera. Sessione 1890–92. Discussioni*, VI, 7875–77, 7902–05, 7912–19, 7925–26, 8391–99, 8448–54; *Sessione 1892–93*, III, 3838–49; IV, 5367, 5796–5803.
83 *Atti. Camera. Sessione 1892–94. Discussioni*, V, 6399–6401, 6402–03.
84 C. Sforza, *Contemporary Italy*, trans. Drake and Denise De Kay (New York, 1944), pp. 110–11; Croce, *Storia d'Italia*, pp. 177, 337. See also A. C. Jemolo, *Crispi* (Florence, 1922), pp. 40–41.
85 *Atti. Camera. Sessione 1892–95. Discussioni*, II, 1620–21; III, 3838–47; IV, 4347–57, 4388–4400, 4478; VIII–IX, 11513–14. See also Crispi, *Politica interna. Diario e documenti*, pp. 30, 155–56, 197–98, 201–02.
86 *Atti. Camera. Sessione 1892–93. Discussioni*, II, 889–91, 2513–15. Chabod, *Storia della politica estera*, pp. 538–62.

CHAPTER FOUR

1 The law of 1860 gave the vote to adult males of 25 or older (this was reduced to 21 by the reform of 1882) on the payment of a 40-lire census or the possession of certain marked intellectual or professional capacities. In 1861, 418,696 eligible voters were listed; this was 1.92 per cent of the population. By 1879, there were 621,896 voters, or 2.15 per cent of the population. The figure reached 2,144,195, or 7.41 per cent, with the reforms of 1882, and by 1892 it stood at 2,934,442, or 9.67 per cent. Eliminating women and minors, about 40 per cent of the total possible electorate could vote. Statistics on the regional distribution of eligible voters show a spread from 14.6 per cent (Piedmont) to 7.65 per cent (Sicily) and 6.82 per cent (Sardinia): L. Palma, "Una pagina di statistica elettorale italiana," *Nuova Antologia*, XLIII (1893), 113–22. For the view that brigandage was a political movement, see C. Scarfoglio, *Il Mezzogiorno e l'unità d'Italia* (Florence, 1953), pp. 440–41. See also E. J. Hobsbawn, *Social Bandits and Primitive Rebels* (Glencoe, Ill., 1959), pp. 5, 10, for an objective appraisal.
2 B. Croce, *Storia d'Italia dal 1871 al 1915* (10th ed. Bari, 1953), pp. 40–41.
3 R. Hostetter, *The Italian Socialist Movement*, Vol. I, *Origins (1860–1882)* (Princeton, 1958), pp. 85–91, 96–98. Cattaneo's thought has had a lasting influence on Italian federalism. His ideas had special importance for regional and political dissatisfaction with the Postrisorgimento. His *Notizie naturali e civili della Lombardia* (1844) was a refutation of unitarian downgrading of the communal structure of the Middle Ages. Municipal clashes were seen as a source of progress and prosperity. This concept, which can be related to Burckhardt's dislike of centrality, plus Cattaneo's republican beliefs, served as a point of departure for many critics of the Piedmontese settlement. Colajanni, Imbriani, and others were fond of citing him as a precursor. Salvemini, too, was indebted to him. His linguistic studies also worked to further regionalism. While Cattaneo was not an advocate of dialectal literature for its own sake, his theory that modern European languages evolved from individual roots that were tending toward unity (as opposed to the theory that ascribed them to a degeneration from an original common tongue) certainly fits in with regionalist ideas. He disdained attempts to create a universal

language artificially, and also attacked the practice of rooting out acceptable localisms from literature, as in Manzoni (*Sul principio istorico delle lingue europee*, 1842). On Manzoni, see his "Dell'uso di nuovi toscanesimi," *Alcuni scritti* (n.p., 1846), in *Scritti critici*, Mario Fubini, ed. (Florence, 1955), pp. 95–105.

Cattaneo was not politically active prior to 1848. He was opposed to cultural chauvinism, as manifested by Gioberti and Schlegel: "Il 'Don Carlo' di Schiller e il 'Filippo' di Alfieri," *Il Politecnico*, V (1842), reprinted in *Scritti critici*, pp. 13–60. Cattaneo hoped to see a federated Austrian Empire, permitting maximum local freedom. He preferred economic ties with Central Europe to those with Piedmont, whose religious policies offended him. When the 1848 revolution broke out, however, he was inspired by the spontaneous demonstration of local vitality. He even shared, momentarily, enthusiasm for the idea of Pius IX as the leader of a federated Italy, despite his previous criticism of Neo-Guelphism, which he found anachronistic: *Stati uniti d'Italia*, N. Bobbio, ed. (Turin, 1945), pp. 129–36. On Balbo and the Neo-Guelphists, see his "Vita di Dante di Cesare Balbo," *Il Politecnico*, I (1839), reprinted in *Scritti critici*, pp. 61–77.

Cattaneo took a very active part in the Milan insurrection of 1848. The outcome of the revolt confirmed the federalist convictions already present in his earlier works. Following the failure of 1848, he condemned the House of Savoy and the municipal provisional government of Milan for having played into Charles Albert's hands. The revolution, a popular uprising, was defeated not by Radetzky but by Turin. In later years, he praised Garibaldi, whose volunteers seemed to express his own faith in the power of the people and in the idea of a militia as opposed to organized professional armies. The rise of Cavour to power met with an expected negative response on his part. In 1860 he hoped to see Sicily and Naples tied to northern Italy by a federal arrangement allowing local administrative and legislative freedoms. The victory of the unitarian settlement thwarted this plan. Cattaneo's writings, therefore, were a stimulation for those who belittled Piedmontese leadership and centralization after 1860. While he was not an anarchist, his faith in popular insurrection, his insistence that liberty and a centralized administration were incompatible, and his tendency to exalt the power of the human will over purely material forces, all helped the cause of the populist critics of the Postrisorgimento. On 1848, see his *L'insurrection de Milan e le Considerazioni sul 1848*, edited and with an introduction by Cesare Spellanzon (Milan, 1926). For his historiography, see B. Croce, *Storia della storiografia italiana nel secolo decimonono* (3rd ed. revised. 2 vols. Bari, 1947), II, 212–21.

4 Hostetter, *Italian Socialist Movement*, pp. 99–103.

5 *Ibid.*, pp. 94, 176, 194–96, 204–05, 211, 287–88; Hobsbawn, *Social Bandits and Primitive Rebels*, pp. 27–28.

6 On Costa's break with the anarchists, see Hostetter, *Italian Socialist Movement*, pp. 418–25, 429.

7 *Nuova Antologia*, CXXXI, Fasc. 18 (September 15, 1893), 340–42.

8 On Turati in particular, see L. Degli Occhi's discerning portrait in his *Storia politica italiana* (Milan, 1946), pp. 114–34.

9 Tasca (A. Rossi), *Nascita e avvento del Fascismo* (Florence, 1950), p.

lviii; R. Michels, "Quelques aperçus sur l'histoire de la bourgeoisie italienne aux XIXe siècle," *Revue historique*, CLXX (1932), 398–425; Marcello Soleri, *Memorie* (Turin, 1949), pp. 18–19; H. Stuart Hughes, *Consciousness and Society* (New York, 1958), p. 42.

10 P. Togliatti, *Discorso su Giolitti* (Rome, 1950), p. 93.

11 C. Sforza, *Contemporary Italy*, trans. Drake and Denise De Kay (New York, 1944), p. 153; F. Turati, *Attraverso le lettere di corrispondenti (1880–1925)* (Bari, 1947), pp. 13–23, 124–42; G. Volpe, *Italia moderna* (2 vols. Florence, 1949), II, 54–55.

12 G. Giolitti, *Discorsi extraparlamentari* (Turin, 1952), pp. 122–23, 174–205; *Atti del parlamento italiano. Camera dei deputati. Sessione 1890–92. Discussioni*, VI, 8086; *Sessione 1892. Discussioni*, I, 121–25.

13 *Atti. Camera. Sessione 1892–93. Discussioni*, II, 970; III, 3849–53; IV, 5177–81.

14 *Atti. Camera. Sessione 1892–95. Discussioni*, VIII–IX, 11414–18, 11520–21.

15 Raffaele Colapietra, *Il '98* (Milan, 1959), pp. 7–31, 60, 196–200.

16 Giolitti, *Discorsi extraparlamentari*, pp. 174–205.

17 Colapietra, *Il '98*, pp. 55–62, 207–11.

18 *Ibid.*, pp. 63–91.

19 *Critica Sociale* (1899), p. 146; Colapietra, *Il'98*, p. 39.

20 *Atti. Camera. Sessione 1898–99 (2^a della XX Legislatura). Discussioni*, IV, 4770–74, 4786–88; *Sessione 1899–1900 (3^a della XX Legislatura). Discussioni*, III, 2054–64.

21 Colapietra, *Il '98*, pp. 96, 99–100.

22 *Atti. Camera. Sessione 1898–99. Discussioni*, IV, 3855–69, 3977–92, 4029–69, 4072–74, 4263–65.

23 *Ibid.*, 4329–33, 4334–43.

24 *Ibid.*, 4559–68, 4591–93, 4645–52, 4688–93, 4697–99, 4704–15.

25 *Ibid.*, 4753–54, 4763–65, 4770–74, 4781–87.

26 *Ibid.*, 4797–99, 4820–22, 4875–81.

27 *Atti. Camera. Sessione 1899–1900. Discussioni*, III, 2041–46, 2054–64.

28 *Ibid.*, 1979–80, 2144–53, 2953–60, 3000.

29 *Ibid.*, 3121–23, 3127, 3130–32, 3143–51, 3154–56.

30 *Atti. Camera. Sessione 1900 (1^a della XXI Legislatura). Discussioni*, I, 341–42, 350–51.

31 L. Albertini, *Venti anni di vita politica* (5 vols. Bologna, 1951), Vol. I, Pt. 1, 37; F. Turati, *Da Pelloux a Mussolini*, A. Schiavi, ed. (Florence, 1953), pp. 9–10; Volpe, *Italia moderna*, II, 14–33.

32 Hobsbawn, *Social Bandits and Primitive Rebels*, pp. 4, 10, 16–17, 23, 30–56.

33 P. Turiello, *Politica contemporanea. Saggi* (Naples, 1894), pp. 47–48, 81.

34 R. Michels, *Storia critica del movimento socialista italiano* (Florence, 1926), pp. 240–44, 247; C. Morandi, *I partiti politici nella storia d'Italia* (2nd ed. Florence, 1958), p. 43; G. Natale, *Giolitti e gli italiani* (Cernusco sul Naviglio, 1949), p. 535.

35 S. Jacini, *Sulle condizioni della cosa pubblica in Italia dopo il 1866* (2nd ed. Florence, 1870), pp. 42–44, 50–52, 64–71, 74–77.

36 A. C. Jemolo, *Chiesa e Stato in Italia negli ultimi cento anni* (3rd ed. Turin, 1952), pp. 262–64; G. Spadolini, *L'opposizione cattolica da Porta Pia al '98* (Florence, 1954), pp. 22–39, 77, 199; V. Gorresio,

Risorgimento scomunicato (Florence, 1958), pp. 276–86. On the history of the non expedit see the article of "Eufrasio" in the *Nuova Antologia* (1904), reprinted in N. Valeri, *La lotta politica in Italia* (2nd ed. revised, Florence, 1958), pp. 111–16.

37 Spadolini, *L'opposizione cattolica*, pp. 43–50, 64–85.

38 Gorresio, *Risorgimento scomunicato*, pp. 150–57. For the circular, see *Petizione di NOVEMILA SACERDOTI ITALIANI a S. S. Pio IX ed ai Vescovi cattolici con esso uniti* (Turin, 1862). Its sponsor was Father Passaglia, with whom Cavour had dealt for an accord with the Vatican.

39 Leo XIII, *The Church Speaks to the Modern World. The Social Teachings of Leo XIII*, edited and with an introduction by Étienne Gilson (4th ed. New York, 1957), pp. 189–98; D. Pantaleoni, *L'idea italiana nella soppressione del potere temporale* (Turin, 1884), pp. 129, 140–41.

40 Leo XIII, *Social Teachings*, introduction, p. 2.

41 *Ibid.*, pp. 189, 192–96.

42 *Ibid.*, pp. 32–33, 46–47.

43 *Ibid.*, pp. 150–53.

44 *Ibid.*, pp. 143, 146–47; Spadolini, *L'opposizione cattolica*, p. 192.

45 Leo XIII, *Social Teachings*, introduction, pp. 14–15; 148–49, 153–54.

46 Jemolo, *Chiesa e Stato*, pp. 402–03.

47 Spadolini, *L'opposizione cattolica*, pp. 174–77.

48 Morandi, *I partiti politici*, p. 20.

49 Spadolini, *L'opposizione cattolica*, pp. 196–97; L. Salvatorelli, *La Triplice Alleanza (1877–1912)* (Milan and Varese, 1939), p. 63.

50 Leo XIII, *Social Teachings*, pp. 163–64, 166–67, 174, 181.

51 *Ibid.*, pp. 168, 178.

52 V. Procacci, *La questione romana. Le vicende del tentativo di conciliazione del 1887 (con documenti inediti)* (Florence, 1929), pp. 7–11, 27–28.

53 *The Memoirs of Francesco Crispi*, trans. Mary Prichard-Agnetti (3 vols. London, 1912), II, 168–70; *Politica estera. Memorie e documenti raccolti e ordinati da T. Palamenghi-Crispi* (Milan, 1912), pp. 136–38; Procacci, *La questione romana*, pp. 20, 30, 35–39, 45–48.

54 Crispi, *Memoirs*, II, 220; Procacci, *La questione romana*, pp. 40–42. On Leo's German diplomacy in general, see F. Salata, *Per la storia diplomatica della questione romana* (Milan, 1929), pp. 83 ff.

55 *Per i caduti di Dogali* (Cremona, 1887); Procacci, *La questione romana*, p. 31; Jemolo, *Chiesa e Stato*, p. 411.

56 Charles de Moüy, *Souvenirs et causeries d'un diplomate* (2nd ed. Paris, 1909), pp. 239–41; Crispi, *Memoirs*, II, 168; Procacci, *La questione romana*, pp. 55–61, 64. For Crispi's overture to the French, see the *Rappel* for February 5, 1887.

57 L. Tosti, *Scritti vari* (2 vols. Rome, 1890), II, 343–63.

58 F. Quintavalle, *La conciliazione fra l'Italia ed il Papato nelle lettere di P. Luigi Tosti e del Sen. Gabrio Casati* (Milan, 1907), pp. 175–344.

59 F. Crispi, *Politica interna. Diario e documenti*, T. Palamenghi-Crispi, ed. (2nd ed. Milan, 1924), pp. 97 ff. Crispi told the Senate in 1889 that Tosti "gave him to believe" that the work had papal approval: Jemolo, *Chiesa e Stato*, p. 412. See also Crispi, "Italy, France and the Papacy," *The Contemporary Review*, LX, No. 308 (August, 1891), 167–69. Croce recalled a discussion of the celebrated pamphlet at his uncle's home.

Silvio Spaventa was well acquainted with the monks of Monte Cassino. It was generally felt that Leo had betrayed Tosti: E. Carloy, "Il tentativo del Tosti nella sua vera luce," *Le Opere e i Giorni*, I, No. 12 (December 1, 1923), 68. See also H. Wickham Steed, *Through Thirty Years, 1892–1922. A Personal Narrative* (2 vols. New York, 1925), I, 172; G. Manfroni in his *Sulla soglia del Vaticano* (2 vols. Bologna, 1920), II, 157 also feels the Pope read it. For the Catholic view, see the *Catholic Encyclopedia* (New York, 1913), XIV, 788; Cardinal Capecelatro, *Problemi moderni* (Rome, 1904), pp. 303 ff. For those who deny any prearranged agreement with the Papacy see V. Fedele, "Leone XIII e l'Abate Tosti (da documenti inediti)," *Nuova Antologia*, LXIX, Fasc. 1490 (April 16, 1934), 562–78; R. de Cesare, "Il padre Tosti nella politica," *Nuova Antologia*, XXXIII, Fasc. 635 (June 1, 1898), 443–62, and his "Il padre D. Luigi Tosti," *La Vita Italiana*, III (1897), 64.

60 Procacci, *La questione romana*, pp. 68–69, 119–21; Crispi, *Politica interna*, pp. 97–116; E. L. Woodward, "The Diplomacy of the Vatican under Popes Pius IX and Leo XIII," *Journal of the British Institute of International Affairs*, III, No. 3 (May, 1924), p. 133.

61 M. Claar, "Kardinal Rampolla als Staatssekretär und Papstweber, 1887–1903," *Europäische Gespräche*, VII (1929), 465–82; Procacci (*La questione romana*, pp. 134–37) agrees. See Jemolo, *Chiesa e Stato*, pp. 419–20, for the article in the *Riforma*.

62 G. Quadrotta, *Il papa, l'Italia e la guerra* (Milan, 1915), pp. 34–36; C. Benoist, *Souvenirs* (3 vols. Paris, 1932–34), I, 155–61.

63 *Osservatore Romano* (July 28, 1887). Tosti was sure he had been betrayed by the Pope: see De Cesare, "Il padre Tosti nella politica," and Crispi, *Politica interna*, p. 117.

64 Jacini, *La questione del papato e l'Italia* (Milan, 1888), passim; *Il principio della neutralizzazione internazionale applicato alla Santa Sede* (Milan, 1888); and "Pensieri sulla politica italiana. Parte seconda," *Nuova Antologia*, XXI, Fasc. 11 (June 1, 1889), 437–44.

65 Benoist, *Souvenirs*, I, 100–111. Benoist, noted theorist of the corporate state idea, editor of *Le Temps* and political editor of the *Revue des deux mondes*, was an ardent Catholic intransigent with excellent sources at the Vatican.

66 Spadolini, *L'opposizione cattolica*, pp. 112–27, 406–08, 463–70.

67 Leo XIII, *Social Teachings*, p. 177.

68 Procacci, *La questione romana*, pp. 23–24, 54, 58, 62, 104–05, 115–16.

69 *Achille Fazzari nelle sue lettere e nei suoi atti* (Rome, 1893), p. 23.

70 Bonghi's article of 1882 appeared in the *Perseveranza*, February 17, reprinted in Valeri, *La lotta politica*, pp. 157–59. On his other statements, see Procacci, *La questione romana*, pp. 5–6, 98–99.

71 Salvatorelli, *La Triplice Alleanza*, p. 133 and n. 3; Procacci, *La questione romana*, p. 123.

72 For another overture by an ex-Garibaldian, General Türr, see *La Réconciliation avec le Pape* (Paris, 1887).

73 Spadolini, *L'opposizione cattolica*, pp. 225–26, 237. According to Claar ("Kardinal Rampolla," p. 470), intransigents at the Vatican wanted the Bruno statue removed as part of the Lateran Pact.

74 Spadolini, *L'opposizione cattolica*, p. 355 and n. 7; F. Chabod, *Storia*

della politica estera italiana dal 1870 al 1896, Vol. I, *Le premesse* (Bari, 1951), pp. 249, 384 and n. 5, 411; W. Steed, *Through Thirty Years*, I, 135–36.

75 "Un Deputato" [S. Sonnino], "Torniamo allo Statuto," *Nuova Antologia* (January 1, 1897), reprinted in Valeri, *La lotta politica*, pp. 251–69.

76 Natale, *Giolitti e gli italiani*, pp. 386–87.

77 A. Labriola, *Storia di dieci anni (1899–1909)* (Milan, 1910), p. 29. The conservative principle of the Alliance was limited to the generic formula in Article I, according to which the three rulers were "animated by the desire . . . to fortify the monarchical principle and thereby to insure the unimpaired maintenance of the social and political order in Their respective states." Bismarck would have been more emphatic, but the Sinistra's Foreign Minister, Mancini, would not accept any conditions impinging on Italy's "internal freedoms" (Salvatorelli, *La Triplice Alleanza*, pp. 62–71).

78 Chabod, *Storia della politica estera*, pp. 360, 384, 524; S. Sonnino, *Il suffragio universale. Discorso pronunziato alla Camera dei deputati nella tornata del 30 marzo 1881* (Rome, 1881).

79 L. Salvatorelli, "Giolitti," *Rivista storica italiana*, LXII, Fasc. 4 (1950), 517–19.

80 G. Giolitti, *Memorie della mia vita* (Milan, 1922), pp. 149–50.

81 Jacini, *Sulle condizioni della cosa pubblica*, pp. 19, 26–28, 66; Bonghi, *L'ufficio del Principe in uno stato libero* (2nd ed. Naples, 1922), pp. 5–13, 15–17, 21–29, 31. First published in the *Nuova Antologia* (January 15, 1893).

82 G. Mosca, *Sulla teoria dei governi e sul governo parlamentare* (Palermo, 1884); Bonghi, "Una questione grossa. La decadenza del regime parlamentare," *Nuova Antologia*, XLV (1884), 482–97.

83 Leo XIII, *Social Teachings*, p. 172.

84 G. Arcoleo, *Il gabinetto nei governi parlamentari* (Naples, 1881), pp. 1–13, 15–16, 21–35, 57–59.

85 *Ibid.*, pp. 57–60, 201–04. Arcoleo continued to write against excessive Crown power under the German constitution: "Il potere imperiale in Germania," extract from Vol. XXXIX of the *Atti della R. Accad. di Scienze Morali e Politiche della Società Reale di Napoli* (Naples, 1909).

86 S. Spaventa, *La politica della Destra. Scritti e discorsi raccolti da B. Croce* (Bari, 1910), pp. 28, 42, 57, 181–90, 199, 274, 474–75. For an analysis of Spaventa's theory of the State, see L. Russo, *Francesco de Sanctis e la cultura napoletana (1860–1885)* (Venice, 1928), pp. 172–95.

87 Croce, *Storia d'Italia*, p. 12; S. Spaventa, *Lettere politiche* (Bari, 1926), pp. 43–44, 117, in Russo, *Francesco de Sanctis*, pp. 267–69.

88 Spaventa, *La politica della Destra*, pp. 125–26.

89 G. Mosca, *Teorica dei governi e governo parlamentare* (2nd ed. Milan, 1925), pp. 39, 27–71, 251–54, 258–59, 267, 300–301.

90 R. De Mattei, "La critica antiparlamentaristica in Italia dopo l'unificazione," *Educazione Fascista*, VI, No. 4 (April, 1928), 197–98; see the interview with Mosca that appeared in *Il Regno* (January 27, 1904). In a note to the second edition of his work, Mosca mentioned the change of mind that had taken place since he wrote the book at the age of twenty-five (*Teorica dei governi*, p. 259 and n.).

91 Giolitti, *Memorie,* pp. 317–18.
92 M. Ball, "The Leadership Principle in National Socialism," *Journal of the History of Ideas,* III, No. 1 (January–October, 1942), 74–93.
93 Russo, *Francesco de Sanctis,* p. 274.
94 Croce, "Come nacque e come morì il marxismo in Italia," in Antonio Labriola, *La concezione materialistica della storia* (Bari, 1953).
95 For a general tendency in Europe, see G. Mosse, *The Culture of Western Europe* (Chicago, 1961), pp. 141–52.
96 M. Grilli, "The Nationality of Philosophy and Bertrando Spaventa," *Journal of the History of Ideas,* II, No. 3 (June, 1941), 339–71.
97 A. O. Lovejoy, "The Practical Tendencies of Bergsonism," *International Journal of Ethics,* XXIII (1912–13), 253–75, 419–43. For works illustrating the revival of Oriani, see above, Chap. I, n. 25.
98 Mussolini was fond of the pose he cultivated, on which see G. Megaro, *Mussolini dal mito alla realtà* (Milan, 1947), pp. 59–65, 146, as well as the discussion below. Nationalists often referred to Crispi as the "tragic hero": Mario Viana, *Crispi, l'eroe tragico* (Milan, 1923), and Chap. VII below. G. Papini, *Un uomo finito* (Florence, 1922), is an excellent autobiographical excursion into this sort of posturing.
99 G. Borgese, "Il ritorno di Oriani," in his *Studi di letterature moderne* (Milan, 1915), pp. 63–71, and "Alfredo Oriani," in his *La vita e il libro* (3 vols. Bologna, 1923), II, 322–27; L. Federzoni, "Un eroe," in his *Paradossi di ieri* (Milan, 1925), pp. 17–27; G. Luongo, *Note di critica,* Vol. I, *Alfredo Oriani* (Naples, 1915), pp. 7–8; G. B. Bianchi, "Il dramma di Alfredo Oriani," *Nuova Antologia,* CCCLXXV, Fasc. 1502 (October 16, 1934), 557–71.
100 G. Gentile, "La filosofia in Italia dopo il 1850. VI: Gli Hegeliani. VII: Angelo Camillo de Meis," *La Critica,* XII (1914), 283–302; Croce, "Note sulla letteratura italiana nella seconda metà del secolo XIX," *La Critica,* V (1907), 348–51.
101 A. Oriani, *La disfatta* (2nd ed. Milan, 1896), p. 51, in Croce, "Note sulla letteratura," *La Critica,* VII (1909), 1–8; H. Frenzel, *Alfredo Oriani. Ein Beitrag zur Geschichte des italienischen Historismus* (Cologne, 1937), pp. 40–41.
102 Borgese, "Il ritorno di Oriani," p. 71.
103 C. Vossler, *Letteratura italiana* (Naples, 1922).
104 A. Oriani, *Fino a Dogali* (Bologna, 1923), pp. 334–39, 355, 357–61.
105 A. Oriani, "Don Giovanni Verità," in *Fino a Dogali,* pp. 33, 82–83, 152–56.
106 A. Oriani, *La lotta politica in Italia: origini della lotta attuale (476–1887)* (2nd ed. Milan, 1895); L. Ambrosini, "Su Alfredo Oriani," *La Voce* (March 28, 1912). See also Croce, "Note sulla letteratura," 1–28.
107 A[madeo] C[rivelluci], *Studi Storici,* I, Fasc. 1 (1892), 286.
108 Croce, *Storia della storiografia,* II, 121–22; Oriani, "Machiavelli," in *Fino a Dogali,* pp. 179–299.
109 Oriani, *La lotta politica,* pp. 354–64, 535–42, 573, 581–91, 612, 618, 634, 670–71, 689–90, 716, 807, 810, 856–58, 882–86.
110 *Ibid.,* pp. 676, 695–704, 856–58, 882–86.
111 A. Oriani, *La rivolta ideale* (2nd ed. Naples, 1908), pp. 34–44, 52–69, 82–83, 133–34, 263–77, 278–93, 340–51, 373–81.

CHAPTER FIVE

1 A. Sandonà, *L'irredentismo nelle lotte politiche e nelle contese diplomatiche italo-austriache* (3 vols. Bologna, 1938), I, 6–7, 10–12, 16–17, 20, 23–26, 29–30.

2 V. Titone, "Una rivoluzione mancata. Palermo nel 1866," *L'osservatore,* I, Fasc. 1 (October, 1954), 12–13. Verga's *I Malavoglia* has a realistic description of Sicilian sailors back from Lissa and the general attitude toward the war.

3 F. Chabod, *Storia della politica estera italiana dal 1870 al 1896,* Vol. I, *Le premesse* (Bari, 1951), 471–75. Crispi agreed, despite his dislike of Austria's treatment of Italians within the Empire: *The Memoirs of Francesco Crispi,* trans. Mary Prichard-Agnetti (3 vols. London, 1912), II, 398–99; III, 152–54. On Balbo, see his *Delle speranze d'Italia* (Paris, 1844); Chap. XI.

4 S. Jacini, "Pensieri sulla politica italiana," *Nuova Antologia,* CV, Fasc. 10 (May 16, 1889), 201–17; Fasc. 11 (June 1, 1889), 428–29.

5 Sandonà, *L'irredentismo,* I, 144–45.

6 *Ibid.,* I, 124. In a separate treaty between Germany and Italy that accompanied the renewal of the Triple Alliance in 1887, under Article IV, the possibility of Italy's acquiring Nice and Corsica was recognized: A. F. Pribram, *Les Traités politiques secrets de l'Autriche-Hongrie, 1879–1914* (Paris, 1923), pp. 64–65. Crispi raised the question of Nice in 1889: *Pensieri e profezie,* T. Palamenghi-Crispi, ed. (Rome, 1920), *Pensiero* No. 191. The French in 1895 suspended the Italian language newspaper *Il Pensiero,* which was published at Nice: A. Billot, *La France et l'Italie. Histoire des années troubles* (2 vols. Paris, 1905), II, 160–63.

7 Sandonà, *L'irredentismo,* I, 270–71; II, 89–90. In 1884, the *Tribuna* launched a press war against Mancini and the Triple Alliance, which had irredentist overtones: *ibid.,* III, 99–106.

8 Crispi, *Memoirs,* III, 128–33, 160–64. For the Durando-Piccoli affair and the more celebrated Seismit-Doda case, see Sandonà, *L'irredentismo,* III, 170–98, 199–201, and Appendix 1.

9 F. Crispi, *Politica interna. Diario e documenti,* T. Palamenghi-Crispi, ed. (2nd ed. Milan, 1924), p. 256.

10 Chabod, *Storia della politica estera,* p. 519 and n. 3; G. Spadolini, *L'opposizione cattolica da Porta Pia al '98* (Florence, 1954), pp. 67–68, 460 and n. 32.

11 *Die Grosse Politik der Europäischen Kabinette 1871–1914* (40 vols. Berlin, 1922 and 1926), III, Doc. No. 541 (Bismarck to Prince Henry VII Reuss, German ambassador at Vienna, December 31, 1881); [A Continental Statesman], "The Savoy Dynasty, the Pope and the Republic," *The Contemporary Review,* LIX, No. 304 (April, 1891), 465–507. For Crispi's reply, see "Italy, France and the Papacy," *The Contemporary Review,* LX, No. 308 (August, 1891), 161–82. This was Crispi's second article in response to the French statement. The first reply caused a reaction in the French press which convinced Crispi that the "vices of Catholic education in France have not been remedied by the work of civilization, and that the demagogues of that country are as intolerable as the Vatican" (pp. 161–62). The first answer appeared in *The Con-*

temporary Review, LIX, No. 306 (June, 1891), 777–93. See also Sandonà, *L'irredentismo*, III, 186, 190, 204.

12 Crispi, *Memoirs*, III, 118–22, 126–27.

13 W. F. Langer, *European Alliances and Alignments* (2nd ed. New York, 1956), pp. 460 ff.; Crispi, *Memoirs*, II, 346–49; III, 145–56, 250–55.

14 In February, 1888, Crispi was not alone in fearing war. Germany also thought France might attack Spezia and advised England to make a show of force at Toulon. The British failed to take the matter seriously (Langer, *European Alliances*, p. 476). In fact, Britain thought France would if anything attack Egypt: Lady Gwendolen Cecil, *Life of Robert Marquis of Salisbury* (4 vols. London, 1922 and 1932), IV, 95. There was little likelihood that France would attack Italy, yet even Billot, the French ambassador at Rome, concedes that Crispi's fears were "sincere" (Billot, *La France et l'Italie*, I, 127–28). But the war scare of 1889 was the result of Crispi's imagination. Giolitti recalled Crispi's almost hysterical fear, based on unconfirmed reports from an agent at the Vatican: *Memorie della mia vita* (Milan, 1922), pp. 46–48. Even Crispi's admirers admit his extraordinary inability to see Italian problems in the larger context of the European balance: G. Volpe, *L'Italia in cammino* (Milan, 1931), p. 70. T. Palamenghi-Crispi's defense of his uncle's diplomacy shows instead that Crispi was ready to rely on any unfounded scrap of information: "La politica estera di Francesco Crispi," *Nuova Antologia* (May 1, 1912), pp. 122–27. Salisbury worried about Crispi's rashness and hoped Italy's financial problems would lead to his downfall (Cecil, *Salisbury*, IV, 105). Crispi mixed feelings of great insecurity with a burning desire to gain a great victory (*Memoirs*, II, 392–93). It was this trait in his makeup that led to Adowa. As to his last ministry, 1893–96, the scare of 1889 and undeniably aggressive French statements account for his claims in the Chamber that a Russian-French-Vatican plot was behind the Sicilian Fasci. He was also worried about the naval base the French were building at Bizerte. This had been the subject of a debate in the Chamber on February 4, 1893, before Crispi came back to power. In his defense, it must be granted that French naval authorities did furnish ample raw material for his suspicious mind; for an example, see P. Fontin and M. J. M. Vignot, *Les Guerres navales de demain, avec une préface de M. le Contre-Amiral Réveillère* (Paris, 1891), preface and Chap. V.

15 F. Chabod, *Storia della politica estera*, pp. 665–67, 674–75; Sandonà, *L'irredentismo*, I, 143; D. Bartoli, *La fine della monarchia* (2nd ed. Verona, 1947), pp. 33–35.

16 In addition to works already discussed, see R. de Sterlich, *Il Re e lo Statuto* (Bologna, 1897); Senator A. Marazio, *Del governo parlamentare italiano* (Turin, 1904); F. Lo Parco, "La parola Statuto nella storia del diritto e nella vita politica italiana," *Il Patriotta* (June 1, 1901); E. Cimbali, *I partiti politici in Italia* (Rome, 1881); L. Stefanoni, *Tristi effetti del governo parlamentare. Fatti e documenti commentati* (Rome, 1902). On the Bonghi incident, see Bartoli, *La fine della monarchia*, pp. 27–28. Mosca's opinion of monarchical sentiment is in his *Teorica dei governi e governo parlamentare* (2nd ed. Milan, 1925), pp. 157–58, 262–66, 273–77.

17 G. Carducci, "Agli elettori del collegio di Pisa" (May 9, 1886), *Edizione Nazionale delle opere di Giosuè Carducci* (30 vols. Bologna, 1935–40),

XXV, 36. For his monarchical poem, see "Alla Croce di Savoia," II, 210–15.

18 G. Goyau, "Le 20 septembre à Rome. Impression d'un témoin," *Revue des deux mondes*, CXXXI (October 15, 1895).

19 A. Oriani, *La lotta politica in Italia: origini della lotta attuale (476–1887)* (2nd ed. Milan, 1895), p. 885. The idea runs through all his work. It is also found in the writings of his Hegelian friend, A. C. De Meis, *Il Sovrano* (Bari, 1927), first published in 1868.

20 Sandonà, *L'irredentismo*, III, 28–29.

21 Volpe, *L'Italia in cammino*, pp. 38–39, 49–50; M. Vaussard, *Sur la nouvelle Italie* (Paris, 1928), pp. 46–92. On Oberdan, see the biography by F. Salata, *Guglielmo Oberdan* (Bologna, 1924).

22 Carducci, "XVIII dicembre," *Opere*, XIX, 191–95, and his speech at the unveiling of a tablet honoring Oberdan, *Opere*, XIX, 205–10; also his "XX dicembre," *Opere*, XIX, 196–97.

23 An extreme example of this sort of literary irredentism may be found in the works of F. Lo Parco, particularly his "I confini della Patria nei canti dei suoi poeti," *Nuova Antologia*, CCXLII, Fasc. 968 (April 16, 1912), and *Lo spirito antitedesco e l'irredentismo di Giosuè Carducci* (Salerno, 1915).

24 H. Wickham Steed, *Through Thirty Years, 1892–1922. A Personal Narrative* (2 vols. New York, 1925), I, 225–26; Chabod, *Storia della politica estera*, pp. 467–73; Sandonà, *L'irredentismo*, III, 265–67.

25 Jacini, "Pensieri sulla politica italiana," 421–22.

26 L. Villari, *Italy* (New York, 1929), pp. 92–97.

27 Sandonà, *L'irredentismo*, I, 106–11.

28 *Ibid.*, 4, 106–13, 141–42, 173, 258–60, 270 and n. 1; II, 27, 134; III, 153, 234.

29 S. W. Halperin, *Italy and the Vatican at War* (Chicago, 1939), pp. 237–38, 336; Crispi, *Memoirs*, II, 86–87.

30 Chabod, *Storia della politica estera*, pp. 690–91.

31 Salata, *Guglielmo Oberdan*, p. 210. Bismarck heard of this analysis and told Vienna he agreed with Robilant (*ibid.*, p. 214).

32 Sandonà, *L'irredentismo*, I, 171; III, 151–54.

33 On Robilant, see Chabod, *Storia della politica estera*, pp. 625–50.

34 Oriani, *La lotta politica*, pp. 885–86.

35 Arturo Labriola, *Storia di dieci anni (1899–1909)* (Milan, 1910), p. 154.

36 Volpe, *L'Italia in cammino*, pp. 43–47. Volpe was a member of the Milan Democratic Liberals for Italian Intervention group, a nonrevolutionary interventionist organization. He took part in several war rallies: see *Corriere della Sera* (April 14 and May 15, 1915) and *Popolo d'Italia* (May 15 and 17, 1915). The experience of the Radiant May has left its mark in Volpe's tendency to play up the "spiritual values" in Italian diplomacy, and the role of the "people." See his *Il popolo italiano tra la pace a la guerra (1914–15)* (Milan and Varese, 1940).

37 A. Pingaud, *L'Italie depuis 1870* (Paris, 1915), a work partial to Pan-Latinism that exaggerates the force behind irredentism and views the Triple Alliance as illogical for Italy.

38 A. C. Coolidge, *The Origins of the Triple Alliance* (2nd ed. New York, 1926), pp. 42, 214–16.

39 Volpe (*L'Italia in cammino*, p. 45) cites the Dante Alighieri Society, founded in 1889, as an illustration of a new trend, since the group was conservative rather than Republican. This is correct. However, its president, Ruggero Bonghi, also made it clear that Austria-Hungary was essential to the balance of power in Eastern Europe. To acquire Italy's natural frontiers at the expense of the Empire's existence, therefore, would create more harm than good. He did not wish to compromise Austrian power over the subject nationalities: P. Fambri, *La Venezia Giulia* (Venice, 1880), preface. For Bonghi's defense of the Triple Alliance, even though he was critical of Bismarck, see Sandonà, *L'irredentismo*, II, 163–66.

40 N. W. Senior, *Conversations with Distinguished Persons during the Second Empire* (2 vols. London, 1880), II, 176–79.

41 Halperin, *Italy and the Vatican at War*, pp. 213–14, 220, 237.

42 Chabod, *Storia della politica estera*, pp. 8, 109, 562–99.

43 Halperin, *Italy and the Vatican at War*, pp. 242–43, 262–65, 316.

44 *Ibid.*, p. 299; Chabod, *Storia della politica estera*, pp. 656–58; V. Gorresio, *Risorgimento scomunicato* (Florence, 1958), pp. 54–64.

45 Halperin, *Italy and the Vatican at War*, pp. 325–27. Given French clericalism, even Luigi Luzzatti approved of the royal tour. Yet Luzzatti was close to French statesmen, especially to Barrère, and was to be active in the post-Crispian period when the anti-French policy was being toned down: see his article, "La conversione della rendita italiana," *Nuova Antologia*, CCCVI, Fasc. 1219 (January 1, 1923), 3–11.

46 The Cardinal himself was suspected at the Vatican of harboring conciliatory views, and of opposing the Jesuits. The Vatican rejected his appointment (Halperin, *Italy and the Vatican at War*, p. 257). He was related to the royal family, being the uncle of the Crown Prince, later William II. In 1876, the Italian clerical press attacked him for staying too long in Germany and for his personal ties with Rosmini and Döllinger. There were rumors that he would leave the Church. Pius IX was disturbed by this. It has been said that Leo XIII prevented his becoming Bishop of Cologne, as he would have wished: see V. Riccio, "Il cardinale Kopp e la sua missione a Roma," *Nuova Antologia*, CLIX, Fasc. 634 (May 16, 1898), 320–21. The post at the Vatican was not filled until 1882.

47 Halperin, *Italy and the Vatican at War*, p. 242; L. Salvatorelli, *La Triplice Alleanza (1877–1912)* (Milan and Varese, 1939), p. 25.

48 Sandonà, *L'irredentismo*, I, 124.

49 Halperin, *Italy and the Vatican at War*, pp. 338–39, 363–65.

50 *Ibid.*, pp. 119–21, 127; Salvatorelli, *La Triplice Alleanza*, pp. 24–25; Chabod, *Storia della politica estera*, pp. 577–78, 579 and n. 6; S. Jacini, *La questione del papato in Italia* (Milan, 1888), pp. 50–53.

51 Sandonà, *L'irredentismo*, I, 97–100, 128–29, 152–53, 233, 238.

52 *Ibid.*, 161, 254 ff.; Alois Ritter von Haymerle, *Italicae Res* (Florence, 1880).

53 Halperin, *Italy and the Vatican at War*, pp. 85 and n. 91, 86–87, 172–73, 175–77.

54 F. Ruffini, "Progetti e propositi germanici per risolvere la questione romana," *Nuova Antologia*, CCXII (May–June, 1921), 24–27; E. Bourgeois, "Les Origines de la Triple Alliance et la question romaine," *Revue de Paris* (January 1, 1926), and his *Manuel historique de politique étrangère* (4 vols. Paris, 1909–26), III. Jacini used the argument of pos-

sible blackmail in order to bolster his plan for internationalization of the Guarantees, which, if done, would prevent foreign exploitation of the Roman Question: "Pensieri, Parte seconda," pp. 438–44. V. E. Orlando, a close friend of Ruffini's, takes the identical view of Bismarck's policy in his *Rome vs. Rome*, trans. Clarence Beardslee (New York, 1937), p. 122.

55 Halperin, *Italy and the Vatican at War*, pp. 87–88, 175; L. Luzzatti, "Le controversie politiche e giuridiche sulla libertà religiosa con speciale riguardo all'Italia," *Bollettino del Circolo Giuridico di Roma*, I (1911), p. 19.

56 Halperin, *Italy and the Vatican at War*, pp. 307–08, 378–82. In 1877, Bismarck complained to Crispi that Italy refused to take part in the *Kulturkampf*, adding that the Guarantees meant that "Vous l'avez emboité dans le coton" (Crispi, *Memoirs*, II, 61).

57 Chabod, *Storia della politica estera*, p. 665, n. 1.

58 Halperin, *Italy and the Vatican at War*, pp. 384 ff.; Salvatorelli, *La Triplice Alleanza*, pp. 25–26 and n. 5; A. J. P. Taylor, *Bismarck: The Man and the Statesman* (New York, 1955), pp. 152–53.

59 Sandonà, *L'irredentismo*, III, 150; F. Salata, "La questione romana e la Triplice Alleanza; secondo nuovi documenti austro-germanici," *Nuova Antologia*, CCXXIII (March–April, 1923), 49–50. Billot, French ambassador to Italy, 1890–98, assumed that there was a guarantee (*La France et l'Italie*, I, 35–36, 61, 338).

60 I. Bonomi, *La politica italiana da Porta Pia a Vittorio Veneto* (Rome, 1944), p. 83; D. Mack Smith, *Italy. A Modern History* (Ann Arbor, 1959), p. 125.

61 Salata, "La questione romana"; see also his *Per la storia diplomatica della questione romana* (Milan, 1929).

62 Ruffini, "Progetti e propositi germanici."

63 Ruffini, "Il potere temporale negli scopi di guerra degli ex-imperi centrali," *Nuova Antologia*, CCXI (March–April, 1921), 289–301; "La questione romana e l'ora presente," *Nuova Antologia*, CCXII (May–June, 1921), 193–206. For the text of the London Treaty, see M. Toscano, *Il patto di Londra* (Bologna, 1934), pp. 183–88. Salata refers specifically to Sonnino's negotiation of this treaty ("La questione romana," pp. 61–62).

64 In 1881, Bismarck decided to restore diplomatic relations with the Vatican. Sonnino feared he wanted to revive the Roman Question, and spoke on the matter in the Chamber, claiming that the Germans might try to internationalize the Guarantees. To parry this imagined threat, he advocated an alliance with Germany. Had Bismarck intended to use the Church-State issue as leverage, Sonnino's remarks would have been most inopportune, as Salvatorelli notes (*La Triplice Alleanza*, pp. 60–61). Bismarck in fact had been working to put an end to the Kulturkampf since the death of Pius IX in 1878, but for reasons quite removed from those that Sonnino persisted in perceiving (Taylor, *Bismarck*, pp. 163 ff.).

65 *Die Grosse Politik*, III, Doc. No. 541.

66 *Ibid.*, Doc. No. 542; Salvatorelli, *La Triplice Alleanza*, p. 63.

67 Salvatorelli suggests that Austria's eventual rejection of a territorial guarantee was also due to the fear that Germany would demand a territorial guarantee of Alsace and Lorraine in turn, something Vienna had refused to give in the Treaty of 1879 (*La Triplice Alleanza*, pp. 65–66). Robilant informed Kálnoky of the Italian position on February 19, 1882.

Yet he himself was by no means an anti-irredentist. Mancini's note to Robilant stated that Italy sought "un patto speciale sulla base della reciproca garanzia territoriale": see G. Volpe, *L'Italia nella Triplice Alleanza (1882–1915)* (2nd ed. Milan and Varese, 1941), p. 43. For Sonnino on irredentism, see the *Rassegna settimanale* (May 29, 1881), cited by Volpe, *L'Italia nella Triplice Alleanza,* pp. 30–33.

68 Salvatorelli, *La Triplice Alleanza,* pp. 66–67.

69 V. Procacci, *La questione romana. Le vicende del tentativo di concilia-zione del 1887 (con documenti inediti)* (Florence, 1929), pp. 55–57.

70 M. Erzberger, *Erlebnisse im Weltkrieg* (Stuttgart and Berlin, 1920), pp. 125–37.

71 Crispi, speaking at Florence in favor of the Alliance on October 8, 1890, attacked irredentism and claimed that the pact had "per i scopo e per base la garanzia territoriale degli stati contraenti" (*Memoirs,* II, 123). For Tittoni's speech of 1908, see *Italy's Foreign and Colonial Policy,* trans. Baron Bernardo Quaranta di San Severino (London, 1914), pp. 83–93.

72 Langer, *European Alliances,* p. 245.

73 Salata, "La questione romana," p. 59–61. Jemolo is correct in writing that Salata's opinions are colored by his irredentism: *Chiesa e Stato in Italia negli ultimi cento anni* (3rd ed. Turin, 1952), p. 376. On the other hand, Jemolo was a neutralist in 1915. His work, therefore, tends to play down both irredentism and the Church-State issue. The two problems are related in the historiography on modern Italy as they were in the evolution of Italian foreign policy.

74 For Mancini's dispatch to Robilant (March 17, 1882), see Volpe, *L'Italia nella Triplice Alleanza,* pp. 47–50. For Bismarck's views, see *Die Grosse Politik,* III, Doc. No. 548.

75 *Nuova Antologia,* December 31, 1883, p. 144; January 14, 1884, pp. 352–54.

76 E. L. Woodward, "The Diplomacy of the Vatican under Popes Pius IX and Leo XIII," *Journal of the British Institute of International Affairs,* III, No. 3 (May, 1924), 134–35.

77 Sandonà, *L'irredentismo,* I, 283 and n. 1, 284–86. Vienna informed the Vatican that the Alliance did not guarantee the city (Salata, *Per la storia diplomatica della questione romana,* pp. 110–25).

78 Salata's opinion, cited by Sandonà, *L'irredentismo,* I, 283.

79 Giolitti, *Memorie,* pp. 223–24.

80 The attempt of the Italian Nationalists to form an alliance with clerical groups will be examined below, Chapters 7 and 8.

81 Langer, *European Alliances,* pp. 35, 246.

82 F. Crispi, *Politica estera. Memorie e documenti raccolti e ordinati da T. Palamenghi-Crispi* (2nd ed. revised, 2 vols. Milan, 1926), I, 128–35, 139–40.

83 Jacini, "Pensieri, Parte seconda" (June 1, 1889), 421–27, 425–26, 432–37; (June 16, 1889), 633, 644.

84 Chabod, *Storia della politica estera,* pp. 182–83; A. P. d'Entrèves, *Italy in Europe,* Montague Burton International Relations Lecture, 1952–53 (Nottingham, 1953), pp. 10–12; R. Michels, "Quelques Aperçus sur l'histoire de la bourgeoisie italienne aux XIXᵉ siècle," *Revue historique,* CLXX (1932), 423.

85 Chabod, *Storia della politica estera*, pp. 542–43; Steed, *Through Thirty Years*, I, 116–19, 150.
86 Volpe, *L'Italia nella Triplice Alleanza*, pp. 43–44.
87 Crispi, *Memoirs*, II, 216–17; III, 257–58. On Spaventa, see *La politica della Destra. Scritti e discorsi raccolti da B. Croce* (Bari, 1910), pp. 201–02. For the rise of the imperialists in the early twentieth century, see below, Chapter 7.
88 Chabod, *Storia della politica estera*, pp. 118, 320–21.
89 Sandonà, *L'irredentismo*, II, 151–52.

CHAPTER SIX

1 R. Hostetter, *The Italian Socialist Movement*, Vol. I, *Origins (1860–1882)* (Princeton, 1958), pp. 376–84.
2 Of the works that fall outside the limits of this study, the most significant are those of Gramsci: see his collected essays on the Mezzogiorno, *La questione meridionale* (Rome, 1951). A recent work devoted to the era of the Postrisorgimento that takes a negative view, largely because of the government's failure to deal with the problems of the South, is M. L. Salvadori, *Il mito del buongoverno* (Turin, 1960).
3 F. Chabod, *Storia della politica estera italiana dal 1870 al 1896*, Vol. I, *Le premesse* (Bari, 1951), p. 542.
4 G. Fortunato, *Il Mezzogiorno e lo Stato italiano* (2 vols. Bari, 1911), II, 332; S. Sonnino, *I contadini in Sicilia* (Florence, 1877), p. 462. The latter is the second volume of the combined study by L. Franchetti and Sonnino, published under the joint title, *La Sicilia nel 1876. Condizioni politiche e amministrative* (Florence, 1877).
5 B. Croce, *Storia del Regno di Napoli* (Bari, 1925), pp. 263–64; Stendhal, *Rome, Naples, Florence*, trans. R. N. Coe (New York, 1960), pp. 28, 121–26, 179.
6 E. Artom, "Il Conte di Cavour e la questione napoletana," *Nuova Antologia*, CLXXX, Fasc. 717 (November 1, 1901), 152; G. Giolitti, *Memorie della mia vita* (Milan, 1922), p. 32.
7 The two began publicizing the question in their journal, the *Rassegna settimanale*, which was first published at Florence in 1878. L. Franchetti had preceded this with his *Sulle condizioni economiche e amministrative della provincie napoletane, Abruzzi e Molise, Calabria e Basilicata. Appunti di viaggio* (Florence, 1875).
8 F. S. Nitti, *Nord e Sud. Prime linee di una inchiesta sulla ripartizione territoriale delle entrate e delle spese* (Turin, 1900), passim, and his *L'Italia all'alba del secolo XX* (Turin and Rome, 1900), pp. 107–49.
9 E. Ciccotti, *Mezzogiorno e settentrione d'Italia* (Rome, 1898), p. 94.
10 *Rivista popolare* (January 15, 1897), p. 243.
11 Salvemini, "La questione meridionale e il federalismo," *Critica Sociale* (July 1, August 1 and 16, 1900), reprinted in *Opere di Gaetano Salvemini*, Vol. I, *Scritti sulla questione meridionale (1896–1955)* (Turin, 1955), pp. 67–107.
12 C. Lombroso, *In Calabria, 1862–1897* (Catania, 1897), pp. 37 ff.
13 A. Niceforo, *L'Italia barbara contemporanea* (Palermo and Milan, 1898), pp. 19–21, 247–62, 294–95; also his *La delinquenza in Sardegna* (Palermo, 1897), p. 109.
14 Salvemini, *Opere*, I, 61; Croce, in *La Critica*, IV (1906), 281–82. For

other southern reactions to race theory, see A. Renda, *La questione meridionale* (Milan, 1900), preface and pp. 1–28, 75–84.

15 Renda, *La questione meridionale*, pp. 33–35, 52–58.

16 Salvemini, *Opere*, I, 17. For Sighele's views see Renda, *La questione meridionale*, pp. 52–58.

17 J. Gay, *Les deux Romes et l'opinion française. Les rapports franco-italiennes depuis 1815* (Paris, 1931), p. 128.

18 G. Goyau, *Lendemains d'Unité* (Paris, 1900), passim. On Goyau, see above, Chapter 2 and n. 15.

19 For clerical use of the regional question, see G. Spadolini, *L'opposizione cattolica da Porta Pia al '98* (Florence, 1954), and C. Benoist, *Souvenirs* (3 vols. Paris, 1932–34), I, 100–103. On Benoist, see above, Chapter 4, n. 65.

20 Lombroso, *In Calabria*, preface and p. 142.

21 See above, Chapter 2, Chapter 3 and n. 3.

22 Stendhal, *Rome, Naples, Florence*, pp. 159–60; E. J. Hobsbawn, *Social Bandits and Primitive Rebels* (Glencoe, Ill., 1959), pp. 13–29.

23 Renda, *La questione meridionale*, pp. 57–58, 187–90.

24 *Atti del parlamento italiano. Camera dei deputati. Sessione 1892–94. Discussioni*, VIII–IX, 11414–15.

25 Franchetti, *La Sicilia nel 1876*, pp. 57, 205–07.

26 Niceforo, *Italiani del nord e italiani del sud* (Turin, 1901), preface, viii, and pp. 16–27, 81; E. Ferri, *L'omicidio* (Turin, 1897). Sergi's work, *Specie e varietà umane*, came out at Turin in 1900.

27 Salvemini, *Opere*, I, 86–94, 96–102, 103–07.

28 *Ibid.*, pp. 159–65. On the Socialists, see "Il Partito Socialista nel presente momento," *La Voce* (October 14, 1910). Salvemini felt that the *Avanti!* had been ignoring his articles, particularly those attacking Giolittian corruption. He accused the Socialist party of being attached to the regime: see *La Voce* (May 11, 1911). He preferred to use the pages of Papini's and Prezzolini's journal, and thenceforth avoided the *Avanti!*: see *L'Unità*, I, No. 3 (December 30, 1911), 9–10. By 1911, he was accusing the party of having done nothing to stop the Tripoli invasion, stating that the war had probably killed the party. The PSI would either reform itself or die. As for the Reggio Emilia congress at which Mussolini led the attack on the reformist wing, Salvemini called it a "joke." "Tripoli e i socialisti," *L'Unità*, I, No. 1 (December 16, 1911); "Socialismo e Tripolismo," *L'Unità*, I, No. 3 (December 30, 1911); "Il Congresso dei conservatori," *L'Unità*, I, No. 31 (July 31, 1912).

29 Salvemini, *Opere*, I, 96–102, 166–82.

30 F. Venturi, "Salvemini storico," *Il Ponte*, XIII, No. 12 (December, 1957), 1794.

31 A. W. Salomone, *L'età giolittiana* (Turin, 1949), preface, ix; Salvemini, "Fu l'Italia prefascista una democrazia? II," *Il Ponte*, VIII, No. 2 (February, 1952), 174; also his *L'autobiografia di un brigante* (Rome, 1915), offprint from the *Bollettino della Società Etnografica Italiana*, III, Fasc. 1 (1914), 61–86. For his later views, see *Opere*, I, 612.

32 Salvemini, "Fu l'Italia prefascista una democrazia? I," *Il Ponte*, VIII, No. 1 (January, 1952), 16–17. By that time, however, it was clear that the Fascists had made good use of the *rivoluzione mancata* theme. Sal-

vemini, a leader of the anti-Fascist underground, attacked the concept, although in his younger days he had helped further the same idea.

33 Salvemini, *Opere*, I, 103.
34 Salvemini, *Il ministro della malavita* (Florence, 1910), pp. 1–64.
35 Salvemini, "Dopo la vittoria giolittiana," *La Voce* (March 10, 1910).
36 G. Fortunato, "I cardini della questione meridionale," speech in the Chamber, July 3, 1896, reprinted in *L'Unità*, I, No. 1 (December 16, 1911).
37 Fortunato, "Le due Italie," *La Voce* (March 16, 1911).
38 Fortunato, "Parlamento e paese," *L'Unità*, I, No. 4 (January 6, 1912).
39 Salvemini, speech at Bagni di San Giuliano, reprinted in *La Voce* (May 11, 1911). See also his "Suffragio universale e clericalismo," *La Voce* (April 27, 1911).
40 Salvemini, "La polveretta," *La Voce* (August 31, 1911).
41 Salvadori, *Il mito del buongoverno*, pp. 115–42, analyzes the work of Turiello, using it to bolster his own negative view of the Postrisorgimento.
42 P. Turiello, *Governo e governati in Italia* (2 vols. Bologna, 1882).
43 *Ibid.*, I, 39, 120–37, 182 ff., 300 ff.
44 *Ibid.*, I, 40 ff., 167 ff., 361–66, 399; II, 307.
45 *Ibid.*, I, 50, 322 ff., 482; II, 131 ff., 230–41, 289, 326 ff.
46 S. Spaventa, *La politica della Destra. Scritti e discorsi raccolti da B. Croce* (Bari, 1910), p. 42.
47 F. Persico, *Governo o rivoluzione* (Naples, 1868), cited in L. Russo, *Francesco de Sanctis e la cultura napoletana (1860–1885)* (Venice, 1928), pp. 160–62.
48 Turiello, *Governo e governati*, I, 411–13, 422–23; II, 180–81. See also his *Politica contemporanea. Saggi* (Naples, 1894), pp. 94–104.
49 Croce, "Dai 'Discorsi politici' non mai raccolti, di Francesco de Sanctis," *La Critica*, XI (1913), 396–405, from a speech in the Chamber, May 30, 1878. But in another speech De Sanctis had expressed his suspicion of military "diversions" that Crispi was then proposing. These, he noted, only obscured real problems and led not to freedom but to "glory," to "Waterloo and Sedan" (*ibid.*, 327–37).
50 Turiello, *Governo e governati*, I, 151, 399; *Politica contemporanea*, p. 106.
51 Turiello, *Governo e governati*, I, 313; II, 139, 245, 311–12.
52 B. Croce, *Storia d'Italia dal 1871 al 1915* (10th ed. Bari, 1953), pp. 260–61. On this aspect of Croce's history of Italy, see Chabod, "Croce storico," *Rivista storica italiana*, LXIV, Fasc. 4 (1952), 518–20.
53 Hostetter, *Italian Socialist Movement*, pp. 13–14.
54 Russo, *Francesco de Sanctis*, pp. 250–54. For Carducci's opinion of the metaphysical state, see his letters attacking A. C. De Meis, reprinted in the Croce edition of De Meis, *Il Sovrano* (Bari, 1927), pp. 22–23, 25–30. During a conversation with Salvemini a few years before his death, the writer happened to use the word. At this, Salvemini bristled and exclaimed, "The 'State,' the 'State'! And what is this 'State'?"
55 Turiello, *Politica contemporanea*, pp. 11–13, 43, 48–49, 85–88; *Governo e governati*, II, 337.
56 L. Salvatorelli, *Nazionalfascismo* (Turin, 1923), pp. 31–42. These essays, written in 1919 and 1920, remain one of the most perceptive treatments of the anarchic right and the rise of early fascism.

CHAPTER SEVEN

1 P. L. Occhini, *Enrico Corradini e la nuova coscienza nazionale* (2nd ed. Florence, 1925), p. 37.

2 Giacomo Barzellotti, "Il pessimismo filosofico in Germania e il problema morale dei nostri tempi," *Nuova Antologia*, XXI, Fasc. 9 (May 1, 1889), 47–66, 274–91.

3 Occhini, *Enrico Corradini*, pp. 69–77. See also Maurice Muret, *La Littérature italienne d'aujourd'hui* (Paris, 1960), pp. 200–03. For Federzoni, see his *Il corruttore* (Bologna, 1900).

4 Occhini, *Enrico Corradini*, pp. 53–66.

5 Muret, *La Littérature italienne*, p. 201.

6 Occhini, *Enrico Corradini*, p. 58.

7 E. Corradini, "Giacomo Vettòri," *Nuova Antologia*, XCI (1901), 211–33; Occhini, *Enrico Corradini*, p. 101.

8 Corradini, writing in the *Germinal*, No. 39 (1892), cited by Prezzolini in *La Voce* (June 3, 1909).

9 G. Volpe, *Italia moderna* (2 vols. Florence, 1949), II, 334; Occhini, *Enrico Corradini*, pp. 119–20.

10 V. Gorresio, "Il congresso dei forti," *Il Mondo* (August 26, 1950).

11 Corradini, in the *Marzocco* (September 14, 1902), in Volpe, *Italia moderna*, II, 334.

12 Editorial, *Il Regno*, I, No. 1 (November 29, 1903).

13 G. Papini, "Per la vita contro la vita," *Il Regno*, I, No. 4 (December 20, 1903).

14 Corradini to Campodonico, *Il Regno*, I, No. 3 (December 13, 1903).

15 Editorial, "Mezze velleità," *Il Regno*, I, No. 4 (December 20, 1903). See also Corradini to Compodonico, *Il Regno*, I, No. 8 (January 17, 1904), and his article, "La politica degli occhi aperti . . . ," *ibid.*, I, No. 26 (May 22, 1904). For an analysis of Turiello's posthumous essays (*Il secolo XIX ed altri scritti di politica internazionale e coloniale*), see M. L. Salvadori, *Il mito del buongoverno* (Turin, 1960), pp. 134–42.

16 Corradini, "La guerra," *Il Regno*, I, No. 14 (February 20, 1904); M. Morasso, *ibid.*, I, No. 19 (April 2, 1904). For Corradini's anticipation of the Futurists see "La nuova bellezza del mondo," *Il Regno*, II, No. 14 (June 3, 1905). The Manifesto first appeared in the *Figaro* (February 20, 1909).

17 G. A. Borgese, "Considerazioni giapponesi," *Il Regno*, I, No. 38 (August 14, 1904); see also "l.a.," "L'anima nazionale," II, No. 18 (September 22, 1905).

18 E. Seillière (Baron Antoine Aimé Leon), *Der demokratische Imperialismus* (Berlin, 1907). Seillière took note of the *Regno*, of the *Leonardo*, and of Morasso's "artistic imperialism" (*ibid.*, pp. 3, 8–9). But he generally ignored Italian currents in favor of French and German. See also his *Introduction à la philosophie de l'impérialisme* (Paris, 1911), *Les Mystiques du néo-romanticisme* (Paris, 1911), and *Mysticisme et domination* (Paris, 1913).

19 F. Flora, *Dal Romanticismo al Futurismo* (Milan, 1925), pp. 76–80.

20 For examples of Papini's mysticism, see the following articles in the *Leonardo*: "Cosa vogliamo. Risposta a Enrico Morselli" (November, 1904); "Athena e Faust" (February, 1905); "Federico Nietzsche" (June–August, 1905); "Dall'uomo a Dio" (February, 1906).

21 "Gian Falco" [Papini], "La coltura e la vita italiana," *Leonardo* (October–December, 1905); also under his pen name, "Campagna per il forzato risveglio," *Leonardo* (August, 1906).

22 Papini, *Un uomo finito* (Florence, 1922), passim.

23 Papini, "Il ministero libero," *La Voce* (September 14, 1911).

24 *Il Regno*, I, No. 19 (April 3, 1904); Prezzolini, "Le due Italie," *Il Regno*, I, No. 26 (May 22, 1904); "La menzogna parlamentare," *Il Regno*, I, No. 29 (June 5, 1904); and his "Come fare l'espansionismo," *Il Regno*, I, No. 30 (June 19, 1904). See also F. Chabod, *Storia della politica estera italiana dal 1870 al 1896*, Vol. I, *Le premesse* (Bari, 1951), pp. 181–82.

25 Papini, "La festa dell'energia," *Il Regno*, I, No. 29 (June 12, 1904), and the editorial on "Le elezioni," I, No. 48 (October 23, 1904).

26 Rastignac, cited in *Il Regno*, I, No. 49 (October 30, 1904).

27 Editorial, *Il Regno*, I, No. 49 (October 30, 1904). Pareto's article on the elections appears in the same number.

28 Corradini, in *Il Regno*, I, No. 43 (September 18, 1904), and his "Tornando sul nostro programma," Part III, *Il Regno*, I, No. 47 (October 16, 1904).

29 Corradini, "La politica degli occhi aperti . . . ," *Il Regno*, I, No. 26 (May 22, 1904); "Tornando sul nostro programma," Part II, *Il Regno*, I, No. 46 (October 9, 1904). See also the editorial, "Verso l'anarchia," I, No. 45 (October 2, 1904).

30 Corradini, "Tornando sul nostro programma," Part III, *Il Regno*, I, No. 47 (October 16, 1904); "La virtù nazionale," *Discorsi politici, 1902–1932* (Florence, 1932), pp. 35–50.

31 G. Gentile, *Origini e dottrina del Fascismo* (Rome, 1929), pp. 22–23.

32 Papini, "Cos'è caduto a Porto Arthur," *Il Regno*, II, No. 2 (January 8, 1905), and his article "Russia e rivoluzione," II, No. 5 (January 29, 1905).

33 Corradini, "Tra la cecità e il sangue," *Il Regno*, II, No. 11 (March 31, 1905); "Il momento presente," II, No. 20 (November 15, 1905).

34 Corradini, "La politica degli occhi aperti . . . ," *Il Regno*, I, No. 26 (May 22, 1904); "Tornando sul nostro programma," Part II, *Il Regno*, I, No. 46 (October 9, 1904); also the *Regno*'s editorial, "Il discorso del Re," I, No. 54 (December 4, 1904).

35 B. Croce, *Storia d'Italia dal 1871 al 1915* (10th ed. Bari, 1953), pp. 260–66. For the Nationalists' use of French political literature, see the following numbers of *Il Regno*: November 29, 1903; June 26, 1904; October 23, 1904; December 16, 1905.

36 Gentile, *Origini e dottrina del Fascismo*, pp. 22–23.

37 Occhini, *Enrico Corradini*, pp. 223–24; Prezzolini, "L'aristocrazia dei briganti," *Il Regno*, I, No. 3 (December 13, 1903). See also G. Papini, *Vecchio e nuovo nazionalismo* (Milan, 1914), p. 29.

38 "Massoneria e Socialismo: colloquio con B. Croce," *La Voce* (November 24, 1910). See also B. Croce, *Cultura e vita morale* (Bari, 1914), pp. 161–68.

39 Stephané Piot, "Le Nationalisme italien," *Revue des sciences politiques*, XXXVII (1912), 204–21.

40 J. W. Meisel, *The Genesis of Georges Sorel* (Ann Arbor, 1951), p. 221 and n. 25.

41 Corradini, in *Il Regno*, I, No. 8 (January 17, 1904); A. Campodonico, "Note di attualità," *ibid.*, III, No. 5 (March 31, 1906).

42 Editorial, "Nazionalismo e anticlericalismo," *Il Regno*, I, No. 52 (November 20, 1904).

43. A. C[ampodonico?], "La politica di Pio X," *Il Regno*, II, No. 15 (June 25, 1905).

44 "Gian Falco" [Papini], "L'ideale imperialista," *Leonardo*, I (January 4, 1903); Corradini, "Il Santo," *Il Regno*, II, No. 21 (December 2, 1905), a review of Fogazzaro's novel which was to be placed on the Index. On Carducci, see his "Alle fonti del Clitumno," *Odi Barbare, Edizione Nazionale delle opere di Giosuè Carducci* (30 vols. Bologna, 1935–40), IV, 23–29.

45 Croce, *Storia d'Italia*, pp. 260–61.

46 L. Russo, *Giovanni Verga* (4th ed. Bari, 1947), pp. 1–12; Occhini, *Enrico Corradini*, p. 42.

47 V. Gorresio, "L'igiene del mondo," *Il Mondo* (September 9, 1950).

48 Pareto, on the outcome of the 1904 elections, in *Il Regno*, I, No. 49 (October 30, 1904).

49 "Regno," unsigned article in the *Leonardo* (June, 1904).

50 Papini, "Nazionalismo," *La Voce* (April 27, 1909). Prezzolini, in *La Voce* (December 27, 1909), took the same stand. For Croce's reaction to the new journal, see his article, "La Voce," *La Critica*, VII (1909), 308. Besides Croce, Pareto, Einaudi, Salvemini, Sorel, Rolland, Amendola, and others made occasional contributions.

51 Gorresio, "Il congresso dei forti," *Il Mondo* (August 26, 1950). See D'Annunzio, *La Nave*, prologue and final chorus "Arm the prow and set sail toward the World." For the Dante quotation, see *Divina Commedia*, Inf. IX, 113.

52 M. Muret, "M. Gabriele D'Annunzio et la critique italienne," *Revue des deux mondes*, LXXXIII (1913), 180–204.

53 G. A. Borgese, *Gabriel D'Annunzio* (Naples, 1909), p. 178.

54 G. P. Lucini, *Antidannunziana* (Milan, 1914), passim. A good collection of anti-D'Annunzian literature, but Lucini's style is that of the Master. Borgese noted that some of the anti-D'Annunzians were worse than the original (*D'Annunzio*, p. 178).

55 W. Eckstein, "F. Nietzsche in the Judgment of Posterity," *Journal of the History of Ideas*, VI, No. 3 (June, 1945), 310–24.

56 For a complete bibliography of Corradini's works, see Occhini, *Enrico Corradini*, pp. 235–63. Muret's judgment appears in his *La Littérature italienne*, p. 202.

57 Gorresio, "Il congresso dei forti," *Il Mondo*, August 26, 1950.

58 Oriani, "Francesco Crispi," *Rivista d'Italia*, IV, vol. 3, Fasc. 9 (September 1, 1901), 48–70; Giulio de Frenzi [Federzoni], "Il dovere di ricordare," *Idea Nazionale* (March 1, 1911).

59 Editorial, "La Tripolitania," *Idea Nazionale* (March 8, 1911); G. Castellini, "Che cosa vale la Tripolitania," *ibid.* (March 29, 1911).

60 Federzoni, "La politica delle alleanze," speech delivered at the first Nationalist Congress at Florence, December 4, 1910, in his *Paradossi d'ieri* (Milan, 1925), pp. 41–77.

61 Editorials, "Gl'interessi italiani minacciati in Tripolitania" and "Quello che non s'è fatto e non si fa ora," *Idea Nazionale* (April 5, 1911).

62 L. Albertini, *Venti anni di vita politica* (5 vols. 2 parts Bologna, 1951), Vol. II, Pt. 1, 96–97. See also Occhini, *Enrico Corradini*, pp. 191 ff. On the internal debate, see the editorial of March 1, 1911, in the *Idea Nazionale* and G. de Frenzi [Federzoni], "Tripoli e l'irredentismo: un dilemma che non esiste," *Idea Nazionale* (June 1, 1911).

63 Sen. T. Tittoni, *Italy's Foreign and Colonial Policy*, trans. Baron Bernardo Quaranta di San Severino (London, 1914), pp. 19–27: speeches in the Chamber of June 4 and 5, 1908, and in the Senate, May 10, 1905.

64 S. Sighele, *Pagine nazionaliste* (Milan, 1910), pp. 238–40.

65 G. Castellini, "Che cosa vale la Tripolitania," *Idea Nazionale* (March 29, 1911). Editorial, "L'illusione tripolina," *La Voce* (May 8, 1911).

66 Corradini, "La richezza aspettante nell'altipiano cirenaico," *Idea Nazionale* (August 31, 1911). Also his books, *Il volere d'Italia* (Naples, 1911), pp. 103–13; and *L'ora di Tripoli* (Milan, 1911), passim. For Bevione's articles, see his *Come siamo andati a Tripoli* (Turin, 1912), pp. 13, 22–25, 32, 38, 55, 58.

67 G. Mosca, *Italia e Libia* (Milan, 1912), pp. 1–67.

68 *Idea Nazionale:* June 1, 1911; Aug. 10, 1911, pp. 1–2; editorial, "Il dilemma tripolino," September 14, 1911; "MANIFESTO," June 4, 1911.

69 Editorial, "Per il Mezzogiorno," *Idea Nazionale* (March 22, 1911); "Quello che non s'è fatto . . ." (April 5, 1911); Corradini, *L'ora di Tripoli*, pp. 227–42; Sighele, *Pagine nazionaliste*, pp. 236–38.

70 G. de Frenzi [Federzoni], "Il dovere di ricordare," *Idea Nazionale* (March 1, 1911).

71 Sighele, *Pagine nazionaliste*, pp. 236–37. Corradini, while insisting that "the Southern Question is above all an African question," that the "Mezzogiorno was more African than European," showed by his analysis of the reasons why Italy had to have the area that the real aim was domestic (*L'ora di Tripoli*, pp. 227–41). Chabod, if he tends to take a "European" view of the impact of the Mezzogiorno on Italian diplomacy, also recognized (citing Turiello) that the "Southern Question" promoted "collectivist" political theories (*Storia della politica estera*, p. 182).

72 Editorial, "Gli assenti dalle feste cinquantenarie," *Idea Nazionale* (April 27, 1911).

73 Sighele, *Pagine nazionaliste*, pp. 217, 233–34.

74 Editorial, "Il Nazionalismo e la realtà politica," *Idea Nazionale* (March 15, 1911).

75 F. Coppola, "Israele contro l'Italia," *Idea Nazionale* (November 16, 1911); also his "Nazionalismo e Democrazia" (December 28, 1911). Others outside the ranks of the Nationalist Association showed traces of antisemitism, as for example G. U. Nazzari, Director of the Liberal Union (*Idea Nazionale*, July 27, 1911). It is also true that Jews were prominent in Italian Freemasonry, violently opposed by the Nationalists. In reaction to the Dreyfus Case, the intransigent clerical press did indulge in antisemitism: G. Spadolini, *L'opposizione cattolica da Porta Pia al '98* (Florence, 1954), p. 457 and n. 29. Though antisemitism was far less in evidence in Italy than in Europe generally, Croce was wrong when he denied its existence (*Storia d'Italia*, p. 97). For Coppola's reply to his critics, see "Il mio antisemitismo," *Idea Nazionale* (November 30, 1911).

76 Sighele, *Il Nazionalismo e i partiti politici* (Milan, 1911), pp. 149–55, 160–85. Also his *Ultime pagine nazionaliste* (Milan, 1912), pp. 149–55.

77 Sighele, *Pagine nazionaliste*, pp. 3–13, 17–65, 143–56, 215–26.
78 Sighele, *Il Nazionalismo e i partiti politici*, pp. 170, 186, 224–25, 233.
79 *Idea Nazionale* (April 25, 1912); editorial, "Il gioco della riforma e la commedia della crisi" (March 22, 1911). See also Sighele, *Il nazionalismo giudicato* (Genoa, 1913), p. 223 and passim.
80 Sighele, *Il Nazionalismo e i partiti politici*, pp. 176, 186, 198–203. For the review of D'Annunzio, see *La Stampa* (July 25, 1910).
81 G. Sorel, *Considerazioni sulla violenza*, trans. Antonio Sarno, with an introduction by B. Croce (Bari, 1909), introduction, p. v. On other Italian editions of Sorel, see above, Chapter 1, n. 38.
82 Corradini, "Sindacalismo, nazionalismo, imperialismo. Conferenza letta nel Dicembre 1909 alla Società 'Minerva' di Trieste, all'Accademia Olimpica di Vicenza, ecc.," in his *Il volere d'Italia*, No. 66, pp. 20–21, 24–27, 29–30, 32–47.
83 Corradini, *Il volere d'Italia*, pp. 157–63.
84 G. Amendola, "Il convegno nazionalista," *La Voce* (October 14, 1910); Sighele, *Il Nazionalismo e i partiti politici*, pp. 208–12.
85 G. Giolitti, *Memorie della mia vita* (Milan, 1922), pp. 288–89; G. Natale, *Giolitti e gli italiani* (Cernusco sul Naviglio, 1949), p. 727; Giolitti, *Discorsi parlamentari* (4 vols. Rome, 1953–56), III, 1366–69.
86 L. Degli Occhi, *Storia politica italiana* (Milan, 1946), pp. 19–107.
87 Giolitti, *Memorie*, p. 292. Although Giolitti's friend Olinda Malagodi, director of the *Tribuna*, had a hand in writing the *Memorie*, the style faithfully captures Giolitti's plain speech; see N. Valeri, introduction to the *Discorsi extraparlamentari* (Turin, 1952), pp. 80–83.
88 Corradini, "Dal parlamento al paese," *Il Regno*, III, No. 8 (June 23, 1906); also his "A che punto siamo," *Idea Nazionale* (April 13, 1911).
89 "La situazione parlamentare," *Idea Nazionale* (July 6, 1911); "Il monopolio della assicurazione" (June 15, 1911). On Salandra's position, see Albertini, *Venti anni di vita politica*, Vol. II, Pt. 1, 75–76. For Giolitti's assessment, see *Memorie*, pp. 297–98.
90 "La situazione parlamentare e l'azione nazionalista," *Idea Nazionale* (July 6, 1911); see also P. Arcari, "Le premesse teoriche dell'azione nazionalista" (May 4, 1911).
91 R. A. Gallenga-Stuart, "Per la direttiva dell'azione nazionalista," *Idea Nazionale* (July 13, 1911); also the editorial, "Nazionalismo, democrazia e partito liberale" (July 27, 1911).
92 *Idea Nazionale* (July 27, 1911), editorial in response to letters from readers discussing future policy.
93 M. Missiroli, "Le nationalisme italien," *L'Indépendance*, I (1911), 419–35. For the Nationalists' answer, see *Idea Nazionale* (August 31, 1911).
94 M. Maraviglia, "Nazionalismo e democrazia," *Idea Nazionale* (December 14, 1911).
95 F. Coppola, "Nazionalismo e democrazia," *Idea Nazionale* (December 28, 1911), and his reply to Livio Marchetti (January 4, 1911). See also m. m. [Maraviglia], "Parlamento e suffragio" (May 9, 1912). For the "democratic" reaction see L. Marchetti, "Guerra e democrazia," *Idea Nazionale* (December 21, 1911), and his "Per intenderci sulla democrazia" (January 4, 1912). Marchetti, like Sighele, was an Irredentist, something often true of the "left" wing of the Nationalist Association.
96 Editorial, "L'Associazione e il Partito," *Idea Nazionale* (July 11, 1912);

Armando Zanetti, "L'indirizzo politico del Nazionalismo" (September 19, 1912), and P. L. Occhini's survey of the party's history (December 12, 1912). For the *Voce's* response, see "La fine del nazionalismo," *La Voce* (May 9, 1912).

97   E. Corradini, *La conquista di Tripoli* (Milan, 1912); Gorresio, "Il primo manganello," *Il Mondo* (September 16, 1950).

98   Occhini, "Nell'imminenza del Congresso di Roma," *Idea Nazionale* (December 12, 1912); see also the editorial, "L'indirizzo politico . . . dopo il Congresso di Roma" (December 12, 1912). For the "democratic" reaction, see Alberto Caroncini, in the *Idea Nazionale* (June 19, 1913). On claims of financial support from industrialists, see Albertini, *Venti anni di vita politica*, Vol. II, Pt. 2, 98.

99   Editorial, "I clericali alla conquista dello stato italiano," *Idea Nazionale* (April 13, 1911); see also Coppola, "Il mio antisemitismo" (November 30, 1911). The same idea was taken up by Paolo Orano (August 7, 1913). See the excellent sections in Gabriele de Rosa, *L'azione cattolica* (2 vols. Bari, 1954), II, Chaps. 8 and 9.

100 *L'Osservatore Romano* (September 23 and November 15, 1911); Spadolini, *L'opposizione cattolica*, pp. 583–84; De Rosa, *L'azione cattolica*, II, 328–37.

101 Albertini, *Venti anni di vita politica*, Vol. II, Pt. 2, 239–45. Gentiloni's interview but did not deny the existence of the Pact (November 9, *d'Italia* (November 7, 1913). The *Osservatore Romano* criticized the interview but did not deny the existence of the Pact, (November 9, 1913). For the Nationalist response see "Nazionalisti, liberali e cattolici," *Idea Nazionale* (November 13, 1913).

102 For the reaction of the Association, see the following articles in the *Idea Nazionale*; editorial, "Nazionalisti, liberali e cattolici" (November 13, 1913); "Nazionalisti e Cattolici" (November 27, 1913); Maraviglia and Federzoni, "Alla vigilia del Congresso" (May 14, 1914); Davanzati, "Un custode dell'Idea'" (June 5, 1914); and the issue of May 23, 1914.

103 N. Valeri, *Da Giolitti a Mussolini. Momenti della crisi del liberalismo* (Florence, 1956), pp. 42–43.

104 E. Corradini, *Le vie dell'oceano* (Milan, 1913).

105 Editorial, *Idea Nazionale* (June 13, 1914); Gorresio, "Il primo manganello," *Il Mondo* (September 16, 1950).

106 See the following articles in *L'Azione*: editorial, "Propositi" (May 10, 1914); A. Caroncini, "Individualismo e nazionalismo" (May 10, 1914); T. Borelli, "Gli avvenimenti" (May 10, 1914); P. Arcari, "Il nazionalismo italiano" (May 17, 1914) and "Il Congresso Nazionalista" (May 24, 1914); Luigi Valli, "Nazionalisti e Cattolici" (May 24, 1914).

107 *Idea Nazionale* (June 13, 1914). De Rosa, *L'azione cattolica*, II, 372–78.

108 *Idea Nazionale* (October 7, 1914).

109 Federzoni, in the *Idea Nazionale* (September 3, 1914); see also the editorial of September 17, 1914, and the issue of November 18, 1914. By November the paper was stepping up its pace, coming out twice weekly, indicative of possible new financial support. By 1915 it had become a daily.

110 *Civiltà Cattolica*, LXV, vol. 4 (1914), 513–43.

111 Editorial, "I moniti della guerra e gli insegnamenti dell' Enciclica," *Civiltà Cattolica*, LXV, vol. 4 (1914), 641–51; also the article, "Nazional-

ismo e amor di Patria secondo la dottrina cattolica," LXVI, vol. 1 (1915), 129–44, 420–35.

112 The letter appeared in the *Tribuna* (February 1, 1915). For the original version see L. Peano, *Ricordi della guerra dei trent'anni 1915–1945* (Florence and Bari, 1948), pp. 16–19. For the Catholic position see "La Provvidenza. Il Papato e l'Italia nell'ora presente," *Civiltà Cattolica*, LXV, vol. 4 (1914), 3–15. On the theme of German blackmail, see above, Chapter 5 and n. 54.

113 See Corradini's article, signed "e.c.," in the *Idea Nazionale* (October 3, 1914). Corradini would destroy clericalism, but tried to distinguish this from "true Catholicism." See also the issue of November 15, 1914.

114 Coppola, "I cattolici e la guerra," *Idea Nazionale* (October 25, 1914). For the edited version see *La crisi italiana* (Rome, 1916), pp. 24–29, where the article is misdated October 26.

115 *Popolo d'Italia* (February 24, 1915). On the monarchy, see Corradini in the *Idea Nazionale*, September 17, 1914, and February 22, 1915, and also the issue of April 13, 1915.

116 *Popolo d'Italia* (April 13, 1915).

117 H. Yarrow, "The Forging of Fascist Doctrine," *Journal of the History of Ideas*, XI, No. 2 (April, 1942), 159–81. Silvio Trentin, in his *Aux Sources du fascisme* (Paris, 1931), noted that the corporate theory, which the Nationalists used, was intended to avoid the charge that fascism was reactionary. On Mussolini's use of the war as the basis for his postwar program, see G. Rumi, "Mussolini e 'il Programma' di San Sepolcro," *Il Movimento di liberazione in Italia*, No. 71, Fasc. 2 (April–June, 1963), 4–26.

CHAPTER EIGHT

1 L. Salvatorelli, *La Triplice Alleanza (1877–1912)* (Milan and Varese, 1939), pp. 395–403. G. Giolitti, *Memorie della mia vita* (Milan, 1922), pp. 327–68.

2 Salvatorelli, *La Triplice Alleanza*, p. 402.

3 G. Ansaldo, *Il ministro della buonavita* (2nd ed. Milan, 1950), p. 365. F. Nitti, *Rivelazioni* (Naples, 1948), preface, xv.

4 Giolitti, *Memorie*, pp. 333–34. C. Askew, *Europe and Italy's Acquisition of Libya* (Durham, North Carolina, 1942), pp. 11–22, 266–74. On economic penetration, see Renato Mori, "La penetrazione pacifica italiana in Libia dal 1907 al 1911 e il Banco di Roma," *Rivista di studi politici internazionali*, XXIV, No. 1 (January–March, 1957), 103–18.

5 G. M. Trevelyan, *Garibaldi and the Making of Italy* (3rd ed. London, 1911), p. 294. By 1911 Trevelyan maintained that Italy had held its place in the family of nations "as securely as France, Spain, or the German Empire" (*ibid.*, p. 2). He was, however, fearful of the consequences of the Libyan war (p. 294, n. 1). For foreign reaction among other scholars see A. Pingaud, *L'Italie depuis 1870* (Paris, 1915), pp. 285–97; and A. Dauzat, *L'Expansion italienne* (Paris, 1914), pp. 69–70.

6 R. Bagot, *The Italians of Today* (Chicago and London, 1913), pp. 22, 167–69. Dauzat, *L'expansion italienne*, pp. 119–21. For Sorel's remark, see G. Volpe, *L'Italia in cammino* (Milan, 1931), p. 170.

7 C. Sforza, *Contemporary Italy*, trans. Drake and Denise De Kay (New York, 1944), p. 160.

8 G. Mosca, *L'Italia e Libia* (Milan, 1912), pp. 84–87. The reference is to Pascoli, who died in 1912.

9 Editorial, "L'Italia si è desta," *Idea Nazionale* (September 28, 1911). A. Labriola, *La guerra di Tripoli e l'opinione socialista* (Naples, 1912). His article, "L'Europa contro l'Italia," which appeared in the *Scintilla* and was the germ of his book on Libya, was reprinted in the *Idea Nazionale* (October 12, 1911).

10 E. Corradini, *Sopra le vie del nuovo impero* (Milan, 1912), pp. 3–12.

11 G. Bevione, *Come siamo andati a Tripoli* (Turin, 1912), p. 186. It should be recalled that Bevione, while an imperialist, wrote for the *Stampa*, whose director, Alfredo Frassati, was a close friend of Giolitti.

12 *Idea Nazionale* (October 26, 1911); see also the article, "Letteratura di guerra" (December 6, 1911).

13 Coppola, "Israele contro Italia," *Idea Nazionale* (November 16, 1911), and his "Redenzione" (October 19, 1911).

14 T. Antongini, *Quarant' anni con D'Annunzio* (Verona, 1957), pp. 219–62, 231; also by Antongini, *La vita segreta di Gabriele D'Annunzio* (10th ed. revised, Verona, 1959), p. 668. For the *Idea Nazionale's* reception of D'Annunzio's war poetry see "La politica del Poeta," February 1, 1912.

15 Ansaldo, *Il ministro della buonavita*, p. 388. On the Poet's clash with the publisher see P. Constantini, "Lettere di Gabriele D'Annunzio a Emilio Treves," *Il Ponte* (October, 1948).

16 Antongini, *La vita segreta*, pp. 669–70.

17 F. T. Marinetti, *Guerra sola igiene del mondo* (Milan, 1915), pp. 153–54.

18 B. Croce, "Ripresa di vecchi giudizii: Oriani postumo," *La Critica*, XXXIII, Fasc. 111 (May 20, 1935), 181–88. At the time, the *Idea Nazionale* reprinted Oriani's article on the death of Crispi, and plugged for a complete edition of his works (March 20 and 27, 1913).

19 Editorial, "L'illusione tripolina," *La Voce* (May 18, 1911); Israele Zangwill, "Perchè non si deve andare a Tripoli," *La Voce* (August 17, 1911).

20 Salvemini, "Il trabocchetto tripolino," *La Voce* (August 24, 1911); "Falsificazioni tripoline. Il rapporto Rohlfs," *L'Unità* (December 16, 1911). On the forgery attributed to the Nationalists, see also *L'Unità* of December 23, 1911.

21 "L'illusione tripolina," and also Prezzolini's article in *La Voce* (August 17, 1911). Salvemini, "La polveretta," *La Voce* (August 31, 1911).

22 Editorials, "Tripoli e Triplice" and "I socialisti," *La Voce* (September 21 and 28, 1911).

23 Editorial, "Tripoli e i Socialisti," *L'Unità* (December 16, 1911).

24 Carlo Maranelli, "I valori morali della guerra," *L'Unità* (October 5, 1912); see A. Di Staso, *Da ciò che insegna la guerra* (Bari, 1912), for another former anti-imperialist who praised the war's beneficial effects. On Fortunato see his "Concordia discors," *L'Unità* (October 19, 1912).

25 *Giornale d'Italia* (April 6, 1910).

26 For the best account of Italy's reaction to the Libyan War see Gorresio, "Storia del nazionalismo italiano. III: L'Italia che vola," *Il Mondo* (September 2, 1950). Dauzat, *L'Expansion italienne*, is a good contemporary source. On the role of the press see M. T. Caracciolo, "L'ufficio stampa . . . durante la guerra," *Nuova Antologia*, CCLIV, Fasc. 1013 (March 1, 1914), 144–45.

27 Dauzat, *L'Expansion italienne*, pp. 122–23; *Il Messaggero* (October 13, 1911).

28 *La Revue* (March 15, 1912), cited in Dauzat, *L'Expansion italienne*, pp. 143–45.

29 *L'Unità* (October 5, 1912), p. 170. Also Salvemini in *La Voce* (September 28, 1912). He granted that his anti-Giolittian stand had lessened somewhat, but refused to retract anything from his *Il ministro della malavita.*

30 Editorial, *L'Unità* (February 24, 1912).

31 R. Hostetter, *The Italian Socialist Movement*, Vol. I, *Origins (1860–1882)* (Princeton, 1958), pp. 13–14, 16–18.

32 G. Giolitti, *Discorsi extraparlamentari* (Turin, 1952), pp. 259–72. That Giolitti's speech was aimed at dampening Nationalist rhetoric was noted at the time by Bonomi, "Il socialismo nella realtà politica," speech at the Modena Congress of the PSI, October, 1911, in *Dieci anni di politica italiana* (Milan, 1923), p. 76.

33 "Il discorso di Torino e il patriottismo dell'onorevole Giolitti," *Idea Nazionale* (October 12, 1911).

34 L. Albertini, *Venti anni di vita politica* (5 vols. Bologna, 1951), Vol. II, Pt. 1, 120–28; Giolitti, *Memorie*, p. 370. Mack Smith, who depends heavily on Albertini, shares his prejudices regarding Giolitti on this and other issues: *Italy. A Modern History* (Ann Arbor, 1959), pp. 277–78.

35 G. Giolitti, *Discorsi parlamentari* (4 vols. Rome, 1953–56), III, 1668.

36 Albertini, *Venti anni di vita politica*, Vol. II, Pt. 2, 126 and n. 1, gives the 100,000 figure; Giolitti set it at over 80,000 (*Memorie*, p. 358). Giolitti, *Discorsi parlamentari*, III, 1668; *Memorie*, p. 371. The *Corriere* itself conceded that colonial wars were likely to run up against such problems (November 28, 1912).

37 Salvatorelli, *La Triplice Alleanza*, pp. 402, 406–08; Giolitti, *Memorie*, p. 373.

38 Salvatorelli, *La Triplice Alleanza*, p. 404; Giolitti, *Memorie*, pp. 377–79.

39 Albertini, *Venti anni di vita politica*, Vol. II, Pt. 1, 138; Golitti, *Memorie*, p. 375.

40 Salvatorelli, *La Triplice Alleanza*, p. 404; Albertini, *Venti anni di vita politica*, Vol. II, Pt. 1, 138–41; Giolitti, *Memorie*, pp. 38–83.

41 Albertini depends on Jagow's dispatches for much of his case regarding Di San Giuliano's position. But these were not always in agreement with other diplomatic reports (Salvatorelli, *La Triplice Alleanza*, p. 404).

42 Albertini, *Venti anni di vita politica*, Vol. II, Pt. 1, 116–17, 121, 141–42. *Corriere della Sera* (November 1 and 5, 1911).

43 M. Soleri, *Memorie* (Turin, 1949), p. 36; Giolitti, *Memorie*, p. 381.

44 "Fatti e non parole," *Idea Nazionale* (November 9, 1911); "La riapertura del parlamento . . ." (February 7, 1912).

45 Giolitti, *Discorsi parlamentari*, III, 1441–42.

46 "Dopo il voto del parlamento," *Idea Nazionale* (February 29, 1912).

47 Salvatorelli, *La Triplice Alleanza*, pp. 413–64; Giolitti, *Memorie*, p. 439.

48 "La pace mediocre e i pericoli balcanici," *Idea Nazionale* (October 17, 1912); "Ora storica" (November 7, 1912); also the editorial of November 14, 1912.

49 Albertini, *Venti anni di vita politica*, Vol. II, Pt. 1, 200–201; and the issue of the *Corriere* of October 17, 1914, on the death of Di San Giuliano, expressing the same idea found in the *Idea Nazionale*.

50 Corradini, "Alla vigilia del Congresso di Roma," *Idea Nazionale* (December 18, 1912). T. Palamenghi-Crispi, *Giolitti* (Rome, 1913), passim. The author relies on Torre's article in the *Corriere* of April 5, 1911 (pp. 158–60).

51 Federzoni, "Il valore nazionalista dell'impresa libica," *Idea Nazionale* (February 26, 1914). (Speech delivered in the Chamber of Deputies, February 25, 1914.)

52 *Idea Nazionale* (January 1, 1915).

53 Mussolini, "Sangue che unisce," *Popolo d'Italia* (December 31, 1914); *Corriere della Sera* (December 31, 1914), in which interventionist propaganda filled page 1, reports of the war's progress being relegated to back pages. See Luigi Barzini, "Sangue italiano nella foresta," *Corriere della Sera* (February 7, 1915). See also the issue of February 4, 1915.

54 Reprinted on page 1 of the *Popolo d'Italia* (January, 1915).

55 Coppola, "Per la democrazia o per l'Italia?" *Idea Nazionale* (October 3, 1914).

56 Editorial, "Il dovere del Re," *Idea Nazionale* (May 15, 1915); see also "L'ora suprema della Dinastia Sabauda" (May 16, 1915); and the two editorials, "Agire" and "Il nemico della Patria," of May 12 and 14, 1915.

57 *Il Messaggero* (October 15, 1911); *Avanti!* (May 8, 1912).

58 *Atti del parlamento italiano. Camera dei deputati. Sessione 1913–15. Discussioni*, VI, 6335 ff.; *Sessione 1912–15. Discussioni*, VII, 6893 ff.; *Corriere della Sera* (May 15, 1915); *Popolo d'Italia* (May 15, 1915).

59 *L'Unità* (October 5, 1912); Salvemini, "Falsificazioni tripoline" and "Il decreto della sovranità," *L'Unità* (December 6, 1911, and October 12, 1912). Also the *Unità's* editorial, "Tripoli e i socialisti" (December 6, 1911).

60 Salvemini, "Sapienti e analfabeti nel nuovo sistema elettorale," *L'Unità* (April 20, 1912); "Gli elettori analfabeti" (May 4, 1912). For Altobelli's speech, see *Atti. Camera. Sessione 1913–14. Discussioni*, I, 154 ff.

61 On the eve of the war, the *Idea Nazionale* printed speeches by Maffeo Pantaleoni, Federzoni, and Davanzati that were favorable to the Triple Alliance (July 31, 1914). When war came, and Italy stayed out, the Nationalists were momentarily confused. Bevione defended neutrality, opposing any aid to the Central Powers. Corradini went into raptures about the beauties of war. Davanzati confessed he was "profoundly disturbed" and obviously regretted that the Alliance had not been put to some active use. He, and all Nationalists, emphasized that those who backed the government's neutralist stand were Socialists, Freemasons, and Democrats (*Idea Nazionale*, August 6, 1914). Fear of being identified with those "degenerates" and with "official" Italy had much to do with the sudden swing to the cause of intervention. There was a counterrevolutionary idea implicit in this shift: see the *Idea Nazionale* (August 13 and 20, 1914). At the time, Mussolini was still a revolutionary neutralist, one of the "degenerates."

62 Salvemini, in reply to an article by Angelo Vivante, *L'Unità* (Dec. 6,

1912); see also his journal's editorial, "La Triplice rinnovata e la questione albanese" (December 13, 1912). For Salvemini's response to the war see *L'Unità* (May 21, 1915); his "Guerra o neutralità," *Problemi italiani*, No. 1 (4th ed. Milan, 1915), and the book *Delenda Austria* (Milan, 1917).

63 *Corriere della Sera* (May 15, 1915); *Giornale d'Italia* (May 15; dateline, Rome, 14th).

64 "La discussione Libica," *Rivista Popolare* (February 15, 1914), pp. 66–70; editorial, "La guerra scellerata e vergognosa" (August 15, 1914), pp. 393–97; also, Colajanni, "Le probabili conseguenze della nostra neutralità," *ibid.*, pp. 397–400; and the editorial, "La guerra scellerata e vergognosa" (August 31, 1914).

65 Editorial, "Il nuovo ministero Salandra," *Rivista Popolare* (November 15, 1914); "La commemorazione di Guglielmo Oberdan" (December 31, 1914), pp. 581–82; Colajanni, *Aspromonte* (Rome, 1912), passim; and his article, "Le colpe della monarchia italiana (la guerra del 1866)," *Rivista Popolare* (January 31, 1915), pp. 30–39.

66 *Atti. Camera. Sessione 1913–15. Discussioni*, VI, 5561 ff.

67 Prezzolini, "Pace giolittiana," *La Voce* (October 24, 1912).

68 Prezzolini, "La vita nazionale," *La Voce* (February 6, 1913); "Parole d'un uomo moderno," *La Voce* (April 24, 1913).

69 Prezzolini, "Le sorprese della storia," *La Voce* (November 7, 1912); editorial, "Programma politico" (October 16, 1913); also the editorial "Le elezioni" (November 6, 1913). V. Fazio-Allmayer, "L'elezione," *La Voce* (June 5, 1913), and the *Voce*'s reply of June 19. Prezzolini, "Parole d'un uomo moderno. V: La disciplina," *La Voce* (September 25, 1913).

70 Prezzolini, "Sciopero giolittiano," *La Voce* (June 28, 1914); also his article, "Cavoli libici rifritti," of October 28, 1914. Luigi Emery, "Verso un altro 'eroico sopruso'?" *La Voce* (November 28, 1914).

71 Editorial, "L'ora," *La Voce* (August 13, 1914); Prezzolini, "Facciamo la guerra" (August 28, 1914); and Emery, "Verso un altro 'eroico sopruso'?"

72 Editorial, "Digrignatori di denti," *La Voce* (April 11, 1912). At the time Papini was running the *Voce*.

73 F. Flora, *D'Annunzio* (Naples, 1926), pp. 85–96, discusses this aspect of the Poet's art. Corradini, "La commemorazione dei soldati morti a Adua," *Idea Nazionale* (March 5, 1914). See also Pr[ezzolini], "Collaborazione al mondo," *La Voce* (April 28, 1914).

74 Papini, "Puzzo di cristianucci," *La Voce* (January 9, 1913).

75 Papini, "Il discorso di Roma," *Lacerba* (March 1, 1913). See also his "Il massacro delle donne," *Lacerba* (April 1, 1914).

76 Papini, "La necessità della rivoluzione," *Lacerba* (April 15, 1913); and his "La vita non è sacra," *Lacerba* (October 16, 1913). When war came, he wanted the "warm blood bath": *Lacerba* (October 1, 1914). The same ideas run through all the issues of the journal, recalling the *Leonardo* and *Regno* phase of Papini's career.

77 Nitti, *Rivelazioni*, p. 318.

78 *Corriere della Sera* (August 14, September 14, October 1, 1914); also the issue of May 15, 1915.

79 L. Gasparotto, *Diario di un deputato* (Milan, 1945), p. 72. *Corriere della Sera* (May 5, 1915), p. 5.

80 *Corriere della Sera* (May 5, 1915), p. 5; Albertini, *Venti anni di vita politica*, Vol. I, Pt. 2, 511–12. According to the terms of the London Treaty, Italy had a month in which to enter the war.

81 *Corriere della Sera* (May 5, 1915). The speech is reprinted in G. D'Annunzio, *Per la più grande Italia* (Milan, MCMXV), pp. 13–33.

82 *Popolo d'Italia* (May 6, 1915).

83 *Ibid.* See also Mussolini's editorial, *Popolo d'Italia* (May 5, 1915), and his "Il monito di Oriani" (March 14, 1915). Antimonarchical passages were deleted in Fascist editions of his writings. The Oriani article, however, was excluded completely: see E. Susmel, *Venticinque scritti e un discorso di Benito Mussolini da lui proibiti, 1915–1919* (Milan, 1950), pp. 41–45.

84 G. Megaro, *Mussolini dal mito alla realtà* (Milan, 1947), pp. 53, 65–86, 91–105, 130–41, 202, 275–77, 328. On his anticlericalism, see also E. Rossi, *Il manganello e l'aspersorio* (Florence, 1959), pp. 23–45.

85 T. Nanni, *Benito Mussolini. Opuscoli della "Voce,"* No. 7 (Florence, 1915), pp. 9–11. The pamphlet first appeared in January, 1915.

86 E. Nolte, "Marx und Nietzsche im Sozialismus des jungen Mussolini," *Historische Zeitschrift*, CXCI, No. 2 (October, 1960), 249–335.

87 Reino Virtanen, "Nietzsche and the Action française," *Journal of the History of Ideas*, XI, No. 2 (April, 1950), 212–13.

88 Jean Variot, *Propos de Georges Sorel* (Paris, 1935), pp. 53–57, cited in Scot H. Lytle, "Croce, il metodo storico e lo storico," *Nuova Antologia*, CCCCLXV, Fasc. 1857 (September, 1955), 31.

89 Megaro, *Mussolini*, pp. 159–60; Mussolini, "Il Trentino," *La Voce* (December 15, 1910).

90 Mussolini, *Il Trentino veduto da un socialista* (Florence, 1911), pp. 36, 66–68. He made clear, however, that the Socialists were autonomists at best (pp. 60–68) and that the proletariat was generally indifferent (p. 32). It is not possible to squeeze much irredentism out of the work, as Finer has tried, in *Mussolini's Italy* (New York, 1935), p. 48, and as Mussolini and his followers later tried to do as well. For a more accurate appraisal see Salvatorelli and Mira, *Storia del Fascismo* (Rome, 1952), p. 20. On Nanni's use of the passages, see his *Benito Mussolini*, p. 13. For the *Voce*'s position on Mussolini see "I Socialisti non sono neutrali" (October 13, 1914).

91 Prezzolini, "Sciopero giolittiano," *La Voce* (June 28, 1914); also in *La Voce*, the article "Partiti e gruppi italiani davanti alla guerra" (September 18, 1914). On the same topic, see G. Dorso, *Mussolini alla conquista del potere* (Turin, 1949), pp. 85–90.

92 *Giornale d'Italia* (October 3, 1914).

93 Dorso, *Mussolini*, pp. 91–92, and the *Voce*'s editorial of October 13, 1914.

94 Dorso, *Mussolini*, pp. 92–94.

95 *Giornale d'Italia* (October 21, 1914).

96 *Corriere della Sera* (October 23, 1914).

97 Missiroli, *L'Italia d'oggi* (3rd ed. Bologna, 1943), pp. 62–65.

98 *Corriere della Sera* (October 25, 1914).

99 Bonomi, *Dal Socialismo al Fascismo* (2nd ed. Rome, 1924), pp. 17 27.
100 *Corriere della Sera* (November 25, 1914); *Giornale d'Italia* (November 24, 1914). See also Mussolini's "Chiodi e Croce," *Popolo d'Italia* (November 20, 1914).
101 V. Vacirca, *Storia d'un cadavere* (New York, 1924), pp. 112–21; G. Salvemini, *Mussolini diplomatico* (Bari, 1952), Appendix A, pp. 419–31; Pietro Nenni, *Sei anni di guerra civile*, translated from the French by Giuliana Emiliani (Milan and Rome, 1945), pp. 44–45; Maria Rigyer, *Mussolini — indicateur de la police française ou les raisons occulte de sa 'conversion'* (Brussels, 1928).
102 *Corriere della Sera* (February 23, 24, 25, 26, 1915).
103 A. Tasca (A. Rossi), *Nascita e avvento del Fascismo* (Florence, 1950), p. 45; Salvemini, *Mussolini diplomatico*, p. 430.
104 T. Borelli, "Gli avvenimenti — Il quarto d'ora dei socialisti rivoluzionari," *L'Azione* (May 10, 1914); editorial, "Nel campo socialista. Il caso Mussolini," *Rivista Popolare* (November 30, 1914); Prezzolini, " 'La Voce' nel 1915," *La Voce* (November 31, 1915). The latter issue also contained the announcement of the *Popolo d'Italia* and advertised Mussolini's book on the Trentino, which had been forgotten until then. Luigi Emery's article on Oriani ("Verso un altro 'eroico sopruso,' " *La Voce*, November 28, 1914) referred to the emergence of Mussolini as indicative of a "more vital" element in the PSI.
105 Editorial, "I Socialisti," *La Voce* (September 28, 1911).
106 Bonomi, "Il Socialismo nella realtà politica," in his *Dieci anni di politica italiana*, pp. 57–84.
107 Bonomi, "Per l'intervento dell'Italia," *ibid.*, pp. 119–24.
108 G. M. Trevelyan, *Scenes from Italy's War* (New York, 1919), pp. 2, 3, 7, 9, 11, 14.

CHAPTER NINE

1 Mussolini, "Audacia!" *Popolo d'Italia* (November 15, 1914); Arturo Concone, "La guerra rivoluzionaria," and the editorial, "I termini del problema," *Popolo d'Italia* (November 16 and 19, 1914).
2 *Popolo d'Italia* (December 28, 1914).
3 Leoncello Bisi, "Incoerenza," *Popolo d'Italia* (November 25, 1914); see also Mussolini's speech at Parma, December 13, 1914, reprinted in *Popolo d'Italia*, December 17; T. Nanni's article of November 14; and Mussolini's Verona speech of December 5, reprinted in *Popolo d'Italia*, December 6.
4 Mussolini, "I morti che vivono," *Popolo d'Italia* (January 8, 1915), and the issue of January 6, 1915.
5 Mussolini, "Fronda," *Popolo d'Italia* (January 11, 1915), and his article of January 12, 1915.
6 Mussolini, article celebrating the anniversary of the Commune, *Popolo d'Italia* (March 18, 1915).
7 Mussolini, in the *Popolo d'Italia* (April 3, 1915); Rossi to the paper, dateline Palermo, March 28, issue of April 3.
8 *Atti del parlamento italiano. Camera dei deputati. Sessione 1913–15. Discussioni*, VI, 6335 ff.
9 Pietro Bertolini, "Diario (agosto 1914–maggio 1915)," *Nuova Antologia*, CCXXII, Fasc. 1221 (February 1, 1923), 214–25.

10 Dorso, to the *Popolo d'Italia* from Avellino, January 1, 1915. See also the following numbers: January 5, 18, and April 9, 1915.

11 Maraviglia, "Bisogna far la guerra anche per il Mezzogiorno," *Idea Nazionale* (December 31, 1914).

12 On this topic, see the following articles from the *Popolo d'Italia*: Mussolini, "Anima e ventre" (December 20, 1914); "I termini del problema" (November 19, 1914); "Guerra di popoli" (December 13, 1914); Rossi in the issue of April 3, 1915; also December 19, 1914, January 20 and 27, 1915, and April 7, 1915. In the *Idea Nazionale*, Coppola's article of October 20, 1914; and N. Fancello," L'ideale contro il ventre," *La Voce. Edizione politica* (May 22, 1915).

13 A. Renda, "I valori della guerra," in *Le pagine dell'ora* (Milan, 1916), pp. 16–20; *Lacerba*, issue of August 15, 1914, passim. Violently anti-Austrian and anti-German articles were censored out of the *Lacerba*, beginning with this issue.

14 G. A. Borgese, *La nuova Germania. La civiltà contemporanea*, No. 1 (Turin, 1909), passim. See also Borgese's speech at Milan, December 27, 1914, in the *Corriere della Sera* (December 28, 1914) and the issue of March 16, 1915. His anti-German book was *Italia e Germania* (Milan, 1915), passim. For Papini on Germany see "Il dovere dell'Italia," *Lacerba* (August 15, 1914).

15 According to Cesare Rossi, Florence was the "Mecca of paunchafism" (*Popolo d'Italia*, March 1, 1915). While southern neutralism was more pronounced, the following dispatches from Tuscany, mostly written by Arcangelo di Staso, show that the area, and its leading paper, the *Nazione*, were clearly neutralist: December 15, 1914; January 21, February 12, 17, 20, 22; March 1, 29; April 21; May 19, 1915.

16 R. Fauro, in the *Idea Nazionale* (April 16, 1914); in the same issue, the editorial, "Il Convegno d'Abbazia"; r[oberto] f[orges] d[avanzati], "Dopo il Convegno d'Abbazia" (April 23, 1914); editorial, "L'ultimo austriaco" (July 3, 1914). On Gayda, see R. Fauro, "Gli italiani irredenti in un libro di Virginio Gayda," *Idea Nazionale* (July 17, 1914); and the issue of July 31, 1914. Gayda's principal work, *La crisi di un impero* (Turin, 1913), was a study of the dissolution of the Dual Monarchy, stressing Austrian use of the Slavs as a weapon against Italians.

17 *Idea Nazionale* (August 13 and September 17, 1914); Salandra and Sonnino, "Carteggio della neutralità: agosto–dicembre 1914," *Nuova Antologia*, LXX, Fasc. 510 (February 16, 1935), 483–504.

18 R. Fauro, in the *Idea Nazionale* (December 12, 1914); see also Mario Alberti (February 19, 1915).

19 Salandra, *L'intervento. Ricordi e pensieri* (Verona, 1930), pp. 108–09.

20 Coppola, in the *Idea Nazionale* (March 12, 1915); and his articles, "Per una coscienza italiana" (March 16, 1915), "Le ragioni politiche" (March 17, 1915).

21 Coppola, "Le ragioni morali . . . ," *Idea Nazionale* (March 25, 1914).

22 Prezzolini, "Austria e Francia," *La Voce* (December 8, 1910); "Basta con la Libia e a Trento e Trieste," *Popolo d'Italia* (November 28, 1914).

23 *Popolo d'Italia* (December 30, 1914); Prezzolini in the issue of January 29, 1915. See Mussolini's comments on Prezzolini's ideas con-

cerning Fiume, which were motivated in part by a speech in which Mussolini referred to future Austrian possession of the city (*Popolo d'Italia,* January 29, 1915).

24 Mussolini, editorial, *Popolo d'Italia* (March 2, 1915); and his "La prima guerra d'Italia" (February 14, 1915); also the issue of March 21, 1915.

25 Mussolini, "La prima guerra d'Italia," *Popolo d'Italia* (February 14, 1915).

26 Editorial, *Corriere della Sera* (April 8, 1915).

27 Stefan Burian, "Risposta ad Erzberger," *Nuova Antologia,* CCXCIII (February 1, 1934), pp. 350–56; B. von Bülow, *Memoirs,* trans. Geoffrey Dunlop (4 vols. Boston, 1932), III, 174–263; M. Erzberger, *Erlebnisse im Weltkrieg* (Stuttgart and Berlin, 1920), pp. 21–41, also his "Memoriale sull'Italia," *Nuova Antologia,* CCXCIII (1934), 343–50; Salandra, *L'intervento,* pp. 256–57; Count Etienne Tisza, *Lettres de guerre (1914–16)* (Paris, 1931), pp. 127–36.

28 G. Giolitti, *Memorie della mia vita* (Milan, 1922), p. 540; Salandra, *L'intervento,* pp. 118–20.

29 *Giornale d'Italia* (May 12, 1915); Editorial, *Corriere della Sera* (May 12, 1915); and the *Corriere* for May 20.

30 Bertolini, "Diario," p. 224.

31 Editorial, *Corriere della Sera* (May 14, 1915).

32 Editorial, "L'unica soluzione," *Corriere della Sera* (May 15, 1915); *Popolo d'Italia* (May 16, 1915). The *Corriere* of May 4 reported from Paris that D'Annunzio had told a reporter on the *Matin* just before leaving for Italy that accords with the Entente had been signed. For Martini's role, see his "Diario," *Il (Nuovo) Corriere della Sera* (July 29, 1958).

33 Editorial, *Corriere della Sera* (May 14, 1915). It may be seen from Barzilai's statement to the press, reported in the *Corriere* of May 15, 1915, that interventionists tried to conceal the fact that the London pact was signed before the Triple Alliance was ended. He stated that obligations were assumed with the Entente "when the impossibility of dignified agreements with the Central Powers forced us to denounce the Austrian alliance." This also proves that the interventionists were being fed state secrets, since Barzilai knew that the Alliance had not been broken with Germany.

34 Editorial, *Corriere della Sera* (May 13, 1915).

35 See the *Corriere della Sera* of September 20, October 10 and 18, 1914.

36 *Corriere della Sera* (February 9 and March 13, 1915). See also Borgese, *Guerra di redenzione, Problemi italiani,* No. 17 (Milan, 1915), passim.

37 *Atti. Camera. Sessione 1913–15. Discussioni,* VII, 7620 ff.; *Corriere della Sera,* editorial of March 23, 1915.

38 *Corriere della Sera* (April 14 and May 8, 1915).

39 J. Destrée, *Figures italiennes d'aujourd'hui* (Paris and Brussels, 1918), gives sketches of the leading Italian interventionists, all of whom Destrée met.

40 Bertolini, "Diario," pp. 214–15; C. Sforza, "Sonnino and His Foreign Policy," *Contemporary Review,* CXXXVI (1929), 724; Carlo Avarna di Gualtieri, "Il carteggio Avarna-Bollati. Luglio 1914–maggio 1915,"

Rivista storica italiana, LXI, Fascs. 2, 3, 4; LXII, Fascs. 1, 2, 3 (1949, 1950). According to C. Benoist, *Souvenirs* (3 vols. Paris, 1932–34), III, 235, no one bought Rome's two pro-German papers, *Concordia* and *Vittoria*. Virgilio Scattolini's *Unser Phlichtgegen Deutschland* (Berlin, 1915) is a rare example of openly pro-German literature. Its arguments, racially based, are no more rational than most interventionist literature on the other side.

41 Editorial, "Ai lettori," *Italia Nostra* (December 6, 1914).

42 *Corriere della Sera* (May 10, 11, 12, 14, 15, 1915).

43 Mussolini, "ABBASSO IL PARLAMENTO," *Popolo d'Italia*, A. II, No. 127 [*sic*], 129 (1915). See also the unsigned editorial of May 14, 1915; Prezzolini, "La rivoluzione antigiolittiana," *La Voce. Edizione politica* (May 22, 1915); *Giornale d'Italia* (May 11, 1915); *Corriere della Sera* (May 13, 1915).

44 Salandra, *L'intervento*, p. 269; *Atti. Camera. Sessione 1913–15. Discussioni*, VII, 7907 ff.

45 "Agire," editorial, *Idea Nazionale* (May 12, 1915).

46 Editorial, *Corriere della Sera* (May 14, 1915), and the issue of May 15. For the perpetuation of the legend of Giolitti's perfidy and cowardice in 1915, see D. Mack Smith, *Italy. A Modern History* (Ann Arbor, 1959), pp. 302–03, 310–13.

47 *Giornale d'Italia* (May 14, 1915).

48 *Atti parlamentari. Legislatura XXIV. Sessione 1913–15. Camera dei deputati. Documenti diplomatici presentati al parlamento italiano dal Ministro degli Affari Esteri* (May 20, 1915) (Rome, Tipografia della Camera, 1915).

49 *Il Libro Verde. Documenti diplomatici presentati al parlamento italiano . . .* (Milan and Treves, 1915), pp. 115–19.

50 *Atti. Camera. Sessione 1913–15. Discussioni*, VII, 7907 ff.

51 *La Voce. Edizione politica* (May 22, 1915).

52 C. de Biase, *L'incolumità di Giolitti e l'assalto a Montecitorio nel maggio 1915* (Rome, 1957), pp. 31–33 and passim.

53 See S. Trentin, *Aux Sources du fascisme* (Paris, 1931), for this interpretation of the rise of fascism.

54 E. Rosen, "Italiens Kriegseintritt im Jahre 1915 als innenpolitisches Problem der Giolitti-Àra," *Historische Zeitschrift*, CLXXXVII, No. 2 (April, 1959), p. 357 and n. 4.

55 G. Volpe, *Il popolo italiano tra la pace e la guerra (1914–1915)* (Milan and Varese, 1940), pp. 250–51.

56 Brunello Vigezzi, "Le 'Radiose giornate' del maggio 1915 nei rapporti dei Prefetti," *Nuova rivista storica*, XLIV, Fasc. 1 (January–April, 1960), 80 and n. 1.

57 *Atti. Camera. Sessione 1913–15. Discussioni*, VI, 5531 ff.

58 A. Concone, "La guerra rivoluzionaria," *Popolo d'Italia* (November 16, 1914); also the issue of November 28, 1914. See also the cartoon of December 2, 1914. Papini, "Rispondo a Benedetto," *Popolo d'Italia* (November 19, 1914).

59 C. Sforza, *Contemporary Italy*, trans. Drake and Denise De Kay (New York, 1944), pp. 198–207.

60 *Corriere della Sera* (September 4, 1914); see also the issues of September 5, p. 3, and October 14, p. 4.

61 *Idea Nazionale* of October 7, 1914, p. 2, and November 18, 1914, p. 2.
62 G. De Rosa, *L'azione cattolica* (2 vols. Bari, 1954), II, 382–88.
63 "La settimana rossa e la guerra," *Civiltà Cattolica*, III (1914), 39.
64 *Idea Nazionale*, October 24, 1914; also Coppola's article, "I cattolici e la guerra," October 25, 1914; De Rosa, *L'azione cattolica*, II, 398–99. The *Idea Nazionale* of October 25, 1914, carried an interview with a "noted Catholic personality" who stated that not all Catholics were neutral while admitting fears of the spread of the Greek Church. More important was the speech of Count Della Torre, head of the *Unione Popolare*, one of Italy's most prominent laymen, given in Rome, January 5, 1915. Della Torre insisted that Italian Catholics were neutral, there being no reason for intervention. His remark that Catholics were also patriots was seized upon by the *Corriere della Sera* (January 6, 1915, p. 3) and by the *Idea Nazionale* (January 7, 1915, p. 1) as indicative of a swing toward war.
65 See the following issues of the *Idea Nazionale*: November 15, 1914, p. 2, and February 22, 1915, pp. 1–2. For the appeal to Catholic patriots against the Pope's authority, see the issues of October 3 and 4, 1914, and especially Alfredo Rocco in the issue of November 22, 1914. The reply came in the article "Nazionalismo e amor dì Patria secondo la dottrina cattolica," *Civiltà Cattolica*, LXVI, vol. 1, Fasc. 1550 (January 8, 1915), 129–38; Fasc. 1552 (February 12, 1915), 420–35.
66 *Corriere della Sera* (April 30, 1914), p. 3; "Lettera del Cardinale Segretario di Stato al Primate del Belgio. Dal Vaticano 13 novembre 1914," in Guglielmo Quadrotta, *Il papa, l'Italia e la guerra* (Milan, 1915), p. 151.
67 Cardinal D. Mercier, *Patriottismo e pazienza. Lettera pastorale, Natale 1914* (Rome, 1915), passim.
68 *Corriere della Sera* (February 21, 1915), p. 3; *Popolo d'Italia* (January 22, 1915), p. 3; Quadrotta, *Il papa, l'Italia e la guerra*, pp. 154, 164.
69 *Civiltà Cattolica*, LXVI, vol. 1, Fasc. 1550 (January 8, 1915), 257–62; *Corriere della Sera* (January 24, 1915), p. 3; *Popolo d'Italia* (January 23, 1915), p. 1.
70 Benoist, *Souvenirs*, III, 235.
71 Coppola, "I democratici e la neutralità. L'equivoco," *Idea Nazionale* (August 13, 1914). On Péguy, see Silvio d'Amico in the *Idea Nazionale* (October 5, 1914).
72 Prezzolini, "Charles Péguy," *La Voce* (March 15, 1915). Eugenio Vajna de' Pava, *La democrazia cristiana italiana e la guerra* (Bologna, 1919), pp. 117 ff., cited in A. Omodeo, *Momenti della vita di guerra* (Bari, 1934), p. 240. Vajna died in battle July 22, 1915.
73 R. Murri, "L'universalismo religioso e la guerra"; lecture delivered December 6, 1914, and printed in *Origini effetti e prospettive della guerra europea* (Milan, 1915), pp. 127–47. De Rosa notes a trend toward idealizing war in the Modernists generally (*L'azione cattolica*, II, 430–31). For the *Civiltà Cattolica's* views, see the issue LXVI, vol. 1, Fasc. 1549 (1915), 114–17.
74 *Civiltà Cattolica*, LXV, vol. 4 (1914), 513–43, 641–51; *Corriere della Sera* (November 17, 1914), p. 2; *Papers Relating to the Foreign Relations of the United States. The Lansing Papers, 1914–1920* (2 vols. Washington, 1939), I, 719.

75 *Civiltà Cattolica*, LXV, vol. 3 (1914), 630–31, 736–49; LXVI, vol. 1 (1915), 8–24.
76 Quadrotta, *Il papa l'Italia e la guerra*, pp. 69–71; F. Scaduto, *Guarentigie pontificie* (Turin, 1889), and his article "Independenza dello stato e libertà della chiesa," *Bilychnis*, II (1913), 251–58.
77 *Corriere della Sera* (September 1, 1914, and May 3, 1915). Luzzatti's articles were in reply to Scaduto, who insisted that Italy take steps to protect itself against papal subversion in case of war.
78 *Atti. Camera. Sessione 1913–15. Discussioni*, VI, 5615 ff.
79 *Corriere della Sera* (April 19, 1915), p. 2.
80 Ruffini, "La Questione Romana e l'ora presente," *Nuova Antologia*, CCXII (May–June, 1921), 202–03; also his article "Il potere temporale negli scopi di guerra degli ex-imperi centrali," *Nuova Antologia*, CCXI (March–April, 1921), 289–301; "Progetti e propositi per risolvere la Questione Romana," *Nuova Antologia*, CCXII (May–June, 1921), 24–40.
81 V. E. Orlando, *Rome vs. Rome*, trans. Clarence Beardslee (New York, 1937), pp. 86–88, 102–04, 132–33. On the background of Article XV see above, Chap. 5 and notes 63, 64.
82 C. de Biase, "Il 'Diario' del Ministro Vincenzo Riccio (1915)," *Nuova Antologia*, CCCCLXV, Fasc. 1860 (December, 1955), 540.
83 Benoist, *Souvenirs*, III, 244–45; *Lansing Papers*, I, 721–22.
84 *Corriere della Sera* (April 25, 1915), p. 5.
85 De Rosa, *L'azione cattolica*, II, 404–06.
86 *Ibid.*, pp. 406–07.
87 Orlando, *Rome vs. Rome*, p. 60.
88 E. J. Dillon, *From the Triple Alliance to the Quadruple Alliance. Why Italy Went to War* (London, 1915), pp. 88–93.
89 G. Ferrero, "La crisi di maggio e la guerra," *La Guerra europea. Studi e discorsi* (Milan, 1915), pp. 222–23.
90 I. Bonomi, *La politica italiana da Porta Pia a Vittorio Veneto* (Rome, 1944), p. 354.

CHAPTER TEN

1 Mussolini, "VITTORIA!" *Popolo d'Italia* (May 17, 1915); editorials in the *Corriere della Sera* (May 17 and 21, 1915); and in the *Idea Nazionale* (May 17, 1915).
2 Mussolini, "Fronda," *Popolo d'Italia* (January 11, 1915), and the issue of January 24.
3 M. Toscano, *Il patto di Londra* (Bologna, 1934), p. 81 and n. 1; A. Pingaud, *L'Italie depuis 1870* (Paris, 1915), pp. 308–09; I. Bonomi, *La politica italiana da Porta Pia a Vittorio Veneto* (Rome, 1944), pp. 350–51, 534.
4 T. Okey, in the *Contemporary Review* (July, 1916), p. 38.
5 Salandra, *L'intervento, Ricordi e pensieri* (Verona, 1930), p. 16.
6 A. Monticone, "Salandra e Sonnino verso la decisione dell'intervento," *Rivista di studi politici internazionali*, XXIV, No. 1 (January–March, 1957), 64–89.
7 Toscano, *Il patto di Londra*, p. 123; also *L'intervento dell'Italia nei documenti segreti dell'Intesa* (Rome, 1923), pp. 125–54.
8 Monticone, "Salandra e Sonnino verso la decisione," pp. 72, 74 and n

18. Nicholas wired his reluctant acceptance on April 8/21, at which time the prefectural survey was halted (*L'intervento nei documenti segreti*, pp. 154–55).

9 Monticone, "Salandra e Sonnino verso la decisione," pp. 74, 76–79 and n. 27, 84, 87.

10 Salandra, *L'intervento*, p. 335.

11 *Giornale d'Italia* (September 25, 1914).

12 [Un ex-diplomatico], "La neutralità," *Nuova Antologia*, CLXXIV (September, 1914), 90–100; M. Ferraris, "Il momento storico," *Nuova Antologia*, CLXXIV (November 1, 1914), 139–42. See also in the same journal the two articles signed "Victor" [Ferraris]: "L'Italia e la neutralità" (January 16, 1915), 316–27, and "L'Italia nella conflagrazione internazionale" (March 16, 1915), i-xx.

13 For a summary of Labriola's letter to the *Patria degli italiani* (Buenos Aires, September 29), see the *Corriere della Sera* (November 21, 1914) and the *Popolo d'Italia* (November 21, 1914).

14 A. Frassati, *Giolitti* (Florence, 1959), p. 6; E. J. Dillon, *From the Triple to the Quadruple Alliance. Why Italy Went to War* (London, 1915), pp. 95–100.

15 G. Giolitti, *Memorie della mia vita* (Milan, 1922), p. 532.

16 M. Soleri, *Memorie* (Turin, 1949), pp. 48–49; L. Peano, *Ricordi della guerra dei trent'anni 1915–1945* (Florence and Bari, 1948), p. 18 and n. 1; Sforza, "Sonnino and His Foreign Policy," *Contemporary Review*, CXXXVI (1929), 721–32; Toscano, *Il patto di Londra*, p. 55.

17 Salandra, *L'intervento*, p. 264.

18 *Atti del parlamento italiano. Camera dei deputati. Sessione 1913–15. Discussioni*, III, 2144 ff.; VII, 6823 ff., 6939 ff.

19 P. Bertolini, "Diario (agosto 1914–maggio 1915)," *Nuova Antologia*, CCXXII, Fasc. 1221 (February 1, 1923), 214–25.

20 Frassati, *Giolitti*, pp. 5–7; F. S. Nitti, *Rivelazioni* (Naples, 1948), pp. 387–88.

21 *Idea Nazionale* (April 7 and November 1, 1914); Coppola, "Il più grande pericolo" (April 9, 1915).

22 G. A. Borgese, *Italia e Germania* (Milan, 1915), introduction, p. xxxvii; *Corriere della Sera* (March 10 and May 5, 1915), p. 5.

23 See the following issues of the *Popolo d'Italia*: November 19 and 29, December 31, 1914; January 20, February 4, March 30, April 2, 1915.

24 Prezzolini, in the *Popolo d'Italia* (January 16, 1915); see also the issue of February 18, 1915.

25 *Popolo d'Italia* (November 23, 1914); *Idea Nazionale* (October 10, 1914, and January 11, 1915); see also Colajanni's speech of December 4, 1914, *Atti. Camera. Sessione 1913–15. Discussioni*, VI, 5561 ff.

26 *Corriere della Sera* (April 14, 1915).

27 *Idea Nazionale* (October 10, 1914); Coppola, "Esame di coscienza," in the issue of October 13; Mussolini, "La prima guerra d'Italia," *Popolo d'Italia* (February 14, 1915); and G. A. Borgese, *Guerra di redenzione, Problemi italiani*, No. 17 (Milan, 1915), passim.

28 Bertolini, "Diario," pp. 218–20; Salandra, *L'intervento*, p. 169. Wickham Steed claims Vienna spread false rumors of a separate peace to keep Italy from intervening: *Through Thirty Years, 1892–1922. A*

Personal Narrative (2 vols. New York, 1925), II, 61. This was a logical move and might have deterred Italy had logic remained in charge of her diplomacy. In fact, tales of a separate peace only urged the interventionists to get in sooner, before it was over.

29 Bertolini, "Diario," pp. 217–18.
30 Monticone, "Salandra e Sonnino verso la decisione," p. 69.
31 On this, see E. Rosen, "Italiens Kriegseintritt im Jahre 1915 als innenpolitisches Problem der Giolitti-Ära," *Historische Zeitschrift,* CLXXXVII, No. 2 (April, 1959), 47–49.
32 *Atti. Camera. Sessione 1913–14. Discussioni,* I, 520 ff., 529 ff.
33 Giolitti, *Memorie,* p. 511.
34 *Atti. Camera. Sessione 1913–14. Discussioni,* III, 2144 ff., 2158 ff.
35 D. Mack Smith, *Italy. A Modern History* (Ann Arbor, 1959), p. 285.
36 *Atti. Camera. Sessione 1913–14. Discussioni,* III, 3975.
37 *Ibid.,* IV, 3861–3924, 3925–75, 4049–56; Giolitti, *Memorie,* p. 511.
38 *Atti. Camera. Sessione 1913–14. Discussioni,* III, 3975; V, 5199 ff.
39 Salandra and Sonnino, "Carteggio della neutralità (agosto–dicembre 1914)," *Nuova Antologia,* LXX, Fasc. 1510 (February 16, 1935), 487, 491–94, 495, 500–01.
40 *Corriere della Sera* (October 10, 1914).
41 Salandra and Sonnino, "Carteggio," pp. 490, 497. Salandra refers to a certain "T" who has become particularly bothersome. This was probably Andrea Torre of the *Corriere.*
42 *Atti. Camera. Sessione 1913–15. Discussioni,* VI, 5531 ff.; *Corriere della Sera* (December 4, 1914).
43 *Atti. Camera. Sessione 1913–15. Discussioni,* VI, 5531 ff.
44 *Ibid.,* 5615 ff., 5825 ff. Ciccotti's book was published anonymously as *Montecitorio. Noterelle di uno che c'è stato* (Rome, 1908).
45 *Corriere della Sera* (December 4, 1914); *Giornale d'Italia* (December 6, 1914); *Idea Nazionale* (December 4, 1914); *Tribuna* (December 6, 1914).
46 *Atti. Camera. Sessione 1913–15. Discussioni,* VI, 5615 ff.; Soleri, *Memorie,* pp. 48–49.
47 *Atti. Camera. Sessione 1913–15. Discussioni,* VII, 7151 ff., 7199 ff.
48 *Popolo d'Italia* (December 13, 1914), p. 3. Beginning with the number July 15, 1914, every issue of *Lacerba* devoted some space to blistering, often obscene, attacks on Salandra's neutralism. Nenni's article "Quale guerra?" appeared in the *Popolo d'Italia* (January 20, 1915). For the *Idea Nazionale,* see the editorials of October 30 and November 4, 1914; also Federzoni, in the issue of October 7; and Coppola, "Il sacro egoìsmo" (October 20) and "La cena della neutralità" (November 13). The last was omitted from his published war articles, *La crisi italiana* (Rome, 1916). Corradini's reaction may be seen from his "La corona e il Governo, *Idea Nazionale* (November 20, 1914).
49 Salandra, *L'intervento,* pp. 26–28. See N. Fancello's description of the quake in the *Popolo d'Italia* (January 17, 1915); see also the issues of January 18, 19, and 22, 1915.
50 Soleri, *Memorie,* pp. 43–44; *Corriere della Sera* (January 20, 1915).
51 *Popolo d'Italia* (January 27, 1915), p. 3; *Corriere della Sera* (January 21, 1915), p. 7.

52 *Corriere d'Italia* (February 2, 1915).

53 *Popolo d'Italia* (February 9, 14, and 24, 1915). G. Dorso, *Mussolini alla conquista del potere* (Turin, 1949), p. xi and n.

54 *Idea Nazionale* (February 12, 1915).

55 For the parecchio letter, in which the accent is more on defending the government than on planning diplomacy, see Peano, *Ricordi*, p. 18. It is also true that Giolitti asked that the letter be published only later, and then for the obvious reason that he saw the attack on Salandra taking a dangerous turn. He may not have recalled the parecchio — or *molto*, as it was in the original — or its ramifications. See also G. Giolitti, *Discorsi extraparlamentari* (Turin, 1952), p. 282, and Rosen, "Italiens Kriegseintritt," p. 337.

56 Giolitti, *Memorie*, pp. 532–33; G. Ansaldo, *Il ministro della buonavita* (2nd ed. Milan, 1950), p. 418.

57 *Atti. Camera. Sessione 1913–15. Discussioni*, VI, 6287 ff.

58 B. Vigezzi, "Le 'Radiose giornate' del maggio 1915 nei rapporti dei Prefetti," *Nuova rivista storica*, XLIII, Fasc. 3 (September–December, 1959), 330–31, denies this. But the report he cites from Turin disproves his own case: *ibid.*, XLIV, Fasc. 1 (January–April, 1960), 88.

59 *Atti. Camera. Sessione 1913–15. Discussioni*, VI, 6441 ff.

60 A. Labriola, "Per il diritto di riunione. Mascherata caduta," *Roma* (March 2–3, 1915); *Popolo d'Italia* (February 27, 1915); and Mussolini's editorial of February 28. For Turati's remark, see *Atti. Camera. Sessione 1913–15. Discussioni*, VI, 6441 ff.

61 [NAR], "Alla vigilia di giorni fatali" (March 1, 1915), and Fancello, "Tradimento" (March 8, 1915), from the *Popolo d'Italia*; Coppola, "Si tradisce l'Italia," *Idea Nazionale* (March 10, 1915). Colajanni's *Rivista Popolare* said Salandra had "lost his dignity" by going to visit Giolitti (March 15, 1915).

62 See the following articles by Mussolini: "Necessità morale" (March 6, 1915); "DISCIPLINA" (April 11, 1915); and the *Popolo d'Italia* for April 7.

63 Editorial, "L'Italia contro il suo Governo," *Popolo d'Italia* (April 12, 1915), and the issue of April 14; also the editorial in the *Idea Nazionale* (April 15).

64 *Popolo d'Italia* (April 15; dateline, Milan, April 14), and the issue of January 29, which covered the meeting of the Milan section of the party. See also the *Corriere della Sera*'s interview with Turati (February 12, 1915).

65 A. Malatesta, *I socialisti italiani durante la guerra* (Milan, 1926), pp. 51–52. Copies of the principal manifestos illustrating the party's dilemma are given on pp. 211–31.

66 G. Megaro, *Mussolini dal mito alla realtà* (Milan, 1947), p. 323.

67 *Atti. Camera. Sessione 1913–15. Discussioni*, VII, 7700 ff.

68 Rosen's view in "Italiens Kriegseintritt," p. 351.

69 Vigezzi, "Le 'Radiose giornate,' " passim.

CHAPTER ELEVEN

1 G. Ansaldo, *Il ministro della buonavita* (2nd ed. Milan, 1950), pp. 418–19; G. Giolitti, *Memorie della mia vita* (Milan, 1922), pp. 534–35;

L. Peano, *Ricordi della guerra dei trent'anni 1915–1945* (Florence and Bari, 1948), p. 21.

2 Ansaldo, *Il ministro della buonavita*, pp. 422 ff.; Salvatorelli, "Giolitti," *Rivista storica italiana*, LXII, Fasc. 4 (1950), 529.

3 Giolitti, *Memorie*, pp. 534–35.

4 E. Rosen, "Italiens Kriegseintritt im Jahre 1915 als innenpolitisches Problem der Giolitti-Ära," *Historische Zeitschrift*, CLXXXVII, No. 2 (April, 1959), 348, 349 and n. 4.

5 *La Stampa's* evening edition for May 8–9 announced that Giolitti would arrive May 9. The May 7 dateline on the report indicates that the decision to go to Rome was made before news of the prorogation reached Cavour. Sobrero, Rome correspondent, had a fairly hopeful interpretation of the prorogation. See also the edition of May 9–10, p. 4.

6 C. De Biase, *L'incolumità di Giolitti e l'assalto a Montecitorio nel maggio 1915* (Rome, 1957), pp. 29–31: Giolitti, *Memorie*, pp. 538–39.

7 A. Frassati, *Giolitti* (Florence, 1959), preface, xi–xii, pp. 14–15; D. Mack Smith, *Italy. A Modern History* (Ann Arbor, 1959), pp. 301–03.

8 P. Bertolini, "Diario (agosto 1914–maggio 1915)," *Nuova Antologia*, CCXXII, Fasc. 1221 (February 1, 1923), 221.

9 Giolitti, *Memorie*, pp. 539–40; Salvatorelli, "Tre colpi di stato," *Il Ponte*, VI, No. 4 (April, 1950), 342–43. Giolitti's memoirs are quite inaccurate on the precise dates of these various meetings.

10 Bertolini, "Diario," p. 221.

11 Salandra, "L'intervento italiano nel primo conflitto. A cura di Giambattista Gifuni," *La politica parlamentare*, X, Nos. 9–10 (September-October, 1957), 62–64; Salandra, *L'intervento. Ricordi e pensieri* (Verona, 1930), pp. 247–48.

12 Fortis and Luzzatti headed the government briefly in 1905–06 and 1909–10 and were looked upon as "lieutenants" by anti-Giolittians. Salandra refers to the *Stampa* in his memoirs as an example of a Giolittian paper that made much of the visit. He did not mention the Turin daily to the King (*L'intervento*, p. 248). But he was hurt far more by the gibes in the interventionist press.

13 Salandra, *L'intervento*, pp. 248–49.

14 *Ibid.*, pp. 249–52, 245–46.

15 Giolitti, *Memorie*, p. 540.

16 Salandra, *L'intervento*, pp. 249–50; Bertolini, "Diario," p. 221.

17 Giolitti, *Memorie*, p. 540.

18 Salandra, *L'intervento*, p. 253.

19 Giolitti, *Memorie*, pp. 540–41.

20 Salandra, *L'intervento*, pp. 253–55.

21 *Ibid.*, pp. 255–56.

22 Bertolini, "Diario," p. 222.

23 Salandra, *L'intervento*, p. 179; M. Erzberger, *Erlebnisse in Weltkrieg* (Stuttgart and Berlin, 1920), pp. 34–36.

24 Salvatorelli, "Tre colpi di stato," passim.

25 Giolitti, *Memorie*, p. 539; Frassati, *Giolitti*, p. 22.

26 S. Burian, "Risposta ad Erzberger," *Nuova Antologia*, CCXCIII (February 1, 1934), 356; M. Erzberger, "Memoriale sull'Italia," *Nuova Antologia*, CCXCIII (February 1, 1934), 347.

27 *La Stampa* (March 22, 1952). For Salvatorelli's latest opinion see "Del nuovo su Giolitti e il patto di Londra," *La Stampa* (December 12, 1957), p. 3.

28 Salandra, "L'intervento italiano nel primo conflitto," p. 62; *L'intervento,* p. 248.

29 Salandra, "L'intervento italiano nel primo conflitto," p. 62; *L'intervento,* pp. 248–49.

30 Salandra, *L'intervento,* p. 248; "L'intervento italiano nel primo conflitto," p. 62. The royal telegrams, except the one to the French Republic, are reprinted in De Biase, *L'incolumità di Giolitti,* p. 40, n. 32.

31 Salandra, "L'intervento italiano nel primo conflitto," p. 62.

32 Salandra, *L'intervento,* pp. 250–51; "L'intervento italiano nel primo conflitto," p. 62.

33 Salandra, *L'intervento,* p. 251. Salvatorelli offers, with obvious disbelief, the suggestion that when Salandra referred to the King as *fiducioso,* in the memoirs, he meant not "confident" but "frank" or "open": *La Stampa* (December 12, 1957). See also "L'intervento italiano nel primo conflitto," pp. 62–63.

34 Salandra, "L'intervento italiano nel primo conflitto," p. 63.

35 Salandra, *L'intervento,* p. 246.

36 Salandra, "L'intervento italiano nel primo conflitto," p. 63.

37 Mack Smith, *Italy,* pp. 302–03.

38 Salandra, "L'intervento italiano nel primo conflitto," pp. 63–64. On Chimirri, see Albertini, *Venti anni di vita politica* (5 vols. Bologna, 1951), Vol. I, Pt. 2, 390–91.

39 Salvatorelli, "Del nuovo su Giolitti," *La Stampa* (December 12, 1957).

40 Salandra, *L'intervento,* p. 254.

41 Giolitti, *Memorie,* p. 540; Bertolini, "Diario," pp. 221–22.

42 Erzberger, *Erlebnisse,* pp. 34–35; Salandra, *L'intervento,* p. 254.

43 Salandra, *L'intervento,* pp. 199 ff.

44 Giolitti, *Memorie,* pp. 541–42; Erzberger, *Erlebnisse,* pp. 32–33; Salandra, *L'intervento,* p. 268.

45 A. Labriola, "Verso le calme discussioni," *Roma* (May 13, 1915).

46 Salandra, "L'intervento italiano nel primo conflitto," p. 64.

47 *Ibid.*

48 *Ibid.*

49 Albertini, *Venti anni di vita politica,* Vol. I, Pt. 2, 464–66; M. Toscano, *Il patto di Londra* (Bologna, 1934), pp. 190–92.

50 Salandra, "L'intervento italiano nel primo conflitto," p. 64.

51 In the published version, the footnotes that were to have gone with what is apparently a missing portion were not taken out when the diary was printed. See following note.

52 Albertini, *Venti anni di vita politica,* Vol. I, Pt. 2, 486. The unmatched notes left in the printed text include one (n. 4) referring to Albertini. The last note (n. 3) for which there is a corresponding passage in the text refers to Admiral Thaon di Revel.

53 G. Quadrotta, *Il papa, l'Italia e la guerra* (Milan, 1915), passim. See particularly the preface by Scaduto.

54 *Corriere della Sera* (April 25, 1915).

55 Orlando, *Rome vs. Rome*, trans. Clarence Beardslee (New York, 1937), pp. 113, 118–19, 139–41.
56 Salandra, *L'intervento*, pp. 245–46.
57 *Ibid.*, pp. 268–70.
58 *Ibid.*, pp. 270–73.
59 Giolitti, *Memorie*, p. 542. The May 11 date is incorrect: Salandra, *L'intervento*, pp. 284–85.
60 T. Antongini, *D'Annunzio* (London and Toronto, 1938), pp. 485–90.
61 *Corriere della Sera* (May 13, 1915; dateline, Rome, May 12).
62 D'Annunzio, *Per la più grande Italia* (Milan, MCMXV), pp. 67–72.
63 The references are to Giolitti's thick lips, and to his trip to Berlin in 1893 following his resignation in connection with the Bank of Rome Scandals. D'Annunzio, *Per la più grande Italia*, pp. 73–78.
64 G. Natale, *Giolitti e gli italiani* (Cernusco sul Naviglio, 1949), pp. 736–37. De Biase insists that Giolitti was never in danger (*L'incolumità di Giolitti*). But Barzilai, on May 25 — when Giolitti was back in Cavour — told Ferdinando Martini that there had been a plot to kill him, "Diario," *Corriere della Sera* (July 29, 1958), p. 3.
65 Bertolini, "Diario," p. 223; *Corriere della Sera* (May 15, 1915), p. 5; also the editorial "La Patria italiana," in the *Idea Nazionale* (May 17, 1915).
66 L. Gasparotto, *Diario di un deputato* (Milan, 1945), pp. 72–73.
67 J. Bainville, *La Guerre et l'Italie* (Paris, 1915), passim. Bainville saw the parallel between 1915 and the French "revolution of contempt" of 1848, with Guizot as Giolitti, Lamartine as D'Annunzio, and the "bourgeois king" as Victor Emmanuel III.
68 Frassati, *Giolitti*, pp. 10–11.
69 Natale, *Giolitti e gli italiani*, p. 739.
70 Bertolini, "Diario," p. 224.
71 F. Turati, *Attraverso le lettere di corrispondenti (1880–1925)* (Bari, 1947), pp. 164–66.
72 *L'Unità Cattolica* (Nov. 15, 1914); G. De Rosa, *L'azione cattolica* (2 vols. Bari, 1954), II, 406–07.
73 Salandra, *L'intervento*, pp. 269–70.
74 Carlo Avarna di Gualtieri, "Il carteggio Avarna-Bollati. Luglio 1914–maggio 1915," *Rivista storica italiana*, LXI, Fasc. 2, 3, 4 (1949); LXII, Fasc. 1, 2, 3 (1950); H. Wickham Steed, *Through Thirty Years, 1892–1922. A Personal Narrative* (2 vols. New York, 1925), II, 64–67; *Papers Relating to the Foreign Relations of the United States. 1915 Supplement. The World War* (Washington, 1928), p. 32.
75 *Red Book*, Doc. No. 2, in E. J. Dillon, *From the Triple to the Quadruple Alliance. Why Italy Went to War* (London, 1915), p. 131.
76 C. Benoist, *Souvenirs* (3 vols. Paris, 1932–34), III, 232–33, 234–49. For an example of Morello's journalism, see *L'albero del male di Rastignac* (Rome, 1914).
77 Salandra, *La neutralità italiana. 1914–15* (Milan, 1928), 370–71.
78 *Corriere della Sera* (October 1 and 3, 1914).
79 Giolitti, *Memorie*, p. 317; *Discorsi parlamentari di Silvio Spaventa* (Rome, 1913), preface; Salandra, *La neutralità*, p. 370.
80 C. de Biase, "Il 'Diario' del Ministro Vincenzo Riccio (1915)," *Nuova*

Antologia, CCCCLXV, Fasc. 1860 (December, 1955), 527–46;
CCCCLXVII, Fasc. 1868 (August, 1956), 513–24; CCCCLXX, Fasc.
1877 (May, 1957), 89–100. Riccio, in 1926, claimed he had not retouched the diary (*Nuova Antologia*, December, 1955, p. 530). But
when he speaks of the events of the time, he sometimes begins, "I
recall" (May 1957, pp. 89–90); and at one point the diary says that
it agrees with what Salandra "has said" (*ibid.*, p. 94).
81 Riccio, "Diario," *passim*.
82 Salandra, *L'intervento*, p. 240; Martini, *Fra un sigaro e l'altro* (Milan,
   1930), pp. 108–14; Martini, "Diario," *Corriere della Sera* (July 13, 17, 22,
   25, 29, 1958).
83 Martini, "Diario," *passim*.
84 Steed, *Through Thirty Years*, II, 58; Bertolini, "Diario," pp. 214–15.
85 Sforza, "Sonnino and His Foreign Policy," *Contemporary Review*,
   CXXXVI (1929), 724.

CHAPTER TWELVE

1 Johan Huizinga, *Men and Ideas. Essays by Johan Huizinga*, trans.
   James E. Holmes and Hans van Marle (New York, 1959), pp. 77–96.
2 H. Stuart Hughes, *Consciousness and Society. The Reorientation of
   European Social Thought 1890–1930* (New York, 1958), pp. 184–85.
3 *Ibid.*, pp. 189, 338–39.
4 "Gian Falco" [Giovanni Papini], "L'ideale imperialista," *Leonardo*, I
   (January, 1903). Also in the *Leonardo* his "Me e non me," I (January,
   1903), and his "Chi sono i socialisti," I (February and March, 1903).
   See as well Giuliano il Sofista [Giuseppe Prezzolini], "La miseria dei
   logici," I (February, 1903).
5 Croce, "Leonardo," *La Critica*, I (1903), 287–91.
6 Croce, review of Prezzolini's *Il linguaggio come causa d'errore. Henri
   Bergson*, in *La Critica*, II (1904), 150–53. Gian N. G. Orsini, *Benedetto Croce. Philosopher of Art and Literary Critic* (Carbondale, Ill.,
   1961), p. 364.
7 Giuliano il Sofista [Prezzolini], review of William James' *La varie
   forme della coscienza religiosa* (Turin, 1904), in *Leonardo*, II (June,
   1904).
8 Ralph Barton Perry, *The Thought and Character of William James*
   (Cambridge, 1948), pp. 321–22. For the Florentine reception of pragmatism, see "Gian Falco" [Papini], "Il teologo del positivismo,"
   Leonardo, II (June, 1904); and Giuliano il Sofista [Prezzolini], replying to
   Mario Calderoni, *Leonardo*, II (November, 1904).
9 For this phase of Italian pragmatism see the following articles in
   Leonardo by "Gian Falco" [Papini]: "Cosa vogliamo," II (November,
   1904); "Athena e Faust," III (February, 1905); "Dall'uomo a Dio,"
   III (February, 1906); and by Giuliano il Sofista [Prezzolini]: "L'arte
   di persuadere," III (February, 1906).
10 See the following articles by Croce in *La Critica*: review of James'
   Pragmatism (New York, 1907), VI (1908), 206; review of Papini's
   Il crepuscolo dei filosofi (Milan, 1906), IV (1906), 140–44; review
   of Mario Calderoni's "L'imperativo categorico," *Leonardo* (April,
   1906), IV (1906), 316–17; "Di un carattere della più recente lettera-

tura italiana," V (1907), 172–90. See also Croce, "A proposito del positivismo italiano," III (1905), 169–72.

11 Croce, "La Voce," *La Critica*, VII (1909), 308. See also Croce's articles in *La Voce*, February 8 and 11, 1909.

12 Croce, "Dai 'Discorsi politici' non mai raccolti, di Francesco de Sanctis," *La Critica*, XI (1913), 56–77, 141–60, 311–38, 395–405.

13 Croce, "Contro l'astrattismo e il materialismo politici," *La Critica*, X (1912), 232–35.

14 Croce, *History as the Story of Liberty* (New York, 1955), pp. 93–95, 96–102.

15 Giovanni Gentile, "La filosofia della guerra," in his *Guerra e fede* (Naples, 1914), pp. 1–24, lecture delivered at the Palermo Philosophical Library, October 11, 1914. For Bergson, see his "La signification de la guerre," *Pages actuelles*, No. 18 (Paris, 1915).

16 Croce, "Ripensando di Giosuè Carducci," *La Critica*, XIII (1915), 320–22. On the *Idea Nazionale*'s attack, see his reply in *La Critica*, XIII (1915), 75–77. For Croce's answer to a similar charge by Mussolini, see his note "Cifre e fatti," *Italia nostra*, I, No. 3 (December 20, 1914).

17 Hughes, *Consciousness and Society*, p. 214.

18 Croce, "Intorno a questa rivista," *La Critica*, VIII (1915), 318–20.

19 "Ai lettori," *Italia nostra*, I, No. 1 (December 6, 1914). On the joining of the two extremes against the Government Croce saw fit to reprint his 1912 analysis of pessimism and its political significance in *Italia nostra*, I, No. 3 (December 20, 1914), 2.

20 Croce, "Le fortune immeritate," *Italia nostra*, II, No. 5 (January 31, 1915). See also his "Cultura tedesca e politica italiana," I, No. 1 (December 6, 1914), and his "Motivazioni di voto" in the same issue.

21 Croce, *Contributo alla critica di me stesso* (Bari, 1926), passim.

22 Prezzolini, *Amici* (Florence, 1922), pp. 99–115. Croce, *L'Italia dal 1914 al 1918. Pagine sulla guerra* (3rd ed. Bari, 1950), pp. 301–11.

23 Alfredo Frassati, *Giolitti* (Florence, 1959), p. 29.

24 For an illustration of this see the fascist paper *L'assalto* directed by Dino Grandi.

25 Croce, "La protesta contro il 'Manifesto' degli intellettuali fascistici," reprinted in *Propositi e speranze (1925–1942)* (Bari, 1944), pp. 7–22.

26 Croce, preface to Gaetano Natale's *Giolitti e gli italiani* (Cernusco sul Naviglio, 1949). Vincenzo Galizzi, *Giolitti e Salandra*, with an introduction by Croce (Bari, 1949).

27 Aldo Scaglione, "Croce's Definition of Literary Criticism," *Journal of Aesthetics and Art Criticism*, XVII (1959), 448, cited by G. N. G. Orsini, *Bulletin of Croce Studies in the U.S.*, No. 1 (November, 1959), pp. 5–6; No. 2 (November, 1960), p. 6.

28 George L. Mosse, *The Culture of Western Europe. The Nineteenth and Twentieth Centuries* (Chicago, 1961), pp. 319–20.

29 Orsini, *Bulletin*, No. 1, pp. 5–6; No. 2, pp. 6–7. Also his *Benedetto Croce*, pp. 275–81. Croce's relation to younger intellectuals is analyzed with similar results by Antonino Gandolfo, *Benedetto Croce. Critico dei contemporanei* (Padua, 1959).

30 G. A. Borgese, "Croce e Vico. Croce e 'I Giovani,'" *La cultura con-*

temporanea, IV, Fasc. 3–4 (March–April, 1912). Giuliano il Sofista [Prezzolini], "La Critica," *Leonardo,* IV (October, 1906), 361–64. See also Prezzolini: "Gentile e Croce," *La Voce* (January 26, 1911); *Amici,* pp. 15–23; and finally his *Uomini 22 e città 3* (Florence, n.d.), pp. 75–85. On the question in general see Mario Sansone, "L'antidecadentismo di Benedetto Croce," *Cultura moderna,* V (November, 1960), 18–22.

31 G. Volpe, *L'Italia in cammino* (Milan, 1931), preface, pp. ix–xxv. Gaudens Megaro, *Mussolini dal mito alla realtà* (Milan, 1947), p. 295.

32 Croce, "Note sulla letteratura italiana nella seconda metà del secolo XIX. Alfredo Oriani," *La Critica,* VII (1909), 1–28. G. Sorel, *Considerazioni sulla violenza,* trans. Antonio Sarno, with an introduction by Croce (Bari, 1909), introduction, pp. v–xxvii. Croce first published the essay in *La Critica,* V (1907), 317–30.

33 Croce, "Notizie ed osservazioni," *La Critica,* XXXII (1934), 90.

34 Orsini, *Benedetto Croce,* pp. 210–23. Croce, *Contributo,* p. 41.

35 Federico Chabod, "Croce storico," *Rivista storica italiana,* LXIV (1952), 508–11.

INDEX

447

DATE DUE

FEB 3 '67			
APR '6			
GAYLORD			PRINTED IN U.S.A.